Neil Fox
Rugby League's greatest points scorer

Neil being presented to the Duke of Edinburgh
at the 1960 Challenge Cup Final

Robert Gate

London League Publications Ltd

To Billy
Best Wishes
Neil Fox
MBE

Neil Fox
Rugby League's greatest points scorer

A CIP catalogue record for this book is available from the British Library.

First published in Great Britain in November 2005 by:
London League Publications Ltd, P.O. Box 10441, London E14 8WR

ISBN: 1-903659-24-8

Cover design by: Stephen McCarthy Graphic Design
                          46, Clarence Road, London N15 5BB

Layout: Peter Lush

Printed and bound by: Biddles Ltd
                          King's Lynn, Great Britain

This book is dedicated by Neil Fox to all his family, especially grandchildren Lisa, James, Daniel and Joshua. Neil and Molly would like to say to all their many friends from all walks of life thanks for all the lovely memories. We will never forget you. We had some great times.

Foreword

Neil played professional rugby league for 25 years. He was awarded two testimonials, and so we decided that two people - both eminent and with strong Wakefield Trinity connections - should contribute to the foreword for this book.

This comprehensive account of the career of a remarkable sportsman is long overdue. It is now 50 years since Neil Fox put pen to paper and signed for Wakefield Trinity RLFC to become the backbone of their highly successful side of the 1960s. The youngest of three brothers who would each distinguish themselves in rugby league, Neil was to develop into a veritable scoring machine, accumulating in a 25-year career a world record 6,220 points - a total which is unlikely ever to be beaten.

I cannot pretend any sense of objectivity in my assessment of Neil Fox's rugby league achievements. The simple fact is Fox was my boyhood hero and perhaps the key figure in my development of a life-long passion for the sport. He was an ever-present in a Trinity side whose successes have never been equalled by those subsequently wearing the famous red, white and blue.

Being just 10 years younger than Neil, my arrival as a youngster on the terraces of Trinity's Belle Vue Ground coincided with the start of his outstanding sporting career. I had the privilege of watching this much talked about young centre develop into one of the greatest rugby players of either code in the world. I have lost count of the numerous matches at club, county and international level - I saw transformed by the prodigious talent of Neil Fox. With his trademark dummy and glorious left boot he seemed to almost single-handedly deliver victory on any number of occasions.

It is a fitting tribute to him that one of rugby league's finest writers – Robert Gate - has, working with Neil, so thoroughly undertaken the challenging task of recording his lengthy and wonderful contribution to the game. The end result is a fascinating reflection on the sporting life of this exceptional player."

David Hinchliffe

My involvement with Wakefield Trinity came after following them on the Challenge Cup trail in 1946, which culminated at Wembley with Billy Stott's match-winning goal against Wigan. I wonder how many became supporters of the club when it graced Wembley in 1960 and created a new record score with Neil Fox breaking goal and points records.

For over 40 years from that first post-war season. I not only became a supporter but a servant of the club in many various ways, eventually becoming a member of the committee for nine years and its vice-chairman in 1971-2.

For around 30 of these years I followed Neil's career probably closer than anyone. I certainly wrote more about him. I saw his first game with Trinity, and almost all of the others he was to play. I saw his first Test match, and was with him at Workington when he played his first game as loose forward after a career at centre. I was with him at his lowest - when injury not only kept him out of a fourth Wembley final but captaincy of Britain's World Cup team to Australia. I penned two testimonial brochures about him, and in the history of Trinity I wrote in 1973 almost five pages were devoted to him. No other player went above two.

This all started when I was joint editor of the Trinity programme in the early 1950s. I started printing the players' records match by match, and later included their career records. This was quite an easy weekly task, but when the teenage Fox arrived it quickly became far more extensive. Not only was there a need to look up existing club records for tries, goals and points, but eventually it required a similar trawl amongst rugby league's all-time record breakers.

Through these years Neil and I have become firm friends and it is a real delight not only to know that his legendary career will now be set down in this biography but also to be able to contribute to it. This book offers those of us who were fortunate enough to see Neil in majestic action a chance to savour many memories, but also it will offer the younger generation of rugby followers the opportunity to read of a player whose remarkable career over four decades will surely never be equalled.

I ended my introduction to his testimonial brochure in 1979 with these words: "His is a truly remarkable career and one, which, over the years, has seen changes. His change of playing position meant a change in style and, of course, there have been changes in the rugby league laws and in the patterns of play. But the person himself has not changed. Neil Fox remains a modest and true sportsman; an ambassador not only for rugby league but for all sport whatever its style and code."

Twenty-six years later, I could not alter one word of that. May this book bring its readers as much pleasure as the 'Big Fella' himself brought both to officials and supporters of the great game of rugby league over so many years. In a way this book is a means of saying 'Thanks for the memory' to Neil, and to wish him, Molly and their family good health and happiness in the years to come.

John Lindley

Special tributes

"It has been a delight and privilege to have played with and be associated with Neil for almost four decades, for he is one of the all-time greats of rugby league."

David R. Garthwaite
Managing Director
H.B. Clark & Co. (Successors) Ltd

"Neil will go down in history as one of the greatest rugby league players of all-time and one of the very best rugby players to come out of the North of England. He will also be remembered as a nice man! It is a privilege to have known him for so many years."

Phillip Hodson
Chief Executive Officer – Oval Insurance
Chairman – R.P. Hodson (Holdings Ltd)

Neil Fox, Robert Gate and London League Publications Ltd would like to thank David Garthwaite and Phillip Hodson for their backing in the publication of this book.

Author's note: One of the things which I most dreaded when I began this book was to find that there had been an error in Neil's grand total of points – accepted now as 6,220. Sometime down the years someone might have misplaced an odd goal or try, or credited him with one or two that were not his. Fortunately, Neil's records for Wakefield Trinity, covering the vast majority of his points, had always been kept scrupulously accurately by John Lindley and Terry Kelly, who produced excellent testimonial brochures for Neil in 1966 and 1979 respectively. Thankfully, everything added up.

The major problem with Neil's assault on the record was not in his own figures, although for a long time the 50 points he scored in South Africa for the Lions in 1962 were a bone of contention among record keepers, the problem was in the figures of the previous record holder, Jim Sullivan. The best guesstimate for Sullivan was 6,206, but there was much suspicion that that figure was too high and included friendlies. In 1979, Neil was declared the official world record holder, the RFL accepting the Rugby League Record Keepers Club's research that Sullivan's total had been 6,005. Unfortunately, by then Neil had long since passed Jim's figure. Retrospectively, it was ascertained that he had scored his record-breaking points for Huddersfield at Doncaster on 4 December 1977.

Unfortunately again, the figures were still slightly flawed. In 1987, the author and Paul Ogden, a Wigan enthusiast and record keeper, finally produced the now accepted figure of 6,022 points for Sullivan. Neil actually set his world record when he kicked his second goal in Huddersfield's 16-5 win at Halifax on 27 December 1977. Neil and Jim Sullivan's figures have been a stimulating trial and tribulation to generations of record keepers. Let us hope we have got it right.

Preface

I didn't ask for this job. I would never dare to approach someone as famous and revered as Neil Fox and ask if he would like to relay his story via me. Actually I wouldn't dare approach anyone, never mind Neil Fox. So it came as quite a surprise when Peter Lush told me that London League Publications were keen to produce a biography of Neil and would I be interested in working on it with the great man – Neil, that is, not Peter? That was 18 months ago, 18 months of hard work, 18 months of wondering if the Halifax to Wakefield buses would turn up anything like on time so I could spend days on end trawling through the microfilms of the *Wakefield Express* at Balne Lane Library, which, for those unacquainted with the Merrie Citie, is next door to Her Majesty's Prison Wakefield. There were times when I began to wonder who had been sentenced to hard labour, me or the neighbours? Then I remembered. They don't sentence criminals to hard labour any more.

Another thing that worried me was Neil. How would I get on with him? Would he take me seriously? Would I take him seriously? I don't know why I was worried. Experience down the years has taught me almost invariably that even the most eminent men I have encountered who have played rugby league have been approachable, amiable and open. Neil fulfils all those descriptions. I still have not encountered anyone with a bad word for him. Eric Ashton, Neil's centre partner and captain on the 1962 Lions tour, told me quite simply, "I can't speak too highly of Neil, as a man or a player" - and I, for one, will not argue with Eric.

I can honestly say that while this book has taken 18 months of hard work to prepare, Neil has made that time an enjoyable experience. It has been a pleasure and an education to share his company, his memories and his thoughts. It appears to me that Neil was not only a supremely gifted rugby league player but that his approach to anything in life has been marked by the right instincts, the urge to act decently and with only his best efforts and intentions. Neil has taken the compilation of this book very seriously. He is blessed with a good memory, a sharp brain and an eye for detail. He is also blessed with a conscience and good manners. For the protection of his grandchildren he told me he did not want any swear words in the book, even from Freddie Trueman. If any have crept in it will be the author's fault!

Neil must have been pretty exhausted by the time he brought down the curtain on a professional career extending over almost quarter of a century and 828 first class matches. I think I know how he felt. I have read accounts of every one of those games in the *Wakefield Express*, the Bradford *Telegraph & Argus*, the *Hull Daily Mail*, the *Yorkshire Evening Press*, the *Pudsey News*, and *Huddersfield Daily Examiner*, not to mention various other newspapers, trade papers and periodicals. Actually, I tell a lie – there was a Trinity game at Workington which was not on the microfilms. However, as I also read the 'A' team reports and multiple versions of accounts of all Neil's major finals, semi-finals and representative matches, I reckon the grand total is near the thousand mark.

In a book such as this, about an icon such as Neil, it is difficult to avoid superlatives. It goes with the territory. Neil's career was built on superlatives. It is impossible to think of Neil without thinking of records. The words 'records' and 'Neil Fox' were probably made for each other. However, after the past 18 months I know that Neil was not just a superlative rugby player but is a superlative man. In that time he has never let me down, never failed to do anything he said he would do, never acted without consideration, never complained and never dodged any questions. He and the lovely Molly have fed and watered me, fussed over me and ferried me to and from their home in Kirkhamgate in order to catch those dreaded Wakefield to Halifax buses. The best tribute I think I can offer to both Neil and Molly is the knowledge that, like the Good Samaritan, they would never walk on the other side of the road if someone needed help. I know we will remain friends and I hope this book will at least come somewhere near to being an adequate and fitting tribute to one of rugby league's greatest players and best possible role models.

Robert Gate
Ripponden, September 2005

Thank you

Many people have contributed to the compilation of this book, other than its subject, the author and the publishers.

I am particularly grateful to David Garthwaite and Phillip Hodson for their support and generosity in regard to this project. Neil is fortunate indeed to have friends like these two gentlemen.

Thanks also go to David Hinchliffe and John Lindley for providing the forewords to the book, while Neil's friend, long-time admirer and career-recorder Terry Kelly has provided a variety of welcome services during the course of its preparation.

Deserving special acknowledgment is Kenny Smith of Photomakeovers, Westfield Road, Horbury. Kenny, another ardent fan of Wakefield Trinity, has helped to enhance this book through his painstaking and intricate work on the vintage colour images within the book and on the cover. I know he has worked long and hard on our behalf. Anyone requiring similar services would benefit from visiting his web-site (www.photomakeovers.co.uk).

Material for the chapter on Neil's time in New Zealand in 1975 has been supplied by Bud Lisle and Bernie Wood. Bernie has gone to considerable time and trouble, I am sure, to provide reports of every match in which Neil played for the Marist club and for Wellington in provincial rugby league. Without that help it would have been impossible to chronicle Neil's exploits in Kiwiland.

Stuart Evans, the York rugby league historian, afforded invaluable assistance in supplying his scrapbook material on Neil's time as a player at Clarence Street. Peter Fox, Neil's brother, was equally useful in providing scrapbook material for Neil's time at Bramley. Tony Collins, the RFL's archivist, provided welcome access to official documents, to much archive information on Neil's sojourn at Hull Kingston Rovers from the late Mick Taylor's carefully compiled scrapbooks, and on the 1962 Lions tour. I am grateful too for the words of wisdom and anecdotes gleaned from interviewing Eric Ashton, Ian Brooke, Peter Fox and Ken Rollin, all men of immense stature and reputation within the game of rugby league and all clearly full of insight into Neil's character, temperament and extraordinary abilities. Graham Chalkley, Graham Morris, Mick Rhodes and the *Huddersfield Examiner*, Brian Robinson, the *Wakefield Express*, Ron Smith and Stuart Smith have also helped in various ways.

Most of the illustrative material in this book has come from Neil Fox's own private collection and some from the author's private collection. If any copyrights have been infringed, it has been unintentional.

Finally, it is fitting that acknowledgement should be made to the men who covered Neil's career in the *Wakefield Express* - John L. Allen, A. G. (Geoff) Cudworth and Frank Jeffrey. Between them they must have written millions of words about Neil and his playing colleagues. Their opinions, articles, criticisms and match reports have been a real illumination on Neil's life and times and a constant delight in the researching of this book.

Robert Gate

London League Publications Ltd would like to thank David Garthwaite and Phillip Hodson for their generous backing for the book. This has enabled us to produce a book that we hope fully reflects Neil's magnificent career and contribution to rugby league.

We would also like to thank everyone who supported Robert in compiling the book, including providing research material, photographs and being interviewed. On the production side, we would like to thank Michael O'Hare for his sub-editing work, Steve McCarthy for designing the cover and the staff at Biddles Ltd, our printers.

We would like to thank Robert for all his efforts and for approaching this book in his usual meticulous way.

Finally, we would like to thank Neil for his full support for the project, and for devoting so much of his time and memories to the book.

Dave Farrar and Peter Lush

nine or 10 I would take him and Don to the top rugby field so I could practice my goal-kicking. They stood behind the posts and I kicked at goal. I wouldn't let them place the ball to kick it back to me as that would take too much time. Instead they had to drop-kick it back to me because it was quicker. I think that's why they both became such fantastic drop-kickers. I also used to get them to play me at touch-and-pass and because I was so much bigger than them, I used to knock hell out of them, even if it was touch-and-pass. That toughened them up and made them effective tacklers.

Of course, in our family all the talk was about rugby so Neil would not have been able to get away from it, even if he wanted to. He became an immense points scorer. He was strong, much stronger than any other centre, and he was difficult to tackle, even for the biggest of opponents. He had brilliant hands, all three of us had. I would say he was phenomenal at every skill in the book, and he was clever and a hard trainer. Some people say he was a bit slow but he wasn't. In his early days at Trinity there was only Freddie Smith who was faster than Neil over 80 to 100 yards. When it comes to judging the really great players you have to take into account longevity at the highest class. Neil fits all the criteria. Sometimes you'll hear someone say about a promising young player, 'That lad is going to be another Neil Fox'. Well, they're wrong because there'll never be another Neil Fox. Since Neil retired, nobody has approached his class and quality as a centre. The only regret Neil has is that he never got to partner Lewis Jones in the centre. He did everything else. Neil never got interested in golf or anything else, so he kept fit to play. I always used to tell players they should play until they died, if they were fit and keen enough. Once you've finished, that's it. Neil lasted such a long time because he was so fit and strong."

Peter is the subject of one of rugby league's most-told anecdotes. His version is: "In the 1961-62 season I was playing for Batley when Wakefield came to Mount Pleasant on the back of 23 straight wins. We had no chance, according to the critics. But I knew we could upset them. Trinity were a team full of stars and were led by Derek Turner, a great loose-forward and a very hard man. I told the Batley lads, 'We can win this. All we've got to do is follow my plan. Don't worry about Turner. I'll take care of him. Rest of you take care of our Neil. I told them to pile into him any time he got near the ball. You couldn't give our Neil any chances or he'd make you pay. Derek got really rattled because Trinity just couldn't score and I was all over him all the time. In the end he got so mad, he flung the ball down and yelled at me, 'Come on then. I'll take thee and thi team on myself.' We drew 0-0."

Another man who holds Neil in high esteem is Eric Ashton, one of Neil's most formidable rivals on the field. Eric played directly opposite Neil on many occasions for Wigan and partnered him in test matches in England, France and Australia. The pair's sublime centre partnership was a major factor in Britain's brilliant Ashes-winning team down under in 1962. He recalls, "In my era the two best centres I played with or against were Neil and Alan Davies. Neil was always a difficult opponent. He was something like Mal Meninga in more recent times. He had tremendous power but he also had the skills and was a good footballer. He was always in the right place at the right time. You can't say that about many players. When I played with him it was a pleasure. Because he had so much ability he was easy to play with. He was a brilliant centre for any wingman. He took the knocks rather than give them bad ball. No matter what anyone says, he did not lack pace. Neil played the game fair and square but he wasn't an angel. He could give you a whack – but within the rules. Another thing to his credit was his ability to remain unruffled despite provocation. His temperament was excellent. In fact I can't really find fault in Neil as a player or as a man. He is a genuinely nice man and still keeps in touch with me. On tour we socialised a lot together. When you are away for such a long period you do form cliques. Neil and I spent a lot of time with Gerry Round and Alex Murphy. We seemed to go everywhere together. In later years I even bumped into Neil in Tenerife. It was a lot less painful than bumping into him at Central Park or Belle Vue."

Ian Brooke was another who had the pleasure of playing alongside Neil in the centres with Trinity and the problems of playing opposite him with Bradford Northern. Ian says: "I have known Neil for over 40 years now and we are best friends. He is as genuine, honest and trustworthy as anyone I have ever known. Neil is a few years older than me and when I got into the Wakefield team as a teenager, he looked after me. I was about 12 stones 3 pounds and Neil was a lot bigger but our styles seemed to complement each other. I always had pace but Neil's pace was deceptive. He travelled faster than most people appreciated. Because he was so big and powerful, opponents had to get up on him as soon as they could. Otherwise they would be smashed out of the way and Neil would make play for others. I really enjoyed playing alongside Neil. Just being with him gave you a lift. Even when things were not going well, you knew that Neil could change things. He would get the team out of tight situations with a break or he would score a try or make one for someone else. It was different when you had to play against him though. I remember one game for Bradford when I couldn't wait for the referee to blow for time. I used to think I was quite good defensively but that day Neil steamrollered me. He threw me around like a rag doll. Anyone who says he wasn't a good tackler doesn't know what they are talking about. Ask anyone who played against him.

I remember playing against Warrington. Neil intercepted and went 60 yards for a try. No one got anywhere near him and Warrington had some fast players. He could take interceptions because he had the ability to read a game. He had a quick mind, which gave him an edge. Like all really top quality players, Neil knew what to do instantaneously in any situation. That's one of the things which set him apart. I'll always be grateful to Neil for the help he gave me in my career. When I was just getting into the team he and Derek Turner always looked out for me. They would soon sort out anyone who got too rough with me. I remember a game against Leeds which was very physical. Their Australian full-back Ken Thornett laid me out with a stiff arm and the referee, I think it was Charlie Appleton, did not even give us a penalty. Not long afterwards Ken was carted off with a cut eye!"

Neil is quick to point out it was not him who gave Thornett the cut. As the Leeds full-back was being taken off, Neil recalls: "Ken yelled back threateningly at Derek Turner, 'Just wait until you come to us on Boxing Day!' When Boxing Day arrived I remember saying to Derek: 'Have you forgotten what Thornett said last time we played Leeds?' Of course, I knew Derek would not have forgotten. He had a long memory. So I asked Derek where he wanted me to put the kick-off. He said, 'Just send it somewhere near to Thornett'. In those days the full-back would stand near his own posts so I kicked the ball straight, so it landed in front of him and he had to come forward collect it. At the same time Derek was heading straight for Ken. There wasn't much threatening from Ken then because he was so alarmed he banged the ball straight into touch on the full."

In April 1979, near the end of Neil's career, Trevor Watson of the *Yorkshire Evening Post* wrote: "Inevitably big Neil has had his critics, mainly from opposing fans. It has often been said he was too slow but on countless occasions he was in the right spot to turn a break by a fast man into a try. Put that down to footballing sense. He always looked after his winger as a centre and since his move to the pack his distribution has improved. There must be very few players... who have not fallen at some time to the Fox dummy."

A more recent appreciation of Neil comes from former Great Britain coach Maurice Bamford's book, *Play to win: Rugby League Heroes*, published in 2005. He writes: "Neil Fox was a massive centre... and because of his physique spectators, mostly those of other clubs, who wished with all their heart that Neil was playing for them, thought that the big man lacked that yard of pace. I say garbage to that. Study the number of long-range tries he scored and then say that he lacked a yard – not in a million years. His great career achievements are a testimony to his brilliant ability."

Bamford also touches on Neil's temperament in saying: "Neil Fox MBE. The fabulous Neil Fox is so unassuming that he may well be embarrassed if he heard anyone call him that, but he was terrific." Eddie Waring wrote succinctly in 1969: "Neil Fox rarely shows his feelings. He was not emotional." Seven years prior to Eddie writing that, Bill Fryer, a witty and acute sports writer for the *Daily Express*, who occasionally made forays into rugby league from his normal territory of soccer, interviewed Neil and wrote: "Neil Fox, a coalmine's gift to Wakefield Trinity, would be in the £100-a-week class if rugby league chaps were on soccer wages. With some of the polish and power of a Denis Law, the football brain, the good temper, and the deadly left boot of a Tom Finney, and the scoring knack of a Jimmy Greaves, Neil has most of the things that matter, if not the lot. Yet listen to this astonishing attitude (for a Yorkshireman!) to wages: 'We are all on the same pay at Wakefield, latest comers to the team and Test men. And that is how it should be. That's what makes team spirit. I know. I was at the bottom once myself'. How this superb specimen can be so unassuming is beyond me."

Neil's own views on why he was so successful confirm much of what the above luminaries have conveyed. He says: "Obviously, I had a head start with my family. Although I had a good deal of success as a schoolboy player, it was only when I was about 15-years-old that I began to think seriously about a rugby career. I knew I didn't want to be down the pits for the rest of my life. I never even thought about playing amateur open-age rugby league as option. I just thought that the next step for me would ultimately be to play professionally. When I did sign for Wakefield I knew that I needed to increase my pace. So I trained at home in Sharlston, kicking and sprinting, as well as doing the normal team training. If I had missed a training session because of work I would run home from Snydale pit to make up for it. I think this regime put an extra two or three yards on my pace. I wasn't a bad trainer but I don't think I was the best. There were aspects of training like lapping that didn't appeal to me. To improve my kicking I would always arrive before the others to get some practice in. I always listened to Peter and Don. They gave me a lot of good advice. They told me how to run at players, how I should run with my head up and never crouch while running, and not to stop when I hit the defenders, just keep running. Also, they told me not to leave my arm out either. If I was going to hand off do it quickly, as if you flapped your arm about before handing off, it was easier for tacklers to bring you down. I became very good at using my hips, thighs and shoulders to knock people off.

I was lucky at Trinity to have Ken Traill as our coach. Ken allowed me to develop my own style. Ken would try to modify an average player's style but he let the lads who had football brains get on with the job their own way. Even on tour no one tried to get me to do things any other way than my own. I'm sure it is a lot different nowadays. Another thing that never happened was anyone trying to influence our diet. I always had fish and chips for dinner before a match when we were at home. There were no diet sheets like today. Perhaps I would have been a better player if we had had them!

Another thing that helped me was the great staff we had at Wakefield. Apart from Ken Traill, we had the benefit of past players like Jack Booth and Harry Wilkinson on the coaching staff. If we were injured we had Paddy Armour to put us right. Paddy was a real godsend as a physiotherapist. He had all sorts of qualifications and was brilliant at getting players fit after injury. Paddy was principal of the School of Remedial Gymnastics and Recreation Therapy at Pinderfields Hospital in Wakefield. He had a great deal of experience, lectured on Football Association courses, wrote manuals on dealing with injuries and was one of the top men in his field. He was appointed as trainer/physio to the 1966 Lions – I think he was the first qualified masseur to tour. Paddy was one of the first people I got to know at Belle Vue, a nice man, who was friendly, well-liked and completely trustworthy. It certainly helps when a club has backroom staff of that calibre."

Alex Murphy's assertion that Neil's temperament was ideal certainly has a resonance for Neil, who says: "I never suffered from nerves. When I first got into the professional game I tended to be a bit quiet in the dressing-room before a game but soon realised that a bit of fun relieved the tension. For some players the pre-match was a trial though. Gerry Round, for example, was always sick before a game and other players had their own ways of coping with the stress. I was lucky, I suppose. I never worried about an opponent. I suppose that meant I was a confident player. Referees could make or break a game but you had to respect them all, although obviously some were better than others. The three best I came across would be Eric Clay, Billy Thompson and Fred Lindop. Eric had a forceful, domineering personality. He more or less demanded respect and he got it. He would not tolerate dissent. He knew he was in charge but he also knew the players and how to handle them. Billy was a very fair man. He always knew what was going off and allowed players the chance to get even if something had happened. But after that they had to keep in line. Fred was more like a modern referee than the other two and very fit. In the latter part of his career he was the best in the game. The RFL should have stuck with Fred as controller of referees. In my day referees always came into the bar and socialised with the players and fans. Nowadays they tend to go around in a team and don't fraternise."

On centre play Neil's view is that "the objective is to make space for your winger. You have to pick the right option as soon as you have possession. Once you have got the winger away you should always follow up for a return pass or for a kick. Centres need to have a good understanding with their wingmen. I was big enough to take two or three tacklers and still make a pass. Centres can also use kicks. I would occasionally put in a grubber-kick for the winger. Sometimes I would kick high over the full-back. If you did it right it gave you time to get to the landing spot and you would have a 50-50 chance of getting the ball. Defence was also a big factor. You need to get up quick on the opposing centre and, if possible, drive him infield to allow the coverers to snuff out the attack. Good defence comes with experience. Sometimes people asked me why I didn't do as much tackling as Alan Skene, when he was so much smaller than me. That was why: who would they rather run at - me or Skeney? At Trinity I was lucky to have Harold Poynton at stand-off. We understood each other. I could rely on Harold not to put me under pressure."

Neil was one of rugby league's greatest goal-kickers. He kicked left-footed in the classical toe-end fashion and with his weight and power gave the ball a mighty thump. He recalls: "I always went through the same routine no matter how far I was kicking and only took a short run. I was always confident about my kicking. Some players lack confidence and it shows. I always reckoned I could score from half-way but didn't try from inside my own half too often. I would attempt really long shots if the conditions or the game warranted it though. Scores were lower and games tighter and goals often meant the difference between winning and losing. I think goal-kickers used to attempt more than they do today and often we played in ankle-deep mud. That's maybe why we missed a few."

So there was much more to Neil Fox than just a points-scoring machine. And it all began in Sharlston, a small village near Wakefield with a great rugby league tradition...

2. Beginnings

Neil Fox was born on 4 May 1939 at 6, Albert Terrace, Sharlston, a council house now long since demolished. Neil was the third son of Thomas and Stella Fox. Tommy Fox was an incomer to Sharlston, spending the early part of his life a couple of miles down the road in Featherstone, but Stella Fox, née Schofield, was a Sharlston girl born and bred. Tommy's working career had begun as a pit head winder but he took over as steward at Sharlston Working Men's Club around 1945, assisted by Stella. It proved extremely handy once their sons were born that the WMC abutted the Sharlston Rovers Rugby League ground. In later life the pair became caretakers of Sharlston County Primary School, where Stella was responsible for cleaning.

Neil recalls: "Our parents were great. They had to bring up three boys on paltry wages but we never went short. Although my mother was stewardess at the club, really she worked full-time looking after us. One thing was certain - there would be a new rugby ball every Christmas. The whole family was rugby mad. We used to practice kicking and catching on Sharlston Rovers' pitch nearly every day. It wasn't far to go – just over the wall. My oldest brother Peter organised these sessions. My other brother Don and I would have to punt or drop-kick the ball back to Peter, who was constantly honing his goal-kicking skills with us as his retrievers. I suppose that was a good grounding for us and why we all became so good at kicking. Being the youngest I also got knocked about a bit. Peter used to have us trying to tackle him, and then it would be Don's turn, and then mine. Obviously being the youngest I would get knocked down a lot. Once, having been clobbered and feeling sorry for myself, I went to complain to my mum but she just told me not to be so soft and get out there again."

Sharlston was, and still is, not a big place. On the map it shows up as a piece of small print wedged between Wakefield and Featherstone straddling the A645, the road which then runs further eastwards to the ancient town of Pontefract. To the south of the village the A638 from Wakefield leads eventually to Doncaster. However, it is a mistake to tell people who come from the village that they are merely Sharlston folk. They may well tell you forcefully that they really come from Sharlston Common, New Sharlston or Old Sharlston. According to the 1991 census Sharlston's population was 2,448. Two years later Sharlston Colliery closed, ending an era which stretched back to 1865, although mining in the area certainly went back even further. The village had depended on the pit for almost 130 years as its major employer. Its closure was a hammer blow to the local populace.

The Sharlston in which Neil and his brothers had been nurtured half a century earlier was a traditional, close-knit, mining community. People knew their neighbours and a good proportion of the wider village population too. Few people went very far from their birthplace and apparently even fewer attempted to rise above their station. Whichever way it was viewed, the pit was likely to dominate their lives.

Apart from mining, Sharlston was known for its prodigious production of rugby players. The village was hardcore rugby league territory with a vengeance. Rugby union had been played in the area in Victorian times but the birth of the Northern Union galvanised competitive rugby in the north of England and Sharlston Rovers embraced the new game wholeheartedly in the first decade of the 20th century. Rovers were the inaugural winners of the Dewsbury, Wakefield & District League in 1906-07, won the Yorkshire Junior Cup for the first time in 1923-24 and were defeated finalists in 1930-31 and 1938-39. In Neil Fox's pre-teenage years Sharlston Rovers won the trophy in 1947-48 and 1948-49 and were runners-up in 1951-52. A whole string of Sharlston players became professionals, the most notable being Jonty Parkin, a scrum-half of pure genius for Wakefield Trinity, who led Lions tours to Australasia in 1924 and 1928, and who was one of the first inductees into the Rugby League Hall of Fame in 1988. His successor as Trinity's scrum-half was another native of Sharlston, the indestructible Herbert Goodfellow who represented Yorkshire and England, won at Wembley with Trinity in 1946 and gave the club 18 years (1933 to 1951) of exemplary service. Parkin and Goodfellow were, however, only the tip of the Sharlston rugby iceberg.

In such an environment it was hardly surprising that Neil would catch the rugby league bug. His family connections with the game ran deep. Stella Fox was a keen supporter of Featherstone Rovers, her father Harry Schofield had played for Normanton and her brother Thomas was a Sharlston Rover. Tommy Fox had been a professional with Featherstone Rovers, playing at loose-forward. He made his first-team debut at Post Office Road on 3 October 1931, when Rovers walloped Bradford Northern 47-0, a game notable for full-back George Johnson's creation of new club records with 10 goals and 23 points. Amazingly, Johnson's records would last until 8 February 1964, when Don Fox broke both in scoring 12 goals and 27 points in a 60-4 victory over amateurs Stanningley in the first round of the Challenge Cup. Featherstone Rovers finished 19th of 28 clubs in the league table in 1931-32 and Tommy scored three tries in 24 appearances. He would play only two more first-team games for Rovers - at Wakefield Trinity on 26 August 1933 and at Hunslet on 2 February 1935. Thereafter, Tommy played as an amateur for Normanton and finally, perhaps inevitably, for Sharlston Rovers.

It was Tommy and the Rovers who provided Neil with his first real recollection of rugby league. Tommy had come out of retirement and had helped Sharlston reach the first round proper of the Rugby League Challenge Cup in 1946. In those days first round cup ties were played on a two-leg basis and Rovers were drawn against Workington Town, who had just entered the Northern Rugby League in that first post-war season. Tommy was skipper of the Rovers for the Workington ties and played at prop. Eleven of his colleagues were under 21 but he was 37. The first leg, on 9 February, was staged at Sharlston's ground, popularly known as 'Back o' t' wall'. Rovers played out of their skins to win 12-7, which added considerably to the excitement which had already been evident in the weeks leading up to the game. Rovers had trailed 2-4 at half-time through two penalty goals from the great Cumbrian full-back Billy Holding against one kicked by second-rower George Green. It was Green who put Rovers ahead in the second half when he converted his own try. Green then converted left centre Dooler's try for Rovers to lead 12-4, before a try from Workington winger George Armstrong concluded the scoring.

Sharlston secretary Tom Chalkley had big problems prior to the game. He had to arrange for a wooden fence around the playing field and to fix a temporary grandstand. Rovers did not have any turnstiles and Chalkley was unable to borrow any. A newspaper reported that "eight stalwart miners guarded the entrance to make sure everyone paid". These were hard times, rationing of all goods following the war was still extremely stringent. The report added: "All the Sharlston team are miners, and it's the women of the village who make them smart for their games. They mend the torn jerseys with patches from their dresses and for the cup ties have stitched home-made numbers on the backs".

Newspaper reports mentioned various notables who were present. They included Jim Brough, the 1936 Great Britain tour captain, who had lectured the Sharlston players on tactics prior to the game. Also present was Jonty Parkin, who put his hand into his pocket and gave each Rover 10 shillings. The colliery management magnanimously gave the players a pound each and granted them a Saturday holiday in recognition of their achievement. The Sharlston vice-president, George Tucker, "to whom the club is financially indebted", according to the *Wakefield Express*, paid for a new match ball.

Neil says of the occasion: "I was only six and saw the game through the legs of the spectators. There seemed to be thousands there. They were coming in across the fields from every direction. They were coming from Crofton and Streethouse and all over the place. I remember before the game workmen had fastened posts which extended above the six feet-high wall down one side of the field and attached a screen of sacking all the way along. That was so people did not get a free view. I don't think they expected kids to pay though. I don't remember any of the actual play but I do remember Billy Ivison, who was playing under an assumed name ('Smith') as a trialist centre for Workington, coming off injured. He asked our Peter to go and get him a packet of cigarettes and Peter did, although the shopkeeper shouldn't have served him! Of course, none of us knew at the time that 'Smith' was Billy Ivison. I think it was Peter who found out later who he was. Billy became a brilliant loose-forward for Workington and played for England but he did not get the test honours he deserved. Amazingly, I played against Billy before he retired. Believe it or not, I played against a few people who my dad played against."

After the match the teams, officials and visitors – some 150 people - were entertained at the Working Men's Club, which must have given Stella Fox a few headaches. The official attendance for the game was 1,200, the gate receipts being about £70, yet there were over 10,000 in attendance for the second leg up in Cumberland on 16 February. Rovers put up a good show but lost the game 2-16, thereby going down 14-23 on aggregate. However, Sharlston were still ahead on aggregate as the game entered its final quarter and it was only a burst of 14 points in the last 15 minutes which finally killed off the gallant amateurs. The *Wakefield Express* noted: "The Rovers stuck to their more experienced opponents like grim death, and at one time it really looked as if they were going to make history and enter the second round". Tom Chalkley had been hard at work, having had permission from the Ministry of Transport to book three motor coaches to transport the team and its most fervent supporters to Workington. Tommy Fox had really impressed the Workington officials, who apparently asked him to sign for them and were only dissuaded when they found out his age. Tommy retired from rugby league permanently not too long afterwards, leaving his three sons to take up his mantle.

The oldest, Peter Gerald Fox, "the brains of the outfit", according to Neil, developed into a loose-forward good enough to win Yorkshire Schools (under-15) honours, scoring his side's only try in a 24-3 loss to Lancashire at St Helens on 24 April 1948. He progressed to Sharlston Rovers and was in their 1951-52 side which reached the final of the Yorkshire Junior Cup losing 5-8 to Middleton Old Boys. Even as a teenager it was evident that Peter had a keen analytical insight into rugby league and thought deeply about how it should best be played. His career as a professional player, from 1953 to 1966, took in Featherstone Rovers, Batley, Hull Kingston Rovers and Wakefield Trinity. It was as a coach, however, that Peter really earned lasting fame. He coached at the highest levels, taking charge at various times of Yorkshire, England and Great Britain. In domestic football he coached Featherstone Rovers, Bradford Northern, Bramley, Leeds and Wakefield Trinity. In the precarious world of rugby league coaching it was a measure of his quality and ability that Peter was almost never unemployed as a professional coach in a career which stretched from 1971 to 1995. Among his many achievements, taking Featherstone to Wembley in 1973 when they won, and 1974, when they were runners-up, and guiding Bradford Northern to consecutive Championships in 1979-80 and 1980-81 may have been the most significant, although his creation of a promotion-winning side at Bramley in 1976-77 on meagre resources was arguably as meritorious.

The middle brother Don – a couple of years older than Neil - was an outstanding schoolboy scrum-half, who played in Yorkshire County Schools trials and was reserve for a Roses match. His small physique at this stage in his development was the only thing which kept him from emulating Peter's achievement of winning a Yorkshire Schools cap. By the time he signed for Featherstone Rovers in April 1953 Don had developed into a 5 feet 9 inches 13-stoner and was the biggest scrum-half in the league. Between leaving school and joining Featherstone, Don had dallied for a time as a centre-forward for Sharlston's soccer club before returning to rugby with Streethouse Intermediates and then Featherstone Rovers Intermediates. His career at Featherstone developed into a catalogue of broken records and by the time he left Rovers in September 1965 he had rattled up club career records for tries (189), goals (594) and points (1,492) in 368 appearances, not to mention numerous other records in individual matches and seasons. Don had also represented Yorkshire, England and Great Britain. He was a match-winner and a delightful footballer.

Small wonder, then, that with such a family background Neil should aspire to becoming a professional rugby league player. His first taste of organised rugby came at Sharlston School, which took pupils from four to 15 years of age. Prior to starting to play for the under-11s, despite being just eight, Neil had received a good grounding in the game, playing many impromptu matches at 'Back o' t' wall' and on the village green. All the Fox boys attended Sharlston School, Don and Neil for their entire school careers. Peter was the exception, going to Wakefield Technical College at 14 to study to become a draughtsman.

Although there was a world war raging for his entire infancy, Neil has little memory of the period, beyond recalling that everything was rationed, especially sweets. He also remembers that omelettes were made with egg powder and water, because eggs were thin on the ground. He certainly did not know who was fighting who in the wider world. Of school Neil says, "I remember not liking school on the first day I went and I took a while to settle in but eventually everything was fine. School was only about 100 yards from home. Obviously, I don't remember too much from my earliest days in Sharlston but I do recall there were some funny goings-off. I used to wonder why large groups of men sometimes gathered in the village and often ended up being chased by policemen. The men used to scatter when the police arrived. I later understood they were gambling. There were also tales of fights being organised between blokes who just wanted to fight each other.

Anyway, at school I enjoyed all the sport – rugby league in winter and cricket in summer. The sports master was Job Musgrave, who we all knew as Joby. Mr Cartwright and Mr Nuttall also helped with the teams. Joby eventually became the headmaster. His wife Betty was also heavily involved. She took the teams to matches all over the region by local bus services and she always made sure that we got home all right, organising our movements to the last detail. Our parents never had to worry about where we had got to. Joby and Betty were lovely people. They took a real interest in both my own and Don's career, giving us a push when we needed it. They seemed almost like a second pair of parents to me, and to lots of other kids.

I always played in the backs at school – wing or centre in the under-11s. I settled at centre though by the time I was playing for the intermediates [under-13], aged 11. I was in the seniors [under-15] by the time I was 13 years old. Sharlston was classified as being in the Castleford district as far as school sport was concerned so we played teams from places like Cas, Featherstone and Normanton. There were some good players at school but the two best left early. Ken Rollin, who played with me at Wakefield for years and then went to Leeds, was a super half-back. He left school to go to Wakefield Tech when he was 13. Ken and I were good mates - we were best men for each other's weddings. Ken was a brilliant batsman who played for Wakefield Cricket Club in the Yorkshire Council competition and could have been a top cricketer. Tommy Smales was another mate. He went to Normanton Grammar School but I later played with him at Featherstone Intermediates. Tommy became a good loose-forward, who played for Wigan and Barrow before winning the Challenge Cup with Featherstone Rovers in 1967. Later he coached Dewsbury to the Championship. Tommy was another good cricketer, an all-rounder. We played cricket together for Streethouse and Old Sharlston. Tommy's wife Kay was bridesmaid for my future wife, Molly. A couple of other Sharlston lads, Tommy Mullaney – Joe Mullaney's cousin – and John Berry, signed for Castleford. Another of my best mates, Terry Caldwell, was the first Sharlston boy to become a professional soccer player, I think. He played left-back for Leeds United, Huddersfield Town, Barrow and Carlisle, so we didn't all become rugby league players. He also went to Normanton Grammar School.

When I was 14 Joby put me and another boy, Gordon Chalkley, into the Castleford Town Schools trial. Gordon was the brother of Barry Chalkley, who signed for Hull KR. Gordon's younger brother Graham played as a professional with Dewsbury and Batley. Our Peter and Joby took us to the trial by car but left early, giving us our bus money for the return journey. I was told that I had been picked for the Town team after the trial but Gordon had not, although he had been the better of the two stand-offs. The day ended badly though. Due to a bus strike we had to walk from Castleford to Sharlston.

At the same age I played in the Yorkshire Schools trial at Burton's Sports Club in Leeds. After it I was selected as Yorkshire captain. The headmaster at Sharlston, Ezra Butterfield, was really pleased and announced the news at assembly. He asked me if I wanted to go home to tell my parents but I said I would wait until home time. So he wrote a letter, which I still have. It says: 'Dear Mrs Fox, Neil has been made captain of the Yorkshire Rugby Team. I wanted him to come home and tell you this morning but he wouldn't. He has made a great name in Sharlston history by this and it is, although I don't deserve it, a great honour for the school. May we thank you for this splendid lad, the very sight of whose modest presence gives us so much confidence and faith in our job. It is boys like him who make a school - not us – and I wish we had a thousand like him. Mr Musgrave, who has the same modesty, is delighted and it is a great honour to him too. I assure you of my eagerness at all times to reciprocate the goodwill which you and your husband and all your boys have shown towards us. Yours very sincerely, E Butterfield.'

It was to be the first really big game I played and, just as when Peter played for Yorkshire, the game was at St Helens. We lost but one thing I remember well was that the two Lancashire half-backs were a bit special – Alex Murphy and Jackie Edwards! The Yorkshire team had some good players too. Ken Hirst, who was only 13, was a tremendous winger. Ken would play alongside me at Wakefield for years. Barry Simms was the hooker and he eventually played for Leeds and became a test player. Dave Elliott became a half-back for Hull KR and played stand-off as a professional for Yorkshire in the same side as me. John Taylor, who toured with me in 1962, was in the pack. He was Hull KR's first tourist. Two of the other forwards, Marshall and Jack Fanning later joined Hunslet but the best forward we had was a lad called Whittaker, who was brilliant. He signed for Batley. I was picked for the following game and this time we beat Cumberland at Dewsbury."

Neil had no opportunity to play association football at Sharlston School until his final year there. A trophy, the Gaskell Cup, had been created for competition between four local schools. Sharlston was deemed too small to compete alone and so was combined with schools from Crofton and Walton. Neil was selected as centre-forward for the combined XI which met Horbury School in the first game. Neil recalls that the teacher's advice to the team consisted of shouting, "Get the ball to the corner and get it lobbed in to Neil Fox". The game plan obviously worked. Neil's team won 9-1 and Neil scored all nine. In the final, against Ossett, the combined schools won 3-1, Neil having to be settle for two goals. Neil recalls that "Sharlston, Crofton and Walton schools each held the trophy for four months. Colin Oldroyd, the sports master at Crofton, organised the team. He later became headmaster at Middlestown and not so long ago was Lord Mayor of Wakefield". Soccer may have lost a second John Charles, when Neil turned professional as a rugby league player.

Cricket also held attractions for Neil. He describes himself as "an all-rounder, a fast bowler and a big hitter". He captained Sharlston School and was in Sharlston Cricket Club's second XI aged 14. At 15 he had progressed to the first XI. He later joined Streethouse CC but gave up the game at the age of 21, more or less when he got married. He was good enough to win a Yorkshire Schools trial at Savile Town in Dewsbury but it was not a happy occasion for him. It was a miserable day and he batted about number eight. The umpire told him there was only one more over to face and, after Neil took a single off the second ball, that was the end of his chance to show what he could do with the bat. It was equally frustrating when his team was in the field. He was given just one over and that was that. He was not picked for the county and was not at all impressed by the selection procedure.

Yorkshire lost to Derbyshire, however, and Neil was selected for another trial at Dewsbury, but decided not to go. When the headmaster called upon him to explain himself, Neil said he had wanted to play for the village team instead where he had scored about 20 runs and taken 4-19 against men. That did not wash too well with the head, however, and Neil admits to feeling awful about his poor attitude after the head had finished with him. His remorse was exacerbated when the head told him the trial he missed was a Yorkshire versus The Rest game. Among the players were Jackie Birkenshaw, who later played for Yorkshire, Leicestershire and England, Barry Stead, later of Yorkshire and Nottinghamshire, and Tony Leighton, who won fame as a prolific centre-forward, scoring 167 goals, with Doncaster Rovers, Barnsley, Huddersfield Town and Bradford City.

Neil enjoyed life at Sharlston School but did not, as he says, "get his exams." This could have had something to do with a decision made by the teaching staff during the time he was in Joby Musgrave's class 6, when he was about 13. Neil remembers: "For my last two years at school I didn't really do any schoolwork, or at least that's how it seemed. One day a girl came into our classroom and announced that 'Mrs Butterfield wants to see Neil Fox'. Mrs Butterfield was the headmaster's wife and took class 9, the top class. When I got to Mrs Butterfield's room, she said, 'I understand you can sing'. I replied, 'I can't'. I did not know what was going off. Mrs Butterfield told me to sing something and then informed me that 'you might be coming into my class'. And I did, for two years. It appeared I had been commandeered for the school's operatic society. I was roped into all the plays and choruses but did not have any big parts. Some of the time Mrs Butterfield had me taking groups of other boys for cricket or rugby. It certainly helped me with my sport. I actually think some of the teachers must have realised my potential and decided that this was the best way they could help me along the path to success."

Neil's future appeared to be mapped out when he left school at 15. He says, "It was obvious I would go to the pit. Everyone got jobs with the Coal Board. I was sent to an interview at Snydale Colliery and the family suggested that I should ask if I could be an apprentice joiner. Our Don was an apprentice joiner at Sharlston Colliery and he spent his entire working life there. Anyway, they said there were no joinery apprenticeships going but I could become an apprentice fitter. That meant that I would get one evening at night school and a day off work each week to attend Whitwood Technical College.

Pit work was not always compatible with rugby schedules, but later on I was lucky. I moved to Sharlston Pit, where they asked me if I would like to become a pipe fitter for miners working at the coal face, but it also meant that I only worked from 9.00am to 4.30pm. In other words, I did not have to do shifts. It suited me better. I remained at Sharlston until I got married and then went to work as a fitter for the Central Electricity Generating Board (CEGB) at Wakefield Power Station."

Leaving schools rugby league behind, Neil joined Featherstone under-18s as a 15-year-old. "The only other choice," he says, "was Wakefield Trinity under-18s but there was never much chance of that. I was a Featherstone Rovers supporter because of my family connections, but when I was a boy I really preferred to watch Huddersfield with their great players like Johnny Hunter, Dave Valentine and Dick Cracknell. Lionel Cooper, their big Australian winger, was my favourite though. I would always try to see Huddersfield when they played in our area at Cas, Featherstone, Wakefield or Dewsbury. At Featherstone, Harold Moxon was the coach of the under-18s. He was very strict and kept good discipline. I think lads need it at that age. We never got any real coaching at school – we just played. I did not do much kicking at Featherstone. Ronnie Armitage, the captain, did the kicking. I played just over a year there and we won all three trophies available to us – the Yorkshire Cup, the Castleford Cup and the Leeds & District Cup. We played all the under-18 sides of the Yorkshire clubs, Hunslet and Leeds usually being the toughest opponents. At the end of my first year most of the team turned professional for Featherstone, although winger Brian Shaw went to Hull KR. They would have been getting something like £200 for signing. I was still young so stayed with the under-18s and was made captain at the start of my second season even though I was only 16. There were only Tommy Smales and myself of the previous year's team left but some good new players came in like Terry Clawson and Jimmy Hunt, who would go a long way."

Although most people assumed that Neil would eventually sign for Featherstone Rovers, like his father and brothers before him, he would not tread that familiar path. Deadly local rivals Wakefield Trinity had designs on the strapping young centre. Neil recalls: "I came home one evening from college and got the shock of my life. My mother told me not to go to bed early that night because Wakefield Trinity were coming round to sign me at 10 o'clock! That was a surprise to me. A lot of folk thought I would be going to Featherstone Rovers to join my brothers but they had never got round to approaching me formally. My mum and dad sent for Peter to come to the negotiations. Eddie Thomas, the Trinity secretary, and committee-man George Wood arrived at the house and offered me £300 at first. We asked for £500 and Eddie gasped: 'We can't pay money like that'. But they did. In the end it was agreed that I would receive £500 plus £100 per annum for the next three years, even if I never got into the first-team. I was also to be given £100 if I represented Yorkshire and £200 if I played for Great Britain. So, in effect, the contract was worth £1,100. The Trinity officials said they would not even need to go back to the club committee and a couple of nights later they came round with the cheque. I was happy enough but Peter asked, 'What about a benefit season for Neil after 10 years?' Eddie Thomas balked at that. Trinity didn't want to put that into the contract but we did get him to sign a piece of paper agreeing to it."

Neil's signing for Trinity was announced in the *Wakefield Express* on Saturday, 15 October 1955. It was given good coverage, a long column not usually considered necessary when juniors were signed. It was headed "Trinity surprise Featherstone" and subtitled "A

13

young centre signed". It read: "The announcement on Wednesday from Wakefield Trinity's headquarters that they had signed on 16-year-old Neil Fox, a centre threequarter with the Featherstone Rovers Juniors team, caused much surprise, especially in Featherstone. There everyone anticipated that Neil would follow his two brothers, Donald and Peter, and become a Rovers player but things did not turn out that way.

It can now be disclosed that on Tuesday of last week, Neil was expected to present himself at the Post Office Road ground and sign forms to attach himself to Rovers playing strength. But Trinity officials moved stealthily and, last week, two of their representatives had a late night visit to Sharlston – at the home of Neil – and obtained his signature.

The secret was well kept although by Monday some Rovers supporters and officials confessed subsequently to having experienced a feeling of apprehension, indicating that something was not going to turn out as they anticipated. They were right, of course, for Neil had become a Trinity player!

Fox, who is six feet in height and over 13 stone, has been a conspicuous player with Featherstone Juniors and has distinguished himself particularly with his goal-kicking."

The announcement finished by stating that Huddersfield had also been interested in signing Neil and relating that three weeks previously on 24 September there had been "a flurry of Foxes at Fartown". Neil had been engaged in an under-18 curtain-raiser prior to the Huddersfield versus Featherstone fixture, in which his brothers played for Rovers' first-team. Neil had amazed the crowd by landing a goal from near the half-way line and news of it had been relayed to Peter and Don as they were preparing for their match. It was noted that although both Peter and Don had similar opportunities in the senior match, neither managed to emulate their younger brother's feat. Neither would have been too bothered, however, as Rovers won a splendid match 25-18, Don grabbing a hat-trick and Peter landing a goal.

Neil remembers: "I had heard there had been some interest from Huddersfield but they had never formally approached me. Oddly enough, even though Huddersfield was my favourite team, I don't see how I could have joined them. The travelling problems would have been awful for me in those days. Catching buses from Sharlston to Fartown would probably have taken about three hours and with having to get up for 5 o'clock shifts at that time, I just would not have been able to mange it."

A week following his signing the Wakefield Trinity programme for the game against Hunslet on 15 October 1955 gave Neil his first of hundreds of write-ups: "Neil Fox is the younger brother of Peter Fox and Don Fox. Neil is another hope of the future for he is as yet only 16 and a half years old. With a weight of 13 stones and a height of close on six feet he should develop into a powerful centre. If he proves to be another of those capable of gaining a first-team place whilst in his middle teens, he will be an immediate help to the club."

The writer was surely a prophet.

3.   1955-56: No rush

Signing for Trinity meant an end to Neil's career with the Featherstone Intermediate (under-18) side. Neil was a big lad but his family was unsure about whether he was ready to play senior rugby league. Trinity promised that they would not rush Neil, who was only 16 years and five months old when he signed for them on 7 October 1955. They said they would not even push him into the reserves. He was, however, immediately made captain of the Wakefield Trinity Intermediate team and made his debut for them at Doncaster on 5 November. The first chance that Trinity supporters had to see him in action at Belle Vue did not occur until 12 December when Trinity under-18s met Rossington.

Within three months Wakefield's promise not to rush him was a memory. He was told he was required for the 'A' team game against Hull Kingston Rovers at Belle Vue on 7 January, 1956. Neil remembers: "I nearly did not make that game. I just could not get a bus from Sharlston. I waited an hour but all the buses which passed were already full. I began to panic and went to phone the club. Paddy Armour, the Trinity physiotherapist, answered. Of course, I did not even know him and he said, 'Just get here as quick as you can', which wasn't very helpful. I ran home – my parents were the school caretakers by then – and grabbed Peter's bike and pedalled off to Belle Vue. I got there 20 minutes before kick-off time, shattered and sweating. There was an amazing crowd, maybe two or three thousand. I don't know if it was because of the big build-up the local paper had given me. I can't remember the score but I soon realised I was playing among old pros, men not boys. They were fitter and faster than anything I had come across before but I did cope."

Trinity 'A' won that game 40-0 and Neil had an entirely satisfactory start to his career among the professionals. Fog, which had shrouded Belle Vue for two days, lifted on the morning of the match but, according to the *Wakefield Express*, it was still "a miserable, dank afternoon with the cold and an oppressive heavy atmosphere thrown in – oppressive that was until Wakefield's back division clicked into gear". The star of the match was Albert Mortimer, Neil's co-centre, who scored a hat-trick and was "streets ahead of any other player on the field". After four minutes stand-off Aubrey Houlden "broke through for Mortimer to romp over near the posts. Fox kicked the goal". By half-time Trinity led 18-0 but Neil had ceded the kicking duties to full-back Dennis Ripley. In the 67th minute Trinity conjured up a spectacular try. It was described thus, "Harry Burton tore away on the right and, when challenged by his opposite, McLeod, kicked inside. Mortimer, striding up in support, relayed the ball out again to Fox, who had no difficulty in finishing off the move". Neil would on countless occasions display that characteristic attribute of being in the right place at the right time. A few minutes later Burton sprinted through again, kicked inside and there was Neil racing onto the ball before sending a lovely scoring pass to second-rower Frank Haigh.

After his debut with the reserves Neil never went back into the under-18 side. He played most of the remaining season in what was probably Trinity's most successful 'A' Team in history. He recalls: "I was lucky to play in such a team. It was a young side but there was also experience in it. The coach was Johnny Jones, who had been Trinity's stand-off when they beat Wigan at Wembley in 1946. The captain was Jack Booth, a big, strapping forward, who had played almost a decade for Trinity and won Yorkshire County honours. He was not the greatest player but everyone looked up to him and he protected the young players if there was any bother. He would say to the opposition, 'If that's the way you want it, that's how you can have it', meaning that he would sort out anyone who took advantage of his young charges. Jack was a big inspiration."

Trinity's 'A' Team swept aside most of their opponents with an open, exciting and efficient style of play during the 1955-56 campaign. They finished third in the Yorkshire Senior Competition behind Halifax and Hull, but in piling up 701 points were easily the most prolific team in the league. Apart from Neil, some other promising players joined the club in loose-forward Les Chamberlain from Leeds amateur rugby league and Streethouse half-back Johnny Bullock. In January, Trinity sold their first-team captain and 1954 World Cup winner Don Robinson to Leeds for £3,000, because they were in financial straits. Part of the deal brought a young winger, Fred Smith, to Trinity. He and Neil soon struck up a deadly partnership on the right flank, which would in due course be replicated in the first-team. There were plenty of other good players in the reserves such as centre Aubrey Houlden, who had been a sensational schoolboy player, while forwards Albert Firth and Dave Lamming would also make a big impression later on. Another of the forwards was Mick Lumb, who would ultimately become club chairman at Dewsbury.

Neil's second game for the reserves was also against Hull KR at Craven Park on 14 January. Trinity won 21-8 and the *Wakefield Express* noted: "A remarkable feature was the fine goal-kicking of Neil Fox who, despite the heavy ground conditions, was successful with six out of seven attempts". Things went swimmingly for Neil in the 'A' Team, where he continued to score freely and impress with his fine temperament. He was selected as a reserve for the first-team against Featherstone at Belle Vue on 2 April, when both his brothers played, Rovers winning 15-4. On 7 April Neil gave the coach and selectors another nudge with six goals in a 30-7 home victory over Halifax 'A' in a fine exhibition of kicking.

A run of bad results and the customary end-of-season fixture pile-up gave Neil his chance in the first-team and he made his debut at Keighley on Tuesday, 10 April. It was a strange looking Trinity team. Skipper Bob Kelly was unavailable, because he had been selected to play for Great Britain against France at Odsal the following day. Keith Holliday was also in the Great Britain team at stand-off partnering Don Fox. Trinity actually played three debutants, Neil for the injured Colin Bell, Mick Lumb for Kelly and Fred Smith for the unavailable Harry Burton. The team for Neil's first-team debut was: Gerry Lockwood; Fred Smith, Don Froggett, Neil Fox, Eric Cooper; Aubrey Houlden, Johnny Bullock; Derek Harrison, John Shaw, Mick Lumb, Les Chamberlain, Ray Jacques and Colin Clifft (captain).

Neil's memories of the game are limited: "It was a miserable day and we lost". Keighley beat Trinity 9-5 but accounts of the game indicate that the 2,500 spectators got their money's worth. It was indeed an awful evening, the local paper saying "It was a pig of a night" but despite the pitch being "an expanse of mud with miniature lakes dotted here and there, it was a fast and often exciting affair". The *Wakefield Express* reported: "Not unnaturally, the individual upon whom eyes were most often glued was Fox. It was hard lines for him that in this, his first appearance in the Trinity elite team, he should have such wretched weather to put up with. Nevertheless, his play afforded considerable satisfaction. For a youth, he did not appear to be as lithe as many expected, but there was no disputing the presence of football ability. Partnering the sturdy youngster, so full of promise, it was reassuring to see the continued splendid form and confidence of Froggett and on both wings Trinity were well served." Losing 3-0 at half-time, Trinity took the lead after 42 minutes when Lockwood converted a try by Clifft. The try was "a pulsating affair. The loose-forward followed up a judicious kick through by Fox and touched down between the posts after a thrilling race".

Neil was left out of the team four days later when Colin Bell returned to the centre as Trinity hammered Huddersfield 26-2 at Belle Vue. On 18 April, however, he was surprised to be informed by Eddie Thomas that he was to play at full-back in the return fixture at

Huddersfield. He recalls: "I had never played full-back before but Mortimer and Lockwood were both injured and there was no goal-kicker so I was selected. Huddersfield had some good backs. Johnny Hunter, Peter Henderson and Mick Sullivan played in the threequarters that day but I was relieved that Lionel Cooper, my favourite player, had retired. I wouldn't have liked to try to tackle him."

The Fartown crowd witnessed an extraordinary turn around in fortunes. Trinity led 13-2 after 25 minutes and 15-5 at half-time. Neil had excelled in booting five penalties and converted a fine try by Bell but Trinity disintegrated in the second half to lose 19-15. The criticism from 'The Pinder' (John L. Allen) in the *Wakefield Express* was withering. He wrote: "The collapse was as disgusting as it was sensational ... Their inept performance was staggering... The rot that has set in among the Wakefield players was unbelievable – another example of tactical blundering and lack of a steadying influence that was astounding to behold." Neil was excused: "Seventeen year-old Fox, in the unfamiliar role of full-back, did not let the side down... His fielding of the ball was good and those six goals out of six attempts in the first half (he missed one after the interval) left a deep impression on the crowd."

The debacle at Fartown was Neil's last taste of senior football for the season but there was plenty of excitement and kudos for him as the 'A' Team concluded its campaign. On 21 April, as the first-team played and won its last game at Dewsbury, Neil booted 10 goals and claimed a try as Trinity 'A' butchered Hull 'A' 41-9 at Belle Vue in the second round of the Yorkshire Senior Competition Challenge Cup. It was reported that "the try scored by Fox was an amazing affair. He took a kick at goal with a penalty award, and when the ball rebounded from an upright, he was in position to catch it and cross the line with a bewildered defence looking on!"

The 'A' Team was demolishing all-comers. On 8 May, four days after his 17th birthday, Neil claimed a try and a goal as York were beaten 31-15 in the Championship semi-final in a fast, thrilling encounter. The victory took Trinity into the Championship Final on Monday, 14 May when they met the league leaders Halifax at Belle Vue. It was a keen struggle which ended in a somewhat flattering 17-4 win for Trinity. Twenty minutes from time Neil made the game safe with a wonderful long range penalty. He kicked four goals from "a host of difficult chances", to add to tries from Fred Smith, Frank Sweeney and Dave Lamming and it was noted that "Fox and Sweeney earned credit for some sterling defensive work". At the close of the game the Yorkshire chairman, Jackie (J. S.) Barritt, presented captain Jack Booth with the Yorkshire Senior Competition Championship Shield and Neil collected his first winners' medal in professional rugby league. Generously, Jack "thanked Halifax for their share in a game of rugby league football at its best".

Neil did not have long to wait for his second medal – just four days in fact. The following Friday the Yorkshire Senior Competition Challenge Cup final took place at Belle Vue with Trinity completing a famous double with a 31-0 success against York 'A'. It was not as easy as the scoreline suggested, however. Trinity were penned in their own quarters for long spells but broke away to score several spectacular tries. Neil's wing partner Fred Smith set the pattern in the first minute when he dashed 75 yards, swerving past three defenders to score a blinder of a try under the posts. He completed his hat-trick in the 35th minute with a repeat performance. The other winger, Frank Sweeney crossed twice and Albert Firth and Aubrey Houlden also scored. Neil's contribution was five goals.

So, barely 17, Neil completed his first season in the professional ranks. He had two winners' medals and had made a couple of first-team appearances. Life was pretty good. He remembers those times with affection but was also aware that he was not the finished article: "It was great. I was being paid for doing something I loved. We got £4 for a win and £2 for a defeat in the 'A' team. That was about the same as my wages. In the first-team it was £7 and £4 and everybody got the same. That's what being a singer did for you! Mind you, I knew that I had to work on my speed. Everything seemed so much faster playing with grown men. I knew I could get faster although I also knew I would never be a 10 second man for the 100 yards. I was not getting any sprint training at Belle Vue though. There were no specialist sprint trainers. We were mostly practising ball skills, doing exercises or lapping. Later on we did have some sessions with Derek Ibbotson, the world mile record holder, and Mike Agostini, a top sprinter, who advised the backs. Freddie Smith was the fastest man at Belle Vue until Berwyn Jones arrived.

The first-team trainer when I arrived was Johnny Malpass, who had been a good footballer with Featherstone and Wakefield. He was a good pro and a decent coach. The first and second teams trained separately and the older players were not particularly helpful to the younger ones. I suppose they thought that their places were at stake. They were all right when you played in the first-team though. All in all, I was quite happy with how my first season had gone. The rugby did not clash with work and I was building up to about 14 stones. The only real problem was that I recognised my deficiency in pace and knew I had to do something about it. So I began my own regime of training at Sharlston and prepared myself for the following season.

During the summer of 1956 I was selected to go on the Rugby Football League's special course for promising players. I also went the following year. The courses were held at Bisham Abbey and were the brainchild of Bill Fallowfield, the secretary of the RFL. The coaches were Alex Fiddes, Russ Pepperell and Laurie Gant. Fiddes and Pepperell had been international players with Huddersfield and Gant had been a Featherstone and Hunslet forward, who had played second-row for Rovers at Wembley in 1952. They were really clued up and imparted a lot of knowledge, sound coaching advice and hints about technique to the eager young players. Three Trinity lads went the first year, Johnny Bullock and Kenny Rollin being the other two, and Kenny went again in 1957 with me. I had a lot of respect for Laurie Gant, both as a coach and as a player. Later Laurie became very helpful to me. He was a cobbler and he used to modify my boots. I was a left-footed kicker and he used to build up my left boot with a square toe, so theoretically I could kick the ball better. It meant I could get a better contact with the ball. Remember, balls were heavier in those days, especially when they got muddy or wet. You needed a hard-toed boot to kick toe-ended. My right boot was always softer. Some years I would get through four or five left boots because eventually the toes would just curl up. Laurie would modify two pairs of boots at a time. I would have the left boots and Gerry Round, who was a right-footed kicker, would have the right boots. Laurie helped quite a few players like that."

Wakefield Trinity 1955-56
Wakefield Trinity finished 17th in the league: P36, W17, L19, For 581, Against 539
Fox scored 6 goals, 12 points for Wakefield

Date	Opponent	Score	Fox	Crowd
10 Apr	Keighley	5-9		1,798
14 Apr	**Huddersfield**	26-2	dnp	4,374
18 Apr	Huddersfield	15-19	6G	3,495
21 Apr	Dewsbury	29-7	dnp	2,233

4. 1956-57: First team progress

Trinity finished 17th in the Northern Rugby League Championship in 1955-56. Their crowds had been falling for a few years and the club was losing money. Even so, there was genuine optimism at Belle Vue at the start of the 1956-57 season. Trinity had a core of good players - Colin Clifft, Bob Kelly, Keith Holliday and Don Froggett were internationals - and, of course, they had a rich crop of youngsters in the double-winning reserve team.

Although Neil had made his first-team debut, he was not really considered as ready for regular first-team duty. Ahead of him in the pecking order for the centre spots were a number of players. The season opened with Don Froggett, a fine player with an unfortunate propensity for picking up serious injuries, and Colin Bell, a former Queen Elizabeth Grammar School pupil, as the centre pairing. The brothers Albert and Frank Mortimer were also more likely to be drafted into the side before Neil, although Frank was really making a big name for himself at full-back.

So it was the reserves for Neil as the season opened. At least everyone – reserves and first-teamers - was pleased that Trinity had new baths and changing rooms for the new campaign. However, there was one thing which irked Neil. He remembers: "When I was asked to train with the first and second teams, Trinity said all training gear would be supplied. After each Tuesday training session all the shirts, shorts, socks and jockstraps were collected and put in a cupboard. The same gear was taken out for the Thursday sessions. It was never washed, was damp and didn't smell good. Then they washed it on the Friday, ready for the following week. Our coach Ken Traill eventually changed this. He made Trinity wash the kit on Wednesdays and Fridays so we could train in clean clothing."

The 'A' team carried on where it had left off – winning handsomely. Neil piled up the points, one of his best performances occurring on 8 September, when he amassed 26 points in a 60-6 win at Doncaster. He kicked eight goals in a thrilling 31-30 victory at Hull 'A' on 22 September, but was missing a week later when Bramley 'A' were massacred 77-2 at Belle Vue. On 3 November there were eight goals and two tries for Neil when Batley 'A' lost 58-5 to the rampant Trinity reserves. He was making it hard for the selectors to leave him out of the firsts.

Meanwhile, Wakefield's first-team had fought their way through to the Yorkshire Cup Final. Neil remembers watching the final on 20 October against Hunslet at Headingley, when 31,147 attended. He says, "I don't care who scored the Trinity tries. What won the cup for us was a vital tackle by hooker Keith Bridges as Hunslet's giant prop Don Hatfield crossed for a certain try. Keith pinched the ball just before he was able to score." Trinity ran out winners 23-5 to take the trophy for the fourth time since the war.

The week after winning the Yorkshire Cup, Trinity were brought back to earth when Hunslet beat them 21-17 in the league at Belle Vue and then another defeat followed at Leigh. Another blow fell when loose-forward Colin Clifft was transferred to Halifax. Consequently, Neil found himself at right centre in the first-team for the visit of Swinton on 10 November. It was his first home game for the senior side and it proved to be one of the toughest games of the season, a match chock-a-block with excitement in which the lead changed hands four times. After 21 minutes Trinity trailed 5-2 at which point Neil scored his first try in senior football. There was an element of luck in the score but as usual Neil was there when it mattered. Peter Armstead put in a shrewd kick to the corner and the ball reared up wickedly. John Allen wrote, "Neil Fox raced through to touch down when most of the Swinton players on the spot could not just make up their minds what to do in such a circumstance. It was all done so quickly that there was reason for ring-side onlookers as well as on-the-spot Swinton players to be staggered." That was the first of Neil's 272 tries for Wakefield. Five minutes from time Trinity were 13-14 down before Ken Rollin won the game with a beautiful dodging run from half-way. John Allen was almost satisfied with Neil, reporting "The sturdy youth gave a most encouraging performance... Young Fox revealed some splendid form on attack but his defence was too susceptible". Neil got on fine with John Allen, who was always ready to give praise, where due, in his *Wakefield Express* columns, but equally ready to offer criticism, if necessary.

Neil retained his place for the next match at Featherstone, where he faced brother Don for the first time as a professional. Wakefield lost 20-21, Neil kicking three conversions and a penalty. He did well, however, Allen noting, "Particularly pleasing was the work of Neil Fox, whose strong, straight running and craft in drawing his man impressed the crowd."

On 10 December Wakefield Trinity met the Australians in a hurriedly arranged game, the last club fixture of the Kangaroos' tour. A 2.30pm kick-off on a Monday meant a low turnout of spectators and the Aussies fielded a second-string XIII. Even so, that game remains fresh in Neil's mind. He says: "I think that was just about the youngest team I ever played in, certainly in the backs. Ken Hirst came in for his debut as my winger and he was only 16. I was 17. The full-back was Ted Wilkins, an 18-year old, who had only played once before in the first-team. The half-backs, Kenny Rollin and Johnny Bullock, were 18 and 19, the other winger Fred Smith was 20 and Keith Holliday, my co-centre was not much older. What a day and what a marvellous win."

The *Wakefield Express* reported: "This was no namby-pamby affair of touch and pass! All the same no one could complain of the fare that was provided". Two men were sent off in the closing minutes. The Australian forward Norm Provan went for striking Peter Armstead. Provan had already been cautioned and so had Trinity hooker John (Joby) Shaw, who Neil recalls, told big Norm as he trudged off, "It's about time, you big silly bugger!" At that point George Philpott, the referee, turned to Shaw and said, "And you can go as well for swearing!" Joby's outburst cost him a three-match suspension, the disciplinary committee's sentence "for voicing his approval of the Australian's dismissal".

The game was a dramatic affair which got off to a spectacular start with a debut try from Hirst. Hirst's score followed a "60 to 70 yards gallop, including a moment when he nearly lost his pants when crashing through a tackle. The kick and follow-up for the touchdown thrilled every onlooker as much as it must have thrilled the ex-Morley RU winger". Neil converted the try and improved another try by Ken Rollin, who snapped up an opportunity when full-back Clive Churchill, playing his last game in England, dropped the ball near his own line. Johnny Bullock scored a third Trinity try straight from a scrum. Neil also had a try at the corner disallowed but pushed his goal tally to four with a couple of penalties. Both the Kangaroo half-backs, Connell and Johnston, claimed tries and Churchill booted three penalties, as Wakefield triumphed 17-12. The victory was hard-earned, Bullock missing the last 18 minutes with concussion and three of the Kangaroos suffering injuries. The crowd were unhappy with some of the Australian tactics, which included voluntary tackles, obstruction and illegally playing nine men outside the scrums at times.

After seeing off the Kangaroos, Wakefield fell 20-18 at home to Oldham, the eventual champions, in one of the best games of the season. Neil landed three goals, put Aubrey Houlden over for a try and played soundly, as Trinity recovered to 10-10 after falling 10-0 behind. The main talking point was a disputed penalty goal kicked by Oldham full-back Bernard Ganley from about 45 yards in the 45th minute. The touch-judges disagreed and it was left to the referee (50 yards away, behind Ganley) to decide that a goal had been kicked. Trinity's players admitted after the game that the ball had just cleared the bar.

A week later, on 22 December, Neil played in a game against Hull KR which the *Wakefield Express* described as "heard but not seen". Conditions were so dreadful – a steady downpour and mist – that only 390 spectators turned up and most of them hardly saw anything but ghostly wraiths flitting in and out of the murk. The training lights were turned on and scorers announced over the tannoy. The referee, Colin Whiteley, finally called off the farce after an hour with Wakefield leading 25-5.

Neil had his first experience of playing on Christmas Day, when Trinity made the short journey to Castleford. A victory was expected because Cas were rooted near the foot of the table but the men from Wheldon Road were not in the mood to give out presents. Neil salvaged a 14-14 draw for Wakefield when he piloted his fourth goal in the 81st minute.

At Whitehaven four days later Trinity lost 21-17 in a gripping encounter to a side which was unbeaten at home. Trinity were 15-12 behind at the interval but were warmly applauded for their enterprising display. Neil contributed a try and four goals. His try on the hour put Trinity ahead and was described thus: "Then came the greatest try of the game. Fox intercepted a Whitehaven pass on his own 25-yard line, burst clear of the Whitehaven team and raced the length of the field for a try under the bar to which he added the goal points". However, two tries in the last five minutes gave Whitehaven victory.

On 12 January another trip to Cumberland brought better fortune when Workington were vanquished 28-16, Neil bagging five goals but perhaps more importantly coming up against one of the most accomplished centres of the period, Eppie Gibson, who dropped a goal. It was something of a compliment for John Allen to comment, "Fox and Bell kept their opposite centres fairly quiet". Neil says: "Eppie was a great footballer, both in attack and defence. He was probably the best centre I encountered in my first full season as a pro."

Trinity had embarked on a seven-match winning run and things were going well for Neil, who was kicking plenty of goals and scoring tries regularly. Luck certainly smiled on him in a 39-13 home win against Castleford on 19 January when he scored a try and six goals. Trinity won easily but Castleford had only 11 men for the last 35 minutes. The *Wakefield Express* reported, "Some of the tries scored were worth going a long way to see but rivalling them for a place of honour was a slick effort by Neil Fox, who provided as great a surprise for his colleagues as he did for his opponents and an incident that provoked keen controversy was a disputed goal from a kick by Fox which appeared to send the ball sailing outside an upright". In this instance Neil missed a sitter under the sticks after a try by Fred Smith. The ball went outside the left post at crossbar level. Neil seemed amazed, hardly able to believe his own eyes, when the touch judges raised their flags and the referee awarded the goal. It said much that the Castleford players and even the Wakefield supporters protested long and loudly. Having missed five (or apparently six) of eight attempts at goal, Neil later prepared to take an angular 20-yard penalty. Whether he was unnerved by his own poor kicking or simply inspired, he suddenly changed his mind, tapped the ball forward, picked it up and proceeded to crash over for a try as the Castleford defenders toed the goal line. Then he missed the conversion.

At York the following week he had a stormer, despite being the youngest player on the field. He contributed two tries and five goals to Trinity's 28-19 win and would have had a hat-trick if he had not been tackled near the line after a 75-yard dash following an interception. 'The Pinder' wrote: "The lad with a great future has, very early in his career, started a habit-forming practice of gathering tries in a most unusual fashion. It is a style, too, that reveals high proficiency as an opportunist. For his first try he quietly snapped up a dropped pass by York's centre Smith, and was over the line, under the shadow of the cross-bar, in the twinkling of an eye! And for his second surprise item, he punted the ball high, followed up and regathered as it bounced out of the grasp of a surprised full-back to finally plant it down in a position from which he kicked his third goal a minute before half-time. It was very bad luck that Fox had not a better goalkicking record than only five successes out of 10 attempts which does him scant justice. His marksmanship and judgment of distance earned him the admiration of the crowd but, somehow, a capricious wind made him fail to find the mark with shots that were most deserving."

Trinity struggled to beat Bramley 18-13 at Belle Vue on 2 February. Neil kicked three goals but most interest was centred on Wakefield's new signing Bob Coverdale, a prop from Hull, who had cost a reported £2,000, a new club record. The signing of Coverdale, one of Great Britain's 1954 World Cup-winning heroes, was a welcome indication that Trinity would become a buying rather than a selling club. Neil was very positive about the capture, "Bob was one of our big signings. He did the work of two men in defence and was a willing worker under pressure. He really helped to stabilise the pack".

On 9 February Wakefield opened their Challenge Cup campaign with a home tie against York. The bookies had Trinity as 33-1 outsiders to win the trophy but they moved easily past York, 37-15. Neil's first Challenge Cup tie yielded him five goals and a try, the latter scored after he chased a kick by Eric Cooper, gathered and "gallantly bashed his way past loose-forward Dawson" when seemingly well held. The following week, in the league, Trinity edged home 6-5 at Hull KR in diabolical conditions to record their seventh consecutive victory. Neil scored a barging try from a well-timed Coverdale pass but failed to convert Joby Shaw's try from in front of the posts.

That missed conversion did not matter, but Neil was to suffer his first major setback a week later when, to all intents and purposes, Trinity had a sure-fire passage to the third round of the Challenge Cup with an easy looking home game against Blackpool Borough. Blackpool had been listed along with Batley, Bramley and Castleford as 1,000-1 shots for the Cup. Nobody was going to back them to win at Belle Vue.

On the scheduled day of the match, 23 February, the Wakefield players assembled at The Three Houses Hotel in Sandal for a pre-match meal and team talk. Neil recalls that they "were so confident that most of the talk was speculation about whom they might play in the third round". Meanwhile snow began to fall heavily and the talk turned to whether the game would actually go ahead. It did not and it was rearranged for the following Wednesday afternoon, when, astonishingly, more than 11,000 fans turned up. It turned out, as Neil says, "A disaster for me and the club. Both sides scored three tries but I didn't kick any goals and we lost 11-9." Neil's discomfort was made especially acute because Trinity had scored a try two minutes before the end and appeared to have snatched a draw. The local paper reported, "The position of the try provided Fox with an easy shot at goal. But to the audible groans of Wakefield spectators he failed just as he had done with four earlier kicks". It was no comfort that Blackpool had also missed four attempts at goal, as the one that full-back Davies did kick made all the difference.

Neil, Colin Bell, Albert Firth and Les Chamberlain felt the wrath of the selectors and were dropped. Neil found his form in the 'A' team, kicking nine goals and scoring a try in a 39-2 home romp against York 'A'. He played in four games for the reserves in March piling up 23 goals and four tries and was restored to first-team duties on 6 April, when he scored a try in a 14-13 success against York. Frank Mortimer had taken over the goal-kicking responsibility for the remainder of the season, however. Frank, who had played full-back in the first two Ashes tests, landed 107 goals for Trinity in the season, falling four short of Sam Lee's club record set in 1938-39. He did, however, set a club record with 229 points.

The campaign ended well for Wakefield who won their final seven games and finished eighth in the league, their highest position since 1945-46. Towards the close of the season Trinity splashed out another club record fee of £3,000 for Featherstone centre Don Metcalfe. Neil could have seen Don's signing as a hindrance to his own ambitions but says: "It was great to have Don in the team. He was very experienced and there was no better tackler than him. He had played at Wembley in 1952 and came from a good footballing family. I did not see how he could fail to succeed and help our team to get better".

Neil's first full season as a professional rugby league player taught him a lot. He realised there could be disappointments and criticism as well as excitement and praise. He had claimed 138 points for the first-team and 163 points for the 'A' team. He was already attracting attention from the wider rugby league fraternity, the *Rugby League Gazette* noting: "Trinity, in their team-building, have shown a long-term policy that has paid full dividends and the hope is there for the future with such talented teenagers as centre Neil Fox, scrum-half Ken Rollin and flyer Ken Hirst. This season Fox has been the side's outstanding back, showing himself to be a most powerful and intelligent player". Much, therefore, was expected of him from the club and the fans. Neil hoped he could deliver but was probably not expecting to go so far so fast in the next couple of years.

However, his career may have been cut prematurely short, if fate had not been kind to him. He recalls: "In the summer of 1957 I was 18 and I got my first car, a Standard 8. After passing my test I changed it for a Morris Oxford. It was during this time that a few of us decided to go to Hornsea for the Bank Holiday weekend to see Ken Rollin and his mates who were staying in his auntie's caravan. I was still a cricketer then, having played with Sharlston and Streethouse after I had left school. I carried on playing until I got married in 1961. Anyway, we were playing cricket at Carlton, near Goole, so it wasn't too far to go to Hornsea after the match. We were joined by two of our other mates, Ken Holmes and Albert Mace, who went in another car. We booked in a bed and breakfast, went to see Ken the next day and spent most of the day playing football, rugby and cricket on the beach.

Later that day Frank, Ken, Albert and I were going back home, but decided to go to Bridlington for the night. We had a few drinks and then left to go back home. On the way home Ken and Albert were following us. We got to a roundabout and we went down one road and Ken and Albert went down another. Ten minutes later we went down a hill and round a bend. But the car hit the kerb and over it went into a field. Luckily, we got out of the car without any injuries, but the car was wrecked.

We walked to the nearest village which seemed miles away. We called at the first house which had a light on to ask for help. A man came to the door and we told him what had happened. He was very helpful and asked us if we knew anyone who lived near. We told him if he could get us to Kenny at Hornsea we would be grateful and pay him for taking us there. It was quite a long way but he said he would drive us there and refused to take anything off us. He dropped us off at the camp site. We went to the caravan and knocked Kenny up. It was about two in the morning. The lads didn't believe us about the car and how we had been given a lift from the Bridlington area.

Next day we went back to a garage in Brid and explained the situation. We took them to the crash scene. When they saw it they couldn't believe we had not been injured. Insurance was sorted out and they arranged to have the car taken back to the garage for repairs. It would have been better to have scrapped it. It took two months to repair. We got back to Wakefield on the train. The worst thing was having to tell mum what had happened. She got over it though. When I got the car back I sold it privately and then bought my first new car, a Ford Popular costing £525 from South Yorkshire Motors in

Wakefield. Coincidentally, the garage rep at that time was Albert Dobson, a famous former rugby league referee."

Wakefield Trinity 1956-57
Wakefield Trinity finished 8th in the league: P38, W23, L14, D1, For 747, Against 545
Fox scored 10 tries, 54 goals, 138 points for Wakefield

Date	Opponent	Score	Fox	Crowd	
18 Aug	**Bradford N**	10-7	dnp	2,789	
20 Aug	Hunslet	14-16	dnp	7,000	
25 Aug	Bramley	7- 8	dnp	3,317	
27 Aug	**Whitehaven**	26-11	dnp	2,361	
1 Sep	**Leeds**	36-15	dnp	12,962	YC1
4 Sep	Dewsbury	15-14	dnp	3,750	
8 Sep	**Workington T**	9-15	dnp	5,606	
10 Sep	**Huddersfield**	13-11	dnp	12,927	YC2
15 Sep	Oldham	15-19	dnp	13,778	
22 Sep	**Leigh**	37-18	dnp	5,932	
25 Sep	**Halifax**	14-13	dnp	17,297	YC Semi
6 Oct	Swinton	18-22	dnp	5,200	
13 Oct	**Batley**	35-9	dnp	4,090	
20 Oct	Hunslet	23-5	dnp	31,147	YC Final (at Leeds)
27 Oct	**Hunslet**	17-21	dnp	6,569	
3 Nov	Leigh	17-24	dnp	5,096	
10 Nov	**Swinton**	16-14	T	4,210	
17 Nov	Featherstone R	20-21	4G	7,500	
24 Nov	**Hull**	13-32	T, 2G	5,112	
27 Nov	Keighley	12-0	2G	777	
8 Dec	Huddersfield	6-22	3G	6,455	
10 Dec	**Australians**	17-12	4G	3,381	
15 Dec	**Oldham**	18-20	3G	4,909	
22 Dec	**Hull KR+**	25-5		390	
25 Dec	Castleford	14-14	4G	2,559	
29 Dec	Whitehaven	17-21	T, 4G	4,622	
5 Jan	**Dewsbury**	23-10	4G	3,540	
12 Jan	Workington T	28-16	5G	3,645	
19 Jan	**Castleford**	39-13	T, 6G	3,134	
26 Jan	York	28-19	2T, 5G	5,256	
2 Feb	**Bramley**	18-13	3G	4,397	
9 Feb	**York**	37-15	T, 5G	12,277	Ch Cup 1
16 Feb	Hull KR	6-5	T	3,087	
27 Feb	**Blackpool B**	9-11		11,142	Ch Cup 2
2 Mar	Hull	24-18	dnp	8,349	
16 Mar	Leeds	12-22	dnp	20,452	
23 Mar	**Keighley**	36-8	dnp	5,585	
3 Apr	**Leeds**	8-18	dnp	11,874	
6 Apr	**York**	14-13	T	4,120	
10 Apr	Bradford N	23-9		2,251	
13 Apr	**Doncaster**	28-12		2,533	
20 Apr	Batley	31-4	dnp	5,000	
22 Apr	**Featherstone R**	18-7	dnp	9,131	
23 Apr	Doncaster	30-11	T	1,200	
27 Apr	**Huddersfield**	20-14		6,450	

+ Match abandoned after 60 minutes

5. 1957-58: Breaking records

"Our ambition, of course, is to finish in the top four and to do it by playing the type of football our local supporters like and demand – the open game, fast and clean... We are ready to enter the transfer market for ready-made players of top class only." Those were the ambitions espoused by the newly installed Wakefield Trinity chairman, Les Pounder, in an interview with the *Wakefield Express* on 17 August, 1957, the opening day of the season. It made good reading for Trinity fans but so did the paper's summary of crazy rumours going round the Merrie City at the same time. Trinity were apparently going to sign Johnny Whiteley, Hull's great loose-forward. Barrow's test centre Phil Jackson was also about to come on board, along with a mysterious new second-rower. Oldham's ferocious back-rower Derek Turner, a local lad who had played as an amateur for Balne Lane, was also definitely going to join the club soon. Johnny Wardle, another son of Wakefield, was certain to take over the Yorkshire Cricket captaincy from Billy Sutcliffe and, of course, pigs could fly. To be fair, the rumour about Turner was eventually borne out – 18 months later.

Some things were true, however. Keith Holliday had been appointed captain and Peter Armstead vice-captain, while Arthur Fletcher, after close on 300 appearances for Trinity, and Colin Bell had retired. Colin, an Oxford University graduate, had qualified as a doctor and consequently had other routes to follow. It was less competition for Neil, however, who also faced no rivalry from the unfortunate Don Froggett, who was to miss the entire season with knee trouble. Even so, Neil was left out of the first-team for the first three games of the season, Frank Mortimer and Don Metcalfe being allotted the centre berths, as Trinity opened in terrific form with victories at Barrow and at home against Hull, followed by a draw against champions Oldham.

While the first-team were walloping Barrow on 17 August, Neil was personally walloping Hunslet 'A' at Belle Vue, where Trinity 'A' won 40-7. Neil scored 22 points (four tries and five goals) and moved the local reporter to write: "Many onlookers shared the view that after Fox's display of good backing-up, strong running and using his weight and speed effectively... he might develop into a top class loose-forward, as so many centres have done". The prediction was accurate enough but its realisation would be a long time off yet.

On 26 August the Trinity first-team rested Mortimer for their game against Bramley at the Barley Mow. Neil took full advantage of his opportunity, scoring another four tries in a 23-2 win. Neil's wing partner, Fred Smith, also in the side because players were being rested, scored the first two Wakefield tries. "Then Neil Fox ran in three in succession, showing excellent finishing power. Then after watching Cooper flash over, he added his fourth try with only two minutes to go. The last was a cheeky effort. Smith, the burly Bramley prop, was trying to burst clear when Fox nipped in, snatched the ball out of his hands, and raced away to outpace the surprised defenders." There was a big shout when Neil converted the last try, because he had missed six previous conversions, all admittedly difficult. It is not recorded what the Bramley prop thought of being robbed by an 18-year-old centre but it is probably unprintable.

There were close on 14,000 at Belle Vue for Wakefield's next fixture, a Yorkshire Cup first round tie against Halifax. Neil was to have a huge impact on the proceedings. In the very first minute he attempted a penalty which bounced back from a post into play at the church end of the ground. Halifax scrum-half Stan Kielty threw a dodgy pass to full-back Garfield Owen, who could not retrieve it but Neil, ever alert, could and did, scoring a try which he converted. Things got even better for Trinity when Halifax hooker Stan Moyser was sent off for tripping Eric Lockwood after 37 minutes but with only five minutes remaining Halifax had crept into a 16-14 lead, Neil having claimed all his team's points. It had been a pretty tough affair and Albert Firth, Trinity's second-rower, was actually still playing while concussed. It appeared that Trinity could salvage a draw when they received a penalty in a very kickable position but instead Neil took a tap. Norman Railton, the referee, decided he had not done so correctly and ordered a scrum. Trinity's hopes seemed to have evaporated when Halifax won the scrum but Les Chamberlain immediately stole the ball back and was grounded near the posts. The ball was flashed out to the right wing where Fred Smith flew over at the corner. Neil converted magnificently from the touchline and Wakefield had made a great escape. A casualty of a torrid encounter was Neil's co-centre Don Metcalfe, who chipped an ankle bone, causing him to miss Yorkshire's game against Cumberland, for which he had been selected as captain.

Trinity's super start to the season continued with an easy win at Castleford, where among Neil's five goals were two stupendous touchliners. A much tougher proposition followed as Wigan came to Belle Vue for a clash of two undefeated sides. At the close of the game Trinity were the last remaining undefeated team in the league, having won a thriller 23-16. Wigan fought back from 18-8 down after 41 minutes to just 18-16 before Neil converted a truly astonishing try from Chamberlain five minutes from time. From 25 yards out, Chamberlain went through four or five Wigan defenders like a demented pinball, bouncing out of tackles which would have floored a less determined man.

This was the first occasion that Neil had clashed with the legendary Wigan duo of Eric Ashton and Billy Boston. Neil recalls: "That game against Wigan was a real tester, coming up against such great players. It was games like that in my early days which taught me how to find openings for my wingers. They also taught me how hard I would have to work in defence. Billy was very hard to tackle. You had to go low on him or he would just bump you off or send you sprawling with that fantastic hand-off. Eric was pure class. He had a football brain second to none and would rarely let his winger have the ball without having at least half a chance, although, even if he did, Billy would not mind - not with his power and pace. They were definitely two of the best I ever played with or against. Another great player from this period was Mick Sullivan, who joined Wigan from Huddersfield soon after that game. Trinity tried to sign him, I think, and would have paid the necessary but Wigan beat us to him. He ranks with Billy as the two greatest wingers I played with or against. How Mick and Eric Ashton are not in the Rugby League Hall of Fame beats me."

Wakefield finally lost for the first time in the season on 16 September when Huddersfield beat them 13-10 at Belle Vue in a second round Yorkshire Cup tie. Trinity's unbeaten run of 15 games went back to 3 April. Amazingly, Neil's last experience of losing with the first-team stretched back even further – to the notorious Cup tie with Blackpool.

Around this time Wakefield was in the grip of the Asian 'flu epidemic and for weeks between five and 20 per cent of the town's labour force was reported to be off work with the virus. Trinity took a severely depleted team to York and gained a creditable 15-6 victory, in a game in which no goals were kicked. Among those who contracted the 'flu were Trinity's half-backs Holliday and Rollin, who both missed Yorkshire's game against Lancashire as a result.

Huddersfield, Featherstone and York all fell to Trinity, whose players were reported to have earned £49 each for their efforts. Wakefield at that point were top of the league, ahead of St Helens, Wigan, Rochdale, Featherstone, Salford and Bradford, and still the only undefeated team in the league. Neil was well up the scoring charts with nine tries and 31 goals from 10 appearances. However, things were beginning to unravel at Belle Vue. On 19

Wakefield Trinity 19 Halifax 16 at Belle Vue, Yorkshire Cup first round, 31 August 1957.
Neil scored 16 points. Back: Albert Firth, John Shaw, Frank Haigh, Don Metcalfe, Bob Coverdale,
Derek Harrison, Les Chamberlain. Front: Neil Fox, Ken Rollin, Fred Smith, Keith Holliday,
Eric Lockwood, Eric Cooper.

October Trinity went to Odsal and met stern resistance from Bradford Northern. They looked like winning, however, when Neil converted a John Shaw try with "a grand shot" 10 minutes from time to give them a 10-8 lead, only for Northern to snatch an 11-10 victory when left-winger Malcolm Davies was on the end of a huge overlap to score the decisive try after 75 minutes. So Trinity lost their unbeaten record in league matches since their 18-8 loss against Leeds on 3 April – a run of 18 games.

Three big home wins against Dewsbury, Bradford and Castleford, in which Neil piled up three tries and 17 goals, were registered in the next month but Trinity's away form cost them the league leadership. On 2 November Oldham, minus five men on test duty, showed Trinity what was necessary to really be top-notchers with some brilliant play in awful conditions at Watersheddings, even though Wakefield were still in the game at 13-12 down after 65 minutes. A fortnight later they were fortunate to salvage a 6-6 draw at Hull KR, Neil's third penalty goal earning a point with only 10 minutes left.

Neil himself had been criticised in some quarters, despite his voracious appetite for amassing points and despite his tender years. Peter Johnson's column, "Talk on Trinity" (*Yorkshire Sports*, 30 November 1957), had this to say: "Fox's physique has been one of Wakefield's greatest attacking assets this season. Yet he has his critics. They say he holds on to the ball too long in those powerful bursts down the middle; that he tends to cut his winger out of the game; and that he is too big and not fast enough for a centre. Against Castleford on Saturday Fox answered all three criticisms in one of the best pieces of centre play seen at Belle Vue for many a season. Anyone who saw him first work an opening, time his pass and then keep pace with his speedy wing partner, Ken Hirst, could come to only one conclusion: that Fox is destined for international honours."

On 30 November there was another defeat for Trinity, completely outclassed at Wigan who played for 55 minutes without the injured Billy Boston. Neil had missed the game as he was groomsman at his brother Peter's wedding, Don being the best man. He recalls, "I pleaded with my mother but there was no way she would let me play that day. I was really keen to play because I had been told that some of the test selectors were going to be at Central Park and there was an Australian tour in the summer."

That Wigan game heralded a disastrous run of six consecutive defeats and by Boxing Day Wakefield had slipped to fifth in the table behind St Helens, Oldham, Hull and Halifax. Neil was back in the side for the visit to Halifax on 7 December. Trinity put up a much better performance with Neil kicking a goal in the first minute and scoring a try on 36 minutes to give them a 5-0 lead, which they held until the hour mark when Colin Clifft, "a discarded Trinitarian", levelled the scores for Halifax with a converted try. 'The Pinder' wrote: "In a surprisingly attractive game in the heavy conditions there were many tense moments, but none more so than that provided by Wakefield's dashing centre Fox. On his young shoulders stood the responsibility for Trinity's defeat just as, paradoxically, to him was rightly attributed credit for the fact that Wakefield ever looked like winning! Who, of those present, will ever forget the sensational threequarters of the length of the field dribble by Fox, who finally left the opposition safely behind as late as the 75th minute? Here was coming the most sensational try of the afternoon as the ball reached the Halifax line near one of the goal-posts. Just another tap and over the line the ball would slide to await the restraining hand of Fox as he touched down! But oh, how could it happen? To the amazement of all onlookers, Fox halted his footsteps, bent down to gather the ball and had the uncomfortable and unforgettable experience of a lifetime crowded into those dramatic seconds in seeing the ball squirm out of his hands, and slide over the dead-ball line. As he sprawled full length on the slimy surface, one could well appreciate his look of utter dejection as he could scarcely have failed with a goal-kick in such a simple position."

Two minutes later the game was lost when Halifax loose-forward Ken Traill claimed the winning try. It proved to be Traill's last significant act for Halifax because he signed for Trinity within days to begin an association with the club which lasted for 12 years and encompassed many of Trinity's greatest days and most significant triumphs. Traill's debut for Trinity in a home game against Leeds on 14 December was inauspicious, although there was plenty of admiration for his "pattern-book passes". Leeds took Trinity's unbeaten home record, winning 21-15, and Neil came in for some criticism for "attempting to do too much on his own". 'The Pinder' attributed to him a "misguided gluttony for work, good as his intentions undoubtedly were", indicating that he had starved his winger, Ken Hirst, of the ball. He did, however, concede that Neil and Keith Holliday had done well in holding their illustrious opposing centres, Lewis Jones and Keith McLellan. This was the first time that Neil had faced Lewis Jones, a genius if ever there was one. He remembers, "The man who did most of the damage was Lewis Jones. What a wonderful player – fast and clever. He had a better change of pace than anyone I ever saw. Against players like him you were left grabbing thin air. You soon learned not to give them room to manoeuvre."

A week later Trinity hit rock bottom. They went to league leaders St Helens. On the way Trinity stopped for a pre-match meal at Brian Snape's pub and during the team talk Ken Traill said his piece. Neil says, "Ken warned us about Nat Silcock, who toured with him in 1954. 'Watch out for Silcock. He's a big lad, six feet two inches. He's 17 stones and comes off both feet like a ballet dancer and he can't half run. Then there's Vince Karalius, Alan Prescott, Alex Murphy, Austin Rhodes and Duggie Greenall and they've also got a South African winger, who is supposed to be pretty quick.' I had never played against as many great players in my life but we were all really stunned when we lost 52-5. That South African, whose name Ken never even mentioned, was Tom van Vollenhoven. Tom scored six tries that afternoon. We soon learned he was something special. Ken tried to blame our defeat on the meal!"

On Christmas Day, Neil came up against Barrow's Phil Jackson, "another Great Britain great, big and strong, with a superb football brain", according to Neil. Trinity copped another defeat and Keith Holliday received a broken jaw in the 41st minute. The following day Christmas was not a merry one as Leeds completed a double over Trinity at Headingley. Neil kicked three goals in an 18-29 loss, while his opposite number Lewis Jones kicked four and helped his winger Garry Hemingway to a hat-trick.

Wakefield's season seemed to be disintegrating around them. Neil remembers, "It was pretty bad. Our forwards were poor in this period and even Ken Traill's introduction did not improve matters much. It made me realise that there was a lot of work to put into being a pro player. We all had to put in a load of work if we were to be successful and it was obvious that new faces were needed."

Two new faces were drafted into the team at Keighley on 28 December in props Mal Kirk and Sam Evans. Kirk arrived via Featherstone Rovers and Evans via Hull KR, to whom Bob Coverdale went, along with £2,000 of Trinity's money. They helped Trinity back onto the winning path at last. Neil had a good afternoon with five goals. Also, in a 19-12 success, he used "his strength to good effect and broke loose from a tackle to cross for his side's first try" after 21 minutes. Another victory followed in a drab affair with Bramley before once more disaster befell Trinity at Hull on 18 January. Trinity were unbelievably inept in going down 2-29 and in the last minute Sam Evans suffered a broken leg.

Two youngsters were signed around this trying time who would, however, make things extremely brighter in the near future. They were stand-off Harold Poynton, a local boy, and full-back Gerry Round, an amateur international, from Hebden Bridge, who was studying engineering at Leeds University. On 30 January Trinity added Reg Parker, Barrow's gangly England second-rower, to their register, the fee being £1,200. Parker's signing was not without repercussions. Trinity played him in a league match before he had been properly registered, also breaking the regulation banning clubs from having more than 50 players on the register at one time. The club subsequently suffered a £50 fine. Still, Reg was a good signing, his experience being invaluable in shoring up Wakefield's struggling pack. At the same time Albert Firth was listed at £3,000 and Ken Traill was reported to be very unsettled, also going on the list at his own request at £1,500. He was immediately dropped from the first-team.

It was with some trepidation therefore that Trinity faced up to St Helens at Belle Vue on 1 February. The new South Stand at the Agbrigg Road end of the ground was officially opened that afternoon with most of its customers probably expecting the worst from their team. Trinity fielded Poynton, Parker and young hooker Geoff Oakes as debutants. "Geoff always got you plenty of the ball and grafted in the loose," according to Neil. It was a sizzling game. Neil kicked Trinity into the lead with a second minute goal, but when half an hour had elapsed, Saints had rushed in four unconverted tries (van Vollenhoven two, Large and Murphy) to lead 12-2. Trinity struck back before the interval with a try by Rollin, converted by Neil. Four minutes after the break Trinity were level after a brilliant try by Metcalfe was also goaled by Neil. In the 55th minute Neil sealed a famous victory when Rollin and Poynton put him over for the final try of the game, to which he added the goal. Trinity thus won 17-12, against all expectations. 'The Pinder' was ecstatic, declaring that the Trinitarians had "earned every halfpenny of the £20 per man received" and eulogised their "remarkable, unforgettable resistance". He was very taken by Harold Poynton, whose astonishing display "revealed pace, guile and all-round natural ability in quantities that marked him as a player who, most certainly, will go far".

Despite such a splendid victory, Wakefield did not capitalise. They won their next game, a Challenge Cup tie against Doncaster, comfortably enough, with Neil scoring 14 points, but then lost another four games on the trot. Three days after the Cup tie Trinity lost 6-5 at Batley. Mount Pleasant that afternoon savagely belied its name for there was continuous rain, strong wind and over-the-ankle-tops mud. It was reported that "for a style of negative football, Batley claimed full marks." It was also noted that "Seldom if ever can a crowd have seen so many players die with their boots on." Batley certainly had no notion of lying down and dying before the conquerors of St Helens.

On 22 February Belle Vue heaved under the strain of accommodating almost 27,000 excited fans, when Wigan arrived for a second-round Challenge Cup match. Trinity were definite underdogs but put up a good show in a game which was unspectacular but decidedly thrilling. Wigan took the lead when Boston scored a try after chasing a kick by Ashton. Fred Smith then scorched over for Trinity and Neil landed a terrific conversion to give his side a 5-3 advantage, only for Jackie Cunliffe to level the scores at 5-5 with a penalty. Billy Boston played havoc on the wing, both Eric Cooper and Harold Poynton suffering injuries in trying to halt his rampaging runs. The only second-half scores were tries to Wigan centres, Ashton and Ernie Ashcroft. Neil's and the Trinity fans' dreams of a trip to Wembley evaporated for another year at least, while Wigan went on to win the Cup.

On 1 March Hull KR surprised Trinity with an 11-0 triumph at Belle Vue, when Gerry Round made his first-team debut. Neil missed that debacle but was back a week later when Trinity went down 8-3 in blizzard conditions at Huddersfield, Frank Dyson's four penalty goals proving fatal. Trinity had dropped to 10th in the league at that point and there was no hope of any tangible reward after such a promising start to the campaign.

There was also considerable off-field controversy in the Wakefield camp. The problems with Ken Traill rumbled on. He had been signed as a player but was also given some responsibility for coaching the forwards and ostensibly was in line for a player-coaching post at some point in the future. The Wakefield committee were heavily berated in the press and by the club members for being secretive about their plans and Traill's future role at the club. All sorts of rumours were bandied around about Ken's terms, but he resumed playing with the 'A' team on 15 March turning in a blinder in a 35-2 hammering of Halifax 'A'. That did not bring an end to the matter, however, as Jim Brough, then in charge at Workington Town, was interviewed for the coaching position, the post being designated as team manager. Eventually Brough turned down the manager's post, which was reported to carry an annual salary of £1,500 plus bonuses - a huge amount.

On 15 March Neil kicked three goals in a featureless 9-4 win at Hunslet. Any win was welcome at that juncture and Trinity suddenly found some form, winning another five games in a row. The victories coincided with Ken Traill's return to the first-team and with a phenomenal orgy of scoring by Neil, who scored a genuinely incredible 106 points in those five fixtures. In the process Neil smashed or equalled no fewer than seven club records.

On 29 March Trinity beat Doncaster 48-13 in a good spirited game at Belle Vue. Despite a slippery surface Neil skated over for six tries and booted six goals to amass 30 points. His six tries equalled Ted Bateson's record set in a 44-3 beating of Castleford on 3 March, 1928, while the 30 points smashed Ron Rylance's record of 24 points (nine goals and two tries) established in a 71-0 massacre of Leeds on 12 September 1945. For good measure, Neil's seventh point of the match took him past Frank Mortimer's points-in-a-season record of 229 set only the previous year. Six days later, on Good Friday, 4 April, Batley were pulverised 61-12 at Belle Vue. While some people were still trying to verify that Neil's 30 points against the Dons was indeed a new club record, he went and broke it again. This time he bagged 31 points, from three tries and 11 goals. The 11 goals also equalled the club record, jointly held by Jimmy Metcalfe in 1909, Charlie Pollard in 1931 and Harry Murphy in 1950. Fred Smith went over for four tries, but prop Henry Sharratt had the misfortune to fracture his leg.

Easter Monday provided sterner opposition in Featherstone Rovers, who were beaten 13-2. Neil was reduced to a couple of goals and "a dashing try from a staggeringly long pass by Ken Traill to Don Metcalfe, which cut out three men". The following afternoon Neil picked up another 19 points in a 40-15 win at Doncaster, whose players must have been sick of the sight of him. On 12 April at Crown Flatt it was Dewsbury's turn to suffer as Neil helped himself to another 19 points with eight goals and one try in a 40-5 romp. His second goal of the game broke Sam Lee's record of 111 goals in a season established in 1938-39. Neil's final achievement came in a 20-8 loss at Hunslet on 19 April, when his try equalled Australian winger Dinny Boocker's club record of 32 tries set in season 1953-54. This last feat was a surprise to Neil, who says, "I did not know about equalling the record until the local press told me. I suppose all eyes were on me for the last game of the season against Halifax at Belle Vue. People were wondering if I could break the record but, sorry to say, I did not make it. I did kick five goals but we lost 13-18. Still, I wasn't too bothered. Thirty-two tries was not bad going for a centre, I thought." Prior to the game Neil was presented with a gold watch for his record-breaking activities, while his winger, Eric Cooper, who was playing his last game for Trinity, received a silver tea service in recognition of his distinguished career at Belle Vue. Neil thought a lot of Eric: "Eric was a nice bloke and a fine winger. He would always go hard for the corner and I used to enjoy watching him strut back to his position after scoring, taking in the applause. He was very popular with the fans."

Neil's season had brought him 32 tries, 124 goals and 344 points in 37 appearances, in only two of which, at York and Huddersfield, he failed to score. In the leading scorers charts only Oldham's Bernard Ganley headed him with 453 points. Ganley, in the process, kicked a world record 219 goals during the season. Neil finished fifth in the goal-kicking lists and 10th in the try-scorers. Perhaps his only disappointment was his failure to gain a place in the touring party to Australasia, for which some critics had been touting his name. In reality the selectors probably considered Neil to be too young and inexperienced – he had still not turned 19. Besides, there could be few quibbles about the centres who were selected – Eric Ashton (Wigan), Jim Challinor (Warrington), Alan Davies (Oldham) and Phil Jackson (Barrow) were a formidable quartet in anyone's language.

Neil had not even been given a run in the tour trials, where there had been places for Dennis Ayres (Oldham), Syd Lowden (Salford), Geoff Palmer (Halifax) and Denzil Webster (York). Even more surprisingly, perhaps, was the omission of Lewis Jones. With competition like that, Neil would have to wait just a bit longer for international recognition.

After the season closed, Trinity announced that Ken Traill had been appointed player-coach for the following season, with Johnny Malpass retained as trainer. After his early fraught dealings with the Wakefield Trinity management, this arrangement might have been expected to cause ructions but the appointment of Traill proved to be arguably Trinity's most astute decision in the club's history. Neil's view was: "Ken Traill made all the difference at Belle Vue. He knew that they had to spend to get a winning team. As a player he was a brilliant on-the-field organiser. He was a magnificent long passer and he was always telling players what to do and where to stand. He was a first-class man-manager, always talking to and advising players. He never fell out with any players and he was good for the club. Mind you, some of the players could wind him up. Harold Poynton, for

31

instance, was always late for training. He'd have Ken tearing his hair out. He'd tell him he couldn't get through the traffic or he couldn't find anywhere to park. Harold never told him he didn't have a car though. Later on some of the older players – Vines, Wilkie and Keith Holliday – would play tricks on him. I remember they would sometimes buy mice from pet shops and leave them in his drawers when we were staying in hotels. Ken hated mice. On training nights we would wait until he was in the bath and then turn the hose pipe on him and that water was icy cold. He took it all in good part though and never held it against you. He was a great bloke. No wonder we had such a good team spirit. That helped us to be successful."

Wakefield Trinity 1957-58

Wakefield Trinity finished 9th in the league: P38, W22, L14, D2, For 729, Against 477
Fox scored 32 tries, 124 goals, 344 points for Wakefield

Date	Opponent	Score	Fox	Crowd	
17 Aug	Barrow	31-11	dnp	5,720	
21 Aug	**Hull**	18-13	dnp	8,095	
24 Aug	**Oldham**	12-12	dnp	11,650	
26 Aug	Bramley	23-2	4T, G	4,885	
31 Aug	**Halifax**	19-16	2T, 5G	13,616	YC1
4 Sep	Castleford	28-9	5G	6,631	
7 Sep	**Wigan**	23-16	4G	13,843	
14 Sep	**Keighley**	17-7	T, 4G	7,127	
16 Sep	**Huddersfield**	10-13	2G	7,801	YC2
21 Sep	York	15-6		6,531	
28 Sep	**Huddersfield**	23-9	G	8,915	
5 Oct	Featherstone R	17-10	4G	11,000	
12 Oct	**York**	40-6	2T, 5G	8,229	
19 Oct	Bradford N	10-11	2G	9,606	
26 Oct	**Dewsbury**	38-6	7G	5,915	
2 Nov	Oldham	12-23	3G	18,505	
9 Nov	**Bradford N**	37-6	3T, 4G	7,909	
16 Nov	Hull KR	6-6	3G	3,313	
23 Nov	**Castleford**	27-10	6G	5,176	
30 Nov	Wigan	10-23	dnp	18,353	
7 Dec	Halifax	5-8	T, G	9,500	
14 Dec	**Leeds**	15-21	3G	11,635	
21 Dec	St Helens	5-52	G	12,907	
25 Dec	**Barrow**	5-16	G	6,489	
26 Dec	Leeds	18-29	3G	20,330	
28 Dec	Keighley	19-12	T, 5G	5,170	
11 Jan	**Bramley**	16-3	2G	4,388	
18 Jan	Hull	2-29	G	9,820	
1 Feb	**St Helens**	17-12	T, 4G	13,442	
12 Feb	**Doncaster**	29-0	2T, 4G	5,132	Ch Cup 1
15 Feb	Batley	5-6	G	4,500	
22 Feb	**Wigan**	5-11	G	26,924	Ch Cup 2
1 Mar	**Hull KR**	0-11	dnp	4,966	
8 Mar	Huddersfield	3-8		4,830	
15 Mar	Hunslet	9-4	3G	7,200	
29 Mar	**Doncaster**	48-13	6T, 6G	1,427	
4 Apr	**Batley**	61-12	3T, 11G	4,001	
7 Apr	**Featherstone R**	13-2	T, 2G	8,883	
8 Apr	Doncaster	40-10	3T, 5G	1,015	
12 Apr	Dewsbury	40-5	T, 8G	4,641	
19 Apr	**Hunslet**	8-20	T, G	5,868	
26 Apr	**Halifax**	13-18	5G	5,828	

6. 1958-59: Caps, medals and Molly

The 1958-59 season started with promising omens for Wakefield Trinity, whose season ticket sales were booming and who were reported to be interested in four South African players – two wingmen, a centre and a second-rower. Trinity, however, had not done any serious recruitment during the close season but were glad to see long term injuries to Sam Evans, Henry Sharratt and Don Froggett cleared up, while prop Wilf Adams returned to action after almost three years out with injury. On the wider front the Rugby Football League had decided on one major change to the laws of the game: that a scrum should be formed if the acting half-back was tackled in possession, a measure designed to prevent the creeping barrage of play-the-balls and runs from dummy half which had begun to dominate the game.

Neil entered the campaign six points short of 500 for the club in just 62 first-team appearances. He passed the milestone in the opening game at Featherstone, when his brother Don scored two tries for Rovers. Neil recalls the game vividly because "I had been on holiday at Butlin's in Pwllheli in North Wales the week before. I was with Joe Mullaney and Willis Fawley, who both played for Rovers, Tommy Smales, who had signed for Wigan, and Ken Rollin. Willis and Joe had been telling Ken and me what they would do to us all week but they got a shock when we beat them 44-16 and I finished with 20 points".

A week later Trinity beat Oldham 23-7 at Belle Vue. Oldham had seven men missing, several of them on tour down under, but it was still a good performance. Neil remains mystified about the Oldham teams of that period: "I think the Oldham team was one of the best sides in the game. How they did not get to Wembley in those days beats me. With stars like Turner, Vines, Davies, Ganley, Pitchford, Little and Winslade, you would have thought they would have got there at least once." Neil landed four goals but the stars of the game were Fred Smith and Ken Rollin, whose hat-trick bordered on perfection.

Two days later, on 25 August, Neil passed the 200 goals mark for Wakefield when Leeds were "licked to a frazzle on their own ground", according to John L. Allen. The 33-13 rout came as a severe jolt to most of a crowd of more than 22,000. Allen reported, "The tremendous strength both on attack and defence of centres Holliday and Fox had a big part in shaping the pattern of the game." He was also impressed with Neil's magnificent kicking, notably a wonderful conversion of a length-of-the-field try by Fred Smith.

Trinity's Yorkshire Cup quest opened against Hunslet, a grim game by any standards. Neil missed seven shots at goal and so did the Hunslet kickers, Langton and Tate. He did, however, have a positive effect on the result. His 34th minute try, after some sharp short passing, and conversion gave Wakefield a half-time lead of 8-5, while his 79th minute penalty goal salvaged a 10-10 draw, for which the Trinity men earned £11 each. The replay, an even more gruelling tie, attracted almost 17,000 to Parkside. Referee Charlie Appleton awarded 41 penalties and cautioned Hunslet forward Harry Poole three times. Neil put Trinity into the lead after four minutes with a penalty and sealed their 15-11 victory with another four minutes from time. The players' reward was a £16 pay packet.

Perhaps unsurprisingly after their exertions, Trinity lost for the first time three days later, when St Helens left Belle Vue with a 24-14 victory. Trinity had done well to hold Saints to 14-14 with 14 minutes left before a Peter Fearis penalty goal gave Saints a late lead, which was flatteringly enlarged with two tries in the last five minutes, one a 60-yard scorcher from van Vollenhoven from only the second pass he received in the game.

On Tuesday 9 September, Trinity went to Hull for a second round Yorkshire Cup tie. Wakefield intimated that they were going to leave Neil out of the team, provided Harold

Poynton was fit to play following an ankle injury. Harold, however, had not recovered and Keith Holliday remained at stand-off in his place, leaving Neil as partner to Don Metcalfe in the centres. A thrilling game ensued and "in the end it really was the survival of the fittest", according to the *Wakefield Express*. Trinity staged a mighty late rally with Neil kicking a difficult last-minute penalty to give his side a 17-16 win and a passage into the semi-final.

An emphatic defeat followed at Oldham on 13 September, when for the first time Neil faced Alan Davies, fresh from his triumphs with the Lions down under. It was loose-forward Derek Turner, however, who was mostly responsible for Oldham's dominance.

But Neil had fresh horizons in view. He had been selected to play for Yorkshire against Cumberland at Whitehaven on 15 September, while Ken Rollin, Les Chamberlain and club skipper Ken Traill had been selected in the shadow team. Traill eventually came in at loose-forward for Johnny Whiteley, who withdrew because of a broken nose. Unfortunately, Neil's county debut went badly. He did kick two goals but Yorkshire lost 29-7.

Neil was amazed at what transpired after the game: "I was injured in the first 20 minutes and had to hobble on the wing because no substitutes were allowed in those days. I was sitting there in the dressing-room worrying about my leg. Bill Riley, the reserve back for Yorkshire, was nearby. A Hull KR committee-man, who was also a Yorkshire selector, came and said to Riley, a Hull KR player, 'Don't worry, Bill. You'll be in next week against Lancashire instead of Fox!' And he was right. He wasn't interested in whether I would be fit for the game. I thought: what a way to carry on and what a start to my representative career". Neil would be perplexed by selectors many more times as his career unfolded.

The Yorkshire team on his debut was:

Frank Dyson (Huddersfield, captain), Del Hodgkinson (Leeds), Derek Hallas (Keighley), Neil Fox (Wakefield Trinity), Terry Hollindrake (Keighley), Brian Gabbitas (Hunslet), Jeff Stevenson (Leeds), Mick Scott (Hull), Alan Holdstock (Hull), Brian Hambling (Hull), Jack Fairbank (Huddersfield), Colin Clifft (Halifax), Ken Traill (Wakefield Trinity).

It was probably of no comfort to Neil that Yorkshire won the County Championship after beating Lancashire twice, with brother Don figuring in the final play-off match.

There were some changes in personnel at Belle Vue around this time. Reg Parker had been transferred to Blackpool Borough for £800, while Trinity had offered £2,000 to Wigan for winger Terry O'Grady, who instead chose to join Warrington. They had, however, been successful in capturing Welsh forward Don Vines from Oldham for a club record £4,500. Don was a blacksmith's striker at a colliery and a very fit man. Neil says, "Don brought a bit of fire to our pack. He was a good handler with plenty of pace and a very good tackler." Also added to the register was stand-off David Mortimer, who had played rugby union for Otley and Huddersfield Old Boys and had been prominent in Army rugby.

Five days after his Yorkshire debut, Neil had another bad experience as Trinity were crushed at home by Leeds. Lewis Jones kicked six goals to Neil's five but that was about as far as the parity went. Leeds were 22-2 ahead at the break and the final scoreline of 33-22 was hardly a fair reflection on the Loiners' superiority. Neil missed Wakefield's next game, a narrow victory at Fartown, when Vines and Mortimer made their debuts. He was back, however, on 1 October for Trinity's seemingly straight-forward Yorkshire Cup semi-final against Batley at Belle Vue. Most critics could see only a convincing win for Wakefield but, as Neil says, "Cup ties are always different". This one certainly was. Batley lost their scrum-half Arthur Talbot in the very first minute with torn knee ligaments but how they made Trinity struggle in a stern, fierce game. Trinity were 12-2 up after 20 minutes by which time Neil had kicked three goals and scored a beautiful try after sending Stan Smith away at top speed and being there for the return pass, when Stan was finally halted. By half-time, though, Batley were only 14-11 down. Traill's try took the lead to 17-11 after 46

34

minutes and Neil's fifth and sixth goals were all Trinity could muster in the later stages. A 21-13 victory saw Trinity into the final but Batley had shaken them rigid. The Batley directors were so pleased with their team that they gave the players winning pay of £9.

On 4 October Trinity beat Dewsbury 29-8 although Neil had a poor day with the boot, landing one from four attempts before handing the kicking to Frank Mortimer, who proceeded to pot three out of four shots. Unforgivably some of the Wakefield supporters, "the boo boys", as the local papers termed them, began to give Neil a hard time, quickly forgetting the match-winning performances they had been applauding so happily over the previous couple of years. Ray Wynne wrote: "This year Fox was considered good enough to play for his county and has already put over 45 goals and scored six tries but soon after the season's start the 'niggling' from the terraces began. Fox is accused of being too slow in attack one minute; too weak in defence the next. Let the jeerers take warning. Fox would not be the first player they have driven away from Belle Vue. Remember international half-back Ron Rylance? He became unsettled at Wakefield for the same reason." Thankfully, Neil's performances would soon silence the idiot fringe, which would have been wiser to have taken note of Neil's sporting reaction in that Dewsbury match, when he was the first to applaud Frank Mortimer's kicking.

On 18 October Neil turned out in his first major domestic final. Odsal housed a crowd of nearly 27,000 for the Yorkshire Cup final against Leeds. Both teams were hovering in mid-table but Trinity were slight favourites. The teams for Neil's first final were:

Wakefield Trinity: Frank Mortimer, Fred Smith, Don Metcalfe, Neil Fox, Stan Smith, Keith Holliday, Ken Rollin; Wilf Adams, John Shaw, Sam Evans, Bob Kelly, Les Chamberlain, Ken Traill (captain).

Leeds: Pat Quinn, Garry Hemingway, Jack Lendill, Lewis Jones, Del Hodgkinson, Gordon Brown, Jeff Stevenson (captain), Tony Skelton, Barry Simms, Colin Tomlinson, Don Robinson, Fred Ward, Alec Dick.

After 15 minutes Neil kicked a penalty to give Trinity the lead but thereafter Leeds took control and at the 60-minute mark led 24-7, having run in six tries, three of them converted. Trinity's only responses had been a try for Metcalfe, created by Neil, and another Fox penalty just before the interval. Fortunately, Wakefield bucked up in the final quarter, Don Metcalfe completing a hat-trick, Ken Rollin claiming a try and Mortimer converting two of the tries. The final scoreline of 24-20 was, however, grossly misleading. Leeds were far and away the better team. George M. Thompson of the *Yorkshire Observer* summed up the game pretty accurately: "Leeds showed a striking power in all sections for three parts of the final... Trinity's backs were too easily put on the wrong foot, and were slack in their tackling. Leeds, always the better tacticians, had a firm grip on the trophy before Trinity had their final fling". The *Wakefield Express* was more scathing, declaring that Trinity had been "very disappointing" and "beaten to a frazzle". It felt that Jeff Stevenson had played havoc with Trinity's defence and that Lewis Jones had been baffling, dummying deceptively, expertly using his wing as a foil and "actually had defenders running away from him in the belief that a pass was in the offing". Nonetheless, it praised Metcalfe's hat-trick and noted: "Fox too had a good game despite the fact that he presented his opponents with a try. His strong bursts split the defence several times but weight of numbers and lack of support on other occasions made his efforts unproductive".

The 44 points scored in the game set a record for a Yorkshire Cup final, while no team had ever scored as many points as Trinity and still lost. The final proved to be John Shaw's last for the club and soon afterwards he transferred to Halifax. Neil says of him, "Joby was a very good hooker, who got you plenty of the ball and was very quick in open play. He did well for Halifax and played in Great Britain's 1960 World Cup-winning team. He also toured with me in 1962. Geoff Oakes took over as hooker when Joby left".

Another notable feature of that 1958 Yorkshire Cup Final was that it was the first time that Trinity wore the sublime kit with which, for a whole generation of rugby league fans, the club became synonymous – pristine all-white with two bands of blue and one of red.

Wakefield got back on track in the next league game, a 39-12 pummelling of Workington Town. Neil had a field day with five tries and four goals. His second try was his 50th for the club and the *Yorkshire Evening News* match report ran: "The greatest thrill for the Belle Vue fans was the brilliance of centre Neil Fox. The lad who, only three weeks ago, was the centre of attraction for the boo-boys is now their hero again. Life is really funny, isn't it?" It was Trinity's first home win against Workington since the Cumbrians entered the league in 1945-46. Sadly, Les Chamberlain suffered a double fracture of his left leg 15 minutes from time, which ended his season.

The Workington game began a run of 11 matches without defeat for Trinity, several of which were by small margins and in most of which Neil's scoring touch had a material effect. On 8 November Fred Smith scored the only try of the game when Trinity beat York 7-0. Neil kicked two penalties and the *Wakefield Express* reported that he "was in top form, his devastating bursts being most disconcerting for the defence to deal with". A week later Ken Traill played his last first-team game for Wakefield, appropriately against Bradford Northern, with whom he had enjoyed his greatest triumphs as a player. On a gloomy day, there was no shortage of thrills but Trinity had to dig deep after trailing 5-0 at half-time and having Don Vines sent off 10 minutes before the final whistle. A 3-1 deficit in the scrums did not deter Northern but they could not cope with Neil. The *Sunday Express* reported, "Trinity's young centre Neil Fox was the star of the afternoon. His powerful thrusts in the centre were something that the visitors' defence, good as it was, sometimes found too much for them". Neil's late drop-goal clinched a 13-8 win. The following Saturday Trinity were heavily indebted to Neil, who claimed all their points in an 11-11 draw at Halifax. There was some controversy when, late in the game, Trinity skipper Keith Holliday elected to let Frank Mortimer take a long straight penalty instead of giving it to Neil.

Since the arrival at St Helens of Tom van Vollenhoven in the autumn of 1957, there had been a headlong rush by English clubs to sign South African rugby union players. Wakefield Trinity were in the vanguard of the movement, bringing over three towards the end of 1958. Jan Lotriet was the first to sign but not the first to appear in the first-team. Lotriet, a six-feet three-inches, 13-stone three-pounds winger, had played six times for Western Province and been a Springbok trialist but he would only figure in three games for Trinity before returning home. His capture was followed by that of Ivor Dorrington, a back-row forward, who had won 47 caps for Western Province and was reported to have signed a contract worth £2,000 over three years. Unfortunately for Ivor (six feet one inch and more than 15 stones), his reputation preceded him. He was reputed to be the "Iron Man of South African rugby". John L. Allen probably upped the anti when he wrote: "Everyone wants a Vince Karalius in their team. Well, here is a tougher South African version". Consequently, as Neil recalls, "Everyone wanted a pop at him. He was supposed to be 28 years old but I think he was probably older than that. He found it hard to adjust to rugby league and he went home after playing about 10 games."

Dorrington made his debut against Hunslet on 29 November in the first ever televised game from Belle Vue. It was thought that he was the first South African to have played for Trinity and he must have wondered what he had let himself in for. It was an extremely misty day and the television viewers hardly got their licence fees' worth although the game was a good one, as far as it could be seen. Dorrington received some criticism for his lobbed passes but Trinity won 23-10. Neil landed three goals and six minutes from time scored "a pearl of a try". Shortly after this game Wakefield Trinity declared they were opposed to live televising of league fixtures.

Neil scored 13 points in an entertaining 19-7 win at Workington. 'A Special Correspondent' wrote in the *Wakefield Express*: "Wakefield can thank their lucky stars that they have such an accurate goal-kicker as Neil Fox, for without him they would almost certainly have returned home with only one point. He worked indefatigably throughout. Fox's try came just when Town supporters were congratulating themselves on their team drawing level through a penalty by Wally McArthur only two minutes after Fox had opened the scoring for Wakefield. Cheers turned to groans as the home fans saw Fox sell a dummy to a confused Wookey, and race through at speed to touch down between the posts. It was a brilliant effort, the like of which has not been seen at Derwent Park for many a day."

Batley were beaten on a Belle Vue mud heap on 13 December before Trinity faced a daunting trip to The Boulevard a week later. Trinity won a fantastic 8-0 victory, the players were dubbed "heroes all" by 'The Pinder' and Hull finished scoreless at home for the first time in six years. Trinity won despite being heavily outscrummaged and, remarkably, there was only one penalty kick at goal – by Hull's Cyril Sykes in the 11th minute. Trinity claimed two tries, the first after 55 minutes being a terrific individual effort by Stan Smith. The second went to Neil in the last minute. Don Vines got a slick pass to Keith Holliday "whose captivating elusiveness cleared a path for Fox to use and go on and score behind the posts without a defender being able to interfere". Neil's conversion wrapped things up.

The 1958 festive season brought Wakefield followers welcome presents, the best being the debut of Alan Skene at Castleford on Christmas Day, Lotriet also making his debut. Skene was the third of Trinity's South African signings and, by many a mile, the most successful. Skene, 26 years old, fair and slightly built, had played for the Villagers RU club in Capetown and was another Western Province representative, having played in more than 50 games for the province. He had been capped by South Africa against France earlier in 1958. His contract was reported to be worth £2,500 for three years, which brought Trinity's expenses on their South African venture to around £7,000, which was good business for Hunslet's South African winger Ron Colin, who had acted as Wakefield's agent in the transactions and was entitled to 10 per cent of the fees. As things turned out, Wakefield would have got more than their money's worth had they paid the entire £7,000 for Skene. Neil says, "Alan was a centre with that extra yard of pace and for a slight man was a great defensive player. Alan and I developed a great centre partnership – probably the best around at that particular time. We were the perfect foils for each other."

Trinity beat Castleford 19-7 and Lotriet scored his first try "a treat that was handed out to him most unselfishly by Fox playing centre to the new player". The best try of the game was bagged by Neil. Unfortunately, many of the spectators had already left as he delightfully used Lotriet as a decoy to bluff the defence. Boxing Day yielded Trinity a double over Hull who were beaten 12-5 at Belle Vue, Wakefield's forwards being at the top of their form. The victory took Trinity to the lofty heights of fifth in the table but they were brought back to earth the following day, when Halifax won 18-9 at Belle Vue. Three games in three days was a punishing schedule in anyone's language but it had been the same for the opposition. Trinity's handling had been positively shocking and their forwards had been overpowered. While Wakefield were again threatening to break into the elite of the game, such results were a reminder that they still had some way to go. That truth was reinforced on 3 January when Wigan crushed Trinity 22-5.

On 24 January 1959, Don Froggett made his long awaited return to the first-team in a 21-2 win at Keighley. A week later Don's testimonial match brought another victory,

Huddersfield being beaten 18-4. On a gluepot pitch Neil and Stan Smith registered wonderful tries but Stan suffered a bad knee ligament injury. Neil recalls, "Don Froggett played well and we thought he had got over his injuries but a week later against Hunslet he broke down again and never played again. I think Don will always be remembered for his wholehearted efforts and for overcoming so many bad injuries." That game at Hunslet pitted the two leading Yorkshire clubs of the moment against each other and was a dour, bitterly fought affair. Two Fox penalty goals were the only first-half scores and two more left Trinity 8-5 up with only four minutes remaining. Trinity could hardly get the ball in the second period, however, losing that half's scrums 16-2. A late try by winger Willie Walker, following a cute diagonal kick by the Hunslet scrum-half over a scrum, won the game for Hunslet and again highlighted some of Trinity's deficiencies.

Coach Ken Traill was trying hard to impose his ideas on the club and the team. Surprisingly, in all his time at Belle Vue, Ken never had full control over team selection, his choice of players always being dependent on agreement from a small caucus of directors. He was particularly vexed in this period by a committee-man who insisted on visiting the dressing-rooms before and after the games. Another thing he was not happy about was Trinity's custom of providing the team with a meal before big games, especially in the Challenge Cup. For the first-round tie against Swinton on 21 February, he announced there would be no such meal. He declared the whole business, not just the meal itself, was unsettling to the players and engendered a tense atmosphere. Trinity held two special daylight training sessions for the tie, the second half of which was televised by the BBC. While Trinity were not wholly convincing in winning 18-2, Neil and Alan Skene had good games and Ken Hirst scored a try which was said to have been right out of the Brian Bevan book – in other words, simply amazing.

On 28 February Neil potted eight goals against Doncaster and helped his winger, Ken Hirst, to four tries. Of more importance that day, however, was the signing of Oldham's test loose-forward Derek Turner, who cost the club a new record of £8,000, which was also a world record for a forward. Trinity had beaten heavy competition from Halifax, Hunslet and Leeds for him. The only problem was that he was ineligible for the Challenge Cup ties. Wakefield's money was well spent, however. Neil was in no doubt about Derek's worth: "Derek is the first player I would choose in any team. Strong, fearless and a great leader, he just hated losing. With him you had to play until the final whistle because he always thought you could still win right to the end. He would never give in. His experience with Oldham, Yorkshire and Great Britain was going to be vital to us if we were going to win trophies. With Derek and Don Vines on our side things were definitely changing for us."

Trinity could certainly have done with Derek Turner's presence on 7 March at The Boulevard, where Wakefield met Hull in the Challenge Cup second round before a crowd of more than 20,000. Trinity escaped with a 4-4 draw in a desultory match but were lucky to do so. Neil was their saviour. He kicked an amazing 40-yard penalty goal into a fierce wind after 30 minutes, expertly keeping the ball low so that it just cleared the bar. It kept Wakefield in the game at 4-2 down at the break. The only other score of the game after 55 minutes was a magnificently struck 30-yard drop-goal by Neil after a sharp back-flip pass from Harold Poynton. It was a gem of a goal and totally unexpected. The replay at Wakefield drew a crowd in excess of 22,000 and was a corker. Trinity led 10-5 after 42 minutes but were pulverised by the Hull pack in the second half and eventually succumbed 16-10. Neil ended up limping on the wing for the last half hour and in the final minute referee Charlie Appleton sent off Trinity prop John Lindley and Hull's fearsome Jim Drake. Neil's Wembley aspirations had gone up in smoke again.

Wakefield now had only Rugby League Championship honours and the Yorkshire League Championship to play for. They had dropped to seventh position but had a good chance of finishing in the top four, if things went well for them. Batley were beaten 28-16 at Mount Pleasant, when Turner made his debut. Neil beat five men to score a tremendous try and added eight goals from 10 attempts. This was also the first occasion on which Neil faced his brother Peter in first class rugby league. Two days later Wakefield made the mistake of resting Neil and Don Vines for their home game against Bramley, who provided an almighty upset by winning 9-6. Ken Hirst dislocated his collar-bone and Trinity paid the price of failing to kick any goals as Bramley's Maori full-back Johnny Wilson landed a decisive three.

On Easter Monday Neil scored 15 points in an 18-14 home success against Featherstone and the following afternoon banged over seven goals in a 47-14 thrashing of Castleford. His partnership with Alan Skene was becoming a thing of beauty and Trinity were back up to fifth position in the table.

Neil had other things on his mind though. He had been selected in the Great Britain shadow team for the test against France at Grenoble on Sunday, 5 April, a sign that he was on the verge of his first cap. Injuries then elevated him to travelling reserve along with Leigh forward Mick Martyn. Suddenly he realised that he had no passport – he had never been beyond north Wales. He recalls, "It was panic stations. I had to get to Liverpool for a passport. So my mate Joe Mullaney, who was Don's half-back partner at Featherstone, drove me over to Liverpool in his car. Joe worked in the saddlery department at Sharlston Pit. I was really grateful to Joe, who incidentally taught me to drive later. And to mark my selection, the Trinity supporters presented me with a travelling clock".

Being travelling reserve was thrilling enough for 19-year-old Neil but when skipper Eric Ashton had to pull out with knee ligament trouble he was amazingly promoted to the test team. The teams for Neil's first test match were:

Great Britain: Eric Fraser (Warrington), Ike Southward (Oldham), Alan Davies (Oldham), Neil Fox (Wakefield Trinity), Mick Sullivan (Wigan), Brian Gabbitas (Hunslet), Alex Murphy (St Helens), Abe Terry (St Helens), Tommy Harris (Hull), Brian McTigue (Wigan), Don Vines (Wakefield Trinity), Charlie Winslade (Oldham), Johnny Whiteley (Hull, captain).

France: Andre Rives (Albi), Marcel Bonnet (Lyons), Raymond Gruppi (Villeneuve), Antoine Jimenez (Villeneuve), Andre Savonne (Avignon), Gilbert Benausse (Lezignan), Rene Jean (Avignon), Angelo Boldini (Bordeaux), Antranick Apelian (Marseille), Jacques Fabre (Albi), Roger Majoral (Perpignan), Robert Eramouspe (Roanne), Andre Lacaze (Villeneuve).

Three weeks earlier Great Britain had murdered France 50-15 at Headingley. Despite lacking three men from the Leeds test side – Ashton, Dave Bolton and Vince Karalius – they were expected to win in Grenoble. However, playing France in those days was always an unpredictable affair and so it proved on that sweltering afternoon of Neil's test debut at the Stade Municipal in the shadow of the Alps. Britain lost 24-15, the first time France had ever achieved a victory over them in official test matches. The scoreline does not seem too bad but the truth was that Britain were completely outplayed, despite Tommy Harris winning two thirds of the scrums, and a referee, Georges Jameau, who was described by Derek Marshall in the *Daily Mail* as "the best and fairest we have seen in France". New captain Johnny Whiteley ran himself into the ground but the response from his team was disappointing. Shoddy defence conceded two tries in the first four minutes and by half-time France were 19-0 ahead. Britain pulled back to 19-12 but had no real answer to the power of the French pack and the scheming of stand-off Benausse.

Marshall wrote: "The test newcomers Brian Gabbitas and Neil Fox need not share in the general remorse. Gabbitas made some brilliant and elusive runs in the second half, and Fox helped himself to two tries. Fox's runs were strong and powerful, and in scoring the opening try he succeeded in pushing off two men and handing off a third. But I don't think he will stay in the test team for his lack of acceleration was a big handicap to the fast moving Sullivan." Jack Bentley (*Daily Express*) agreed with Marshall, saying: "Fox will have to speed up to challenge for another test chance. But in his debut he at least showed determination, bumping off a couple of defenders and handing off another to score Great Britain's first try after 47 minutes. He gave a repeat performance six minutes later." Jack Bentley would return to his theme of questioning Neil's pace over the next few years but would ultimately be convinced that the game had produced few better centres. Two tries on a test debut and in a poor team performance was certainly an encouraging start – and Neil could get faster. Incidentally, he was not called upon to kick for goal in this test, Eric Fraser landing three, while Brian McTigue claimed Britain's third try.

Neil's cross-Channel trip meant he missed Trinity's league fixture at Bradford, where they went down 12-9, an ultimately very costly reverse. Wakefield supporters who took the *Sunday Express* must have found Phil King's remark that "Trinity badly missed the thrust and the steadying hand of 19-year-old 'veteran' Neil Fox" somewhat amusing. His return to the team on 8 April was a triumph. He bagged 19 points from three tries and five goals, in a 46-0 home win over Hull KR. His first goal broke his own club record of 124 set just the previous season. Three days later Neil's five goals won a close encounter at York 13-7 and with the fifth he broke his own club record for points-in-a-season, also set the previous year. Neil was having a wonderful time, his next distinction coming when he won Trinity's Player of the Year award, ahead of Skene and Vines.

Trinity had entered the transfer market again and returned to Oldham to sign their veteran wingman John Etty, who had made his debut in the game at York. There appeared to be unanimity in league circles that for a mere £500 Trinity had made the bargain of the season, even if it was nearly at an end. Etty became a very effective wing partner for Neil, who remembers him with affection: "What an impact he made for us. John was extremely strong in defence and such a good finisher. He was also one of the nicest blokes you could wish to meet. He gave us all a bit of a scare, though, when he intimated that he was going to retire but luckily for us and himself he changed his mind. He went on to play at Wembley and so coming to Wakefield brought a good ending to his career". Apart from Etty, there were rumours that Jim Sullivan was coming to Wakefield as coach and that Ken Traill would be his assistant but these came to nothing. Nor did the rumour that Don Fox was heading for Belle Vue, a theory which regularly reared its head over the years.

On 18 April Neil rattled up his 100th appearance for Wakefield and celebrated by claiming 13 points in a 31-4 victory at Dewsbury. His century of games had yielded 850 points (68 tries and 323 goals). The following Wednesday Trinity met Wigan before the biggest crowd of the season at Belle Vue – 21,900. A lot rested on the outcome because both teams could finish second to St Helens, if they won their remaining matches, and thereby gain home advantage in the Championship semi-finals. The game was an absolute thriller. By half-time Wigan led 10-2, thanks to two Billy Boston tries, one of them gifted to him by Neil, whose inside pass to Etty went into the wrong hands. It was not Neil's day although Trinity rallied to just fail 13-12. He missed a relatively easy penalty and narrowly failed with two drop-goal attempts in the closing minutes. Wigan had been fortunate to secure a 13th consecutive victory but good teams always ride their luck. Trinity had defended gloriously but it would probably have been scant consolation if Neil had known that his third goal equalled Frank Mortimer's post-war record of 856 points for the club.

On Saturday, 25 April, Neil left Frank's record behind with four goals in a 38-0 home drubbing of Keighley. However, the star of the show was flying Fred Smith, who had started the game on 30 tries, two short of the club record jointly held by Neil and Dinny Boocker. Fred smashed the record to smithereens with seven tries, which also broke Neil's and Ted Bateson's old record of six in a match. Two days later Trinity, minus Neil, went to Hull KR for their final league fixture, a game which could have catapulted them into a top four spot, provided Oldham lost to St Helens. The destination of the Yorkshire League Championship was also at stake, Trinity needing a draw to pip Hunslet for the title. Rovers made Trinity fight all the way and with ten minutes remaining led 6-4 before a three-try burst gave Wakefield a 17-6 victory and their first Yorkshire Championship since 1945-46. The dream of a Championship semi-final was dashed, however, when it was learned that Oldham had defeated St Helens 15-14. Wakefield were thus squeezed into fifth place in the league behind Saints, Wigan, Hunslet and Oldham. It must have been particularly galling for coach Ken Traill, who had been promised a £100 bonus for a top four finish.

Even so, Neil could hardly complain about his season. He had attained Yorkshire and Great Britain status. He had extended his own club records to 146 goals and 370 points and had become Trinity's most prolific scorer in post-war football. Only Wigan's Fred Griffiths with 394 and Oldham's Bernard Ganley with 383 had scored more points than Neil, who had tied with Hunslet full-back Billy Langton on 380, while he had finished fifth in the goal-kicking chart. He had also picked up his first winners' medal at first-team level. It was not a bad performance for a young man, who had still not reached 20 years of age.

Trinity were now almost there. They had taken the Yorkshire Championship, been runners-up in the Yorkshire Cup and nearly made the Championship semi-finals. The 790 points they had gathered in league fixtures was a new club record and they had been the meanest defenders of the season, conceding only 393 points in 38 matches. Champions St Helens conceded 450. Recruitment of star players was beginning to show results. More than £21,000 had been spent on players in 1958-59, far more than any other club had paid out. Money was also flowing in, though, as Trinity's pools scheme was a huge earner. Trinity's attractive style of rugby was also bringing in the fans, home crowds as often as not now being counted in five figures, and Trinity were a big draw on away grounds. Ken Traill was fostering a fine team spirit, the players were receiving better pay than most other teams and ground improvements were taking place. All the vibrations were good.

Neil's personal life was looking up too. He had met an attractive young lady named Molly Bentley: "I met Molly around March 1959 at the Embassy dance hall in Wakefield. We had a couple of dances and then returned to our respective friends. The following week we saw each other again and danced and talked more, finding out about where each other lived and worked and what interests we had. Molly worked for the Yorkshire Electricity Board and also modelled for them. She was quite famous because there were life-size cut-outs of her in the YEB shops and showrooms advertising cookers, fridges and other electrical items. We got on very well and I liked her a lot but then had to tell her that I couldn't see her the next week because I would be playing for Great Britain in France. So I would see her in a fortnight, I told her. Of course, Molly was pleased for me but, for some reason, our paths did not cross again until long afterwards. When we did meet again everything fell into place. We became an item, got married a couple of years later and are still happily married all these years on. In a career as long as mine there were ups and downs, but Molly has always been there to help."

Wakefield Trinity 1958-59

Wakefield Trinity finished 5th in the league: P38, W27, L10, D1, For 790, Against 393
Fox scored 26 tries, 146 goals, 370 points for Wakefield, and 2 tries, 2 goals, 10 points in representative games

Date	Opponent	Score	Fox	Crowd	
16 Aug	Featherstone R	44-16	2T, 7G	7,945	
23 Aug	**Oldham**	23-7	4G	12,247	
25 Aug	Leeds	33-13	T, 6G	22,029	
30 Aug	**Hunslet**	10-10	T, 2G	12,948	YC1
3 Sep	Hunslet	15-11	3G	16,926	Replay
6 Sep	**St Helens**	14-24	4G	14,632	
9 Sep	Hull	17-16	4G	17,788	YC2
13 Sep	Oldham	11-28	G	14,543	
20 Sep	**Leeds**	22-33	5G	14,092	
27 Sep	Huddersfield	15-14	dnp	8,868	
1 Oct	**Batley**	21-13	T, 6G	11,595	YC Semi
4 Oct	**Dewsbury**	29-8	T, G	4,909	
11 Oct	St Helens	8-15	dnp	12,407	
18 Oct	Leeds	20-24	2G	26,927	YC Final (at Odsal)
25 Oct	**Workington T**	39-12	5T, 4G	6,920	
1 Nov	Bramley	21-7	T, 3G	5,491	
8 Nov	**York**	7-0	2G	7,573	
15 Nov	**Bradford N**	13-8	G	5,365	
22 Nov	Halifax	11-11	T, 4G	10,550	
29 Nov	**Hunslet**	23-10	T, 3G	4,223	
6 Dec	Workington T	19-7	T, 5G	5,082	
13 Dec	**Batley**	13-4	2G	5,202	
20 Dec	Hull	8-0	T, G	9,167	
25 Dec	Castleford	19-7	2T, G	5,694	
26 Dec	**Hull**	12-5	3G	10,200	
27 Dec	**Halifax**	9-18	3G	10,187	
3 Jan	Wigan	5-22	G	18,877	
24 Jan	Keighley	21-2	T, 3G	5,867	
31 Jan	**Huddersfield**	18-4	T, 3G	6,556	
7 Feb	Hunslet	8-10	4G	10,600	
21 Feb	**Swinton**	18-2	3G	12,857	Ch Cup 1
28 Feb	**Doncaster**	52-2	8G	4,111	
7 Mar	Hull	4-4	2G	20,210	Ch Cup 2
11 Mar	**Hull**	10-16	2G	22,296	Replay
14 Mar	Batley	28-16	T, 8G	6,000	
23 Mar	**Bramley**	6-9	dnp	4,687	
28 Mar	Doncaster	28-11	dnp	1,587	
30 Mar	**Featherstone R**	18-14	T, 6G	10,702	
31 Mar	**Castleford**	47-14	7G	6,524	
4 Apr	Bradford N	9-12	dnp	6,933	
8 Apr	**Hull KR**	46-0	3T, 5G	4,224	
11 Apr	York	13-7	5G	6,771	
18 Apr	Dewsbury	31-4	T, 5G	6,371	
22 Apr	**Wigan**	12-13	3G	21,900	
25 Apr	**Keighley**	38-0	4G	3,383	
27 Apr	Hull KR	17-6	dnp	5,882	

Representative appearances

15 Sep	Yorkshire 7 Cumberland 29 (Whitehaven)	2G	
5 Apr	Great Britain 15 France 24 (Grenoble)	2T	

42

An omen for the future: Neil dives for a try in a curtain-raiser at Belle Vue. He was playing for Castleford Town Schools against Wakefield City Schools at under-15 level.

The Featherstone Rovers Intermediate (under-18) team which swept all before it in 1954-55.
Back: V. Guy, G. W. Ward, Harold Moxon (coach), John Reynolds, Neil Fox, Peter Stocks, Walt Colwood, Gordon Graham, Ron Armitage, Alan Field, Unknown, E. Cooper.
Seated: Barry Nock, Matthews, Les Evans, Tony Jukes, Brian Shaw, Tommy Smales (kneeling).
Front: Mick Reynolds, Alan Marchant

Neil breaks through Ian Walsh's tackle (above) and then scores a crucial try (below) for Great Britain against Australia in the second test at Headingley, 21 November 1959.

7. 1959-60: The Kangaroos and Wembley

Early in July 1959 Stuart Hadfield succeeded Les Pounder as chairman of Wakefield Trinity. He had taken the job at just the right time in the history of the Trinitarians, who were about to enter the most successful period the club ever experienced, at least in its time as a rugby league club. A few weeks earlier Wakefield had announced a profit of £2,419 on the preceding year, despite its massive outlay on new players. Home gate receipts, at £30,357, had risen by nearly £7,000 and the development fund (Wakefield Trinity's pools) had brought in £24,000.

On the playing side Derek Turner was appointed club captain for the 1959-60 season, replacing Keith Holliday, who became his vice-captain. Holliday had been a revelation in the latter part of the previous campaign, when he had moved to the scrum-half position. Neil regarded Keith very highly, wherever he played, but especially when he took possession of the number seven jersey, rating him as "one of the best in the league. It was like having another forward on the pitch, when the work had to be done". Turner, then a bricklayer's labourer, was reported to have lost a stone building his own bungalow in Ossett during the summer. Neil must have been making up for Derek's loss of weight for, at the pre-season weigh-in, he was easily the heaviest back at 14 stones 11¾ pounds and he was heavier than most of the forwards. Neil's centre partner Alan Skene was, in contrast, at 11 stones almost four stones lighter.

The city of Wakefield was expecting much of its rugby league team for 1959-60. It was time for Trinity to deliver. Season ticket sales doubled on the previous season and the club announced that the players would be on generous bonuses if they were successful. Ken Traill was promised a bonus of £200 for a top four finish. Playing terms for the players were set at £6 for a defeat, £10 for a home win, £11 for an away win and £12 for a win against Lancashire opposition. Bonuses could radically inflate those figures. If 10 points were reached in a game £1 was added and then another £1 for each additional 10 points. Of course, when the cup ties came round, bonuses were bigger. All this was music to young Neil's ears. Sensibly he had been putting all his rugby earnings aside for the future, proving he had plenty between the ears off the field, as well as on it.

Wakefield had signed a clutch of youngsters from the Trinity Intermediate side, including Tony Thomas, an under-19 international stand-off, and three forwards, Trevor Sampson, Geoff Steel and Bob Steele. They had not, however, made any major signings and if there were any real misgivings in the camp, they centred on the lack of reserve strength. Consequently, when a practice match of two 20-minute periods was played before the public and refereed by local official Ron Gelder, it seemed like a good idea gone wrong when both Harold Poynton and John Etty suffered injuries which kept them out of action for four and two months respectively. It was not a promising start to the season.

Nonetheless, Trinity got off to a flying start. Challenge Cup holders Wigan were the first visitors to Belle Vue on 15 August and 17,000 were provided with a treat. Trinity led 16-2 at one point but were pegged back to 16-14 with only 10 minutes left. It was Neil who settled the issue after 74 minutes when he burst through a posse of Wigan defenders to touch down under the sticks, before landing the conversion to give Trinity victory by 21-14. It had been Turner though who had been the architect of the win. If any man had ever won a game on his own, it had been him on this occasion. He had scored terrific tries in the 4th and 28th minutes and bullied his team into rising above itself. The importance of the victory was evident in the size of the Trinity players' wage packets of £22.

Two days later Trinity faced a stiff test at Featherstone, where the crowd was 12,687, a record for a league match at Post Office Road. With 25 minutes gone Rovers led 9-0. Neil kicked a penalty and then in the 32nd minute, according to the *Wakefield Express*, "His strength and coolness in an emergency were amply demonstrated when, despite the close attention of three defenders, he released himself from custody to provide Skene with a try-producing pass". He then kicked the touchline conversion and three minutes later levelled the scores with a similarly difficult penalty. Trinity took control and raced away to a comfortable 25-11 success, earning £21 each for their efforts.

St Helens at Knowsley Road was the next obstacle and Trinity were utterly routed 40-7. Had they won they would have received £30 rather than their £6 basic losing pay. In such circumstances though it hardly mattered what the remuneration was. Trinity had been humiliated, "the severity of defeat beyond belief", according to John L. Allen. Saints' full-back Austin Rhodes did a Neil Fox in piling up 25 points from three tries and eight goals.

Trinity got back on the winning path four days later against Leeds at Belle Vue but were not at all convincing. A rib injury kept Leeds full-back Pat Quinn off the pitch for the entire second half but the Loiners were still level, 17-17, as the game entered the last 15 minutes. However, two late converted tries sealed the game for Trinity. Neil's contribution was six goals, from 14 attempts, and a try, which the *Wakefield Express* described thus, "Fox, with one of his superman efforts, crashed his way through almost the entire Leeds side in a run from near the halfway line to finally plant the ball down behind the posts".

On 29 August, Trinity went to Halifax for a first round Yorkshire Cup tie. Together with Hunslet, Wakefield were favourites for the trophy. The game was televised on BBC's *Grandstand* and was the first one to be screened from Thrum Hall. By half-time Trinity were effectively beaten as Halifax led 15-4, having won the first-half scrums 11-2. Trinity fought back but went down 17-14. Neil booted four goals and scored a lovely solo try with a cute dummy. However, a good thumping at St Helens and dismissal from the Yorkshire Cup in the first round was not what Wakefield's players and supporters had anticipated.

Trinity moved quickly to strengthen the side, buying fiery Halifax prop Jack Wilkinson for £4,500. Wilkie was thought to be past his best. He had toured Australia in 1954, played in Wembley Cup finals in 1954 and 1956 and in three Championship finals for Halifax, all as losers. Moreover, he had not played since the previous April, so he was not yet as battle-hardened as he would have liked to have been. Trinity wanted Jack in their front row to help deliver more and better possession for their talented backs, who were often on short rations. They had already let Bob Kelly go to Batley on a free transfer and would soon offload three more props in John Lindley to St Helens for £2,000, Derek Harrison to Batley for £800 and Sam Evans to Hull. Trinity were pinning a lot on Wilkie's success. They would not be disappointed as he proved the doubters wrong.

On 5 September, Trinity went to Wigan, giving debuts to props Wilkinson and Trevor Sampson. They still contrived to lose the scrums 18-4 but won a sensational 27-19 victory. Referee Eric Clay handed out 27 penalties and 10 cautions and after the game Stuart Hadfield complained that the Trinity players were spat upon when leaving the field. Early in the game the crowd had slow-handclapped Neil as he took his kicks, but the *Wakefield Express* wrote triumphantly: "Neil Fox highlighted the sparkling victory with some touchline goalkicking (four gems they were!) that melted the hearts of the crestfallen locals and led them to applaud". Neil also scored the last try of the match three minutes from time to put the issue beyond doubt.

Up one week, down the next. On 12 September, St Helens came to Belle Vue intent on repeating the same medicine they had ladled out three weeks earlier. In heat wave conditions Trinity gained parity in the scrums for a change and held the Saints to 5-2 on the hour mark, Neil landing a penalty. The last 20 minutes was all Saints, however, and they ran in three more tries to win 16-2. Neil and Derek Turner were injured and consequently had to withdraw from Yorkshire's team to meet Cumberland at Hull the following Wednesday, Trinity's only representative being Albert Firth.

Neil missed Trinity victories over York and Dewsbury but was back in action for Yorkshire's encounter with the touring Australians at York on 28 September. Jack Wilkinson and Derek Turner were also in the county side. Neil had a field day: "It was a match I'll never forget. I finished with 10 goals and a try with us winning 47-15. Because Australia played a lot of their test team, all our lads got a tremendous boost". Neil equalled the Yorkshire record of 10 goals kicked by Vic Yorke against Lancashire at Craven Park, Hull, just one year earlier, but his try gave him 23 points, a new all-time record for Yorkshire. Oldham stand-off Alan Kellett starred with a stunning hat-trick and Neil did well enough for Jack Bentley of the *Daily Express* to write, "Another Yorkshire lad who did his test chances a deal of good was centre Neil Fox. If only for his goalkicking – 10 goals from 12 attempts – he rates consideration."

On 3 October, Neil returned to action with Trinity, who had a good 35-19 win over Hunslet, of which Neil provided a try and four goals. His form though, however good, was not enough to sway the test selectors into picking him for the first Ashes test at Swinton on 17 October. Derek Turner was chosen at loose-forward and Neil and Don Vines were travelling reserves. Eric Ashton and Alan Davies were the preferred centres, with Neil and Jim Challinor as shadows.

On 24 October, Neil did his test aspirations a good turn at Fartown in a rough game, punctuated by moments of sublime rugby. He scored three goals and an interception try in a 27-5 win but, as John L. Allen noted: "On a day when most of the team earned laurels, Fox stood out as a great personality – a player whose performance impressed friend and foe alike. His physical power is well known to Wakefield followers. And if it wasn't so well known to Huddersfield supporters, the way he buffeted his way through three defenders to send Skene away for a try afforded the home crowd an opportunity of passing judgement on the 20-year-old's claim to a place in the Great Britain side."

Alfred Drewry in the *Yorkshire Post* was equally enthusiastic: "Fox did a lot of damage, but those who took exception to his methods had no right to be watching rugby football. He gave a textbook demonstration of the legitimate uses of weight and strength; powerful charges in which hips and shoulders were used without mercy – but also without malice, which is the important point. And there was more to him than that. The dummy and acceleration that wrong-footed half-a-dozen defenders and led to the first of Trinity's seven tries was a clever piece of centre play."

Another journalist behind Neil's test cause was Arthur Haddock of the *Yorkshire Evening Post*, who wrote: "Fox has every natural advantage to make top test grade. He is six feet tall... 14 stone eight pounds, gets his knees well up in the gallop, handles neatly and can go powerfully into an opening. I also rate him as a crushing tackler. These are the attributes of a world beater. What, then, does Neil possibly lack to put him in such class? I would say that two more yards of speed and a bit more assertiveness (or shall we say confidence to go through?) could earn him this label. He is Yorkshire's nearest approach to Lewis Jones as a scoring machine, goalkicker and try snatcher, but that alone is not sufficient. At the age of 20, however, a wonderful opportunity spreads itself before Fox with one of our test team centre berths there to be grabbed... Many good judges think that

Fox could... become as big a scourge to the Aussies as was Ernest Ward, his illustrious predecessor in the Yorkshire team at left-centre."

Comparisons with great men such as Ward, Great Britain's captain on the 1950 tour to Australasia, were a sure sign that Neil was really beginning to be taken seriously as one of the men upon whom Great Britain would depend for continued success over the coming years. He still had to get past the incumbent test centres, Alan Davies and Eric Ashton, however, and they were not likely to stand aside meekly. In the meantime Neil had to continue turning in eye-catching performances. He carried on doing what he did best – breaking records and passing new milestones. On 31 October he plundered Hull KR's defence for 20 points from two tries and seven goals, in a 44-9 home win. His fifth point brought him his 1,000th in all matches in first-class rugby league. An unnamed reporter wrote: "His two tries were typical. In both he used his weight to shoulder aside the opposition as he strode for the line. Had he been selfish, Fox could have increased his personal score. On several occasions when there was a possible try for him he passed to make certain of a try for Trinity." Alan Skene also enjoyed himself with a hat-trick.

On 7 November, Neil's second goal in a 28-7 romp at Bramley took him past Frank Mortimer's post-war Trinity record of 377 goals, while four days later he was man of the match in Yorkshire's 38-28 triumph in the Roses Match at Leigh. Playing alongside Halifax centre John Burnett, Neil made hay in opposition to Ashton and Davies, scoring yet another interception try, making three others and booting seven goals. On 14 November Trinity pasted Huddersfield 31-6 at Belle Vue, Neil landing eight goals from 11 attempts, his fourth taking him past the 1,000 points mark for his club. The game was also notable as the debut of Malcolm Sampson in the Trinity second-row.

Great Britain had lost the first Ashes test 22-14 at Swinton on 17 October. That scoreline disguised Australia's dominance and the British selectors were clearly rattled by the quality of the Australians' performance. They were particularly nonplussed by the Kangaroo centres, Reg Gasnier and Harry Wells, who scored all four of Australia's tries. Gasnier's hat-trick was stupendous, as he displayed speed and elegance of running which has rarely been matched. Wells was as big and powerful as Neil, and the pairing of Gasnier and Wells seemed made in heaven. For the second test at Headingley on 21 November, Britain made eight changes, including bringing in Neil for Eric Ashton, who was relegated to travelling reserve. In the event, Eric was to partner Neil in the centre, because Alan Davies had to withdraw when his employers, the National Coal Board, refused to allow him time off for daylight training.

Neil recalls: "I was surprised at our low-key preparation for the test. We got together at Parkside, Hunslet's ground, on the Thursday afternoon. Then we warmed up with a couple of laps round the field, half-a-dozen sprints, worked a few moves and finished with some touch and pass. Then it was back to the Griffin Hotel in Leeds, where we were staying. On the Friday we went back to Parkside after breakfast to do a bit more training and went through the moves we had done the day before. After dinner we just went for a stroll around Leeds and then to bed.

After breakfast on the morning of the match we had a team talk about what to expect from the Aussies early on in the game, because one more win for them meant the Ashes would be theirs. We talked about the danger men, which meant most of the threequarters. But it especially meant Reg Gasnier, who was on his first tour but already a star. Alongside him was Harry Wells, a seasoned campaigner and one of the hardest and strongest centres in the world. The two wingers, Brian Carlson and Eddie Lumsden, had enough pace to score from anywhere on the field. The conditions would not favour the Aussies as they were used to harder, drier pitches but they were still a class act. Keith Barnes, the captain, was a fine full-back and kicker and they had good, tough halves in Brian Clay and Barry Muir. Their pack was solid, led by Ian Walsh and Rex Mossop, and then there was Johnny Raper at loose-forward, whom I rated very highly, but he missed the Leeds test. So, I thought, we could be in for a difficult time. Mostly, though, I was thinking that I hoped we could win and that I could play well and not let anyone down. After lunch, I remember, were we waiting to get off to Headingley, when into the room came the one-and-only legend of Yorkshire cricket, Fred Trueman. Fred was reporting the match for the *Sunday People*. I had met him before and he came over to me and asked about our chances. Then he asked me what our pay would be. I said, '£20 if we win'. His reply was, 'By Jove, I wouldn't even take my coat off against those chaps for that, let alone play'. Except he didn't say 'By Jove' and he didn't call the Aussies 'chaps'!"

A crowd of 30,184 packed into Headingley, a ground on which Australia had not won an Ashes test in six attempts. Conditions, as well as history, favoured the British. A dull day and a soft playing surface was just what was required to take the edge off the Aussie speedsters. The teams for Neil's Ashes debut were:

Great Britain: Frank Dyson (Huddersfield), Ike Southward (Oldham), Eric Ashton (Wigan), Neil Fox (Wakefield T), Mick Sullivan (Wigan), Dave Bolton (Wigan), Jeff Stevenson (York, captain), Abe Terry (St Helens), Tommy Harris (Hull), Don Robinson (Leeds), Brian McTigue (Wigan), Don Vines (Wakefield T), Johnny Whiteley (Hull).

Australia: Keith Barnes (captain), Brian Carlson, Harry Wells, Reg Gasnier, Eddie Lumsden, Brian Clay, Barry Muir, Billy Wilson, Ian Walsh, Garry Parcell, Rex Mossop, Elton Rasmussen, Brian Hambly.

Harold Mather in the *Manchester Guardian* was well pleased by the encounter, writing, "This was the match of a lifetime between two brilliant sides and Great Britain's victory means that all now depends on the third and last test at Wigan on December 12. To ask for a better game then would be asking for the almost impossible; to hope for one as good may be hoping for too much; to think that either may happen only gives credit to two splendid teams." Not all the critics went as far as Mather, although George M. Thompson in *Yorkshire Sports* described it as "one of the greatest post-war test matches I have seen". All agreed, nonetheless, that the test was a genuine thriller.

Britain got off to the best possible start, scoring a try after 55 seconds, when Stevenson sent Robinson crashing over following a swiftly taken tap penalty. Neil missed the conversion. Barnes reduced the lead when he kicked a splendid 45-yard penalty goal in the 11th minute but damaged his hamstring in so doing. There was no further scoring until the 32nd minute. After intense pressure McTigue, Whiteley and Bolton worked the ball wide to Ashton, who deftly gave Neil a reverse pass which enabled him to burst past Walsh and through Lumsden's tackle to score the first three points of the 61 he would rack up in tests against the Kangaroos. Britain led 6-2 at the interval but by the 48th minute they were 10-6 behind, as the Australians ripped through for two wonderful tries from Carlson, the first created by Wells and the second by a mesmerising effort from Gasnier. Carlson converted the first try. Shortly afterwards he stuck the post with a penalty – a fatal miss. Britain began to regain the initiative, thanks in considerable part to Harris's 17-6 pull in the scrums. Sixteen minutes from time a scrum went down near the Australians' goal. Stevenson fed, Harris struck quicker than Walsh, Stevenson picked up and in the twinkling of an eye worked a reverse pass to the onrushing Whiteley, who stormed over under the posts. It was a sucker punch but it killed the Kangaroos. Neil was given the burden of kicking the conversion, having failed with four previous shots. His nerve held and the ball sailed straight and true to give Britain an 11-10 lead, which they preserved heroically to referee Ron Gelder's final whistle.

Tom Longworth in the *News Chronicle* wrote, "In the after-match inquest both Eric Ashton and Neil Fox were criticised and Eric Fraser was preferred by some to Frank Dyson at full-back. Personally, I saw nothing really amiss with the team, and shall be surprised if there are many changes". Phil King in the *Sunday People* said, "Fox made a few mistakes – who wouldn't against Wells and Gasnier? – but I rated him a success. Stars in a solid pack which had no failure were McTigue and Whiteley". There was still some doubt, particularly from Lancastrians, as to whether Neil was really up to test standard and whether his partnership with Ashton could cope with Wells and Gasnier. A week after the Headingley test he showed them.

The Australians visited Belle Vue on 28 November with a team containing nine of the men who played in the Leeds test, including Wells and Gasnier. Trinity, second in the league behind St Helens, were up for it. 'The Pinder' reported, "It was tough, keen, occasionally vicious, thrilling, spectacular, but all the Wakefield men finished in the pink of condition." Neil's memories of the game are clear: "We were lacking Skene and Turner and Harold Poynton was playing his first game of the season but we cut them down to size, winning 20-10. I finished with four goals and a try. I remember the try well, breaking a double tackle from Wells and Gasnier, then rounding the full-back and going under the posts. This was probably my best game of the year, against the best opposition."

The *Wakefield Express* noted, "Fox, regarded as too slow for a test match place by some critics, satisfied at least two test selectors with his forceful display. It was the type of football most favourable to a match in which strength and skill might have a big advantage over pace alone". Neil converted all four of Trinity's tries.

They led 10-5 at half-time, Firth and Vines powering through for tries. On 45 minutes Neil bagged the third try – "a Fox special after slick handling in which Vines figured prominently. The final burst by the centre blasted a gap at a point near where three opponents had been promenading a second before". Five minutes later Firth crossed for his second try. Prior to kick-off Stuart Hadfield had presented test caps to Neil, Derek Turner and Don Vines. So, with winning pay and plaudits all round, it had been a pretty good afternoon's work for Neil.

The victory over the Australians was Trinity's 11th in a row but the week afterwards they went down 14-10 at Swinton. Fortunately, the following week they began another winning run of 12 matches, beating Halifax 24-13 on 12 December. Prop Joe Smith, recently signed from Keighley, made his debut, kicking six goals. Neil was missing, however, because he was chosen for the Ashes decider at Wigan. Also in the side were his team-mates Jack Wilkinson and Gerry Round, who was making his test debut. They were effectively the only two changes from the second test, Wilkie coming in for Don Vines, which meant Don Robinson moved from blind-side prop into the second-row. Australia retained their entire back division but brought in Dud Beattie for Parcell and Johnny Raper for Rasmussen. The Great Britain team was taken to Southport to prepare for the test, training at the local soccer club on the Thursday and Friday before the game.

Interestingly, Alan Prescott, the 1958 tour skipper, wrote in his preview to the Wigan test, "On packs and half-backs test triumphs are founded, and that is one reason why I think Australia will go home with a pocketful of well-earned and welcome cash – but without the prize of the Ashes trophy. Fox, in the first half at least of the second test, showed he could stand up to Wells, although he slipped from his pedestal after the interval. Now he has had two games' experience against the Aussies. Fox will be all the better for that experience and with less excuse for stage fright this time, I expect his goalkicking to be more up to standard. Ashton knows that he must not give Gasnier an inch… Ashton must be his constant companion."

Prescott must have had remarkable intuition for the page-wide headlines of the *Sunday Pictorial* of 13 December 1959 blared, "Fox flays 'em now" and Eddie Waring opened his account of the Ashes deciding test with, "It's test justice that Neil Fox, the man condemned by [some of] the critics after the second test, should win off his own left foot the decisive game and the Ashes for Britain at Wigan yesterday. Fox scored 15 of Britain's 18 points".

Neil had certainly lit up a grey Wigan afternoon and a drab, dour match played in cloying mud. In the *Sunday People* Phil King wrote, "Neil Fox played a sound game and covered himself with glory". Tom Banks in *Empire News* said, "Australia got the best two tries of the game – one from a pippin of a run by that wonder boy Reg Gasnier. But this will go down as Fox's match …Great Britain had the team for the day and the heavy going. They had the weight in the pack, and they had Fox, whose goals made all of the difference". Even Jack Bentley in the *Daily Express* acknowledged Neil's performance: "Having criticised the choice of centre Neil Fox, I must now applaud his 15 point performance which justified his selection. Forced into the goalkicking job by the withdrawal of Eric Fraser, this shy, modest Wakefield lad hit a five-minute 50-yard beauty then followed up with another five to give Britain their winning margin. I still think he needs more pace – and again it showed on occasions – but he chased one of his up-and-under kicks to score Great Britain's first try in grand style. Haven't Wakefield got a sprint expert to help Neil shorten and quicken that giant stride of his? It's all he needs to put him in the top centre bracket". Perhaps Neil would have been most gratified by the remark of his skipper, Jeff Stevenson, who said, "When Fox made it 6-2 I knew we had the Aussies on the run. Fox has had his critics. Let's hope he made 'em eat humble pie after this grand show".

Forty-five years later in 2004, the Central Park crowd of 26,089 and the millions of viewers who watched the game on BBC's *Grandstand* – at least those of us who are still alive – are still waiting to see Great Britain win a competition against Australia on British soil. For those who were witnesses, that occasion really was Fox's match. Neil banged over three first half penalties in the fifth, eighth and 27th minutes against a solitary penalty by Barnes in the 18th. He extended that 6-2 lead to 13-2 within eight minutes of the second half, landing a penalty and converting his own try. That try followed a typical piece of canniness. From 30 yards out he lofted a high kick, which bounced badly for both the British chasers and for several of the Aussie defenders. Neil was on hand to calmly gather the ball and touch down under the posts. Australia struck back with a try by Raper after some Gasnier magic, and Barnes's conversion brought the score to 13-7. Neil then calmed British jitters by kicking his sixth goal and after 70 minutes the score was Neil Fox 15 Australia 7. Gasnier's creation of a try for Carlson, improved by Barnes, was answered by a final try from Ike Southward and Britain had won 18-12.

Neil had played in four games against the 1959 Kangaroos – for Trinity, Yorkshire and twice for Britain – and had been a winner every time. He had rattled up four tries and 21 goals (54 points) in the process.

In the week after the third test Neil received a pleasant early Christmas present when he was elected Wakefield Sportsman of the Year, a trophy that had previously been won by such notable stars as Johnny Wardle, the Yorkshire and England cricketer, and the champion motorcyclist Dennis Parkinson. Among the opposition had been his colleague Don Vines and referee Ron Gelder.

Neil's return to league action brought him a 21-point haul against Bramley on 19 December and the Christmas period brought more success. Christmas Day presented

Trinity and Castleford with a gluepot pitch and conditions which 'The Pinder' described as "inhuman". Even so, a good game, played in good spirit, ensued with Neil kicking four goals in a 20-2 victory. Boxing Day again brought terrible ground conditions at Headingley and for the first 20 minutes nothing separated the two teams, who were level at 5-5. Thereafter Trinity simply astonished the onlookers, racing to a 20-5 half-time lead and blitzing Leeds in the second half to win 39-5, Neil's share being a couple of tries and six goals. Derek Turner and Trevor Whitehead were sent off in the 70th minute for fighting, although the game had been a very clean affair. Trinity's players picked up £34 for winning their Christmas games.

The New Year of 1960 brought a significant change in the laws of the game with the abolition of the tap penalty and of playing the advantage at scrummages. The new regulations did not bother Wakefield, however, who opened with another top performance when Hull were hammered 34-9 at Belle Vue. Neil landed eight of 12 attempts at goal but the highlight was a prodigious long-distance try by 'Budgie' Firth. Even more meritorious, however, was the following Saturday's 14-8 win at third-placed Oldham. The Trinity pack was in formidable form and Neil's only scoring contribution was a goal but he played so well that Phil King in the *Sunday People* remarked, "Neil Fox's masterful centre performance should silence his 'too slow' critics". 'The Pinder' was delighted to report that Neil had been quite the equal of the man he faced, the redoubtable Alan Davies. By this time Trinity, with six straight victories, were on £25 a man.

The following week, 16 January, things were a little less glorious but Trinity kept on the winning trail at Batley. The *Wakefield Express* headlined its match report: "On Batley's Icy Mountain". In freezing winds and intermittent sleet and snowstorms, Wakefield won 8-2 but were losing until Neil nosed them ahead in the 44th minute. The Batley full-back dropped the ball 30 yards out and Neil was quickest to react, grabbing the leather and racing to the posts for a try which he converted. Fred Smith scored the only other try of the match. Fred scored another four the following week when Doncaster were swept away 41-0 at Belle Vue. Neil also scored four tries and landed a couple of goals.

After a 12-0 home victory over Hull KR on 6 February, Wakefield were still second in the league behind St. Helens, closely followed by Oldham and Featherstone. At that point attention turned from the league to the Challenge Cup. Saints were hot favourites with the bookies at odds of 3-1, Wigan were 5-1 and Oldham and Trinity at 7-1. Sod's Law was obviously operating because Trinity were drawn away at St Helens in the first round on 13 February. It was going to be as hard as it could get to win at Knowsley Road but history would show that this cup tie would be the beginning of the most glorious period of Wakefield's long and illustrious existence. The St Helens coach Alan Prescott probably cranked up Neil's resolve when he told Derek Marshall of the *Daily Mail*, "Our centres have always played pretty well against Wakefield and Fox has never had a good game against us. Fox is big but Ken Large is greased lightning, and Skene is marking a good kid in McGinn... You only have to run through the players in our pack [Terry, Bowden, Prescott, Briggs, Huddart and Karalius] to see what Wakefield are up against."

Just short of 30,000 filed into Knowsley Road for a game which fulfilled all expectations, especially if you were a Wakefield fan. The weather had been decidedly wintry all week and the playing surface was slimy, yet the game proved terrifically robust but clean. The *Wakefield Express* was ecstatic: "Wakefield had only one plan. That was to go in and beat St Helens by the best brand of football, a mission that was accomplished in a fashion earning full marks". Neil started the scoring with a penalty after three minutes, helped send John Etty over for a try after 10 minutes and booted another penalty on 22 minutes. Saints reduced the lead to 7-5 three minutes later, when McGinn scored a converted try. Trinity looked to be in deep trouble on the half hour when full-back Gerry Round and stand-off Harold Poynton crashed sickeningly into each other trying to field a high ball. They were both knocked cold. Round had suffered a double fracture of the jaw and Poynton received four stitches as an ugly chunk of raw flesh was exposed over his left eye. There were no substitutes in those days, so Gerry and Harold simply soldiered on. Trinity's response was virtually immediate with Etty again scoring after more wonderfully daring play. At half-time Trinity led 10-5 and made the game safe after 45 minutes, when Jack Wilkinson, along with Vines and Turner the outstanding forwards on the field, crashed through McGinn's tackle to score his first try for the club. Neil converted for 15-5 and although Rhodes claimed a try and a goal for Saints, Trinity safely proceeded to the second round.

Alan Prescott took back his pre-match comments and declared, "Fox was brilliant". Another of Neil's critics, Jack Bentley concurred: "Poor little Large took a terrific hammering. Besides Etty's body-bruising tackles, he bore the brunt of Fox's thundering bursts and though Ken clung courageously to the mighty Neil he could never halt him". Neil's and John Etty's smothering tackles made Large's life so difficult that the ball hardly got as far as Tom van Vollenhoven, Saints' most dangerous threat.

On 20 February Wakefield had an important 11-5 home win over Oldham, reinforcing the belief that they really could beat the best the game had to offer on a consistent basis. It was a poor game, however, with the defences snuffing out attempts to play an open game. Mischievously, 'The Pinder' suggested that the highlight for some would have been the sight of Miss Wakefield Trinity, Gwenda Savern, kicking off. Amazingly, she probably had as much luck as Neil and Bernard Ganley, two of the greatest kickers in the game's annals, who could muster just one goal apiece from nine attempts each.

Trinity, now joint favourites with Wigan at 5-2, had pulled another tough nut out of the Challenge Cup hat and drawn Widnes away in the second round. The team was taken to Southport on the preceding Friday to train on the sands, as they had for the St Helens game. A crowd of 18,773 packed Naughton Park for the tie. Neil recalls, "This was another hard game, as Widnes had beaten Warrington in the first round. I remember breaking through twice early in the match and feeding Keith Holliday but he was brought back both times for forward passes, or at least the referee thought they were. It was only in the second half that John Etty finally scored the try which won the match and I converted it." It had certainly proved a tough tie to win – "almost continuously exciting though dour", according to 'The Pinder'. Trinity were, however, better than the 5-2 scoreline because Keith Holliday had those two Fox-instigated tries ruled out in the fifth and 23rd minutes and the Trinity forwards had the upper hand in tight and loose. 'The Pinder' added, "The performance of Fox provoked some controversy. He probably was rather quieter than in some matches. But that did not lead close observers to overlook the tremendously effective touches he provided, even if he did not produce his powerful bursts to scatter defenders."

Neil had been in prime form for months now and there was no surprise when he was selected for Britain's next test against France at Toulouse on Sunday, 6 March. Also in the side were Wilkinson and Turner, the latter brought in at the last moment when Johnny Whiteley withdrew injured. The test match was fairly typical of Franco-British clashes at this period, at times brilliant, at others brutal. Britain rushed to an 11-0 lead after 23 minutes through tries by Eric Ashton, Neil – a 20-yard power burst after receiving from skipper Jeff Stevenson – and Mick Sullivan, the first of which Neil converted. However, by half-time France had taken a 12-11 lead. In the 48th minute it was Neil who put Britain ahead again, racing 50 yards for a superb try, which he converted. The scoring continued to fluctuate and by the 67th minute Britain led 18-17, Neil having added another goal. Then everything blew up. Derek Turner tackled French scrum-half Georges Fages "heavily but fairly", according to several British press reports. Fages patently disagreed and kicked Turner under the chin. Derek retaliated and the upshot was a massive brawl – "the biggest single brawl I have seen in several mêlée-marred matches in this country", according to Jack Bentley. Feet and fists flew and when things calmed down only Turner was sent off by the referee, Georges Jameau. Turner refused to go, clearly believing that Fages would be joining him. After five minutes of confusion Bill Fallowfield escorted Turner away and the game continued before the nonplussed crowd of 15,308. France then won the match 20-18 with a try six minutes from time from prop Aldo Quaglio, described by Harold Mather in the *Manchester Guardian* as "the culmination of some of the finest backing-up – the ball went right, left, right, left, through 11 pairs of hands – it is possible to imagine".

In the Trinity trio's absence Wakefield had lost their first game since 5 December, going down 11-5 at Hull. They returned to form at Hunslet on 12 March, inflicting a 15-8 defeat on the Parksiders, their first at home since April 1958. Then it was back to Challenge Cup fare and a problematic third round tie at Whitehaven. The Trinity players were whisked off to a Keswick hotel on the preceding Wednesday. The *Wakefield Express* reported, "Country walks and complete relaxation, it is hoped, will blow away staleness members of the committee have detected in the players". Club chairman Stuart Hadfield handed over sprigs of shamrock to skipper 'Rocky' Turner as the players left Wakefield – 'little bits of Ireland' provided by a Roman Catholic Priest, Father R. C. Finn, a diehard Trinity supporter, who commentated on Trinity's games on the Wakefield Hospitals Relay Service and later wrote for the *Rugby Leaguer* under the *nom de plume* of 'Leftfooter'.

The game was all-ticket and Whitehaven housed its record crowd – 18,619. 'Haven put up a good show but as the *Wakefield Express* observed, "It was an occasion on which class told, for Whitehaven were never in the same category as their attractive visitors". The early exchanges were furious with the referee handing out seven cautions. Whitehaven full-back John McKeown, another deadly kicker, gave his side the lead before tries by Fred Smith and Malcolm Sampson put Trinity 8-4 up at half-time. A super try from Turner extended the lead before Whitehaven pulled back to 11-10 after 53 minutes with three penalty goals. Five minutes later Turner calmed Trinity fans' nerves with a second blockbusting try from a play-the-ball, with Neil adding a touchline conversion. Alan Skene rounded it off with a late try, again goaled from touch by Neil and Trinity won 21-10. The *Wakefield Express* noted, "Fox made a big impression on his first appearance against the Cumbrian side. What they thought of him could best be described in the words of a local director who said Fox was the biggest sensation they had had at Whitehaven for a long time!"

Trinity won at Castleford on 26 March, when referee Matt Coates sent John Etty off after 35 minutes for striking his opposing winger, Colin Battye, with what 'The Pinder' described as "a short, crisp right hook". It was not amusing, as a suspension could have cost John a place in the Cup semi-final. With his record of never having been dismissed in over 600 games, the disciplinary committee eventually decided that sending-off was sufficient punishment and there was a collective sigh of relief throughout Trinity's ranks.

While John had been indulging his new-found aptitude for pugilism, Neil had been otherwise engaged playing for Great Britain in the return test against France at Knowsley Road. The crowd of more than 13,000 saw a much cleaner match than the Toulouse affair with referee Eric 'Sergeant-Major' Clay keeping a firm grip on proceedings. However, they went away disappointed by Britain's inability to again hold on to a 10-point lead. The game was drawn 17-17 and few Brits came out of it with much credit. Neil was one who did.

After a quarter of an hour he set up the first points, snapping up a loose ball before sending Mick Sullivan sprinting 50 yards for a try, which Neil converted. The French drew level within seven minutes after a flowing move, which ended with a try from centre Antoine Jimenez, goaled by full-back Pierre Lacaze. Neil restored Britain's lead with a 35-yard penalty in the 28th minute but Lacaze's drop-goal three minutes later levelled the scores 7-7 at the break. Three minutes after half-time Neil kicked another penalty and then scored a try after combining well with Derek Turner. The *Rugby Leaguer* wrote, "In scoring Britain's second and most decisive try in the 56th minute Neil once again demonstrated the unusual knack of having players all around him yet, at the same time, making them all look so ineffective". When Dave Bolton ran in a stunning 40-yard try in the 67th minute, goaled again by Neil, Britain seemed impregnable with a 17-7 lead. At that juncture France sprang irresistibly to life. Ten minutes from time second-rower Robert Eramouspe clattered over for a try and three minutes from time a sensational touchdown by centre Jean Verges saved the game for France. Lacaze converted both and almost snatched victory with a last gasp drop at goal. The British press corps were scathing of the team but almost unanimously acclaimed Neil as Britain's best. The representative season had now ended. Neil's four test matches had yielded five tries and 14 goals and he was regarded as one of half-a-dozen or so men, who would certainly be picked for Great Britain's 1960 World Cup squad, barring mishaps.

In club football Neil and Trinity faced a hectic end-of-season schedule. Eight league fixtures and a Challenge Cup semi-final had to be negotiated in only 30 days but there was a real prospect of winning either the Cup or the Championship, or both if fortune was on their side. The Wakefield management certainly believed the future was bright. Their confidence in coach Ken Traill was shown when they extended his contract for another two years with a weekly wage of £8, which with match bonuses would probably amount to £14, making him arguably the highest paid coach in the game. He had to agree to stop playing, however, having continued to turn out occasionally for the 'A' team.

League victories over Dewsbury and at York preceded Trinity's Challenge Cup semi-final against neighbours Featherstone Rovers at Odsal on 9 April. There was much media interest in the fact that Neil and Don would be on opposing sides in the semi-final. Graham Chalkley was a schoolboy at Sharlston at the time and recalls: "Eddie Waring came to Sharlston School with the television cameras to interview Neil and Don. They picked two sides from the kids who were playing in the playground – one side for Neil Fox and the other for Don Fox – and we had a game of touch and pass for the cameras. I can only remember myself, Vic Loxton and Colin Chalkley playing though. The programme was shown on BBC's *Sportsnight*, I think."

Trinity were clear favourites to win the Cup by now but the committee were still keen to allow the team special preparation time. On this occasion they were despatched to the Granby Hotel in Harrogate. Trinity were reported to be on £45 per man if they won. A massive attendance of almost 56,000 poured into Odsal. Rovers were playing in the semis for the third consecutive season and Don Fox was at scrum-half for them. Of course, this was Neil's first Challenge Cup semi-final so he was in unknown territory. Unfortunately for Rovers, injuries conspired to deprive them of the services of winger Frank Smith and half their pack – Joe Anderson, hooker Willis Fawley and Colin Clifft.

Despite the fierceness of local rivalries the semi-final turned out to be less heated than expected and not much of a spectacle. First blood was drawn by Rovers when Terry Clawson kicked a prodigious 45-yard penalty after 32 minutes. Four minutes later Trinity took a lead they would never lose. Phil King in the *Sunday People* wrote: "Wakefield scored an amazing try which put them on the road to Wembley, with 20-year-old Neil Fox the brains behind the move. Rovers lost the ball in midfield and Poynton fly-kicked ahead. Winger Fred Smith gained possession and was tackled. From the play-the-ball Fox burst on to a pass like an outsized meteor and swept his way pugnaciously towards the far touchline, pushing off two Featherstone players en route. Before Rovers' defence could rally, Fox let the ball go to Turner and Etty was finally over in the corner." Thereafter, however hard Rovers tried, they were never going to win. After 44 minutes Alan Skene performed one of his characteristic swallow dives to score wide out and on 58 minutes Etty crashed through Mullaney and Jackie Fennell for another try at the corner. Neil sealed an 11-2 victory with a 78th-minute penalty goal.

One of Neil's great ambitions was thus attained: "I knew it was not going to be easy, especially with Don and Joe Mullaney in the opposition. I was chuffed that we had won but disappointed for Don and Joe. But that's what games are all about. Winning big games and going to Wembley for the first time was something I always wanted. In between the semi-final and Wembley the next four weeks at the club were very exciting. We were measured for club blazers and flannels and shirts from Double 2. Then there were the team photos for the Cup Final programme. I really couldn't wait for the final."

Hull beat Oldham 12-9 in the other semi-final at Swinton, so an all-Yorkshire final was assured for Wembley on 14 May, when the Queen was due to attend her first rugby league match. Although Trinity were almost certain to finish second to St Helens in the league, they still needed to win a few matches to ensure that they secured a home game in the Championship semi-finals and the Yorkshire League Championship was also there for the taking. Two days after the Odsal match Trinity overcame Swinton 13-2 and the following Saturday beat Keighley 26-0, when Neil supplied 14 of their points. They were now assured of a place in the top four play-offs.

There were, however, setbacks. Malcolm Sampson and Albert Firth were involved in a car accident. Budgie was unhurt but Malcolm, a real revelation in the Trinity pack, fractured his left wrist so badly that he missed the rest of the season. On Easter Monday, 18 April, Wakefield came a real cropper in losing 10-7 at home to Featherstone, who were fielding half a team of reserves. Don Fox played magnificently in a game which was a timely reminder to Trinity of the sin of overconfidence and ended an eight-match winning sequence. The following afternoon Trinity went to Odsal and defeated Bradford Northern 28-17. The game was second-rower Geoff Steel's debut but its outstanding incident was a fabulous 85-yard try from Fred Smith, who beat practically all the Bradford side in a labyrinthine run. Neil had a good day too. He scored the game's first try in the fourth minute. 'The Pinder' was impressed: "It was a particularly cheeky affair by Fox, who stepped smartly forward into a round of passing by Bradford and actually took the ball out of centre Plenderleith's hands! Incredible, but real, nevertheless, as was proved when Fox, having put the finishing touches to a pulsating [45 yards] effort, added the goal points from a position two yards inside the touchline." That try was Neil's 400th point of the season in all games, an achievement previously managed only by Jim Sullivan, Lewis Jones and Bernard Ganley, none of whom was as young as Neil when they did it.

Defeat followed at Thrum Hall, something of a bogey venue for Trinity. The *Wakefield Express* described the game as a yawn but something must have happened, at least in the first 15 minutes, when referee Eric Clay cautioned eight players, including Neil. The final league match at home to Bradford Northern followed on Wednesday, 27 April, with Trinity needing only to draw to retain the Yorkshire League Championship. Neil had a dreadful day with the boot, failing with all his seven shots at goal. However, with the ball in hand he was magnificent, scoring two tries in a 28-5 victory. The *Wakefield Express* noted he was "the leading figure in several scintillating movements. His second-half try, in collaboration with Etty and Smith, was a brilliant affair".

Trinity had therefore clinched the Yorkshire League title but it had been a close-run thing, as runners-up Hull finished only one point behind them. Wakefield finished second in the Northern Rugby League table, five points adrift of St Helens, which gave them a home Championship semi-final, ironically against Hull, their opponents in the Challenge Cup Final. The semi was played on 7 May and caused something of a stir as it clashed with live television coverage of the FA Cup Final between Blackburn Rovers and Wolverhampton Wanderers. St Helens and Wigan had decided to play their game in the evening. Trinity had also put up the price of admission for the game, which did not go down at all well with their supporters. Consequently, the relatively low attendance of 16,283 was disappointing, but hardly unexpected. The game turned out to be uninspiring too. Trinity won 24-4 against an injury-ridden Hull but did not impress, scoring 13 of their points in the last 19 minutes, 10 in the last four. Neil provided such fireworks as there were. Trinity led 9-4 at half-time, Neil kicking them ahead on 12 minutes before Bateson equalised on 22 minutes. "Then", related Ray Oddy in *Yorkshire Sports*, "in remarkable fashion Fox dropped a brilliant goal. Gathering a loose ball over on the left, he dummied to his right and turned round to drop an angled goal which brought the house down. One minute later, Trinity were there again. That man Fox found the gap and Hull were beaten to a frazzle by his kick through. Skene won the race for the ball to dive triumphantly for a try." Bateson added a second penalty but that was cancelled out when Neil kicked his third goal. He kicked a fourth after 49 minutes and 13 minutes later pounded 40 yards for a snap try to give Trinity a 14-4 lead. In the dying minutes he converted tries by Firth and Etty.

Trinity's victory over the Airlie Birds had carried them to their first ever Championship final. Their opponents would be Wigan, who had surprised St Helens 19-9 in a stormy encounter at Knowsley Road.

First, however, they had to negotiate their Challenge Cup Final against Hull on 14 May. The team left Wakefield on the Thursday morning and travelled south by train, making their headquarters at the Aldenham Lodge Hotel in Radlett, Hertfordshire. Trinity were overwhelming favourites to win the Cup. Their only absentees were Malcolm Sampson and Harold Poynton, who had not recovered from a shoulder injury sustained in the Championship semi-final. Hull, on the other hand, were reduced to scraping about for a representative team. Their goalkicking full-back Peter Bateson had been heavily concussed in the game against Trinity and was ruled out. Even worse, however, Hull's formidable pack was shorn of Bill Drake, Jim Drake, Cyril Sykes and Peter Whiteley. It was hard to see how they could compensate for such heavy depletion. So hard pressed for forwards were the Boulevarders that they gave a first-team debut to second-rower Mike Smith, a unique occurrence in a Challenge Cup Final. Sam Evans, the former Wakefield prop, was drafted into the blind-side prop position to face his old team-mates. Neil, who had celebrated his 21st birthday just 10 days earlier, can rarely have played in a game in which the four centres came from such disparate sources – a Sharlston lad, partnering Alan Skene who was a South African, in opposition to Nan Halafihi, the first Tongan to play at Wembley, who had come to England ostensibly as a boxer, and one of the few Scots in rugby league, Stan Cowan. Neil was somewhat surprised at Trinity's casual approach to the final, recalling that just a few hours before the game the team were happily frolicking in the hotel swimming pool. But it was a glorious, sunny afternoon at Wembley, where a crowd of just fewer than 80,000 saw the teams line up as follows:

57

Wakefield Trinity: Gerry Round, Fred Smith, Alan Skene, Neil Fox, John Etty, Ken Rollin, Keith Holliday, Jack Wilkinson, Geoff Oakes, Don Vines, Albert Firth, Les Chamberlain, Derek Turner (captain).

Hull: Jack Kershaw, Gordon Harrison, Stan Cowan, Nanumi Halafihi, David Johnson, Frank Broadhurst, Tommy Finn, Mick Scott, Tommy Harris, Sam Evans, Tom Sutton, Mike Smith, Johnny Whiteley (captain).

Prior to kick-off the teams were presented to the Duke of Edinburgh and he had barely taken his place in the royal box before Neil had kicked his side into a 2-0 lead with a 40-yard penalty after Hull were penalised at the first scrum by referee Eric Clay. By the time three minutes had elapsed Trinity were 5-0 up. From his own '25' Ken Rollin suddenly found a gap, raced clear, kicked past full-back Kershaw, and won the race with his Hull pursuers to score a wonderful 75-yard try. Neil missed the goal. If anyone expected the floodgates to open, however, they were badly mistaken. Hull fought back ferociously and many judged they had the better of the rest of the first half. On 12 minutes they won a scrum 20 yards from Wakefield's line and worked a smart move between the half-backs, which sent Cowan twisting past Round for an equalising try, which Evans goaled. Cowan, consistent with Hull's bad luck, broke a rib in the process but bravely played on to the end. Two minutes later Neil restored Wakefield's lead with another penalty goal and half-time arrived with Trinity in front 7-5. Hull had been aided by a scrum and penalty count well in their favour, but, ominously, their live-wire hooker Tommy Harris had taken a battering and collapsed in front of the royal box on the half hour. He was badly concussed and ended up in hospital, although he played blind in one eye until the 65th minute when he was finally taken off. He literally ran himself into the ground and was rewarded for his skill and courage with the Lance Todd Trophy.

Neil and his Wakefield team-mates trooped into the dressing rooms at the break fully aware that they had not performed anywhere near their best. Coach Ken Traill tore into his team, insisting that they play to their strengths: their superior speed and handling skills. It was essential that they moved the ball. "I didn't half give it them", Traill told reporters, "and look how it improved Turner's play. Open football is the only answer at Wembley." Certainly Derek Turner led the cavalry charge as Trinity completely eclipsed the brave but hapless Hull men in the second period. Although the Hull supporters tried to buoy up their team with a rendition of their anthem *Old Faithful*, within 10 minutes Trinity were out of sight. Neil started the rout striding mightily for the corner flag to finish off a crisp handling movement involving Vines, Rollin and Skene. He missed the conversion, nor could he convert the next try a few minutes later, when Skene flew majestically to the line from around 65 yards. In the 59th minute Turner burst the defence and sent Holliday racing in from half-way. Neil goaled and Trinity led 18-5. Wave upon wave of attacking football climaxed with another Skene try after good work by Wilkinson and Turner on 65 minutes. Neil improved it, as he did his own second try on 72 minutes, with a storming charge from half-way after Round had begun the move on his own '25'. In the last three minutes he added further conversions to scores by Smith and Holliday, as Trinity ran out victors by a then record Challenge Cup Final score of 38-5.

For such a one-sided game, this final was one of the most entertaining in the history of the Challenge Cup. Neil had shattered all the records for a final with his seven goals and 20 points, the latter still being unbeaten in 2005. For Neil it was another ambition fulfilled. He says: "The 1960 Challenge Cup Final was one of the real highlights of my career. There was not a lot of open play in the first half. We knew that with Tommy Harris concussed just before half-time we had to make that pay in the second half and we did. The second half was open rugby at its best. Tommy won the Lance Todd Trophy for his guts and determination and he was the only Hull player who troubled us on the day. Actually he ran into me twice in heavy tackles, which probably didn't do him much good. I couldn't have got all those points without the other boys. I always felt we had the beating of Hull and I, personally, didn't have a tough time. Of course, the whole thing was made more special because the Queen presented the Cup."

After their triumph Trinity decamped to their new London accommodation at Bailey's Hotel on Gloucester Road, where they enjoyed a celebratory dinner. While they were in the capital Neil recalls, "We went to London Zoo and were watching the lions. Ken Rollin teased one of them and it obviously didn't think much of Ken's antics. As it moved away from his vicinity it peed all over his trouser legs and wet him through. On the Sunday evening we went to see Nat King Cole at the London Palladium. The players' wives and girlfriends were invited down for the weekend but stayed at a different hotel and their husbands and boyfriends had to pay the hotel bills for their two nights there. We got £100 for winning the Cup, less one third in tax and the bills for the wives and girlfriends. We finished up with about £40 but it was well worth it, having them share the experience with us."

The return to Wakefield on Monday was fantastic. The *Wakefield Express* finally dispensed with its traditional front page of adverts and emblazoned across it were the headlines: "Home with the Rugby League Challenge Cup after 14 years – Wakefield has never seen anything like it! – Trinity receive breathtaking welcome from 40,000 crowd."

"Cheering Wakefield Trinity home from Wembley began 10 miles away from the city and culminated in an awe-inspiring, surging, roaring crowd of flag-waving men, women and children numbering over 40,000 offering a welcome right out of the pages of a fairy tale."

Having arrived at Westgate station, the Trinity heroes boarded an open brewery lorry, which was led through the streets by the Nostell Colliery band. The lorry was decorated with more than 200 yards of red, white and blue ribbons. On the front was a rosette, a yard wide, made by local shop girls. The crowds lining the streets to the town hall were 20 or 30 deep and police struggled to hold them back. Eventually the team reached the town hall, Derek Turner brought the cup out onto the balcony and Neil and his colleagues shared the crowd's adulation. Later the mayor, Councillor L. Moore, presided over a reception in the team's honour.

It had certainly been a good week for Neil and Trinity. It would be even better if Wigan could be vanquished the following Saturday at Odsal. Trinity had never won the Championship but they were confident that would be rectified. The bookies made them favourites but, oddly, many of the rugby league writers favoured Wigan, even when they announced a completely re-jigged back division. Fiery test winger Mick Sullivan had been dismissed along with Alex Murphy in Wigan's semi-final victory over St Helens and was suspended for the Championship final. Wigan consequently brought Billy Boston in from the wing to centre in order to counter the threat posed by Neil. Eric Ashton moved from centre to stand-off and Dave Bolton, the current test stand-off, went to scrum-half.

None of that seemed to worry the Wakefield fans, who were keen to see Trinity complete a rare and historic Cup and League double. An estimated 16,000 were going to Odsal. Every available bus in Wakefield and the surrounding villages had been booked and the West Riding Automobile Company reported that more than 40 'specials' had been hired. Wigan were reported to be taking 10,000 supporters but Odsal would cope with the capacity set at 80,000.

At Wembley Neil had taken his points total for Trinity for the season up to 370, equalling his own club record. He would surely break that record, given any sort of luck. Fred Smith's try at Wembley, his 37th, had also brought him level with his own try-scoring record for the club. Maybe he too would be celebrating smashing his own record. Trinity's XIII was the same as at Wembley, while their opponents fielded the following team:

Wigan: Fred Griffiths, Frank Halliwell, Billy Boston, Keith Holden, Syd Fenton, Eric Ashton (captain), Dave Bolton, John Barton, Bill Sayer, Frank Collier, Brian McTigue, Geoff Lyon, Roy Evans.

The referee at Wembley, Eric Clay, was again in charge. The teams were introduced to Lord Derby before the game and there was a bigger attendance than for the Challenge Cup Final. Despite the stated 80,000 capacity, a record Championship Final crowd of 83,190 covered the slopes and filled the stands and what they witnessed was a complete surprise.

Just as at Wembley, Trinity opened with a bang. In the second minute wonderfully dextrous handling stretched the Wigan defence to breaking point. Vines made the initial break in midfield, Kenny Rollin shot 40 yards diagonally and put Fred Smith over for his record-breaking 38th try of the season. Neil failed with the kick but it was an almost perfect start for Trinity. But instead of things getting better, they got worse and Neil was the central figure.

After eight minutes Griffiths landed a penalty from a scrum offence and four minutes later Neil was incapacitated by a bad injury to his left thigh. From then on he was merely a passenger hobbling painfully on the left wing, unable to offer much more than nuisance value to his side. Wakefield's tactics appeared to change from running the ball to trying to master the Wigan pack and they simply did not work. Although Neil's injury was a blow to Trinity it did not detract from Wigan's ultimate 27-3 victory. The Wigan forwards were masterful, Brian McTigue playing one of the supreme games of his great career. On 22 minutes Griffiths kicked a difficult 35-yard penalty for another scrum offence, the ball hitting a post before going over the bar and Wigan never looked back. Gerry Round made two miraculous tackles on Boston to keep Trinity interested but just before half-time, Billy finally got the better of Gerry to score wide out, from where Griffiths goaled superbly and Wigan led 9-3. Neil had four pain-killing injections at half-time but to no avail. Wigan had a problem too as their left-centre Keith Holden played much of the game with concussion and was later put on the wing opposite Neil. Poor tactics and bad luck continued to dog Trinity and Wigan added four tries, through an Ashton brace, Sayer and Boston in the second-half, with Griffiths adding another three goals.

Skipper Derek Turner told Arthur Brooks of the *Sunday Pictorial*, "They hit us like a bomb. We expected it would be close and after that try by Fred Smith we looked favourites. Disaster came with that injury to Neil Fox. It was the leg he lands goals with. No use bringing him up for kicks with a knee twice its normal size. We were well licked". Phil King in the *Sunday People* graphically wrote, "With Fox limping pitifully on the wing... Wakefield always looked like a leaderless legion". Neil recalls: "Wigan made a lot of positional changes, including putting Billy Boston to watch me. Regarding the injury, I took the ball at speed and went between Billy and Frank Halliwell but caught Frank's knee right on my thigh. So I finished up limping on the wing and from then on we were no match for a rampant Wigan. Their pack dominated our six. Eric Ashton and Dave Bolton dictated play and Wigan won in style. It was a match too far for us. But it was still a great season for the club and me."

Although the season ended in injury and disappointment – Neil failed to break his club points record and failed to score in a game for the first time in 95 matches (87 for Trinity), since March 1958 – he had made his mark. He finished fifth leading try-scorer in the league with 37; jointly with Austin Rhodes of St Helens he led the goalkickers with 171 and topped the points scorers with 453 – 54 more than second-placed Rhodes. Only Lewis Jones with

496 in 1956-57 had ever scored more points in a season, although Bernard Ganley had also amassed 453 points in 1957-58.

Although 35-try Alan Skene took the Wakefield Trinity Player of the Year Award, Neil was widely regarded as the game's outstanding player of the season. He won the National Federation of Supporters Clubs' Player of the Year Award, a huge accolade. Tom Longworth of the *News Chronicle* wrote: "I can without delay nominate Neil Fox as the outstanding centre and Tom van Vollenhoven and Billy Boston as the premier wing threequarters". Lewis Jones in the *News of the World* was certain that Neil would win the award, regarding his only rivals as van Vollenhoven, Whiteley and Jeff Stevenson. He wrote, "Early this season the wiseacres said that Fox was too slow and ponderous to be a successful centre. But he has quickened up, and, combining a footballer's brain with handling ability and 14 stone 10 pounds of thrust, has undoubtedly come to stay in the big-time".

Eddie Waring, in his *Rugby League Annual*, declared: "Neil Fox is my Player of the Year. All Wakefield, most of Yorkshire and lots of fans in Lancashire and Cumberland will agree that the Trinity centre did more in 1959-60 than any man in the game... If any player is capable of breaking Lewis Jones's all-time record in a season... it must be Neil Fox. He has the ideal build, temperament and skill for a centre. His critics say he is not fast enough and that he will finish as a forward. Time will tell. I only know that he is Britain's best centre and, given freedom from injury, will be a World Cup force in 1960 and a dominating figure in Australia in 1962."

Back on 11 March 'JEB' had issued his "Rugby League World Ratings" in the *Rugby Leaguer*. He had named Neil as the number one left-centre in the game, ahead of Johnny Riley (Australia), Antoine Jimenez (France), Lewis Jones and Alan Davies. Neil must have been doing something right.

Wakefield Trinity 1959-60

Wakefield Trinity finished 2nd in the league: P38, W32, L6, For 831, Against 348

Fox scored 30 tries, 140 goals, 370 points for Wakefield, and 7 tries, 31 goals, 83 points in representative games

Date	Opponent	Score	Fox	Crowd	
15 Aug	**Wigan**	21-14	T, 3G	17,000	
17 Aug	Featherstone R	25-11	5G	12,687	
22 Aug	St Helens	7-40	2G	19,122	
26 Aug	**Leeds**	27-17	T, 6G	14,000	
29 Aug	Halifax	14-17	T, 4G	12,508	YC1
5 Sep	Wigan	27-19	T, 6G	23,774	
12 Sep	**St Helens**	2-16	G	19,000	
19 Sep	**York**	14-8	dnp	7,733	
26 Sep	Dewsbury	29-3	dnp	7,500	
3 Oct	**Hunslet**	35-19	T, 4G	12,575	
10 Oct	Doncaster	42-12	6G	3,000	
17 Oct	**Batley**	16-9	dnp	8,500	
24 Oct	Huddersfield	27-5	T, 3G	7,570	
31 Oct	**Hull KR**	44-9	2T, 7G	7,721	
7 Nov	Bramley	28-7	2T, 2G	4,930	
14 Nov	**Huddersfield**	31-6	8G	6,476	
21 Nov	Keighley	21-14	dnp	6,226	
28 Nov	**Australians**	20-10	T, 4G	17,615	
5 Dec	Swinton	10-14	2G	7,700	
12 Dec	**Halifax**	24-13	dnp	4,829	
19 Dec	**Bramley**	48-9	3T, 6G	4,600	
25 Dec	**Castleford**	20-2	4G	5,370	
26 Dec	Leeds	39-5	2T, 6G	14,441	
2 Jan	**Hull**	34-9	8G	9,839	
9 Jan	Oldham	14-8	G	16,694	
16 Jan	Batley	8-2	T, G	9,336	
23 Jan	**Doncaster**	41-0	4T, 2G	5,487	
6 Feb	Hull KR	12-0	3G	7,732	
13 Feb	St Helens	15-10	3G	29,371	Ch Cup 1
20 Feb	**Oldham**	11-5	G	14,926	
27 Feb	Widnes	5-2	G	18,773	Ch Cup 2
5 Mar	Hull	5-11	dnp	13,175	
12 Mar	Hunslet	15-8	3G	17,500	
19 Mar	Whitehaven	21-10	3G	18,619	Ch Cup 3
26 Mar	Castleford	10-2	dnp	8,500	
28 Mar	**Dewsbury**	17-0	T, 4G	5,900	
2 Apr	York	21-8	3G	8,208	
9 Apr	Featherstone R	11-2	G	55,935	Ch Cup semi (at Odsal)
11 Apr	**Swinton**	13-2	2G	10,348	
16 Apr	**Keighley**	26-0	2T, 4G	8,660	
18 Apr	**Featherstone R**	7-10	2G	18,171	
19 Apr	Bradford N	28-17	T, 5G	7,500	
23 Apr	Halifax	5-9	G	10,909	
27 Apr	**Bradford N**	28-5	2T	8,463	
7 May	**Hull**	24-4	T, 6G	16,283	CH semi
14 May	Hull	38-5	2T, 7G	79,733	Ch Cup Final (at Wembley)
21 May	Wigan	3-27		83,190	CH Final (at Odsal)

Representative appearances

28 Sep	Yorkshire 47 Australians 15 (York)	T, 10G
11 Nov	Yorkshire 38 Lancashire 28 (Leigh)	T, 7G
21 Nov	Great Britain 11 Australia 10 (Leeds)	T, G
12 Dec	Great Britain 18 Australia 12 (Wigan)	T, 6G
6 Mar	Great Britain 18 France 20 (Toulouse)	2T, 3G
26 Mar	Great Britain 17 France 17 (St Helens)	T, 4G

8. 1960-61: A curate's egg of a season

Even after such a successful season as 1959-60, the Wakefield management was keen to strengthen its side. Within a week of losing to Wigan in the Championship Final they splashed out £5,000 for St Helens's second-rower Brian Briggs. Neil had plenty of time for Brian: "He was a Wakefield lad who had first signed for York, then Huddersfield and onto St Helens. He had got Yorkshire caps and went on the 1954 tour. So his capture made our pack a lot stronger. He was a willing worker and probably the best cover tackler in the game. When Brian came to Trinity I got him a job working with me at Sharlston pit doing pipe-fitting. He had just taken over the Fox and Grapes pub in Eastmoor. At first his wife Mary ran the pub during the day, while he worked with me. That lasted for about six months until he went full-time at the pub. In later years Brian took the British Oak, and John Ridge, one of our chairmen at Trinity, replaced him at the Fox and Grapes".

Trinity were really on the crest of a wave at this period. On 16 June they announced a whopping profit on the year of £4,629 and found that season tickets were flying out of the office doors at a staggering rate. All the main stand seats were sold and the club boasted about 4,000 members, branches of the Supporters' Club flourishing at Belle Vue, Lupset, Netherton & Middlestown, Normanton, Outwood and Ryhill, with a General Post Office branch and a British Ropes Limited branch. The next couple of years would see additional branches established at East Ardsley & Thorpe, Hopetown, Kettlethorpe, Ossett and Primrose Hill. The club had good reason to be grateful for the Supporters' Club raised many thousands of pounds for Trinity, at a time when in many cases rugby league gates were in steady decline. For the time being, however, Trinity were bucking the trend as they developed into one of the most entertaining teams the game has seen.

The season began with Neil reporting for duty at 15 stones four pounds – he was obviously still growing. His partner Alan Skene had also put on weight at 11 stones 9½ pounds. The only fly in Trinity's ointment appeared to be the continued absence of the injured Malcolm Sampson, although Wilf Adams had been sold to Hunslet for £1,000.

On 13 August, Trinity kicked off with a 17-7 home success against Swinton in a tough game, illuminated by Skene's brilliance. Alan made a try for Neil – "a fitting reward for the young international centre who showed touches of his greatness and his great strength". Four days later Trinity won 26-9 at Castleford with Neil booting four goals and claiming his 100th try for Wakefield. They had made hard work of winning though, being behind until the 57th minute. Worse followed at Wilderspool where Warrington hammered Trinity 26-5, Neil recalling, "That was the first time I came up against Brian Bevan and Jim Challinor. What a wonderful player Bevan was. He scored after two minutes and got another later. He and Challinor were a very good combination, Jim finding room and Brian finishing things off. It was Wakefield's first game at Wilderspool for 13 years and we found out how hard it was to win there. I also remember Keith Holliday getting his jaw broken just before half-time. Brian Briggs cracked a rib too. It was a bad day all round".

Two days later Wakefield won easily at Keighley but the *Wakefield Express* observed that neither Gerry Round nor Neil had yet found their true form. There was better fortune for Neil on 27 August, when Trinity faced Halifax in the first round of the Yorkshire Cup at Belle Vue, but even then there was a downside, although there was no way he would ever forget that day. The *Wakefield Express* headlined their match report "Fox tips the balance". The afternoon was truly horrendous. There were thunderstorms, driving rain and horizontal hail. The pitch became "a water polo pool-cum-skating arena" and John L. Allen wrote that few would forget "the Homeric nature of the struggle under conditions which tested the endurance of every player". Neil's hip was crocked in the 16th minute and he went out onto the left wing for the rest of the game, a passenger but still a useful one. In a tremendous game chances were few and far between and only one was made to pay. In the 34th minute Ken Rollin found a rare gap and created an overlap, at the end of which hobbled Neil. He had enough space and time to limp over for the only score of the game and Trinity progressed 3-0. It had been quite a day for Neil because that morning he had announced his engagement to Molly. All-in-all it was quite an eventful few hours.

Neil's injury put his place in the Yorkshire team to meet Lancashire on 31 August in some doubt but he recovered in time. Also in the team were Fred Smith, Jack Wilkinson and Rocky Turner. Neil may have wished he had not recovered because Yorkshire threw away a 17-0 lead (Neil had kicked four goals) established by the 32nd minute and lost 21-20, when Wigan forward Frank Collier snapped up two tries in the last four minutes. The *Wakefield Express* reported, "In the centre Alan Davies caught the eye and Burnett was not far behind, but Neil Fox, although showing a big improvement on his recent club form, seemed slow in comparison to Davies and Challinor". It was important for Neil to show up well in such games because selection for the 1960 World Cup squad was on the horizon.

Things improved when his six goals went a long way towards a welcome 18-5 win at St Helens on 3 September. All his goals were kicked from difficult angles or long distances, while his wing partner John Etty completely blotted out the threat posed by Tom van Vollenhoven. There was bad news for Trinity fans just before the game, however, when it was announced that Don Vines had been transferred to St Helens for an £8,000 fee.

On 7 September Wakefield routed Bramley 40-6 in the Yorkshire Cup second round. Neil was in fine fettle, kicking eight goals from 12 attempts and scoring a try. John L. Allen noted, "He revealed a turn of speed that confounded his critics, and his powerful lunges backed by plenty of skill were a treat to see".

Three days later, Neil clocked up his 150th appearance for Trinity in a 25-9 revenge victory over Warrington at Belle Vue. He claimed a try and five goals, the fourth his 500th for the club. He and Alan Skene outshone their opposite centres, Jim Challinor and Ally Naughton, and Neil's try was the outcome of sheer artistry when he took Harold Poynton's back-flip from a cross field run from a scrum. Neil must have been very gratified and hopeful of a place in the 18-man World Cup party when he read the following newspaper report: "The more I see of Neil Fox the more I think he is going to be one enormous headache for Britain's World Cup opposition. True, the side hasn't been picked. But it would be calamitous if this 14½-stone centre were left out. I grow tired of people – mostly from Lancashire – telling me he isn't fast enough. Let them get a real close-up of Fox in full cry for the line as man after man tries to claw him down! They will then discover just how fast Fox is. Granted, he's not an even-timer. But what do you expect from such a hefty guy? Fox is fast enough. Ask Warrington! It was often as much as they could manage to down him at the third attempt as he pounded through. Fox scored just one try. Poynton... worked it with a superb back-flip that reached Fox on the burst. Now, you slow Fox-trot wallahs, ask Warrington how Fox raced through their defences in jig-time for that try!"

Two days later Neil turned out at left centre alongside Eric Ashton for Great Britain against the Rest of the League at St Helens in an official World Cup trial. Their direct opponents were Challinor and Davies. Everyone knew that only three centres would be chosen for the tournament so a good performance was vital. Britain won 21-16 and Neil kicked a couple of goals but missed a few more. None of the centres won critical acclaim, largely because none of the wingers got the opportunity to run. At least that meant that no-one had stolen a march on him in the selection stakes, or so it could be assumed.

Two days after the trial the selection committee met in Manchester. Neil's team-mates Turner and Wilkinson were in the World Cup squad but there was no place for a disappointed Neil. Ashton, as captain, Challinor and Davies all got the nod. Neil, who along with Geoff Oakes was selected as one of six World Cup squad reserves, was crestfallen: "The selectors obviously thought I had not done enough to secure a place in the final squad. It was very sad news for me as I thought I had done enough up to the trial to warrant inclusion. I didn't like to think one indifferent game would mean I lost out but that's how it appeared. Of course, Britain went on to win the World Cup. After the shock of not being picked, I think the decision seemed to spur me on to prove the doubters wrong."

Matters did not improve immediately though. Just hours after the World Cup selectors met, Neil turned out for Yorkshire against Cumberland at Whitehaven, accompanied by fellow Trinitarians, Smith, Poynton, Wilkinson and Turner. Yorkshire lost 43-19. Neil kicked five goals and played pretty well, but opposing centres Dick Huddart and John O'Neil had a field day, the latter bagging four tries. It was a costly game for Poynton, who suffered a bad shoulder injury, and Wilkie, who missed 20 minutes of the game with a cut eye.

On 17 September, Trinity went to Batley and lost 5-2. Batley's defence was magnificent affording Trinity only one chance to gain a try, when Alan Skene almost scored after Neil hit the post with a penalty. It was ironic that the Batley pack contained three former Wakefield men in Armstead, Harrison and Kelly, not to mention Neil's brother Peter.

The following Wednesday Neil was outstanding in a 46-10 win over Bramley, amassing 22 points and being captain for the first time, Turner being on World Cup duty. The club also experimented with playing the Australian centre fashion with Neil at inside centre over the next few games. The Bramley match must have created some sort of Wakefield club record as eight pairs of shorts and seven jerseys were ripped during the game and had to be replaced. Neil was captain again at Hull, where Trinity ground out an 8-3 win, thanks to four penalties from the skipper. "Fox's goal-kicking from long distance angular shots brought appreciation from even the Hull partisans", according to the *Wakefield Express*.

On Wednesday, 12 October, Trinity met Keighley in the semi-final of the Yorkshire Cup. The venue was Odsal, Keighley giving up home advantage to play a rare game under floodlights. Trinity were red hot favourites but in the words of their chairman, Stuart Hadfield, "were the luckiest team in the world to win" 5-4 in a real cliff-hanger. Keighley deservedly led from the 8th to the 78th minute, when Les Chamberlain barged over from a play-the-ball and Neil held his nerve to land an easy but match-winning conversion. John L. Allen described Trinity's fans as "delirious with relief" when the ball passed over the bar, while Allan Cave in the *Daily Herald* remarked that "Trinity will need to play 1,000 per cent better to beat Huddersfield in the final". It was certainly rough justice for Keighley, whose directors decided to pay their players the normal winning pay of £9 anyway.

Trinity performed a lot better in winning 19-8 against Hunslet at Belle Vue three days later, Neil booting five goals, but the next week they went down 11-7 at Swinton. Former Oldham forward Des McKeown made his debut for Trinity, who found it hard to break down a cast-iron defence. Neil landed a monster penalty from his own half and set Rollin up for Wakefield's only try but had a tough time opposite Peter Smethurst. The *Wakefield Express* declared, "Seldom has he been so effectively marked as he was on this occasion by forward-cum-centre Smethurst, a chunky piece of footballer, who was a real live-wire".

Next up was the Yorkshire Cup final at Headingley on 29 October. Huddersfield, their opponents, were 19th in the league, 16 places below Trinity. Moreover, they were shorn of several regulars and had to bring back Dave Valentine at loose-forward after an absence of three years. Valentine, captain of the 1954 World Cup-winning side, had retired in 1957 with ankle problems. He had been one of Neil's heroes as a youngster: "What a privilege it was to play against him, a very hard man and a wonderful footballer". Needless to say, few beyond Huddersfield expected anything but a victory for Wakefield. It did not help the Fartowners that they only arrived at Headingley 20 minutes before kick-off due to traffic problems and their winger Aidan Breen cut it even finer, arriving seven minutes before the teams entered the field on a typically dull and murky autumnal day.

The ensuing game was not particularly attractive, but there was plenty of excitement as Huddersfield strove mightily to cause an upset. Trinity struck the front after nine minutes when Fred Smith took advantage of a poor pass from centre and captain Ernie Ashcroft to Breen to intercept and race 40 yards for the touchdown. Neil landed a fine conversion. Within six minutes Huddersfield retaliated with the best try of the game, a seven-man move which saw Breen crash over at the corner. Frank Dyson's conversion attempt hit the post and bounced out. As the game approached half-time, Neil capitalised on some severe pressure applied by Trinity. George M. Thompson wrote in *Yorkshire Sports*: "The big centre was checked in a handling move but was able to get in a high kick directed towards the Huddersfield posts. Dyson missed the ball as it dropped awkwardly for him, and it bounced well nigh ideally for Fox, who gathered it and ran three yards before touching down behind the posts and adding an easy goal". Lucky, or what? It was amazing how fortunate Neil seemed to be with such kicks, particularly for one said to be lacking in pace.

The second half did not go at all according to the script. Dyson kicked a penalty, when Skene obstructed Don Devereux and then referee Norman Railton allowed Huddersfield to benefit from an advantage, which ended in stand-off Don Lockwood scoring an opportunist try, which was converted by Dyson. With six minutes remaining a 10-10 draw seemed the likely outcome. Neil had missed three penalties and Trinity had made the fatal error of settling for a forward battle, ignoring the clear superiority of their backs. Finally, the penny dropped and Trinity drove to within 10 yards of Huddersfield's line before Rollin and Briggs opened the defence to send Etty crashing over at the corner. Neil failed with the kick but it did not matter. Two minutes from time he applied the *coup de grâce* when he intercepted a pass from Lockwood to dash 15 yards before banging the ball down for his second try, enabling Trinity to win 16-10 and to take their tally of Yorkshire Cups to seven.

Neil's and the team's form noticeably improved following their success in the Yorkshire Cup. The following Saturday there was a close call at York. Neil and Alan Skene put Fred Smith over for an equalising try to make it 3-3 after nine minutes but thereafter could not cross York's line again. Trinity owed their 11-10 victory to Neil's magic boot, which piloted four goals, including three crucial second-half penalties. On 12 November Wigan visited Belle Vue and went away defeated 12-7. Neil reckoned he played his best game of the season against the cherry and whites. He was certainly on form with his kicking. Trinity led 10-0 at the break. Neil was over the line early on, but failed to ground the ball, according to the referee, Charlie Appleton. Gerry Round eventually gave Trinity the lead with a superb try at the right corner flag. "Fox made it all the more memorable with a beautiful touchline goal that found the target as accurately as a guided missile," according to 'The Pinder'. Neil also converted Harold Poynton's first half try. After 68 minutes Neil coolly dropped a goal from a pass by Derek Turner to end the scoring, as Trinity gained some of revenge for their defeat in the Championship Final six months earlier.

The following Saturday Wakefield won 7-3 at Hunslet, thanks to a stupendous effort in defence and Neil's match-winning instincts. The victory came at a price – Oakes, Wilkinson, Chamberlain and Round all picking up injuries. Neil opened the scoring after two minutes with a touchline penalty, which took him past 1,500 points in first-class rugby league. On

14 minutes he produced the spark for the decisive score. The try was scored by Chamberlain and "sprang from a wizard one-handed pick-up of a loose ball by Fox, now happily back in international form. The centre despatched the ball smartly inside to Holliday, who in turn passed to Chamberlain". Neil's conversion rounded off Trinity's scoring for the afternoon. All Hunslet could muster was a 41st-minute try by Geoff Gunney.

Around this time Trinity signed a 19-year-old loose-forward, David Blakeley, from Westtown ARL, Dewsbury and with Jack Wilkinson's injury requiring a knee cartilage operation, the club was also scanning the rugby league landscape for a replacement prop. After sounding out the possibilities of acquiring Norm Herbert of Workington, Ken Roberts of Swinton, Don Robinson of Leeds and Mick Scott of Hull, they eventually settled on a short-term fix by buying the veteran Frank Moore from Featherstone for £200.

December opened with wins against Bramley and Batley, but Neil was missing from the latter. He had gone to Bordeaux for the first test against France on Sunday, 11 December. He admits: "The way the selectors operated baffled me. Great Britain had just won the World Cup and I hadn't been good enough for that team, but I was good enough for this French test. It all seemed a bit strange to me and I often wondered who pulled the strings when it came to picking the test teams. I suppose politics must have been involved."

Neil's form had certainly been improving, but it was Eric Ashton's absence due to a cartilage operation which opened the door for Neil's re-entry to test rugby. Neil took Ashton's right centre berth, and for the first time partnered Billy Boston. Alan Davies and Mick Sullivan formed the left flank. Full-back Eric Fraser took the captaincy, while the half-backs were the World Cup wizards Frank Myler and Alex Murphy. The forwards were Abe Terry, John Shaw, John Barton, Derek Turner, Brian Shaw and Vince Karalius. For a change a test in France was free of unpleasant sensations and Britain gave one of their best performances in test match rugby league. Despite the French winning the scrums 19-7, Britain played some wonderful, open rugby when in possession and defended demonically.

Loose-forward Andre Lacaze opened the scoring with a penalty after 18 minutes and stretched France's lead to 5-0 after 23 minutes, when right centre Jean Foussat stepped out of Davies's tackle to claim a fine try. Seven minutes before half-time Billy Boston intercepted high French passing and a move between Myler, Turner and Myler again, took the stand-off over for a try, which Fraser converted. France edged ahead almost immediately with another Lacaze penalty and were 7-5 up at the interval. Britain never touched the ball for the first 15 minutes of the second half but denied the French at every turn and then, as Harold Mather in the *Manchester Guardian* reported: "Gradually, Britain turned the tide much more surely and effectively than did Canute ...During, so to speak, a lull in the French storm Murphy made the break, Karalius carried on the move, and Fox, having evaded a determined attempt to tackle, scored a try which put Britain's nose in front. Like a good thoroughbred horse scenting victory, the team thereafter steadily increased the margin with tries by Fox, Murphy and John Shaw, and two goals by Fox, to which France's only reply was a [second] try by Foussat – and there was a doubt about even that". Britain thus ran out 21-10 winners and Neil had given the selectors a firm reminder of what he could offer at test level.

His return to domestic football was truly anticlimactic. Trinity lost 5-3 at home to Huddersfield, Neil missed seven shots at goal, including a relatively easy 77th minute conversion to draw the game, and 'The Pinder' described the team's performance as "impotent", "alarming" and "lamentable". Neil, who at this juncture was leading the league's goals and points-scoring charts, failed to score for the first time that season. It was the first time he had not scored in a game at Belle Vue since 27 April 1957, also against Huddersfield.

On Christmas Eve, Trinity beat York 29-19 at Belle Vue. Neil scored a try but did not kick any goals, leaving the marksmanship to Joe Smith, who landed four. Trinity perked up tremendously on Boxing Day, when they went to league leaders Leeds with a weakened team and gained a wonderful 14-9 victory before a crowd of almost 30,000. Poynton and Rollin were outstanding, while Albert Firth, playing on the left wing was something of a nightmare for his opponent, the flying Springbok Wilf Rosenberg. Frank Moore made his debut and helped win Trinity enough ball to build a platform on which to base their victory. The teams were level at 9-9 before Brian Briggs scored the winning try, which Neil converted for his only goal of the game. Turner, Poynton and Ken Hirst were the other try-scorers, although Ken may remember the game more vividly for the stiff-arm tackle which removed three of his teeth. New Year's Eve brought Castleford to Belle Vue and at half-time it was 7-7. Neil set Trinity on the way to a 21-7 win, however, after 55 minutes with a characteristic interception try, to add to his three goals.

So, as 1961 dawned, Wakefield Trinity shared top spot in the league with Leeds, both having gained 32 points from 20 games. They were followed by Halifax on 31, with Warrington, St Helens, Swinton and Leigh, all on 26, chasing hard. Despite their lofty position, they had serious problems with injuries and Ken Traill and his charges knew it would take a Herculean effort if Trinity were to maintain the challenge for honours.

Matters took an unfortunate turn for Neil in the next few months. Trinity opened the new year with a comfortable 15-4 win at Dewsbury, Neil claiming a try, but missing with six attempts on goal, Joe Smith missing another three. There was considerable entertainment value from "a black mongrel with inexhaustible energy", which cavorted about the field for most of the match, but Neil was probably not amused because he spent the last 25 minutes on the wing having damaged knee ligaments and injured his thigh. For several weeks his kicking had been distinctly below par and the newspapers had reported that extra practice was failing to get him back to his normal accuracy. This injury was most unwelcome, particularly because it also cost him a test appearance against France at St Helens on 28 January for which he had been selected. Derek Hallas of Leeds took Neil's place, while the other centre was Mick Sullivan – a fairly unlikely pairing just months after Great Britain's World Cup success. However, Britain won 27-8.

In the meantime Neil missed scratchy victories over Hull KR and Doncaster. He returned against Hull at Belle Vue on 4 February, when he partnered Trinity's latest signing from St Helens, Springbok winger Jan Prinsloo, who had cost a club record £9,000. Trinity lost 11-5 and Neil aggravated his thigh injury. He missed Trinity's next two games, a first-round Challenge Cup tie win against York and a league victory at Keighley, when newly signed Roy Bell from Featherstone made his debut in Neil's position. Derek Turner's dismissal in that game would prove costly when he received a three match ban.

Trinity had begun the Cup campaign as joint second favourites with Warrington at 5-1, behind St Helens who were listed at 5-2. The second round brought them the toughest of tasks, however, especially in view of all their injury problems. They drew Wigan, conquerors of Leeds in the first round, at Belle Vue and the game was so attractive that it had to be declared all-ticket. Trinity were so desperate to determine the fitness of Neil, Wilkie and Les Chamberlain that they arranged to play an 'A' team match against Doncaster on the Monday preceding the cup tie, a most unusual arrangement. Trinity 'A' won 37-0. Jack and Neil came through satisfactorily but Chamberlain's ankle injury prevented him from finishing the game. Neil bagged a couple of tries but did little kicking.

A crowd of 28,681 jammed into Belle Vue on 25 February, despite strong winds and persistent rain. Trinity faced the elements in the first half and to compound their discomfort Wigan's reserve hooker Jack Gregory won the first half scrums two to one. The only score was an easy penalty kicked by Wigan full-back Fred Griffiths after Rollin was penalised for feeding at a scrum in the 11th minute. Neil had a chance to equalise two minutes later, his only shot of the game, but missed. The second half saw no further scoring as Wigan played perfect safety first rugby to deny Trinity the benefit of Oakes's second half scrum superiority. Their stick-it-up-their-jersey tactics brought the slow handclap from the Belle Vue faithful, but in the circumstances Wigan, brilliantly marshalled by Brian McTigue, could afford to laugh. They had deserved their 2-0 victory. Trinity's consolation would have to be their share of record gate receipts of £3,755.

Out of the Cup, Trinity fans were keen to hear what Stuart Hadfield was up to in South Africa in the hope that reinforcements might restore Trinity's waning fortunes. The rumour was that Wakefield – and Wigan – were in the hunt for Doug Hopwood, a brilliant Springbok back-rower. In the event neither got him but Wakefield intimated that they had signed a star back, although Hadfield was strangely reticent about naming him.

On 4 March, Trinity began their quest to clinch a place in the top four play-offs with a comprehensive 36-6 home win over Dewsbury. They gave debuts to forwards Eric Payne and David Blakeley and welcomed back Keith Holliday, whose season had been scarred by injuries. This game also provided the finale to the long and distinguished career of John Etty, who had been Neil's wing partner for the last couple of seasons. Neil's strong running helped John to a two-try finish to his career, while the former's six goals were a welcome sign that he had regained his kicking touch. The following two Saturdays proved calamitous, however. Trinity were absolutely dreadful in going down 19-2 at Hull KR and then were put through the wringer at Central Park, losing 25-9 before almost 22,000 fans. Neil captained the side in this encounter, but it was far from a good afternoon for him. After 15 minutes he injured his ankle and spent the remainder of the game on the wing. Remarkably, he scored Trinity's only try from an interception.

That injury kept him out of Trinity's next five games, three of which were won but two losses – at home to Featherstone and at Huddersfield – were injurious to their hopes of a Championship semi-final although they still held fourth spot. They had already, however, lost their hold on the Yorkshire League Championship which had been taken by Leeds.

Neil was eased back into action with the 'A' team on 8 April in a 20-5 home success over Bradford Northern 'A'. He made a quiet return but produced occasional bursts, one of which resulted in a try for Joe Smith. He was restored to first-team duty in what looked like a probable romp at Tattersfield against Doncaster. It was a lovely day and the football was excellent. Doncaster gave as good as they got and were leading 9-8 after 35 minutes. By the 50th minute Trinity were ahead 15-9. At that point the game exploded. Brian Briggs and Doncaster forward Alan Hepworth were sent off for fighting. At the next scrum Derek Turner, the Trinity captain, asked referee Jack Senior why he had sent the two players off, because he thought there had been nothing much in the incident. Senior immediately sent Derek off and when seconds later Jack Wilkinson also made an attempt to engage the referee, he was dismissed, both of them for dissent, according to Senior. Three minutes before the end he also sent off Don Metcalfe and Colin Price, the Dons' full-back, for an "affray near Wakefield Trinity's line". Six men had been sent off but Trinity finished with a flourish despite being reduced to nine players, Jan Prinsloo completing a hat-trick and Gerry Round kicking seven goals in a 32-9 win. To this day Neil cannot explain the events of that game at Tattersfield: "There did not seem to be any reason for all the bother and as for Don Metcalfe doing any punching, well, it would be the first time in a long, long career."

A week later Neil was much more like his old self, scoring three tries and three goals in a 34-11 win at Bradford. His 15 points took him past the 200 mark for Trinity during the season. Even more significantly, those 15 points made him the highest scorer in Wakefield Trinity's history, as he passed Charlie Pollard's old record of 1,434 set between 1919 and 1931. There remained one game to play – against champions-in-waiting, Leeds at Belle Vue on 29 April. Remarkably, Wakefield still had a mathematical chance of finishing in the top four, provided they won and Warrington, St Helens and Swinton all lost their last games. Trinity's prospects dimmed when the RFL Disciplinary Committee met and suspended all four of Trinity's players who had been sent off at Doncaster. Turner and Briggs got two matches each and Metcalfe and Wilkinson one each. All four had made personal appearances before the committee, but to no avail. More than 16,000 fans saw Trinity's chance disappear despite a valiant attempt. Leeds were never behind and won more easily than the 15-8 scoreline suggested. In any case, Warrington, Saints and Swinton all won, so Trinity would still have failed to qualify if they had beaten the Loiners. They finished seventh in one of the tightest scraps for the top four places on record.

In most seasons Trinity would have been delighted to finish seventh, win the Yorkshire Cup and finish runners-up in the Yorkshire League Championship. Expectations had, however, changed over recent times and most people connected with Belle Vue were disappointed. Neil's season had certainly been like the curate's egg – good in parts but not really fulfilling. The injuries, his failure to make the World Cup squad and loss of form with the boot were personal disappointments, which he would have to overcome but which would make him stronger for the great challenges of the future.

Anyway, there was the small matter of his marriage to Molly to take his mind off rugby league. They were married on 3 June 1961 at St George's Church, Lupset. Talking to Neil, it is clear the occasion was much more memorable than many of his sporting experiences: "Just about all the first-team squad, plus wives or girlfriends attended. All the committee members and their wives came too, not forgetting many relatives and friends. My best man was Ken Rollin and the groomsmen were Frank Dix and Tommy Smales. Tommy's girlfriend and future wife, Kay Southern, was one of the bridesmaids and the others were Molly's cousin Joan Bentley, Molly's friend Mary Holmes and our Peter's little daughter, Karen. After the reception at Lupset Working Mens Club, Molly and I went off on honeymoon to Blackpool for a week. We stayed at the Cumberland Hotel. We arrived late, so we picked up a barbequed chicken, took it to our room and ate it because we were really hungry.

The next morning we went down for breakfast and came across two Oldham players, Johnny Noon and Frank Pitchford, who were also there for the week with their wives. They didn't realise we had just got married until later that week. They only noticed when we gave two ladies from the hotel a lift down into town and they saw the confetti on the floor of the car. The next day all the guests and staff had a collection and bought us a present. We had a great time – as you do on honeymoon! We took in a lot of shows. One starred Ken Dodd. He was on stage for two hours and had everyone in gales of laughter from start to finish. We also saw Al Read, another very funny man. After the show we went to the Lobster Pot restaurant and he walked in for a meal. He had the diners in stitches. It was just as if he was still on stage.

The Saturday we left was Molly's 21st birthday, 10 June. I bought her a leather coat. On returning home Molly's mum and dad had organised a welcome home party for her 21st."

Wakefield Trinity 1960-61

Wakefield Trinity finished 7th in the league: P36, W26, L10, For 576, Against 326

Fox scored 18 tries, 81 goals, 216 points for Wakefield, and 2 tries, 13 goals, 32 points in representative games

Date	Opponent	Score	Fox	Crowd	
13 Aug	**Swinton**	17-7	T, 4G	10,759	
17 Aug	Castleford	26-9	T, 4G	10,600	
20 Aug	Warrington	5-26	G	13,056	
22 Aug	**Keighley**	24-6	3G	7,823	
27 Aug	**Halifax**	3-0	T	14,053	YC1
3 Sep	St Helens	18-5	6G	13,126	
7 Sep	**Bramley**	40-6	T, 8G	9,856	YC2
10 Sep	**Warrington**	25-9	T, 5G	14,105	
17 Sep	Batley	2-5	G	7,100	
21 Sep	**Bramley**	46-10	2T, 8G	5,694	
26 Sep	Hull	8-3	4G	8,312	
12 Oct	Keighley	5-4	G	6,892	YC semi (at Odsal)
15 Oct	**Hunslet**	19-8	5G	11,855	
22 Oct	Swinton	7-11	2G	8,000	
29 Oct	Huddersfield	16-10	2T, 2G	17,456	YC Final (at Leeds)
5 Nov	York	11-10	4G	5,239	
12 Nov	**Wigan**	12-7	3G	18,224	
19 Nov	Hunslet	7-3	2G	9,000	
3 Dec	Bramley	19-4	2T, 2G	1,906	
10 Dec	**Batley**	12-2	dnp	7,656	
17 Dec	**Huddersfield**	3-5		8,562	
24 Dec	**York**	29-19	T	8,081	
26 Dec	Leeds	14-9	G	29,226	
31 Dec	**Castleford**	21-7	T, 3G	9,818	
7 Jan	Dewsbury	15-4	T	5,600	
11 Jan	**Hull KR**	18-15	dnp	4,807	
14 Jan	**Doncaster**	19-9	dnp	7,142	
4 Feb	**Hull**	5-11	G	10,546	
11 Feb	**York**	11-3	dnp	11,058	Ch Cup 1
18 Feb	Keighley	18-5	dnp	5,160	
25 Feb	**Wigan**	0-2		28,681	Ch Cup 2
4 Mar	**Dewsbury**	36-6	6G	9,333	
11 Mar	Hull KR	2-19	G	4,869	
18 Mar	Wigan	9-25	T	21,904	
25 Mar	**Bradford N**	26-0	dnp	7,728	
27 Mar	**St Helens**	4-2	dnp	18,841	
1 Apr	Featherstone R	10-2	dnp	10,800	
3 Apr	**Featherstone R**	2-11	dnp	16,927	
8 Apr	Huddersfield	13-17	dnp	10,172	
15 Apr	Doncaster	32-9		1,850	
22 Apr	Bradford N	34-11	3T, 3G	3,800	
29 Apr	**Leeds**	8-15	G	16,279	

Representative appearances

31 Aug	Yorkshire 20 Lancashire 21 (Wakefield)	4G
12 Sep	Great Britain 21 The Rest 16 (St Helens)	2G
14 Sep	Yorkshire 19 Cumberland 43 (Whitehaven)	5G
11 Dec	Great Britain 21 France 10 (Bordeaux)	2T, 2G

Wedding day: Neil and Molly with their parents, Tom and Stella Fox and Dora and Hubert Bentley.

The happy couple

9. 1961-62: The greatest season

The close season of 1961 at Belle Vue did not pass off quietly. The club announced a profit on the previous season of £1,267 – but considerably down on 1959-60. Gate receipts had dropped by £3,153, which was a big worry for the management, who now knew what it took to maintain a winning team.

None the less, team strengthening remained the priority. In June it was revealed that the mystery South African who had been pursued earlier in the year by Stuart Hadfield was Colin Greenwood, who had accepted a fee of about £4,000. Greenwood was a 25-year-old centre or stand-off, who had played for the Villagers club, Western Province and South Africa. He had played one test in 1961, when he scored two tries in a 24-8 win against Ireland at Cape Town on 13 May, a month before signing for Trinity. He was clearly a big loss to the Springboks. A couple of weeks later Trinity signed hooker Milan Kosanovic from Bradford Northern for £2,000 in hope of rectifying the recurring problem of lack of scrummage possession. Neil regarded Milan as "a good ball-getter and did his tackling when needed". A signing for the future was amateur international stand-off or centre Ian Brooke, while just before the new season started Don Vines returned to Wakefield from St Helens for a fee approaching £7,500 – a popular move with Trinity diehards.

There was disappointment, however, when it was announced that Malcolm Sampson's injury had caused him to retire extremely prematurely. Trinity also issued a list of 11 players for whom they would consider offers. Among them were David Wakefield and Eric Lockwood, who departed for Doncaster. Overall, though, locals believed that the strength of the side was as good as in 1959-60. There was a scare when Ken Traill's contract renewal caused problems, but things were smoothed over and Ken then took over some duties in connection with Trinity's pools scheme, for which he was to be paid by results.

There was certainly plenty to play for in 1961-62. Crucially, the RFL had decided that two divisions would operate the following year in 1962-63 and that the top 16 clubs from 1961-62 would form the First Division. Failure to qualify did not bear thinking about but Trinity were aiming much higher. Neil too had plenty to aim for. There was a Kiwi tour in 1961 and Neil wanted a crack at them and his test jersey back. Even more appealing was the prospect of winning a place on the 1962 Australasian tour.

The season began as usual with a fixture against Castleford and a resounding 42-9 victory. Neil scored a try and five goals, the second of which was the 600th of his first class career. He also had to have two stitches in a cut above his eye, inflicted by the head of Keith Holliday as they combined in a tackle. Kosanovic made his debut at Wheldon Road and in the next game against York at Belle Vue, Greenwood made his debut and Vines reappeared in Trinity's colours. Neil had the novel experience of being the only native Englishman in a threequarter line containing three South Africans – Greenwood, Skene and Prinsloo. Neil kicked three goals in a scratchy 18-12 win and put Greenwood over for his first try after selling a beautiful dummy to the York defence.

On 30 August Trinity failed in their first big test of the campaign, going down 10-5 before more than 21,000 in a gruesome game at St Helens. The match was played in bad spirit with referee Eric Clay giving a virtuoso performance, as the players appeared intent on breaking all the rules. The only surprise was that he sent off only Harold Poynton, on 48 minutes, for tripping, and Austin Rhodes three minutes from time, for butting.

For Neil there were repercussions which went further than just losing a match. He was dumbounded when he learnt he had been left out of Trinity's team for their first-round Yorkshire Cup tie against Bradford Northern on 2 September. He recalls: "I got a shock when I heard I had been dropped. I asked the committee why. They said they were resting me. I replied, 'What, after only three games? Plus the fact that it is a cup tie!' My form could not have been so poor as I had been selected for Yorkshire against the New Zealanders just a couple of days earlier." The newspapers were quickly on the case. The *Wakefield Express* said that Stuart Hadfield had told Neil, "You have been dropped because of your loss of form." Neil's response was reported, citing his assertion that if he was below par, it was because the forwards were too slow in getting the ball to the backs. There was also talk of Neil intending to request a transfer but nothing came of it. John Lindley in the *Rugby Leaguer* was probably right when he wrote: "Fox was dropped through 'loss of form'. Yet the man who replaced him has no form to assess – one RL game, and that on the wing, hardly suggests that Greenwood is a 'must'. By making this lone change, the implications automatically made Fox the scapegoat for the St Helens match... But whatever the selectors think of the centre berths... they can ill afford to unsettle a player of Fox's calibre... One hopes that Fox's philosophical remarks after Saturday's match that 'there will be plenty more games' will be the last words on an incident which should never have arisen. There will be plenty more games; games in which Trinity will look to Fox for inspiration amongst the backs as they have so often done."

Ironically, Trinity broke the club record with a 73-5 slaughter of Bradford and Gerry Round equalled the club goalkicking record, jointly held by Neil, by landing 11 goals, although he also missed nine. Neil put the recent fracas behind him by helping Yorkshire to beat the New Zealanders 21-11 at Craven Park, Hull on Wednesday, 6 September. Fred Smith, Jack Wilkinson, Albert Firth – in wonderful form for Trinity at blind-side prop – and Derek Turner were also in the Tykes' XIII. Smith bagged two tries and others came from Turner, hooker Alan Lockwood and Neil. It was Neil who scored the opening try after 30 minutes, when he latched onto a high pass from stand-off Alan Kellett and powered over from 10 yards. Cyril Kellett was kicking the goals for Yorkshire and landed three.

Three days later Neil was back in Trinity's first-team, kicking four goals in a 29-15 home win over Hull. The *Sunday People* reported, "Fox figured in the play of the Trinity backs like the giant he is, both in stature and performance, and great co-operation from Springbok centre Alan Skene gave a thrust down the middle that had Hull all at sea". Prop Albert Firth did his bit too with spectacular tries from 30 yards and 70 yards.

On 11 September Neil was in the Yorkshire side which was defeated 23-8 by a rampant Cumberland at Belle Vue. It was a bad evening for stand-off Alan Hardisty's Yorkshire debut, but Neil performed well enough and claimed a try and a goal. Two days later five goals and a try were Neil's share of Wakefield's 55-5 crushing of Doncaster, while all three of the other threequarters – Smith, Greenwood and Prinsloo - scored try hat-tricks.

A potentially difficult fixture at Swinton on 16 September ended in a 22-7 victory which took Trinity to the top of the league alongside Wigan and Workington. Trinity scored 15 points in the last 20 minutes. Among them was Neil's 1,500th for Trinity, while his five goals were landed despite the vagaries of a strong wind. The following Tuesday another daunting task was successfully negotiated. Wakefield went to The Boulevard for a second-round Yorkshire Cup tie and silenced 14,000 baying Hull fans with a 13-7 victory. It was a real drama. Hull led 7-4 after an hour and it looked like curtains for Trinity when Jack Wilkinson was sent off after 63 minutes. However, Neil's third penalty goal dragged Trinity to within a point and four minutes from time a fourth penalty gave them an 8-7 lead. At that stage Hull received a kickable penalty, which full-back Peter Bateson essayed to win a place for Hull in the semi-final, but instead, according to 'The Pinder', "the scene changed with dynamic swiftness and staggering effect". Bateson's attempt failed, the ball did not even go dead and loose-forward Dave Lamming pounded forward from his own line with the ball. He linked with Fred Smith, who set off on a bewildering run. By the time he passed to Skene, the defence had been completely demoralised and the South African skipped over under the posts. Neil's conversion was his fifth goal. The game had always been near flashpoint but 'The Pinder' reported that "even the notorious Boulevard rowdies were stunned and rendered speechless". After the game one Wakefield forward declared, "It was one of those games where everybody had to work. They couldn't dodge it!"

Trinity parted with two good servants during the next week, as Les Chamberlain and Neil's old wing partner Stan Smith moved to Bramley. Neil was probably more concerned with the test selectors' decision to only name him as reserve back for the first New Zealand test at Headingley on 30 September. His brother Don was named as the shadow scrum-half and, surprisingly, the only Trinitarian in the side was Derek Turner. The centres were Eric Ashton and Derek Hallas. There was not much Neil could do, except produce performances which would convince the selectors they had picked the wrong men.

He had a gilt-edged chance to do so on 23 September, when Trinity took on Leeds at Belle Vue. Neil's direct opposite was Derek Hallas, who had taken his test place. More than 21,000, including 2,134 children, who paid sixpence each, turned up expecting a close game. At half-time Trinity led 5-4, but the second half was one-way traffic and Trinity surged away to win 21-4. J. C. Lindley in the *Rugby Leaguer* wrote: "Prinsloo's two tries kept him at the head of the league scoring list and Skene's classical effort was a scorching affair from near half-way. The first and last tries went to Fox, who constantly showed his cool craft at centre and was obviously intent on proving Britain's selectors wrong."

On 4 October Trinity swept York aside 24-4 in the Yorkshire Cup semi-final. Neil contributed three goals and the *Wakefield Express* noted, "Neil played the game that suits him best – movements in which his strength, in the shape of powerful thrusts, were combined with skill. He certainly shaped like an automatic choice for an Australasian tour". He starred in the next game too, a 31-10 thrashing of Leigh. Trinity gave a debut to Dennis Williamson, another big signing - £4,000 from Whitehaven - but it was Neil who took the Belle Vue crowd's breath away. Trinity scored seven tries and Neil had a hand in six of them, adding five goals. Allan Cave in the *Daily Herald* wrote, "Leigh certainly knew they had a few brushes with Fox before they'd finished, for he swept through them majestically time after time... It was grand to see the zest this 22-year-old put into his game."

Neil's hectic schedule saw him at Leigh two days later, 9 October, for Yorkshire's encounter with Lancashire, team-mate Keith Holliday appearing at scrum-half. For much of the game it seemed that Neil was playing Lancashire on his own, for he was undoubtedly the game's leading light. In the 10th minute he gave Yorkshire the lead, engineering a dazzling try covering half the length of the pitch, being the middle man in a seven-man move he started and finished himself. He added a penalty but Yorkshire trailed 11-5 at half-time. Neil then proceeded to win back the lead with a coruscating display. In the 58th minute he sent winger Gary Waterworth over at the corner and landed a towering conversion. Five minutes later his howitzer 50-yard penalty gave the Tykes a 12-11 lead, only for Lancashire to finally steal the spoils 14-12 when stand-off Dave Bolton scored a superb try 13 minutes from time.

The following day the test selectors wielded the axe on the team which had been murdered 29-11 by New Zealand in the first test at Headingley. For the second test at Odsal on 21 October they announced eight changes. Neil was restored to left centre with his partner something of a surprise in Widnes's Frank Myler, who had recently been moved from stand-off. Eric Ashton had been demoted to travelling reserve.

By coincidence, Neil was at Odsal the week before the test, wreaking havoc in Bradford Northern's defence. Trinity beat Northern 38-7, Neil kicking seven goals, several of them spectacular efforts. It was his winger Jan Prinsloo, who took most of the plaudits though with a tremendous haul of six tries, none of which was a walk-in.

On 21 October Neil played his first test against the Kiwis. His originally selected co-centre Frank Myler badly damaged his ankle in training and had to withdraw. Eric Ashton subsequently regained his position alongside Neil. The teams at Odsal were:

Great Britain: Eric Fraser (Warrington, captain), Billy Boston (Wigan), Eric Ashton (Wigan), Neil Fox (Wakefield Trinity), Mick Sullivan (St Helens), Dave Bolton (Wigan), Alex Murphy (St Helens), Abe Terry (St Helens), Bob Dagnall (St Helens), Brian McTigue (Wigan), Dick Huddart (St Helens), Johnny Whiteley (Hull), Roy Evans (Wigan).

New Zealand: Jack Fagan, Graham Kennedy, Reg Cooke, Roger Bailey, Brian Reidy, Jim Bond, Billy Snowden, Sam Edwards, Jock Butterfield, Maunga Emery, Don Hammond (captain), Mel Cooke, Bruce Castle.

Britain had all the play in the first 20 minutes as Fraser, twice, and Neil attempted penalty goals but failed to hit the target. Completely against the run of play, New Zealand took the lead the first time they breached the home '25'. From a close-in scrum the ball was swung swiftly to the right flank and when Sullivan slipped in trying to tackle Reg Cooke, the centre handed on to Bailey who casually sauntered through a huge gap to score and Fagan goaled. Britain regained parity within eight minutes. Neil opened their scoring with a penalty goal and was then involved in a sweet move with Fraser and Huddart, which sent Sullivan over for an unconverted try. Shortly afterwards Neil put his side into the lead with a penalty and on 35 minutes Murphy hared through and kicked inside for Sullivan to dive for a second touchdown to give Britain a 10-5 half-time lead.

New Zealand pulled back to 10-7 with a penalty early in the second half but thereafter offered little real threat to a solid Great Britain side, which sometimes appeared to be capable of exquisite rugby and at other times of playing well within its capabilities. Whiteley and Huddart combined well to put Evans in for a try, which Neil converted. Neil and Sullivan opened up the Kiwi defences for the next try, enabling Bolton to sprint 35 yards down an unprotected touchline for a smashing try near the flag. New Zealand responded with a smart try from Bailey to reduce Britain's lead to 18-10. "Then," wrote George M. Thompson in *Yorkshire Sports*, "came an unexpected little thrill for the crowd [of 19,980] when Fox, three yards from midway inside the New Zealand half, kicked a goal at the success of which even some of the New Zealanders showed their appreciation by clapping their hands." Just before referee Eric Clay blew for time Ashton sealed a 23-10 victory with his side's fifth try after juggling with a sharp pass from Murphy.

The following Saturday, Neil again came up against the Kiwis as Trinity entertained the tourists before a crowd of 16,558. By half-time Wakefield were home and dry, having outplayed the New Zealanders to lead 15-2. Neil set the rout in motion after 15 minutes. Round made a great break from his own '25' and linked with Prinsloo. The winger shot along for another 25 yards before turning the ball inside to Neil who thundered 40 yards to touch down under the bar and added the conversion. Five minutes later Neil swooped on a loose ball, swatted off Kiwi winger Ford, beat two more defenders and parted to Prinsloo, who sailed unmolested to the goal-line for another try. Neil made the score 10-0 minutes later with a 45-yard penalty and a spectacular third try by Alan Skene, converted by Neil, stretched the lead to 15-0 before New Zealand got on the scoreboard with a Fagan penalty goal. The second half was much more attritional, as the New Zealanders resorted to negative methods to stop the Trinity machine and referee George Philpott did well to keep 26 players on the field. Both Neil (knee) and Prinsloo (groin) picked up injuries and the only Trinity try of the half came on the hour when Holliday scored off Turner's pass, Round adding the goal. New Zealand finally claimed a try through loose-forward Castle after 78 minutes, improved by Fagan. Trinity's 20-7 victory was their first ever over the Kiwis.

Jan Prinsloo, Neil's wing partner, had scored 23 tries in 14 games for Trinity before he was injured against the Kiwis and was the league's leading try-scorer at that time. Though an exceptionally fast and determined winger, Jan would have to give credit to Neil for some of his scores because his centre had rarely exhibited better form and had become a winger's delight. Neil, recalls, "We saw the best of Jan when he scored those six tries at Bradford. What a sight he was at full speed. After that injury against New Zealand he only played one more game until March and didn't really find his form again. But he did finish as Trinity's top try-scorer with 30 for the season."

Neil's knee injury did not stop him from appearing for the third consecutive Saturday against New Zealand. The selectors stuck with the same side for the third test at Swinton on 4 November. Abe Terry had to drop out through injury, though, and was replaced by a new cap, Norm Herbert of Workington Town. New Zealand made three changes, bringing in Bill Harrison, Tom Hadfield and Brian Lee for Fagan, Kennedy and Castle.

The 22,558 crowd expected the worst when the Kiwis led 4-0 with two Reg Cooke penalty goals after only six minutes. However, after 14 minutes Britain took the lead and never lost it. Ashton broke through in midfield, beat three men and sent a delighted Herbert over for a try to which Neil added the goal. From then on there was only one team in it. By half-time Britain led 18-6, following two tries from Sullivan and a magical one by Alex Murphy, Neil converting Sullivan's second try and landing a penalty. New Zealand could only muster a third goal from Cooke. They were unable to cope with the British pack in the scrums, Dagnall heeling from 10 of the 11 first-half scrums. The Kiwis did not win a scrum until the 33rd minute by when Britain were in total control.

The second half began with a lovely solo kick-and-chase try from skipper Fraser, goaled by Neil. On 53 minutes New Zealand grabbed a try through prop Edwards, which Cooke converted and the same player added a penalty. At 23-13 there was a brief glimmer of hope for the Kiwis but Neil landed another penalty and then kicked a perfect conversion of an Ashton try from the touchline. Dagnall scored Britain's seventh try to which Neil added his seventh goal, equalling the Great Britain record for a test against New Zealand, set by Eric Fraser in Auckland in 1958. Winger Hadfield got through for two tries in the last four minutes but Britain's 35-19 victory was no less than they deserved. Neil had played perhaps his best test football so far, a judgment endorsed even by Jack Bentley.

Neil remembers an interesting repercussion from his sixth goal of the test: "Mackeson had offered a golden Rolex watch for all the members of the side which scored most points against the Kiwis. Up to the third test, the last game of the tour, Wigan were expecting the watches. They had beaten the Kiwis 28-6. But when I kicked that goal from touch [to make the score 30-13], Billy Boston charged over from the opposite side of the field and hugged me as though we had won the Cup. Then he told me we had won the watches. He was really pleased because he had missed the Wigan game against the New Zealanders. This made up for it."

Neil's match fee for the win against New Zealand was £15. It would have been only £11 if Britain lost. The Kiwis, being amateurs, received no monetary rewards. On the same afternoon Wakefield won 36-10 at Swinton and Neil's club-mates picked up £27 each.

While Neil was exerting his considerable influence on his triple encounter with the New Zealanders, his club chairman, Mr Hadfield, had caused some consternation at Belle Vue by resigning from the selection committee, of which he was also chairman. The Trinity team was picked by a four-man committee and the coach in those days and Mr Hadfield took umbrage at the team choice for the game against the Kiwis. Fortunately, the problem was resolved in a few weeks, Mr Hadfield resumed his leadership of the selectors and peace returned to Trinity's administration.

Attention now turned to the Yorkshire Cup Final on 11 November at Odsal. Leeds were underdogs, with some key players missing and indifferent league form, but they proved to have more bite than the experts anticipated. A grey afternoon started badly for Leeds, who arrived at Bradford without their boots. Their baggage man was escorted to Leeds and back by the police to collect them. The match kicked off 12 minutes late, which probably upset the producers of BBC's *Grandstand*, where the second half was to be shown.

Leeds got off to a flyer, however. Gerry Round caught a Leeds kick and began a clearing run but then threw a careless pass which was intercepted by Leeds winger Garry Hemingway, who flew to the corner for a simple try and Leeds were 3-0 up in four minutes. After 20 minutes Trinity were level when Derek Turner scored the best try of the final following a scrum near Leeds's goal-line. Turner feinted to go one way, went the other and crashed through two defenders. Lewis Jones restored Leeds's lead with a penalty but Neil levelled with a magnificent penalty of his own. At half-time it was 5-5 and Trinity knew they were in a hard struggle. Jack Nott in the *News of the World* summed it up pretty well: "Trinity had bags of class. Their handling was crisp; their passing rippled. But for rugged determination and for hunting the half chance they took second place". 'The Pinder' said of the game, "It was tough, close and exciting but not much else".

The second half was played in increasing murk, causing the Odsal floodlights to be brought into rare action as the rain began to teem down. In the end it was Neil who decided the issue with his left boot, aided by Milan Kosanovic's scrum supremacy. Neil pushed Trinity ahead with "two superb penalties fired almost from the same blade of grass," according to Brian Batty of the *Daily Express*. Around the hour mark Harold Poynton put in a kick which seemed to paralyse the Leeds pair of Ken Thornett and Eddie Ratcliffe, who left each other to deal with it. Alan Skene swept in where Leeds feared to tread and scored near the corner. Neil whacked over a beautiful conversion and Trinity led 14-5. Jones replied with a penalty but Trinity stretched their advantage to 17-7 when Jones mortifyingly sent a drop out straight to Fred Smith, who ran through a non-existent defence to score. Jones kicked a third penalty but Neil had the last word with a well struck drop-goal and Trinity took the Yorkshire Cup with a 19-9 victory.

It had not been a pretty game – for example, Don Vines had been lectured five times by referee Tom Watkinson – but Neil's unerring left foot had ensured that Trinity took the spoils. The *Wakefield Express* made no bones about it: "Without any doubt the brightest feature of this Cup final was the goal-kicking of Fox". Eddie Waring's *Sunday Pictorial* report was headlined "Golden Boots Fox bang on!" in one inch high capitals. No one noticed, however, that Neil's second goal had been his 600th for Trinity.

The Yorkshire Cup win was Wakefield's 13th consecutive victory of the season, a post-war club record. So well were Trinity performing that talk began to be heard of a possible 'All Four Cups' season. Such talk may have been extremely, even foolishly, premature but there was a feeling abroad that Trinity had what it took to accomplish that rare feat. There was no question now that they were one of the game's glamour teams. They had match-winners, none better than Neil, steel in the pack and, crucially, strong reserve players.

Trinity's winning run had reached 18 matches by Christmas. On 18 November there were six goals for Neil in a 33-12 home win against Bradford Northern. A week later he could only muster two tries and a goal in a 20-9 success at York in an exciting but bad-tempered affair. John L. Allen railed that Neil "had one of the worst days of his career so far as goal-kicking went. Out of ten shots he only succeeded with one!" However, he conceded that Neil's second try, the last and decisive one of the game, was the highlight. The movement started almost on Trinity's line. Holliday and Firth put Turner away on his own '25'. Derek hared to the York '25' and who should be there to take the ball the last 25 yards to the line but that so-called slow coach Neil Fox, flaunting his 'lucky' habit of being there when needed.

On 2 December, Neil bagged 13 points in a 24-13 win against Batley but Trinity suffered a blow when Kosanovic dislocated his collar-bone. The following Saturday Wakefield came up against much sterner opposition in St Helens at Belle Vue in a match that did not contain a dull moment. The *Wakefield Express* reported, "Fox was in great form, his power-packed, straight running being a thrilling feature of his work which will, without much doubt, be entertaining the Australian crowds in the fairly near future." Neil kicked Trinity into the lead with a penalty, the only score of the first half, gave Trinity a 7-5 lead with another penalty and stretched the advantage to 9-5 on the hour with a fine drop-goal, after kidding the Saints into believing he was going to pass the ball wide. To prove he was fallible, however, with only eight minutes left and Trinity leading 12-5, Neil threw a pass to Skene which Saints winger Pimblett intercepted ridiculously easily to touch down under the posts with Northey's conversion making the score 12-10. As a result of this victory Wakefield retained their joint league leadership with Wigan and Workington.

On 23 December, Dewsbury visited Belle Vue and were drubbed 58-5. Jan Prinsloo reappeared in the Trinity ranks but retired at half-time with a recurrence of his groin injury. As Dewsbury centre Riley also retired at the break, the second half was played 12-a-side. Not that it mattered to Neil, who equalled his own club record by kicking 11 goals out of 12 attempts, failing only to convert the first of three Fred Smith tries.

Bad weather caused the postponement of all Wakefield's Christmas and New Year fixtures but there was good news for Neil and his team-mates, who were hopeful of a coveted place on the summer's Australasian tour. Club chairman Stuart Hadfield was chosen as senior tour manager, the first time that such a role had been created, as previous tours had worked a joint-manager arrangement between two officials. The 1958 tour, though ultimately tremendously successful, had been dogged by friction between the managers and coach. The RFL was anxious that such problems should not arise again.

Neil's tour prospects could hardly be overlooked this time. He entered the New Year as the league's leading goalkicker and points-scorer and his all-round performances had often been almost superhuman. All the newspapers had him marked out as a certainty to tour.

He and Trinity returned to action on 13 January with a good 29-13 win over Hunslet at Belle Vue, Neil scoring 11 points. It was a hot tempered clash and Skene, Turner, Vines and Oakes were all in the wars. Turner suffered bruised ribs, a damaged knee and had three stitches in his right eyelid – no wonder he was dubbed 'Rocky'.

The following week Trinity faced a real toughie at Featherstone. Neither team had been beaten in the Yorkshire League and such was the local interest that Rovers had a record league crowd and took record receipts for what turned out to be an epic struggle. Trinity fielded a weakened pack as a result of the bruising battle against Hunslet and included debutant hooker Roy Hawksley, yet they led 5-2 at half-time, thanks to a titanic defensive effort. Rovers lost the plot in the 41st minute when hooker Willis Fawley was sent off for striking Neil. Even so, it was not until the last 20 minutes that Trinity finally pulled clear to win 18-4, with Neil having the satisfaction of becoming the first player in the league to pass a century of goals for the season.

On 27 January, Wakefield met Keighley at Belle Vue, seeking their 21st straight victory to equal the post-war record set by Warrington between April and November 1948. By half-time the mission was accomplished as Trinity led 18-2 with Ken Hirst scoring three tries on his first appearance since 6 September. He added another in the second half and Trinity won 27-7. Neil was in imperious mood. Apart from collecting six goals, he set up three of Hirst's tries in moves covering 50 or more yards.

That week the *Wakefield Express* revealed that Belle Vue was to be used for much of the rugby league content of local author David Storey's novel *This Sporting Life*, which was being turned into a film by the famous producer Lindsay Anderson. Anderson and the star of the film Richard Harris were both present at the Keighley match. Neil and his team-mates would be seeing a lot of the pair over the next few months.

On 3 February, Trinity were faced with a daunting trip to Thrum Hall where they would attempt to surpass Warrington's 1948 record. Halifax were having an indifferent season and engaged in the struggle for a top 16 place to ensure First Division football in 1962-63. Even so, only Wigan had won at Thrum Hall that season and Trinity had won only once at Halifax since the war. Consequently it was likely to be a difficult match, particularly with the record at stake. By now every team wanted to knock Wakefield off their perch and Halifax were certainly not ready to lie down and die. A howling gale played havoc with Neil's kicking, restricting him to one goal in nine attempts, but the Halifax defence had more influence on matters. By half-time Trinity were 2-0 down to a Ronnie James penalty on 32 minutes, just a minute after referee George Wilson had marched hookers Joby Shaw and Milan Kosanovic for persistent technical offences. Three minutes after the break loose-forward Charlie Renilson scored a converted try for Halifax and at 7-0, with a seemingly impenetrable defence baulking them at every turn, Trinity seemed destined to fail in their quest to create a new record. Then fortune smiled on them. Halifax second-rower Wynford Phillips was sent off after 54 minutes after a tackle on Albert Firth and Halifax were compelled to pack three forwards against Trinity's five. The game got ever more hectic, players were cautioned, some were laid out – and still Trinity could not break through. Finally they did after 64 minutes, when Holliday crossed from the blind-side of a scrum five yards out. Neil kicked the goal and the blitz on the Halifax line continued, but it was not until the 78th minute that Halifax capitulated and Neil was the spark. Hemmed in on the Halifax '25' and with all exits apparently blocked, Neil suddenly spotted the possibility of unlocking the defence. He turned the ball in completely the opposite direction to the move Wakefield had begun. It was shipped across field to Alan Skene whose do-or-die spurt to the line won the game 8-7 and gave Trinity their record-breaking 22nd consecutive victory. Stanley Pearson in the *Bradford Telegraph & Argus* declared that "this was undoubtedly the most exciting 80 minutes of rugby I have ever seen".

By coincidence, the following Saturday Trinity met Warrington, from whom they had taken the record, in the first round of the Challenge Cup at Belle Vue. Wakefield were 4-1 second favourites for the trophy behind Wigan at 3-1, but no cup tie against Warrington could be regarded as a foregone conclusion. Neil has happy memories of the match: "That was a game I will always remember. In the morning papers Jim Challinor, my opposing centre, said he was not worried about me. He said he would let me pass him and catch me from behind. He did a couple of times but that was after I had placed the ball over their line four times. We won the match 40-18. It was a great game. I also kicked five goals. I wonder what Jim thought after the game?"

That match, played before almost 20,000 enraptured fans, was undoubtedly a wonderful contest and completely different from the type of game expected in a Challenge

Cup match between two top-line teams. Neil had a beano. The *Wakefield Express* eulogised, "Neil Fox's two tries in the first half... will be talked about for a long time. In the old style of classic centre play – straight down the middle and no frills – he demolished opponents as if they weren't there... in both cases he scattered three defenders in a pulsating charge which forced a passage to the line as efficiently as a scythe... On this occasion he excelled himself. The Australians are certainly going to see a player fit to join the legendary figures of the past." The Wire defenders must have wondered what had hit them because in Alan Skene, Neil had the perfect partner, who exhibited pace, skill, twinkling feet, body swerve and a debilitating change of pace.

On 17 February, Trinity went to the opposite end of the spectrum drawing 0-0 at Batley, thus bringing their winning run to an end after 23 games. They played inexplicably awful football in "a show that did them great discredit". 'The Pinder' moaned, "Batley were the better of two wretched teams". No doubt the *Batley News* reported it in a different way and Neil's brother, Peter, propping for Batley, would also have viewed it very differently.

Fortunately, Neil was many miles from Mount Pleasant, playing for Great Britain against France at Wigan. It was an important test with the selections for the Australasian tour looming. Britain had stuck with the tried and tested threequarters – Boston, Ashton, Fox and Sullivan – and Bolton and Murphy at half-back. Gerry Round had been restored to full-back after last appearing in the final Ashes test of 1959. The forwards, however, were relatively unknown at this level. Debuts were given to hooker Barry Simms of Leeds and the Featherstone pair Mal Dixon at prop and Terry Clawson in the second-row. Abe Terry, Dick Huddart and Johnny Whiteley were, however, seasoned test men.

The first half saw Britain playing superb rugby. Sullivan, Huddart and Ashton scored tries, two of which Neil converted. They led 13-2 at the break but after it went totally off the boil. France began to gain the forward ascendancy, brilliantly led by loose-forward and skipper Jean Barthe and fearsome prop Marcel Bescos, and rattled up 13 points in a 10 minute barrage. Claude Mantoulan and Gilbert Benausse, the latter scoring two, roared in for tries as the French backs "threw the ball about with gay abandon". In this period the only British reply was a long range penalty from Neil and the scores were tied at 15-15. Eight minutes from time more scintillating rugby put winger Jacques Dubon over for the winning try, to which Benausse added his fourth goal. For the rest of the game *Les Chanticleers* tackled everything, causing Neil to tell Eddie Waring of the *Sunday Pictorial*, "It looked as if there were 26 Frenchmen on the field, they plugged the holes up so well".

The following Saturday, Trinity hosted Wigan, their main rivals for the game's major prizes, in a game which drew a crowd of 27,614, a post-war record for Belle Vue. Hundreds were locked out and hundreds more climbed over walls to gain admission. There was no doubt that this was the game of the season so far in every respect. Trinity's unbeaten run now stood at 24 games, while Wigan had 17 consecutive victories behind them. It was also the stage for one of Neil's greatest performances.

After four minutes Neil landed a prodigious goal from three yards inside the Wigan half when their opponents ran offside. Nine minutes later Trinity opened out play in classical fashion following a scrum. Poynton whipped the ball to Neil, who delayed his pass until Alan Davies tackled him, then adroitly fed Round, who shot down the left wing and threw the ball inside to winger Hirst, who careered over. Neil converted and Trinity led 7-0 - and went 9-0 up after 21 minutes when Neil landed another penalty goal. After 27 minutes Fred Griffiths put Wigan on the scoreboard with a penalty. Then the game assumed a different complexion. Neil took a drop-out from his own goal-line. The ball went high but short. Wigan second-rower Norm Cherrington leapt for the ball and knocked it backwards. Neil was on it immediately and broke into the open field with a surge of 30 yards and sent Griffiths the wrong way. He had two men in support and a certain try in the offing only to be brought back for what the referee decided was a knock-on. Amid a torrent of slow handclapping, Wigan won the resultant scrum and winger Frank Carlton scored a magnificent try from the ensuing movement. Fred Griffiths struck a fine conversion and Trinity held a precarious 9-7 lead, when it could have easily been a match-breaking 14-2. Wigan now held the whip hand, dominating the scrums and mounting incessant attacks.

The handling by both teams had been remarkable considering the game was played almost throughout in drizzle. Griffiths kicked penalty goals after 51 and 67 minutes for Wigan to lead 11-9. It would have been more if Neil had not stopped Billy Boston head on in one of the winger's crash-bash runs. As Trinity's hopes were fast receding, they conjured up a glorious match-winner with six minutes remaining. Trinity took a scrum and worked the ball via Poynton, Neil and the jet-heeled Skene, who set Fred Smith racing past three men down the flank. As frantic Wigan defenders buried Fred it looked all over but, according to the *Rugby Leaguer*, "Fox, sensing the victory chance, went with him for the return pass. It came 20 yards out and the centre took it to move in for a try without a defender getting near him". He converted and Wakefield scraped home 14-11.

Trinity's next fixture was potentially much easier – an away tie at Blackpool Borough in the Challenge Cup on 3 March. It was also, as those whose memories stretched back to 1957 conceded, potentially the most slippery of banana skins. If that disaster was preying on Neil's mind it did not show. However, it was no cake-walk. On a minimum-sized pitch and with majority possession going Trinity's way, Blackpool fought hard enough. After 20 minutes they led 2-0, courtesy of a penalty by Arthur Pimblett, which was cancelled out by Neil five minutes later. A second penalty by Neil after 30 minutes put Trinity 4-2 in the lead. It also took Neil past Charlie Pollard's club record of 654 goals between 1919 and 1931, but that was another of those records which no-one noticed at the time. Borough held out until the third minute of first-half injury time. They were attacking the Trinity line when, as George Lunn in the *Rugby Leaguer* reported, "Suddenly a Borough player dropped the ball. It was snapped up by Fox who, more in desperation than as a planned move, put in a long kick down the centre of the field. The Borough full-back, Pimblett, had to chase back to recover, but although he appeared to have ample time to gather the ball, which was bouncing awkwardly, he failed to do so, and Fox who had followed up fast managed to gather and sailed over the line near the posts for a simple try, which he also converted". Was it a simple try, George? The *Yorkshire Evening News* reporter may have been fairer in describing it as "a triumph of individual effort".

In the second half Pimblett and Neil exchanged penalties before the stubborn Blackpool defence finally broke again in the last quarter. Derek Turner cleverly punted out to the left wing. Prinsloo raced after the ball and practically ripped it from winger Doug Iredale's grasp as it bounced. Jan then hoisted the ball back infield to Neil who won a thrilling sprint to score his second try, which he also improved. Neil certainly took revenge for 1957, the final score being Blackpool Borough 4 Neil Fox 16.

The following Monday, a 50-strong unit under Lindsay Anderson arrived at Belle Vue to start filming the rugby scenes for *This Sporting Life*. He needed 200 locals to act as extras and spent the next two weeks shooting around Wakefield before returning south to Beaconsfield Studios. A month later he would be back in Wakefield. Neil recalls: "The players were asked to get two weeks off work to act as extras. That was fine as we were paid £20 a week for it and got well fed into the bargain. The male stars – Richard Harris, Jack Watson and Colin Blakeley – did most of their scenes at Belle Vue but we didn't see the actresses like Rachel Roberts. It was interesting seeing how they filmed but it was also boring sometimes just waiting to be involved. Richard Harris became a fan and never missed a cup match. He would come up and join us in the dressing room and was thrilled when we won the Challenge Cup. I remember he swapped his sheepskin coat for Keith Holliday's jersey, jumped in the bath with us and drank champagne. Later, when I was away down-under on tour, most of the players who could get time off work did a lot of filming when the dance and pub scenes were shot. Ken Traill was on a different contract to the rest because he had a speaking part. Ken and Richard stayed in touch with each other long after the film was made and Richard always kept in touch with Trinity's progress."

On 11 March, Neil travelled to Perpignan for Britain's return test against France. The French game was something of a disaster. Everything went wrong for Britain. France beat them 23-13 after blitzing their opponents 21-5 in the first half. The British team and officials felt that referee, Jean Queroli, allowed his countrymen to play offside for most of the game, to spoil and to make a mockery of the play-the-ball and scrummaging laws. Manager Stuart Hadfield, obviously gearing up for what was to follow in Australia, bellowed at the British press: "We have been playing 14 people. I think the referee was diabolical". On the other hand, he admitted, "Some of the tackling by our forwards was shocking and we never played up to form". Skipper Eric Ashton plaintively asked, "Why does it always happen when I'm captain?" Ashton, nonetheless, was one of the few Brits who emerged with much credit, although Gerry Round was thought to have played himself into the touring party. Neil, who kicked a couple of goals, was not exempt from criticism. Alfred Drewry in the *Yorkshire Post* wrote, "Fox had one of those games in which his lack of speed is more noticeable than his strength and his quick football brain".

Three days after the debacle at Perpignan, Neil made his 200th appearance for Trinity at Bramley, kicking five goals in a 25-11 win. Two of his successes were from the touchline and two from massive distances. Playing his third game in six days at Hull on 17 March, Neil reminded the selectors of his value as Trinity won a hard, relentless, exhausting game 13-4 and took over top spot in the league from Wigan. Derek Turner scored Trinity's first two tries to give his team a 10-2 lead. The second in the 53rd minute was scored almost at the flag next to Hull's infamous Threepenny Stand. The *Wakefield Express* commented on "the senseless behaviour of the crowd", and as Neil prepared to take the conversion he recalls, "The try was scored right in the corner so it was a hard kick. I didn't take a long run for my kicks at the best of times but there was not much room between the touchline and the crowd. As I backed onto the fence the fans kept pushing me in the back and putting me off balance. Just as I was ready to kick some Hull fans came over the fence and one of them booted the ball." The referee had the police to take the culprit away and Neil, unsurprisingly, went on to miss the conversion. He had the last laugh though 12 minutes later, when one of his tremendous surging runs took three Hull defenders over the line with him for a try which finished the scoring.

Two days later, on Monday, 19 March, Neil was one of eight first-teamers rested for Trinity's visit to Central Park. It did not stop more than 30,000 turning up to watch Wigan beat Wakefield 28-9 to regain the league leadership. Trinity had chosen to send a weakened team because they were to meet Wigan again at Belle Vue on the Saturday in the third round of the Challenge Cup. It was unquestionably going to be the game of the season – even more important than the game the two had played just a month earlier. This time the fixture was made an all-ticket affair.

Just two days before it though was the small matter of the announcement of the Australasian tour party, upon which Neil pinned so much hope. The selectors had clearly discounted the poor exhibition at Perpignan for 11 of that team were in the squad, including Neil. Not only was Neil about to fulfil his dream, but so was his brother Don, who had won the second scrum-half spot alongside Alex Murphy. Trinity also provided tourists in Gerry Round, Harold Poynton, Jack Wilkinson and Derek Turner, who was vice-captain to Eric Ashton. It was the first time since 1928 that a pair of brothers had been selected to tour together. Back then Jack and Bryn Evans of Swinton had made history as the first brothers to tour together, and by coincidence one was a centre and the other a scrum-half. Trinity's provision of five tourists was easily a record for the club.

Tour selection assured, Neil's focus turned to the all-important Cup quarter final against Wigan on 24 March, a game televised on BBC's *Grandstand* and also filmed for and used in *This Sporting Life*. Almost half the tourists were on show in this clash, as Wigan fielded six men who had been chosen, but lacked stand-off Dave Bolton, a seventh tourist. Just as they had done in the 1960 Championship Final, Wigan moved Billy Boston into the centres and pushed Eric Ashton to stand-off. It appeared that they had targeted Wakefield's centres as their most potent threat. The post-war ground crowd record was again broken with 28,524 squeezing into Belle Vue.

The game was a stern struggle with few spectacular passages of play. There was very little scoring, the first half restricted to two penalty goals. Neil kicked the first on 25 minutes and Fred Griffiths replied on 32 minutes. Trinity were out-hooked 2-1 in the first-half scrums. The second half saw possession going 2-1 in Trinity's favour and they made it pay, with Dennis Williamson giving a towering performance in their pack. It was, however, Wigan who struck first five minutes after the break. Ashton dropped for goal from 30 yards. The ball hit first one post, then the other, before dropping on to the bar and over for two points. Wigan's lead lasted a mere five minutes before Fred Smith dived over at the corner in the face of some fiery defence to claim the final – and winning - score of the game, a 5-4 victory for Trinity. At the time Fred was swallow-diving to glory, Alan Skene was off the field for the second time after being laid low by high tackles. He played the last 33 minutes concussed. Wigan had certainly bottled up Trinity's centres, one way or another, for "Fox was never quite able to throw off the unyielding strait jacket imposed by his vigilant opponent", stated the *Wakefield Express*. However, this concentration on Fox and Skene allowed Trinity's half-backs to shine and Poynton effectively blotted out Ashton. Wakefield were in fact much the better team and fully deserved their £45 winning pay.

The price of success was once again a fixture pile-up of major proportions. Trinity faced 11 league matches and a Cup semi-final in the next 35 days. Neil played in all but the last of the 11. The first three – games at Hunslet, Keighley and Doncaster - were negotiated without difficulty with Neil contributing 31 of the 61 points Trinity scored in them.

Trinity's opponents in the Challenge Cup semi-final were again Featherstone Rovers. For the first time in peace-time rugby league all four semi-finalists came from Yorkshire, presenting the authorities with a unique problem. They decided to play both semis at Odsal. Huddersfield and Hull KR were allotted a Saturday fixture but the Trinity versus Rovers game was to precede it on Wednesday, 11 April. Neither club was happy about the situation because the arrangement was bound to reduce the attendance. Even so, more than 43,000 flocked to the match. Neil's summary of the game is pretty succinct: "Although we were in command all through, we did not play to the best of our ability. We won 9-0 and I kicked three goals and Ken Hirst scored our only try. So it was another disappointment for Don and Joe but back to Wembley for us". Hirst's try came after 24 minutes and Neil kicked three penalties in the 34th, 45th and 65th minutes. His brother Don's offside offences gave him the first two opportunities. The measure of Trinity's dominance was perhaps best gauged from the fact that the only chance Rovers had to score came from a 50-yard penalty attempt by Terry Clawson. The *Wakefield Express* commented, "At times Neil Fox showed traces of his great power as a test centre but mostly he was an individual whose every movement attracted considerable attention from his brother's playing-mates. And that was a happening which cramped Neil's style somewhat."

Trinity followed their Odsal triumph by hammering Castleford 23-3 at Belle Vue and then, with half a team of reserves, Hull KR 30-0 at Craven Park. Neil was in fabulous form. Allan Cave wrote in the *Daily Herald*, "The man who really showed his outstanding international skill was Wakefield heavyweight centre Neil Fox, who in this form is going to be one heck of a headache for Australia... He scored two thunderous tries from half-way. For the first, Fox carried on an excellent move by Steel and ever alert half-backs Poynton and Holliday to sweep aside every attempt to tackle him." He also booted six goals.

Two days later, on Good Friday, Trinity had a blip at Leigh, who, desperately fighting for a place in the new First Division, were good value for their 10-6 victory. Wigan were so happy that Trinity had been beaten that they telephoned congratulatory messages to Leigh. The defeat allowed Wigan to maintain their league leadership.

Trinity would not slip up again in the league, however. The day after the Leigh defeat, they saw Halifax off 20-3 at Belle Vue and two days after that dispatched Hull KR 23-5. The latter game saw Neil shatter his own club goal-kicking record, his fourth and final goal taking him past his old record of 146. He did not just kick goals, either, as Derek Marshall of the *Daily Mail* reported, "Neil Fox showed a defence-wrecking combination of craft and crunch to leave Hull KR's championship semi-final chances dangling by a thread. He sold a perfect dummy to give Briggs the opening try, drew the cover to provide another for Prinsloo, and finally thundered over himself after a scrum break by Poynton". The game also clinched the Yorkshire League Championship for Trinity with four matches still to play. That in turn opened up the real possibility that they could perhaps win all four cups. Trinity created a record too by going through their entire 28-game Yorkshire League programme undefeated, the only blot on their copybook being the scoreless draw at Batley.

Records continued to tumble to Neil. At Headingley on 25 April, Trinity beat Leeds 21-6, despite losing Fred Smith after 45 minutes. Smith was sent off for a bad high tackle on opposing winger Eddie Ratcliffe, whose collar-bone was broken. Neil landed six goals, his first taking him past his club points-in-a-season record of 370. Also in the same game were his 700th goal for Trinity and his 2,000th point in all first-class games.

Neil's last league game of the season brought him four goals in a 20-13 win at Dewsbury. He missed the last league match, a 17-9 home win against Featherstone, although he remembers, "I was rested and making his debut was Ian Brooke, who later became my regular partner in the centre, replacing Alan Skene".

At the conclusion of the league competition the top four finished thus:

	P	W	D	L	Pts	For	Agst
Wigan	36	32	1	3	65	885	283
Wakefield Trinity	36	32	1	3	65	822	288
Featherstone Rovers	36	28	1	7	57	621	370
Huddersfield	36	25	2	9	52	494	351

Trinity had to get past Featherstone Rovers in the Championship semi-final at Belle Vue on the evening of 5 May to maintain the quest for all four cups. They lacked Fred Smith, suspended, but Rovers were short of the injured Don Fox. More than 20,000 piled into Belle Vue and many went away feeling justice had not been done when the 80 minutes were over. Neil did plenty of damage in the first half, as Rovers full-back Jackie Fennell would testify after being heavily dazed in one confrontation with him. Neil also created the first try after 17 minutes, brilliantly sending Round over in the corner. A Carl Dooler try, converted by Terry Clawson rocked Trinity, who did not regain the lead until the 39th minute. Following a scrum on Rovers '25', Neil took Poynton's reverse pass, banged down Gary Cooper's attempted tackle, left three other defenders standing and put Ken Hirst over for a try. Neil's touchline conversion hit the post and ricocheted out. Shortly after the interval Rovers lost prop Cliff Lambert but the 12 remaining Rovers did not give up. Neil extended Trinity's lead to 8-5 with a long-range penalty but with 20 minutes left, Gary Jordan scored a superb try to level matters. It was not until the 74th minute that Trinity sealed victory when Jack Wilkinson launched himself over triumphantly for a try, goaled by Neil. There was considerable doubt about the score, however, because most people on the ground believed that Brian Briggs had blatantly knocked on before Wilkie touched down. Fortunately for Trinity, the man who mattered, referee Matt Coates, disagreed.

Most unexpectedly, Huddersfield won at Wigan in the other semi-final. Trinity would therefore have to meet the Fartowners in both the Challenge Cup final and the Championship final on consecutive Saturdays. The critics expected Wakefield to win both games. All four cups were now within their grasp.

In the meantime Neil had to cope with the preparation, both in training and social terms, for two massive games. He also had to go through the ritual of travelling to Leeds for the kitting-out operations necessary for all Australasian tours. He had to be measured for his tour outfit, listen to the advice about what was expected of the Lions and collect the itinerary for the tour games. He was also expected to go to work every day at the CEGB, and he had been married for less than a year. It must have seemed at times to Neil that there were hardly enough hours in a day.

For the 1962 Challenge Cup Final Wakefield – on £85 to win - made their headquarters at a West End hotel and used a training ground in Hayes. The wives and girlfriends joined them at the hotel after the final.

Few expected Huddersfield to win at Wembley but Ken Traill and his players knew that they were in for a hard game. Huddersfield were no mugs. After all, they had defeated Wigan in the top four play-off and in the second round of the Cup had won at St Helens. Moreover, they had qualified for the Championship final despite playing in the Lancashire League, which was regarded as a tougher competition than the Yorkshire League. They had discipline, a tough defence, which had conceded only one try in reaching the final, and some good players in key positions. Their captain, scrum-half and leading light, Tommy Smales told the press, "We know Wakefield are a good side but I think they have only three players we need really worry about – their centres, Neil Fox and Alan Skene, and loose-forward Derek Turner. As far as the other forwards are concerned, I have no worries at all. Just weigh up our pack man for man with Trinity's and I think you'll agree. We shan't try anything that we've not done previously and I expect we'll play it up the middle where we are strongest and then fan it out when we can."

The teams on an uncharacteristically dull May afternoon at Wembley were:
Wakefield Trinity: Gerry Round, Fred Smith, Alan Skene, Neil Fox, Ken Hirst, Harold Poynton, Keith Holliday, Jack Wilkinson, Geoff Oakes, Albert Firth, Brian Briggs, Dennis Williamson, Derek Turner (captain).
Huddersfield: Frank Dyson, Aidan Breen, Leo Booth, Ray Haywood, Mike Wicks, Harry Deighton, Tommy Smales (captain), Ted Slevin, Don Close, Ken Noble, Mick Clark, Ken Bowman, Peter Ramsden.

Neil describes the game in characteristic matter-of-fact style: "This turned out to be another good final for me. Early in the game I dropped a goal from about 30 yards. This was when our captain, Derek Turner, was being treated for injury. Then I got Ken Hirst away on our 25-yard line. He galloped up the wing and went inside Dyson, the Huddersfield full-back. I backed Ken up and shouted for the ball. He threw it back inside and I went the last 40 yards to score in the corner to give us a lead of 5-0. People used to say I couldn't run but I think that proved otherwise. Huddersfield came back to make the score 5-3 at half-time. Tommy Smales scored a good try.

In the dressing-room during the interval we realised there wouldn't be many points scored. So Derek and I decided that when we got near to their posts, I would try dropping another goal. Halfway through the second half a chance came and we scored another two points from my boot. Then we got another try from Hirst and were 10-3 up. Ramsden scored for Huddersfield to make it 10-6. Then I dropped another goal to make it safe at 12-6 and victory was ours. Both Frank Dyson and myself missed some goals but I had secured the win with those three drop-goals. That had never been done before. Along with the try I scored, those kicks won me the Lance Todd Trophy. Celebrations were in order."

Neil's performance in dropping those goals, in the 17th, 63rd and 80th minutes, had proved to be a novel way of winning the Challenge Cup. They were certainly necessary as Huddersfield had given Trinity a torrid time and really made them work for their success. There was no counter to the drop-goal, though, especially when Neil had been given so much time to take his shots after well set-up play-the-balls, the first from Geoff Oakes' pass and the second and third from Brian Briggs. Briggs had been the best forward on the field and taken the reins when Derek Turner had been clattered by Peter Ramsden in a tackle which left Rocky off the field for eight minutes and in a daze for half the game.

After the game a euphoric Ken Traill told reporters, "Fox is the greatest footballer I have ever seen... It was not a spectacular game from the crowd's point of view. It was a game for the connoisseur."

On the Sunday evening after the final, Trinity took the Challenge Cup with them to the London Palladium. Neil recalls: "Derek Turner and I were lucky because we were invited backstage to meet the star of the show, Shirley Bassey, and the compere, comedian Norman Vaughan." The triumphal return to Wakefield on the Monday followed the pattern of 1960, tens of thousands filling the city centre, as the team received a civic reception.

Only 80 minutes of rugby stood between Trinity and immortality now. No team had got nearer to emulating the four cup seasons of Hunslet (1907-08), Huddersfield (1914-15) and Swinton (1927-28), than this Trinity side. They knew they had the beating of Huddersfield in most circumstances but also knew that rugby could be a funny game. Trinity went off to Bridlington on the Tuesday before their date with destiny, to relax and prepare. Neil and his fellow tourists were allowed to stay at home until Thursday, because they would soon be a lot further from family and home than the harbour at Brid.

For the Championship Final, on 19 May, Trinity brought in Kosanovic for Oakes and Vines for Williamson. Theoretically they were even stronger than at Wembley. Huddersfield replaced Deighton with Gwyn Davies at stand-off, moving Deighton to centre in place of Haywood, while in the pack Austin Kilroy took over from Mick Clark.

Unfortunately, the weather was foul, a factor which kept the attendance down to 37,451, most of whom were thoroughly sodden. There was a strong wind and rain fell throughout, turning the pitch into a morass. There was no doubt that such conditions would be more welcome to the Fartowners than to Trinity. Wakefield, however, had the elements in their favour in the first half and, perhaps ill-advisedly, tried to play too much football in the first half hour. In those 30 minutes Kosanovic won the scrums 10-5 but Trinity went behind to a 27th-minute penalty by Dyson. Finally their enterprise paid off in the 29th minute when they scored a magnificent try. Briggs suddenly broke into an open field, passed to Neil, who battered his way past a couple of tacklers and sent Fred Smith scooting down the wing. Fred could have gone for the corner and might have made it but instead turned the ball inside for Neil to stride imperiously to the posts for a try which he converted. Trinity led 5-2 but that was as good as it got for them. Huddersfield began to win their share of possession and a couple of minutes before half-time took the lead with a dubious try. Jack Nott, writing for the *News of the World*, did not mince his words: "Huddersfield got away with the most doubtful touchdown I have ever seen. An exploratory kick through sliced wingward from the middle. It was the most innocent thing you ever saw. Gerry Round coasted across to cover it, but two yards short he was grabbed by a Huddersfield player, and, with his hands pinioned to his sides, he could do nothing other than look on helplessly as Fartown flier Mike Wicks streaked up to gather and cross. And the astonishing thing was that referee Norman Railton awarded a try". Dyson's great touchline conversion added insult to injury and at the break Huddersfield led 7-5.

The second half saw Huddersfield impose a vice-like grip on the game. Their forwards were remorseless – "like hounds in pursuit of their quarry", while Dyson constantly drove Trinity back with long kicks. The *Huddersfield Examiner* reported, "Long before the end the ferocity of the Huddersfield tackling had so sapped the strength and confidence of Trinity's attack that wild passes were being thrown and centres Alan Skene and Neil Fox were receiving ball and man at the same second." Dyson kicked a penalty in the 47th minute and just before the final whistle, Davies worked an opportunity for Smales to race 20 yards to the corner for a stunning try. The crowd erupted and hundreds of ecstatic Fartown supporters careered on to the field. The police eventually cleared them and Dyson bounced an unlikely conversion onto the bar and over and Trinity had lost 14-5, their all four cups ambitions drowned in Odsal's mud and rain. There was no question that Huddersfield deserved their victory. The unnamed *Rugby Leaguer* correspondent wrote, "When Huddersfield were cheered to the echo as they came up the steps to receive their medals and the cup, I noted with real pleasure how Derek Turner and Neil Fox, at the foot of the steps, clapped each Fartown player. The other Trinity players were lost in the crowd."

For Neil an extraordinarily long and successful season had ended in disappointment but he had much to remember and much to be proud of. Materially, he had three more winners' medals and a losers' in his growing collection, while he had drawn losing pay just three times in 42 appearances for Trinity. He had won the Lance Todd trophy and finished as the league's leading points scorer with 456 - 66 more than Wigan's Fred Griffiths. He and Griffiths shared the leading goalkickers' spot with 183 and his 30 tries in all games gave him joint sixth place in the leading try-scorers' lists, along with his team-mate Jan Prinsloo and Featherstone winger Gary Jordan. For Trinity he had extended his points-in-a-season record from 370 to 407 and his goals-in-a-season record from 146 to 163. However, as for the wicked, there was to be no rest yet for Neil and his fellow Lions.

Wakefield Trinity 1961-62

Wakefield Trinity finished 2nd in the league: P36, W32, L3, D1, For 822, Against 288
Fox scored 27 tries, 163 goals, 407 points for Wakefield, and 3 tries, 20 goals, 49 points in representative games

Date	Opponent	Score	Fox	Crowd	
19 Aug	Castleford	42-9	T, 5G	9,000	
26 Aug	**York**	18-12	3G	11,000	
30 Aug	St Helens	5-10	G	21,109	
2 Sep	**Bradford N**	73-5	dnp	10,942	YC1
6 Sep	**Bramley**	14-2	dnp	6,700	
9 Sep	**Hull**	29-15	4G	13,278	
13 Sep	**Doncaster**	55-5	T, 5G	7,019	
16 Sep	Swinton	22-7	5G	13,410	
19 Sep	Hull	13-7	5G	14,000	YC2
23 Sep	**Leeds**	21-4	2T, G	21,362	
4 Oct	**York**	24-4	3G	12,167	YC semi
7 Oct	**Leigh**	31-10	5G	12,117	
14 Oct	Bradford N	38-7	7G	5,636	
28 Oct	**New Zealand**	20-7	T, 3G	16,558	
4 Nov	**Swinton**	36-10	dnp	11,904	
11 Nov	Leeds	19-9	5G	16,329	YC Final (at Odsal)
18 Nov	**Bradford N**	33-12	6G	8,554	
25 Nov	York	20-9	2T, G	6,295	
2 Dec	**Batley**	24-13	T, 6G	6,464	
9 Dec	**St Helens**	12-10	3G	12,696	
23 Dec	**Dewsbury**	58-5	T, 11G	6,688	
13 Jan	**Hunslet**	29-13	T, 4G	9,454	
20 Jan	Featherstone R	18-4	3G	14,990	
27 Jan	**Keighley**	27-7	6G	10,999	
3 Feb	Halifax	8-7	G	12,715	
10 Feb	**Warrington**	40-18	4T, 5G	19,330	Ch Cup 1
17 Feb	Batley	0-0	dnp	6,000	
24 Feb	**Wigan**	14-11	T, 4G	27,614	
3 Mar	Blackpool B	16-4	2T, 5G	6,000	Ch Cup 2
14 Mar	Bramley	25-11	5G	6,672	
17 Mar	Hull	13-4	T, 2G	14,530	
19 Mar	Wigan	9-28	dnp	30,674	
24 Mar	**Wigan**	5-4	G	28,254	Ch Cup 3
26 Mar	Hunslet	25-8	5G	8,600	
31 Mar	Keighley	17-2	4G	5,000	
7 Apr	Doncaster	19-6	3T, 2G	4,850	
11 Apr	Featherstone R	9-0	3G	43,627	Ch Cup semi (at Odsal)
14 Apr	**Castleford**	23-3	4G	11,888	
18 Apr	Hull KR	30-0	2T, 6G	7,440	
20 Apr	Leigh	6-10	T	8,341	
21 Apr	**Halifax**	20-3	4G	7,185	
23 Apr	**Hull KR**	23-5	T, 4G	15,772	
25 Apr	Leeds	21-6	6G	27,741	
28 Apr	Dewsbury	20-13	4G	7,400	
30 Apr	**Featherstone R**	17-9	dnp	15,077	
5 May	**Featherstone R**	13-8	2G	20,215	CH semi
12 May	Huddersfield	12-6	T, 3G	81,263	Ch Cup Final (at Wembley)
19 May	Huddersfield	5-14	T, G	37,451	CH Final (at Odsal)

Representative appearances

6 Sep	Yorkshire 21 New Zealand 11 (Hull KR)	T
11 Sep	Yorkshire 8 Cumberland 23 (Wakefield)	T, G
9 Oct	Yorkshire 12 Lancashire 14 (Leigh)	T, 3G
21 Oct	Great Britain 23 New Zealand 10 (Odsal)	4G
4 Nov	Great Britain 35 New Zealand 19 (Swinton)	7G
17 Feb	Great Britain 15 France 20 (Wigan)	3G
11 Mar	Great Britain 13 France 23 (Perpignan)	2G

It's the start of something big. Knowsley Road is bursting at the seams for a first round Challenge Cup tie between Saints and Trinity in February 1960. Almost 30,000 were there to see Trinity win 15-10 to kick-start a run which brought them three Challenge Cups over the next four seasons. In this classic shot Neil has left spring-heeled Ken Large floundering before tearing away with winger John Etty in support.
(Photo: Wakefield Express)

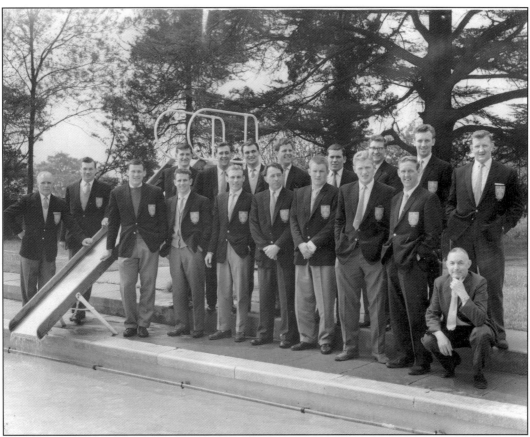

Relaxing before the big day – the Wakefield team before the 1960 Challenge Cup Final.

Derek Turner and Neil take the Challenge Cup backstage at the London Palladium to meet star of the show Shirley Bassey after Trinity's victory over Huddersfield at Wembley in 1962.

Trinity celebrating their 1962 Challenge Cup victory over Huddersfield.

10. 1962: On tour with the Lions

Despite Great Britain's indifferent form in the test matches of 1961 and 1962 and the misgivings of many pundits, the squad of players which was selected for the 1962 Lions tour of Australia, New Zealand and South Africa turned out to be one of the most successful that ever left British shores.

As usual, there were some surprises. Neil had been a cast-iron certainty, along with skipper Eric Ashton, for a centre spot, but the selectors sprang a couple of real shocks with the other centre choices. Neither Featherstone's Gary Cooper nor Castleford's Peter Small had yet won any representative honours at senior level, yet both were chosen. Among the other backs the most surprising choices to many critics were the selections of Harold Poynton at stand-off and Don Fox at scrum-half. Don got the nod ahead of Oldham's Frank Pitchford and Huddersfield's Tommy Smales, while among those disappointed not to have been selected were Frank Myler of Widnes and Ken Gowers of Swinton, both of whom would have provided versatility in several positions. Among the forwards, Huddersfield's Ken Noble and John Taylor of Hull KR were shock selections and two men of great experience with Wakefield connections, Jack Wilkinson and John Shaw, who might well have thought their representative days were behind them, found themselves back in the limelight. John was only 28 years old, but he had lost his test place over a year earlier and was apparently behind Bill Sayer, Barry Simms of Leeds and Bob Dagnall of St Helens in the selectors' rankings before the selection meeting. Perhaps the most notable omission from the forwards was that of Hull's great loose-forward Johnny Whiteley.

Despite the normal smattering of shock choices, the 1962 Lions squad was brimming with experience, as no fewer than 12 of them had toured previously. Of the 26 players, a dozen were Yorkshiremen, 10 Lancastrians and three Cumbrians, while Billy Boston was the lone Welshman. In charge of them all was tour manager Stuart Hadfield who, of course, was no stranger to Neil and his four fellow Trinity tourists. On previous tours there had always been a joint managership, which had sometimes been a cause of friction, so Hadfield was breaking new ground. His assistant manager was Arthur Walker of Rochdale Hornets, a box manufacturer who had been a paratrooper in the Second World War. The position of trainer-baggage man was taken by Hull KR's Colin Hutton who had won the post in competition with Ken Traill and Dave Valentine. In reality Colin was the coach, as well as having many other roles, but the RFL strangely was reluctant to designate him as such.

Neil recalls: "Of course, I was absolutely thrilled to have been picked for the tour, especially as our Don was going too. It is certainly one of the top honours in the game. There was a bit of a shock for me though when I was selected. My employers, the CEGB, asked me to resign, but told me that I would get my job back when I returned. That was so they wouldn't have to pay me while I was on tour. It's funny that they didn't want to pay me but they were very happy to use me for publicity in their magazines.

It was great that there were so many Trinity players and Stuart Hadfield in the party, but it did cause a bit of a problem. The tour party was due to leave on 15 May but Trinity still had to play Huddersfield in the Championship Final on 19 May. So all the Wakefield men and Huddersfield prop Ken Noble had to leave on Monday 21 May, along with Stuart Hadfield, which meant we would certainly miss a couple of games in Australia. What a journey we were in for. We left Wakefield on the Monday morning, taking the train to London to catch the night flight from Heathrow. Eddie Waring and Phil King were also with us, having had to cover the Championship Final for their papers. The plane that was to fly us out broke down in Singapore before it reached London and our flight was put back 24 hours. Then when we were finally airborne we were delayed in Marseille because of a cracked window on the flight deck. They replaced the window and we left France late on Wednesday night. There was a stop in Bahrain for refuelling and another in Singapore. We finally reached Sydney around 8pm on Friday 25 May. There to meet us were brother Don, Joby Shaw and Arthur Walker. We were tired out, but were straightaway whisked off to one of the Leagues clubs, where the rest of the players were at a function. When we arrived at the airport, I remember, an Australian press man ran up to Phil King and asked 'Would you be Eddie Waring?' to which Phil replied, 'Not for all the tea in China!' I don't think Eddie and Phil got on. I remember Eddie travelled first-class on this trip. The rest of us were in tourist class. Eddie kept inviting Stuart up to his section for meals."

Apart from Don, Neil was obviously best acquainted with his fellow Trinitarian tourists. He says of Stuart Hadfield: "He was a good businessman, a coal and fuel distributor, and he had certainly done well for Wakefield. He was always happy to back Ken Traill's judgment on players, when it came to signings for Trinity. He didn't really have any problems on tour so discipline was never an issue. He was a fair man and all the players got on well with him and respected him. He helped make it a happy tour. Stuart and Arthur Walker picked the teams, with Eric Ashton and Derek Turner, who was the vice-captain.

Derek always led from the front, always did the work. It didn't matter whether it was an easy game or a hard game, he just hated losing. He was a good handler and a brilliant kicker to touch and he was very thoughtful about the game. He relished taking the ball up and knocking the Australians down. I remember there were tears in his eyes when he knew he wouldn't be able to play in the second test because of injury. We all knew that it would be so much harder without Rocky.

Jack Wilkinson was probably lucky to tour. Wilkie had come to Wakefield at the right time, which would certainly have improved his chances. He probably surprised himself that he was selected for the squad but he had played well all season. Jack was almost 32 though and wasn't really in line for the test prop spots, although he would always be up for the chance if it came along. He had toured in 1954.

Full-back Gerry Round was as safe as houses in defence, was a good fielder of the ball and ran it out well. He could make the breakthrough and was a good strong kicker. He did most of the touch kicking for Wakefield. He was a better punter of the ball than me. He was a decent goalkicker too but had a problem with confidence – goalkicking worried him sometimes. I think Gerry was the best full-back around at that time.

Harold Poynton was one of the shock choices but not to anyone who had played with him or had watched him for a long time. He was a real workaholic. That was funny because he was a really bad trainer. Somehow, though, he was always remarkably fit. It didn't matter who ran at Harold, he would tackle them. Although he looked frail, he was out of this world with the ball in his hands. He did not have the pace of Dave Bolton but he was more of a footballer. He never stopped running, with or without the ball. When Dave was ruled out of the second Ashes test no one worried about Harold's ability to replace him."

By the time Neil arrived in Sydney the Lions had already played twice. They won 39-12 against Western Australia in Perth, where rain fell for the first time in nine months and Eric Ashton rattled up six goals and two tries. They were equally successful at Wagga Wagga, beating Riverina 34-7. Once more conditions were helpful, rain again falling, this time after a three month drought and Ashton helped himself to five goals and a hat-trick of tries.

The first real crunch match of the tour was against Sydney at the SCG on 26 May, the day after Neil and his fellow late-arrivals hit town. Neil recalls: "I couldn't believe the interest in this game. Spectators were arriving from 10 o'clock in the morning. They were

94

walking past the hotel down to the match so early because of the other things which were going on in and around the ground – athletics, mini-rugby, curtain-raisers, all sorts of things, which staggered the arrival times of the spectators, so they did not all arrive at once like they tended to do in England. I was down to play against Sydney but because we had been so delayed, I didn't think I could do justice to myself, so I was given another day to get over the journey. Gerry Round was the only late-arrival to play in the game. We won 21-13, which was a good result because playing Sydney was almost like playing a test match. They fielded mostly test players and there was a crowd of 57,000."

The victory against Sydney was a big psychological victory for Britain, who trailed 5-0 at half-time but swept into a 23-5 lead by the 70th minute. Billy Boston and Brian Edgar both scored twice and there was a try for Dick Huddart and three goals for Laurie Gilfedder.

The following day the Lions had a fixture against Western New South Wales at Bathurst, when all the late-arrivals were fielded and for the first time as professionals Neil and Don played together in a team. Neil was one of the players whose reputation had preceded him to Australia and spectators and the press were eager to see him perform. He recalls: "The day after the Sydney match I had to turn out with the 'ham and eggers', as the second teamers were traditionally called. Usually two or three of the test team would be included to strengthen it. In the opposing team was Tony Paskins, the famous Workington Town centre of the early 1950s, who was the captain and full-back. Our older players couldn't believe he was still playing, and apparently in with a chance of playing for Australia, because he must have been in his late 30s."

Britain gave the least impressive performance of the tour so far but won 24-10. Neil had an off-day with his kicking, succeeding with three from 11 shots, but he scored the first try on 21 minutes, when Don Fox prised open the defence. Don, who scored two tries, was one of the British stars and Harold Poynton also had a bright start but suffered an injury to his foot, while Derek Turner suffered bruised ribs.

The tourists were based in Sydney for the first part of the tour. Neil says: "Our hotel was the Olympic on Moore Park Road, opposite the Sydney Cricket Ground. The Show Ground, where we trained, was also next door which was very handy. All we had to do was cross the road and walk a couple of hundred yards to the changing rooms. This was the same for all the matches at the SCG and the hotel was a good location for supporters calling before or after the games. Most of the earlier tour parties stopped at this hotel. It was very basic. There were no mod cons and there was no security cover in the area from the bar to our rooms. So we had to make sure that any valuables were hidden away.

During our stay there I don't think the menu ever changed. You could have bacon, egg, sausages, steak and beans every morning with bottles of milk, tea and coffee. The same menu came out for dinner with just a couple of extra items. Alex Murphy was always shouting out, 'It's thumb soup again!' That was because one of the older waitresses always had her thumb in the dish. It got to the point later where everyone joined in when anyone asked what the soup of the day was. They would all shout out 'Thumb soup!'

The next game was against New South Wales, a side packed with test players such as Johnny Raper, Billy Wilson, Ken Irvine, Ian Walsh, Brian Clay and Mike Cleary, while Tony Paskins was in at centre alongside Bob Honeysett, opposite me and Eric Ashton. From early morning the crowds gathered again around the hotel, shouting and singing what they were going to do to us. When it was time to go to the game, we all walked down to the ground, taking the banter in our stride. Playing on an oval took some time to get used to. At English grounds the spectators are only five or 10 yards away, but at the SCG they are a long way off, although there was still a lot of noise with 60,000 people shouting."

The encounter with New South Wales on 2 June produced just about everything a game of rugby league could. To say it was sensational would be a gross understatement. Phil King's report in the *Sunday Express* was headlined "Another Battle in Sydney". It began, "Six players sent off... many more punch-ups... and 11 scintillating tries". Peter Muszkat, of the *Sydney Daily Mirror*, reported: "The Menzies-Macmillan feud over the European Common Market should pale into insignificance on Saturday, when Britain and Australia wage full-scale war at rugby league. An ominous warning of things to come was sounded before 60,000 fans yesterday when the British tourists survived a gory second half Donnybrook to beat New South Wales by 33 points to 28." The famous former Kangaroo Jack Reardon described the affair as "the wildest rugby league match for several years... The only comparable major match was in 1954 when the game between Britain and New South Wales was abandoned because of fighting."

Stuart Hadfield condemned referee Cliff Brown's handling of the game in the press, fulminating, "I do not think the referee had any control at all. The trouble could have been avoided if he had given the players a good talking to early on". Mr Hadfield would go on to criticise Australian referees on several more occasions, incurring the wrath of the Australian press corps – much as previous managers have done from the earliest tours. It was true that Mr Brown could have taken a firmer line early on. For example, he cautioned Rocky Turner on three, maybe four, occasions and issued other warnings. It was not until the 54th minute that he sent off rival wingers, Billy Boston and Ken Irvine, neither of whom had been cautioned. Boston, everyone agreed, had merely been trying to protect Brian Edgar, who had been crocked in a ferocious double tackle. Then with five minutes remaining a scrum on Britain's '25' erupted and a huge free-for-all followed. Jack McNamara in the *Manchester Evening News* observed, "Edgar ducked a shattering haymaker that would have hit him over the stands if it had connected. Sullivan gave chase, slugging it out, while most of the forwards were engaged in a roughhouse nearby". Mr Brown then sent off both of the other wingers, Mick Sullivan and Mike Cleary, Britain's hooker Bill Sayer and NSW prop Billy Wilson.

The warfare gained the headlines but detracted from some wonderful rugby played by the British, who led 23-14 at half-time on the back of Sayer's 11-2 scrum superiority. Eric Ashton scored a hat-trick of tries, despite having to play at stand-off for half the game, following the brilliant Dave Bolton's departure with a shoulder injury. Jack McNamara was also impressed by Neil, writing, "Hefty centre Neil Fox had a grand Sydney debut, bashing his way through all but the toughest tackles. His goalkicking was also first-rate, landing six". Round, Sullivan, Cooper and Bolton were other try-scorers for the Lions, who sometimes appeared capable of scoring at will. It was just as well that NSW full-back Don Parish was in such excellent kicking form, with eight goals to add to his try. After the defeat of Sydney, this latest exhibition of power, pace and class against NSW was clearly another psychological blow to Australian test hopes.

The NSW judiciary committee severely cautioned Boston and Irvine and suspended the remaining four defendants until the following Tuesday, which amounted to a slap on the wrist for all but Cleary, who missed a club fixture.

Two days after the fracas at the SCG, the Lions sent a second-string side to Newcastle for what was traditionally a tough fixture. Of the players picked, only Ashton and Turner were likely to make the test team. Neil and the remaining players stayed in Sydney and were probably lucky. The Lions lost 23-18 and had two more men sent off. Hooker John Shaw was dismissed after 55 minutes by Keith Lyons for striking after being bitten over his right eye. Shaw told Jack McNamara, "I didn't complain to the referee, because what's the use here?" In the last minute Jack Wilkinson was sent off for a stiff-arm tackle on scrum-half Neville Hannah, which provoked a youth from the crowd to attack him. After the police, stewards and the players had sorted out the riot, it was discovered that the youth was a relative of the unfortunate Hannah. Wilkinson picked up a one-match suspension. Don Fox copped a shoulder injury, which rendered him a passenger for most of the second half, when Derek Turner moved to scrum-half, and Harold Poynton was replaced by Ashton after suffering a ligament injury.

The first test was scheduled for 9 June at the SCG. Neil recalls, "For this game Eric and Derek, plus the two managers, picked the team, which was the best team I had played with so far in my career. For a change of scenery 16 of us were taken about 20 miles to Coolangata, right on the beach, for two days training. It was great getting away from Sydney. We didn't need much training, just loosening up, going through the moves and the game plan. Then on the Saturday we set off back to Sydney for the big game."

Australia were desperate to beat Great Britain, who had won three consecutive Ashes series - in 1956 and 1959 in England and in 1958 in Australia. Moreover, they had beaten the Aussies to win the 1960 World Cup. Elements in the Australian press were intent on depicting Britain as roughhouse merchants, forgetting that it takes more than one to fight. The *Sydney Daily Mirror* columnist Frank Browne's pre-test article was typical of the media hype launched at the Lions. He wrote venomously: "This is a typical English League side, artists alike at football and mayhem, talented plug-uglies who will win at any price with no interest in anything but victory. On Friday I discounted the sanctimonious nonsense of English manager Stuart Hadfield, who said he wouldn't tolerate his men playing dirty football. I can imagine Messrs Turner, Murphy and Sullivan at the Hadfield lecture murmuring, 'Listen to yon old goat'."

More reasoned articles addressed the real issue – who was going to win. Rex Phillips of the *Sydney Morning Herald* wrote, "Britain start favourites because they have greater strength and mobility in the pack and centres [where] Neil Fox and Ashton are expected to prove too sturdy for the Australians". Britain were 6-4 on to win with Phillips adding the rider, "provided Murphy and Sayer can satisfy ace referee Darcy Lawler with their scrum feeding and hooking".

The teams which turned out for the first Ashes test were:
Australia: Don Parish (Wests), Mike Cleary (Souths), Reg Gasnier (St George, captain), Bob Hagan (Townsville), Ken Irvine (Norths), Arthur Summons (Wests), Barry Muir (Brisbane Wests), Gary Parcell (Ipswich), Ian Walsh (St George), Dud Beattie (Ipswich), Elton Rasmussen (St George), Ron Lynch (Parramatta), Johnny Raper (St George).
Great Britain: Gerry Round (Wakefield Trinity), Billy Boston (Wigan), Eric Ashton (Wigan, captain), Neil Fox (Wakefield Trinity), Mick Sullivan (St Helens), Dave Bolton (Wigan), Alex Murphy (St Helens), Norm Herbert (Workington Town), Bill Sayer (Wigan), Brian McTigue (Wigan), Dick Huddart (St Helens), Brian Edgar (Workington Town), Derek Turner (Wakefield Trinity).

The 69,990 spectators, who paid record receipts of £29,576, got the start they wanted as Australia took a seven-point lead within the first five minutes, Parish converting a superb try by Irvine created by Summons, and then adding a penalty when Neil was deemed offside. That was as good as it got for Australia, however. By half-time Britain led 9-7, despite being on the wrong end of a 10-2 scrum count in that half. The Lions forwards were simply irresistible in the loose, led by the mighty magician Brian McTigue, ably supported by the crashing runs of Edgar, Huddart and Turner and the industry of Sayer and Herbert. Britain scored their first try after 18 minutes, when Turner bluffed his way over following some wonderful combined play. Eleven minutes later Turner broke through some astonished Australian tacklers and released Neil, who pushed off Parish, held off

Cleary and Hagan and sent Sullivan diving in at the corner. Three minutes before the interval Sullivan was over again following sublime handling by McTigue, Herbert, Bolton, Ashton and Neil. Neil failed to convert any of the tries but made amends in the second half by converting all four tries scored by his side and adding a 35-yard penalty. Britain's superiority in the last 40 minutes was breathtaking and Australian fans flocked to the exits well before full-time, knowing that there had been only one team in it after the first 10 minutes. Britain's second-half tries came from Ashton, with two, Boston and Huddart. Australia only added a try, albeit a scintillating one, by Gasnier, converted by Parish.

Britain's 31-12 victory was probably flattering to Australia, who could have lost by more if Britain had experienced a bit more luck and had not had to contend with Mr Lawler's 20-8 penalty count against them and Walsh's 17-10 pull in the scrums. Rampaging Dick Huddart won the official man-of-the-match award but did not remember most of the game after being dazed in a collision with Brian Edgar. Although the forwards were so dominant, the British backs were in dazzling form too. The [British] *Daily Telegraph* reported, "Though Murphy had a somewhat quiet game, especially in the last 15 minutes when he hurt his right arm slightly, Bolton, typical of him in test matches, showed such thrust and broke through and made gaps so often that, having straightened his run, overlaps were there. And how well Ashton and Fox supported him on either side and how stringently Boston and Sullivan were always in position for taking passes." It said much for Britain's dominance that Gerry Round at full-back was seldom troubled. It also said much for both teams' discipline that there were none of the bloody exchanges forecast by the doom-mongers. The game was played in the best of spirits.

Neil could hardly have been happier. He remembers: "After the game we went to the bar to celebrate. There were plenty of English people there who were living locally and chuffed we had won, especially as they had been taking ear-bashings about how Australia would beat us. Then it was back to the hotel for more drinks. Unfortunately, I was then told that I, Alex Murphy and Mick Sullivan would be helping out the ham and eggers the following day against North Coast at Lismore." It might have comforted Neil, post-celebration headache notwithstanding, to read Jack Reardon's comment before the Lismore game: "Eric Ashton impresses in every match with his polished centre play and great leadership and yesterday we saw Neil Fox at his best, breaking tackles and running with purpose previously lacking".

Reardon's next report back to the *Daily Express* of Britain's 33-13 victory over North Coast probably reflected the effects of the previous night's celebrations. He began: "The British played like a team of spare parts at Lismore today but still won comfortably. Three of yesterday's test side, Alex Murphy, Neil Fox and Mick Sullivan [at stand-off], had their second game in two days [and were] content to send the ball on to the men outside." Neil kicked two goals but shared the kicking with Gilfedder, who potted four and grabbed two tries. Neil admits he "can't remember much about that game but do remember that the team got back late to their Sydney hotel to pack our cases because we were leaving for 18 days in Queensland."

Those 18 days would involve eight games, including the second test at Brisbane. The team made the Australian Hotel their headquarters for this section of the tour. Neil recalls: "Our hotel was in the middle of Brisbane above a very noisy bar. It was about the same standard as the Olympic in Sydney but it had a veranda on two sides overlooking the main streets. It was definitely not ideal for a rugby team." Stuart Hadfield concurred with Neil's view of the accommodation. In one of his reports to Bill Fallowfield back in England, he stated that "the Olympic at Sydney is very third rate, as also is the Australian Hotel in

Brisbane", while later he was furious about the hotel in Rockhampton, where one player refused to sleep in his bed because it was full of ants. He recommended that in future the tourists should be afforded better accommodation, never mind the cost. Neil would have been interested to know that, in a letter of 12 June, Hadfield wrote to Fallowfield, "Neil Fox is just coming into his own but had a poor start and is affected by hard grounds and leg weariness". By that time Neil had only played four games in Australia and the grounds were getting harder, particularly in Queensland, but by the end of the tour Neil had played more games than any other back. His legs certainly must have been weary by then, if Mr Hadfield's assessment was accurate.

The Fox brothers had a small family reunion while they were in Brisbane. Their uncle Harry, Tommy Fox's brother, who had been born in Bridlington, and his wife Mary had moved from England to Perth, Western Australia, 10 years before. When the Lions touched down in Brisbane they were waiting to greet Neil and Don, having driven 3,343 miles from Perth. Harry told the press, "The last time we saw these lads was 15 years ago and they were still in short pants. But they recognised us as soon as they stepped off the plane."

Neil recalls: "Some strange things happen on every tour. One of the strangest happened in Brisbane. I came back to the hotel alone while nearly everyone else was still out. As I headed upstairs for my room, I suddenly heard a rumpus and someone shouting, 'Keep bloody still, will you!' I hadn't a clue what was happening but the noise was coming from Colin Hutton's room, so I looked in to see what was going on. Colin had this bloke in his room and was struggling with him, trying to stitch his eye. He yelled at me to give him a hand. We held him firmly and Colin proceeded to put a couple of stitches in the wound. I don't know if he was qualified to stitch people but he did. Apparently this bloke had banged his head and was in a right state. He came back the next day to say thank you."

The Lions opened their tour of Queensland with a floodlit game against Brisbane at the Exhibition Ground on 13 June and crept home 16-14. Neil did not play. The game was won in the dying seconds when Ashton, scorer of 10 points, converted his second try. Sullivan scored Britain's other two tries.

Three days later there was another big game against Queensland at Lang Park. Almost 30,000 fans saw Britain win 22-17 in another sensational clash. The Lions had the game won by half-time having run up a 20-5 lead. In one spectacular four-minute period they swept in for 15 points, but their success was marred a few minutes before half-time when Brian Edgar was injured and replaced by Laurie Gilfedder. In the second half Britain lost their composure and confidence as Queensland began to tackle harder and more often. Referee Jack Casey dished out no fewer than 30 penalties in the second half – 17 to the Lions. Just before the final whistle Derek Turner was sent off after an affray with Dud Beattie and for a moment hundreds of people seated behind the barriers began moving towards a group of struggling players, but the quick action of Casey prevented serious consequences. Neil's performance had been one of his best on tour. He had converted all four tries and landed a second-half penalty, besides racing over from Gilfedder's pass to score the fourth British try.

The following day Neil was in action again at Toowoomba, when Alex Murphy was given the captaincy. Toowoomba gave the tourists a hard fight in the first 40 minutes, restricting them to an 8-2 lead. The turning point came in the 32nd minute when Derek Turner replaced the injured Gary Cooper. He made all the difference, scored three brilliant tries and engineered a few more as Britain stretched away to win 36-12. Neil was in good kicking form with six goals.

On Wednesday, 20 June, the Lions travelled to Rockhampton to play Central Queensland and stayed at the hotel mentioned earlier where ants were found in the beds. Neil says: "Rockhampton was not a pretty place. The hotel was on a par with the others we had used — not in any way luxurious but at least it was quieter, except when the train roared through the middle of the town." Neil was a substitute for the game and during it replaced Billy Boston, who took a knock on the knee in the first half. Another casualty was Jack Wilkinson, who suffered a cut head and was replaced by Norm Herbert. Playing in high humidity and with the temperature at 80° Fahrenheit, Britain ran up their biggest win of the tour so far: 55-8. Neil had time to score a try and three goals, while winger Frank Carlton grabbed four tries. Neil also picked up a leg injury. Fortunately, it did not persist.

Neil recalls: "There was good news after the Rockhampton game. Seven players were going to be billeted in Townsville the following day rather than travelling on to Cairns for the match against Far North Queensland. I was to be one of them. The others were Eric Ashton, Billy Boston, Alex Murphy, Brian McTigue, Bill Sayer and Dave Bolton. This meant we were on our own for three days. Mr Hadfield told Eric to make sure we trained every day. We did too - around the swimming pool on the beach, where the Australian Olympic swimming team used to train. What a welcome break that was, after playing so many games in such a short time and on hard grounds. The news that we were to be left behind was music to our ears."

The Lions who went to Cairns scraped home 33-31. After 78 minutes they trailed 31-28, but Gerry Round equalised with a try and Gilfedder's conversion won the match. They had a good excuse for their below-par showing, other than injuries to Peter Small and Don Fox. On the morning of the match the team had gone by boat to Green Island, a beauty spot on the Great Barrier Reef. The sea had been rough and all the party, apart from skipper Derek Turner, seemed to have suffered badly from the experience, some of the team complaining that when they took to the field the ground was dipping and swaying beneath them.

Neil recalls, "When the lads returned to Townsville, they looked completely shattered and they couldn't believe how tanned were the seven of us who had remained after spending only three days in the sun. The rest had done us no end of good and freed us from aches and pains and grazes. Unfortunately for our Don, the management had forced him to play at Cairns. He knew he was not right to play. He was injured again and that was his last game on tour." Don's injury was to his left shoulder joint.

On Sunday 24 June, Great Britain fielded their test team for the game against North Queensland, the strongest side in the state outside Brisbane, at Townsville. The clash was fast and fiery but Britain were far superior and won 47-14. Brian McTigue was in top form and Billy Boston crashed over for four tries. Neil rattled up 20 points with two tries and seven goals and Bill Sayer dominated the scrums 27-9. However, Dave Bolton retired at half-time with an injured knee, which caused him to miss the second test.

In the run-up to the second test, the Australian press, at least its tabloid sector, had abandoned criticising British rough play and turned to encouraging Australia to get rougher. The British chose to keep well away from controversy. Neil remembers: "After the game at Townsville the test squad went to the Gold Coast to train away from the hustle and bustle. The hotel, the Pan Pacific, was right on the beach with miles of sand in both directions. It was an ideal spot to prepare for the test. Our only doubts were Dave Bolton and Derek Turner. When the day of the test dawned both were ruled out and Harold Poynton and Laurie Gilfedder came in. Both were making their test debuts. For a man of such courage and determination, I've never seen a more distraught player than Derek when he realised he was missing a match of such importance. Tears came into his eyes when he was told he

The 1962 Lions tour to Australia

Top: An example of Neil's immense power. Neil bumps off the tackle of scrum-half Arthur Summons in the second test, when Britain beat Australia 17-10 at Brisbane to clinch the Ashes.
Above left: Neil and his great rival Reg Gasnier in Ashes action.
Above right: Neil attempts to escape an Australian tackle.

was not going to be risked. The other players were disappointed not to have him in the side, but the two players who were selected in their places played out of their skins."

A ground record 34,760 piled into Lang Park, paying record receipts of £20,204. Britain's team was the same as the one which had won the first test, apart from Poynton and Gilfedder. Australia, in panic, had completely rejigged their side, which was:

Keith Barnes (Balmain, captain), Eddie Lumsden (St George), Alan Gil (Cairns), Reg Gasnier (St George), Ken Irvine (Norths), Bob Banks (Toowoomba), Arthur Summons (Wests), Dud Beattie (Ipswich), Ian Walsh (St George), Bill Carson (Wests), Mick Veivers (Brisbane Souths), Billy Owen (Newcastle), George Smith (Lithgow).

Britain hit the front after seven minutes when Neil landed a penalty. Eleven minutes later Britain swept from their own '25' almost to Australia's goal-line, after McTigue sent Huddart scorching downfield. From the play-the-ball Poynton sent out a pass which struck the ground before Boston gathered the ball to score wide out. Neil hit a fine goal and Britain were seven up. Irvine pulled back a 25th-minute try, but there was no mistaking which team was on top. The Aussie defences creaked and groaned before inevitably cracking in the 34th minute. Gilfedder and Ashton released Boston, who fended off Irvine and Veivers, before taking Summons over the line for an extraordinary try. Billy's try was his ninth in Ashes tests which was a record. Britain went into the break 10-3 ahead and clearly in command. Barnes landed a penalty in the 44th minute, but the Lions stretched their lead three minutes later when Murphy exploded through from a scrum without a finger being laid on him. Neil converted and the lead was 15-5. Just when they looked like swamping the home side Britain lost Murphy after 55 minutes. With no substitutes in this fixture, Ashton moved to stand-off and Poynton to scrum-half. Even against 12 men the Australians could make no inroads. Ashton potted a drop-goal and it was almost full-time before Australia claimed a try by Summons, improved by Barnes. Britain's 17-10 victory was far more comprehensive than the score suggested and they had won the Ashes in Australia after only two matches – for the first time since 1928.

The *Daily Telegraph* observed: "The forwards as a whole were so much in command that they almost toyed with the opposition in both the tight and the loose. Huddart with his powerful running, McTigue with his ball distribution and Edgar with his quite remarkable sidestepping, all worried the Australian defence. In the backs, Murphy, until injured, Poynton, Ashton and Fox formed such an effective combination that often their counterparts did not know which way to turn for the best. On the wings, Boston particularly and Sullivan needed only to back up well and the chances would come, and at full-back Round, though still not properly tested, did all that was asked of him."

Neil remembers the aftermath, "With the Ashes won, our celebrations lasted nearly all night. The feeling was great – the best I had known. It was even better than when we won in 1959 in my first Ashes series. The confidence of the team was sky-high. Luckily, I wasn't down to play at Maryborough, the day after the second test, against Wide Bay. Some of the test team had to play though. Even after such a late night we won 84-20. Then it was back to Sydney for the remainder of the Australian part of the tour." Neil would have had a field day against Wide Bay for the team racked up 20 tries and Laurie Gilfedder booted 12 goals. Boston got five tries and Ashton four, while Huddart and Carlton bagged three each.

On 7 July, the Lions were pitted against New South Wales for a second time at the SCG. Just how much confidence had drained from the Australians was witnessed in the size of the crowd. Only 28,000 turned out compared with the 60,000 who had watched the first clash. Britain were just too good for NSW, winning 20-5. Neil converted all the Lions' four tries. The only blemish was a further injury to Dave Bolton, who appeared with his knee heavily strapped and had to be replaced by Peter Small after half an hour.

Neil being tackled in the Lions match against Toowoomba

Neil had to back up the following day against Southern NSW at Wollongong, along with eight others. Britain were so strapped by injuries that the half-backs were Eric Fraser and Gary Cooper. It was another of those controversial clashes with too much needle and not enough football. Referee Jack Jewell told the press that the Brits wanted to fight rather than play and a full-scale brawl broke out just before the end. Jewell was reported to have had such a fiery exchange of words, plus a bit of jostling, with a British forward that he had offered to "settle matters later behind the grandstand". For their part, Britain were appalled by the pitch they had to play on. It resembled a furrowed paddock. Arthur Walker fumed, "I have never seen anything like it in my life. It is downright dangerous." In the circumstances it was not too surprising that the Lions lost 18-10, Neil kicking two goals to add to tries by Boston and Noble. Typical of Britain's luck was the extraordinary try conceded in the first half. Eric Fraser took a drop-out from under the posts and somehow contrived to hit the cross-bar causing the ball to ricochet straight down allowing Armstrong to score a most bizarre try. There were also injuries to Roy Evans and Gerry Round. Neil's view was that "playing games like that took its toll on players. There should have been a better system than continually playing on successive days. I also remember that Graeme Langlands played that day and had a great match. No wonder he went on to become one of Australia's star players. After that game it was back to Coolangata for training for the third test. The ham and eggers stayed in Sydney."

The third test was played on the SCG on 14 July before a crowd of just over 42,000, most of whom probably expected a clean sweep by the Lions. Before the game the players were introduced to Robert Menzies, the Australian Prime Minister. The teams were:

Australia: Frank Drake (Brisbane Souths), Eddie Lumsden (St George), Alan Gil (Cairns), Peter Dimond (Wests), Ken Irvine (Norths), Johnny Lisle (Souths), Arthur Summons (Wests, captain), Dud Beattie (Ipswich), Ian Walsh (St George), Bill Carson (Wests), Mick Veivers (Brisbane Souths), Elton Rasmussen (St George), Johnny Raper (St George).

Great Britain: Round, Boston, Ashton (captain), Fox, Sullivan, Poynton, Murphy, Herbert, Sayer, McTigue, Edgar, Huddart, Turner.

The first half was a thrilling affair. Australia took an 8-0 lead within the first 15 minutes with a magnificent try by Summons, followed by another by Drake after a glorious move, which Irvine converted. Drake thus became the first full-back ever to score a try in an Ashes test. Despite these concessions and Walsh's ability to win the scrums, Britain were still playing confidently. After 25 minutes Poynton and Murphy worked an exquisite move, culminating in Murphy's back-flip which sent Neil careering over for a try, which he converted. In the 36th minute, Murphy struck again to send Ashton 40 yards for a try under the sticks. Neil converted and added a penalty but Australia scored through Irvine on the stroke of half-time, when Britain led 12-11.

The second half was a very different kettle of fish. On 46 minutes Sullivan was sent off by referee Darcy Lawler following a tackle on Dimond. Huddart went out onto the wing but Australia seemed incapable of making their extra man pay. In the 56th minute Dud Beattie, already suffering from a rib injury, provoked Turner into a fight and the pair were dismissed. With 15 minutes remaining Britain extended their lead with an astonishing 50-yard try from Murphy straight from a scrum. Neil's conversion gave Britain a seemingly winning 17-11 lead, despite their depleted numbers. However, Australia were offered a lifeline when Irvine landed a simple penalty. With barely two minutes to play Summons and Carson worked the ball to Irvine, who shot away for a try at the corner to make the score 17-16. Although not a first-line goalkicker, Irvine stroked over a wonderful conversion from the touchline. Even then there was a chance for Britain to win. A scrum went down 30 yards out to the right of Australia's goal and there was an opportunity for Neil to drop a goal, if Sayer could win the ball. Summons fed the ball into his second-row and the chance was gone. At the next play-the-ball Poynton was penalised, Drake booted the ball into touch, the hooter went for the end of the game and somehow the Lions had lost 18-17.

The repercussions of the game reverberated loud and long. Neil says: "When the final whistle was blown, we knew we had been cheated out of winning but credit to Ken Irvine. He did kick that difficult goal to win the game. The last pass for the final try was forward. Billy Boston went up to the referee and told him it was a yard forward. Lawler said, 'If it had been three yards forward, I would still have given it!' Still, it was nice to run around the field celebrating our Ashes win and again the celebrations continued until the early hours back at the hotel."

After the match Beattie and Turner received cautions, but Mick Sullivan was banned from the two remaining games in Australia. He had not taken his dismissal well and had reportedly abused both the referee and the judiciary. Stuart Hadfield had not taken the defeat well, either. He wrote to Bill Fallowfield on 16 July, saying, "Well, you will know by now we lost the third test by 18 to 17. I have never known in all my life such a diabolical performance by Lawler. He did everything. The players were disgusted. We were leading 17 to 11 six minutes from time. He then penalised us in front of the posts for putting the ball in the second-row and we were packing three forwards at the time... How could we put the ball in the second-row under those circumstances? An easy goal was kicked and there were only three minutes to go when Carson broke through, passing Poynton, who had a broken thumb, and then sending a pass at least three yards forward to Irvine, who scored and kicked the goal. Lawler told our chaps that they must not kick at the play-the-ball and the man playing it must be able to play it without any interference. After 15 minutes Poynton was playing it [the ball] and was kicked on the thumb breaking it, which more or less put him out of the game and nothing was done about it. Sullivan was sent off for retaliation and Turner retaliated against Beattie. Harry Bath [Australia's coach] had told Beattie (cracked rib) he had to go out after half-time and take someone off with him."

Hadfield also asserted that the referee took penalties as far to the centre as he could whenever he awarded them in the Lions' half to give Australia easier shots and that Raper was continually allowed to play off-side. He also said that Alex Murphy told him that Summons kept throwing the ball in behind his pack and got away with it. Hadfield concluded by writing, "I think Lawler must have got his instructions that Australia must win this match at all costs... This was the most blatant case of cheating I have ever seen."

Stuart Hadfield was certainly an unpopular figure in the eyes of the Australian press, refereeing societies and some Australian board members. Indeed Peter Muszkat, of the Australian *Sunday Mirror*, writing an article for the British *Daily Mail* on 23 July, said, "Hadfield, the least popular British team manager to visit Australia since the war, has already been rebuked by Board of Control chairman Buckley for his criticism of Australia's team before the third test. And in a television interview tonight, referee Lawler said Hadfield 'could have picked up a lot of diplomacy from such fine English managers as Tom Hesketh and Hector Rawson.' Correspondences from Bill Fallowfield to Mr Hadfield repeatedly advised him not to criticise Australian referees but to little avail."

Even though the test series was over, Britain had to face arguably their hardest fixture of the tour on the following Wednesday. Their opponents were the perennial NSW Premiership winning club St George, whom many thought a better side than the test team. A massive crowd of 57,895 - 15,000 more than for the third test at the same venue - crammed into the SCG, a fair indication that the locals expected a hard contest. And so it seemed as the game remained scoreless until the 27th minute when St George took the lead after Gasnier cut out a try for Lumsden, goaled by Graham. The jubilant crowd was soon stunned, however, as Alex Murphy, playing with painful arm and ankle injuries, began to run the Dragons ragged. By half-time Huddart, Ashton and Murphy had shredded the defence for three tries and Britain led 13-5. Britain suffered a huge blow when Ashton was carried off and replaced by Carlton, with Boston moving into the centre alongside Neil. Even so, the second half merely emphasised the real greatness of the 1962 Lions, who scored 20 unanswered points to run out 33-5 winners, further tries coming from Murphy, Edgar, Boston and McTigue, the last named's only try of the tour. Peter Muszkat's report to the *Daily Mail* added, "Immaculate goal-kicking by Fox was another feature of the match. Fox landed six from acute angles."

Only one fixture remained for the Lions in Australia against Northern New South Wales at Tamworth on Sunday 22 July. Neil was honoured by being given the captaincy and concluded his personal contribution to the Lions' cause in Australia with a truly spectacular performance. One reporter noted: "Neil Fox, who, although aged 23, is already considered one of the all-time rugby league greats, scored a personal tally of 32 points, made up of four tries, nine conversions and one penalty goal... The splendidly built Fox gave the crowd a full review of his many talents. Owing to his genius, the match was virtually all over after the first nine minutes. In that period the Tourists scored 15 points. It was all started by the alert Fox intercepting a pass and going over for a try, which he converted after four minutes. He then made strong runs which resulted in tries for Carlton and Taylor." The Lions signed off with a 56-13 victory, their 18th in a 21-match itinerary: a brilliant record. They had scored 679 points, including 151 tries, and conceded 303, and only 61 tries. Neil

105

had played in 14 games, scoring in them all and racking up 165 points from 11 tries and 66 goals. His 32 points against Northern NSW was the biggest haul of his first-class career.

At the commencement of the tour the chairman of the Australian Board of Control, Bill Buckley had written in *Rugby League News*, the official programme of the NSWRL: "Britain's newest weapon and one which is by no means on the secret list is big Neil Fox, the record-scoring Wakefield Trinity centre. English players enthused over Fox when they reached Sydney this week and obviously Neil is a centre right out of the bag. He and Eric Ashton should make the tussle with our centres a highlight of all games. It is a long time since Britain brought one player who stood out as Fox does for this tour. When the quality of the other back-line stars is remembered, the brilliance of Fox must be exceptional for him to have such a high rating."

Neil definitely fulfilled expectations. At the close of the Australian section of the tour Stuart Hadfield reported back to the RFL potted comments on each individual player. His entry on Neil read: "Took some time to find his best form but has for some time now played very well indeed and lived up to his reputation. A very good tourist indeed."

Neil had certainly enjoyed the tour so far. He recalls the Lions' routine in Sydney: "After breakfast every morning we trained from 10 o'clock until 11.30. Then it was back to the hotel for lunch. We would receive mail every day, which Arthur Walker had collected. Molly's letters came nearly every day, keeping me up to date with news back home. Then we might write home, after which we would go into Sydney, have a drink in the Leagues Club in Philip Street, look around the shops and return for dinner. In the evenings we would go to the pictures or to the local for a drink. We were always made welcome in the clubs and the drinks were paid for. We went to lots of functions and civic receptions, where the locals would always want us to sing *Mardi Gras*. It had become a sort of Lions anthem and Alex Murphy was always our conductor. We were also invited to a lot of stores to sign autographs and photos. The stores in return would give us a cash donation for the players' fund and small gifts such as cufflinks, badges and tie-pins. The man-of-the-match awards were usually cigarettes, so the non-smokers gave them to the smokers, even though there were not many of them."

On to New Zealand and South Africa

The tourists left Sydney for New Zealand on 23 July, but not without more controversy. Stuart Hadfield further incensed the Australian press by pointedly refusing to be photographed shaking the hand of Harold Matthews, the secretary of the Australian Board of Control, although he did shake hands with Bill Buckley, the chairman. Eric Ashton was more diplomatic, telling the press, "We had wonderful hospitality from your officials and supporters during the tour. I, personally, will never forget it".

Ashton, a towering figure on the tour, had his lower left leg encased in plaster – the result of his injury against St George, which turned out to be severely torn ankle ligaments. Eric was flown back to England the next day - a crushing blow to the tourists. Don Fox's shoulder injury had not responded to treatment and he too was flown home. On arrival he was reported to have told the press, "The Australians seemed to think we were the best-disciplined and most well-behaved side that had gone out there". It had been a great shame that Don had only been able to play in five tour games. The Australian fans would have certainly been enthralled if he had been able to show his talents more often, especially if he had been fully fit.

Derek Turner took over the captaincy and Alex Murphy was made vice-captain. However, Alex's tour had also effectively finished with the game against St George. His arm injury prevented him from playing and he was on the plane back to England on 4 August. The loss of Ashton and Murphy was a colossal detriment to the test team, while the fact that Murphy and Don Fox had departed meant that there were no specialist scrum-halves in the party and the two players who could fill in for them, Poynton and Bolton, were themselves carrying injuries.

There was also a problem over Jack Wilkinson. In 1954, he had been sent off in the last game in New Zealand and banned for a month. The suspension was still current and had to be lifted to allow him to play. A deal was done between Bill Fallowfield and the New Zealand RL, which cleared Jack for action. Billy Boston was initially denied entry to New Zealand because of his colour, but was later sent a letter of apology by the New Zealand Immigration Office for any embarrassment caused by their demanding an entry permit to allow him into the country. The rule did not apply to the white British players.

Billy did not let it bother him too much and scored two tries in the opening fixture on 25 July, when the Lions beat Waikato 59-20 at Huntley. Neil did not play but was in his usual number nine jersey for the first test in Auckland three days later. Neil wore the number nine shirt because the Lions' jerseys were numbered in alphabetical order, beginning with Eric Ashton (number 1) and ending at Jack Wilkinson (number 26).

The first test was played at Carlaw Park and heavy rain made for a treacherous surface. The Lions had become used to playing on firm pitches and so may have been a little disadvantaged, although it was the same for both teams. Injuries were now becoming an almost intolerable burden for the tourists and they had to turn out a strange-looking side. The teams were:

New Zealand: Tony Smith, Brian Reidy, Reece Griffiths, Graham Kennedy, Neville Denton, Jimmy Bond, Billy Snowden, Maunga Emery, Jock Butterfield, Sam Edwards, Ron Ackland, Don Hammond, Mel Cooke, (captain).

Great Britain: Gerry Round, Ike Southward, Laurie Gilfedder, Neil Fox, Frank Carlton, Dave Bolton, Mick Sullivan, Norm Herbert, Bill Sayer, Brian McTigue, Dick Huddart, Roy Evans, Derek Turner, (captain).

On the day Britain simply failed to perform and the New Zealanders took full advantage. The Kiwi forwards thoroughly outplayed their opposites and five tries were scored in their 19-0 victory. The Lions never seemed likely to score a try and Neil had only one penalty kick at goal, from an awkward position. Mick Sullivan played at scrum-half for the first 35 minutes with little success and thereafter switched positions with Bolton, but the British backs remained almost spectators. Turner and Round excelled in defence but overall it was a performance which was best forgotten.

On 31 July, the Lions went to Wellington to meet a Maori XIII, expecting a tough struggle. Again the conditions were awful. It was freezing, windy and wet, but the Lions ran out easy winners 35-5. Neil was in fine form, scoring 20 points from four tries and four goals. Britain took an 8-0 lead in the first quarter and added 27 points in the second half. The Maoris only scored a late try by Emery, goaled by Rata Harrison. Jack McNamara in the *Manchester Evening News* reported, "The first try came when Jack Wilkinson cleverly switched play, giving Fox the chance to use his strength and sidestep to beat two men to score near the posts. Fox was unlucky with the kick, one touch-judge raising his flag and the other wiping out the goal decision, supported by the referee."

There were more good tidings for Neil, who recalls, "It was during our stay in New Zealand that Molly gave me some wonderful news. She was expecting a baby. I was chuffed to bits and couldn't wait to tell my team-mates from Trinity." Under the terms of the tour contract, players' wives received £3 and 10 shillings (£3.50) per week, while their husbands were away, plus £1 for each child. The players were paid 60 shillings (£3) a week in Australian or New Zealand currency for the duration of the tour and were given a £20 lump sum in Australia. Their major source of income for touring would come later, when they were to receive equal shares of 30 per cent of the tour profits, which was usually a considerable amount. Before the tour Neil and his fellow Wakefield tourists had all been given £100 by the club in recognition of their selection and Brian Briggs had arranged a raffle at his pub which raised £60, which meant an extra £12 each. On one occasion on tour Neil recalls, "There was this chap, Inspector Pierce at the Bondi Icebergs club, who invited the Lions to visit the bowling club at Vaucluse. Only Dick Huddart and I went. We went on stage and the audience asked us questions and presented us with a few mementos. It was a nice occasion and afterwards the club secretary asked us what we did for spending money. We told him we received £3 a week and he was amazed. He gave us £5 each, almost a week's wages and said, 'If you run short come back'. But we never did."

The tourists flew to the South Island to play Canterbury at Christchurch on 2 August and came away with a 26-5 victory from a fairly drab game. The penalty count was 18-6 against the Lions but Sayer took the scrums 23-10. Neil kicked four goals, one a touchline beauty to convert Gilfedder's try in the 70th minute, and claimed a smart try after interpassing with Frank Carlton and then being on hand to gather the winger's infield kick. His 11 points took him to 199 for the tour.

Two days later, also in Christchurch, the Lions were faced with a fixture against a New Zealand XIII, a game Neil regarded as a virtual test match. The tourists played their best rugby of the New Zealand tour so far in winning 31-17. John Shaw won the scrums two to one and there were outstanding displays by full-back Eric Fraser and makeshift scrum-half Peter Small, while Brian McTigue gave glimpses of his amazing ball-handling expertise. Derek Turner was unfortunate to be dismissed in the second half, with the Lions 16-9 ahead. He appeared merely to be making sure of a tackle on Bruce Castle and considerable confusion followed until his team-mates persuaded him that he had been sent off. The NZRL Council did not suspend Derek but cautioned him for "over-vigorous tackling", even though Castle had told the press that the incident hardly warranted a dismissal. Neil had a good game and added 13 points to his ever-growing tally.

Neil says: "Next day I was rested along with several of the first-teamers. The remainder caught an early morning train across to Greymouth on the West Coast. They won 66-8 and came back on the last train out of Greymouth. It had been a really gruelling journey for them." Neil would have probably gathered a lot of points had he played against West Coast, who were the New Zealand provincial champions, because the Lions ran in 16 tries, with Cooper and Small both scoring four. There was speculation that Neil, already with 212 points on tour, might approach Lewis Jones's 1954 record of 278 points but he would have needed to play in all the games in New Zealand to have had a realistic chance.

The Lions returned to the North Island and met Bay of Plenty at Rotorua on 7 August. On the driest ground they had experienced in New Zealand they ran riot, scoring 17 tries and 15 goals in an 81-14 massacre. The Bay side include only one Paheka (white man) and the crowd was almost all Maori. Neil came on as a substitute for Mick Sullivan and claimed a try and four goals. Eric Fraser had booted 11 goals before Neil took over the kicking and there were three tries each for John Taylor, Gerry Round and Peter Small.

On Saturday 11 August, the Lions entered the final test of their tour at Carlaw Park, Auckland. By then their injury list had risen to crisis proportions. The cock-a-hoop Kiwis made just two changes from their first-test victory, bringing in Jack Fagan at full-back and replacing Griffiths in the centre with Roger Bailey, changes which actually strengthened their team. The Great Britain team was: Round, Boston, Gilfedder, Fox, Small, Bolton, Poynton, Wilkinson, Shaw, McTigue, Huddart, Edgar, Turner (captain).

The forwards were severely depleted, McTigue and Edgar being forced to play when not really fit. Edgar, in particular, was handicapped by a damaged thigh, being barely able to move at more than walking pace. Boston was also far from fit, his troublesome knee injury being heavily strapped. Small was pressed into service on the left wing simply because no one else could be considered because of injuries. During the game Bolton received a broken nose and Round suffered a broken thumb. In the circumstances it was hardly surprising that the Lions struggled against a very fine New Zealand team.

By half-time New Zealand led 8-0. Britain had only engineered one scoring chance but Gilfedder dropped Neil's pass when he had a clear run for the line. Neil opened Britain's account after 49 minutes when he sprinted 50 yards for a try but they were 27-3 behind before they scored the final try of the game, through Small, converted by Gilfedder. The Kiwis' 27-8 victory gave them their first series success against Great Britain since 1950. Winger Brian Reidy was their star, while the introduction of Bailey, who scored two tries and Fagan, who kicked six goals, was clearly successful. New Zealand had been the better side in both tests but injuries had taken such a toll on the Lions that a comparison between the teams was academic. The *Daily Telegraph* observed, "The British backs, especially Bolton and Poynton, did their best to rally the side, as did Fox, until he suffered an eye injury late in the game, but what zest there might have been never materialised because too many legs and bodies were unable to respond." Neil ruefully says, "The conditions were awful. We were up to the ankles in mud and that suited the Kiwis' pack. I think everyone in the squad was ready for home after all the matches we had played."

The tour was not yet complete, however. Two days after the test match the Lions had to face Auckland at Carlaw Park. The Auckland fixture was traditionally as hard as any test and the Lions were not in any fit state to rise to the challenge. Neil had to have two stitches in his eyelid and Wilkinson had needed stitches in the back of his head, after being hit by flying glass as a shattered window in the dressing-room struck him after the test, while, Bolton, of course, had a broken nose. All three had to play against Auckland. By now the Lions had no full-backs, no wingers and no scrum-halves available. Neil's centre partner was Dick Huddart and the wingers were Gilfedder and Bolton. Peter Small was scrum-half for the seventh time on tour and hooker John Shaw was in the second-row. Unsurprisingly, they lost 46-13 to suffer the worst defeat any Lions side had experienced in New Zealand. Things deteriorated so much that at half-time Huddart went into the second-row, Gilfedder moved to centre and poor John Shaw was put on the wing, opposite a real speed merchant in Neville Denton, who scored a hat-trick. The Lions' cause was not helped by a back injury to Wilkinson and a knee injury to Noble, which left him hopping around on one leg. The Lions claimed tries by Poynton, with two, and Small, to which Neil added a couple of goals. Stuart Hadfield was typically forthright in talking to the press, merely asking them, "What could you expect with a team of crocks?" It had been a desperately sad ending to a great tour. Even so, the Lions had won six of their nine fixtures, scoring 319 points and conceding 161. On the complete tour of Australia and New Zealand, they had lost just six of their 30 fixtures and piled up 998 points against 464. Overall, it was a record which compared favourably with most of the tours in Lions' history.

Neil recalls, "The big games in New Zealand went horribly wrong for us. The people in New Zealand were great and very friendly but we were very disappointed with our performances. We flew back to Sydney for four days to try and recuperate, because we were going to South Africa for three more games on our way home."

The South African venture had been exercising Stuart Hadfield's mind for several weeks. Rugby league was just being introduced to the South Africans and the plan was for 17 players to play some exhibition games and fly the rugby league flag. Early in the New Zealand section of the tour he had reported to Bill Fallowfield that injuries were going to be a real problem. He thought he would be able to mobilise enough forwards but was desperately short of backs. He told Fallowfield, "Most of the players are ready for home now, never mind New Zealand. They are no longer enjoying the trip but want to be home."

Fallowfield wrote back: "The Wakefield Trinity tour was a bit of a fiasco as opposition was rather weak and it is more than ever essential that the games against Rugby League South Africa (RLSA) take place. This organisation appears to be the stronger of the two [there were two rival rugby league organisations in the country at the time] and is the more likely to succeed. If we fail to send our touring team then we can say goodbye to rugby league football in South Africa. Furthermore, we would be breaking our agreement. It is appreciated that players get homesick during a long tour and that is why I brought this subject up in Leeds. They were all dead keen to go at that meeting. In fact one player, I think it was Neil Fox, said it would be difficult to get players to stand down. I know the players will enjoy themselves when they are over there."

The 17 players who went on to South Africa were Bolton, Carlton, Cooper, Evans, Fox, Fraser, Gilfedder, Huddart, Noble, Poynton, Shaw, Small, Southward, Sullivan, Taylor, Turner, who was also the captain, and Wilkinson. Stuart Hadfield had decided not to go. He had been plagued by a nervous rash nearly all the tour. He believed the hot climate of South Africa was liable to aggravate the condition and Arthur Walker was delegated to lead the tour with Colin Hutton continuing his duties as trainer.

Billy Boston, of course, would not have been allowed into South Africa. The country, under president Dr Verwoerd, espoused apartheid and had just withdrawn from the Commonwealth. It was a very sensitive time to be embarking on missionary sporting tours, as the United Nations had called for sanctions against South Africa.

Neil recalls: "After our short rest in Sydney, the Lions set off on one of the longest journeys I have ever made. We went from Sydney to Perth in six hours, where we refuelled before flying to the Cocos Islands which took another eight hours. Then it was on to Mauritius which took 12 hours, where we stayed for three nights. The flight from there to Johannesburg took another six hours and we stayed in South Africa for 10 days."

The three games the Lions played were all against sides designated as Rugby League South Africa – at Pretoria on 23 August, Durban on the 25 and Johannesburg on the 31. All were of an exhibition nature with Britain winning 49-30, 39-33 and 45-23. Neil played in each game and rattled up 50 points from four tries and 19 goals. In the game at Durban the Lions were so short of bodies that Colin Hutton came on as substitute for Ike Southward and had the pleasure of playing wing to Neil. Colin had been a fine full-back for Widnes and Hull but had never played for Great Britain. Neil says, "Colin didn't let us down. In fact he scored four tries, although he did admit he only had to catch the ball and put it down to score. It would be something he would never forget, although I think he was pushing his luck in saying that he would have broken the world record if he had been doing the kicking as well."

While the Lions were in Durban, Gary Cooper had an unpleasant experience. Neil recalls, "We were all swimming in the sea, when Gary got caught in an undercurrent and was struggling to keep afloat. Luckily, Peter Small swam out and helped him back to the beach. Both of them were completely out of breath when the beach patrol came and asked if they were all right. Gary spluttered, 'Yes, but no ***** thanks to you!' I don't think Gary went swimming again. I also remember the overnight train journey from Pretoria to Durban. It took about 10 hours. While we were having a meal and a few beers, someone must have been wandering the train and saw a tour blazer hanging up in one of the compartments. He obviously took a fancy to the Lions badge and ripped the whole pocket off. The blazer was Joby Shaw's. So for the rest of the trip he went to receptions minus his pocket and badge."

Neil says: "I remember, after we flew in we travelled through some of the townships to Johannesburg. We couldn't believe the conditions people were living in – tumbledown shacks and tin huts. There used to be groups of African people washing down the streets with hose-pipes and selling cheap watches on street corners. The crowds at the games were multi-racial though. In the evenings most of the players went out in groups, maybe to the pictures, or stayed in the hotel. We were warned not to go out alone when it was dark. In Johannesburg we stayed at the same hotel as Jim Reeves, the American singer, but the only time we saw him was when he was leaving with his entourage for a concert. We were given a civic reception in Pretoria but we were so tired of travelling that we turned down the offer of a trip to one of the national parks when we were in Durban. The experience in South Africa was a good one but by then we really did want to get back home. We had been away for more than three months and I just wanted to see Molly. Yet, after we set off for England we were delayed in Athens for about eight hours. Instead of being in Manchester around midday, we didn't arrive until about 8 pm. All the wives and girlfriends had a long wait to meet us. It was great being back with Molly after all that time and talking about our impending addition to the family."

The tour had been a wonderful experience for Neil. He had played in 21 games in Australia and New Zealand. Only Laurie Gilfedder and Dick Huddart – with 24 each – had made more appearances and he was, of course, the leading scorer with 227 points from 19 tries and 85 goals. He had played in all the tests. The 1962 Lions have gone down in history as one of the best teams ever to have toured Australia, and their Ashes test performances were magnificent, fit to rank with the wonderful deeds of the Lions of 1928, 1946, 1958 and 1970. Neil's view is that the 1958 Lions probably had a better squad than the 1962 Lions but that the 1962 test team was stronger. However, sheer weight of injuries by the time they reached New Zealand took some of the gloss off their achievements.

Tour captain Eric Ashton wrote of his team in his 1966 autobiography, *Glory in the Centre Spot*, "We were a well-balanced, fine, successful side. The lads were well-behaved off the field. There were no trouble-makers... I had to issue remarkably few 'dos' and 'don'ts'... there were no moans from any of them... no skipper could have asked for more". In picking his world team in the autobiography, Ashton selected Reg Gasnier and Neil as the centres, saying of Neil, "He's there because of his supreme strength, his goal-kicking prowess, and because, as a big-match player, he can run straight through the rugby league football alphabet from A to Z. In fact, on the '62 Australasian tour we went together like lumps of sugar in the same teacup. I couldn't have asked for a more efficient partner in the middle. Fox has the ideal build, temperament and skill for a centre".

When the tour finances were finalised, the Lions players' 30 per cent share of the profits came to £571/14/9 (£571.74). However, by the time tax, national insurance and deductions for blazers, badges, slacks, ties, scarves and photographs had been applied, Neil reckons the final pay-out was a little over £300.

1962 Lions Tour record

The 1962 British Lions played 30 games in Australia and New Zealand, winning 24 and losing six. They scored 998 points and conceded 464.
Neil scored 19 tries, 85 goals, 227 points in 21 appearances (2 as a substitute) in Australia and New Zealand.

Date	Venue	Opponent	Score	Fox	Crowd
20 May	Perth	Western Australia	39-12	dnp	2,842
23 May	Wagga Wagga	Riverina	34-7	dnp	5,191
26 May	Sydney	Sydney	21-13	dnp	57,142
27 May	Bathurst	Western NSW	24-10	T, 3G	10,000
2 June	Sydney	NSW	33-28	6G	60,016
4 June	Newcastle	Newcastle	18-23	dnp	22,750
9 June	Sydney	AUSTRALIA	31-12	5G	69,990
10 June	Lismore	North Coast	33-13	T, 2G	5,240
13 June	Brisbane	Brisbane	16-14	dnp	22,650
16 June	Brisbane	Queensland	22-17	T, 5G	29,102
17 June	Toowoomba	Toowoomba	36-12	6G	10,491
20 June	Rockhampton	Central Queensland*	55-8	T, 3G	5,000
23 June	Cairns	Far North Queensland	33-31	dnp	4,769
24 June	Townsville	North Queensland	47-14	2T, 7G	8,278
30 June	Brisbane	AUSTRALIA	17-10	3G	34,760
1 July	Maryborough	Wide Bay	84-20	dnp	4,386
7 July	Sydney	NSW	20-5	4G	28,042
8 July	Wollongong	Southern NSW	10-18	2G	10,527
14 July	Sydney	AUSTRALIA	17-18	T, 4G	42,104
18 July	Sydney	St George	33-5	6G	57,895
22 July	Tamworth	Northern NSW	56-13	4T, 10G	9,000
25 July	Huntley	Waikato	59-20	dnp	3,461
28 July	Auckland	NEW ZEALAND	0-19		14,976
31 July	Wellington	Maoris	35-5	4T, 4G	3,091
2 Aug	Christchurch	Canterbury	26-5	T, 4G	2,500
4 Aug	Christchurch	New Zealand XIII	31-17	T, 5G	5,000
5 Aug	Greymouth	West Coast	66-8	dnp	2,758
7 Aug	Rotorua	Bay of Plenty*	81-14	T, 4G	1,852
11 Aug	Auckland	NEW ZEALAND	8-27	T	16,411
13 Aug	Auckland	Auckland	13-46	2G	10,444
23 Aug	Pretoria	RL South Africa	49-30	2T, 8G	10,000
25 Aug	Durban	RL South Africa	39-33	T, 6G	3,000
31 Aug	Johannesburg	RL South Africa	45-23	T, 5G	10,000

* Fox came on as substitute. The Lions' score is given first.

NB. The three games against RL South Africa are not included in the statistics for the Australasian tour but are included in Neil's career records.

11. 1962-63: Winning the Cup again

Neil and his fellow Lions arrived back in England on 1 September. Plenty had been happening while he had been on the other side of the globe.

Wakefield Trinity had been a hive of activity during the summer. The club had undertaken a ground-breaking six-match tour of South Africa at the end of June and into July, winning all of them. They had beaten Johannesburg Celtic 52-6, Boksburg Vikings 42-15, Bloemfontein Aquilas 48-9 and a South African Invitation XIII 59-3, 38-25 and 42-8, the last three games being played at Durban, Benoni and Pretoria. Keith Holliday had generously allowed Alan Skene to skipper the Trinity side in his native country. Wakefield had been reinforced by four South African guest players – Wigan's Fred Griffiths, St Helens's Tom van Vollenhoven, Hull's Wilf Rosenberg and Leigh's Ted Brophy.

Once the tour was over, however, troubles seemed to beset the club. On 24 July Jan Prinsloo told the club he wanted to return home to South Africa. It was a bolt from the blue for Trinity, who had paid a huge sum of money for him and had anticipated a great deal more service. For the time being his request to be released was shelved and he began the season as usual on Trinity's left wing. Don Metcalfe announced his retirement and there was news from Cumberland that Dennis Williamson, who had been on tour to South Africa, had developed a serious problem with his urinary tract and was likely to miss the whole season. Another casualty of the South African tour was Colin Greenwood, who had sustained a severe groin injury and thus missed the first three months of the season.

With the five Great Britain tourists still away when the season opened, Trinity found themselves in the unexpected position of barely being able to field two sides for the opening first-team and 'A' team fixtures. The only new signing of note had been loose-forward Roger Pearman, who had played rugby union for Sandal, Headingley and Loughborough College. Trinity had also transfer-listed 15 players, so despite their brilliance during 1961-62 the club found itself in a sticky position as the 1962-63 campaign kicked off. Additionally, the players' terms had been altered. They would now receive £14 for a win, £10 for a draw and £7 for a defeat, home or away. There was a rise in admission charges too. The minimum charge for adults had been raised to two shillings and sixpence (12½p), while children now had to pay nine pence, although OAPs were still to pay sixpence (2½p). There was also tragedy at the club when chairman Bill Simpson died just weeks after being elected. Ronnie Rylance, the vice-chairman, took his place temporarily.

The 1962-63 season began with the newly introduced Eastern and Western Division Championships which were to precede the commencement of the First and Second Division campaigns. Trinity were in the Eastern Division, which comprised the 16 Yorkshire clubs. The top four clubs from the previous season's Yorkshire Championship met the bottom four home and away, while the two middle groups of four similarly met each other. Theoretically, even with their personnel problems, Trinity should not have much trouble qualifying for the top four play-offs of the Eastern Division when their opponents were Batley, Bradford Northern, Dewsbury and Doncaster. By the time Neil returned, however, Trinity had played five games but had failed to impress. Don Vines had failed to attend a training session before the season began and was disciplined by being dropped for the first five games, which exacerbated Trinity's problems unnecessarily. They had even lost 11-2 at Dewsbury and one more defeat would probably exclude them from the play-offs.

Gerry Round had not been among the 17 players who went to South Africa with the Lions. Consequently, he had arrived home on 17 August and was back in action with Trinity after a week's rest. The other tourists arrived a fortnight later but straight away one of

113

their number dropped a bombshell on the Trinity committee and supporters. Derek Turner, a real hero to the fans, asked to be released from his club commitments in order to allow him to seek a player-coach or coaching appointment in Australia. Newspaper reports said he had been offered £50 a week, a house and a job. The story rumbled on for weeks but Derek ultimately remained a Wakefield player.

John L. Allen reported, "Rumours that Neil Fox might also return to Australia can be forgotten. He told me that while he had not received any direct offers he had been approached several times to consider returning to that country. Neil said there were some decent lads among the new players in South Africa" and he thought that if the two rival organisations running the game there could unite, league might take off in that country.

When Neil got back to Wakefield he got a big shock, "Molly and I lived at Royston Hill, East Ardsley, next door to our Peter and his family. It was our first house together. Before that we had spent a few months at Molly's mother's. On tour I had been writing to Molly and asking what she was doing with herself. She would tell me she had been out ice-skating, going to the pictures with her friends, keeping the garden tidy and going out to work. So when I got home, I couldn't believe what I saw. Molly, with some help from her dad, had completely redecorated the house. One door had been bricked up, a wall had been knocked through and dividing doors installed and there were now fitted wardrobes upstairs. She had certainly been busy. It was amazing."

On 8 September – just a week after leaving South Africa – Neil was demonstrating his undiminished appetite for the game by turning out for Wakefield in their first round Yorkshire Cup tie at Hunslet. It was not an auspicious occasion. Trinity's misfortunes continued to pile up. They were well beaten 34-9 and after only eight minutes lost Alan Skene with a dislocated shoulder and broken collarbone. Alan was due to leave for South Africa in December at the end of his contract and this injury kept him inactive almost until his departure. John L. Allen was scathing about Trinity's performance, calling it "a floor-wiping disgrace" and predicting that "it seems odds-on the Belle Vue sideboard being merely full of dust when the season ends". He exonerated Neil, though, who kicked three goals and put Gerry Round in for his side's only try after 77 minutes. He wrote, "A glimmer on the bleak horizon was the form of Fox, whose work in his first match for Trinity this season indicated that he may be an even more powerful force this term than last season, staleness permitting. He simply bristled with aggressiveness and determination."

The following Saturday Trinity's interest in the Eastern Division Championship evaporated when they went down 13-11 at Batley, increasingly an unhappy hunting ground for them. Neil landed four goals and inspired a late rally with a rampaging 50-yard burst but was disallowed a try from a tap penalty, when his foot was ruled to have been in touch. In injury time Prinsloo scored in the corner, but Neil could not convert and then he missed with a desperate last-second attempt to drop a goal.

On 19 September Neil, Fred Smith and Brian Briggs played for Yorkshire against Cumberland at Workington. Yorkshire won 11-2 and in the 36th minute, according to Alfred Drewry in the *Yorkshire Post*, "Fox set Yorkshire on the road to victory... He scattered O'Neill and Baker in turn to score a try after passing from a scrum". He also converted a 75th-minute try by Smith to seal the win. Three days later he scored 15 points in a 45-11 home romp against Bradford, a game which saw the return of tourists Poynton and Turner and the debut of second-rower Bob Haigh. On 26 September Neil and Briggs appeared in the Roses Match at Belle Vue. Neil kicked five goals, the second of which was the 900th of his career, as Yorkshire won 22-8 to lift the County Championship for the first time since 1958-59. His centre partnership with Geoff Shelton of Hunslet was reported to be much steadier than that of their direct opposites, Alan Buckley and Alan Davies. An ankle injury he received in this match was not enough to keep him out of action, however, when he landed another four goals in Trinity's last game of the Eastern Division campaign, a 29-0 win at Doncaster. John L. Allen's headline of the match report in the *Wakefield Express* disparagingly proclaimed "The final practice match!", meaning that the real business of First Division rugby was about to begin. Trinity had found the Eastern Division hard enough but, with the return of the tourists, hope sprang eternal that Trinity could negotiate the tougher challenge ahead successfully.

They had, however, already lost Jan Prinsloo for the foreseeable future as he was reported to be suffering from a rheumatic problem. On the positive side, Stuart Hadfield had been elected as club chairman once again.

Trinity's first league game at home against Hull on 6 October produced a somewhat lucky 21-20 victory, with Hull almost snatching a win after being 14-2 behind at half-time. Keith Holliday showed his courage and tenacity after his left eye had sustained a cut in one corner after 32 minutes. He was taken off and stitched up, returning to the fray after the break. He was then kicked in the ribs, carted off, bandaged and came back to see out the 80 minutes. Keith's injury meant Neil had to move to stand-off and the *Wakefield Express* asked the pertinent question: "Where would Trinity have been without the six goals from Neil Fox?" The next week saw Wakefield win well at Swinton, with Neil and Round the pick of the backs. Neil booted four goals and Swinton were described as "more like a flock of lambs than the kings of the jungle", a disparaging reference to their Lions nickname. A stark contrast was highlighted between "the immense power of Trinity compared with the feeble opposition". The writer may well have choked on his words as the season unfolded and Swinton took the Championship.

The Prinsloo saga came to a head when Jan announced he was definitely going home in mid-December. Neil consequently lost his wing partner fairly early into the season. For the time being he was partnered by the promising ex-amateur international Gerry Mann, a well-built and speedy wingman, who could be a real handful for opposing players. Meanwhile, Stuart Hadfield was extremely put out by Prinsloo's decision. Trinity had paid out £9,000 for his services, taking over his contract after he had signed from St Helens. Mr Hadfield railed that Jan's appearances had cost Wakefield more than £187 each, which was decidedly over the odds. Tragically, Jan Prinsloo, who away from rugby was a classical music buff, died aged only 31 on 28 July, 1966.

Mr Hadfield was also disturbed by Trinity's finances. Although the club had announced a profit of £4,183 in the off-season, that had only been possible because of a £5,000 donation from the Supporters' Club. The club was facing a bill of £12-14,000 for its proposed ground developments and upgrading of facilities. There was concern that the ground capacity had gradually been lowered from 37,000 to only 28,000 and, for a club with Trinity's ambitions, Mr Hadfield was adamant that was not enough. He believed that they should be able to accommodate at least 40,000. The only thing which would allow such ambitions to be fulfilled was a winning team which played attractive football.

Trinity were currently not supplying that level of success and entertainment, certainly not with any consistency. They were assuredly going to be faced with much tougher opposition over the next extraordinary eight months, because there were very few easy games in the new Division One. The home game against Widnes on 20 October was an example. The match was bright, entertaining and incident-packed. Trinity were behind 5-0 after only eight minutes but Neil pulled them back into contention, scoring a timely try after 29 minutes for which he "ran brilliantly, kicked ahead and beat all-comers for the touchdown". Trinity finally got ahead 10-7 in the 43rd minute when Neil converted a try by Holliday. Two minutes later though Widnes winger Bobby Chisnall equalised and second-rower Jim Measures scored another try after 68 minutes. Widnes held on to their 13-10 lead to the end, although the last few minutes of the game were played in "an absolute frenzy as Trinity tried to steal the points", according to John L. Allen.

The following Saturday Wakefield had better luck, winning a rugged match 15-3 at Oldham, who were one of the weakest teams in the league and had resorted to uncharacteristic negative spotting and spoiling tactics. Early in the second half with the score 3-3, Oldham's prop Alf Mumberson was sent off after a clash with Don Vines but three minutes later Vines was also dismissed after a dust-up with Charlie Bott. Ken Rollin was the star of the show with two beautiful tries, while Albert Firth also got a typically crashing try. Neil converted the last two tries from the touchline.

At this time Trinity were seeking to strengthen the centre position with Alan Skene's imminent departure. They were reported to have tried to tempt Halifax's Geoff Palmer out of retirement to play alongside Neil, while Newport rugby union wing forward Alan Thomas also rejected their overtures, turning down a £3,000 fee. There was better news, however, with the return to action of Malcolm Sampson after two years out of the game.

On 1 November Neil appeared for an Eastern Division XIII against France in Carcassonne. The Eastern Division team was:

Ken Thornett (Leeds), Graham Paul (Hull KR), Geoff Shelton (Hunslet), Neil Fox (Wakefield Trinity), Ron Cowan (Leeds), Lewis Jones (Leeds), Tommy Smales (Huddersfield), Len Hammill (Featherstone Rovers), Peter Flanagan (Hull KR), Brian Tyson (Hull KR), Ken Bowman (Huddersfield), Terry Clawson (Featherstone Rovers), Derek Turner (Wakefield Trinity, captain).

Neil recalls: "This was the only time I ever played in the same team as the great Lewis Jones. He was picked at centre alongside me but when Harold Poynton cried off with 'flu in France, he moved to stand-off. He drew men with ease and found gaps for all the players. It was a brilliant display from Lewis." The Eastern Division team had a hard struggle in the first half but shortly after the interval they suddenly burst into unstoppable action to transform a deficit of 10-11 into a 23-11 lead. The French scored a last-minute try but were beaten 23-16. Neil added four goals to tries from Bowman and Paul, who scored two each, plus one from Smales. Jones and Fox – what a combination that would have been for some team made in heaven. Although their careers overlapped for around eight years before Lewis left to play in Australia for Wentworthville, they were never afforded another opportunity to play together.

Alan Skene addressed the Wakefield & District Rugby League Referees Society in late October about his experiences of English rugby league and declared Neil Fox to be "the greatest player in the world" and "Derek Turner, Billy Boston and Alex Murphy as the world's best in their respective positions". He also said that he would have stayed at Trinity if a second signing-on fee had been legalised by the RFL, a change in the laws which some clubs had suggested. Skene would certainly have enjoyed playing in Trinity's next game on 3 November, a 27-27 draw against Featherstone at Belle Vue, a scoreline which was completely alien to the game in that epoch, if not exactly uncommon at the start of the 21st century. The game was Keith Holliday's benefit match. While the defences obviously left something to be desired, the *Wakefield Express* commented, "The entertainment value of this fixture was almost beyond belief". The lead changed hands four times and the teams were level on four occasions. Neil kicked six goals but could not win the match when he attempted to convert Gerry Mann's try scored half a minute from time. "Neil Fox never ceased in his efforts to pull the game round but was heavily spotted", noted John L. Allen.

On 10 November Wakefield went to Hull, another of the weaker teams, who were also beset by injuries. Both sides scored four tries but Trinity had a truly horrendous afternoon and lost 14-20. The forwards were completely outplayed and the whole side's handling was appalling. Colin Greenwood picked a bad match to make his return to first-team football. Neil helped Gerry Mann to two tries but his kicking was wayward, although the touchline conversion of his own try was a beauty.

The big problem with Trinity during this period, according to the press and fans, was a real lack of cohesion between the forwards and the backs and it was not easy to see how Ken Traill was going to rectify matters. Things were not improved when, almost unbelievably, Wakefield suddenly appeared happy enough to let half-backs Keith Holliday and Harold Poynton go to Whitehaven and St Helens respectively. Saints were reported to have agreed terms for Poynton for £8,000, an indication that the club's financial state was still causing concern. Fortunately, both players remained at Wakefield, but the signs were ominous and suggested that Trinity needed success and they needed it quickly.

Neil's next appointment was for England against France at Headingley on 17 November. With five new internationals (Ken Gowers, Bill Burgess, Tommy Smales, Peter Flanagan and Bill Drake), England struggled for the first 20 minutes, when French stand-off Gilbert Benausse potted three penalty goals. It was Neil who brought England back into the game, when he galloped up in support of Norm Herbert to score the first of four English tries. Burgess scored two and skipper Eric Ashton grabbed the last. Neil's three goals helped England to an 18-6 win.

Although obviously happy to be playing for England on 17 November, Neil had some regret at not being able to appear for Trinity against Swinton at Belle Vue. The international coincided with Alan Skene's last appearance for Wakefield. It had been more than two months since Alan had been injured in the Yorkshire Cup disaster at Hunslet. At least he was able to make a curtain call as Swinton were beaten 16-3, his colleagues chairing him from the field at the final whistle. Neil says: "Alan made a great centre partner for me. He was one of our best buys. In his 136 appearances he scored 69 tries and made plenty more for his winger, Fred Smith. He was certainly going to be missed." In the *Rugby Leaguer* John Lindley wrote, "From the moment he made his debut, on Christmas Day 1958 at Castleford's home, Skene showed his great potential. The ease in which he made the change of code under different weather conditions was remarkable. This lithe and talented player brought much to Trinity's attack and he and Neil Fox formed a centre partnership which has been the most outstanding combination in club football in recent times."

A year or so earlier, Lewis Jones in the *News of the World* commented, "A number of Wakefield supporters have asked me if I agree that Skene and Fox are the best centres in the game and whether I've ever seen their equal. It can be unwise to over praise or condemn... Football is full of ups and downs... Having said that, however, I must admit that Skene and Fox are a truly great, effective combination, a pleasure to watch and difficult to play against. They are similar in style and make-up to Welshmen Jackie Matthews and Bleddyn Williams, the best pair of centres I ever saw in rugby union. A big strong 'un, with a fast, crafty, ball-playing type alongside, has always been the ideal centre blend. Williams and Matthews provided this, and so do Fox and Skene. On present-day prices the value of the Trinity pair must be sky-high."

Skene returned to South Africa at the beginning of December, but spent the summer of 1963 playing for Souths in Sydney, as well as representing South Africa, who made a pioneering tour of Australia and New Zealand.

Meanwhile Trinity went down to a bad home defeat against Widnes on 24 November. Neil kicked Trinity into a 6-3 interval lead with three penalties but that was about as good as it got. The Trinity forwards were woeful and Neil and Colin Greenwood were provided with "slow, useless ball", according to John L. Allen, as Widnes won 12-6. Worse followed on 1 December when bottom-of-the-league Oldham left Belle Vue with a 19-12 win. Fortunately for Neil, he was on Great Britain duty in Perpignan. Having said that, Britain too were losers, 17-12 to a fired–up French team. Again the referee, Edouard Martung, came in for severe criticism. Bill Fallowfield, the RFL secretary, complained, "Had we been able to play real rugby we would have won. I believe our team is superior to the French, but today we were prevented from playing. This game was too rough".

France led 7-2 at half-time and 17-2 with only 10 minutes left. A Reuter's reporter wrote of Britain's late comeback, "Fox... led the Britain rally, and finished with nine of his side's points. He landed a first-half penalty goal, improved a try by Ashton 10 minutes from the end, and with only three minutes to go he crashed through to score a try himself and kick the goal. That was the only period of the match in which Britain were on top."

Returning to domestic rugby, Neil enjoyed two superb victories with Trinity. On 8 December Trinity went the few miles to Post Office Road and came away with a magnificent win. Trinity lost the scrums 10-18 and had Derek Turner sent off after 24 minutes. Half-backs, Holliday and Poynton showed exactly why Trinity would have been fools to part with them, while the remaining five forwards played as if their lives were at stake. Ken Hirst scored a tremendous 50-yard try in the 13th minute after an interception, but Rovers struck back to lead 8-3. "The marvellous goalkicking of Neil Fox" decided the issue. He hit a stunning long shot into a strong wind in the 31st minute and kicked a fine angled penalty in the 42nd minute to make the score 8-7 to Featherstone. He then won the match with a massive penalty from half-way in the 51st minute.

After the success at Featherstone – regarded by many as one of Trinity's best wins of the post-war period – Wakefield registered another powerful performance on 15 December. For the first time all season they were able to field the same team for two matches running when they met St Helens at Belle Vue. A very exciting game ensued. A terrific solo try by Holliday, who bluffed three defenders in a 25-yard dash down the blind-side of a scrum, gave Trinity a 13th minute lead they would not surrender. Neil's super conversion from near touch and his improvement of a Hirst try gave Trinity a 10-2 interval lead. A try by van Vollenhoven with seven minutes remaining brought Saints back to 10-7. When Dick Huddart strode over the Trinity goal line in the 73rd minute it looked all over for Wakefield but he tried to make ground in-field to simplify the conversion for Kel Coslett to win the game. Neil's co-centre Roy Bell hounded Huddart so effectively, however, that the great second-rower was forced over the dead-ball line and Saints paid the ultimate penalty, when they would have had at least a draw if he had touched down immediately.

Although no one could have anticipated it, that game was the last that Wakefield would play for almost three months. Shortly afterwards the big freeze of the winter of 1962-63 virtually wiped out sport in the north of England. It was the worst winter since 1947 and there has certainly been nothing to approach it since. Only seven scheduled games took place in the period between 29 December and 2 March.

Before the snow and ice gripped the nation, Trinity transfer-listed Dennis Williamson, who had not made any appearances at all during the season, at £4,000 and sold Budgie Firth to York for £3,000. Neil respected Albert Firth as a player and colleague, "Albert left because he was finding it hard to get into the first-team. I will always remember him from when I first started in the 'A' team as a 16-year-old. He was a very solid player with plenty of speed and strength. We progressed together in the first-team. I'll never forget that day when Ken Traill picked him to play on my wing at Leeds in 1960, opposite the flying Springbok, Wilf Rosenberg. Wilf didn't do much flying that afternoon."

Clubs tried all kinds of methods to get games on during this new ice age. Some, such as Castleford, Hull, Hull KR and St Helens tried thawing out their pitches by massive use of braziers with men being paid to stoke them through the night. Huddersfield tried to use a road repair machine to defrost the playing surface but, once the heat had passed over it, the ground simply froze again. Widnes used chemicals with some success – four games were staged there - but no one really knew what the consequences for the pitch or the players might be, while Castleford and Barrow tried sand and salt, which were guaranteed to ruin the playing surface. Leeds decided that they would invest in a £10,000 underground electric heating system for future years. The cost would be £5 an hour to run and many critics said it would never pay for itself. Leeds had the last laugh, however, as history proved. Neil recalls, "Wakefield continued to try to train at Belle Vue but that just compacted the ice even more. They came up with a plan to pump hot water from the power station across Doncaster Road to use as underground heating. I don't really think the idea was at all feasible. It never got off the ground, never mind under the ground."

By the time February arrived no games at all had been played. Consequently, the Challenge Cup first round was put back until 2 March. Castleford and Leeds managed to play their first round tie on 9 February, as did Liverpool City and Barrow amateurs Roose, at Widnes. Wigan were installed as 5-1 favourites, with Trinity and St Helens at 6-1 and Workington Town at 7-1. Trinity's opponents, Bradford Northern, who were bottom of Division Two, were 2,000-1 no-hopers.

Meanwhile, Neil had other matters to address, "On 16 February Trinity should have been at Workington Town for a league match but it was frozen off. Instead I had a lovely surprise because Mandy, our daughter, was born that day. So I was thrilled to be at home when I got the call from Benton Hill Nursing Home, in Horbury, telling me she had been born. I couldn't wait to get in the car to see Molly and Mandy [Amanda Jayne]. She weighed nine pounds and there was a picture of Molly and her on the front page of the *Wakefield Express* the following week."

There was also a film première to attend. Neil and his team-mates had been invited to attend the reception prior to the Leeds première of *This Sporting Life* at the Odeon Theatre and Restaurant on Sunday evening, 24 February. Molly was unable to attend for obvious reasons. There were nearly 200 guests at the showing but Richard Harris and Rachel Roberts were absentees. Harris sent a letter of apology and a tape of the song *Keep right on to the end of the road*, which had everyone singing along. His excuse for not attending was the fact that he was rehearsing for *Diary of a Madman*, for which he admitted he was suitably cast. His letter ran: "I hope you enjoy the picture which you and everyone up north helped to make a success, and to show the world where the blood and guts of England really is. On reflection I personally feel some of the happiest moments of my career were spent on the field of Belle Vue – not to mention those late-night sessions at Ken's [Traill] or Brian's [Briggs] and, of course, not forgetting Fred Smith's great try versus Wigan, which he so kindly 'lent me' for the picture. When the play comes off I hope to travel up north to see you again – or better still to take a bath with you all again at Wembley after your next victory. So 'Keep right on to the end of the Road'. May God bless you all, Richard."

This Sporting Life ran for 137 minutes. It was not on general release until 17 March 1963 but it was on view at Wakefield Playhouse from 10 March onwards. The 11 March performance was declared a civic occasion with the Mayor and Mayoress in attendance.

Apart from births and premières, Neil's enforced lay-off saw the arrival of a new wing partner. On 22 February, John Ridge, Eddie Thomas and Colin Greenwood travelled to Manchester airport to greet a new South African trialist, Gert 'Oupa' Coetzer. Gert was to have a trial terminating on 16 April. He had played rugby league for Johannesburg Celtic against Trinity and had appeared 44 times for the Orange Free State rugby union side. John Ridge told the press, "He's like Tom van Vollenhoven in appearance and I hope he's as good." Almost miraculously, Wakefield managed to fulfil an 'A' team game at Castleford the next day and Coetzer was introduced to the joys of winter rugby league in England within 24 hours of his arrival. If the mud and penetrating cold were hard enough to bear, the result was equally depressing - a 9-7 defeat. Still, Neil would have no complaints about the new South African winger, who would grace the Belle Vue turf for the next five years.

The deep mid-winter break served to reinvigorate Wakefield Trinity and for Neil and his fellow Lions in particular the break must have come as a welcome tonic after 16 months of continuous rugby. It also allowed Trinity's walking wounded to recover and the season essentially began anew on 9 March, when for the first time in 1963 there was a full programme of games. Before the shut-down Trinity had been none too impressive overall but were still good enough to be in fourth place in the First Division, behind Widnes, Wigan and Castleford. However, the levelling out effect of two division rugby was obvious – only 13 points separated leaders Widnes from the 16th and bottom team Oldham.

The backlog of postponed fixtures was so great that the season was extended to 1 June and, with the Wembley final being set in stone for 11 May, priority had to be given to playing the Cup ties. Trinity had to play 25 games over the next three months.

They began with a home game against Workington Town, potentially a hard proposition. In the event it was no-contest. Despite squally and heavy rain, Wakefield played delightfully to win 41-5. Neil was quickly into form. His first kick of the 'new season' was a great touchline conversion of a Don Vines try and he added another six goals.

Two days later Trinity went to Odsal for the formality of knocking Bradford Northern out of the Challenge Cup. It proved no formality. Wind and rain combined to make conditions virtually impossible, especially for goalkicking. Northern took a shock fourth minute lead with a try by winger Goulam Abed and were level 3-3 at half-time. Trinity scored four unanswered tries in the second half, including one from Neil, but not a goal was landed in the match, as Trinity ground out a 15-3 win. Five days later Trinity had another apparently easy second-round Cup tie against 600-1 outsiders Liverpool City at Belle Vue. The Wakefield selectors clearly thought it was safe enough to give Coetzer his first-team debut and to experiment with Fred Smith at right centre for the first time. Before the game Neil, Brian Briggs and Fred Smith were presented with Yorkshire caps and County Championship medals by club president Alderman Frank West.

Like Bradford, Liverpool had not read the script. They scared Wakefield rigid and lost only 14-12. Like most of his team, Neil did not play particularly well, but his four goals to Wilf Hunt's three was the difference between the teams. John L. Allen described Trinity's display variously as "casual", "reckless" and "careless" but deemed "the play of the South African trialist as most encouraging. He showed commendable dash, and with proper treatment should prove a great favourite at Belle Vue". Neil says, "This game could easily have been lost. Late on a Liverpool player broke through and with support on the outside he drew our full-back Gerry Round. Had he passed, the game would have been over for us but he dummied. Gerry smothered him and we won a very tight match. It just showed again how cup ties can produce shocks."

On 23 March Trinity flogged Leeds 33-8 at Belle Vue. Neil was in prime form. He kicked prodigiously, three of his six goals being touchliners, scored a try and helped his winger, Coetzer, to his first hat-trick. Neil's touchline conversion of Gert's last try brought him his 2,000th point for Trinity. Neil was partnered in the centres by Ian Brooke, who was beginning to hold down a permanent place in the team. Ian also had a brilliant game despite being pole-axed by a Ken Thornett tackle. Four minutes after that tackle the Australian full-back was stretchered off with a bloody head wound.

There was no joy at Warrington, however, the following Saturday. A gripping game in the mud was replete with terrific tackling and Trinity went down 5-0 with Jim Challinor scoring the only try in the last minute. Worse than the result were injuries to Gerry Round with a broken finger and Bob Haigh who sustained a broken wrist bone. Haigh's injury ended his season. A small consolation was the winning of the fourth period of the Mackeson Points Scoring Contest - all the team collecting a silver tankard.

On 3 April Neil played for Great Britain against France at Wigan and scored half of the points in a 42-4 massacre. He kicked nine goals from 11 attempts and grabbed a superb try from 40 yards out, benefiting from a cunningly disguised reverse pass from full-back Ken Gowers. His 21 points equalled Lewis Jones's record for a British test player, also set against France at Leeds in 1957. His eighth point of the test brought up his 2,500th in first-class rugby league.

Wakefield's good fortune in the Challenge Cup continued in the third round draw. Once more they had drawn the rank outsiders, 20-1 York, who were currently fourth in the Second Division. The game was played on 6 April at Clarence Street and was a sell-out all-ticket match, 13,500 paying record ground receipts of £2,492. Once again, though, the underdogs came out biting. After only 12 minutes Trinity were nine points down. Vic Yorke had landed three goals and Budgie Firth had scored a try. By the interval it was 9-7, Neil having kicked a penalty and improved a try from Fred Smith. Towards the end of the game Neil missed a relatively easy penalty but redeemed himself on 74 minutes when he was successful with a much more difficult shot from wide out. Blood pressure rose all round as Yorke missed a penalty two minutes later and Neil also failed with one in the last minute. York, who had lost Firth with a broken collar-bone on the hour, fully deserved their 9-9 draw, their defence being staggering throughout.

The replay four days later drew almost 19,000 to Belle Vue on a miserable evening. It proved to be another rousing game but Wakefield were too good this time for the gallant Minstermen. Neil booted five goals and there were dazzling tries from Coetzer and Holliday as Wakefield won 25-11. Coetzer's performance went some way to provoking the Wakefield administration to sign him permanently for a contract worth £4,500. Unsurprisingly, 24 hours later Trinity lost 17-7 at Halifax.

On Easter Saturday ABC televised the second half of Trinity's home game against Hull KR. It was a poor game in mud and rain and both teams seemed more interested in their Challenge Cup semi-finals the following week. Wakefield won 12-5, Neil providing nine of the points. The *Wakefield Express* reported the highlight of the game was "a majestic run by Neil Fox to complete a splendid handling movement midway through the first half. He sold a dummy which indicated he was to pass to Coetzer but, seeing the defenders had been caught on the wrong foot, the centre turned inward, very sharply and acutely, to provide himself with a clear run behind the posts." On Easter Monday the two sides met again at Craven Park. Neil kicked a penalty after 10 minutes but that was all Trinity scored in a feeble performance, going down 24-2 in their fifth game in nine days.

Five days later, on 20 April, they were to meet Warrington at Swinton in the semi-final of the Challenge Cup. Wakefield took the players to Southport for training on the preceding Thursday and they stayed until Saturday at a Birkdale hotel. Neither team's progress thus far had been impressive but Trinity were slight favourites. The conditions again influenced the nature of the encounter. A muddy ground and two unyielding defences decreed that it should be an unspectacular match but nonetheless interesting and gripping. Neil effectively won the game in the 8th minute. Both sides got a solitary chance to score a try. Trinity took theirs while the Wire missed theirs 11 minutes from time. The *Wakefield Express* described the match-winner: "Fox's delightful effort from Poynton's pass inside the Warrington half was as sparkling a piece of play as there was in the entire game. After escaping the clutches of two would-be tacklers the race he started for the line, after kicking ahead, had the crowd jumping and shouting in uncontrollable excitement. And need it be added what a sensation it was when the man who has been referred to as 'rather slow for a centre' beat all-comers in the sprint to cross the goal-line; and then on to within inches of the dead ball line before diving for the touchdown? It was perfect justice when he added the goal points".

In scoring that decisive try – his 150th for Wakefield - Neil had badly hurt his hip. After beating full-back Tommy Conroy he had crashed into husky winger Brian Glover as he slithered for the touchdown. At half-time he had received a pain-killing injection but was a passenger for most of the game. Laurie Gilfedder kicked a penalty for Warrington 20 minutes into the second half but, more importantly, had missed four in the first half. There was no more scoring and Warrington's only chance to score a try was dashed when centre Joe Pickavance tried to emulate Neil's manoeuvre but was beaten to the ball by Fred Smith. Trinity owed much to Milan Kosanovic's scrum superiority and a stirring display from the rest of the pack, particularly Brian Briggs and David Blakeley.

Neil recalls: "The Warrington game was always going to be very hard, with a pitch as heavy as that one was. From the kick-off Brian Briggs hit Charlie Winslade just as he was catching the ball. He meant business. Charlie struggled after that big hit and from then onwards it was a matter of which pack of forwards got on top. I'm pleased to say it was ours. My try and conversion put us 5-0 up but the injury meant I had to play the rest of the game on the wing. I could hardly move because of the pain and I don't think I got the ball again. We were back at Wembley though, so I didn't worry too much that the injury caused me to miss the next two games."

Trinity lost both those games – 8-6 at Leeds in a lively clash, won by four Lewis Jones penalties and, alarmingly, 26-3 at home to Warrington just a week after the semi-final. Neil returned on 29 April for an absolute thriller at St Helens, which Wakefield won 16-15. He bagged five goals and a try in a sizzling display. The *Wakefield Express* reported his 51st minute try thus: "A cute back-flip from Harold Poynton served Fox as he tore through on the burst and scored. The centre strode out to the right and confused the defenders still more when he suddenly straightened out and sprinted directly to the line, as the cover was sweeping towards the wing." Trinity survived a last-minute scare when Kel Coslett failed to land a penalty.

The Championship had by then developed into a straight struggle between Swinton and Widnes. But although Trinity had reached Wembley again, there was briefly some concern that five defeats in six league games prior to the Knowsley Road triumph had placed them almost in the relegation zone. However, a 23-8 home win against Castleford on May Day effectively banished any thoughts of a relegation struggle. Neil's four goals included his 800th for Wakefield. On 4 May, Neil's 23rd birthday, they played their last game before the Challenge Cup final at Bramley with a reserve pack and lost 19-10.

On Sunday 5 May, Molly and Neil had Amanda Jayne christened and the newspapers were full of Neil's promise: "Next week I'll bring her home the Cup". The critics were unconvinced. Most of the rugby league *cognoscenti* predicted a victory for Wakefield's opponents Wigan. They argued that Wigan's pack would be too powerful and experienced for Trinity's and that their backs would be too fast and clever – five of Wigan's forwards and six of their backs were test men, while Wakefield's Wembley team contained six test players. They also agreed that a Wakefield versus Wigan final was the perfect vehicle for rugby league. After all, they were the Wembley specialists – Wigan had won there in 1958 and 1959 and been runners-up in 1961, while Trinity had lifted the Cup in 1960 and 1962 – and both were capable of playing sublime rugby.

Trinity's preparation began on the Tuesday with a trip to the Turkish baths in Leeds, followed by some light training at Belle Vue on Wednesday morning. On Thursday the Wakefield players journeyed by train to London to their headquarters at Bailey's Hotel. Their final training session was a game of association football at Queen's Park Rangers' ground. Wigan's team was injury–free but Trinity were still not absolutely sure of their line-up, having queries over the fitness of several men. A victory would reward the Wakefield players with £65 winning pay.

'Ramon Joyce' (now better known as Raymond Fletcher) summed up the prevailing mood among the journalists in his *Rugby Leaguer* preview: "Wigan for the Cup! Is that clear enough! Now for the whys and wherefores. If it becomes a battle of wits between the backs Wigan have probably the greatest tactician in the game to swing everything the way he wants it, namely Eric Ashton. And if it turns out a forward battle who can deny that Brian McTigue is the Number One schemer-in-chief? Even 'Monty' will learn something about field marshalling from these two. Almost as intriguing as the match itself will be the personal duel between Eric Ashton and Neil Fox for the unofficial 'Centre-threequarter Championship of the World'. Yet, I reckon Fox will find the 'Boston Bounce' is the Wigan plan to blot out the Wakefield colossus. And when those two collide – stand well back."

Alfred Drewry in the *Yorkshire Post* was cagier. He wrote: "Either side could have an off day today. If Wakefield win the chances are that the decisive blows will be struck by Fox or by Poynton, for stand-off half seems to me the one position in which Wakefield should have a clear advantage." The *Daily Mirror's* Joe Humphreys was more forthright, declaring, "Wigan to beat Wakefield... It's as simple as A B C D".

A new-look Wembley housed a crowd of 84,492 under its ultra-modern fibreglass roof which covered all the spectators, while the press corps was accommodated in a gigantic new press box slung from girders over the Royal Box. The main guest was Viscount Montgomery, whose allegiance decidedly veered towards Wakefield. Although it was his first visit to a rugby league match, Monty was a Freeman of the City of Wakefield and it was revealed after the final that he had given Derek Turner strict orders that Trinity must win. He would soon become a patron of Wakefield Trinity.

True to Wembley tradition, the afternoon was a fine, pleasant one after the threat of rain cleared, although it was quite windy. The teams were:

Wakefield Trinity: Gerry Round, Colin Greenwood, Ian Brooke, Neil Fox, Gert Coetzer, Harold Poynton, Keith Holliday, Jack Wilkinson, Milan Kosanovic, Malcolm Sampson, Don Vines, Derek Turner (captain), Roger Pearman.

Wigan: Dave Bolton, Billy Boston, Eric Ashton (captain), Alan Davies, Frank Carlton, Stan McLeod, Frank Pitchford, John Barton, Bill Sayer, Brian McTigue, Frank Collier, Geoff Lyon, Roy Evans.

Neil remembers the final thus: "Wigan were odds-on favourites. We had to make changes. Colin Greenwood came in on the wing for Fred Smith. Brian Briggs was suffering from gout and Roger Pearman came in at loose-forward with Derek Turner moving to second-row. It was only Pearman's seventh first-team match. Ian Brooke, only just turned 20, came into the centre for his first appearance at Wembley and Malcolm Sampson was also making his debut at Wembley after missing the 1960 and 1962 finals through that bad car-crash injury. My winger, Gert Coetzer had to have a secret pain-killing injection into a shoulder injury an hour before kick-off. Wigan had their full team out, just about everyone an International. They gave us the run-around in the first 20 minutes but somehow we held out. Eric Ashton had a try disallowed in that period because of a double movement. Luckily, the referee, D. T. H. Davies, saw it.

After that we started to get more possession and settled down. Two minutes before half-time we went 5-0 up, when Keith Holliday cleverly fed Malcolm Sampson, who charged over under the posts and I kicked the goal. Then Dave Bolton was carried off after taking a very hard tackle from me. The second half opened with Frank Pitchford scoring a really good try, making the score 5-3 and it was still anyone's game. Then Coetzer scored in the corner and I kicked another goal and it was 10-3. Ashton kicked a penalty for Wigan and Bolton returned but was still looking groggy. I kicked a penalty but so did Ashton to make it 12-7. It was then that the sucker punch was delivered. Bolton made a break and Harold Poynton intercepted his pass which was meant for Billy Boston. He raced 30 yards for a try and my conversion made it 17-7. That was when we knew we were going to win the Cup.

Wigan hit back with a try from Frank Carlton but Gert Coetzer scored his second try for us and we led 20-10. The final nail in Wigan's coffin was an Ian Brooke try, which I converted and we had won 25-10. I thought this was our best Wembley win, beating such a talented side as Wigan. We were the first Yorkshire side to win the Cup in consecutive seasons at Wembley and the feeling was great. Harold Poynton got the Lance Todd trophy and there was no question that he deserved it."

There was general satisfaction with the standard of play in the 1963 Challenge Cup Final, but great surprise at the margin of Trinity's victory. In his preview in the *Daily Telegraph*, Bob Pemberton had surmised that Roger Pearman could have been a weak link in Trinity's armour. He retracted his view in his match report, "Tactically speaking, Wigan made the mistake of concentrating too much attention on Fox. Pearman got over a nervous start to play like a veteran". The *Daily Mirror's* Joe Humphreys candidly admitted, "Wakefield played the football that was expected of Wigan", while Jack Nott in the *News of the World* declared Trinity's last three tries "turned Wigan into a rabble and this Wembley final into a rout". John L. Allen, who had sat on the fence in his pre-match views, announced to *Wakefield Express* readers, "In this great event Wakefield's chances were widely rated as nil! But Trinity accomplished the 'impossible' in such competent style that no impartial onlooker could have been left in any doubt that the better team had won". Eddie Waring blared in the *Sunday Mirror*: "Harold Poynton smashed Wigan to dramatic and utter defeat".

Trinity's was a superb performance. Much credit went to Milan Kosanovic, who beat the redoubtable Bill Sayer 9-4 in the first-half scrums, allowing Trinity to negate the power of the opposing pack. Remarkably, there were only four second-half scrums, all of which were won by Sayer but Trinity's defence was so overwhelming that the cherry and whites coughed up mounds of possession to the eager Belle Vue men. Wakefield's half-backs Holliday and Poynton played magnificently, making a mockery of Trinity's apparent willingness to dispose of their services a few months earlier. The Wakefield forwards earned enormous praise, Derek Marshall of the *Daily Mail* said that their dominance "marked the end of a once-great Wigan pack". Derek Turner became the first man to captain three Wembley Challenge Cup-winning teams – if he had not, Eric Ashton would have earned the distinction. Jack Wilkinson became the first man to play in five Wembley finals, having appeared there with Halifax in 1954 and 1956, as well as in Trinity's trio.

Neil had set further records. His five goals had raised his aggregate in Wembley finals to 39 points, a record which lasted until 1995, when Frano Botica raised it to 46 points, having played in five finals. One notable statistic which appeared to have escaped everyone came with Neil's conversion of Sampson's try. It was the 1,000th goal of his first-class career. His kicking at Wembley started off shakily, for both he and Ashton missed three first-half penalties before that 1,000th goal bisected the posts. His second-half tally of four out of six attempts really served to undermine Wigan's morale, while his brilliant touchline conversion of Coetzer's first try was a crucial score.

On the Monday after the final Trinity returned to the Merrie Citie with the Cup for the third time in four years. The triumphal return before 25,000 ecstatic men, women and children in the streets from Westgate to Wakefield Town Hall and the ritual civic reception went like clockwork and then it was back to clearing the backlog of league fixtures. Eight games were to be played between 14 May and 1 June. Of course, there was no chance of glory in the league, so the euphoria of Wembley would have to sustain the team in what would inevitably be an anticlimactic wind-down to another memorable season.

However, Neil's season finished suddenly. After scoring 11 points in a 32-0 romp against Bramley at Belle Vue on 14 May, Neil lined up again four days later at Central Park against Wigan. Wigan took a 7-0 lead but in the 21st minute Keith Holliday scored a try which Neil converted for his 100th goal of the season for Trinity. A couple of minutes later Neil made a break and kicked ahead. Bolton and Trevor Lake knocked each other out in going for the ball and David Blakeley cantered over for a try, Gerry Round converted to give Wakefield a 10-7 lead. Unfortunately, Neil had also been injured in this passage of play and retired from the game in the 26th minute. Trinity survived a violent second-half hailstorm and Neil's absence to win 21-13. He had severely damaged a thigh muscle and missed the last six games. Trinity lost half of them but inflicted a third defeat, 21-8, on Wigan at Belle Vue on 25 May, to reinforce their superiority over the men from Central Park.

Wakefield eventually finished fifth in Division 1 - 12 points behind champions Swinton. It was respectable enough but the big freeze and the monumental fixture pile-up had made the Championship a lottery for some of the clubs who, like Trinity, had put all their eggs into the Challenge Cup basket. For Trinity it had worked and another glorious chapter found its way into the club's history. Injuries apart, the season had been splendid for Neil. In all games he had amassed 292 points to finish runner-up by 29 to St Helens's Kel Coslett in the points-scoring chart. In the goalkicking list he was fourth with 125, behind Coslett (156), Hull KR's Cyril Kellett (142) and Hunslet's Billy Langton (134).

Wakefield Trinity 1962-63

Wakefield Trinity finished 5th in Division 1: P30, W16, L13, D1, For 432, Against 359
Fox scored 10 tries, 100 goals, 230 points for Wakefield, and 4 tries, 25 goals, 62 points in representative games

Date	Opponent	Score	Fox	Crowd	
18 Aug	**Batley**	18-9	dnp	9,470	ED
21 Aug	Dewsbury	2-11	dnp	6,000	ED
25 Aug	Bradford N	19-10	dnp	2,756	ED
27 Aug	**Doncaster**	39-0	dnp	7,542	ED
1 Sep	**Dewsbury**	30-11	dnp	7,981	ED
8 Sep	Hunslet	9-34	3G	9,500	YC1
15 Sep	Batley	11-13	4G	4,900	ED
22 Sep	**Bradford N**	45-11	T, 6G	6,741	ED
29 Sep	Doncaster	29-0	4G	3,525	ED
6 Oct	**Hull**	21-20	6G	9,216	
13 Oct	Swinton	19-5	4G	10,600	
20 Oct	**Widnes**	10-13	T, 2G	13,718	
27 Oct	Oldham	15-3	3G	9,349	
3 Nov	**Featherstone R**	27-27	6G	12,772	
10 Nov	Hull	14-20	T, G	8,500	
17 Nov	**Swinton**	16-3	dnp	8,821	
24 Nov	Widnes	6-12	3G	7,074	
1 Dec	**Oldham**	12-19	dnp	8,888	
8 Dec	Featherstone R	9-8	3G	5,671	
15 Dec	**St Helens**	10-7	2G	9,560	
9 Mar	**Workington T**	41-5	7G	8,013	
11 Mar	Bradford N	15-3	T	2,069	Ch Cup 1
16 Mar	**Liverpool C**	14-12	4G	10,173	Ch Cup 2
23 Mar	**Leeds**	33-8	T, 6G	17,995	
30 Mar	Warrington	0-5		7,338	
6 Apr	York	9-9	3G	13,500	Ch Cup 3
10 Apr	**York**	25-11	5G	18,718	Replay
11 Apr	Halifax	7-17	2G	4,330	
13 Apr	**Hull KR**	12-5	T, 3G	10,021	
15 Apr	Hull KR	2-24	G	10,572	
20 Apr	Warrington	5-2	T, G	15,565	Ch Cup semi-final (at Swinton)
24 Apr	Leeds	6-8	dnp	17,172	
27 Apr	**Warrington**	3-26	dnp	9,853	
29 Apr	St Helens	16-15	T, 5G	12,830	
1 May	**Castleford**	23-8	4G	11,762	
4 May	Bramley	10-19	T, 2G	4,707	
11 May	Wigan	25-10	5G	84,492	Ch Cup Final (at Wembley)
14 May	**Bramley**	32-0	T, 4G	9,960	
18 May	Wigan	21-13	G	16,194	
20 May	Huddersfield	5-11	dnp	7,353	
22 May	Castleford	8-21	dnp	9,500	
25 May	**Wigan**	21-8	dnp	9,028	
27 May	Workington T	18-10	dnp	4,500	
29 May	**Huddersfield**	8-3	dnp	9,002	
1 Jun	**Halifax**	7-16	dnp	7,406	

Representative appearances

19 Sep	Yorkshire 11 Cumberland 2 (Workington)	T, G
26 Sep	Yorkshire 22 Lancashire 8 (Wakefield)	5G
1 Nov	Eastern Division XIII 23 France 16 (Carcassonne)	4G
17 Nov	England 18 France 6 (Leeds)	T, 3G
2 Dec	Great Britain 12 France 17 (Perpignan)	T, 3G
3 Apr	Great Britain 42 France 4 (Wigan)	T, 9G

Wakefield Trinity versus Wigan: Neil supporting Fred Smith

Wembley 1963: Another Trinity Challenge Cup triumph.

Family life

Top left: It always seemed to take two to bring Neil down. Jonathan and Mandy
seem to be more than enough to stop the Big Fella.
Top right: The young Foxes – Neil and Molly with Mandy and Jonathan.
Bottom: Molly and Neil introduce Amanda Jayne to the Rugby League Challenge
Cup in May 1963. Neil had told the press that he would bring the Cup home for his
new-born daughter and fulfilled his prediction.

12. 1963-64: Turning down the Australians

There were changes at Belle Vue in the 1963 close season. Neil recalls, "There were two departures after the 1962-63 season and they were both great people. Johnny Jones, my coach when I was in the 'A' team, left, as did Johnny Malpass. He was my coach when I made the first-team. Both gave tremendous service to Trinity and I will always be grateful for the help they gave to me while I was still learning the game. Johnny Jones had 26 years with Wakefield and played in the 1946 Wembley final. I think Johnny Malpass served the club for 27 years as player, coach and as assistant coach to our great team of the early 1960s. When he left Wakefield he went to Featherstone as their first-team coach."

On the playing front Trinity made no major signings for the new season, but Don Metcalfe came out of retirement to play again. Trouble was brewing, however, as the result of the RFL's ruling that clubs could no longer pay bonuses for league fixtures and that winning pay could not be more than double losing pay. This was an early version of salary-capping and was a response to the fall in attendances, a trend which was beginning to accelerate alarmingly in rugby league, as it was across all spectator sports. Despite winning the Cup and playing in the more competitive First Division, Trinity's gate receipts for 1962-63 had fallen by £6,000 on the previous season, when only one league was in operation. Without their pools scheme even such a successful club as Wakefield would have been in trouble. The pools had grossed a phenomenal £242,303 over the last eight years, which had brought in net income of £93,490 directly to Trinity.

The terms the Wakefield players were offered for 1963-64 were £20 for an away win, £16 for a home win, £10 for an away defeat and £8 for a home defeat. The Trinity players stated that they stood to lose £60 each over the season and wanted higher losing pay. By 15 August there had been no agreement and the players continued to refuse to sign on those terms. A group of clubs, the "big five" (Leeds, St Helens, Wakefield, Widnes and Wigan), as they were dubbed, held a meeting and decided to act in concert. There was talk of the players forming a union and even mention of a "super league". However, Leeds quickly settled their affairs and the three Lancashire clubs held another meeting without Trinity. The Trinity players realised that their stance had not gone down well with the fans and eventually accepted the club's terms by the start of the new campaign. The RFL's Management Committee agreed that bonuses for points-scoring would be allowed.

On 24 August the season got off to a bad start with a 33-7 loss at Castleford, Neil kicking a couple of goals. John L. Allen, who had now dropped his nom de plume of 'The Pinder' after many years, was sarcastically forthright, writing, "Mercifully for the Wakefield visitors, the game had to come to an end, thanks to the time limit!" Two days later they made some amends with an 18-7 home victory over Workington, the highlights being a wonderful try from Ken Hirst and storming games from Bob Haigh and Brian Briggs, the latter now operating at open-side prop. Allen commented that "Fox and Greenwood brought their wingers into action most entertainingly." Neil added three goals.

The following Thursday Trinity caused a stir by transfer-listing Fred Smith and Jack Wilkinson. Wilkie responded by announcing his retirement.

On 31 August Neil and his wing partner Gert Coetzer put on a master class in a 20-15 win against Hull at Belle Vue. Trinity led 15-5 at the interval and, according to the *Wakefield Express*, "This was largely due to two tries coming from Fox, who burst through a menacing looking gang of defenders in fantastic style and the other by Coetzer who beat three men in an astonishing run after turning inside from the wing". By the 68th minute Hull had levelled at 15-15 and so "It was left to Fox and Coetzer to pull their side out of the hole by providing between them another wonder try. This arose from the super driving force of Fox, who left a couple of hitherto alert looking defenders rather limp after he had passed them by, and Coetzer's remarkable skill in completing a most satisfactory movement". Neil sealed his team's success with a last-minute penalty.

On 4 September, Trinity went to Halifax and lost 7-5. Wilkie had abandoned his short-lived retirement by now and the game at Thrum Hall was Neil's 250th for Wakefield. He started the move which afforded Ian Brooke the chance to score Trinity's only try and kicked a 55th-minute penalty. However, he sustained an injury to a shoulder joint and spent much of the game on the wing. The injury caused him to miss a superb 9-4 Trinity victory in the Yorkshire Cup at Hunslet where his deputy, debutant David Sampson, had the misfortune to break his collarbone after only 10 minutes. Two days later he was also absent for Trinity's 25-14 win at Bradford in the first of Trinity's Eastern Division fixtures. The RFL had decided to intersperse the Eastern Division fixtures throughout the season rather than play them en bloc at the start of the campaign. The Bradford game had seen second-rower Malcolm Storey's debut, who had been signed from Hull for a reported fee of £4,800. On the other hand, Trinity had listed two more forwards – Briggs and Blakeley.

Neil returned to action at Featherstone on 14 September and scored 11 points in a stirring 14-7 win. In shades of Trinity's previous visit to Post Office Road, Derek Turner was sent off after 17 minutes, Harold Poynton suffered a knee injury and Storey broke two toes. By half-time Neil had kicked two penalties but Rovers led 5-4. Six minutes into the second half Neil exploded into irresistible action. The *Yorkshire Evening News* 'Green Final' reported, "Neil Fox treated the packed house to one of the finest tries ever seen at Post Office Road. There seemed no great danger as the international picked up in midfield just to the left of the Featherstone posts but by brilliant acceleration and the use of the dummy he beat at least five defenders before touching down in the right corner." No-one even laid a finger on Neil. Four minutes later he booted a penalty. Gerry Round got a fine try and Trinity led 12-5. Neil and brother Don exchanged penalties to conclude the scoring.

Four days later Neil was in Yorkshire's team which met the Australians at Craven Park, Hull. Derek Turner was the skipper and Brian Briggs was at blind-side prop. Yorkshire were never in danger and Neil was the best player on view. He kicked four first-half penalties and a try by Keighley stand-off Roy Sabine stretched Yorkshire's lead to 11-0. Australia did not reply until the 72nd minute when winger Ken Irvine streaked over and converted his own try. Alfred Drewry in the *Yorkshire Post* noted: "Fox, whom the Australians will meet in the tests, was head and shoulders above any other back on the field. The Australians, for all their sturdy spoiling, would have been in a bad way had he seen more of the ball." In the *Daily Express*, Jack Bentley wrote, "Twice... Fox showed the tourists what they can expect from him in the tests with magnificent bursts up the middle and he gave the tourists an example of his kicking prowess too". Although the Australians were far from impressive, Neil says, "This Australian side developed into the best I had played against. They were certainly better than the team we played against down under in 1962".

On 21 September Wakefield saw off promoted Keighley 33-5 at Belle Vue, the highlight being a length-of-the-field try by Ian Brooke. Neil landed six goals, but Gert Coetzer received a shoulder injury which kept him inactive for a month.

Two days later it was a different story as Trinity entertained Halifax before a crowd of almost 10,000. The *Wakefield Express* blasted, "Not for the vast majority of those who have frequented Belle Vue for many years will it be possible to recall a more humiliating experience than this one 'earned' by the team on Monday night in the second round of the County Cup." Everything seemed hunky dory when Halifax second-rower Ken Roberts was

130

sent off after 15 minutes for kicking in the scrum. Trinity fans thought their passage into the semi-finals was assured three minutes later, when Halifax prop forward Wyn Phillips was also dismissed for kicking recklessly at a play-the-ball, especially after Neil kicked the resultant penalty. Within 20 minutes Halifax had been reduced to 11 men, but by half-time led 10-2. Trinity could not break their defence down and became more and more frustrated. Their only reward was a 62nd-minute penalty by Neil and that was cancelled out by full-back Ronnie James as Halifax went on to a famous 12-4 victory.

Their expulsion from the Yorkshire Cup in such ignominy was a real shaker and Neil picked up a knee injury which cost him his place in Yorkshire's team to play Cumberland at Wakefield on 25 September. There were no Trinity players in the Yorkshire side as skipper Derek Turner was also ruled out by suspension. The team's next performance at Hull KR was no better. Fox played brilliantly. Unfortunately for Neil, it was his brother Peter in the Rovers' pack! Trinity lost 22-7, Neil scoring all Trinity's points, including a last minute try.

This was a disturbing period for Wakefield, whose form prompted some to query the fitness of the side since the loss of Johnny Malpass. Stuart Hadfield went so far as to call a 'pay parade meeting' at the Thursday training session following the Hull KR debacle and told the press what they already knew: that Trinity were in "a bad patch and had a lack of confidence". Don Vines had not turned up at the meeting and was dropped for the home game against Batley, an Eastern Division fixture, on 5 October. Thankfully, Trinity won 30-6 with Turner in rampaging form and Neil potted six goals. But more unsettling news came when it was reported that Derek Turner was in the frame for the coaching job at Leeds.

On 12 October, Hunslet went down 27-5 at Belle Vue but again it was an unconvincing display by Trinity. Hunslet's scrum-half Garforth was sent off after 20 minutes for persistent offside and by half-time Trinity could only muster a 6-0 lead, courtesy of three goals from Neil, who finished with a tally of 15 points. Keith Holliday was outstanding but Trinity owed the margin of their victory to a purple patch of 12 minutes when they ran in four tries.

Despite Trinity's indifferent form Neil was playing well enough to be selected for the first Ashes test on Wednesday, 16 October. The RFL had decided to try an enterprising move by taking the test to Wembley Stadium and staging a test under floodlights for the first time. The teams for the Wembley Ashes test were:

Great Britain: Ken Gowers (Swinton), Bill Burgess (Barrow), Eric Ashton (Wigan, captain), Neil Fox (Wakefield T), Norman Field (Batley), Dave Bolton (Wigan), Alex Murphy (St Helens), John Tembey (St Helens), Bill Sayer (Wigan), Brian Tyson (Hull KR), Ken Bowman (Huddersfield), Jim Measures (Widnes), Vince Karalius (Widnes).

Australia: Ken Thornett (Parramatta), Ken Irvine (Norths), Graeme Langlands (St George), Reg Gasnier (St George), Peter Dimond (Wests), Earl Harrison (Gilgandra), Barry Muir (Wests, Brisbane), Peter Gallagher (Brothers, Brisbane), Ian Walsh (St George, captain), Noel Kelly (Wests), Dick Thornett (Parramatta), Brian Hambly (Parramatta), Johnny Raper (St George).

Unfortunately, wintry and wet conditions helped neither the handling of a rugby ball nor Wembley's ability to attract a crowd. Only 13,946 rattled about the cavernous stadium, lending a somewhat eerie atmosphere to the proceedings. Neil had not really been impressed by the team selection. He says, "I could not believe only five of the 1962 Lions had been picked for the game. That was the old problem we had when a selection committee decided test teams."

A Langlands penalty goal gave the Kangaroos an early lead and from the 18th minute Britain were a man short when Bolton had to retire with a sprung shoulder. The other half-back Murphy struggled for 66 minutes with a broken nose. Soon after Bolton departed Britain equalised when Neil landed a prodigious 50-yard penalty goal, the ball bouncing on the bar. In the last six minutes of the half Australia rushed to a 10-2 lead with tries from

Thornett and Langlands. The second half saw a depleted Britain concede another four tries and they lost 28-2. The star of the show was Reg Gasnier, who scored three dazzling tries and in so doing became the first man to score a hat-trick in two Ashes tests.

Neil's next game was not much happier. On 19 October, Trinity journeyed to Wigan. Neil opened the scoring with a sixth minute penalty and closed it in the 78th when he converted his own try. In between Wigan ran in 31 unanswered points, all seven of their tries coming from the threequarters. It was a genuine good hiding for Trinity.

Neil came up against the Australians again on 26 October, when 15,821 were present and hoping for another famous Wakefield victory over the tourists. After the game the Kangaroos received a civic reception at the Town Hall and the half-time interval was extended from five to 10 minutes for a gathering and photograph of Trinity's old Lions, including Tommy Newbould, who toured in 1910, and Jonty Parkin, who skippered the Lions in 1924 and 1928. Neil and his 1962 Lions colleagues were also in the photograph but heaven knows what they were thinking in view of what happened in the match itself.

The *Wakefield Express* reported, "There was football of excellence, equalled by some fighting that might have been great entertainment in less civilised places." In the 70th minute the game erupted in a disgraceful brawl. Play was seven or eight yards from Trinity's goal line when "All of a sudden, as if they had heard a starter's pistol shot, half a dozen or more players from each side broke into riotous conduct, with fists swinging merrily, but apparently not too skilfully for there were no severely damaged casualties. Nevertheless, it was pandemonium, or, in other words, the 'abode of demons' was a most appropriate description for the loathsome affair." As the players scrapped half a dozen policemen, including an inspector and a sergeant, moved in to break up the proceedings. Six minutes later another flare-up between the packs occurred and this time the referee, Mr D. S. Brown of Dewsbury sent off the Kangaroos' hooker and captain, Ian Walsh, who refused to leave the field for the best part of two minutes.

When the players were not fighting there was some classic rugby especially from the Australians, who triumphed 29-14. Neil gave a superlative exhibition of goalkicking, with seven goals from seven attempts, and was often dangerous on attack. However, this was another game which showcased Reg Gasnier's genius. He scored two tries, as did winger Ken Irvine, while Graeme Langlands scored a try and kicked seven goals from nine shots.

Off the field there was a boost for the club when Derek Turner was appointed assistant coach to Ken Traill but that was tempered by the need for Turner to undergo surgery on his knee ligaments. Trinity were still in the hunt for a centre partner for Neil and were reported to be interested in St Helens's Brian McGinn but the only movement was that of Trinity's own centre Roy Bell, who left for Featherstone.

Wakefield got back on the winning path on 9 November with a narrow victory at Workington where Neil, most unusually, failed to score, and the following week convincingly beat Huddersfield at Fartown. Neil was missing from the latter match as he was in the Great Britain centre for the second test at Swinton. Happy Australia made just two changes from their Wembley team, Paul Quinn replacing Peter Gallagher at prop and Ken Day coming in for Brian Hambly in the second row. Britain were forced to make several changes and their situation was made worse when three original pack choices – Derek Turner, Dick Huddart and Brian Edgar – had to withdraw. Mick Sullivan of York and Swinton's John Stopford were brought on to the wings, while Frank Myler replaced the injured Bolton at stand-off. Of the Wembley pack only the Widnes pair, Measures and Karalius, survived. An entirely new front row of Bill Robinson of Leigh, Len McIntyre of

Oldham and Cliff Watson of St Helens was introduced and Ron Morgan of Swinton came into the second row.

If the crowd of 30,843 expected better things of Great Britain, they were sorely disappointed. Britain's luck was non-existent. Once again they were savagely hit by injury. Myler lasted only 20 minutes before rib damage caused his retirement and another rib injury caused the loss of skipper Ashton, who missed some of the first half and all the second. As substitutions were not allowed, Australia had a field day, cruising to a record 50-12 victory and to the Ashes for the first time in Britain since 1911-12. Langlands bagged an Ashes record-equalling 20 points from seven goals and two tries, while the other Kangaroo threequarters, Irvine with three, Gasnier and Dimond, with two each, contributed another seven tries. Harrison, Kelly and Thornett added further touchdowns.

Neil had actually sparked Great Britain into a 10th-minute lead when he dashed 60 yards, and was caught by Irvine but managed to pass to Stopford who scored as fine a try as could be imagined. Just before the break Neil converted another try by Measures. Unfortunately, by this time it only brought the score back to 31-8. All Britain could muster in the second half was two penalties from Neil. Neil has unhappy memories of the game. He says, "There were another seven changes in the team. This seemed to happen in most test matches I played in. Too many selectors chose their own men. Consequently, we often failed to put out our best side. And with no substitutes being allowed it was no wonder Australia got their record score. I was dropped for the final test at Leeds three weeks later, along with nine other players. Our Don was picked at loose-forward and with no injuries for a change Britain won a ferocious match 16-5."

A heavy cold kept Neil out of Trinity's narrow loss at Widnes on 23 November, by which time Trinity had signed Geoff Wraith, a 17-year-old star of the future from Belle Isle Youth Club and captain of Leeds City Juniors. They had also sensationally agreed the transfer of Hull centre Dick Gemmell for a fee amounting to £11,000, which would be a record for both clubs. However, just when it seemed that an experienced and talented co-centre had been found for Neil, the deal fell through.

After a month without a game Neil reappeared on 7 December for St Helens's visit to Belle Vue. It was a desperately close encounter with all the try-scoring in the first half, Gerry Round claiming one for Trinity, who trailed 8-3 at the break. Saints, however, scored two tries within four minutes, the first from Peter Harvey in the 27th minute, quickly followed by a stunner from Alex Murphy, who stole in to intercept a pass from Holliday to Vines at a play-the-ball. Trinity players and fans protested that he must have been offside because no one was so quick. Neil dragged Trinity back to 8-7 with two penalties but failed to win the game with two drop-goal attempts. The first struck one post, ricocheted onto the opposite post and agonisingly dropped on the wrong side of the crossbar.

At this stage in the season Trinity occupied seventh position in Division One and were boosted by three excellent victories in the remaining weeks of December. At Keighley Neil shone in a 26-14 success marked by excellent teamwork and a refreshing monopoly of possession. Neil banged over four goals and scored a try, his 200th in first-class games. On Boxing Day Wakefield went to Headingley for an 11am kick-off. The newly installed electric under-soil heating ensured the game went ahead although the pitch was very muddy. The mud did not bother Trinity or Neil. In a delightfully brisk and entertaining fashion Leeds were despatched 32-8. The *Wakefield Express* wrote, "Fox provided some of the afternoon's greatest sensations. The way this supposedly 'slow' player several times left the 'speed' men in the opposition trailing when in pursuit of his four tries which, with four goal kicks, afforded him 20 points was something as laughable as it was productive." Although the game was described as "pleasantly contested", Leeds's centre Ron Cowan's nose was broken in a brush with Rocky Turner.

Two days later Trinity and Leeds, minus the dropped Lewis Jones, met at Belle Vue. Trinity were again imperious, with Colin Greenwood registering three tries in a 24-2 triumph. Neil landed three goals but just before half-time tore his knee ligaments. He went to full-back but finally left the field after 68 minutes. He missed the next four games.

There was a fair amount of coming and going at Belle Vue in January. Rudy Hasse, a South African forward, was signed from Bradford Northern, the club that had recently given up the ghost and resigned from the league. More forward power was added with the signing of second-rower Fred Turnbull from Halifax, but on the debit side Roger Pearman left for Australia to take up a teaching post, while Malcolm Sampson was transfer-listed at £6,000. In Neil's absence Trinity lost three out of four games in January at Warrington, astonishingly at Doncaster in the Eastern Division, and at Hunslet. In between, on 11 January, there was a fine 9-8 win at home to Castleford when Turnbull, Geoff Wraith and prop Derek Plumstead made their debuts. It was also Pearman's finale, with Roger filling in at left centre for Neil. Ken Rollin made his last appearance for Wakefield in this game while Fred Smith ostensibly played his last game but, after playing amateur rugby league, made a comeback in October 1965. Finally, Milan Kosanovic, the answer to Trinity's prayers as a ball-winner, was transferred to Featherstone just before the Challenge Cup register closed.

Neil was deliberately left out of the team so that he could be fit for the Challenge Cup ties. He reappeared for the televised home game against Wigan on 1 February, when he was partnered in the centres by Willis Rushton, who had cost £4,250 from Bramley. Rushton was an excellent footballer, who would give some outstanding performances in Trinity's colours. Unfortunately, the Wigan game was narrowly lost and Trinity went into the Challenge Cup having lost four out of their last five games. Viscount Montgomery sent the club a letter prior to the first-round tie at Hunslet on 8 February ordering the Trinitarians to retain the Challenge Cup. Cup fever was definitely in the air and Parkside's biggest crowd for years, just fewer than 20,000, paid record ground receipts of £2,707. A bright, sunny afternoon seemed to favour Trinity and they did deserve to win, but had to settle for a 4-4 draw, their replay being owed to Neil, who calmly kicked a penalty nine minutes from time. Lack of possession probably cost Trinity the tie although the old guard of Wilkinson, Briggs and Turner had played themselves into the ground.

Trinity paid their players £25 for their draw at Parkside and they had high hopes of making ground advantage pay at Belle Vue, where victory would have meant pay packets of £32. This time Wakefield won the scrums but found themselves down 5-2 at half-time, after Neil's penalty goal had drawn first blood. In the second half Hunslet's forward power and some fine football proved too much for Trinity, who were finally beaten 14-7. It was reported that "Neil Fox occasionally promised to pull the game out of the fire but Hunslet's tackling was too good." The dream of a third consecutive Wembley victory was dashed at the first hurdle and it was a chastened Trinity side which drew their £8 losing money.

The Hunslet cup tie proved to be Jack Wilkinson's last appearance for Wakefield and more bad news followed when Don Vines and Ken Rollin announced they were retiring, while Colin Greenwood revealed that he was going to join North Sydney. Neil was very sorry to see Ken Rollin bow out of Belle Vue. Ken had been a great player, in both half-back positions, for Trinity with more than 200 appearances to his credit. They had been friends since childhood and in 1963 Neil had been best man at Ken's wedding. He recalls, "During my speech I presented Ken with a box. On opening it he found a pot lion. All the players who were present fell about laughing. The rest of the guests just looked blank, though, until I explained about the incident with the peeing lion after Wembley in 1960. I think Ken had forgotten all about it until he opened the box."

On 15 February, Neil had a big part in Trinity's 18-0 home win over Dewsbury in the Eastern Division, claiming two tries and three goals. He was, however, disappointed not to be selected for Great Britain's trip to Perpignan on 8 March, nor was any other Wakefield man. The centres were Warrington's Keith Holden and Swinton's Alan Buckley, while the travelling reserve back was Hunslet centre Geoff Shelton. Don Fox was selected at loose-forward. By a strange quirk of fate, Don had to withdraw from the test team, while Neil was promoted to travelling reserve, after Holden pulled out and Shelton took his place.

On 29 February, because of postponed fixtures, Trinity fielded a strong 'A' Team at Hull, when Neil kicked three goals in an 18-11 win.

The following week, while Neil was in France watching Britain win 11-5, Trinity beat Hull KR 35-8. Colin Greenwood captained the side in his last appearance for Wakefield. Neil's next appointment was for Great Britain against France at Leigh on 18 March, when he was restored as centre partner to Shelton. Neil had another field day against the French, who were thumped 39-0, despite holding the British to a 7-0 half-time lead. Neil equalled his own test record with 21 points, giving another master class in goalkicking with nine goals from nine attempts. He also bagged a try – "a block-buster replete with dummy – carved out by Tommy Smales", according to Allan Cave in the *Daily Herald*.

Trinity were in the middle of another three-week break and so once again Neil had an outing with the 'A' team, kicking four goals in a 45-0 hammering of Batley's 'A' team at Belle Vue on 21 March. His dynamic centre play carved out chance after chance for the wingers, Gerry Mann and Dennis Atkinson, who scored seven tries between them. His first game for six weeks for Trinity followed on 28 March at Dewsbury in an Eastern Division fixture. Trinity won 23-8 in extremely miserable weather conditions of cold, wind and rain but Neil was in mesmeric form. Trinity scored four tries in the first half to lead 18-0 and Neil's potent mixture of deception, dummies and destructiveness had produced three of them for Rushton, Coetzer and Round, while he also added three goals. One reporter was moved to note: "Brave tacklers bounced off him like peas off armour".

Two days later at Fartown there were no tries for anyone, not even Neil. The only points of an incident-packed match came from Huddersfield full-back Brian Curry's 65th-minute penalty goal. A young amateur hooker, George Shepherd, made his debut for Trinity and, strangely, the Wakefield forwards had seemed intent on making it a game in which backs were mere spectators. Neil's usual left winger Gert Coetzer was moved over to the right wing for this match and Neil was given the responsibility of looking after 'Walker', a trialist from Wales. 'Walker' hardly got a sniff of the ball until the 70th minute, when he was put in possession and flew like the proverbial bat out of hell, completely taking the crowd, officials and players by surprise. He outstripped everyone on the field but just as he seemed certain to score, Curry, running a much shorter distance, somehow managed to nudge him over the touchline. Neil says, "He was the fastest man I had ever seen on a rugby pitch. The next day we played at Doncaster, winning 44-3 in an Eastern Division game. The trialist scored a good try but we did not see much of the ball on our wing. He did show though that he could make it in rugby league, even though he had never played the game before." 'Walker' scored his try in the 19th minute, going like a bolt from a crossbow for the corner, but it was Gert Coetzer on the right wing that really caught the eye with five tries in his own inimitable style.

Wakefield signed 'Walker' after the Doncaster match and the *Wakefield Express* of 4 April blared: "A Super Speed Merchant Arrives at Belle Vue". The new signing was definitely big news, a genuine sensation. He was Berwyn Jones, at that time the fourth fastest man in the world. He had traded the possibility of a gold medal at the Tokyo Olympics for a fee of between £6,000 and £8,000. Jones had run 9.4 seconds for the 100 yards and was joint British record holder for the 100 metres at 10.3 seconds. He was the AAA champion and had represented Great Britain in the European Games and Wales at the Commonwealth Games, where he took a bronze medal. He had run in seven internationals for Great Britain and was a member of the British 4 x 110 yards team which set a new world record in 1963. A PE teacher in Birmingham, he had a good, sturdy physique and had played rugby union some years before for Rhymney, so he was not a complete novice.

The full glare of publicity now descended upon Wakefield for Jones's next match against Halifax on 4 April. Trinity reaped the benefits almost immediately with the first league gate of the season to produce receipts of more than £1,000 at Belle Vue. The Halifax cover ensured that Jones did not touch the ball in the first 40 minutes, after which Trinity led 8-5. In fact it was not until the 71st minute that he handled it from a misdirected Halifax pass. In the meantime Wakefield crushed their opponents 38-10. John L. Allen noted: "One of the afternoon's most thrilling features [was] seeing the majestic power and sometimes extraordinarily convincing artistry from the stolid Fox. He was at his best in the second half when Halifax was routed... There were times when it was quite obvious Fox was to send a pass to Jones – and then he didn't do anything of the sort! There were occasions when he could have passed to Jones and left the Welshman to sort things out when he was simply covered. But the crafty Fox was alert enough to the prevailing circumstances. He appeared to be a thought reader as far as the Halifax defence was concerned! It was a great display by the man on whom much attention is being focused at the moment on account of rumours emanating from Australia... His 20 points, from seven goals and two tries, was fitting reward for a great show."

The rumours from Australia were just as sensational, in Wakefield at least, as had been the signing of Jones. Writing in the *Yorkshire Evening News*, Arthur Haddock ran an article under the headline, "Not less than £15,000 for Fox – Chairman". He wrote, "As Wakefield Trinity today announced the signing... of Berwyn Jones... the Sydney club Parramatta stepped in with an inquiry about Neil Fox, Trinity's test centre. The approach... came this morning. It was made, said Wakefield chairman Mr Stuart Hadfield, by a contact on behalf of the Parramatta club. Mr Hadfield was asked if Trinity would put a price on their 24-year-old record scorer. 'I told the contact that Trinity would not take a penny less than £15,000 sterling. We certainly do not want to lose Fox, but if we have to let him go through emigration we would not dream of accepting less than that amount'. The contact, I understand, is a Leeds solicitor who has handled nearly all the Australian deals."

Neil explains his situation thus: "After the Aussies had won the test series I got a telephone call from Ronnie Teeman, a Leeds solicitor acting as an agent for Parramatta, asking if I would be interested in going to Australia for a couple of years. He wanted to know if I could find out how much Wakefield would want for a transfer fee. I went to Mr Hadfield to find out and he said, '£10,000 but why do you want to go?' I told him, 'I am very interested and it would be a good experience for me and a great challenge'.

I contacted Ronnie and told him what the chairman had said. I left it with him and he later came back saying that the fee would be OK and that I would get a £5,000 signing fee for two seasons, plus match fees and a job. This would have been a really good contract for me as I would only be earning about £1,000 a season with Trinity. So with this offer I was able to go back to the chairman and tell him I was very interested in accepting it. Mr Hadfield then asked me to ask Ronnie to contact him. Then the chairman changed his mind and asked for £15,000. But Parramatta would not pay so much with my contract money on top of it. I must admit I was disappointed with Mr Hadfield for changing his mind on the fee. So I just went away to get on with the job in hand, which was helping Trinity, as I have always done. I did not want to rock the boat, because in another 12 months I was due a benefit at the club."

The relief among Wakefield fans that Neil would be staying was almost palpable. J. C. Lindley was happy too, writing in the *Rugby Leaguer*: "Fox's form since he returned to the international scene against France... has been tremendous. Back with all his old confidence, using that power and skill, which combines into such an awesome sight for defences, his partnership with Jones could grow into one of the greatest our game has known ... His work at present is such that he looks to be emphasising his value to the club with every move. Certainly it makes a fee of £15,000... look very small compensation indeed for the tremendous loss Trinity would suffer." Lindley also pointed out that a future with Trinity may well hold the probability of captaining the club and Great Britain, selection for the scheduled 1965 World Cup and for the 1966 Australasian tour, not forgetting "a chance to carve his name even deeper into the records of rugby league football. Those chances are bright – and so indeed is a benefit of record-breaking proportions".

When all the fuss died down, Trinity got back into action at St Helens on 11 April but went down 24-10. Neil's long pass put Coetzer over for the opening score but by the 48th minute they trailed 24-3. Saints scored two tries from interceptions, the first by forward Ray French being something of a surprise. The second, less surprisingly, was from Alex Murphy and effectively won the match. There was better luck, for a change, at Batley. Trinity's 38-11 success meant that they qualified for a play-off place in the Eastern Division Championship. Gert Coetzer produced another five-try performance but the highlight was a stupendous try from Berwyn Jones. He snapped up a loose ball near Trinity's goal-line and kicked ahead. His pace left everyone gasping as he regathered and dived under the posts after a sprint of almost 100 yards, but there were no television cameras or hordes of press photographers present. Previously they had been following him around to each game. Neil claimed a try and kicked four goals, the third of which was his 900th for the club.

On 18 April Neil touched his best form in a 24-8 home win against Warrington, when Rudy Hasse made his first-team debut. Six days later Trinity surprisingly went down 21-16 at Hull. The lead changed hands five times but, to many observers, Trinity only stayed in the game because of Neil's brilliance. Bob Haigh was stretchered off after 35 minutes and Hull, who had won only twice in the league, had overwhelming possession and a great leader in Johnny Whiteley. Neil twice scattered the Hull defence for tries and made another for Rushton. His two conversions meant that Trinity led 13-9 at one point but two late long-range penalty goals from Eric Broome finally killed off Wakefield.

A 20-10 victory over Widnes at Belle Vue followed, to which Neil contributed 11 points before Trinity got their final chance of silverware at Halifax in the semi-final of the Eastern Division Championship on 2 May. Although Trinity led 12-8 at the break, Neil having kicked three goals, there was to be no fairytale ending to the season. Halifax struck back with 13 unanswered points within nine minutes of the restart to win 25-12 and reinforce the reputation of Thrum Hall as Wakefield's bogey ground. J. C. Lindley wrote in the *Rugby Leaguer*: "Fox... must have been sadly frustrated by the service from half-back... It is a sad thing to see such match-winning talent as his and Jones's wasted."

On 13 May, Swinton visited Belle Vue, hot on the trail of a second consecutive First Division Championship. They beat Trinity 12-7 after a ferocious encounter, punctuated by some disgraceful scenes. The referee, F. J. Howker of Rochdale, was described as "the most tolerant referee seen this season". The *Wakefield Express* fumed, "The outstanding performer on the field was Fox. He was in the honours class. Without his brilliant exhibition during most of the game, what role Trinity would have played in this unsporting affair would, perhaps, best be left to the imagination rather than described in words." Neil kicked two goals in the first half, the first his 100th of the season for Wakefield.

A week later Trinity faced Featherstone Rovers at Belle Vue. Although neither team had anything tangible to play for, much interest focused on the struggle between Neil and his brother Don, because they occupied the top two positions in the leading scorers' list. Prior to the clash Don had 301 points and Neil 296. Unfortunately for Don he was forced off the field after 31 minutes with a groin injury when Trinity led 3-0 after a try by Gerry Mann. Eight minutes later Keith Holliday snaffled a fine try which Neil converted. Two minutes into the second half Neil converted his own try, taking him to 303 points and past Don's total. He added a further penalty goal and Trinity ran out easy winners 21-0.

The final game of a long season on 23 May took Trinity to Swinton, who had retained their league title. Unlike their torrid clash of 10 days before, this was a spectacularly bright and open game with the result always in the balance. After half an hour Trinity led 4-0, thanks to two goals from Neil, but scintillating tries from Ken Gowers and Bobbie Fleet pushed the Lions into a 12-4 lead. Just before the interval Willis Rushton wove his way through for a brilliant try, equally brilliantly converted by Neil from the touchline. On 45 minutes Ted Campbell bulldozed over for a try and Neil converted for a 14-12 lead. Swinton skipper Albert Blan levelled with a penalty after 66 minutes and then Neil was a victim of a baffling decision by the referee, J. Hebblethwaite. Neil was in full flight for the Swinton line when his ankle was clipped by a tackler and down he went. Neil was quickly back on his feet and passed to Roy Hawksley who would have scored. The referee seemed happy with the pass, indicating that Neil had not been held by the tackler but, on the intervention of a touch judge, Mr Hebblethwaite penalised Neil and the chance of victory dissipated. Five minutes from time Blan dropped a match-winning goal for the champions.

The 1963-64 season had seen Trinity finish seventh in Division One and third in the Eastern Division Championship, not disastrous performances at all. However, with their early dismissals from the Yorkshire and Challenge Cups, Trinity had failed to win a trophy for the first time since 1957-58. By their own standards, this was failure. Neil's personal performances had often been splendid and Australian taunts that he was 'over the hill', emanating from the departing 1963 Kangaroos' tour manager, rang curiously hollow for those who had seen him play regularly. He finished top of the league's scorers with 313 points, 12 ahead of Don and 22 ahead of Kel Coslett of St Helens. Coslett topped the goalkickers' list with 138, followed by Oldham's Frank Dyson on 135, Don on 131 and Neil, Wigan's Laurie Gilfedder and Hunslet's Billy Langton, who all landed 125.

Unfortunately for Wakefield there was an excess of over-the-hill personnel at Belle Vue, as the great team of previous years grew older, retired or left. There was great disappointment at the close of the season when Derek Turner, leader of the great Trinity sides of the period, retired. That was indeed a major loss. Also leaving the club to join the newly reformed Bradford Northern were Jack Wilkinson, as player-coach, and Ian Brooke, who cost the Odsal club £2,750. Neil considered the departure of Brooke as a real blow to the club, recalling, "Ian had a couple of pulled muscles during this season and was told this was always going to be his let down. But he proved people wrong because he later went on to tour Australia in 1966 and also played with me for Great Britain in the centres."

Wakefield Trinity 1963-64

Wakefield Trinity finished 7th in Division 1: P30, W16, L14, For 488, Against 339
Fox scored 20 tries, 108 goals, 276 points for Wakefield, and 1 try, 17 goals, 37 points in representative games

Date	Opponent	Score	Fox	Crowd	
24 Aug	Castleford	7-33	2G	10,200	
26 Aug	**Workington T**	18-7	3G	8,514	
31 Aug	**Hull**	20-15	T, 4G	10,200	
4 Sep	Halifax	5-7	G	7,466	
7 Sep	Hunslet	9-4	dnp	7,800	YC1
9 Sep	Bradford N	25-14	dnp	1,686	ED
14 Sep	Featherstone R	14-7	T, 4G	10,453	
21 Sep	**Keighley**	33-5	6G	8,631	
23 Sep	**Halifax**	4-12	2G	9,954	YC2
28 Sep	Hull KR	7-22	T, 2G	8,811	
5 Oct	**Batley**	30-6	6G	6,767	ED
12 Oct	**Hunslet**	27-5	T, 6G	9,832	
19 Oct	Wigan	7-31	T, 2G	15,075	
26 Oct	**Australians**	14-29	7G	15,821	
2 Nov	Workington T	9-2		3,940	
9 Nov	**Huddersfield**	28-2	dnp	5,540	
23 Nov	Widnes	3-7	dnp	5,065	
7 Dec	**St Helens**	7-8	2G	8,137	
14 Dec	Keighley	26-14	T, 4G	1,675	
26 Dec	Leeds	32-8	4T, 4G	10,729	
28 Dec	**Leeds**	24-2	3G	8,163	
1 Jan	Warrington	12-21	dnp	7,152	
4 Jan	Doncaster	6-9	dnp	1,680	ED
11 Jan	**Castleford**	9-8	dnp	8,656	
25 Jan	Hunslet	7-12	dnp	7,675	
1 Feb	**Wigan**	8-12	G	9,534	
8 Feb	Hunslet	4-4	2G	19,932	Ch Cup 1
12 Feb	**Hunslet**	7-14	2G	20,822	Replay
15 Feb	**Dewsbury**	18-0	2T, 3G	5,065	ED
7 Mar	**Hull KR**	35-8	dnp	4,856	
28 Mar	Dewsbury	23-8	4G	3,600	ED
30 Mar	Huddersfield	0-2		5,472	
31 Mar	**Doncaster**	44-3	T, 4G	5,440	ED
4 Apr	**Halifax**	38-10	2T, 7G	10,696	
11 Apr	St Helens	10-24	2G	11,122	
15 Apr	Batley	38-11	T, 4G	3,500	ED
18 Apr	**Warrington**	24-8	3G	8,412	
24 Apr	Hull	16-21	2T, 2G	8,000	
29 Apr	**Widnes**	20-10	T, 4G	7,541	
2 May	Halifax	12-21	3G	7,961	ED semi
13 May	**Swinton**	7-12	2G	7,773	
20 May	**Featherstone R**	21-0	T, 3G	8,282	
23 May	Swinton	14-16	4G	8,350	

Representative appearances

18 Sep	Yorkshire 11 Australians 5 (Hull KR)	4G	
16 Oct	Great Britain 2 Australia 28 (Wembley)	G	
9 Nov	Great Britain 12 Australia 50 (Swinton)	3G	
18 Mar	Great Britain 39 France 0 (Leigh)	T, 9G	

Great Britain training: Neil Fox, Eric Ashton, Mick Sullivan and Billy Boston.

Neil scoring against Leeds, as Ken Thornett attempts to tackle him.

13. 1964-65: Captain Dreadnought

The 1964-65 season presented fans, officials, clubs and players with a new landscape. Back in February the clubs had voted 23-4 in favour of reverting to one league and scrapping the divisional championships. Most clubs were in financial difficulties and their situation had not been helped by the formation of two divisions. Bradford Northern, of course, was the most extreme example of the fall in fortunes of the game. However, they had reformed and were included in the fixtures for 1964-65. Even at a club as successful as Wakefield, the danger flags were hoisted when they announced a loss on the past season of £3,748. In order to create more interest for more teams, a top-16 competition was instituted to decide the champions, and the Lancashire and Yorkshire Championships were also revived.

The minimum admission fee was raised from half a crown (12½p) to three shillings (15p) but clubs were still able to set their own tariffs for pensioners, women and schoolchildren. On the field there was also to be considerable change. Substitutes would be allowed but only two per team, they were to be used only for genuinely injured players and only before half-time. This also meant that many Yorkshire clubs, including Trinity, could no longer allow loose-forwards to wear number 14 jerseys instead of 13. After a score had been registered, all kick-offs were now to be place kicks. Previously a drop-kick was taken if a try had not been converted. The draconian measure of conceding a penalty was introduced if any kick-off (from the centre, '25' or goal-line) did not travel 10 yards forward or if the kick went straight into touch. At penalty kicks the offending team now had to retire 10 yards from the mark, reversing the previous practice. Finally, the tap penalty was no longer permitted. These changes had the effect of increasing the number of scrums and increasing the number of goals kicked.

There were also alterations to the law regarding dead-balls. The five yard scrum was abolished and in its place there was to be a drop-out from under the posts, if the defending team had made the ball dead, or a 25-yard drop-out, if the attacking side had done so. The scrummaging laws were altered to ensure that the ball emerged from between the second-row and loose-forward – theoretically.

There was also plenty of change at Belle Vue. Most significantly, Derek Turner's retirement meant the elevation of Neil to the captaincy. Don Vines, having abandoned retirement, became vice-captain and pack leader. Neil says: "Replacing Derek Turner was going to be impossible. For the last decade he had been the best forward in the game and that was not just my opinion. A lot of players who had come up against him would agree. Being captain was a real honour for me. Don Vines, the vice-captain had plenty to do around this time. He had taken up professional wrestling and sometimes did work as an extra on television. He was also a bailiff and I don't think he would have had any trouble collecting outstanding debts."

Neil was certainly a popular choice as the new captain. 'Leftfooter' (alias Father Finn) in the *Rugby Leaguer*, wrote: "A pleasing feature is the appointment of Neil Fox as captain, as I feel he will respond to the responsibility and will bring out his best qualities. His intelligent approach to the game will blossom forth into new fruit. There are still one or two heights left for Neil to assail and shrewd captaincy can lead to these". One of Neil's main targets was to earn selection in Great Britain's World Cup squad for New Zealand and Australia in May and June of 1965. A more immediate aim, however, was to help Ken Traill mould a new Trinity capable of reaching similar standards to the recent past. He had a very young pack, which would obviously take time to gel, but there was a good nucleus of talented players on which to build success. Thankfully, there was no pay dispute to deal with, the players having accepted terms of £14 for a home win, £16 for an away win and £6 for a defeat. There was, however, a strange variation in team selection procedure. As usual the team would be selected on Tuesday evenings but instead of a fixed four-man (plus the coach) selection committee, all committee-men who were on the spot at training sessions would now be allowed a say instead of being silent observers. It was a system which did not last very long.

Although Neil was still only 25 years-old, he was now the leading points scorer still playing in the British game, having amassed 2,913 points in first-class rugby league. The previous holder of this distinction, Lewis Jones, had joined Wentworthville in Australia. Lewis had departed with a tally of 3,445 points to his credit. Remarkably, only three other men in the entire history of the game had scored more points than Neil – Jimmy Ledgard (3,279), Gus Risman (4,055) and Jim Sullivan (6,022). Ledgard, Jones and even Risman were clearly in Neil's sights but no-one seriously considered Sullivan's monumental total to be threatened, even by a player as prolific as Neil.

Trinity's first game on 22 August was a tough encounter at Castleford. The *Wakefield Express* did not mince its words, denouncing it as "a game of many handling mistakes, interminable scrummage infringements, poor goal-kicking and vicious tackling". That aside, Trinity were unlucky to merely draw 7-7. Harold Poynton was sent off in the 58th minute with his team 7-4 in front. Harold had retaliated against a Castleford forward but the referee only saw the retaliation. Castleford's equalising try was scored nine minutes from time. Trinity's earlier try came after Neil had kicked, followed up and tackled full-back Derek Edwards so hard that the ball came loose for Willis Rushton to score. Neil converted and added a 47th-minute penalty but had to be happy with the draw.

Two days later Trinity's new scrum-half signing from Widnes, Ray Owen, made his debut against Dewsbury at Belle Vue. Neil recalls, "Ray was a really good buy for £2,000. We couldn't understand why Widnes let him go." Ray had a good debut but Wakefield were abysmal, losing 12-10 to a converted try three minutes before the final whistle. Neil could certainly have expected a better start to the new campaign.

There was an improvement against Doncaster on 29 August. Trinity won 28-4 and Neil claimed 13 points. John L. Allen noted, "It was good to see Fox, after a quiet start to the season, coming more into his own." Neil sent Gert Coetzer over for the first try and then scored himself from an interception to set up a 12-4 interval lead. Interestingly, Wakefield had moved Berwyn Jones from left wing to the right, having realised that he had a natural side-step off his right foot, which had previously caused him to step into touch on occasions. From now on Coetzer would be Neil's regular winger. Jones certainly benefited from the change, scoring two tries and gaining Neil a couple of penalty goals after Jones was obstructed.

On 2 September it was back to square one as Halifax beat Wakefield 10-6 at Thrum Hall, Trinity's only scores being three penalties from Neil. Three days later and there was almost another disaster at Crown Flatt in the first round of the Yorkshire Cup. Despite a big advantage in possession Trinity were "too bad to be true", according to the *Wakefield Express*. George Shepherd scored their only try after 57 minutes. Neil's conversion, his third goal of the afternoon, brought Trinity back into contention at 10-9 but it was not until the 76th minute that the great escape materialised. At that juncture Wakefield received a highly debatable penalty, when a Wakefield player appeared to run offside at a Dewsbury play-the-ball. Dewsbury fumbled a pass as a consequence and scrum-half Alvin Newall picked up the ball in an offside position. Referee R. L. Thomas of Oldham awarded Trinity a penalty, which Neil coolly converted to win the tie 11-10. As so often, the *Wakefield*

Express mused, it was "left to Neil Fox to drag his side out of the doldrums". Dewsbury were far from happy and immediately after Neil kicked the goal, the referee sent off their stand-off Gwyn Davies, who allegedly abused and threatened to hit him. Stones were thrown by infuriated Dewsbury supporters and police had to escort the referee from the field. Davies received a *sine die* ban, despite never having been dismissed before, although it was lifted on appeal in April 1965.

On 9 September, Neil was the solitary Wakefield representative in Yorkshire's 14-6 win against Cumberland at Whitehaven. He put Yorkshire into the lead with a penalty in the eighth minute but failed with three other shots before Cyril Kellett took over the goalkicking. After Yorkshire had fallen 3-2 behind it was Neil who swept over for their first try after good work by Alan Hardisty. Three days later Wakefield crushed Keighley 46-5 at Belle Vue. Berwyn Jones scored a scintillating hat-trick, his first for Trinity, Gerry Round played majestically at full-back and Neil had a new centre partner in debutant Derek Woolley, a former England under-19 captain. More significantly, Neil bagged 25 points, equalling his own shared club record by kicking 11 goals from 13 attempts. He would have broken the record if one of his shots had gone in instead of out when it smacked the post.

A tough second-round Yorkshire Cup tie followed at Featherstone on 16 September. Rovers led 5-2 at the break but five minutes into the second half Jones recorded a truly staggering try which brought the crowd to its feet. He received a pass on Rovers' '25' and, as a posse of coverers arrived, he shot inside with a mind-blowing burst of speed, leaving four men for dead and scoring under the posts. Neil converted and Trinity never lost the lead again, despite losing the scrums 20-7. Twelve minutes from time Neil and Harold Poynton put Bob Haigh in under the posts and then Neil put the seal on a 15-5 victory with a typically thunderous 50-yard try.

A routine 31-15 home win against York proved costly for Neil. He claimed a crashing try in the 10th minute but then tore a hamstring and retired on the hour. The injury deprived him of the honour of captaining Yorkshire for the first time in the Roses Match at Hull on 23 September, when Yorkshire clinched the County Championship. He also missed Trinity's next league match at Bramley but was declared fit for the Yorkshire Cup semi-final at Huddersfield on 30 September. Trinity were clearly desperate to have their match-winner on the field but might have been better advised to have left him out. The result was fine. Trinity won 7-0 and Neil's 27th-minute 50-yard penalty goal was a real morale booster for Wakefield. However, his leg went again and he retired just before the interval. Trinity performed heroics in the second half and displayed outstanding team spirit, despite being unable to get any possession. John L. Allen was so impressed he wrote, "Not for years has a Wakefield side tackled so well". In injury time Keith Holliday, now enjoying an Indian summer at loose-forward, sliced through for the only try of the tie and Round converted.

Neil was ruled out of the next three games, a narrow loss at Featherstone, yet another disaster at Mount Pleasant where a weakened Batley held Trinity 4-4, and a tense home victory over Halifax. It was not good form and Trinity officials became voluble about affairs at Belle Vue. Stuart Hadfield went on the rampage to the press about the dreadful obstruction tactics teams were employing to stop Berwyn Jones from running, while Ken Traill went public on his concerns about some players' poor attitudes towards training and called a players' meeting to address the problem. Complicating matters further was speculation that Traill was to take over the coaching role at Bradford Northern although this proved unfounded when he signed another extended three-year contract with Trinity.

Neil was clearly beginning to appreciate that captaincy was not a bed of roses and it was probably fortunate that he had other things to distract him from its worries and from his injury. This was because he had embarked upon a career as a bookmaker, as Neil Fox Turf Accountant Ltd. He explains: "I got a telephone call from a life-long Wakefield supporter asking if he could come and meet me. He was Trevor Woodward, who in his youth had been the office boy at Trinity. He had just come out of the public house trade and had opened a betting shop in Ossett. Having read about my situation regarding the offer from Australia for me to play there, he decided he did not want me to leave Trinity so he came up with the idea of making me a partner in his bookmaking business and extending it into Wakefield. Molly and I listened and thought the idea through before I agreed to it. I didn't know anything about horse racing but Trevor said he would show me the ropes and show me how to work out bets.

So I left the Central Electricity Generating Board and started up with Trevor. The first thing I had to do was to apply for a betting office permit, which was granted. Then we found a plot of land to rent on Vicarage Street in Wakefield. We put in an application for a purpose-built betting shop. That was passed and the next step was to apply for a betting licence. At that point the newspapers got hold of the story and helped me along by suggesting that if I didn't get the licence I might be heading for Australia. Thankfully, I got it but every other bookie in town objected to the application. They said there were enough bookies in Wakefield already.

On receiving the good news, we built the office and started Neil Fox Turf Accountants Ltd. We changed the name of the office in Ossett to that too. In a short period of time we opened another shop in Wakefield, much to the disgust of the other bookies. Then shops were opened in Castleford, Mirfield and Dewsbury. Trevor and I quickly had six shops. So, not going to Australia turned out to be a blessing in disguise. Trevor later became chairman of Wakefield Trinity and held that position when Trinity lost to Widnes at Wembley in 1979."

Neil was back playing on 24 October but it was not a happy return. Wakefield went down 7-3 at Keighley and Neil was completely out of touch, handling badly and missing four kicks, but there was one flash of his usual self when a terrific cross-field run almost put Jones over. The following Saturday Fartown was the scene of the Yorkshire Cup Final between Trinity and Leeds. Wakefield's form was not indicative of a team destined to win trophies, although they had certainly ridden their luck to get to the final. They were deservedly languishing at 14th in the table, but Leeds were not much more impressive and were just two places higher. Trinity went through their normal big-match ritual, having daylight training sessions and a meat pie supper on the Thursday evening preceding the final. With his bookmaker's hat on, Neil would probably have made Leeds slight favourites, especially as he knew that he was taking a gamble with his own fitness. He had to have an injection before the game.

However, on a dark, misty autumnal afternoon, Wakefield confounded their critics with a display reminiscent of their very best days and Neil was once again a towering figure. After four minutes he landed a fine 30-yard penalty after the ball was stolen from Don Vines, the best forward on view. After 10 minutes Wakefield delivered a hammer blow. Neil and Harold Poynton combined with some sizzling passing to open up a two-man overlap. Right centre Tony Thomas presented Berwyn Jones with a perfect pass and the winger shot 40 yards diagonally to score behind the sticks. Jack Paul in the *Sunday Express* remarked that it "was the fastest 40-yard dash I've seen on a rugby field". It was a pity that the live coverage of the game on BBC's *Grandstand* had yet to begin, as the programme was only showing the second half. Neil potted the conversion and the only other score of the first half was a penalty to Leeds kicked by full-back Robin Dewhurst.

The BBC cameras captured some dazzling entertainment from Neil's team in the second half. Neil had aggravated his injury only 10 minutes into the game and at half-time there was concern over whether he could carry on. He told Jack Paul, "We thought it might boost the Leeds morale if I didn't appear, so I kept going". Paul added, "And how he kept going! The burly Wakefield star romped in for two second-half tries, and, with his three goals, altogether accomplished more on one sound leg than 13 two-legged Leeds lads did together". In the 50th minute Neil administered the *coup de grâce*, when he surged past three defenders to make the score 10-2. Six minutes later a trademark Poynton reverse pass enabled Neil to skittle another three tacklers for another touchdown, which he converted to make it 15-2. Two minutes from time Vines beautifully prised open the Leeds defence to send Jones haring away before rounding Dewhurst and sending a photographer flying for his second try. Trinity thoroughly deserved their 18-2 win. Harold Poynton was probably the best man on the field but Neil, despite his handicap, had been magnificent. He is quick to praise his team-mates, though: "It was a grand victory. The team spirit was great and the younger players gained valuable confidence from this match. Obviously I was delighted to have led Trinity to their first trophy under my captaincy but I had damaged my leg muscle again and missed the next five games". Neil's second try had brought him the 3,000th point of his first class career.

The Yorkshire Cup triumph was soon overshadowed by tragedy. On 5 November club chairman Stuart Hadfield died of a heart attack, aged 64. Just a few hours earlier at Leeds, he had been elected vice-chairman of the Rugby League International Selection Committee. His loss to the club was impossible to exaggerate. He had been a pivotal figure in Trinity's rise to prominence and had become one of the most well-known and respected administrators in the game. One of his last acts at Belle Vue had been to help select the Yorkshire Cup-winning team. Stanley Milner was a unanimous choice as his successor, with Les Pounder taking over as vice-chairman.

There was more bad news for Neil when the scheduled 1965 World Cup competition was called off at the instigation of the Australian RL Board of Control, although the New Zealanders were prepared to stage the tournament alone. Australia were disappointed at the standard of the 1964 French touring team and asserted that France were not good enough to take part in the World Cup. Within a month of the decision to defer the next tournament to 1967, and subsequently to 1968, France defeated Great Britain. The World Cup became one target Neil never hit, purely because bizarre circumstances, such as the aforementioned Australian unilateral action, seemed to crop up unexpectedly.

Before Neil returned from injury Trinity had sold prop Eric Payne to York for £1,500, transfer-listed five more forwards and given a debut to Australian prop Noel Dolton, formerly of Newtown and Parramatta. Trinity had paid a transfer fee of £500 but also had to pay Noel £1,000 a year.

Neil returned to action on 12 December, kicking three goals in a poor performance by Wakefield at Hunslet, who won 20-6. The following week he had a run-out in the 'A' team, who beat Doncaster 'A' 23-3. At Christmas Trinity were 15th in the league table with only 16 points from 17 games, a long way behind leaders St Helens - who had won all 15 of their fixtures - Castleford, Wigan and Hunslet. A fully fit Neil Fox was necessary if Trinity were to climb the table and have a say in the destination of the game's major honours.

Boxing Day at Headingley indicated that a happy New Year might follow, although the kick-off had been delayed for half an hour until 11.30am to allow the underground heating to thaw out the pitch. In the Yorkshire Cup Final Neil had outshone ace Leeds centre Dick Gemmell but now Leeds had acquired Australian centre Bob Landers, a 15-stoner from

145

Eastern Suburbs, who kicked goals too. He had played for New South Wales and was reckoned by some Loiners to be the antidote to Neil Fox. Neil showed them the error of their ways, turning on a virtuoso display, brushing his much-vaunted opposing centres aside and landing seven goals from nine attempts. Trinity were on fire and led 21-0 by the break, Neil having booted six goals. Leeds managed to batten down the hatches but Neil's try at the corner after a Bob Haigh break killed them off stone dead. Leeds could not muster a try and perished 29-6.

In fact no-one was going to score a try against this Trinity team of dreadnoughts for some considerable time. On 2 January Trinity went to Dewsbury and were again stretched to the limit in their third meeting of the season. It was a rugged affair, played with the intensity of a cup tie. The *Wakefield Express's* headline ran: "Bull's-eye Fox kicks Trinity to victory", as his five penalties decided the issue 10-0. A week later one was just enough to beat Warrington 2-0 at Belle Vue. This time the headline was "Match-winner Fox does it again". Conditions were awful and defences established an unbreakable stranglehold. Breaks of even 20 yards were rare and Neil's winning kick came after only 10 minutes, when the Wire were penalised for feeding at the scrum, although a minute before half-time Neil hit the post with a penalty. John L. Allen wrote, "Fox led the side intelligently and was easily the most penetrative back".

On the same day as the Warrington match, 9 January, a *Wakefield Express* headline announced, "Trinity are £5,500 in the red: No silly money to be spent – chairman". Stanley Milner was spelling out Wakefield's financial problems. They needed £800 from each home game, which meant an attendance of 8,000, which they were not getting. The 'A' team cost £2,000 a year to run but brought in less than £300. He added that winning the Yorkshire Cup had only brought a profit of £200 and that was because of the television fee. On a brighter note, he informed readers that Halifax had an overdraft of £12,000. Season ticket sales and income from the pools continued to plummet but at least Mr Milner was positive about Neil's team, which he described as "a good and young team". Neil must have been glad to have had other matters to occupy his thoughts. He was hitting the headlines because of his bookmaking career. One paper declared "Neil Fox in court three times this week" – which didn't exactly explain that he was there to sort out various licences, while in the *Yorkshire Evening News* Arthur Haddock ran an article describing Neil as "the Terry Downes of Northern Rugby League football. Downes has cashed in on his boxing fame by opening a chain of betting shops that have made him one of the wealthiest bookies in the London area; Fox aims to do much the same in and around Wakefield, where he is the local sporting idol".

Perhaps playing rugby league was much simpler, if more dangerous, than the world of finance, which appeared to be turned on its head when Trinity, contrary to their recent financial warnings, suddenly declared they were offering the team a bonus incentive for getting into the top eight and proceeding through the subsequent rounds, at a time when most clubs were reported to be cutting wages.

On 16 January, Trinity extended their winning run with a 10-2 success at Hull KR in a very exciting game, marked once again by Trinity's own version of the iron curtain. Reserve half-backs Trevor Ward, on his debut, and Terry Hopwood played exceptionally well and Neil converted tries by Thomas and Vines, the latter from an extraordinary 40-yard interception. The four recent victories had taken Wakefield up to 10th in the table and prospects were brightening with each win.

On 23 January, Neil was restored to the test team for the return clash with France at Swinton. On 6 December France had beaten Britain 18-8 at Perpignan, when Dick Gemmell and Frank Myler had been the centres and Berwyn Jones had made a try-scoring test debut. Alex Murphy captained the side in both tests but perhaps even the volatile Alex was amazed by what unfolded at Station Road. The game was televised – unfortunately but memorably – and played on a mud heap. In the first half the French played some magnificent rugby and after 16 minutes led 7-0. Jack Nott in the *News of the World* waxed exceedingly lyrical: "Their handling was delicate like rare perfume, and their tactics were daring like 'Les Folies'. But then they ruined everything with a 60th-minute exhibition of childish petulance that I have never seen before, not even on the playing fields of the kindergarten". Bob Pemberton in the *Daily Telegraph* described what happened as "this miserable display of bad-tempered rule breaking", while Alex Murphy complained, "We have rarely taken so much boot".

By half-time Neil had landed two goals to reduce the deficit to 7-4 and, by the time the affair really boiled over on the hour, he had added two more for Britain to lead 8-7. At that point, following two free-for-alls, several cautions for butting, kicking and punching, referee Dennis Davies ordered off French skipper Marcel Bescos. The French prop, known as *L'ours* (The Bear), refused to retreat after a penalty had been awarded to Britain. He had tried Mr Davies's patience once too often. However, he refused to leave the field and was soon seemingly supported by every other French player, official and fan. Eventually the French touch-judge, Monsieur Jameau, escorted Bescos to the sidelines after police and officials had removed all the extraneous bodies. The incident was not over, however. Bescos suddenly decided to return to the field. At that point the referee departed, followed by most of the French team and chaos reigned. In the end, Arthur Walker, the chairman of the RFL, pleaded with the French to return "for the sake of international football". After about eight minutes the game resumed minus Bescos, who stayed in the dressing room with tears running down his cheeks. Even with the history of games against France, this was all pretty amazing.

Within three minutes of the resumption Jones scored a simple try, touching down a kick through from prop Brian Tyson, although the crestfallen French merely stood and watched. Neil converted and then added two more penalties. His seven goals from eight shots was another example of his match-winning prowess, most of them being long-range efforts.

After these extraordinary events it must have been a relief for Neil to return to Belle Vue for the visit of champions Swinton on 30 January. Trinity maintained their progress with a 6-0 victory and the *Wakefield Express* pronounced "This was great stuff". Neil was the match-winner yet again with three first-half penalties in a game played in a magnificent spirit. The players marked Sir Winston Churchill's recent death by wearing black armbands.

On 6 February, Wakefield opened the Challenge Cup campaign with a tie at Dewsbury and, true to form, another gruelling encounter ensued. One report described the game as "slogging but fascinating". Dewsbury took a third minute lead with a penalty goal but by half-time Neil had kicked his side into a 4-2 lead. In the 42nd minute the game was made safe when Hopwood scored after supporting a fine break by Holliday, Neil adding the goal. Neil concluded the scoring with a final penalty after 62 minutes. Don Metcalfe played magnificently but there was bad luck for Bob Haigh who suffered a broken jaw. Neil also passed two milestones with his 1,200th goal in all games and his 2,500th point for Trinity.

During the week of the cup tie Neil had been to 10, Downing Street to meet Prime Minister, Harold Wilson, along with other sporting celebrities, including rugby league men, Bill Fallowfield, Alex Murphy and Eric Ashton. Alex and Eric travelled to London by train, while Bill took Neil down in his sports car. The four met up at the plush Russell Hotel in Russell Square and after the reception went out to dine with the jockey Terry Biddlecombe and boxer Howard Winstone. Alex and Eric caught the train back to Lancashire the next day, but Bill Fallowfield and Neil were invited to lunch at the residence of the owner of the Russell Hotel, who was a friend of Bill. Neil recalls, "It was the first time I was ever served by a servant in someone's house."

After Downing Street, Neil's next appointment was at Swinton, where Trinity kept their line intact for the seventh game in a row. Ray Owen, back after a collarbone fracture, scored the only try of the game after 17 minutes, Neil converting. There was no more scoring until the last minute when, wrote John L. Allen, to waste some time, Neil "audaciously placed the ball for a penalty shot in the teeth of a gale force wind. Aye, and what's more, he surprised everyone when he kicked it. The effort was worth a lot more than two points!"

Neil made his 300th appearance for Wakefield in a 16-2 victory at Hunslet on 20 February. It was a most entertaining affair until the 52nd minute when Trinity were 5-0 ahead. At that point Ted Campbell and Hunslet's great veteran forward, Geoff Gunney, were sent off, followed very quickly by Hunslet's other second-rower Bill Ramsey. Gunney had never been sent off before in 14 years with the Parksiders. This aside, Trinity's first try by Coetzer was the game's highlight. It was started by Owen and ended after an exquisite scissors movement with Neil.

The following Saturday Trinity were engaged in a second-round cup tie at Odsal, in which Keith Holliday was making his 400th appearance for the club. Northern, who were well down the league, put up a good fight but Trinity finally struck the front after 31 minutes, when Neil bluffed the defence into taking his dummy before sending Coetzer away for a try. Terry Clawson and Neil exchanged penalty goals before half-time and 10 minutes after the break Trinity had a shock when Coetzer was sent off for tripping Ian Brooke, when he looked a likely scorer. Wakefield, however, stretched their advantage to 10-2 with a spectacular try from Jones and a goal from Neil. Two minutes from time Wakefield finally conceded a try for the first time since 12 December when former Wakefield star Ian Brooke crossed their line. Trinity's 10-7 victory was more emphatic than the scoreline suggested and the critics were coming round to the view that Neil's team really were Wembley candidates.

Neil missed Trinity's 17-4 victory at York on 6 March but was back for the third round of the Challenge Cup on 13 March. Trinity, who had now risen to sixth in the league, had a home tie against bottom-of-the-league Blackpool Borough. If ever there was a certainty, this must have been it. Once again, however, Blackpool rocked Trinity rigid. At half-time there was no score and John L. Allen marvelled at the Borough defence, "It was stern and efficient enough to have taxed Wakefield's skill at its best". Trinity were not at their best, but Borough's resistance was incredible. What they could not successfully withstand was the power of Neil's boot. Within four minutes of the restart Neil had landed two prodigious penalties and secured Trinity's entry to the semi-finals via a 4-0 victory. Blackpool had certainly deserved a draw. Before the game one Yorkshire bookmaker had Trinity as 9-4 cup favourites, with Blackpool at 1,000-1.

Three days after the struggle to overcome basement Borough, Neil took his team to St Helens for a floodlit league fixture. Saints were top of the league, having lost just twice, and had not been beaten at Knowsley Road. This time it was Trinity's turn to display their defensive prowess in a rousing match. At the break Wakefield led 6-2 despite losing the first-half scrums 11-6. The *Wakefield Express* recorded, "Once again it was the prodigious kicking of Neil Fox which was responsible for those six points". In the eighth minute he potted a simple goal when Bob Dagnall was penalised for a loose arm in the scrum. A minute later he landed a monstrous penalty from half-way and in the 14th minute he sent a drop-goal steepling high over the Saints' posts. That other truly great kicker, Saints' Len Killeen had an unhappy time in contrast, missing with four shots in the first half hour before eventually landing one. In an incident reminiscent of the famous Challenge Cup tie back in 1960, Harold Poynton was injured in a collision with his team-mate Tony Thomas. While Harold was receiving attention Don Vines and debutant hooker Peter Barlow combined to send Jones flying on his way to a try, leaving Ray French and Cliff Watson wondering where he had gone. It was the last score of the game, Trinity's 9-2 victory being one of their best performances of the season. The *Wakefield Express* noted that "Fox and Vines were mighty figures in steadying Trinity".

Four days later, on 20 March, the two sides met again at Belle Vue in wretched conditions. Persistent sleet turned the pitch into a quagmire but Trinity rose above the conditions, handling the treacherous ball excellently. There was only one try in the match, which was Berwyn Jones's first score at Belle Vue since 12 September. It was a stunner. The ball was whipped from the left wing to the right wing through at least six pairs of hands. When it arrived in Jones's grasp on the Saints' '25' he appeared to have no chance but astonishingly outstripped the covering defenders with ease. John L. Allen said, "He won the pulsating sprint by a second". Neil added a penalty and although the final score was only 5-4 to Trinity, they had been clear masters of the league leaders. Apart from leading Trinity to this tremendous double over St Helens, Neil had more to celebrate that day. Molly gave birth to their second child, Jonathan, who weighed in at nine pounds four ounces. Life was being good to the Fox family.

The run of closely fought games Trinity had experienced had been phenomenal and frayed the nerves of all involved at Belle Vue. There had been no doubting the sheer efficacy of Wakefield's tackling. It had now carried them to 13 straight victories since Boxing Day. In that time Trinity had conceded just one try, an almost unbelievable achievement for this era, and Neil's staggering ability to land game-breaking goals had been the other main weapon in their armoury. The nagging doubt for some critics, however, was Trinity's own apparent inability to score tries themselves. Sooner or later, they would be on the losing end of some of the close encounters they were constantly experiencing. In the meantime, though, they just wanted to keep on winning.

On 24 March they defeated Bramley 26-4, scoring the highest number of points they had recorded since the Boxing Day rout of Leeds, and once again they conceded no try. Neil booted seven goals from eight shots and bagged a try in a game that became so robust that the referee stopped it after 65 minutes to calm the players down. Three days later Wakefield were almost beaten at Doncaster, who held them to 12-12 at half-time. Trinity eventually triumphed 22-17 but John L. Allen asked pertinently, "Where would Trinity have been without Neil Fox's five goals?" – not to mention his try. Neil's first goal brought up his 1,000th for the club. On the other hand, the Dons' winger Peter Goodchild must have been disappointed to have been on the losing side despite scoring three tries, the first against Trinity since the cup tie at Odsal.

Wakefield chalked up their 16th win in a row on 29 March, beating Hull 21-7 at Belle Vue. Neil gave them the lead with a fifth minute interception try under the Hull posts and went on to score 13 points in a sometimes classic display of open football which delighted the crowd. Team spirit among the Trinity players was tremendous, as evidenced by Malcolm Sampson's readiness to cut short his Windermere honeymoon to play against Hull. A 17th consecutive win followed on 3 April with a fabulous performance against table-topping Castleford at Belle Vue. Wakefield ran their opponents off their feet and all seven of their tries in a 27-7 success went to the wingers. Berwyn Jones, "the human form of jet propulsion", produced amazing speed for his two first half tries but the star was Gert Coetzer, supplied by Neil, who claimed the other five. Four of them came in the second half when "change of pace, deception... and strength in bursting out of tackles, were qualities exhibited in glorious fashion". The *Wakefield Express* also noted, "Particularly pleasing was the power-packed show by Neil Fox, alongside his fast and elusive partner Tony Thomas. The two centre stars, along with wingers in such devastating form, must have presented a club threequarter line second to none". The fans were also returning to Belle Vue, the attendance of 15,314 being the best of the season.

With 17 straight victories to their credit, Wakefield Trinity definitely entered their Challenge Cup semi-final against Hunslet at Headingley on 10 April as clear favourites. They had climbed a fluctuating league table to be second behind Warrington. Hunslet were currently 12th in the league and had won just three of 10 league fixtures since the New Year. However, they had put Oldham, Batley and Leeds out of the Cup and conceded only a solitary try, against the Loiners, in that run. They had also been the last team to defeat Trinity, back on 12 December. They were not mugs, nor would they act as sacrificial lambs. Trinity had moved to Harrogate on the preceding Thursday to prepare for the semi-final and fully expected to play Wigan again at Wembley, the cherry and whites having already disposed of Swinton in the first semi-final. Wakefield were at full strength, apart from missing scrum-half Ray Owen, whose season had been ended by injury at Doncaster.

Trinity also got what they prayed for – a fine, sunny afternoon. Most of the 21,262 present at Headingley believed the good conditions would suit the faster, more mobile Wakefield players, provided they could gain enough possession. Hunslet's hooker Bernard Prior beat George Shepherd 13-8 in the scrums but Trinity had the better of the early stages. Neil missed a straight 25-yard penalty after seven minutes and failed to land an acutely angled drop-goal after 20 minutes and half-time arrived with no score. There was still no score with only 12 minutes remaining and chances had been almost non-existent. Hunslet had played to their strengths – their pack and a monotonous cycle of drives from the play-the-ball – and were driving Trinity to distraction. When the breaks finally came they fell to the Parksiders, who scored "two splendidly cunning tries" by Alan Preece and John Griffiths and sealed an 8-0 win when Billy Langton thumped over a magnificent 50-yard penalty in the last minute. Neil's hopes of leading Trinity to Wembley in his first season of captaincy had been ground to dust by the masterly way Hunslet had exploited the play-the-ball rules. It was not a pretty sight but on this occasion it worked.

John L. Allen was at his fulminating best. He fumed about "this awful type of rugby league", about "this appalling play-the-ball rule" which deprived Trinity of possession, and about "Hunslet's bullocking and barging" which "exposed how brutal and unattractive the game can be". Many other critics and fans supported his views but others had relished the extreme drama of the encounter. Ramon Joyce in the *Rugby Leaguer* dared to declare: "If Hunslet's exploiting of the play-the-ball... turns out to be the last act before the signing of the death warrant for that rule then I, for one, will consider it died a glorious death. Like many others, I have blamed the play-the-ball rule for much of what is wrong with the game. But, I have to admit, I enjoyed last Saturday's match almost as much as any I have seen this season. The tension and drama compensated for the lack of open football." Of course, no one connected with Hunslet complained.

Two days later Trinity won 12-7 against Bradford in a bright game, scarred by an ugly brawl in the 52nd minute. Trinity recorded all their points in the first half, Neil scoring a try and landing three goals. In the next fixture, a 16-13 defeat at Hull, he kicked brilliantly –

five goals from five attempts, "all of them a credit to this goalkicker whose allowances for the capricious wind were really marvellous".

At half-time of the last league game of the season at home to Leeds on Easter Monday, 19 April, Neil was presented with a stainless steel tea service and a framed photograph of himself in recognition of his achievement in kicking his 1,000th goal for Trinity the previous month. Leeds, fielding mostly reserves, gave Trinity a good run for their money however, and Neil's 11 points were a major factor in a 20-7 Wakefield victory. Jack Austen made his Trinity debut outside Neil but hooker Peter Barlow was unfortunate enough to fracture a leg 10 minutes before the end.

Trinity had done splendidly to finish in fourth position in the league and hopes were high that the new top 16 play-offs could see them finish as champions at last. It would be an ideal way for Neil to climax his debut season as captain. They began with a scratchy 15-9 home win against Hull, when Gerry Round reappeared after an absence dating back to October. It was a rough, bad-tempered affair and Trinity had six Neil Fox goals to thank for their passage through to the quarter-final, another home game against Warrington on 1 May. Trinity won this 17-8 and again had much to thank Neil for. He created a try for Rushton and then was instrumental in another for Coetzer, and landed four crucial goals.

Through to a semi-final against league leaders St Helens at Knowsley Road, matters appeared to be proceeding according to plan. For most of the first half Trinity were on top. Neil converted a try by Rushton and they led 5-2. Their prospects seemed even brighter when Saints lost forward John Warlow, who was sent off after 30 minutes. However, Saints continued to win the scrums and Trinity were unable to control Alex Murphy, who ultimately won the game for his team. In the 35th minute he split Trinity wide open before sending van Vollenhoven over under the posts for a try converted by Killeen. This appeared to demoralise Trinity and the game became very niggly with referee Eric Clay dishing out numerous cautions – even issuing one to Ken Traill on the touchline. A long pass from Murphy which created a try for Killeen was the final blow to a brave Trinity, who lost 10-5.

Neil's first season as captain of the club had been a success. Trinity had done well to finish fourth in the league, behind St Helens, Wigan and Castleford, while only St Helens could boast a better defensive record. Neil had led his team to victory in the Yorkshire Cup and taken them to the semi-finals of the Challenge Cup and Championship. It was a good start, especially as team rebuilding was still in progress and, if the truth was told, few people would have really have expected such success so early. Neil's own form, after recovery from his early season injuries, was as impressive as ever and his glorious goalkicking in so many low-scoring battles had probably never been more important to his side. He was arguably the greatest out-and-out match-winner in the game. Despite his long lay-offs, Neil had finished third in the leading scorers with 281 points, behind St Helens winger Len Killeen (360) and Hull KR full-back Cyril Kellett (306). His 121 goals placed him sixth behind Kellett (150), Killeen (141), Hunslet's Billy Langton (132), Halifax's Ronnie James (125) and Huddersfield's Brian Curry (123).

To say that the months between August 1964 and May 1965 had been momentous for Neil would be a colossal understatement. At the age of 25 he had become captain of one of the country's most successful clubs, completely changed his employment, immeasurably enhanced his life prospects and been blessed by the birth of his second child.

Wakefield Trinity 1964-65

Wakefield Trinity finished 4th in the league: P34, W24, L8, D2, For 486, Against 228

Fox scored 12 tries, 113 goals, 262 points for Wakefield, and 1 try, 8 goals, 19 points in representative games

Date	Opponent	Score	Fox	Crowd	
22 Aug	Castleford	7-7	2G	11,000	
24 Aug	**Dewsbury**	10-12	G	7,772	
29 Aug	**Doncaster**	28-4	T, 5G	5,707	
2 Sep	Halifax	6-10	3G	5,359	
5 Sep	Dewsbury	11-10	4G	6,500	YC1
12 Sep	**Keighley**	46-5	T, 11G	6,557	
16 Sep	Featherstone R	15-5	T, 3G	5,000	YC2
19 Sep	**York**	31-15	T	5,805	
26 Sep	Bramley	13-7	dnp	3,930	
30 Sep	Huddersfield	7-0	G	9,371	YC semi
3 Oct	**Featherstone R**	5-8	dnp	8,319	
10 Oct	Batley	4-4	dnp	3,900	
17 Oct	**Halifax**	10-7	dnp	7,244	
24 Oct	Keighley	3-7		2,450	
31 Oct	Leeds	18-2	2T, 3G	13,527	YC Final (at Fartown)
7 Nov	Featherstone R	12-6	dnp	6,200	
14 Nov	Warrington	10-16	dnp	7,463	
21 Nov	**Hull KR**	14-7	dnp	8,499	
28 Nov	Bradford N	0-3	dnp	7,658	
5 Dec	**Batley**	29-5	dnp	3,509	
12 Dec	**Hunslet**	6-20	3G	5,921	
26 Dec	Leeds	29-6	T, 7G	10,736	
2 Jan	Dewsbury	10-0	5G	4,500	
9 Jan	**Warrington**	2-0	G	4,378	
16 Jan	Hull KR	10-2	2G	8,430	
30 Jan	**Swinton**	6-0	3G	6,579	
6 Feb	Dewsbury	11-2	4G	8,513	Ch Cup 1
13 Feb	Swinton	7-0	2G	6,200	
20 Feb	Hunslet	16-2	2G	6,200	
27 Feb	Bradford N	10-7	2G	19,905	Ch Cup 2
6 Mar	York	17-4	dnp	3,503	
13 Mar	**Blackpool B**	4-0	2G	12,986	Ch Cup 3
16 Mar	St Helens	9-2	3G	14,106	
20 Mar	**St Helens**	5-4	G	5,958	
24 Mar	**Bramley**	26-4	T, 7G	5,392	
27 Mar	Doncaster	22-17	T, 5G	2,600	
29 Mar	**Hull**	21-7	T, 5G	8,301	
3 Apr	**Castleford**	27-7	3G	15,314	
10 Apr	Hunslet	0-8		21,262	Ch Cup semi (at Leeds)
12 Apr	**Bradford N**	12-7	T, 3G	7,219	
17 Apr	Hull	13-16	5G	7,000	
19 Apr	**Leeds**	20-7	T, 4G	7,569	
24 Apr	**Hull**	15-9	6G	8,172	CH1
1 May	**Warrington**	17-8	4G	10,580	CH2
15 May	St Helens	5-10	G	21,870	CH semi

Representative appearances

9 Sep	Yorkshire 14 Cumberland 6 (Whitehaven)	T, G
23 Jan	Great Britain 17 France 7 (Swinton)	7G

152

Neil takes the Challenge Cup into the losers' dressing room after Trinity beat Huddersfield at Wembley in 1962. Fartown skipper Tommy Smales quenches his thirst, while his coach Dave Valentine, right, looks on. (Photo: Photomakeovers).

Neil practising his goalkicking in Sydney on the 1962 Lions tour.
(Photo: Photomakeovers)

Peter, Don and Neil pose together after Peter had become the third Fox brother to join Wakefield Trinity in 1966. (Photo: Photomakeovers)

This unique photo was taken at half-time during Wakefield Trinity's game against the Australians in 1963. Trinity's surviving Australasian tourists were gathered together for the occasion.
Standing: Tommy Newbould, Ernest Pollard, Jack Lynch (Kangaroo manager), Stuart Hadfield, Bill Horton, Jonty Parkin, Mick Exley, Harold Poynton, Gerry Round, A.J. Sparks (Kangaroo manager), Charlie Pollard. Front: Derek Turner, Jack Wilkinson, Neil Fox. (Photo: Photomakeovers)

Four studies of Neil by renowned rugby league artist Stuart Smith.

Wakefield Trinity versus Warrington.
Top: Neil crashes over for a try in Trinity's 40-18 victory over Warrington in the
Challenge Cup first round tie in 1962. Derek Turner is up in support.
Bottom: Neil is over again against the Wire. Full-back Ernie Ashcroft is flat on his back
while Brian Bevan and Joe Pickavance (4) cannot stop Neil touching down.
(Photos: Photomakeovers)

Neil joins in the Rugby League's centenary celebrations at Huddersfield in 1995 with fellow Hall of Famers Billy Boston, Alex Murphy and Gus Risman.

Neil receives his Hall of Fame medal from Lord Derby in 1989.

All dressed up and somewhere to go. Molly and Neil are about to leave for the
Queen's Silver Jubilee Dinner at Leeds Civic Hall in 1977.

Neil and Molly, summer 2005.

Family photos

All the family gather for Neil's 65th birthday, 4 May 2004, with great-granddad Bentley in the centre.

Neil's daughter Mandy and her family, husband Mick, daughter Lisa and son James.

Neil's son Jonathan and his family, wife Sue and sons Daniel and Joshua.

160

benefit season. I've captained Trinity often enough and was picked to skipper Yorkshire but had to cry off. I've played in France four times before and feel this is a good side which, given the chance, will play plenty of football. I believe the French team is playing pretty well this season, so it will be a hard match."

There were still matches to be played before the test, however. New Year's Eve took Trinity to Grange-over-Sands, where they stayed overnight at Reg Parker's hotel prior to the following day's game at Workington Town. Neil marshalled his team to a good 12-5 win, leading the way with nine points. A week later Trinity demolished Doncaster 33-5 and Neil only had time to register a try and a goal before he was forced from the field after 22 minutes with a damaged left knee. The injury made him a doubtful starter for the test in France. In the event he was able to lead the test team on 16 January but in hindsight he may well have wished his injury had been slower to heal. The team Neil skippered was:

Ken Gowers (Swinton), Berwyn Jones (Wakefield Trinity), Geoff Shelton (Hunslet), Neil Fox (Wakefield Trinity, captain), John Stopford (Swinton), Cliff Hill (Wigan), Alex Murphy (St Helens), Ken Roberts (Halifax), Colin Clarke (Wigan), Cliff Watson (St Helens), John Mantle (St Helens), Bill Holliday (Hull KR), Dave Robinson (Swinton).

Jack Bentley in the *Daily Express* sounded a warning note in the first paragraph of his match report, writing, "Two Great Britain aces, former captain Alex Murphy and new captain Neil Fox, put their test futures in the selectors' melting pot at the Stade Gilbert Brutus here today where France snatched victory in the last 11 minutes". Murphy played sensationally, scoring Britain's first try, providing the kick-through from which Berwyn Jones scored the second and giving the pass which launched John Stopford on a 45-yard run for the third try. Neil converted Murphy's try and added a penalty and Britain led 13-12 after 64 minutes. In the 69th minute referee Eric Clay penalised Murphy following a tackle on second-rower Georges Aillères and full-back Pierre Lacaze landed a fine 40-yard angled goal to give France a one point lead. Four minutes later Lacaze potted another penalty after Alex had hoofed the ball straight into touch from a '25' drop-out. Unbelievably, Neil repeated the same mistake three minutes from time and Lacaze's sixth goal of the afternoon gave France an 18-13 victory. Britain's prospects were not helped by a 16-6 pasting in the scrums, but in truth France had been the better side.

Neil's first national captaincy had not been the success he had hoped for but there was no need for panic. There was still a home test against the French at Wigan on 5 March before the selectors met to pick the tour party on 23 March.

Wakefield had a three-week break before resuming activities with a vital game at Central Park on 29 January. The encounter was lively, robust and sporting and Wigan should have won by 20 points but had to be satisfied with a 7-5 victory. Trinity lost the scrums 19-8 and did not score until the 75th minute when Neil, Gert Coetzer and Ken Batty produced a sparkling movement which sent Neil under the posts for a try, which he converted. Earlier Neil had made a tremendous 40-yard break after intercepting, from which he would normally have scored, but was easily caught from behind by Eric Ashton, an indication to some observers that Neil was not really firing on all cylinders.

Two days later Neil had a happier time at a sportsman's ball held for his testimonial fund at Unity Hall, where comedians Ted Rogers, Mike and Bernie Winters, singer Ronnie Hilton and test cricketer Brian Close were among the guests. Molly was presented with a bouquet and Neil recalls, "I met Ted Rogers later when he was performing at the Theatre Club in Wakefield and went backstage for a drink. I also met Diana Dors, when she appeared there and later in the same week I was a guest judge with her and Fred Trueman at the Miss Great Britain heats in both Leeds and Wakefield".

Five days later he was happier still, booting six goals out of the mud at Keighley, Trinity winning 36-2. Trinity had a more difficult time on 12 February in beating Dewsbury 13-5 at Belle Vue, when Don Fox finally reappeared after his injury at St Helens back in November. Unfortunately, poor Don suffered a recurrence of the injury and required surgery.

Neil's benefit match against St Helens followed on 19 February. There was a complication when it was realised that the BBC intended to televise the game. Wakefield knew that would mean a reduction in the crowd, and asked the RFL to request that another game was televised instead. Trinity, it should be noted, were one of the teams supporting Wigan in their campaign against live television coverage, believing that it reduced gates. The fact that Wakefield had drawn a home Challenge Cup tie against Saints the following week came to their assistance, because the clash between the league's two leading teams was just what the BBC wanted for *Grandstand's* live Challenge Cup coverage. So, all was well. Neil's testimonial fund got the benefit of a near 10,000 crowd despite hours of rain which made the pitch a morass. In spite of the conditions a thrill-a-minute match was served up and Neil played up to test-match standard, kicking four goals in a splendid 20-12 win. Prior to the game, Neil and his team-mates received tankards for winning the season's third section of the Mackeson top-scorers competition. The game also brought up the 100th appearance of Neil's wing partner Oupa Coetzer in a Trinity shirt.

The following Saturday the Challenge Cup tie was an altogether different kettle of fish in front of a crowd exceeding 20,000. Neil played directly opposite Alex Murphy, who was playing centre under sufferance, as he preferred his normal half-back role. Trinity had first use of a strong wind but St Helens's forwards gained the ascendancy and half-time arrived without any score. In the second half Saints dominated, scored tries through Tommy Bishop and Tom van Vollenhoven, Len Killeen added two goals, and Saints won 10-0. Murphy murdered Trinity in the second half, using the wind to aid his tactical kicking.

Bundled out of the Challenge Cup at the first hurdle, Neil's and Trinity's aspirations now settled on the Championship. Running second, they had every reason to believe that the league title was within Wakefield's grasp for the first time in history. On 5 March, Trinity went to York and ran away with the game 24-0. The former Hull KR prop, John Bath made his Trinity debut but the highlight was an amazing try by Don Metcalfe, whose labyrinthine run took him through half the York team and left the last three defenders mesmerised. Neil was very prominent, claimed two tries and three goals and gave a telling reminder to those who were writing him off for the tour. On the same afternoon Britain, led by Alex Murphy, had lost 8-4 to France at Wigan, in one of the worst test matches anyone could remember. Perhaps, for Neil, Clarence Street was a better place to be than Central Park that day.

The following week Neil put in another formidable performance in a 17-2 win against Workington Town at Belle Vue. Despite losing the first-half scrums 9-4, Trinity led 4-2 thanks to two penalties from Neil. He sailed over for the first try in the 54th minute and added a towering conversion, which killed off Town's challenge. Unfortunately he picked up strained lower abdominal muscles which caused him to miss the next two games against Hull, when Keith Holliday played his last game for the club, and at Halifax. Keith Holliday had been at Wakefield for the whole time Neil had been at the club and Neil had great admiration for him, "Keith will always be remembered at Belle Vue for his workmanlike performances at centre, scrum-half and loose-forward. It was a sad day for Wakefield folk when he left to become player-coach at Bramley."

The tour selectors met in Leeds on 23 March and emerged with their decisions after a meeting which lasted two hours and 40 minutes. Trinity had realistic hopes that Neil, Berwyn Jones and Bob Haigh would be selected and club physiotherapist Paddy Armour had already been appointed as the Lions' physiotherapist and trainer. The news that only Berwyn had been picked came as a real bombshell to Neil, who says: "After playing for and captaining Great Britain just a few weeks earlier, I was overlooked for the tour. It was a real disappointment. I couldn't believe I was not in the 26 chosen. Could it have been that one little mistake in Perpignan had cost me a tour place, I wondered. My mate Alex Murphy was picked at centre along with Buckley, Myler and Shelton. Alex thought he should have been captain but they gave Harry Poole that position. So Alex decided not to go. Eric Ashton was approached to go in Alex's place but turned the offer down and then Bill Fallowfield rang me to see if I was available. I said I wasn't. That made me sixth choice centre. In the end they brought my old team-mate Ian Brooke into the squad and he turned out to be one of the successes of the tour, appearing in all the tests and playing in 18 games and scoring 13 tries."

The touring party was a conundrum to many observers, who were immediately struck by the inexperience of the squad. Only two, Brian Edgar and Alex Murphy, had toured before and Alex, of course, pulled out. The captaincy was an even bigger mystery. The main contenders were reckoned to be Neil, Alex, Swinton's Ken Gowers, who went as vice-captain, and Tommy Smales of Bradford Northern. Tommy had been captain in all three of the 1965 Kiwis tests, none of which had been lost, but was not even in the party, while Neil and Alex had been in charge for the two French tests. To many, the selectors seemed to be in a parallel universe. Eric Ashton, who definitely could have been a candidate for the captaincy, had formally retired from test rugby after the 1963 Ashes series.

Another glaring omission was the absence of match-winning goalkickers. Only the full-backs Ken Gowers and Arthur Keegan of Hull were regarded as competent goalkickers and there was certainly no-one in the class of Neil Fox. Remarkably, the only man to have played in all five tests during the season, Hull KR second-rower Bill Holliday, a first-rate kicker, was omitted from the squad.

There was plenty of sympathy for Neil in his time of trial. Even Jack Bentley in the *Daily Express* came to his defence. He wrote: "I think Holliday is extremely unlucky to be left out. Stand-off Alan Hardisty is equally lucky to be in. For while Hardisty on top form would be an almost automatic choice, he has been hampered by a series of injuries and has not hit anything like peak form. Presumably he has then been selected on reputation. If so, why has not Wakefield's Neil Fox had similar consideration?" Roland Tinker in the *Halifax Courier & Guardian* noted: "Naturally, there are many disheartened and disappointed men, particularly two, who have captained Great Britain this season – Tommy Smales and Neil Fox... Such has been the baffling behaviour of the selectors (all 15 of them) that the 'privilege' of being given the game's top honour – captaincy of Great Britain – has proved a handicap." He also wondered how Frank Myler of Widnes, great player though he was, had been selected in the centres after only recently returning from three months' absence after a back injury. In the *Sunday Express* Phil King revealed that "Surprisingly, this season's Great Britain captain in France, centre Neil Fox, hooker in the Wigan test, Bernard Prior (Hunslet), and back substitute in the Wigan test, Ian Brooke (Bradford Northern), never got to the voting stage." Norman Gaulton, noted in the *Rugby League Magazine*, "Many will feel that the strength and marksmanship of Neil Fox may be missed in the back division." The *Rugby League Magazine* had run a tour selection competition among its readers and reported, "Of the players not chosen by the Tour committee Neil Fox, Holliday, Smales and Johnny Ward [of Castleford] had by far the highest proportion of our readers' votes."

Of course, all tour selections throw up controversy - though very few were as controversial as in 1966 - and those who do not gain recognition just had to get on with the rest of their careers. Neil was no exception and buckled down to his task with Trinity.

Ironically, his first game for Trinity after the tour party was announced was at Bradford on 28 March and Ian Brooke was his direct opponent. Bradford allowed Ian the honour of leading his team out but Wakefield routed Northern 20-2. The *Wakefield Express* reported, "Wakefield packed the game with highlights, none of which provided bigger thrills than the mastery Neil Fox held over former Belle Vue player Ian Brooke. The Australasian tourist, selected for a position not offered to Fox at the selection meeting, was never in the same class as the Trinity centre, either as an attacker or a defender." Trinity's second try was described as "a picture-book effort by Coetzer, who rounded off a sensational thrust by Fox, which knocked his would-be tackler Brooke aside". Neil had earlier brilliantly converted Coetzer's first try from the touchline and John L. Allen remarked that his performance "left the crowd wondering how Neil Fox could have been left out of the tour".

Wakefield had three games left and were engaged in a tight struggle for the Yorkshire League Championship with Leeds and Castleford, both of whom had bigger schedules to negotiate than Trinity. They made a good start with an 8-3 win at Hunslet, a match played throughout in driving snow. Neil missed that game but was back for a vital clash under floodlights at Castleford on Good Friday, 8 April. A gripping game in grim conditions ended in a 6-6 draw, with Neil claiming Trinity's second try. The Easter Monday clash with Leeds at Belle Vue provided another fine game. Coetzer scored a hat-trick and Neil kicked seven goals. Trinity's 35-16 win almost assured them of the Yorkshire League title but all doubt disappeared the following day when Castleford lost 2-0 at Keighley.

Trinity finished fourth in the league table behind St Helens, Swinton and Wigan. This gave them a home tie against Hull in the play-offs on 30 April. Prior to the game Neil received the Yorkshire League Championship trophy from the 1966 tour manager, Wilf Spaven, and on a gloriously sunny afternoon Wakefield turned on a sparkling show in winning 36-6. Neil, playing in his 400th first-class match, booted six goals and had his benefit fund boosted by £44-14-0 from a collection held at the ground. It was not such a happy day for Derek Turner, who had his ear almost ripped off just after the interval.

Trinity certainly missed Turner when they met Hull KR in the Championship quarter-final at Belle Vue. Rovers had finished 12th in the league but defeated Trinity 10-9. Wakefield could offer some excuses – Cyril Kellett had been awarded a 44th-minute penalty goal by referee Harry Hunt, when his attempt had seemed to dip below the bar and one touch-judge had ruled no-goal, and Trinity had lost second-rower Derek Plumstead with a broken jaw in the 41st minute. There was no dispute that Rovers were the better team. Neil had dropped a beautiful goal from 35 yards after 30 minutes to reduce Rovers' lead to 3-2 and had kicked a 48th minute penalty to make the score 5-4 to Rovers, while his conversion of Don Metcalfe's late try was the last score of the game and the season.

The campaign had seen both frustration and disappointment for Neil and the club. He had led Trinity to the Yorkshire League Championship, their fourth since 1958-59 and they would never win it again. In view of their terrible injury list, their final position of fourth was pretty good. There was little wrong with the defence – only Castleford with 233 had conceded fewer than Trinity's 239 points. Moreover, Trinity scored 562 points in the league; only Wigan with 604 managed more. For only the second time since his establishment in Trinity's first-team Neil failed to land 100 goals for the club, but he did pass the 200 points mark for Wakefield for the ninth year running. He finished seventh in the leading goalkickers' list and sixth in the leading points-scorers.

168

Wakefield Trinity 1965-66

Wakefield Trinity finished 4th in the league: P34, W25, L7, D2, For 562, Against 239
Fox scored 11 tries, 94 goals, 221 points for Wakefield, and 4 goals, 8 points in representative games

Date	Opponent	Score	Fox	Crowd	
21 Aug	**Castleford**	5-24	dnp	10,414	
23 Aug	Hull	7-16	dnp	7,000	
28 Aug	Dewsbury	22-7	dnp	4,500	
31 Aug	**Halifax**	7-14	dnp	9,129	
4 Sep	**Hull**	4-8	dnp	7,038	YC1
11 Sep	Batley	23-7	dnp	2,400	
18 Sep	**Bradford N**	7-2	dnp	10,121	
25 Sep	Doncaster	10-8	2G	2,350	
2 Oct	**Batley**	13-2	2G	6,098	
9 Oct	**Keighley**	43-7	T, 8G	6,525	
16 Oct	Featherstone R	22-7	4G	7,307	
23 Oct	**Hull KR**	21-10	2T, 3G	5,722	
30 Oct	**New Zealand**	16-4	T, 5G	7,484	
6 Nov	Bramley	13-2	2G	7,250	
13 Nov	**Hunslet**	6-0	3G	6,330	
20 Nov	Hull KR	8-6	G	5,900	
27 Nov	St Helens	9-9	2G	12,764	
4 Dec	**York**	20-3	4G	5,452	
11 Dec	**Bramley**	33-4	6G	5,367	
18 Dec	**Wigan**	10-13	2G	9,736	
27 Dec	Leeds	9-11	3G	20,877	
28 Dec	**Featherstone R+**	27-7	3G	6,081	
1 Jan	Workington T	12-5	T, 3G	2,670	
8 Jan	**Doncaster**	33-5	T, G	4,888	
29 Jan	Wigan	5-7	T, G	13,771	
5 Feb	Keighley	36-2	6G	3,750	
12 Feb	**Dewsbury**	13-5	2G	4,266	
19 Feb	**St Helens**	20-12	4G	9,606	
26 Feb	**St Helens**	0-10		20,317	Ch Cup 1
5 Mar	York	24-0	2T, 3G	3,311	
12 Mar	**Workington T**	17-2	T, 4G	6,151	
14 Mar	**Hull**	0-15	dnp	4,682	
26 Mar	Halifax	18-0	dnp	4,718	
28 Mar	Bradford N	20-2	4G	11,706	
1 Apr	Hunslet	8-3	dnp	2,050	
8 Apr	Castleford	6-6	T	9,400	
11 Apr	**Leeds**	35-16	7G	11,451	
30 Apr	**Hull**	36-6	6G	8,291	CH1
7 May	**Hull KR**	9-10	3G	12,086	CH2

+ Played at Headingley

Representative appearances

10 Nov	Yorkshire 16 Lancashire 13 (Swinton)	2G
16 Jan	Great Britain 13 France 18 (Perpignan)	2G

Neil's first captaincy of Great Britain was an 18-13 defeat against France at Perpignan on 16 January 1966. Back: Bill Holliday, Alex Murphy, Cliff Watson, Ken Roberts, John Mantle, Colin Clarke, Bill Bryant (sub), Dave Robinson. Front: Neil Fox, Ken Gowers, Berwyn Jones, Geoff Shelton, John Stopford, Cliff Hill, Roger Millward (sub).

Eight months after first captaining Great Britain Neil led Yorkshire for the first time in a 17-17 draw with Cumberland at Workington on 7 September 1966.
Back: Peter Flanagan, Mick Shoebottom, Terry Clawson, Terry Major, Frank Fox, Terry Ramshaw, Jack Scroby. Front: Carl Dooler, Arthur Keegan, Neil Fox, Ian Brooke, Geoff Wriglesworth, Peter Goodchild.

170

15. 1966-67: Champions at last

For sheer confusion the beginning of the 1966-67 season reached new heights. For years there had been problems with the play-the-ball laws. Teams had developed the ability to hold on to the ball for interminable lengths of time, largely because referees were unable to ensure that the ball was played properly. This sometimes led to sterile play with little variety and an unwillingness to move the ball unnecessarily or take risks. Of course, there was absolutely nothing wrong with the sport and the spectacle when teams played the game in the right spirit and referees applied the laws. Another bugbear for the administrators was the number of scrums and their attendant problems. It was also felt that the current mode of play contributed to an increase in violence on the pitch. All these factors were thought to be contributing to the general fall in rugby league attendances.

The laws of the game have always been tampered with and rugby league fans were used to change - but only in small doses. Bill Fallowfield, Secretary of the RFL and its most powerful voice, had long been determined to alter the play-the-ball system to one which allowed more fluidity of possession. In 1966 he finally got his way as there was a general consensus that something had to be done.

Before the season began the clubs had agreed to reintroduce the tap-kick after a penalty kick to touch rather than a scrum, in order to cut down deliberate offside and to reduce the number of scrums. In addition, a decision at the International Board meeting in Australia in July had resolved that defences should retreat five yards at the play-the-ball rather than the current three yards. Australia and New Zealand had played the five-yard rule during their 1966 seasons. However, Britain and France decided to carry on with the old rule for the moment. The RFL allowed the season to start under the three-yard rule but suddenly decided to introduce the five-yard rule from 1 September.

At local level in Wakefield there were changes too. Three players, Dave Sampson, Jack Austen and Terry Hopwood, had moved to Bramley but the only additions to the playing staff had been four junior players – half-back Ivan Spawforth and forwards David Hawley, John Godfrey and Brian Cooper. Trinity had expressed an interest in Halifax's second-rower-cum-centre Colin Dixon but nothing had come of it. Among the backroom staff Harry Wilkinson had retired after giving 36 years of service to the club, while Johnny Malpass had returned from Featherstone after three years coaching at Rovers. Derek Turner was made assistant to Ken Traill and became vice-captain to Neil.

The *Wakefield Express* said: "Neil is putting in some hard spells of training and is keen to shake off the memory of the sub-normal form he showed in some matches last season. … he can put down his loss of form to the illness which kept him out of football during the early part of the last campaign. He underwent an operation and never seemed to pick up to produce the sparkle of which a normal Neil Fox is known to be capable. This season will be all so different. Neil is determined to make it so!"

Off the field Wakefield officially opened their new luxurious social club on Wednesday 31 August, although it had been in operation for several weeks already. Trinity's most distinguished Honorary Patron, Viscount Montgomery had been invited to open it but was unable to attend. He did, however, send one of his now customary messages to Trinity President, Alderman Fred West, "Dear West, I had hoped to see the team at Wembley last May but as the team did not reach the final I did not attend it. But if you can battle your way through the early rounds and reach Wembley for the Rugby League Cup Final in May 1967 – I will be there to see us win the cup. So give my orders to the club: Wembley in May 1967, and no nonsense about it. Yours sincerely, Montgomery of Alamein."

Another Honorary Patron of the club, Ronnie Fell, took Monty's place and performed the opening ceremony. The Social Club had cost a massive £40,000 but soon had more than 1,000 members to enjoy its facilities. In addition, a huge car and bus park was to be developed on the east side of the ground, where the malt kilns currently stood, and five new turnstiles were to be erected on Doncaster Road. Ronnie Fell, who owned Fell Construction and was a renowned racehorse owner, became a very good friend to Trinity, helping finance many projects at the club and represented the club on the Rugby League Council, an unusual arrangement for a rugby league club, as he was not a club director.

The season began on 20 August and it was not a happy start. Trinity lost 8-4 at Castleford and John L. Allen noted, "Apart from supplying evidence that in glorious summer sunshine with a temperature climbing towards the 80s, rugby league is out of place, there was little else to mention about this unattractive and often boring affair." He did, however add, "Harold Poynton often caught the eye... and some encouragement was forthcoming when Fox was seen running with confidence and power at a pitch indicative of his return to full physical fitness." It seemed that the new tap penalty rule reduced the number of scrums, which Trinity won 8-5, but the most significant thing in this first game of the season was the shoulder dislocation, his fourth, which ended Derek Turner's career.

Four days later it looked as if Trinity might not get a much better result at Featherstone. However, the Fox brothers made sure that Wakefield fans made the short journey home in good spirits. Neil opened the scoring with a touchline penalty after 17 minutes and then added another on the half-hour to give his side a 4-2 half-time lead. Seven minutes after the break Don hurled himself over from a play-the-ball and Neil converted but with only four minutes remaining it was 9-9. Rovers' fans were dismayed but probably not surprised when Don won the match with a dazzling solo try, throwing the defence on to the wrong foot, rounding the full-back and diving under the posts for Neil to convert.

If anyone thought there were too many Foxes at Wakefield they were to be disappointed. Another arrived when Peter landed at Belle Vue from Hull KR and played for the reserves against Hull 'A' on 27 August. It was also reported that Trinity were interested in St Helens stars Ray French and Alex Murphy. John L. Allen pointedly noted, "It can be added that locally the probable signing of Murphy was received with mixed feelings." Nothing came of the approach, but the Murphy saga was to drag on for many months.

On 27 August, Trinity met Wigan at Belle Vue in a game notable for being Don Metcalfe's 200th for the club and for the debut of Michael Hunte, a Barbadian, who learned his rugby league as an amateur with Lockwood in the Huddersfield area. His son, Alan, played briefly for Trinity in the late 1980s and ultimately became a Great Britain winger. Trinity overturned a 7-4 half-time deficit with three cracking tries to emerge victorious 19-7. Neil bagged a try and five goals and in doing so passed Lewis Jones's career record of 3,445 points. Only Gus Risman and Jim Sullivan now stood above him as points scorers. The *Wakefield Express* remarked on "Fox giving additional proof that his stamina and skill are edging back up to a standard that has captivated onlookers so often".

Two days later the other Lancashire giants, St Helens, arrived at Belle Vue for the last game Trinity would play under the three-yard rule. Trinity's forwards were totally dominant and the team's display evoked memories of the club's palmiest days. Neil rattled up 16 points in a 28-15 win and John L. Allen was suitably impressed, writing, "Fox treated the crowd to some exciting power-packed running as well as introducing classical touches to lift his performance into top grade international class".

A first-round Yorkshire Cup tie at Dewsbury on Saturday 3 September, brought Wakefield back to earth. The new five-yard rule should in theory have favoured Trinity's classier style but Dewsbury played all over them. Their tactics were unattractive but effective. Three minutes from time Dewsbury led 13-10 but Trinity were saved when Garthwaite went over at the corner flag after juggling with Neil's high but game-saving pass. A 13-13 draw was as much as Trinity deserved. The *Wakefield Express* reported, "Fox worked tremendously hard in the centre, but when you are a player of his reputation, it makes it all the more difficult to sidetrack the extra attention received from opponents." Two days later in the replay Neil made his 350th appearance for the club and Dewsbury again gave Trinity a hard time. Around the hour mark the score was 9-9 before Neil crashed through and was grounded just short. Don Fox bashed over from the play-the-ball and Neil converted. He finished with a match-winning six goals as Trinity progressed 18-11.

Neil's form had been good enough to earn him selection for Yorkshire's game against Cumberland at Workington on 7 September. He was also able to fulfil his ambition of captaining the county after being denied the chance through injury in previous years. Don Fox was the substitute forward and Neil's centre partner was Ian Brooke, one of five 1966 Lions in the side. Things looked bleak when Yorkshire fell 12-0 behind after only 23 minutes but they got onto the scoreboard just before the break, when Mick Shoebottom scored from a break by 'Flash' Flanagan. A goal from Neil reduced the arrears to 12-5 and in a five-minute spell in the second half Yorkshire gathered 10 points, thanks to two tries from Geoff Wriglesworth and two goals from Neil. In a see-saw thriller, Cumberland seemed to have secured victory when loose-forward Frank Foster grabbed a lovely try, converted by Bill Holliday. However, Neil brought Yorkshire level at 17-17 with a colossal 35-yard drop-goal as the game neared time and then just failed to snatch victory with another 40-yard effort.

Meanwhile, Trinity's fortunes nose-dived for a while. On 10 September Neil booted four goals against Hull, but the Humberside club left Belle Vue 19-14 winners. The following Monday, Huddersfield despatched Wakefield from the Yorkshire Cup, grinding out a turgid 11-6 success against a side which could not gain enough possession to worry the limited but fired-up Fartowners. Another defeat ensued on 17 September at Swinton. Neil, with a groin injury, and Don both missed the game. It was most unfortunate, for brother Peter made his debut for Trinity that afternoon, as did Gary Cooper, who Trinity had signed from Featherstone for £3,000. The game also represented Noel Dolton's last for Trinity. Neil recalls, "It was a pity Don and I missed this match with injuries. It would have been the first time the three of us would have played together and unfortunately we would never get another chance. Peter tore his Achilles tendon, which finished his playing career. Signing Gary Cooper was good for us though. He had been on tour with me in 1962 as a centre but now usually played full-back. He had played with Don at Featherstone for a long time and they understood each other's games."

Neil returned to action for Yorkshire's clash with Lancashire at Headingley on 21 September, a game which saw the ground's new floodlights switched on. Neil was not captain of Yorkshire this time, however, because tour skipper Harry Poole won back the position. The game was a very entertaining affair for the 10,528 paying customers, although most would have preferred a different result. Amazingly, with just minutes to go, the score was again 17-17 with Neil having landed another four goals, the last of which appeared to have earned Yorkshire another draw. A determined Lancashire side, inspired by Frank Myler, stole the spoils – deservedly on the night – with a last-gasp try by winger Brian Glover, converted by Colin Tyrer. With his second goal Neil had notched up his 3,500th point in first-class rugby league.

173

Neil's groin injury was aggravated in the Roses Match and he missed Trinity's next two games, victories against Keighley and Doncaster. He was given a run-out with the 'A' team against Keighley 'A' on 1 October and scored three tries and a goal, in a 14-7 win. In the Doncaster game Trinity gave a debut to Bernard Prior, a 31-year-old hooker from Hunslet. Bernard had been out of the game for several months after being injured on his test debut against France at Wigan and had actually announced his retirement. He certainly knew how to hook and was seen as the answer, albeit perhaps not for long, to Trinity's long-standing problems in gaining possession. At a mere £750 he proved a rare bargain.

Possession was about to become even more important than ever because the RFL had suddenly decided on another ground-breaking change to the laws of the game. Their revolutionary idea was to trial the four-tackle rule in that season's BBC2 Floodlit Trophy competition, with effect from the beginning of October.

Trinity had not yet acquired floodlights and so were, for the time being, unaffected. The game was now in the patently nonsensical situation of playing under two different sets of rules in the league and floodlit competitions. Moreover, as the trials progressed, the RFL decided on 26 October to institute the four-tackle rule for all games as from 29 October, thus initiating a change of seismic proportions for the sport, the results of which are still being felt in the 21st century. To complicate matters even further consenting clubs were allowed to play the four-tackle rule even before 29 October. Trinity were not among them.

Back on Saturday 8 October, Trinity played one of the most amazing games of their existence prior to the introduction of limited tackles football. It was against Hunslet at Belle Vue where, within a fortnight of signing for Trinity, Bernard Prior came up against his former team-mates. Neil claimed his 200th try for Trinity but that was just a footnote to this extraordinary affair. Neil recalls, "By half-time we were losing 17-0 but in the second half we pulled back to 17-16. Even so, with only seconds to go, defeat was staring us in the face. It must have been the last scrum about 45 yards out and 10 yards in from touch. Don was loose-forward but didn't pack down this time and stood to the side of the scrum. He shouted to our scrum-half Ray Owen, 'Pass that ball to me. I'm going to have a drop at goal'. Ray told him not to be so daft but when the ball came out, he did as he had been told. Don kicked the ball straight between the sticks for an amazing goal. We won 18-17. I think this had been the best fightback during my career so far. The spectators couldn't believe what they had seen. This just showed what a great player Don was."

The following Friday, Trinity went down 18-15 at St Helens in a fast, exciting encounter. The turning point came when Gert Coetzer was dismissed after 58 minutes in an incident after van Vollenhoven had scored a try to give Saints a 12-10 lead.

Soon after the defeat at Knowsley Road, Neil hit the headlines by resigning from the captaincy. The *Wakefield Express* ran the following account: "The international centre's action is, however, typical of the individual, who has always given Trinity most loyal service. This commendable attitude he is obviously anxious to continue as is indicated by his statements to colleagues which disclose that Neil's greatest concern is for the interests of the club and not personal glory to be achieved by retaining the distinguished position of captain... Fox acknowledged that the step had been taken 'because of criticism by supporters who are used to a winning side. You have to accept these things... I am going to see if giving up the captaincy will improve my play. It will be nice to concentrate on my own play for a change, instead of thinking about the other lads most of the time'."

Harold Poynton was awarded the captaincy with Don Fox as his vice-captain. A second sensation hit the Wakefield supporters almost immediately, when Berwyn Jones was dropped for the game at Hull KR on 22 October. Berwyn then announced his retirement, to which Trinity responded by transfer-listing him at £5,000.

The game at Craven Park was Trinity's last under unlimited tackles and, under Sod's Law, was a veritable feast of all that was best in the game. Rovers had won their last 12 games and beat Trinity 25-11. Don Fox captained the team in the absence of Harold Poynton and Neil kicked a solitary goal in his last club game under the old rules. According to John L. Allen, "Neil had a very sound game against players whose eagerness to keep a grip on the powerful centre was very evident." This game so enchanted the onlookers that the crowd remained behind to applaud both sides off the field.

Playing under the old rules, with the addition of the tap after a penalty to touch and the extension of the three-yard rule to five yards at the play-the-ball, had radically reduced the number of scrums. The average had dropped from 28 to 14 per game, the Rovers versus Trinity game being absolutely typical of the trend, with Trinity winning them 9-5. Under the new four-tackle rule the number of scrums increased again because after each fourth tackle a scrum was formed, an effect completely at odds with the avowed intent of the reformers prior to introducing limited tackles. The other major consequences of the change were the increase in general kicking and the proliferation of drop-goal attempts.

Whatever laws the legislators brought in, two things were certain. They could not please everyone and nothing could stop Neil Fox from piling up points. He had already amassed more than 3,500 points in 10 years of unlimited tackles rugby. Few could have dreamed that he would add another 2,700 points over the next 13 years.

At first the new rules did not go down too well at Belle Vue. The game against York on 29 October was Trinity's introduction to the new order. On a lovely day Trinity served up some poor stuff, which was miserable to watch. There was much frenzied play leading to collisions between colleagues and some shoddy defence. Trinity won 17-10 and Neil claimed 11 points, as well as creating the match-winning try, described as "a mighty lunge by Fox [which] demanded the attention of three opponents. They stopped his progress but did not prevent a nicely timed pass being sent out to David Garthwaite to canter in at the corner – too far out for Neil to round off his thrilling move with a goal". Malcolm Sampson made his last appearance as a Trinitarian before being transferred to Bramley.

At this game there was a collection for the victims of the Aberfan disaster, where over 100 children had been killed in South Wales when a coal-tip slid onto a primary school, which realised a penny short of £74 - a poignant gesture of generosity from one mining community to another.

Neil missed the next game – a 15-13 win at Wigan with a depleted team. Don Fox exhibited the family match-winning trait by dropping yet another 40-yard goal in the closing minutes. At this point in the season Wakefield stood 10th in the league, which was headed by the Yorkshire triumvirate of Hull KR, Leeds and Bradford Northern, the last two of whom were reported to be seeking Berwyn Jones's signature.

On 12 November, Trinity beat high-flying Bradford Northern 16-10 at Belle Vue. Both hookers were sent off but the spectators saw a very entertaining match. Neil dropped a peach of a goal from 30 yards. He landed five goals in total, as did Northern's kicker, Terry Clawson. However, after the Lord Mayor's show display against Bradford, Trinity infuriatingly hit rock bottom and lost 6-5 at Dewsbury, having forward Geoff Steel sent off after only 14 minutes. In the 59th minute Neil dropped a goal to give his side a 5-4 lead but the *Wakefield Express* described the game as "a black day for Neil", who missed six penalties and two drop-goal attempts. Don also failed with two drops but Dewsbury full-back Bob Hirst won the game with a drop in the 61st minute.

Trinity's up-and-down form continued on 26 November, when they ended Hull KR's run of 17 consecutive victories in a game televised from Belle Vue on BBC's *Grandstand*. It was a magnificent game in which Neil, Gary Cooper and Harold Poynton were outstanding and "Don Fox produced some of his famous guile". Neil booted four goals in a 22-14 success and "was at his best whether he was engaged in pulling opponents down or tearing through them in some pulsating gallops". The game marked the debut of hooker Dave Hawley, deputising for the suspended Bernard Prior.

By the time that Trinity went to Halifax on 3 December, the RFL had brought in another new rule, deciding that if the acting half-back was caught in possession there would no longer be a scrum. Thrum Hall presented the players with diabolical conditions. Half of the pitch seemed to be ankle-deep in mud while the other half resembled a skating rink. Both sides managed to score only one try, Poynton getting Trinity's in the 21st minute, while Halifax had to wait until the 76th for theirs. None the less, Trinity's forwards were dominant and laid the foundations for an impressive 17-3 victory. Neil's goal-kicking – seven successes out of 10 attempts - bordered on the miraculous under the vile conditions.

The following week Wakefield won 13-0 against Swinton, becoming the only team to nil the Lions that season. John L. Allen wrote, "Happiest memory of this encounter for Belle Vue fans would undoubtedly be a return to the glory of international form of Neil Fox. Victory was largely due to his most impressive work – some robust tackling and spirited running... He scored the third and last try with a characteristic burst and dummy that completely bluffed the defenders."

Doncaster were despatched 29-7 on 17 December, despite the Dons winning the scrums 20-11. Loose-forward Brian Cooper scored a sixth minute try on his debut for Trinity but Neil again stole the show with seven goals.

On Boxing Day morning Trinity, now sixth in the league, went to Headingley, where league leaders Leeds gave them a good hiding, 28-6. Trinity lost Prior concussed after 14 minutes and prop John Godfrey was sent off in the 69th minute but they were comprehensively outclassed. However, they must have learned some salutary lesson for defeat was to become a stranger over the coming months.

The following afternoon Wakefield hammered Featherstone 27-0 at Belle Vue. Neil scored two tries and three goals and passed the 3,000 points mark for his club. On New Year's Eve Wakefield ground out an important 9-7 victory at Bradford, where "ground conditions provided a striking resemblance to a farm stockyard – all mud and straw". Neil contributed a 15th-minute try described by the *Wakefield Express* thus: "Neil Fox was put in possession some 10 yards inside his own half. Off the centre went in a devastating run in which he either bluffed or bumped off a succession of would-be tacklers before crossing the line to end a thrilling run which stood out as the afternoon's highlight." Two minutes before the interval Ken Hirst, who had just returned to the game after a long absence through illness, scored another astounding try with an incredible feint and change of direction from a standing start, which left Crawshaw and Roberts "grovelling their way through the mud, completely off course". Trinity had a half-time lead of 9-0 but by the 60th minute Northern were back in contention at 9-7 and Trinity did well to hold out. The *Wakefield Express* moaned, "As a rugby league offering between two of the code's top four aspirants it was little more than a burlesque". Trinity were happy enough though. They had met most of the best teams on their fixture list and were close to the top four, facing an easier second half to the season than any of their major rivals – in theory, at least.

Meanwhile the Alex Murphy saga went on. Alex was still officially a St Helens player but was coaching Leigh. Wakefield committee men went to see him at the Huddersfield versus

Leigh game on 27 December. Trinity had reportedly agreed a fee of £6,500 with St Helens but Alex was reported to be on £30 a week with Leigh, did not want to cross the Pennines and said "I am happy at Leigh and am not in the least bothered if I never play again". John L. Allen reported: "I'm told authoritatively that if Murphy had come to Wakefield he would have worn the number 3 jersey". Neil and Alex in the centres - fancy that?

Actually the two future Hall-of-Famers were united a few days later on 4 January at Wakefield Trinity's new social club. The occasion was the presentation of Neil's benefit cheque. It was an all-ticket affair and at half-a-crown a head it sold out. Ronnie Fell presented the cheque to Neil. Among the guests were his parents, Stella and Tommy, Bill Fallowfield, Ian Brooke and the ubiquitous Murph. Also present were Yorkshire cricketers Brian Close, Doug Padgett and Freddie Trueman, local legend Denis Parkinson - thrice winner of the Manx Grand Prix, Sam Hall - arguably the north's most notable racehorse trainer and Joe Sime - the North's leading jockey. Neil's benefit raised a new rugby league record of £2,150, beating the previous record, held by Alex Murphy, by £50.

That same evening Wakefield Trinity re-signed Ian Brooke from Bradford Northern for around £8,000. He and Neil would forge a deadly centre partnership over the coming months. Ian was certainly one of the fastest players in the game. John L. Allen posed the question, "Will he bring to the Trinity middle backs the thrust and pace some of us remember so well when that talented man Alan Skene was partner to Neil Fox, who is without much doubt the best rugby league centre there is in Great Britain?" The short answer to that question was 'yes'.

Helping to fund the Brooke transfer was Trinity's decision to raise the price of admission to Belle Vue from three to four shillings. The committee told the fans that they were only bringing Wakefield's charges into line with all the other clubs. The decision brought in an extra £300 for the game against Halifax on 14 January, when Brooke made his second debut for Trinity. Ian helped repay some of the fee with a typically stylish try as Wakefield, on top form, raced away to win 23-3. It was reported that "Neil Fox, now back in his majestic, old-time form, scored the first and third tries". The report did not, however, note that they were his 200th and 201st tries for the club, or that his third of four goals brought him his 1,200th for Trinity.

A week later Trinity won 18-5 at Hunslet but failed to land any of their 11 attempts at goal! Neil was hundreds of miles away, however, having been restored to the Great Britain side for the test match at Carcassonne. Bizarrely, the game was played under the unlimited tackles laws, because France had not yet adopted four-tackle rugby league. Britain upset the odds in beating France 16-13 with some lovely, enterprising rugby. After going behind to a drop-goal, they took the lead after 13 minutes, when Neil snapped up a loose ball and despatched his winger, debutant Clive Sullivan, on his way to his first try in test football. Just before half-time Neil converted a try by new skipper Alan Hardisty to give Britain an 8-6 lead. Five minutes after the break Neil and prop Brian Tyson got Hardisty sidestepping over from 20 yards for a second try to lead 11-6. The French countered so strongly that by the last minute they led 13-11. Britain deservedly pulled the game from the fire, however, when Tyson and Terry Fogerty deftly worked the ball to Neil, who unceremoniously pushed off his opposite Guy Andrieu and flung the ball to Sullivan around the half-way line. The winger flew past three men on the outside, turned inside to wrong-foot two more tacklers and touched down triumphantly under the posts. Neil added the *coup de grâce* with the conversion. It was a very satisfactory return to test rugby for '*Monsieur Renard'*.

On 28 January Neil was back for Trinity's somewhat scratchy 21-11 home win over Bramley, who fielded six former Trinity players and were only 13-11 behind on the hour.

Neil had had better days, kicking only three goals from 10 shots and losing the ball in scoring 10 minutes from time. Cumbrian prop Nia Vaughan, an amateur international signed from Whitehaven, made his debut, while Tony Thomas played his last game for Wakefield before transferring to Castleford for £2,750.

February 4 presented Trinity with a potentially tricky first-round Challenge Cup match at Hunslet, where they had never previously won a cup tie. Although both scrum-halves were sent off after a dust-up, the game "wasn't a bit like a cup tie", according to John L. Allen. Ken Batty and Gary Cooper were in scintillating form and Neil kicked five goals as Trinity won 28-2. Allen was sufficiently enthusiastic to comment that there was "enough evidence to indicate that a side capable of reaching Wembley was there on view at Parkside".

A septic heel kept Neil out of Trinity's 18-11 home win against a spirited Dewsbury but he was back on 18 February for a sparkling 31-6 success at York, kicking five goals and scoring a try after Gert Coetzer had made an interception. Berwyn Jones played his last game for Wakefield and was transferred to Bradford Northern for £3,000 within a fortnight.

Wakefield had risen to third in the league at this stage, behind Leeds and Hull KR. They were therefore not too perturbed to draw an away tie at 21st-placed Featherstone in the second round of the Challenge Cup on 25 February. History also pointed to a Trinity victory, as Rovers had not beaten them in any cup tie since the war. The match was declared all-ticket and 12,502 fans squeezed into Post Office Road, taking no notice of the teams' respective league positions. Trinity were at full strength, apart from missing full-back Gary Cooper. A treacherous muddy pitch did not seem to be a hindrance to Wakefield who dominated the first quarter. After 16 minutes Don Fox put Poynton over under the bar, for Neil to convert. Then Ted Campbell crashed over but was prevented from grounding the ball. Rovers pulled back with a try from Ken Greatorex on 22 minutes but Trinity led 5-3 at the break. The second half confirmed why Post Office Road was such a graveyard for favourites though, as Rovers, adapting much better to the conditions, turned the screw to win 11-7, Trinity's only score being a penalty from Neil.

Oddly enough, the following week's *Wakefield Express* headlines proclaimed "There's still another Cup to be won: Trinity for the League Championship Trophy?" Perhaps the headline writer had inside information or had psychic powers. The cup tie defeat had ended Trinity's eight match winning run, but they would not taste the bitterness of defeat again during the remainder of the campaign.

Neil would experience defeat, however, in his next outing. While Wakefield were accounting for Batley 26-11 at Belle Vue, Neil was wearing Great Britain's number four jersey in the return test against France at Wigan on 4 March. He was also reacquainted with the unlimited tackles rule for the last time. The test was fairly typical of Anglo-French encounters, especially when refereed by a Frenchman. That is to say that they were punctuated by glorious passages of play, individual pieces of genius, confusion, bloody-mindedness and bouts of mayhem, in varying proportions from both sides.

Britain made five changes from the side which won in Carcassonne, Neil having a new winger in Huddersfield's combative Ken Senior. Phil King in the *Sunday People* was not enamoured at all, describing the game as "a spasmodic and often pathetic and scrappy spectacle under the old play-the-ball rule". He concluded his match report with this sentiment: "I sincerely hope that is the last I'll ever see of that old play-the-ball rule". Jack Paul, writing in the *Sunday Express* was equally dismayed and reported, "Great Britain, as poor and pathetic as the size of the crowd – 7,448, the smallest for a match of this kind at Wigan – went down to a shock defeat. But spare them no sympathy". The fact that Britain had lost a game they seemed likely to win for a long time probably coloured King's and

Paul's verdicts. They should surely have made more allowance for the misfortune that struck Britain with injuries, at a time when no substitutes were allowed after half-time. King did point out forcibly that "the Frenchmen played their usual short-tempered game with the boot and the clenched fist coming often. But many of Marseilles gendarme Georges Jameau's refereeing decisions were hard to follow".

Britain had begun brilliantly. Full-back Arthur Keegan went over after 16 minutes and Neil kicked a grand conversion. In the 23rd minute Alan Hardisty executed a beautiful kick and gather try from 30 yards and Britain were 8-2 ahead. However, France hit back with a try from loose-forward Jean-Pierre Clar and two more goals from full-back Pierre Lacaze to lead 9-8 at the interval. Lacaze popped over two drop-goals early in the second half to extend the lead to 13-8 but Britain levelled after 52 minutes, when loose-forward Dave Robinson strode over for a try to which Neil added the conversion. Britain had the initiative but were shattered five minutes later when Clar clattered second-rower Bill Bryant with a vicious stiff-arm tackle, which laid him out like a log. Bryant's leg was broken just above the ankle, as his 17-stone body collapsed awkwardly. Bill missed the rest of the season and the crowd was infuriated when the referee merely cautioned Clar. Things got worse after 66 minutes when scrum-half Keith Hepworth was taken off with a broken bone in his hand, valiantly sustained in trying to prevent second-rower Henri Marracq from scoring a try which, with Lacaze's conversion, gave the French an 18-13 lead. Down to 11 men and with captain Alan Hardisty suffering with a torn finger tendon, Britain conceded a final try to centre Jean-Pierre Lecompte and a seventh goal to Lacaze to lose 23-13.

Neil was probably relieved to be merely faced with a trip to Hull's Boulevard the following Saturday, where Trinity gained a well-merited 21-7 victory. Neil dropped a goal in the first minute, landed a penalty in the fifth minute and converted a 75 yard Coetzer interception try in the ninth minute, but hit the post with a touchline shot when attempting to improve Gert's second, even longer, interception try after 30 minutes. In the second half Coetzer completed his hat-trick, Neil landed two penalties and Don Fox was ordered off in the 53rd minute for a high tackle. Full-back Don Metcalfe made his last appearance in this game and Neil was sure he would be missed: "Don had been a very valuable player to Wakefield, playing in 212 games and scoring 33 tries. He was probably the best defensive player we had in this period but he was unlucky when it came to the big games like our appearances at Wembley, when Gerry Round was full-back or Alan Skene and Ian Brooke kept him out at centre." There was a fitting reward for Don at the season's close, when he was awarded the coveted James Harrison Trophy, presented to the fairest and most loyal player in the county by the Yorkshire Federation of Supporters' Clubs.

A patchy victory at Keighley left Trinity with just the rash of Easter fixtures to complete – four games in seven days – as they chased a top-four position. On Easter Saturday a very weak Castleford were crushed 35-10 at Belle Vue. The *Wakefield Express* noted, "Neil Fox starred with some accurate goal-kicking that earned him seven successes out of nine attempts". A similarly weak Leeds team, preparing for a Challenge Cup semi-final and containing only two first-teamers, was overcome 27-9 on Easter Monday before Belle Vue's biggest crowd of the season, 12,736. Neil landed another half-dozen goals. The following day Trinity met a much sterner challenge from Bramley on their first visit to the Villagers' new ground, McLaren Field. Bramley led 3-0 at the break. Neil kicked a penalty after 56 minutes but it was only a 69th-minute try out of the blue from Coetzer, his 100th for Trinity, which enabled them to snatch a 5-3 victory.

The last league game of the season brought a 17-2 win at Batley. Neil contributed four goals and the *Wakefield Express* lauded his performance, "Neil Fox caused the Batley defence no end of trouble with his power-packed bursts and was easily the most penetrative back on view". Neil recalls: "I remember this game particularly well. A young man we signed from Featherstone was making his debut. Although we signed him as a centre, he played on my wing. He'll not forget it either. He had a nightmare, knocking on four times with the line at his mercy. Coming off the pitch after the game a young Batley supporter ran up to our debutant and said, 'The way tha' played today, tha'd be good enough to play for us'. That wouldn't do his confidence any good, I thought. But eventually he developed into a very good forward, scored plenty of tries, represented Yorkshire and went on to play for England in the 1975 World Championship. In 1981-82 he scored a record number of tries for a prop forward in a season when he got 25 playing for Carlisle. It was Mick Morgan, who became one of Wakefield Trinity's supporters' all-time favourites."

Trinity had finished third in the table and had a fortnight's rest before the top sixteen played off for the Championship. In that period Trinity made a third attempt to sign Alex Murphy but failed, signed another promising centre from Trinity Juniors in Terry Crook and gave their player-of-the-year award to skipper Harold Poynton, who had been in wonderful form. Trinity had not been beaten in the league since Boxing Day and had won their last 14 league fixtures. They had adapted to the new rules better than most teams, having most of the requirements necessary for success under the different conditions. They had a very mobile pack and, crucially, a hooker in Bernard Prior who would guarantee plenty of ball. Poynton and Owen at half-back were an excellent combination and the other backs Cooper, Hirst, Brooke and Coetzer had a rare combination of experience, skill and, above all, pace which complemented Neil's power, nous and dynamism perfectly. This was a team which could win the Championship.

The play-offs opened with a visit from Salford on 15 April. Before the game Trinity players were presented with tankards for winning the fifth and final period (13 March to 29 April) of that season's Mackeson Trophy, their high-scoring over eight games (averaging 23.50 points) earning the reward. Trinity had also won the fourth period (16 January to 11 March) with an average of 21.25 points per match. After the first 40 minutes against the Red Devils, Trinity looked anything but Championship material. Although they led 8-5, Wakefield had been totally unconvincing. After the break they brought on substitute Don Fox and everything changed. The turning point occurred in the 47th minute. Salford were attacking Trinity's line and threatening to go in front, when Ian Brooke got his boot to a loose ball and play rapidly moved to the other end of the field, where Ken Hirst took advantage of a lucky bounce to score. Neil's conversion gave his side the lead and was the signal for a truly bewildering display by Trinity. They ran Salford ragged with 40 unanswered second-half points to win 48-8. Neil contributed 22 of those points, with eight goals and two tries. The *Wakefield Express* said: "In the second half Neil was at his best... By judicious use of a powerful frame and great skill, his brilliance stood out prominently".

On 22 April, Workington Town, who had finished sixth, journeyed to Belle Vue for the quarter-final. They offered sterner resistance than Salford. Trinity led only 7-2 at half-time but were clearly the better team. However, yet again, the second half produced some wonderful play from the Trinitarians' backs, while Don Fox and Bob Haigh were at their best in the pack. Again Trinity conceded no points in the second half but added 15 of their own. Neil collected four goals. On this performance the team had every right to fancy their chances to become the first Trinity side to be hailed as champions.

First, however, they had to visit Hull KR in the semi-final. Rovers had pipped Trinity for second place in the table on points average and the memory was still fresh in many minds of their success at Belle Vue in the play-offs the preceding season. Moreover, Rovers had not lost at Craven Park since 20 November 1965, when Trinity had been their conquerors. In the event it was no contest. Harold Poynton played one of the greatest 40 minutes of his career. He dropped two early goals and in the 33rd minute made a try for Hirst with one of his trademark back-flips. Neil converted and at 9-0 Rovers were hard-pressed to get back into the game. Poynton did not reappear for the second half, but Don Fox took over where he had left off. The power of his pack "allowed Don Fox to exercise his fascinating, unorthodox way of teasing the foe to an extent that was most unsettling to the Rovers front department", according to John L. Allen. Neil recalls, "Prop John Bath, playing for Trinity against his old team, had his best game of the season. He was told just to run as hard as possible at the opposition – mainly at Frank Foster. We knew Frank would go high in the tackle and we would be able to pick up some points from penalties. John was not a pretty sight when he came off but had done a great job provoking the Hull KR pack." Neil, who kicked four goals, had done a pretty good job himself. The *Wakefield Express* said, "Neil Fox was always an outstanding performer. Whenever he was in possession his forceful tactics and deceptive movement left his opposite number, the highly rated [Alan] Burwell, completely outclassed." Neil's combination with Ian Brooke worked to perfection and Trinity ran out winners by 18-6, Rovers collecting two late consolation tries.

Wakefield had qualified for only their third Championship Final. Neil was hoping for better luck than came his way in the losing finals of 1960 and 1962 but Trinity's opponents were the formidable St Helens. Saints were the reigning champions and had won the Lancashire League. They had, however, only finished fourth in the table, seven points behind Wakefield. Their greatest asset was the power of their forwards, while Trinity appeared to have an advantage in the backs. There were no favourites for the final. It was anybody's guess who would win. Unfortunately, Neil had a shock earlier in the week, when a break-in at his office had cost him £200. Things could only get better, he hoped. The teams that took the field at Headingley for the showdown on 6 May were as follows:

St Helens: Frank Barrow, Tom van Vollenhoven, captain, Tony Barrow, Wilf Smith, Len Killeen, Peter Douglas, Tommy Bishop, John Warlow, Bill Sayer, Cliff Watson, Ray French, Brian Hogan, John Mantle. Substitutes: John Houghton, Joe Robinson.

Wakefield Trinity: Gary Cooper, Ken Hirst, Ian Brooke, Neil Fox, Gert Coetzer, Harold Poynton, captain, Ray Owen, John Bath, Bernard Prior, Ted Campbell, Geoff Clarkson, Bob Haigh, Don Fox. Substitutes: Ken Batty, Dave Hawley.

No one who was present at Headingley for the 1967 Championship Final is likely to forget it. For sheer drama it had everything. Many people were amazed that it took place at all because the elements threw every nasty thing imaginable at Headingley. The 1968 Watersplash Final at Wembley is often cited as a game which would never have taken place, if it had not been such an important event and part of the television schedule. Well, this Championship Final was probably just as sorely afflicted by the weather but for much longer and in a greater variety of awfulness. Ask anybody who was at both! Eddie Waring's report in the *Sunday Mirror* ran with the headlines "The Thunder and Lightning Final: Fox robbed of glory chance". Eddie wrote, "What a day! And, boy, what a game! Thunder, lightning and torrential rain combined to make a dramatic back cloth to the rugby league championship final at Headingley. And St Helens and Wakefield matched the elements with some real blood and thunder rugby." He forgot to mention the tremendous hail storms, the pitch that seemed more suitable for aquatic sports and the periodic bouts of sunshine.

Under the circumstances the game was better than anyone had any right to expect, absolutely gripping and surrounded by controversy. It was clear from the first whistle that Saints were determined to make it a forward battle, while Trinity were keen to risk dry-weather tactics despite the conditions. Some of Saints' tackling was of the strong-arm variety and it was obvious that Neil and Harold Poynton were in for some rough treatment. Early on Harold was knocked out, while Neil remembers, "Because of the conditions we knew that this was going to be a very physical match. I got an elbow into my chest bone and could hardly breathe but carried on. Harold Poynton had been taken off and by the time he returned I had kicked a penalty". That was after 12 minutes. A few minutes later referee George Philpott of Leeds put the cat among the pigeons when he disallowed a try claimed by Tony Barrow because of a debatable knock-on. On 23 minutes Saints did take the lead with a well worked try from the outstanding prop Cliff Watson after good play by van Vollenhoven, Bishop and French. Killeen converted and Wakefield were three points behind, which became five after 28 minutes when Killeen piloted a fine 40-yard penalty.

Half-time arrived with Saints deservedly 7-2 ahead but with many spectators wondering why the game was being played at all and when it might be abandoned. They were, however, equally entranced by the whole dramatic spectacle of brave, fit and rugged men battling so hard against one another in such a terrible maelstrom. Neil goes on, "At half-time I had treatment to my chest injury and then we went out again into the rain, thunder and lightning. I kicked a goal and made it 7-4." That was in the 50th minute after hooker Bill Sayer had obstructed Neil.

In the second half Trinity appeared to be running their opponents into a frazzle, but Saints' tackling was a source of wonder to all present. It seemed that Wakefield would never breach their defence and the trophy would return to Knowsley Road but, with seven minutes left on the clock, they grabbed an unexpected lifeline. A scrum went down near the St Helens line. Sayer heeled the ball but Bishop could not control it and Ray Owen was on to it in a flash, poking it over the goal line only to be held back by Douglas. The referee immediately awarded an obstruction try to level the scores, much to the disgust and disbelief of the St Helens fans and players who doubted that Owen would have been first to the ball. Neil took the kick which could have brought the Championship to the Merrie Citie for the first time. More than 20,000 spectators and a million or more ABC television viewers fell silent as he placed the ball for a wide-angled shot at the posts. Neil has not forgotten the moment, "I knew this was the chance to win the game. But as I placed the ball, the snow, the wind and the rain all blasted into my face and I could hardly see the ball, never mind the goal, as I kicked. The ball smacked into the post and bounced out."

Unbelievably, Neil got another chance to win the game in the last minute when Mantle obstructed Ken Hirst as he tried to regather a kick through. It was not far out but it was acutely angled and his shot just passed outside the post. In the final analysis most critics felt justice had been done. Neil says, "I was just glad we had another chance in a replay. I think we were a bit lucky to get it though because I don't think that Ray Owen would have got to the ball for that penalty try." Towards the interval Trinity had been awarded some penalties which many journalists thought were kickable by a man as capable as Neil but Wakefield kicked for touch instead. Ken Traill put them right after the game, saying, "After that early knock he got, Neil was suffering from double-vision. Even with the shots he did take, he could see two rugby balls as he was kicking."

There was one unfortunate repercussion from the Headingley game. Referee George Philpott withdrew from the replay after his wife had received threatening letters from some fool or fools aggrieved at the awarding of Owen's obstruction try. Bill Fallowfield told the press, "Hanging is too good for such a dastardly act." Joe Manley of Warrington replaced Philpott for the replay at Swinton on Wednesday evening, 10 May, when the weather and conditions were perfect. Interest was extremely high for the first Championship Final to be replayed since Huddersfield and Leeds went through the process at Halifax in 1930. A crowd of 33,537 attended the game, which was contested between two unchanged sides. Neither Neil, with his chest injury, nor John Bath, with a bad shoulder, were fully fit but decided to play with the aid of injections.

The teams took the same attitudes into the replay as they had to the game at Leeds, where Saints had won the scrums 20-12. On a firm, dry pitch Trinity's approach was bound to be more productive if they could win enough possession. Saints once again tried to dominate through their pack but were unable to produce the same amount of fire and brimstone as they had at Headingley. Trinity's style of play was made for the warm and windless conditions and Bernard Prior's amazing monopoly of the first-half scrums – he won eight of the first nine – allowed their play-makers to dictate.

Wakefield started off in whirlwind fashion. Hirst and Coetzer both got over but had tries disallowed and Poynton hit the bar with a drop-goal attempt. It took only eight minutes before Owen gave them the lead, scooting over from a play-the-ball. Neil missed the conversion and failed with a penalty from half-way before Killeen landed a 45-yard goal after quarter of an hour. Four minutes later, Don Fox adroitly switched play to send Brooke over at the corner and Trinity looked comfortable at 6-2. Saints were not done though and a 25-yard Bishop drop-goal was followed by a 27th-minute try from van Vollenhoven at the corner flag. Saints were 7-6 up against the run of play but Wakefield were equal to the challenge. Cooper sent Coetzer over in the 33rd minute but a forward pass denied the score. After 36 minutes Poynton broke the defence and flung a long pass to Hirst, who almost got in at the corner. From the play-the-ball Owen sent Poynton over for a try as easily as he might shell peas. Neil converted and Trinity led 11-7. Early in the second half Wakefield appeared vulnerable when Bishop almost scored from a kick and chase but Owen got to the ball first. Killeen made the score 11-9 after 51 minutes with an easy penalty for offside. Thereafter Trinity took control. After 53 minutes Poynton sent Haigh crashing through and when eventually he was brought down, Owen sent Brooke dummying over from the play-the-ball. Neil converted and Trinity led 16-9. A few minutes later it was all over bar the shouting, when Hirst avoided the clutches of Watson and Frank Barrow to score a splendid try after typically clever work from Poynton. Seven minutes from time Neil finished the scoring with a fine-angled penalty and Trinity had triumphed 21-9. Ray Owen won the Harry Sunderland Trophy and after Harold Poynton became the first Trinity skipper to collect the Championship Cup, John L. Allen remarked, "No wonder the team left the field to a standing ovation, with some supporters moist-eyed!"

Wakefield's players were well rewarded for their historic victory. They received £76 from the club and £50 each from an anonymous well-wisher, who most fans assumed was Ronnie Fell. Ronnie certainly provided the lads with a five-day break in Spain for their efforts and there was the customary civic reception for the team. The *Wakefield Express* leader writer proudly proclaimed, "Trinity do more than any other organisation to put Wakefield on the map". It was definitely a glorious end to a wonderful season.

Neil had finally completed his collection of all the game's major medals and was looking forward to a break before trying to add a few more. He had certainly had a good season, finally captaining his county and regaining his test place. His 309 points for Wakefield were his best return for the club since 1961-62. In all games he had 336 points, placing him behind only Len Killeen of St Helens on 353 and Leeds's Bev Risman on 347. His 144 goals were beaten only by Risman with 163, Killeen on 148 and Hull KR's Cyril Kellett with 145.

Wakefield Trinity 1966-67

Wakefield Trinity finished 3rd in the league: P34, W27, L7, For 631, Against 339
Fox scored 15 tries, 132 goals, 309 points for Wakefield, and 1 try, 12 goals, 27 points in representative games

Date	Opponent	Score	Fox	Crowd	
20 Aug	Castleford	4-8	2G	8,000	
24 Aug	Featherstone R	14-9	4G	5,170	
27 Aug	**Wigan**	19-7	T, 5G	6,957	
29 Aug	**St Helens**	28-15	2T, 5G	8,514	
3 Sep	Dewsbury	13-13	2G	6,800	YC1
5 Sep	**Dewsbury**	18-11	6G	8,013	Replay
10 Sep	**Hull**	14-19	4G	6,901	
12 Sep	Huddersfield	6-11		7,473	YC2
17 Sep	Swinton	13-27	dnp	5,600	
24 Sep	**Keighley**	42-6	dnp	5,198	
1 Oct	Doncaster	19-0	dnp	2,020	
8 Oct	**Hunslet**	18-17	T, 2G	5,885	
14 Oct	St Helens	15-18	3G	11,976	
22 Oct	Hull KR	11-25	G	9,500	
29 Oct	**York**	17-10	T, 4G	4,831	
5 Nov	Wigan	15-13	dnp	10,473	
12 Nov	**Bradford N**	16-10	5G	8,440	
19 Nov	Dewsbury	5-6	G	4,500	
26 Nov	**Hull KR**	22-14	4G	6,121	
3 Dec	Halifax	17-3	7G	6,037	
10 Dec	**Swinton**	13-0	T, G	6,010	
17 Dec	**Doncaster**	29-7	7G	3,779	
26 Dec	Leeds	6-28	2G	16,368	
27 Dec	**Featherstone R**	27-0	2T, 3G	4,996	
31 Dec	Bradford N	9-7	T	9,852	
14 Jan	**Halifax**	23-3	2T, 4G	7,759	
21 Jan	Hunslet	18-5	dnp	5,250	
28 Jan	**Bramley**	21-11	3G	5,240	
4 Feb	Hunslet	28-2	5G	8,813	Ch Cup 1
11 Feb	**Dewsbury**	18-11	dnp	7,227	
18 Feb	York	31-6	T, 5G	5,190	
25 Feb	Featherstone R	7-11	2G	12,502	Ch Cup 2
4 Mar	**Batley**	26-11	dnp	3,664	
11 Mar	Hull	21-7	5G	6,200	
18 Mar	Keighley	16-12	2G	2,500	
25 Mar	**Castleford**	35-10	T, 7G	7,067	
27 Mar	**Leeds**	27-9	6G	12,736	
28 Mar	Bramley	5-3	G	3,250	
1 Apr	Batley	17-2	4G	3,000	
15 Apr	**Salford**	48-8	2T, 8G	8,381	CH1
22 Apr	**Workington T**	22-2	3G	7,543	CH2
29 Apr	Hull KR	18-6	4G	12,776	CH semi
6 May	St Helens	7-7	2G	20,161	CH Final (at Leeds)
10 May	St Helens	21-9	3G	33,537	Replay (at Swinton)

Representative appearances

Date		Fox
7 Sep	Yorkshire 17 Cumberland 17 (Workington)	4G
21 Sep	Yorkshire 17 Lancashire 22 (Leeds)	T, 4G
22 Jan	Great Britain 16 France 13 (Carcassonne)	2G
4 Mar	Great Britain 13 France 23 (Wigan)	2G

16. 1967-68: Ecstasy and agony

On 5 August 1967 the *Wakefield Express* reported that "Wakefield Trinity's international centre, Neil Fox, has sold his shares in his turf accountant's business to Midlands bookmaker, Mr Jack Woolf, but he and his partner, Mr Trevor Woodward, will continue to run the business for him. Neil, who has six betting offices, told the *Express* yesterday, 'We are hoping to extend the business further up North'." Neil's business activities were prospering. He recalls, "We sold out to Jack Woolf Turf Accountants Limited, with a nice profit. They had shops around Birmingham and were buying shops in other areas, hoping that they could become a public company one day. This did not transpire and they later sold their shops. Trevor and I started up again in 1969 with three shops in South Yorkshire, built them up for three years and then sold them to a local guy. It was good business."

However, Neil's club Wakefield Trinity represented something of a conundrum. As champions they had certainly done the business on the field and the gate takings for the 1966-67 season had shot up from £15,929 to £23,376, largely because of the increase in admission charges. They had nonetheless contrived to lose £2,960 on the season and Trinity's average home league attendance had fallen from 8,067 in 1965-66 to 6,725 in the championship-winning campaign. Nineteen of the 30 clubs had recorded increased attendances in 1966-67, which made the Trinity decline so much more mystifying.

During the close season John Ridge was elected as club chairman and Neil's former playing colleague Brian Briggs won a place on the committee. Match earnings were agreed at £16 for an away win, £14 for a home win and £6 for a defeat, home or away. The players were assured that if they performed as well as they had in the previous season they would definitely make more than £1,000 each.

Changes in playing personnel were not far-reaching. The club had signed winger Eddie McDonagh from Huddersfield St Joseph's, who was said to be a real flyer, and Bernard Ward, a Yorkshire under-19 half-back from Normanton. Departures included Derek Plumstead, who joined a host of Trinity old boys at Bramley, and scrum-half Terry Gorman, who went to Batley. Don Metcalfe had taken the coaching role at Keighley. A novel addition to the Belle Vue personnel was the introduction of two young women as cheerleaders.

After introducing so many changes in the playing rules in 1966-67, there were thankfully only two more minor alterations for the start of the new season. Firstly, a failed drop at goal now resulted in a '25' yard tap kick to the defending side. Secondly, all penalty tries were now to be followed by a conversion from under the posts, instead of where the offence was deemed to have been committed. If the latter rule had applied at Headingley in the previous year's Championship Final, Trinity would almost certainly have not required a replay. The new rules had brought about an 18 per cent increase in the number of tries scored, according to RFL figures, and an unspecified but probably astronomical rise in the number of drop-goals and attempts at drop-goals.

Wakefield opened the season with a 31-11 trouncing of Castleford. The *Wakefield Express* commented "Trinity can reserve places on the club sideboard for a row of trophies." Harold Poynton was so good that his colleagues hardly knew what he would do next and the *Express* remarked, "Neil Fox was not consistently at his best but when he did find his true standard, he revealed that with his two tries and five goals he is still about the finest scoring machine in the game. His crashing runs and hand-offs were a treat to see." The third of his goals was the 1,500th of his first class career.

The following Wednesday it was back to the drawing-board as the team had a collective off-day at Swinton, going down 27-13 after being level 10-10 as half-time approached. Neil kicked two goals but had a beano in the next fixture, a home game against Batley on 26 August. All manner of records went by the board. Trinity won 78-9 to beat their previous record score, while Neil broke his shared club record by landing 12 goals. He also scored three tries to extend his own club points-in-a-match record to 33. That also beat his personal record of 32 points against Northern New South Wales on the 1962 Lions tour. Agonisingly, Neil had to wait until the last minute to break the goal-kicking record, when full-back Richard Payley registered his own hat-trick following a breath-taking solo run.

Two days later Trinity travelled for a crunch encounter at St Helens, who were bent on avenging their Championship Final defeat. It was certainly a lively game. Trinity lost the scrums two to one but, remarkably, had most of the territorial advantage. Neil kicked them into an 11th-minute lead with a penalty which went over after striking the post. Gert Coetzer's try four minutes later was converted from wide out by Neil, but tries by Peter Douglas and Ray French brought Saints back to 7-6 after 45 minutes. On the hour Douglas got a second try after Billy Benyon intercepted a George Shepherd pass and the conversion meant Trinity trailed 11-7. Neil banged over two penalties but Saints won 13-11 after Kel Coslett landed a massive penalty from just inside his own half with five minutes remaining.

Neil claimed nine points in a 23-5 victory at Keighley in the first round of the Yorkshire Cup. He missed the second half, the *Wakefield Express* noting, "When scoring a great try seven minutes before half-time he penetrated a wall of five defenders and damaged his hip in the process". He was more fortunate than Bob Haigh, who tore knee ligaments after seven minutes. Neil had a few days' holiday in Blackpool and was fit for the visit of Hull KR on 9 September. An injury-hit Trinity did well to draw 12-12, Neil booting three goals.

The two teams met again at Belle Vue on 13 September in the Yorkshire Cup second round. Trinity took the risk of fielding Bernard Prior, who had been injured in pre-season training. Unfortunately, the hooker lasted only 13 minutes before limping off. The game became "a terrific, tough struggle" with an 8-8 interval scoreline. In the 68th minute Rovers stand-off Roger Millward scored after a dramatic 70-yard run. At 11-8 down Trinity were awarded a kickable penalty. Neil knew there was no point in kicking for goal and began a passing move which ended in Hirst haring over at the corner. Neil's nerve held and he converted magnificently from a very difficult angle. But in a real nail-biter Rovers equalised with an injury-time penalty from Cyril Kellett.

The replay took place at Craven Park two days later but Trinity were well beaten 14-5. They did not score until three minutes from time when Neil got over from a long pass by Poynton, converting his own try. Rovers and Trinity would be sick of the sight of each other before the season closed.

Less than 24 hours after the defeat in Hull, Wakefield won 17-5 at Batley. Neil scored nine points but Trinity again suffered injury blows. His wing partner Gert Coetzer dislocated a shoulder joint, causing his absence for seven games, while young hooker Dave Hawley (cut head) had to be replaced by debutant Michael Lig, who scored a try within two minutes of taking the field. Neil recalls, "There were an awful lot of injuries at that time. Not only that but our prop John Bath found the pressure of travelling all the way from home in Bridlington to train and play too much and called it a day after the Batley game and joined York. To replace John, we signed another front-rower, David Jeanes, from Wakefield RU club, along with his playing colleague Ray Spencer. David Jeanes was a big man – 6 feet 2 inches and 16½ stones – just the type you needed in our game. He was strong and could run and he did just that on his debut against Featherstone, coming on to balls at speed sent out by our Don. We won that game 22-5 and David must have been pleased with the way his first game went. He became an important player for us." Neil kicked five goals against Featherstone, including his 1,300th for Trinity.

There had been a minute's silence before the game against Featherstone in remembrance of club patron Ronnie Fell, who had died suddenly. His generosity and drive would be missed.

On 29 September, Trinity played Hull KR for the fourth time in three weeks but met with even less success than in the previous encounters. There was a distinct lack of cohesion and pace and all the luck seemed to run Rovers' way. Neil was described as "the dominant figure in the threequarter line", landed two goals and made a try for Ian Brooke but the result was a 25-7 beating.

Neil was playing well enough to be selected as captain of Yorkshire for their game against the 1967 Kangaroos on Wednesday 4 October, along with Trinity second-rower Geoff Clarkson. It was a great occasion in more ways than one. Trinity had joined the ever growing band of clubs who had installed floodlights and Belle Vue saw their inauguration on the occasion of the tour fixture. The lights had cost Wakefield £11,000 and consisted of four pylons down each touchline, with 15 lights to each pylon. The great driving force behind Trinity's acquisition of floodlighting had been the unfortunate Ronnie Fell, who had not lived to see his project completed. In every sense the game was a brilliant spectacle for the 19,376 crowd – the biggest of the season so far in Yorkshire. Most people who saw the game would unquestionably regard it as one of Neil's finest performances.

The Australians lost fiery prop John Sattler in the 25th minute after laying out Yorkshire prop Dave Hill at a scrum and full-back Graeme Langlands was taken off before the interval with a rib injury and replaced by second-row forward Dennis Manteit. Skipper Reg Gasnier moved to full-back in his place and had a fairly unhappy game. Neil took full advantage. Yorkshire led 6-0 at the break. Jack Bentley of the *Daily Express* wrote, "It was Fox who tore away from a Peter Small pass to push off two defenders in a touchline burst and plunge over at the corner in a flurry of tacklers for Yorkshire's first try in the 16th minute. It was Fox who thundered 60 yards, backed up by winger Bill Francis, to lay on Yorkshire's second try in the 35th minute for scrum-half Carl Dooler." In the second half Neil landed a couple of superb penalty goals but the Australians gradually gained impetus and led 14-10 after 68 minutes, through tries from Elwyn Walters and Ron Coote, plus four goals from Ken Irvine. Yorkshire's cause seemed lost as the game entered its final minute but it was the Aussies who were doomed to defeat. Alfred Drewry in the *Yorkshire Post* declared, "The man who beat them was Neil Fox, without a doubt... It was from his last minute burst that Millward scored. Fox lost the ball as he was tackled and the Australians claimed a knock-on, but the referee ruled that Irvine had had a chance to derive advantage from Fox's slip and muffed it." Millward hacked the ball on, followed up and touched down. Neil was left with the last act of the match, the conversion which would win or lose the game for Yorkshire. His nerve held, his aim was true and the Tykes triumphed 15-14."

After the match, the teams and the Mayor of Wakefield attended a reception, at which Alderman Frank West, Trinity's president, thanked both captains for a splendid game. It had been notably clean, apart from the Sattler incident. The *Wakefield Express* noted that "the Yorkshire skipper, Neil Fox, with his customary modesty, promptly replied that he did not require any thanks. Instead, he thanked the county officials for picking him!" Nowadays Neil regards that game as one of his career highlights, saying, "It was really wonderful to be able to lead out Yorkshire in front of our own Wakefield supporters and fantastic to gain such a marvellous win under the new floodlights".

Neil had been the outstanding player on the field and it was no surprise that the selectors chose him to captain Great Britain in the first Ashes test at Headingley on 21 October. Neil had picked up an ankle injury in the Yorkshire game and missed Trinity's 21-19 win at Keighley on 11 October but was back for the game at Hunslet three days later, when another recent captain of Great Britain, scrum-half Tommy Smales made his debut for Trinity, after joining the club on a temporary transfer until Christmas. Hooker Geoff Oakes returned to Trinity on a month's trial from Warrington and also made his reappearance at Parkside. Trinity won 9-2 in driving rain but paid a heavy price. Prop Nia Vaughan was sent off just before half-time and Geoff Clarkson followed him in the 76th minute, while Harold Poynton spent the last 25 minutes limping on the wing. Worst of all, Neil had to retire at half-time with a recurrence of ankle trouble and was unable to play in the test at Leeds, which Britain won 16-11. It was a hard blow. The injury kept Neil out of home games against Halifax and Hull KR – yet another drawn game, in the Floodlit Trophy – and deprived him of leading Yorkshire against Cumberland.

To prove he was fit for the second test, Neil was back for Trinity's encounter with the Australians on 28 October. Three high-ranking Kenyan Government officials attended the game at Belle Vue, although the newspapers did not report why. They were probably not impressed with Wakefield's performance but would certainly have admired the Kangaroos' speed and skill, as they overwhelmed Trinity 33-7 before a crowd of more than 10,000. Neil kicked a couple of goals but Wakefield did not score their solitary try until the 77th minute when Ken Batty got over. To be fair to Trinity, only four of the 1967 Championship-winning team played and they were reduced to 12 men with almost half an hour left.

The second Ashes test took place at the White City stadium in London and was played under floodlights on Friday 3 November. Neil was one of only two changes from the side which won at Leeds, replacing Rochdale Hornets' Malcolm Price, the other being the introduction of Frank Foster at loose-forward instead of Swinton's Dave Robinson. The selectors decided to retain Bill Holliday as captain after Britain's success at Headingley. Australia lacked three major stars through injury in Reg Gasnier, Billy Smith and Johnny Raper. Britain consequently were well fancied to clinch the Ashes. The teams were:

Great Britain: Arthur Keegan (Hull), Chris Young (Hull KR), Ian Brooke (Wakefield T), Neil Fox (Wakefield Trinity), Bill Francis (Wigan), Roger Millward (Hull KR), Tommy Bishop (St Helens), Bill Holliday (Hull KR, captain), Peter Flanagan (Hull KR), Cliff Watson (St Helens), Bob Irving (Oldham), John Mantle (St Helens), Frank Foster (Hull KR).
Substitutes: Malcolm Price (Rochdale H), Dave Robinson (Swinton).

Australia: Les Johns (Canterbury), Johnny Greaves (Canterbury), Graeme Langlands (St George), John McDonald (Toowoomba), Johnny King (St George), Tony Branson (Nowra), Johnny Gleeson (Brothers, Brisbane), Peter Gallagher (Brothers, Brisbane, captain), Noel Kelly (Wests), Noel Gallagher (Bundaberg), Ron Lynch (Parramatta), Elton Rasmussen (St George), Ron Coote (Souths).
Substitutes: Ken Irvine (Norths) and Dennis Manteit (Brothers, Brisbane).

The first half was tense and try-less, the only points coming from a penalty by Langlands and a drop-goal by Bishop. Fifteen minutes into the second half Britain hit the lead when Brooke sliced deep into Australian territory before falling to a superb cover tackle by Coote. The ball was quickly shifted to Bishop, who, though tackled, got up and played the ball to himself before touching down. Neil added the goal for a 7-2 lead. On the hour Australia replied with a Langlands penalty and a couple of minutes later were level, when Branson opened up the British defence to enable Langlands to score near the posts. Unbelievably, he failed with the conversion and Neil made Australia pay by landing a penalty within two minutes of Langlands's miss. On 67 minutes Langlands brought the score to 9-9 with a successful penalty attempt and three minutes later, amid steady rain,

Australia went ahead. Holliday made a clearing run from the '25' and threw a reckless pass to Brooke, which hit him on the shoulder and the ball went to ground. Aussie winger King swept on to the slippery ball and did well to score. Langlands's conversion gave Australia a 14-9 lead, which was cut by two five minutes from time when Neil landed his third goal. Australia sealed a 17-11 victory when Coote scored a hotly debated try in the 78th minute.

Neil entered the test match needing just eight points to surpass Jim Sullivan's record of 62 points in Ashes tests. He was now stuck on 61 but his selection for the third test at was expected to provide him with the opportunity to break Sullivan's record.

Neil and Ian Brooke rushed back from London to play for Trinity against Keighley the following afternoon. Both contributed substantially to an 18-2 victory, Ian scoring twice and Neil making a try for Hawley and kicking three goals. Unfortunately, injury overtook Neil again and over the next seven weeks he would only play in one first-team game, a 7-5 loss at Huddersfield on 18 November, when he suffered a knee injury falling on a hard pitch. He was ruled out of the deciding Ashes test, which was lost 3-11, and never had another opportunity to break Jim Sullivan's record.

In Neil's absence Trinity went out of the Floodlit Trophy, losing to Hull KR, and exhibited very patchy form in their league games. They were certainly not producing anything like Championship form and there appeared to be some unrest among the players with George Shepherd, Don Fox and Bernard Prior all being transfer-listed. By the time Neil was fit Trinity were a long way off the pace, languishing at 16th in the league after a 21-4 defeat at Leeds on Boxing Day. It was their lowest position for a decade. Neil had made his return in that defeat at Headingley, where Syd Hynes had eclipsed him and Mick Shoebottom had run Trinity ragged. Matters had to improve quickly or Trinity's season could be written off.

Mercifully, players who had been long term absentees began to return. Wakefield also acquired the services of two useful players from Whitehaven as the New Year passed in second-rower Matt McLeod for £1,750 and scrum-half Joe Bonnar for £3,250. The club was again in dire financial straits as gates continued to fall and the much lauded social club failed to make money for Trinity. Ultimately, the social club was taken over by C. Bartle Promotions Ltd, enlarged to accommodate 1,500 members and renamed the Wakefield Theatre Club. Trinity now had no connection with the club but were grateful for the £5,000 in part-payment for it, which paid for the transfer fees of the two Cumbrians.

On 30 December, Trinity went to Doncaster and won a hard game 15-2 with Neil scoring nine points. The win was expected but somehow its manner seemed to hint at better times ahead. Barney Ward made his first-team debut at scrum-half but the most significant feature of the game was the appearance and performance of Don Fox in a new incarnation at blind-side prop. This unremarkable game at Tattersfield heralded another of those long unbeaten sequences Trinity had so routinely clocked up during the 1960s. They would not lose another game until April and a season which had seemed destined to end in mediocrity took a turn towards glory.

On New Year's Day, Trinity entertained Dewsbury in a game played under the new floodlights. The ground was covered in snow and reporters remarked on its Christmas-card appearance. Trinity won 34-3 and gave a truly uplifting performance. Neil contributed a try and five goals. The underfoot conditions made it hard labour for the forwards among whom Hawley, Haigh and Jeanes shone, while there was some inspired back play from Batty, Coetzer and Cooper. The *Wakefield Express* noted, "This display of the Wakefield backs was splendidly balanced by the skilful distribution of the ball and all-round efficiency of centres Ian Brooke and Neil Fox."

189

A week later, Matt McLeod made his debut in a comprehensive 26-8 victory over Swinton. Trinity played gloriously in the second half after taking an 8-2 interval lead. The *Wakefield Express* seemed ecstatic: "While all four of the tries were impressive to see, the first, in which the Fox brothers figured conspicuously, would perhaps strike onlookers as the one to remember best. Don, appearing as a prop, still found time to bring into play his fascinating handling of a ball that so often has left opponents guessing. It was in one of these episodes that he made the break and, after teasing the defenders with his cute handling, he whipped a pass out to the left, where brother Neil was up in support and was quickly over for a try to which he landed the goal... Neil, celebrating his 400th appearance with Trinity, played with his old-time skill and strength to give his wingman Coetzer some running chances."

At Hull a fortnight later Wakefield put on their best away performance for a long time, despite losing Poynton with a gashed lip after only 13 minutes. Neil and Ian Brooke gave a superb display of centre skills, all the more exceptional because they faced a fine Hull pairing in Dick Gemmell and John Maloney. Four days later Huddersfield were beaten 17-7 at Belle Vue but Neil was captaining Yorkshire against Lancashire at Widnes. Neil gave Yorkshire the lead with a penalty and went on to kick four goals but Yorkshire were overwhelmed in the forwards and had no answer to scrum-half Tommy Bishop, who led them a merry dance. The Lancastrians won 23-17 to take their first County Championship since 1960. Harold Mather in the *Manchester Guardian* wrote, "Lancashire were considerably more in command than the score suggests... Certainly this was not a night on which Yorkshire will look back with any kind of pleasure." Neither the venerable Mather nor Neil himself knew that the Naughton Park Roses Match was to be the last Neil would play in the white jersey of Yorkshire. His county career had lasted almost 10 years and encompassed 17 caps. He had scored in all 17 matches - nine tries, 60 goals and 147 points, the latter two figures remaining records for Yorkshire, which will almost certainly never be broken. Of Neil's appearances, nine ended in victories and one in a draw. Remarkably, he was never in a side which lost to a touring team, enjoying successes against the Australians of 1959, 1963 and 1967 and against the 1961 New Zealanders.

Neil must have performed well enough against Lancashire because he was selected as Great Britain's captain for the test against France on 11 February, his co-centre being Ian Brooke. 'Left Footer' of the *Rugby Leaguer* wrote: "Most people these days are noting the improved form of Neil Fox. His intensive training, plenty of play and reduced weight have all contributed to earn Neil once again the top honour of being chosen captain of Great Britain." A couple of days later he confirmed his good form with 14 points in a 40-15 home win over York. There was more good news for Trinity when Don Fox came off the transfer list and Gert Coetzer agreed to stay at Belle Vue for another two years.

Trinity faced a difficult first round Challenge Cup tie at Barrow on 3 February. A crowd of 10,437 was held on tenterhooks until the final whistle blew. Trinity led 5-2 at the break, Neil having converted a lovely solo try by Joe Bonnar but Barrow were only 5-4 down until the 58th minute, when Don Fox bluffed his way over to make it 8-4. The last 20 minutes saw a tremendous barrage on the Wakefield line but Trinity's defence bordered on the miraculous to repel all of Barrow's furious efforts.

Neil shifted his attention from Craven Park to the Parc des Princes in Paris the following Sunday but before that the authorities had bizarrely arranged for Great Britain to have a run out against Salford on the Monday night, 5 February. Sod's Law struck. Snow began falling several hours before kick-off and the game was abandoned by referee Eric Clay after 35 minutes with Britain leading 12-0. Harold Mather in the *Manchester Guardian* remarked that "in the centre Fox and Brooke combined well" but had to admit that "it was an achievement merely for the players to keep their feet, let alone to run or to try to turn... Nevertheless the form of some players was both a surprise and in terms of team-work, as far as Great Britain were concerned, a pleasure. Indeed, considering that the British players previously had had only one training session together, they blended surprisingly well."

The good team-work carried over to the Paris test, which Great Britain won 22-13, giving as good a performance as they had produced for some time. Neil led the team well and a 15-0 lead was quickly established. Neil did not kick, the admirable full-back Bev Risman of Leeds taking the scoring honours with five goals and two tries on his test debut. It was the first time in 14 tests against the French that Neil had not scored and only the second time in his test career, which now stretched to 26 games for Great Britain.

Neil helped Trinity to a splendid 27-9 victory at Featherstone on 17 February. The following Saturday, Wakefield travelled to Salford for a televised second round Challenge Cup tie. Salford took the lead after half an hour when David Watkins dropped a goal. Neil re-started with a well-placed kick which bounced between two Salford forwards, who appeared to leave the ball for each other. Ken Batty nipped in and served Neil, who burst through a bemused bunch of defenders to score a try, which he converted. Batty claimed a try four minutes into the second half before Ron Hill finished the scoring for Salford with a penalty in the 52nd minute. Although the score was only 8-4, Wakefield were much the superior side. The threequarter line functioned sweetly with Neil its prime mover and the *Yorkshire Post* described him as "a tower of strength at centre". It added presciently, "It was a fine team effort by Trinity, one with a Wembley look about it." Salford seemed to have no other plan than to attempt drop-goals and hoist up-and-unders. However, referee Ronnie Jackson upset Wakefield chairman John Ridge so much with a 17-2 penalty count against Trinity that he sent a letter of complaint to the RFL.

Following the second round Cup ties the RFL brought in another refinement to the laws of the game, decreeing that following a kick dead by an attacking team, the defending team would receive a tap on the '25', instead of dropping out. Teams had been deliberately hoofing the ball dead on the fourth tackle in the near certainty that they would regain possession from the resulting drop-out.

Neil retained his position as captain of Great Britain for the return test against France at Bradford on 2 March in an unchanged XIII. As for the Paris test, the selectors gave the side the opportunity of some match play together by arranging a game against Leeds on Monday 26 February and recorded a 25-7 victory. However, it was by no means easy. Leeds went 7-0 up after only four minutes, causing Alfred Drewry of the *Yorkshire Post* to comment, "What might have become merely a training exercise became a desperate struggle for self-respect". Britain scored three of their tries after Syd Hynes had left the field injured in the 50th minute, leaving his side to cope with only 12 men. Britain, however, had at least shown plenty of resolve against one of the game's top teams and the selectors seemed content. Neil was pleased that his team-mate David Jeanes had been drafted in as a substitute and played half the game – a sure sign that he was going to make the grade a lot quicker than anyone had imagined. Although David was not selected in the 1968 World Cup party, he did go on to win eight Great Britain caps and was a member of the team which won the World Cup in France in 1972.

Compared with their performance in Paris, the Great Britain team did not live up to expectations at Odsal, despite their 19-8 victory. France were first to score, led 8-6 at half-time and did not lose their lead until the 50th minute. Britain only made the game safe with two converted tries in the last four minutes through Alan Burwell of Hull KR and Arnie

Morgan of Featherstone Rovers. Neil again left the kicking to Bev Risman, whose only successes were those last two conversions. Neil made a few powerful bursts and lofted the high kick, which caused confusion before Burwell scored the fourth of Britain's five tries. His handling was sometimes faulty. In Britain's defence, much of their problem stemmed from Monsieur Lacaze, a referee who had unusual interpretations of the offside laws and foul play. Roland Tinker wrote in the *Halifax Courier & Guardian*, "I reckon the Frenchmen made more head tackles in that one game than in all those I have seen previously this season. Naturally, when players are wondering whether they are going to be concussed at any time, they take precautions, tending to watch the man rather than the ball."

During Neil's absence at the test match Trinity extended their winning run to 10 games with a 20-4 success against Hull at Belle Vue. A heavy cold prevented him playing in a 21-0 victory at Bradford on 6 March, which lifted the club from sixth to fourth in the league.

On 9 March Trinity won 18-7 at Dewsbury. John L. Allen described the clash as "this game of alternating splendour and drabness". Neil contributed nine points, which took him past the 200 mark for Trinity for the season, but he had a try disallowed after he had stormed half the length of the pitch. Ken Traill was so incensed at the decision that he let the referee hear his opinion and was reprimanded. A week later the third round of the Challenge Cup brought arch rivals Castleford to Belle Vue for a game attended by more than 19,000. Castleford came determined to tame Trinity and within a minute Don Fox had been relieved of three of his teeth. Trinity's response was to carry on playing football – superb and restrained football. The forwards were wonderfully effective, with McLeod outstanding. The Wakefield centres, Neil and Gert Coetzer, produced some inspired groundwork which enabled full-back Gary Cooper to run riot, creating tries for Coetzer and two for Ken Batty, as they ran out 18-5 victors. The *Wakefield Express* headline proclaimed "Trinity the magnificent!" and asked "Is the praise too generous for a side supplying top quality football in face of early provocation enough to lead most teams to descend to the level of a thumping exhibition?" The bookies were certainly impressed by Trinity's display and installed them as 7-4 favourites for the Cup.

On 22 March, Neil got some news for which he had been hoping. The test selectors chose him among the group of players probably going to Australia and New Zealand for the 1968 World Cup in the summer. They did not release the names of the players to public scrutiny, however, and had notified more players than the 19 who would eventually make up the squad. All the players were to undergo the necessary inoculations, even though they would not all be going down under. It was all part of a plan the selectors had hatched after the loss of the Ashes earlier in the season. The press was later told, "The selectors decided to settle on one team and try to improve it by giving it more chances to play together instead of by chopping and changing". Hence the decision was made to retain the same team for the two French tests and also to play extra fixtures against club sides.

Neil was investing a lot of effort, thought and hope into the possibility of selection for the 1968 World Cup party. He had suffered the disappointment of being left out in 1960 and the cancellation of the 1965 tournament had been a bad blow. Realistically, 1968 would be his last chance to take part in a World Cup. His selection as captain in the French tests was a good indication that his ambition might at last be fulfilled. He recalled, "I don't think that any Great Britain teams had ever been asked to play games against club sides like we were in 1968. Bill Fallowfield, the World Cup tour manager, kept telling us, 'Win these games and you'll all be going down to the World Cup'. Well, we did keep winning them but these games were all played in between our club games and the tests. It became a really heavy workload but at least we knew we were liable to be picked for the World

Cup." The final selection was to be made on 10 April and the party would leave on 18 May and receive £250 each if they won the trophy.

In the meantime a lot of water would flow under Neil's bridge. On 23 March, Trinity had a gloriously improbable 23-3 home win against St Helens with a weakened team. This was in spite of the fact that hooker Geoff Oakes broke his fibula after 15 minutes and Trinity subsequently lost the scrum battle 16-30. Neil landed four goals, his last bringing him his 4,000th point in first class rugby league. However, in the 42nd minute he was forced to retire from the match with an injured groin. Ironically the injury, caused when he fell over on his leg in a tackle, might never have occurred had he decided not to play the second half. He had received a bump in the first half and had contemplated not returning for the second half but changed his mind. To say that it was a bad time to sustain an injury was an understatement. A week later Trinity were to play their Challenge Cup semi-final against Huddersfield at Odsal and he could not afford to miss too many games or his place in the World Cup party might be jeopardised.

On the Monday preceding the semi-final the notorious Odsal pitch consisted of seven inches of mud and both Trinity and Huddersfield requested that the game be transferred to Headingley. The RFL told them to play at Odsal, where, according to John L. Allen, "conditions were just right for a shabby burlesque of rugby league". The mud won hands down and Neil watched a 0-0 draw. In fact Neil never did play in a scoreless game, certainly at professional level. The words "scoreless" and "Neil Fox" could probably be defined as a contradiction in terms. The replay, ironically at Headingley, the following Wednesday produced an enthralling game which Trinity won 15-10, Don Fox being Wakefield's star performer. All of a sudden Wakefield were looking at the possibility of achieving that elusive Cup and League double which they had so nearly pulled off in 1960 and 1962. Neil's priority was to recover from the injury as soon as possible.

He missed Great Britain's 20-5 win against Salford on 5 April and a shock 10-12 home defeat for Trinity by Bramley three days later. The defeat was Wakefield's first in 17 matches. On 10 April, though, there was great news for Neil, when he was named as captain of the Great Britain World Cup squad. His club-mates, Ian Brooke and Bob Haigh also earned selection. Neil recalls, "Of course, that was a great moment for me. Although the groin problem was causing me to miss games, the Rugby League was happy for me to take it steady and not rush me to get ready. We had the tour team photographs taken and were kitted out and it was another of those exciting times for me."

Neil missed victories at Castleford on Good Friday and at home to Leeds on Easter Monday, the latter being Harold Poynton's benefit match. He was persuaded to play at Bramley, however, on Easter Tuesday, 16 April. He kicked a goal in a fiercely fought affair which Trinity won 7-6 to secure second place in the league, but it was a Don Fox penalty in the 68th minute which sealed the win. Neil had only played to help the club out but his groin injury flared up again and it was now touch and go whether he would be fit for Wembley and the Championship play-offs. The top-of-the-table places were extraordinarily closely contested, the leading four being:

	P	W	D	L	For	Agst	Pts
Leeds	34	28	0	6	720	271	56
Wakefield T	34	24	1	9	600	295	49
Hull KR	34	24	1	9	620	348	49
St Helens	34	24	1	9	472	334	49

Neil was ruled out of the first play-off game on 20 April in which Trinity beat Huddersfield 20-11. He was also absent from the quarter-final against Castleford three days later, when Trinity triumphed 17-14 in a desperately close finish. Ominously, on Saturday, 27 April, the *Yorkshire Post* reported, "Neil Fox yesterday had a recurrence of the groin injury which has affected him for over a month and had to withdraw from the team [to play Wigan in the semi-final]. Unless Trinity win today he will thus have no chance of meeting the demands of Britain's selectors that he prove his match fitness by next weekend. The selectors will in that event have to arrange a special test for him or replace him." Neil and Geoff Oakes had visited the remedial baths in Leeds on Friday morning and on leaving the baths Neil had felt more pain in the injury. Both the RFL and Wakefield Trinity were anxious that he prove his fitness.

Trinity gave Neil a lifeline by easily accounting for Wigan 26-9 in the Championship semi-final with Don Fox kicking six goals from six shots. The game was Billy Boston's last for Wigan. Wakefield now faced two consecutive Saturdays playing for the game's biggest domestic honours. Their opponents in the Championship final on 4 May, Neil's 29th birthday, were Hull KR, whom they had failed to beat in six attempts during the current season. Trinity had to decide whether to risk bringing Neil back. They had been doing well enough without him, Gert Coetzer playing at left-centre. However, they fully appreciated that his match-winning qualities would be invaluable and gave him an option to play in the Championship final or miss Wembley. Neil says, "I found that hard to swallow. I felt that Trinity were forcing me to play against my will and better judgment. I told them I was not 100 per cent fit but would risk it. I still thought that they would pick me for Wembley whether Trinity won the Championship Final or not. Really, they put me under a lot of pressure." Meanwhile, the RFL had their own priorities and wanted him to prove his fitness by playing for Great Britain at Halifax less than 24 hours before the game against Hull KR.

Neil duly turned out at Thrum Hall on the eve of the Championship Final and helped Great Britain beat Halifax 28-2. He completed the first half and was then withdrawn. The following morning the *Yorkshire Post's* match report was headlined "Fox proves his fitness". Derek Gledhill wrote, "He pronounced himself 'quite all right' but Wakefield will wait to see whether he suffers any reaction... before deciding whether to include him". In the event he was passed fit and took his place as Wakefield's left centre at Headingley. The teams were:

Hull Kingston Rovers: Dave Wainwright, Chris Young, John Moore, Alan Burwell, Paul Longstaff, Roger Millward, Colin Cooper, Les Foster, Peter Flanagan, Brian Mennell, Phil Lowe, Terry Major, Frank Foster (captain).
Substitutes: Phil Coupland and Bill Holliday.
Wakefield Trinity: Gary Cooper, Gert Coetzer, Ian Brooke, Neil Fox, Ken Batty, Harold Poynton (captain), Ray Owen, David Jeanes, George Shepherd, Don Fox, Matt McLeod, Bob Haigh, Dave Hawley.
Substitutes: Ken Hirst and Ted Campbell.

There were 22,586 spectators filling the Headingley stands and terraces as Trinity defended their Championship title. It hardly seemed credible that after waiting for so long for their first title, the chance of a second should so swiftly follow. The game that ensued was worthy of the occasion, although Trinity always seemed to have the advantage. Indeed they were never behind. Neil tells the story of the game succinctly, "We knew that we had not beaten Hull KR in six attempts before the final, so the cards were against us. But we were confident we would get the right result this time. We took the lead when Ray Owen scored the first try and I kicked the goal. Roger Millward replied with a penalty and before half-time Rovers got level, when Longstaff scored at the corner after a kick by Foster. It was 5-5 at half-time but we were definitely on top. After the break we had the wind behind us and made it pay. David Jeanes gave us the lead back when he scored a great try, knocking three defenders out of his way. I kicked the goal and we led 10-5. Rovers put us under a lot of pressure for a while and Millward dropped a goal to make it 10-7. At that point I was given the ball about 30 yards out and went for the line beating a couple of men. Just before I touched down for the try my groin went again. Don kicked the conversion and it was 15-7. Moore got a try for Rovers but Harold Poynton dropped a goal to make the final score 17-10. Gary Cooper won the Harry Sunderland Trophy for man-of-the-match and we had won back-to-back Championships. It was wonderful but I had paid the price for playing."

Neil had done well to finish the game. All the critics had noted his difficulty in moving smoothly, despite the fact that he scored the decisive try. The *Wakefield Express* noted: "It was sad to see a star of the dazzling brightness of Neil Fox playing such an inconspicuous part in a match of such great importance. Very sad, too, to know that his lack of fire was due to his troublesome groin injury. That he was not as fit as he was thought to be was evident when he handed over the responsibility for some early penalty kicks to brother Don. Neil kicked the goal to his own try and that of Jeanes earlier on, but those successful efforts apart, he was hardly in the game."

Naturally, Neil knew how the injured groin had affected him. He says, "Going up for the winners medal after the game, Colin Hutton the Hull KR coach and the coach for the World Cup team, was congratulating our players. When I reached him, I whispered that I would have to cry off from the World Cup. He said, 'Don't do it yet. Let's talk with Bill Fallowfield after you get changed.' I did but with only two weeks left before the tour, I didn't think I would be right. Maybe I could have gone but my conscience wouldn't let me. They brought John Atkinson in for me and Bev Risman took over the captain's job. It has always been a real disappointment for me that I never played in a World Cup."

The elation of winning a second Championship was tempered for Neil by the near certainty that he would not be able to play at Wembley. If he had been able to play, he would have had the chance to become the first player to win four Challenge Cups at the great stadium. On the Monday after the Championship triumph Neil and Paddy Armour consulted an orthopaedic surgeon, who confirmed Paddy's diagnosis of severely torn groin muscles. Fortunately, there was no rupture and surgery was not needed. However, he was informed that he must have a month's complete rest and only return very gently to training. There was no earthly chance of that fourth Wembley Cup Final.

Trinity's opponents at Wembley on 11 May were Leeds, a clash of the Champions against the League leaders, second versus first. A crowd of 87,100 expected a classic. Certainly they saw an unforgettable game. Neil recalls, "I did not enjoy the fact that I was not in the team for Wembley. I felt down, not being able to join in the preparations and wondering if I had not played in the Championship Final, would I have been playing in the Cup Final. Would the committee have stuck to their word? I'll never know now."

Of course, anyone with any knowledge of rugby league will be aware of the extraordinary circumstances surrounding the 1968 Challenge Cup Final, which has become enshrined in the game's folklore as "the Watersplash Final". An hour before kick-off the heavens opened and flooded the stadium, leaving it resembling a shallow lake. In normal circumstances the referee would have deemed that the game should not have gone ahead but it would have been a brave man who told the 87,100 fans that they would have to come back another day, not to mention the millions intent upon watching the match on television. Trinity's made two changes from the team which had taken the Championship at Headingley. Gert Coetzer replaced Neil and Ken Hirst came in on the wing.

The game was much better than anyone could have anticipated, as the players aquaplaned over the hallowed, but submerged, turf. Three tries were scored but in no case did the scorer actually carry the ball across the goal line. All the tries were the product of the unpredictable surface. By half-time Wakefield had established a 7-4 lead through a Ken Hirst try, augmented by a conversion and a penalty from Don Fox. Leeds had replied with two penalties from Bev Risman. As the game entered its final stages Leeds suddenly appeared home if not dry, when they were awarded a controversial penalty try for obstruction on winger John Atkinson. Risman converted and then landed a penalty to give his side an 11-7 lead. The game and the coveted double had apparently been snatched from Trinity's grasp. There was barely time to restart the game. There was, however, one final, heart-stopping twist to this, the most extraordinary Cup final imaginable. Don Fox, who had 10 minutes earlier been awarded the Lance Todd Trophy as the game's outstanding player, kicked off towards the right touchline. The ball fell invitingly into Ken Hirst's flight path. Ken hacked the ball on and dived for an insanely improbable match-winning try just to the side of the posts. But everyone knows the ending was not of the fairytale variety. Don Fox, whose kicking in every form had so far been immaculate, dragged the simple conversion wide, the Cup was lost and television commentator Eddie Waring uttered the immortal phrase "poor lad", as the whistle went and the relieved and jubilant Leeds players swept up-field past the kneeling and mortified Trinity prop.

Neil was thunderstruck. Despite his own misfortune, he had been so pleased that Don had finally achieved his ambition of appearing at Wembley in a Challenge Cup final. Now this! He recalls, "With us leading 7-4 with about 12 minutes to go, I didn't think Leeds could win. Then they were awarded that penalty try. In those conditions that was an injustice. When Ken Hirst scored his try in injury time, I sat there, deafened by cheering Wakefield supporters and I thought we had won. I was actually sitting on the bench and thinking I wish I was taking the kick. I don't mean this because I wanted the accolades for kicking the winning goal. But being a kicker and with the conditions being so terrible, I realised the pressure was being put on Don. What if he missed? What effect would it have on him? All I hoped was that he would kick it. But he didn't and we are never allowed to forget it. He did win the man-of-the-match award for his brilliant performance. Only Ken Hirst with his two tries came near him, I think."

So a season which had begun so indifferently, then transformed into a triumphal procession, turned sour in the end. The Championship had been retained. In any other season that would have been seen as a fantastic achievement and indubitably it was. However, it was to be forever overshadowed by Wembley. Neil's personal ambitions also rose and fell with that nagging groin injury. The game's biggest prizes – a Wembley final and captaincy of a Great Britain World Cup tour – had been snatched away from him.

Wakefield fans turned out in force on the Monday after Wembley to welcome the team home. As the players made their way to the civic reception, 5,000 people, 10-deep, lined Wood Street. They carried banners urging Don Fox to carry on playing – prior to Wembley he had intimated he might retire. They proclaimed he was "the greatest", there were cheers for him and chants of "Fox, Fox, Fox". Some people always find it difficult to forgive. But most of the fans probably thought Don had nothing he needed to be forgiven for.

Neil had missed 21 Trinity games and some representative fixtures through injuries, but still kicked 98 goals to finish fifth leading goal-kicker, while his 250 points placed him fourth in the points-scorers list, behind Bev Risman on 332, Wigan's Colin Tyrer on 298 and Hull's John Maloney on 255. One is tempted to wonder if Neil had played in all the games open to him, how near to Lewis Jones's record of 496 points in a season would he have got?

Wakefield Trinity 1967-68

Wakefield Trinity finished 2nd in the league: P34, W24, L9, D1, For 600, Against 295
Fox scored 17 tries, 88 goals, 227 points for Wakefield, and 1 try, 10 goals, 23 points in representative games

Date	Opponent	Score	Fox	Crowd	
19 Aug	**Castleford**	31-11	2T, 5G	6,720	
23 Aug	Swinton	13-27	2G	5,700	
26 Aug	**Batley**	78-9	3T, 12G	4,533	
28 Aug	St Helens	11-13	4G	11,474	
1 Sep	Keighley	23-5	T, 3G	3,889	YC1
9 Sep	**Hull KR**	12-12	3G	7,829	
13 Sep	**Hull KR**	13-13	G	9,207	YC2
15 Sep	Hull KR	5-14	T, G	11,200	Replay
16 Sep	Batley	17-5	T, 3G	3,100	
23 Sep	**Featherstone R**	22-5	5G	6,594	
29 Sep	Hull KR	7-25	2G	11,875	
11 Oct	Keighley	21-19	dnp	2,500	
14 Oct	Hunslet	9-2	G	3,738	
20 Oct	**Halifax**	7-9	dnp	5,975	
24 Oct	**Hull KR**	5-5	dnp	5,786	FT1
28 Oct	**Australians**	7-33	2G	10,056	
4 Nov	**Keighley**	18-2	3G	3,665	
6 Nov	Hull KR	10-13	dnp	8,266	Replay
11 Nov	**Doncaster**	20-2	dnp	3,033	
18 Nov	Huddersfield	5-7	T, G	5,231	
25 Nov	**Bradford N**	5-6	dnp	9,797	
2 Dec	York	12-8	dnp	1,530	
16 Dec	Halifax	9-16	dnp	4,060	
22 Dec	**Hunslet**	6-3	dnp	3,519	
26 Dec	Leeds	4-21	2G	13,378	
30 Dec	Doncaster	15-2	T, 3G	1,275	
1 Jan	**Dewsbury**	34-3	T, 5G	3,418	
6 Jan	**Swinton**	26-8	T, 4G	5,378	
20 Jan	Hull	20-8	4G	5,600	
24 Jan	**Huddersfield**	17-7	dnp	5,542	
27 Jan	**York**	40-15	2T, 4G	4,138	
3 Feb	Barrow	8-4	G	10,437	Ch Cup 1
17 Feb	Featherstone R	27-9	3G	7,331	
24 Feb	Salford	8-4	T, G	14,079	Ch Cup 2
1 Mar	**Hull**	20-4	dnp	4,956	
6 Mar	Bradford N	21-0	dnp	8,839	
9 Mar	Dewsbury	18-7	T, 3G	6,400	
16 Mar	**Castleford**	18-5	3G	19,115	Ch Cup 3
23 Mar	**St Helens**	23-3	4G	7,446	
30 Mar	Huddersfield	0-0	dnp	21,569	Ch Cup semi (at Odsal)
3 Apr	Huddersfield	15-10	dnp	20,983	Replay (at Leeds)
8 Apr	**Bramley**	10-12	dnp	5,582	
12 Apr	Castleford	5-4	dnp	8,799	
15 Apr	**Leeds**	10-5	dnp	13,760	
16 Apr	Bramley	7-6	G	5,500	
20 Apr	**Huddersfield**	20-11	dnp	10,630	CH1
24 Apr	**Castleford**	17-14	dnp	12,894	CH2
27 Apr	**Wigan**	26-9	dnp	13,318	CH semi
4 May	Hull KR	17-10	T, 2G	22,586	CH Final (at Leeds)
11 May	Leeds	10-11	dnp	87,100	Ch Cup Final (at Wembley)

Representative appearances

4 Oct	Yorkshire 15 Australians 14 (Wakefield)	T, 3G
3 Nov	Great Britain 11 Australia 17 (White City)	3G
24 Jan	Yorkshire 17 Lancashire 23 (Widnes)	4G
11 Feb	Great Britain 22 France 13 (Paris)	
2 Mar	Great Britain 19 France 8 (Odsal)	

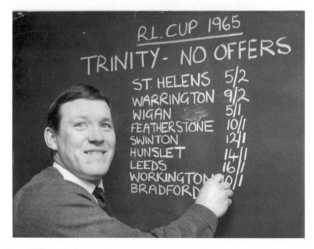

Life off the pitch:
Top: The food was good! Neil, Roy Bell and Fred Smith enjoy a break
from filming *This Sporting Life* at Belle Vue in 1962.
Bottom left: Early working life as a miner.
Bottom right: Neil pictured early in his career as a turf accountant. On this occasion
he did not quite get it right. Wigan went on to beat Hunslet at Wembley in one of
the game's greatest finals.

17. 1968-69: Goodbye tests and the swinging 60s

The close season of 1968 produced mostly good news for Wakefield Trinity. Ken Traill signed a new three-year contract and an old Trinity favourite and captain, Don Robinson, joined the training staff as coach to the under-17 team. The club announced a profit of £2,238 on the previous season and reported that gate monies had risen from £23,376 to £38,344. Wages had, however, risen £3,500 on the previous season. The RFL had decided that the minimum admission charge would rise from four shillings to five shillings and that OAPs and boys would have to pay half charges. Trinity declared themselves strongly against the increases but had no alternative but to implement them. They also vehemently reiterated their opposition to live televised games and wanted broadcasts to be stopped as soon as practicable. As a members' club Trinity always seemed to act reluctantly and changed slowly. By now Sunday rugby had made its appearance, but chairman John Ridge had said that the club would never countenance playing on a Sunday. Playing terms were raised to £18 for an away win, £16 for a home win and £8 for a defeat, home or away.

Trinity had signed two exceptionally promising youngsters in Yorkshire under-17 prop George Ballantyne and stand-off David Topliss who had played for Normanton and England under-19s. Also signed and due to arrive in September was Queensland second-rower Peter Hall, while there was welcome news that Geoff Wraith had returned to training after a season's absence. Another big signing just as the season opened was second-rower Terry Ramshaw from Bradford Northern, who was exchanged for Geoff Clarkson plus a fee. On the debit side there was a blow just before the season started when Gary Cooper became unsettled and was transfer-listed at a club record £8,000. Even more discouraging was the enforced retirement of winger Gert Coetzer, who had formed such a potent partnership with Neil. Gert's succession of shoulder injuries had ended his career after 191 appearances and 122 tries for the club. Neil regarded Gert as "a great 100 per cent player, who never let us down. Of all the wingers I played with, Oupa would be in the top six. He was good in defence and scored plenty of important tries for Trinity. He was not a really big man but he had tremendous power, which helped him to break out of tackles. The first tackler hardly ever got him down and he could get out of the trickiest situations." Neil was also sorry to hear that hooker Geoff Oakes had decided to give up playing, saying, "Having got over his broken leg we thought he would come back but he obviously thought enough was enough. Geoff was a real workhorse for us. He played 193 games for Trinity."

As the season opened the *Wakefield Express* reported, "Clearly much will depend on the form of Fox after his troublesome groin injury." Chairman John Ridge told the newspaper, "Neil has gone well in training. He was training on his own before the official call-up and we have high hopes of him." Needless to say, Neil also had high hopes. He wanted to regain his Great Britain place and was doubtless interested to learn that after the 1968 World Cup had taken place, the competing nations had agreed to stage another World Cup in October 1969 in France and England. However, he also knew that his groin was not yet properly mended and did not appear in Trinity's opening two fixtures against St Helens and Castleford, both of which were lost.

His first appearance was against Salford at Belle Vue on 24 August, when Ramshaw made his debut and scored the team's first try. The only scores of the first half were five penalties, which translated into a 6-4 lead for Trinity. In the second half Trinity ran away to a 31-12 victory and the *Wakefield Express* noted, "Fox distinguished himself mostly with some really top class goal-kicking by succeeding with eight out of nine shots." His fifth goal took him to the 1,600 mark in all games. Unusually Neil caused a rumpus when Salford players took umbrage at a tackle of his on David Watkins but the fuss soon calmed down.

There was a storm in another teacup off the field for Neil too. After Trinity had lost 24-8 at St Helens on 28 August the *Wakefield Express* carried a huge headline shouting, "Clouds remain stationary over Belle Vue – The gloom thickens as Neil Fox is dropped". Neil had missed training on the Thursday night after the Knowsley Road defeat and had consequently been selected for the 'A' team against Hull 'A'. It was all a misunderstanding. Neil had rearranged a long standing social engagement from the Wednesday to the Thursday in order to play in the game at St Helens. Somewhere some wires had obviously been crossed but the club rule had to be observed – no training on Thursday meant no first-team place on Saturday. It applied even to Neil. Unfortunately, rumours began to circulate that Neil had fallen out with the committee, wanted a better contract, wanted a coaching position, escalating to the point where he probably wanted to become secretary of the Rugby Football League. In the 14 September edition of the *Wakefield Express* loyal followers of Trinity were relieved to read, "One of the biggest talking points of recent times has concerned international centre Neil Fox. It will come as pleasant news to be assured by club chairman John Ridge that Neil will stay with Trinity until the end of his career which it is hoped will last for another three seasons". It was a reassuring assertion but anyone concerned with rugby league would treat three-year forecasts with some scepticism.

Back on the playing scene Neil's injury was still a concern and he missed defeats at Warrington and Halifax. The game at Wilderspool was lost to a converted try in injury time and at Thrum Hall, Trinity's stand-in kickers missed six kicks. The game at Halifax was notable for David Topliss's debut. John L. Allen noted that it was, "A trying experience for 18-year-old David Topliss to make his debut on the right wing but he came through quite well in the circumstances." It was the launch of a wonderful career and Neil recalls, "David was our brightest prospect at that time. Although he was still learning the game, you could see from the start that he was going to be one of the great players of the future."

Neil returned to action on 7 September in the televised Yorkshire Cup first-round tie against Hull KR at Belle Vue, a lively, pleasant encounter, which saw Trinity collapse in the second half, when they leaked 24 points in a 20 minute spell to lose 30-18. It was the largest home defeat to a club team for a decade. Neil kicked three goals but embarrassingly gave away two points to Roger Millward when he forgot one of the new rules. After Rovers had missed a penalty attempt, he tried to restart with a tap kick, forgetting that such a situation required a 25-yard drop-out so Rovers got another penalty. Two days later Trinity suffered another home defeat, going down 11-15 to Castleford, now coached by Derek Turner, in the first leg of the preliminary round of the BBC2 Floodlit Trophy. Again Trinity went to sleep as Cas hit them with a magical eight-minute period when they scored 13 points. Neil scored all Wakefield's points.

Trinity's performances were far from what had been expected of a team which had won consecutive championships. Only one of their first eight games had been won, they were 24th in the league and were already out of the Yorkshire Cup. The past two seasons had seen Trinity as slow starters and they had surged through to glory but it would surely be asking too much for a third miracle. No-one was ready to press the panic button yet but the outlook appeared bleak.

A second league victory was achieved at Batley on 14 September, when Neil had a new wing partner in Stuart Carlton, who was making his debut. Neil contributed two tries and two goals to his side's 22-3 success. A week later there was a repeat of the Watersplash final at Belle Vue, when repeated squally showers made the ball extremely hard to handle.

Trinity led Leeds 7-3 at the break, Ray Owen having scored a try and Neil a couple of goals. Neil had to retire at half-time with a thigh injury and Leeds squared the game 7-7 when Barry Seabourne dropped a 74th-minute goal.

Trinity continued to disappoint. Castleford hammered them 18-0 in the second leg of the Floodlit Trophy tie and a 14-20 loss followed in the league at Hull KR. The critics were scathing of Trinity's performances, citing poor support play, lack of ideas, dreadful defence, with the notable exception of Dave Hawley - and the perennial problem of a lack of ball from the scrums. Trinity had tried to remedy this last fault by trialling Barry Anderson of Halifax and Roy Firth of Dewsbury but did not retain either. They finally took the plunge and signed Whitehaven and Cumberland hooker Tom Hill, who soon proved well able to get the ball. There was also a glaring weakness on the wings, where there was really no cover for the incumbents, Ken Hirst and Ken Batty. Trinity caused a stir by signing Keith Slater from Headingley RUFC at a reported £3,000 signing-fee. Slater, a Cambridge Blue, had been in line for an England rugby union cap.

The new men made their debuts in the home game against York on 5 October. Slater showed plenty of speed and guts in scoring a try in each half as Trinity won 29-5. Topliss, now at stand-off, excelled but it was Neil who won the newly introduced man-of-the-match award. His seven goals were only part of his contribution. He followed with four crucial goals the following week in a hard earned 14-9 win at Bramley. He also created the 76th-minute match-winning try for Batty. Neil had put on one of his one-man band shows, moving the *Wakefield Express* to report, "Without the four goals by Fox, one of which was a mighty effort from well inside his own half that lifted the ball high over the social club premises and out of the ground, it would have been a most uncertain future for Wakefield".

A third consecutive victory was achieved on 16 October when Batley were beaten 14-5 at Belle Vue. The comedian Charlie Drake, who was appearing for the week at Wakefield Theatre Club, kicked off. The game saw the long-awaited debut of the Australian forward, Peter Hall, and Ken Hirst returned for his first game of the season after illness and scored a splendid try. Wakefield's prospects seemed to be on the ascendant when Warrington were beaten 22-15 on 26 October, Neil supplying two goals and a typically crashing, power-driven try. A fifth win in a row, 18-14 against Halifax at Belle Vue on 9 November, raised the team to 13th in the table. Trinity's performance in this thrilling game, in which the lead changed hands six times, had the stamp of champions and Neil turned in a virtuoso display. Alfred Drewry wrote in the *Yorkshire Post*, "Every now and then Neil Fox gives notice that after 11 years at the top of the rugby league tree he considers himself to have squatter's rights and that attempts to dislodge him are a waste of time... If any other centre has given a better display this season I have not seen him. The born footballer's gift of being in the right spot at the right time, the deft, delicate handling so much at odds with his bulk, and the explosive match-winning qualities which have made him a legend were all in evidence... It was Fox who took the wind out of [Halifax's] sails with a goal dropped almost from within touching distance of the crossbar, and it was Fox who sank them with a try in the grand manner, bustling past half-a-dozen defenders in a determined run of 30 yards."

Neil missed encouraging Trinity successes at home against Hunslet (21-10) and at Bradford Northern (17-16). In the latter game a 40-yard Don Fox penalty goal in the 68th minute was the match-clincher but much of the attention was on Northern full-back, Terry Price, a big money signing from Welsh rugby union the previous season. Price kicked five goals from 15 attempts − not up to his usual standard. The *Wakefield Express* remarked, "If Price is worth £10,000, Neil Fox must be worth £40,000." In those days no one had dreamt of such a transfer fee and Neil was by then heading for his 30th birthday. His form was so good though that Great Britain chose him for the test against France at St Helens on 30 November, although the captaincy was awarded to Tommy Bishop. Les Scarlett in *Yorkshire Sports* observed, "The recall of Neil Fox to the Great Britain ranks comes as no surprise to the followers of Wakefield Trinity. It has been obvious for some weeks that the 'Big Fella' has been getting a second wind, as it were. His displays have steadily improved and if... the selectors feel that there is still no better centre in the game today – of his type – I, for one, am not going to argue with them. In the game against Halifax I was asked to select the man of the match and my choice of Fox seemed to be that of all present, judging by the cheer which greeted the announcement."

The test against France proved a comfortable ride for Great Britain. They won 34-10 and earned general critical acclaim for a job well done. The threequarter line was particularly impressive, rattling up 28 points between them. Winger Bill Burgess grabbed a fine hat-trick, centre Dick Gemmell crossed twice and there was a try for the other wingman, Alan Burwell. Neil landed five goals, converting only one of his side's four first-half tries but improving all four added in the second half. His tally against France in test rugby now stood at 53 goals and 10 tries.

Unfortunately, the test at St Helens left Neil with a knee ligament injury, which proved troublesome for several weeks. During this time Trinity extended their sequence of victories to 10 to attain the lofty heights of fifth position in the league. However, that was as high as they would rise in 1968-69. Defeats at Hull and Salford burst Wakefield's bubble and Neil's absence from the latter game had unexpected repercussions.

The day after the game Neil's name was plastered all over the rugby league columns of all the newspapers. They were reporting on the shock news that Wakefield Trinity had transfer-listed Neil at £10,000. Trinity said it was a disciplinary measure, informing the press that "The committee had been concerned about Fox's approach to training and his attitude towards the coaching staff". Neil had been selected to play against Salford but had withdrawn after a fitness test because his knee was not yet recovered. Neil told Arthur Haddock of the *Yorkshire Evening News*, "[The Committee] had me before them on Tuesday night about my knee injury, and I told them I had never shirked in my life. I knew some of them thought I had shirked last season when my groin trouble caused me to miss a number of games. But if I had been fit would I have missed the Cup Final at Wembley and the chance of captaining Great Britain in Australia, plus about £500? I would have gone on the Australian tour without pay rather than miss it, but I have always been honest about fitness. When I play I have to be fit. I have always been happy at Wakefield and I told them that as soon as I got fit, I would play as well as ever for them." He told Joe Humphreys of the *Daily Mirror*, "In all the 14 years I have been at Wakefield, I have never given any trouble. They are being most unfair over this. I don't want to leave Trinity, but there are members on the committee who are forcing me to go. Putting a £10,000 fee on me is ridiculous. I think £4,000 would have been more reasonable. It looks as if they want to keep me not sell me."

The impasse ended within three weeks. Neil's injury healed and he came back at his own request for an 'A' team game against Keighley on 3 January 1969, when the gate amounted to £31/2/6 (£31 12½p), the biggest of the season, reserve matches yielding an average gate of only £14. His name was removed from the transfer list on 9 January and two days later his five goals were a crucial element of a 16-11 win at Keighley. A week later Bramley pushed Trinity to the limit before going down 15-12 at Belle Vue. Apart from putting in an enormous amount of work, Neil kicked three goals and passed two more milestones – his 1,400th goal for Wakefield and his 3,500th point for the club.

On 25 January, Trinity set out on the Wembley trail with an intriguing first round tie against local amateurs Ackworth. The amateurs were quoted at 25,000-1 and a miner from Ackton Hall Colliery was rash enough to place a £1 bet on Ackworth getting to Wembley. They tried hard enough, defended stoutly but could not cope with the Brooke-Slater wing partnership in particular, Slater bagging four tries. Neil had a pleasant afternoon with 10 goals to his name from 12 attempts. The amateurs included future RFL chairman Bob Ashby in their team. Their share of a £1,580 gate was £673 plus about £200 from the Challenge Cup pool.

Two days after the Cup tie Trinity went down 23-14 at home against Hull KR, who seemed to have the Indian sign on them in this period. There was never a dull moment and the lead was exchanged half a dozen times. Neil gave a sound performance and kicked four goals. His form since his return to the team had been excellent and he was rewarded with selection for the return test against France at Toulouse on Sunday, 2 February. Neil consequently missed another Wakefield defeat at Huddersfield on the Saturday but the day was much blacker for all at Belle Vue, when it was learned that Gerry Round, the club's test full-back, who had successfully switched to the pack, had been killed in a road accident.

Meanwhile, the test at Toulouse proved an enormous disappointment. Britain had four changes from the team which had played so well at St Helens, and gave a test debut to loose-forward Ray Batten. Neil gave Britain an early 4-2 lead with a couple of penalty goals but by half-time France were 7-4 ahead. Neil added another goal in the second half and Colin Dixon scored a try but Britain finished losers by 13-9. The game proved to be Neil's last for Great Britain. It was his 29th test match, which remains a record for a Great Britain centre. He had passed the previous record for a centre of 25 tests, jointly held by Phil Jackson and Eric Ashton, in Paris in 1968. His 93 goals and 228 points also remain British test records to this day. Neil never formally announced that he had retired from test rugby, as did Eric Ashton. He says the selectors simply stopped picking him.

The British players returned to a mini ice age and there were wholesale postponements for three weeks. On 7 February Neil had the melancholy task of bearing Gerry Round's coffin, along with Ken Traill, Derek Turner and Jack Wilkinson at his funeral in Hebden Bridge. Neil and Gerry were very good friends. Neil recalls, "Gerry had been a wonderful servant to Wakefield. He had earned eight Great Britain caps, won lots of medals and toured with me in 1962. We always shared rooms wherever we went as players, so I was really upset when I heard he had died. I remember driving over to the funeral with Geoff Oakes, Harold Poynton and Ian Brooke. Harold suddenly pulled out a bottle of whiskey and said, "This is what Gerry would want us to do – have a drink to him and remember the good times we all shared. There's no point in being miserable."

By the time the weather relented, the Challenge Cup ties were in a state of chaos. Some teams had progressed to the third round. Others, including Trinity, had still not managed to play their second-round games. Wakefield had drawn an away tie at Bradford but it proved impossible for it to be played at Odsal. It was postponed three times and the teams finally met at Headingley under floodlights on Wednesday, 26 February, after hurried negotiations. Northern had won 11 games in a row, while Trinity had slipped to ninth in the league and were not inspiring confidence in their followers, but a crowd of 15,077 witnessed a thrilling Cup tie. Neil missed a penalty in the second minute but two minutes later Don Fox created an unconverted try for Gary Cooper. Terry Price booted two penalties to give Northern a 4-3 lead but after Berwyn Jones had tackled Ken Hirst without the ball in the 39th minute, Neil kicked a stunning touchline penalty over the bar to give his side a 5-4 lead. On the hour he landed another penalty and Trinity, displaying encouraging staying power and resilience, looked capable of holding their 7-4 lead. Nine minutes from time, however, Berwyn Jones came back to haunt them. After being starved of passes he finally got a chance on Bradford's own '25' line and shot like an arrow for a truly magnificent try. Neil recalls, "Berwyn ran about 70 yards to score but instead of making for the posts he ran in a straight line and placed the ball halfway between the corner and the posts. Terry Price came up for the conversion. Normally it would be an easy kick for him but he surprised us all by missing and so we had to replay." A 7-7 draw was a little less than Trinity had deserved on the run of play.

Astonishingly, but unavoidably, the replay was set for the following evening at Belle Vue. Trinity were on £65 to win the tie by now and a remarkably good crowd of 11,701 spent an exciting Thursday evening watching a gripping game played on a greasy surface at a frantic tempo and punctuated by intermittent snow showers. Neil was the outstanding performer and had tremendous support from Dave Hawley and Bob Haigh, as Trinity always had the upper hand. Even so, there had been no score after an hour. Inevitably, it was Neil who shattered the deadlock. Ken Batty almost scored just before Neil crashed over near the posts and converted. The huge roar which greeted his try indicated the Trinity fans' relief. A few minutes later Batty made the game safe, when he dribbled over from a spilled Bradford pass. Neil converted from the touchline and Wakefield won 10-0.

There was no respite for Trinity though, who played their third Cup tie in only four days, when they met Rochdale Hornets in the third round at Belle Vue on Saturday 1 March. Trinity were on a £35 bonus to win but must have been horrified to see the pitch on which they were expected to play. It was ankle deep in mud. Wakefield were on top in the first half and led 10-0. Cooper and Hirst claimed tries, both of which Neil converted, the latter almost from touch. Fatigue caught up with Trinity in the second half as Hornets blitzed them. Tries by Pratt and Tees, both converted by Graham Starkey, levelled the scores and Trinity were fortunate when Tees's 74th-minute drop-goal attempt just missed.

So Wakefield went to the Athletic Grounds for another replay the following Wednesday. Neil was making his 500th appearance in first-class rugby league, including the two he had made as a substitute on the 1962 Lions tour. Trinity's bonus had risen to £45 and they produced a ruthless performance. There was some dazzling football before Rochdale's biggest crowd in 10 years - 10,830 - and Neil was in superb form, as were Hawley, Haigh, Batty and Don Fox. Neil set Trinity on the path to the semi-finals in the 16th minute, when he intercepted, broke clear and sent Keith Slater away for the opening score. Batty and Don Fox added further tries and Neil landed three magnificent goals to earn a 15-2 victory.

On 8 March, Trinity played their first league game for five weeks at York. The home side had almost all the play but lost. Neil kicked two goals, one a touchline conversion and won the player-of-the-match award, as Wakefield scraped home 10-5. The *Wakefield Express* reported: "It was reassuring to see the rise to lofty heights of Neil Fox. His long distance relieving kicks must have set the opposition bemoaning his presence. In addition his all-round generalship served the Trinitarians exceedingly well." An 11-0 home win against Dewsbury followed with Trinity playing well within themselves, obviously with an eye on the following week's semi-final. Neil scored a sensational second-half try, surging through on a devastating 20-yard run for a touchdown "to rank with any he had ever scored", according to John L. Allen. Neil was made captain for the rest of the season, as Harold Poynton had struggled all season with injuries.

The Challenge Cup semi-final drew 21,497 fans to Headingley for Trinity against Castleford, whose coach was Derek Turner. Trinity were aiming for a fifth Wembley final in the 1960s. Castleford, second in the league, were 10 places higher than Wakefield and were 2-1 favourites for the Cup. Tim Ashcroft reported in the *Rugby Leaguer*: "This will surely be marked down as one of the finest shows in the post-war history of the game - a display which must have stirred all England and viewers in the remotest places. On a keen, blustery day it was obvious that whichever side best harnessed the high wind would take command and when Trinity got first use of it, that is exactly what they achieved. The brothers Fox alternately pin-pointed raking shots to touch and lofted shots to the clouds that cost Cas acres in the first half and they did supremely well to contain Trinity to a 10-2 lead as the break approached. Trinity's tries came from clinically efficient rounds of great rugby. First Neil Fox burst out of a midfield tackle and sent Hirst roaring in at the corner. Five minutes later Hirst touched down through the skill of Ian Brooke in picking up a pass at ground level and from almost precisely the same spot Neil Fox thumped a great goal to give Trinity an edge that would have seen them through on any normal day."

Unfortunately for Wakefield, this was not to be a normal day. Neil observes, "With Derek Turner as their coach Castleford had instilled into them what he had instilled into Wakefield Trinity as our captain. You haven't lost until the final whistle blows – and this game was no different." Just before half-time, Trevor Briggs strolled through for a try, which second-rower Mick Redfearn brilliantly goaled, despite a turbulent wind, and at 10-7 Castleford were back in the game. The second half saw Castleford stifling all Trinity's efforts but all they had to show was another goal from Redfearn. With five minutes to go Trinity looked Wembley-bound in spite of Cas's control. At that point they conceded a penalty. It was a long way out but this was Mick Redfearn's day and the ball went straight over from his boot to give his team an 11-10 lead. Trinity were done. In the dying minutes Hardisty scored the clinching try, Redfearn hoofed his fifth goal and Trinity had lost 16-10. It was scant consolation that it had been one of the all-time great Challenge Cup ties. Their pay was a reminder of defeat - £8 for losing, instead of almost £100 had they won.

By coincidence, Castleford were Trinity's next opponents in the league and they repeated the dose with a 13-4 win at Belle Vue on Good Friday. Neil missed the game with another knee injury. Easter Monday brought another defeat, 19-17 at Dewsbury, where Trevor Lowe dropped a late goal for the winners. Neil played very well, desperately trying to rally his tired team-mates and grabbing a couple of tries and a goal, which took him past the 200 points mark for the season. The next day Trinity seemed to be heading for another defeat when they were held 4-4 in the 39th minute by Huddersfield at Belle Vue but they turned on a great second-half performance to run out 25-4 winners. Neil kicked five goals. He did not score at all four days later but Trinity beat Bradford Northern 6-4 at Belle Vue.

Wakefield Trinity finally played on a Sunday on 13 April at Featherstone. It was not a good day for Trinity, who lost 15-5, or Neil, who fractured his thumb. He missed Trinity's remaining league fixture at Hunslet and Trinity's attempt to retain the Championship for a third consecutive season. They went out at Swinton in the first round of the play-offs.

A few weeks later the International Board announced that there would be no World Cup competition in 1969, a further disappointment for Neil to add to many others of the 1968-69 campaign. Unusually he had failed to land a century of goals, falling five short and was only 13th in the leading goalkickers' list. His 217 points left him 12th in the points listing.

The 1968-69 season was the end of Trinity's halcyon days. They had been the most successful team of the 1960s but all good things come to an end. The sixties had certainly swung for Wakefield Trinity and for Neil. The future was going to be different for both.

Wakefield Trinity 1968-69

Wakefield Trinity finished 12th in the league: P34, W19, L14, D1, For 473, Against 375
Fox scored 9 tries, 87 goals, 201 points for Wakefield and 8 goals, 16 points in representative games

Date	Opponent	Score	Fox	Crowd	
14 Aug	**St Helens**	0-5	dnp	6,630	
16 Aug	Castleford	6-15	dnp	7,400	
24 Aug	**Salford**	31-12	8G	6,869	
28 Aug	St Helens	8-24	G	8,301	
31 Aug	Warrington	20-24	dnp	4,916	
2 Sep	Halifax	6-15	dnp	4,686	
7 Sep	**Hull KR**	18-30	3G	5,545	YC1
9 Sep	**Castleford**	11-15	T, 4G	6,044	FT Prel, 1st leg
14 Sep	Batley	22-3	2T, 2G	2,900	
21 Sep	**Leeds**	7-7	2G	7,965	
23 Sep	Castleford	0-18		6,666	FT Prel, 2nd leg
28 Sep	Hull KR	14-20	4G	6,650	
5 Oct	**York**	29-5	7G	6,072	
12 Oct	Bramley	14-9	4G	2,950	
16 Oct	**Batley**	14-5	G	4,256	
26 Oct	**Warrington**	22-15	T, 2G	5,791	
9 Nov	**Halifax**	18-14	T, 3G	6,254	
13 Nov	**Hunslet**	21-10	dnp	4,280	
16 Nov	Bradford N	17-16	dnp	6,823	
23 Nov	**Featherstone R**	15-9	3G	6,245	
30 Nov	**Hull**	22-2	dnp	4,887	
7 Dec	**Keighley**	24-0	dnp	4,407	
14 Dec	Hull	2-4	dnp	5,400	
20 Dec	Salford	3-17	dnp	7,969	
4 Jan	Leeds	12-16	dnp	9,642	
11 Jan	Keighley	16-11	5G	3,000	
18 Jan	**Bramley**	15-12	3G	4,449	
25 Jan	**Ackworth**	50-7	10G	6,380	Ch Cup 1
27 Jan	**Hull KR**	14-23	4G	5,712	
1 Feb	Huddersfield	2-10	dnp	3,547	
26 Feb	Bradford N	7-7	2G	15,077	Ch Cup 2 (at Leeds)
27 Feb	**Bradford N**	10-0	T, 2G	11,701	Replay
1 Mar	**Rochdale H**	10-10	2G	7,950	Ch Cup 3
5 Mar	Rochdale H	15-2	3G	10,830	Replay
8 Mar	York	10-5	2G	3,184	
21 Mar	**Dewsbury**	11-0	T, G	4,720	
29 Mar	Castleford	10-16	2G	21,497	Ch Cup semi (at Leeds)
4 Apr	**Castleford**	4-13	dnp	8,898	
7 Apr	Dewsbury	17-19	2T, G	3,200	
8 Apr	**Huddersfield**	25-4	5G	4,741	
12 Apr	**Bradford N**	6-4		5,043	
13 Apr	Featherstone R	5-15	G	5,333	
18 Apr	Hunslet	21-12	dnp	1,950	
26 Apr	Swinton	5-9	dnp	4,254	CH1

Representative appearances

30 Nov	Great Britain 34 France 10 (St Helens)		5G
2 Feb	Great Britain 9 France 13 (Toulouse)		3G

18. 1969-70: Off to Odsal

The omens were not good for Wakefield Trinity as they entered the 1969-70 season. The last campaign had seen them finish only 12th in the league, their lowest position since 1955-56. For only the second time since 1957-58 the team had not won at least one major trophy. There had been no major signings for the new season and the club started the season lacking long-term injury absentees in Don Fox, David Jeanes, Dave Hawley and Terry Ramshaw. Ray Owen had been transferred to Rochdale Hornets, while Ken Hirst had retired. Ian Brooke was appointed as captain and Bob Haigh vice-captain. Financially matters were parlous too. The club had made a profit of £1,677 on the 1968-69 season but that was largely because they had not had to pay out winning money so often. Gate money had fallen by £12,000, so new chairman Les Pounder faced a difficult set of problems.

The season began uncommonly early on 7 August when Trinity went down 27-15 at Halifax in the Yorkshire Cup first-round. Neil scored nine points and was the only Trinity player to have played anywhere near well enough. A knee problem kept him out of the opening league fixture when Trinity lost 16-0 at home to Castleford. On 19 August the horror start continued with a 17-9 loss at Dewsbury, despite leading 4-3 at the break, thanks to two penalties from Neil. The *Wakefield Express* was scathing, "Wakefield provided the crowd with some third-rate football as they were taught the value of enthusiasm, skill and teamwork by the home side." Only Neil and Gary Cooper were exonerated.

Trinity supporters were then subjected to a bombshell. Neil says, "When the season started I didn't think I would be leaving the club after only three games. Out of the blue I was placed on the transfer list at £6,000. I couldn't believe it. They said I hadn't been trying, so on the list I went. After 13 seasons with the club, I was shocked, stunned. I rang Ken Traill at home and he hadn't heard the news. They had done it without his permission. He said, 'If you go, I go. Keep me in touch if anything transpires'. The next day I got a telephone call from Harry Womersley, the Bradford Northern chairman. He asked if they could talk to me. Trinity had done a deal with them - £3,000 down and the remainder later. So it looked like they didn't want me at Trinity. After talking to Harry, he sold the club to me and I agreed to sign. Five minutes after I signed, Tommy Smales, the Castleford coach, rang me to ask if he could see me with a view to signing for them. I had to tell him, 'Sorry, I have just signed for Northern'. He just said, 'Oh, dear' but wished me the best of luck. I rang Ken and he seemed shocked and told me, 'I don't think I'll stay now'. But he did. Unfortunately for Ken that season was the worst at Trinity for over 30 years. He resigned at the end of the season after 12 years with the club. He was the most successful coach Trinity ever had."

"Looking back," Neil adds, "Castleford would have been a better move for me. With the players they had at the time, I think I would have fitted in well. If I had waited 24 hours I might have been a Castleford player or at least I would have had two options. Cas did go back to Wembley that season."

For the record, Neil's playing figures for Wakefield Trinity stood at 441 appearances, 238 tries, 1,442 goals and 3,598 points, when he was transferred. His career figures were: 507 appearances plus two as a substitute, 283 tries, 1,696 goals and 4,241 points.

Trinity received £3,000 on Neil signing, with Bradford undertaking to pay the rest of the fee – something in excess of £2,500 – by December 1970. Wakefield's overdraft was currently running at around £10,000, which influenced their decision to part with arguably the greatest player in the club's history, and certainly one of the most popular.

If Wakefield were a declining club, Bradford were going in the opposite direction. Barely six years previously they had been playing in front of three-figure crowds and had resigned from the league in December 1963. They were revived for the 1964-65 season, had won the Yorkshire Cup in 1965-66 and had gradually become the best-supported team in the league, at a time when almost every other club was experiencing falling attendances. What they really needed, though, was success in the Championship and the Challenge Cup to cement their resurrection. They clearly felt Neil was going to help them achieve this.

When Neil arrived at Odsal the man in charge of coaching was the redoubtable Albert Fearnley, who was also the general manager. Skipper of the team was the fearsome Frank Foster, a test forward who could play the game any way the opposition wanted. His vice-captain was Dave Stockwell, a wily player who operated at stand-off or centre.

Bradford were notorious in this era for dipping in and out of the transfer market in their bid for success. The policy made things interesting for the fans and press but did not do much for the stability of the team. Their biggest signing had been full-back Terry Price, the former Wales rugby union star, who had cost them £10,000 in 1967. Terry was a phenomenal goal and field kicker, a gifted attacking player and a genuine match-winner, when in the mood. He was, however, a touch erratic, not particularly quick and inclined to appear too laid back. Northern did not stop at Wales either, for they had brought over a handful of Australians, who, unfortunately, did not really live up to expectations. However, the Bradford pack was definitely big and tough. Not many teams took liberties with the likes of Jim Mills, Tony Fisher, Dave Hill, Foster, Geoff Clarkson and Stan Fearnley. The backs, though clever and experienced in many cases, lacked overall pace.

Neil made his debut for Northern on 23 August 1969 in a 35-12 home win against Dewsbury. Douglas Hird, writing in the Bradford *Telegraph & Argus*, noted: "Northern's gamble in stretching their pocket to buy Wakefield Trinity's human scoring machine, Neil Fox, looked like a wonderful investment with the first glimpse of his power on Saturday. The former Great Britain captain could not have wished for a better Northern debut – two tries and a hand in others, plus the player-of-the-match award. If his first try was something of a gift, when Dewsbury's passing broke down, his second was a gem. Fox, in his powerful, swerving manner, raced more than 40 yards through the Dewsbury defence to score under the posts. He also moved the ball well to give his wingers the chances they need and Northern's seven-try spree gave them a convincing victory."

This excellent start was reinforced four days later when Oldham were eventually despatched 25-9 at Odsal. Brian Smith reported in the *Telegraph & Argus*: "Neil Fox is making the sort of impact Odsal officials must have dreamed about... Northern were trailing 9-3 shortly before the interval when Fox took a pass from Diabira and, almost contemptuously, shrugged off two would-be tacklers to cross for a try. Within 10 minutes of the restart, after Northern had done all but score in a series of hectic raids, he beat three men in a 35-yard run to put Hill in for a try which, with a goal by Price, put them 11-9 in front. Then, for good measure, he came short off another Diabira pass from the scrum to send in Stockwell for a try which virtually settled the issue."

Neil and Molly had arranged to take a week's holiday at St Anne's after the game at Hunslet on Saturday 30 August but Neil had also arranged to return for the Bank Holiday Monday match at Keighley, a local derby. Neil was so keen to do well and keep fit that the *Wakefield Express*, still anxious to follow his progress, reported, "Neil asked Bradford Northern officials to contact Blackpool Borough for permission to train on their ground next week in order to be ready for the tit-bit of their season on September 6, when Trinity visit Bradford!" The game at Hunslet was won 20-5, even though Northern wasted many chances. Unfortunately, wingman Les Thomas broke his collarbone, which kept him out for a couple of months. Brian Smith in the *Telegraph & Argus* observed, "If Fox didn't quite have the devastating effect of his first two games, he still did a lot of useful work which should have brought at least one other try".

The game at Keighley drew a crowd of 8,500 and a Northern side missing six regulars had a hard struggle before winning 19-7. Queenslander Col Reynolds made his debut for Bradford on the wing and another debutant, second-rower Graham Joyce, showed up well. It was Foster who ran the show, however, with a couple of drop-goals, a try and as fine a display of forward skills as could be imagined, while Price booted a penalty from his own half. Neil was kept relatively quiet by his opposite number Terry O'Brien.

The much-awaited clash with Trinity drew 10,230 to Odsal and Neil was made captain for the day, Foster being absent. An entertaining game ended in an easy 27-7 success for Northern. Neil had a rather subdued game and was replaced 10 minutes before the end, after straining a muscle. The *Telegraph & Argus* remarked, "A 20 point win over Wakefield isn't the triumph it would have been a year ago, for Trinity these days are but a shadow of their former selves." Northern fans did not care about Trinity's problems. They were just glad that the win took Bradford to the top of the league.

On 13 September, Northern's winning run came to an end before a crowd of 12,160 at Leeds, who beat them 22-11. Neil had to come off after only 10 minutes. He recalls, "Everything had been going so well for me at Bradford until that Leeds match. I remember, I was being tackled by two men. While I was held on the ground another player came in and deliberately jumped on my knee. It was a dirty thing to do. Anyway, that was the end of me for five weeks. I was out with knee ligament trouble."

In Neil's absence Bradford lost four out of five games, including the return at Wakefield. Northern slipped from top to 14th in the league in that time. Something had to be done and when Albert Fearnley took over the secretary's job in addition to being manager, the club appointed Neil's old Yorkshire and Great Britain wing partner Mick Sullivan as coach.

By the time Neil returned to duty at Doncaster on Saturday, 1 November, Northern were confident of a return to winning ways. Neil's absence had coincided with a long suspension for Frank Foster. Now the two of them, plus the unfortunate Les Thomas, were all back in action. At least the visit to Tattersfield put them on the victory path but their 12-7 win was unimpressive and Thomas suffered further injury to his shoulder. A better performance followed with a 22-13 victory at Bramley the following afternoon. Almost on full-time Neil made a try for co-centre Alan Rhodes, who was returning for the first time since breaking a leg the previous Easter.

Two defeats at Odsal followed, however. Featherstone won 22-13 in a televised game watched in appalling conditions by the first crowd of less than 5,000 on the ground since December 1965. Terry Price scored all Northern's points - a try and five goals - and Brian Smith bemoaned the fact that there was "no authority among the middle backs". The following week against Huddersfield, Sullivan moved Price in to the centres as partner to Neil but Northern's performance was absolutely awful. The 16-0 loss seemed to precipitate a crisis. Geoff Clarkson and scrum-half Paul Daley requested transfers and Bak Diabira was listed against his wishes at £5,000. A clear-the-air meeting was arranged, attended by players, coaching staff and directors and there were newspaper reports that Bradford might be signing Billy Boston, who was 35 years old and in retirement.

There was some good news at last when Northern announced a profit of £2,424 on the previous year's accounts. That was followed by a well earned 18-12 victory at Barrow.

After only six weeks in the job, Mick Sullivan resigned as coach. Mick lived in Dewsbury but during the week was working in the Warrington area as a pipe-fitter on the building of a new power station. Travelling to training and to games was proving too much, both in terms of time and money, so 'A' team coach Stan Kielty took over training on a temporary basis. Then, on 5 December, the *Telegraph & Argus* ran an article under the headline "Foster, Fox Share Odsal Job". The two former test players had agreed to jointly coach the side. Harry Womersley announced, "In the past both players have proved themselves good leaders on the field. This is an opportunity for them to establish themselves as coaches. It is not a stop-gap appointment; it's entirely up to them. Obviously, they will stand or fall on their own ability... Both will be consulted regarding team selection but the final say will rest with the football committee." Frank Foster remained as team captain.

Bradford's first fixture under the new dual coaches was at Batley on Sunday, 7 December. Frank Foster could not play because of flu and Northern lost ingloriously, albeit narrowly, 9-8. Neil's sometimes depressing experiences with Wakefield at Mount Pleasant did not make this one any more bearable. Northern seemed incapable of doing anything but playing down the middle and Brian Smith facetiously remarked, "Without Foster, the Northern pack had about as much pattern as crazy paving, and the backs just didn't have the pace to make any better impression. Fox was in the picture more than he has been for weeks, but, hard as he tried, he just could not channel Northern's hard work in the right direction." Batley had prop Tyson sent off after 32 minutes but Northern did not get to within touching distance of winning until Neil created a try for Price late on but the latter missed the conversion. Terry missed four of his five shots at goal and both he and Neil failed with last-gasp attempts to drop a goal.

On 13 December, Northern put up an infinitely better show against Leeds at Odsal but still lost 12-10 in an enthralling game. It was arguably Northern's best performance of the season but in the end class told. Neil told the press, "Better... but not good enough". Neil had his best game since the early season but Northern were outsmarted, particularly at half-back, where Mick Shoebottom and Barry Seabourne dominated. Nonetheless, it took a 76th-minute drop-goal by second-rower Bill Ramsey to finally account for Bradford.

There was more disconcerting news for the Bradford faithful when the press informed them that Barrow had made a £5,000 offer for Frank Foster. Northern said he was not for sale and entered the market themselves by signing Glen Beaumont, a winger with Leeds and Carnegie College RU. Beaumont was a welcome addition to Bradford's register for he had the genuine pace so badly required.

Beaumont made his debut at Hull KR on 20 December. Rovers won 13-7 but Northern again put up a good show. Unfortunately, Les Thomas broke his collar-bone yet again and did not play again that season. Ironically, Thomas had actually been moved to centre because Neil had arrived late, having been given a garbled message about the game being off. Neil consequently missed the first half and came on as a substitute for the first time in domestic rugby. Having arrived on the field, he soon pulled a muscle and had to come off.

On 23 December, Bradford accepted £6,000 from Barrow for Frank Foster, leaving Neil as sole coach, something he had definitely not bargained for when he arrived at Odsal. Part of the Foster transfer involved Barrow agreeing to play their league fixture on a Sunday at Odsal. The Barrow players had been opposed to Sunday games but agreed that signing Foster was so important to the club that they would sacrifice their principles.

Neil's first games in sole charge were the Christmas derbies against Halifax. On Christmas Day at Odsal, Neil had to retire at half-time with Bradford leading 12-6 but Northern's forwards and half-backs played brilliantly in a 29-11 win. Terry Price had a wonderful game with the boot, landing seven goals. Neil missed the Boxing Day fixture at Thrum Hall, when two late tries by winger Col Reynolds snatched a 17-9 win. Northern were now 12th in the league with a 50 per cent record and room for much improvement. Unfortunately their next game, three weeks later thanks to postponements, at home to Batley produced a sorry display. Chance after chance went begging as Batley won 16-6 to inflict Northern's fifth home defeat in their last six appearances at Odsal.

The first addition to the club's playing strength under Neil came in the shape of winger or centre Mike Lamb, who cost £2,000 from Leeds. He provided some welcome pace to the side, who were so short of match practice because of the weather and the lamentable Odsal pitch, that Northern arranged a practice match at Hunslet's Parkside on 24 January. A week later, Lamb made a try-scoring debut in a 28-5 home win against Doncaster.

Northern had a tough draw in the Challenge Cup at St Helens on 7 February. Bradford put up a stern struggle but lost 16-3. Saints had too much class and pace and scored three tries from inside their own half. Terry Price injured a thigh and could not play the second half, which afforded Neil his first attempt at goalkicking since August, albeit unsuccessfully. The injury to Price cost him his place in the Wales team to meet England.

On 19 February, Bradford signed the Keighley player-coach Alan Kellett, a veteran player, who had been a fine stand-off and centre but who Northern expected to operate at loose-forward. He was not available for the home game against Barrow on 22 February, when Bradford overcame atrocious conditions to win 14-4. Neil converted a try by Lamb in the first half with a beautiful kick from the sideline – his first goal for Bradford. Otherwise Neil's kicking in the game was pretty poor and he took extra kicking practice, telling the *Telegraph & Argus*, "I have never kicked so badly in my life". To put matters into perspective, Brian Smith told his readers, "No other club possesses two goalkickers of the calibre of Price and Fox". Neil concedes that "with Terry Price doing all the kicking, I was not getting much practice and my timing was not as good as it used to be. So I thought I had better put in some extra sessions in training."

Kellett made his debut on 28 February in a 13-2 victory over Bramley at Odsal. He won the man-of-the-match award, giving an excellent display of distribution but appeared "more of a floating midfield player than a loose-forward". Neil had a good game and landed a couple of goals. The following day, in a 19-8 defeat at Hull, Neil dropped a goal which was the 1,700th of his career. Again he had a poor day with the boot "but in general play he worked hard to keep Northern going".

On 5 March the Great Britain selectors named Northern's Welsh trio of Jim Mills, Tony Fisher and Terry Price in the 1970 Lions party to tour Australasia. The selection of Price was perhaps the biggest shock to rugby league fans outside Bradford. Terry thought so too. He said he had not been playing well. In fact he had not been playing at all for the last month and would not reappear in Northern's colours until 31 March. In view of his own problems with injuries and tour selectors in the past, Neil must have wondered once more at the mysterious ways of selection committees. Incidentally, Jim Mills quickly turned his tour place down, preferring to emigrate to join North Sydney.

Bradford again entered the transfer market, exchanging Neil's usual wing partner Paul Litten for Hull forward Jim Macklin. Macklin made his debut on 10 March at Castleford in a controversial clash. The *Telegraph & Argus* noted, "Northern, boosted by two unbelievably casual 40-yard drop-goals from Fox early on, must have thought a shock win was in their grasp." Northern were in fine fettle but Castleford's speed began to tell and by half-time they led 7-4. Unfortunately, the first 40 minutes were merely the prelude to "a second half of savagery", according to Brian Smith. In the 45th minute a furious free-for-all broke out.

211

Northern prop Dave Hill was left prostrate on the ground and taken to hospital for treatment to his eye, hooker Tony Fisher was cautioned and Castleford prop Dennis Hartley was sent off. Then more controversy arose when Neil attempted a long-range penalty which appeared to creep inside a post. The touch judges were divided and referee Ronnie Jackson decided it was no goal, much to the ire of the Bradford fans. Five minutes from time Castleford secured a 10-4 win when Hardisty made a try for Briggs.

An exciting game against Hull at Odsal followed on 15 March. Northern trailed 7-5 at the break, Neil having converted a Paul Daley try. On the hour a drop-goal from Neil levelled the scores but a penalty goal from Hull centre John Maloney appeared to have won the game for his side. Six minutes from time Northern snatched a hard-earned 10-9 victory when Dave Stockwell scored a wonderful try, completely wrong-footing the Hull defence and beating three men to score at the corner flag.

Two days later the papers were full of the news that Ken Traill had resigned as coach at Wakefield with a year of his contract still to run. He was reported to have had differences of opinion with members of the committee, who a fortnight previously had decided to alter his terms of employment, resulting in a 25 per cent pay cut for him.

For now Neil had other things on his mind. Northern were still not sure of a place in the play-offs. Their trip to Featherstone on 22 March did not help their prospects. Terry Price was at last fit to play but turned up 15 minutes late – for the third time that season – and consequently was left out. Northern played very well and might have won with better finishing. Neil kicked a solitary goal and finished off some crisp passing for his first try since 27 August but his team went down 8-16. He also suffered another groin strain and missed two good away wins at Keighley and Huddersfield, which virtually assured Northern's presence in the play-offs.

A terrific struggle at Oldham on 3 April brought a 12-7 victory. It was a good day for Terry Price, who made his 100th appearance for Northern and landed his 100th goal of the season. Neil revealed some good form too. He broke strongly to put Price over for a fine try just before the interval. Neil then converted from the touchline to give his side an 8-7 lead. On the hour Oldham prop Gardiner went high on Neil and was sent off, before two goals from Price wound up the scoring. On 12 April, York visited Odsal on a foul day. The pitch was a mixture of puddles and mud, there was persistent heavy rain and it was freezing cold. It did not seem to bother Neil's men, however, who led 15-0 at half-time, with Kellett and Clarkson leading the charges. However, in the 63rd minute with Bradford 18-5 up, referee Harry Hunt abandoned proceedings. He told the press that he believed that some players were suffering from exposure and decided to abandon the game.

Northern had finished the season well to finish 12th, seven places higher than 1968-69. Their reward was a first-round play-off game at Hull KR, where they lost 26-13 with Neil landing one goal. A season which had promised so much came to a spluttering conclusion.

Neil, at 31, was naturally concerned about his future prospects. He recalls: "I asked Harry Womersley and Albert Fearnley what would be happening next season. Was I going to be player-coach or not and would there be a contract? They said, 'No, just let's see how things work out'. That wasn't very helpful and, to tell the truth, I had not been very happy at Bradford. There were players coming and going all the time and we never seemed to have a settled squad. Trinity asked if I would come back to Wakefield. There had been a lot of changes at Belle Vue and the new members of the committee wanted me back. So I had another talk with Harry and Albert and told them about Wakefield's approach. They said that if Wakefield would waive the £3,000 still owed on my transfer, they would not stand in my way. So I was happy to be going back home, back to Wakefield Trinity."

Wakefield Trinity 1969-70

Wakefield Trinity finished 21st in the league: P34, W13, L19, D2, For 521 Against 452
Fox scored 1 try, 6 goals, 15 points for Wakefield before signing for Bradford Northern

Date	Opponent	Score	Fox	Crowd	
7 Aug	Halifax	15-27	T, 3G	3,282	YC1
13 Aug	**Castleford**	0-16	dnp	5,942	
19 Aug	Dewsbury	9-17	3G	3,000	

Bradford Northern 1969-70

Bradford Northern finished 12th in the league: P34, W19, L15, For 511, Against 404
Fox scored 4 tries, 11 goals, 34 points for Bradford

Date	Opponent	Score	Fox	Crowd	
8 Aug	Leeds	6-20	dnp	9,518	YC1
20 Aug	York	5-10	dnp	3,373	
23 Aug	**Dewsbury**	35-12	2T	6,218	
27 Aug	**Oldham**	25-9	T	7,270	
30 Aug	Hunslet	20-5		4,375	
1 Sep	Keighley	19-7		8,500	
6 Sep	**Wakefield T**	27-7		10,230	
13 Sep	Leeds	11-22		12,160	
20 Sep	**Hull KR**	14-22	dnp	7,385	
27 Sep	Dewsbury	11-17	dnp	4,700	
4 Oct	**Hunslet**	22-19	dnp	6,600	
11 Oct	Wakefield T	13-28	dnp	6,290	
25 Oct	**Castleford**	17-18	dnp	7,026	
1 Nov	Doncaster	12-7		1,800	
2 Nov	Bramley	22-13		3,600	
8 Nov	**Featherstone R**	13-22		4,471	
15 Nov	**Huddersfield**	0-16		4,655	
22 Nov	Barrow	18-12		3,348	
7 Dec	Batley	8-9		4,061	
13 Dec	**Leeds**	10-12		8,419	
20 Dec	Hull KR*	7-13		3,732	
25 Dec	**Halifax**	29-11		6,949	
26 Dec	Halifax	17-9	dnp	5,688	
17 Jan	**Batley**	6-16		4,892	
31 Jan	**Doncaster**	28-5		4,549	
7 Feb	St Helens	3-16		7,062	Ch Cup 1
22 Feb	**Barrow**	14-4	G	4,236	
28 Feb	**Bramley**	13-2	2G	5,275	
1 Mar	Hull	8-19	G	5,300	
10 Mar	Castleford	4-10	2G	5,954	
15 Mar	**Hull**	10-9	2G	7,322	
22 Mar	Featherstone R	8-16	T, G	4,672	
28 Mar	Keighley	24-7	dnp	5,884	
31 Mar	Huddersfield	11-4	dnp	5,085	
3 Apr	Oldham	12-7	G	2,377	
12 Apr	**York**	18-5		4,498	
18 Apr	Hull KR	13-26	G	4,977	CH1

* Substitute

213

Wakefield Trinity Champions 1968
Back: E. Thomas, J.C. Lindley, E.W. Sugden, S. Milner, J. Townend, C.H. Glossop, L. Pounder,
B. Briggs, D.W. Armitage. Standing: K. Traill, R. Haigh, E. Campbell, G. Shepherd, G. Round, N. Fox,
D. Jeanes, M. McLeod, J. Malpass. Seated: D. Hawley, D. Garthwaite, R. Payley, F. West, H. Poynton,
J. Ridge, D. Fox, J. Bonnar, G. Cooper, I. Brooke, K. Batty. Insets: G. Oakes, K. Hirst, G. Coetzer,
W.J. Armour, R. Owen, G. Clarkson, G. Steel

Neil playing for Wakefield against Halifax in 1971, passing to Ken Batty.

19. 1970-71: Bouncing back at Belle Vue

If Neil thought that things had been deteriorating at Wakefield before he was transferred to Bradford, he discovered they were even worse when he returned to Belle Vue. From being champions in 1968 Trinity had slumped to 21st in the league table in 1969-70. Financially, matters were dire. The club lost £2,090 on the 1969-70 season, had an overdraft of £12,906, total liabilities of £29,049 and had taken only £11,438 in gate money during 1969-70, compared with £26,469 the previous season. Things had got so bad that the reserve team had played unpaid for much of 1969-70.

While Neil was at Bradford there had been key changes in personnel at Wakefield. Harold Poynton had retired and Don Fox had transferred to Batley, where he finished his playing career. Bob Haigh had been transferred to Leeds in April for £6,500 and, of course, Ken Traill had ended his great career as Trinity's coach. Ken briefly coached Barrow and Keighley before fading from the coaching scene altogether. There had even been changes at the *Wakefield Express*, which was now published each Friday instead of on Saturdays. John L. Allen had retired as its Trinity correspondent, the club's affairs now being covered by Geoff (A. G.) Cudworth and Frank Jeffrey.

Another missing face was David Garthwaite. Neil says, "David was really unlucky with injuries. His fourth bad shoulder injury had finally forced him to retire in 1969. Trinity had signed David from Wakefield RUFC around the same time as they signed Geoff Clarkson and he was our substitute back for the 1968 Wembley final. He played 64 matches for Trinity and scored 23 tries but it could have been a lot more but for injuries. He was a very fine player, equally good at centre and wing and a very good finisher. Later on he became a committee member at Belle Vue. David is still a good friend of mine. He went to Silcoates school as a boarder, which always seemed a bit strange to me because he only lived a short distance from the place. David's family owned HB Clark's brewery in Wakefield near the prison and David became managing director in the late 1980s. The firm is one of the north of England's biggest independent wholesalers. David has since done an awful lot for sport in Wakefield and sponsored lots of sporting organisations and causes."

Neil had signed a three-year contract as player-coach in May and had the players in training almost immediately. Trinity had received 11 applications for the post of coach, which they had whittled down to four in Don Froggett, Jack Scroby, Peter Fox and Tommy Smales. Neil was a last-minute applicant. He had help on the training side from two stalwarts in Johnny Malpass and Don Froggett. Neil recalls: "After the disappointment of the previous season, all the lads were raring to go and seemed pleased to have me back. Gary Cooper helped me with the training and the players were jumping out of their skins by the start of the season." Although Neil was aware that not all the committee were in favour of his appointment, Chairman Les Pounder guaranteed him the committee's full backing. It was agreed that there would be a small selection committee of four, including the chairman, with Neil having the major say.

On 7 August the *Wakefield Express* ran an interview with Neil, in which Geoff Cudworth reported, "He feels he can be an effective force in the game for another two or three seasons. So far as his coaching is concerned, he feels his probationary six months at Odsal provided him with a very useful insight into the job's peculiar problems. 'I am not so conceited to think that I know it all,' he ventured, 'in fact, I take note of ideas from whatever club I visit. If I think any of them are worth adopting I shall do just that. But I have played the game long enough now to appreciate the basic demands of the game physically and mentally, and have in my mind tactical theories which I feel are sound'."

215

Neil's main concern was the lack of forward strength on Wakefield's books so the first deal he presided over was the exchange of Stuart Carlton for Bradford's big second-rower Bob Oswald. He also recalls the signing of another forward, "During the close season some committee men went down to Northampton to sign union player Bryan West, who had played eight times for England and toured South Africa in 1968 with the British Lions, as a replacement. He was about six feet four inches tall and weighed about 14 stones. I asked them to wait until I could see him but they took it into their hands to sign him. They paid £6,000 for him, £3,000 down and £3,000 to follow. When I heard the news, I asked one of them what he was like and the answer was, 'He's a smashing fellow' but, sadly, he played bloody awful. He was recommended by a former Trinity player and they took his advice and signed him. In his two years with us he struggled. Being tall and slim he couldn't break tackles. He once said to Mick Morgan, 'When you pass the ball to me, make sure I'm running into a gap', to which Mick replied, 'Tha got £6,000, thee put me into gaps'. Bryan played 30 times for us. He later played at York for a short spell under Gary Cooper. He broke his wrist and packed in after he was paid the remainder of his contract. We did sign another union player, who did well. That was John Hegarty, a centre from Hawick. He was a very hard tackler, good with the ball and had a good physique, ideal for rugby league."

Rugby league had a new fixture format for the 1970-71 season. The old established Lancashire and Yorkshire League Championships were abandoned and fixtures were based on the league positions for 1969-70. The top 15 clubs played each other home and away, plus three teams from the bottom 15, and vice versa. In effect there were two leagues within one. Trinity, who had finished in the bottom 15, therefore had a comparatively easy schedule, having to meet only Hull KR, Salford and Wigan of the top clubs.

Neil took over the club captaincy with Dave Hawley as his vice-captain. The season opened with a 51-0 run-out against the Wakefield & District Amateur League. Neil scored 11 points and there was a hat-trick for Dave Topliss, while new signings West and Oswald also scored tries. The real business, however, began at Rochdale on 22 August with a cracking 35-9 victory. Frank Jeffrey observed: "Not for years have I seen a Wakefield side looking so fit and sharp in the opening fixture... It was a great comeback for Neil Fox, who led the side superbly. He had a hand in several tries and repeatedly bamboozled his opponents in a classy display. He seemed to revel in his new role as captain and coach and was constantly urging the side to greater efforts, even when they had 30 points on the board." Neil kicked six goals and there was another hat-trick for Topliss.

Two days later Trinity had a fine 27-5 home win over Hull KR. Their forwards and half-backs were on top form but Neil took the man-of-the-match award. The *Wakefield Express* noted: "Almost all the flair of this master of the game was apparent from time to time. His points contribution was prodigious with nine successful kicks from 11 attempts. And his leadership ranged widely from the subtle to the plain storming."

There was, however, sad news at Belle Vue when the club president, Alderman Frank West died. A Conservative councillor and former mayor of the city, he had been a member of the Wakefield committee since 1945. His trademark was to always wear a flower in his button hole. He was succeeded as president by Ernest Corscadden, an accountant, who had been the club's auditor for 20 years.

On 29 August, Trinity took on Leeds at Belle Vue in the first round of the Yorkshire Cup – one of the hardest tests they could face. The game was almost as torrid as the late summer weather, the first half in particular being "a sordid, niggling affair", according to Frank Jeffrey. There was an ugly incident after 25 minutes when Mick Shoebottom bowled over try-scorer Dave Topliss well after he had touched down. Referee Harry Hunt sent both hookers off in the 46th minute for technical offences. That seemed to calm matters down but helped Leeds more than Trinity, who were leading 7-5 at the 55-minute mark, only to concede 15 points in 16 minutes and lose the tie 20-10. It had been a good performance. Neil had landed two goals, made a try and been the mainspring of Trinity's attack.

After three such good opening displays there was considerable disappointment when Dewsbury won 10-7 at Belle Vue on 31 August, although playing four games in only nine days certainly had an effect on the Wakefield performance.

Neil's boys got back to winning ways at Workington Town on 5 September, after an overnight stop at Cockermouth. Hegarty and West made their debuts. Neil remembers this game for a particular reason - for the first time in his career he played in the forwards. He says: "I probably confused Workington because I picked myself at number 4 but played in the pack. My opposite centre must have wondered, 'Where has Foxy gone?' Anyway, I must have done well enough because I won the man-of-the-match award. Phil King had always told me that if I moved to loose-forward I would play there for Great Britain, but I think I left it a bit too late for that. Phil wrote in my benefit brochure that I should tour as a threequarter in 1966 and then mould myself into a back-row forward."

Workington were beaten 22-12, Neil kicked five goals and the *Wakefield Express* reported that "he had an extremely busy afternoon in and around the scrums; was obviously at some pains to ensure that Trinity's moves were sustained with precision and, at the same time, skilfully found room amid the forward skirmishing to drop two goals".

Neil turned out at loose-forward again, kicking six goals and winning the man-of-the-match award in a 30-13 home win over Doncaster, in an entertaining game played in near gale-force winds. He was totally dominant in the first half but, perhaps understandably, faded in the last quarter. Les Scarlett of *Yorkshire Sports* was an interested observer of Neil's transformation from backs to pack. He wrote: "Until now Fox has always steadfastly refused to play in the pack – a move I suggested here more than three years ago, when it was becoming apparent that his speed was beginning to desert him. What Neil said to me after my views appeared were unrepeatable then and still are! What did emerge from our conversation at the time was that he would retire when his days at centre were numbered and on no account would he move up front. However, different days, different ways, and now that he has been appointed player-coach no doubt he has developed a different attitude of mind. Now the team comes first. It is his job to produce a winning side and if, as coach, he can set an example then it is up to him to do so.

So, at Workington, for the very first time and on Wednesday for the first time in front of his own crowd, we saw the Big Fella playing at loose-forward. And those who came to scoff, quoting those nonsensical clichés we have heard from them so often – such as 'Fox isn't hard enough' or 'Fox can't tackle' – surely stayed to cheer. He made a tremendous impact on the game, using his weight to the best advantage and tackling as well as the next. But it was his perfectly timed long passes, which always found his man and opened up the way for many attacks, which caught the eye. In fact, his passes reminded me of those which made Ken Traill, Fox's predecessor as Trinity's coach, famous as an international loose-forward. No praise could be higher than that."

Neil must have been doing something right, because he was chosen in the shadow team for Yorkshire's game at Cumberland, along with Terry Ramshaw, while winger Keith Slater was awarded his first county cap.

Trinity's rich seam of form resulted in a 46-18 win at York on 12 September, their highest score in an away game since the war. Neil scored a try and landed five goals, two from the touchline, and the *Wakefield Express* remarked that Wakefield "displayed a mastery reminiscent of their golden days". Derek Marshall wrote in the *Daily Mail*: "If Neil Fox... is still feeling a little strange in the unaccustomed position of loose-forward the records don't show it. Since moving there he has twice been voted man-of-the-match and if he couldn't quite make it a hat-trick... he certainly shouldered a dominating role in the 46-18 win over York. He produced touch kicks that devoured the ground the frustrated York attack had won. He quickened his stride to produce breaks of thunderous power, and he distributed the ball with a speed and length of pass that gained Wakefield yards of space. Instead of disrupting his generalship, York, it seemed, stood back to admire it. Wakefield responded with a display full of spectacle."

On 15 September, Doncaster gave Trinity a hard time at Tattersfield before losing 9-2. At half-time Trinity led 6-2, thanks to three penalties from Barney Ward, while the only score of the second half was a try to Keith Slater. The *Wakefield Express* noted, "They clearly missed the skill and leadership of Fox, who got the biggest cheer of the night when he came on as a substitute 10 minutes after the interval, Ramshaw having been injured. He had been a doubtful starter owing to injury. He had a quiet game but sent out some shrewd passes and restored the confidence of the team."

A handsome 30-14 victory followed at Barrow, when Neil made his 450th appearance for Wakefield. Trinity then performed in lacklustre fashion while beating Keighley 20-8 at Belle Vue and were grateful that Neil was on the field to win the game. He landed four goals, created two tries for Ian Brooke with superb long passes and scored the decisive try in the 63rd minute, when a pass from Dave Hawley allowed him to beat two defenders to touch down near the posts, provoking a great roar of relief from Trinity's edgy fans. Neil's performance brought him his fifth player-of-the-match award of the season, worth £6 to him. He and another old-stager, Alex Murphy, were leading the player-of-the match awards at this point in the season, while Trinity were at the top of the league alongside St Helens. Neil was at the top of the league's goalkickers' list, with 42 in 10 matches.

He added another half dozen to his tally on 26 September, when Huyton were blitzed 63-0 at Belle Vue. Geoff Cudworth remarked that Neil may have broken his own club record if he had not missed 33 minutes of the second half with a knee injury he picked up early in the game. Cudworth was one of several critics who at this time suggested that the Great Britain selectors could do worse than pick Neil at loose-forward for the World Cup team in the forthcoming tournament to be held in England.

Neil's knee injury kept him out of the side for the next two games, which included Wakefield's exit from the BBC2 Floodlit Trophy in the preliminary round. It was becoming noticeable that Trinity struggled when Neil was not on the field and he should perhaps not have put himself at risk on 7 October, when an unbeaten Wigan visited Belle Vue. Trinity gave a good account of themselves and were only 4-2 down as late as the 54th minute. However, they had no answer to Wigan centre Bill Ashurst, who gave a virtuoso display and personally sank Trinity scoring nine points in the last eight minutes, with a penalty, a drop-goal, a try and a conversion, as Wigan won 18-5.

Trinity splashed out £4,500 for Huddersfield test second-rower Rob Valentine and £750 for Halifax hooker or utility forward Stuart Kelley in an effort to bolster their pack. Valentine was a hard-working forward who would stiffen the defensive screen considerably, while Kelley was brought in to add more fire.

Neil missed a comfortable home victory over Rochdale Hornets, when Valentine made his debut, but returned at centre for another home win against Batley. Dave Topliss starred with another hat-trick, but Valentine looked unhappy at loose-forward. Neil was in top kicking form, landing six goals, and scoring a try from a dropped pass before taking himself off in the 68th minute. Two days later, Neil moved back to loose-forward for a tough away fixture at Salford. Trinity were soon 7-0 down but in the 13th minute Neil fired a perfect long pass from a scrum to get Slater over and on 26 minutes cleverly wrong-footed the defence with a dummy to cross near the posts, converting to give his side an 8-7 lead. Thereafter, however, Trinity fell away, probably feeling the effects of playing four games in nine days, to lose 25-10 – their first loss on away territory that season.

After a 10-day break Wakefield played at Oldham on 26 October. It was a wet night and there were far too many penalties and scrums but there was a thrilling finish. Dave Topliss produced a gem of a try and Neil passed the 1,500 goals mark for Trinity with the second of his three successful kicks. Wakefield trailed 15-12 by the 73rd minute, when Slater took a pass from Hegarty, found a slight gap, beat a man and took two men over with him for an equalising try at the flag. Neil's conversion just missed and then he failed with penalties from 40 yards and half-way before missing with a last-gasp drop at goal.

Things were definitely looking up at Trinity since Neil's return. Even the finances were in better shape, £2,000 having been lopped off their overdraft. The team was entrenched near the top of the table and Neil's leadership qualities were shining through. Trinity were also unlikely to be affected by any potentially damaging late-season fixture pile-up, because they had already played 16 league fixtures – more than any other team, some of whom had only played 10 games. Even so, Neil called a players' meeting, directing some team members to watch their diets in order to keep match-fit. Extra Sunday training was introduced while the World Cup was taking place and fixtures were on hold. There was also exciting news about the capture of South African winger David Barends, who had been recommended to the club by Ivor Dorrington. Barends had represented a South African 'Coloured' XV in rugby union and was expected to add greatly to Trinity's threequarter strength. Jim Windsor, who had represented Trinity in negotiations for Barends, described him as "tremendously fast, good on defence and a great prospect. He will be another Billy Boston type of player". However, there were difficulties with getting him a passport and his arrival was delayed for a month.

On 14 November, the World Cup having ended, Trinity despatched Oldham 38-2 at Belle Vue. Neil, now playing at centre again, opened the scoring with a try and conversion and added another six goals. A comprehensive 28-4 win at Hunslet followed. Just before half-time Trinity hooker Hill was sent off for technical offences and nine minutes into the second half, when a dubious tackle on Ramshaw went unaddressed by the referee, Stuart Kelley and Hunslet skipper Geoff Crewdson were sent off after a scuffle. For all that, it was not a violent encounter. David Jeanes stood out with two storming try-scoring runs and Neil got the last try and kicked five goals.

There was a remarkable game at Thrum Hall on 29 November on a rainswept day. One critic described the match as "a wonderful advertisement for the game – clean and entertaining in vile conditions". Neil had combined smartly with Geoff Wraith to score the opening try after four minutes and later kicked a penalty but on the hour Halifax led 11-5. Trinity struck back hard and Frank Jeffrey was moved to declare, "They rallied superbly to score three tries in what I regard as their finest recovery effort for a long time". Ken Batty scored the first two tries in the recovery. Neil converted the second from a wide angle to give them a 13-11 lead, before Ramshaw smashed his way over in the 73rd minute to seal a spirited 16-11 win. Referee Eric Lawrinson went to the dressing rooms after the game to compliment the players. He said the match ranked among the best and cleanest of some 700 games he had handled.

David Barends arrived in Wakefield to a temperature 40° Fahrenheit lower than Johannesburg and moved into a house shared with fellow winger Michael Hunte. At around the same time it was announced that Ken Batty would soon be emigrating to Australia to play for St George in Sydney. Neil immediately praised Ken's readiness to assume the role of utility back, saying, "I would like younger players to take a leaf out of Ken's notebook. He has never grumbled wherever Trinity have switched him to play".

Barends made his first-team debut in a home game against Blackpool Borough on Sunday, 13 December, Trinity by now having given up their resistance to playing on Sundays. Trinity won easily 44-8, and Barends was an immediate hit. He scored his first try for the club in the 32nd minute when Neil put him through and he brushed off the fullback to score at the flag. He got a second on 56 minutes, when the crowd erupted after he beat two men to score again in the corner. Yet, despite Barends's grand debut, Neil was the game's star and won the man-of-the-match award. Just before half-time he scored off a loose ball and shortly after the break he bamboozled the defence at a play-the-ball before crashing over near the corner flag. His goalkicking was spot-on too with seven successes. His 20 points against Blackpool meant he had scored 60 points in the last four games, with six tries and 21 goals.

The following Saturday at Belle Vue he was at it again against Workington Town, who as sixth placed team in the league were expected to give Trinity a stern test. Trinity won 42-6 and Neil walked off with yet another man-of-the-match prize. Former test cricketer Freddie Trueman, who reported rugby league matches for the *Sunday People* in the cricket off-season, wrote, "Neil Fox might be getting on a bit now – but as a points-gatherer he is still way out on his own. He proved that his golden left foot is still as lethal as ever. He landed 12 goals to equal the club record set by himself – who else – three years ago. His team-mates tried hard in the dying minutes to pave the way for the record-breaker. But twice he failed with drop-goal attempts... Between his kicking feats Fox managed to do a few other things which put a poor Workington side well and truly on the rack. He made four of the six tries with snappy passes and altogether the scene is looking rosy for Trinity's player-coach." Neil had kicked six penalties, four conversions and two drop-goals in his record-equalling display and during the game had passed his 200th point of the season, and left behind the landmark of 3,800 points for the Trinitarians.

On Boxing Day, Wakefield went to Mount Pleasant on an unpleasant afternoon, replete with biting winds and snow flurries. Only Leeds had won there during that season and Batley offered their usual stern brand of resistance to table-toppers Trinity. Neil gave Trinity the lead with a 36th-minute penalty, the 1,800th goal of his career and converted a magnificent try by Keith Slater. However, as the game entered its final 10 minutes Trinity were clinging to a 9-4 lead, when Batley passing broke down 30 yards from their own goal. Neil was quickly onto the ball, booting it forward for Barends to gather and score the clinching try for a 12-4 victory. Trinity thus entered the New Year still on top of the league, ahead of Wigan, who remained unbeaten after 18 games, St Helens and Leeds, who both had games in hand over Wakefield. Despite the fact that Trinity had been blessed with a weaker list of fixtures, Neil was to be congratulated on the team's remarkable resurgence.

Unfortunately, the New Year began with a cruel defeat at Hull KR on 2 January. It was a marvellous game on a snowbound pitch. Neil had reverted to loose-forward for this fixture and appeared to have earned Trinity a well-deserved 10-10 draw when he landed a drop-goal in the 79th minute. However, Rovers were awarded a penalty at a scrum 30 yards out in the fourth minute of injury time, which Terry Clawson put over the bar to win the game.

On Sunday 10 January, Neil moved back to centre for the home game against star-studded Salford. A spring-like day drew a crowd of 10,606 to Belle Vue, the biggest there since the Easter fixture against Leeds in 1968. In an absorbing contest the man-of-the-match award went to Rob Valentine but Neil was again the match-winner, the *Wakefield Express* observing, "Fox's generalship played a big part in his side's success". During the course of the game Neil passed yet another milestone – his 4,500th point in first-class games. He had given Trinity the lead with a drop-goal but David Watkins levelled with a penalty after 15 minutes. Three minutes later Valentine claimed the first try of the game. Watkins almost immediately landed a second penalty before Neil responded with a 40-yard penalty in the 22nd minute and Trinity led 7-4 at the break. Maurice Richards levelled the scores again with a try in the 50th minute, only for Neil to restore Trinity's advantage with a 57th-minute penalty. Eight minutes from time Topliss and Marston engineered the decisive try for Slater before Neil's injury-time penalty goal – his 100th goal of the season – ended the scoring at 14-7, for one of Wakefield's best victories of recent years.

A week later Halifax visited Belle Vue for a game which was the very antithesis of the sporting encounter the two teams had played out at Thrum Hall so memorably in November. Trinity players Hill (knee), Hawley (shoulder), Spencer (broken nose) and Valentine (shoulder) were all injured and after 35 minutes the referee, George Wilson, lectured the whole Halifax team about rough play. In the 51st minute, Ian Brooke and Halifax forward, Terry Fogerty were sent off after a wild free-for-all. Neil was in the wars too, breaking his thumb but returning to the field after treatment. The *Yorkshire Post* had this to say, "One day Neil Fox will have to stop winning games for Wakefield Trinity, and clubs other than Halifax will no doubt be very relieved. They were the victims of Fox's special magic in yet another financially successful Sunday game at Belle Vue. After an hour Halifax were hanging on grimly to a slender 5-4 lead gained in a bitter and bruising atmosphere. Their tenacious tackling had rattled Trinity, but captain-coach Fox shocked them with seven points in two minutes. He sold an outrageous dummy before ambling between the posts, converted the try, and then kicked a 35-yard penalty goal two minutes later." A David Jeanes try 12 minutes from time sealed a great 14-8 Wakefield victory.

Neil's thumb fracture came at the worst possible time. On 24 January a weakened Trinity had to face Salford without him in a Challenge Cup first-round tie at The Willows. Despite their handicaps, Trinity achieved a wonderful 6-6 draw before a crowd of more than 14,000. Barney Ward had kicked Trinity into a 6-4 lead after 70 minutes of a spine-tingling tie but a baffling penalty award at a play-the-ball allowed David Watkins to rescue his side in injury time. The replay, which attracted a crowd of 11,733 to Belle Vue, was never going to go Wakefield's way, but they put up a brave fight before going down 15-8. Stuart Kelley joined Neil in the broken thumb club.

Neil was still absent on 6 February when a hapless Hunslet side were overwhelmed 72-8 at Belle Vue. Barney Ward equalled Neil's club record in landing 12 goals and Keith Slater emulated Fred Smith's club record of seven tries in a game. Ward could have broken Neil's record but missed with a last-minute conversion of Slater's seventh try. Keith Slater was dropped for Trinity's next game – a 12-5 win at Blackpool. Neil dropped him because he had failed to meet the team bus from Wakefield on the Friday afternoon, Wakefield having planned for an overnight stay at Blackpool.

Neil returned to action at centre with the 'A' team on 19 February in a 39-5 win against Huddersfield 'A' at Belle Vue, landing six goals, while Bryan West claimed a hat-trick of tries. Neil was at loose-forward, though, for Trinity's visit to Wigan on 6 March. Wigan had now overtaken Trinity at the top of the league but had finally suffered their first league defeat, at Hull KR on 12 February. Trinity were not able to emulate Rovers, however, and in an uncharacteristically drab match were beaten 11-5. Much worse followed when Trinity went to lowly Huyton and lost 5-0. Frank Jeffrey posed the inevitable question – was this Trinity's greatest humiliation? Huyton, of course, played heroically and tackled Trinity out of the game. Trinity's excuse was a crippling injury list, which was so severe that they had to field six of those who had played in the 'A' team game at Keighley just 24 hours previously, when Neil had been a substitute. There was hardly the same pressure or excuse the following week when another totally unexpected 22-11 defeat was suffered at home to Barrow. Neil scored the opening try – his 250th for Wakefield – and at half-time they led 11-5, only to collapse dramatically in the second half.

Neil was unable to play in any of the last four league games, which brought home wins against Bramley and York and defeats at Keighley and Dewsbury. He had suffered an ankle injury in training and had other things on his mind on 3 April, when he attended Trinity's 'A' team fixture at Featherstone, a second round Yorkshire Senior Competition Challenge Cup tie, which Rovers won 11-2. Frank Jeffrey in the *Wakefield Express* described the encounter as "one of the most depressing games it has ever been my misfortune to watch". He called it "a shameful affair" and "a black day" and it made him "sick at heart". To call the game a roughhouse would perhaps be understating it. Trinity were on the wrong end of a lopsided penalty count and matters came to a head when referee Edward Hill of Bradford sent off Trinity players Gary Cooper and Mick Lig five minutes from time. Cooper had been kicked in the mouth while on the ground and when he asked the referee for some protection he was dismissed for "mouthing". Lig protested that Cooper should not be sent off for complaining and was immediately dismissed too. Trinity scrum-half Harkin then suggested that the whole team might as well go off, at which point Mick Morgan began to lead the team off. They never actually left the field because Neil stopped them from doing so. Instead they returned to take up their positions for play. Unfortunately, by this time, the referee had abandoned the match. It had certainly been a fractious and rough game and Trinity officials were adamant that weak refereeing in the face of an intimidating Post Office Road crowd had been the cause of the trouble. Both teams were censured by the RFL's disciplinary committee and Trinity were fined £6.50 – 50 pence per player. Cooper was banned for three matches and Lig for two.

Coaching obviously carried more problems than merely putting players through training sessions. Nine days after the Post Office Road fracas, Neil saw another fiasco, when Trinity lost 22-15 at Dewsbury, unbelievably surrendering a 13-point lead and playing ineptly. Neil was so disappointed that he ordered extra Wednesday training. Geoff Cudworth reported that "Neil told me this week he would like to concentrate on coaching. He felt that the dual role of player-coach could result in less than 100 per cent effectiveness in one role or the other, though he was quite prepared to carry on in Trinity's team."

Meanwhile, Neil just got on with his job. Despite their late season slump, Wakefield finished fifth, behind Wigan, St Helens, Leeds and Leigh. Only Leeds scored more tries and points than Trinity and only Wigan and St Helens had better defensive records.

Towards the end of the league season Trinity received a transfer fee of £1,750 from St George in Australia for Ken Batty, who had made the last of his 184 appearances for Trinity against Hunslet on 6 February. Coming into the Belle Vue set-up was Peter Harrison, for whom Trinity paid £1,000 to Featherstone Rovers. He made his debut in the second-row at Keighley on 2 April. Neil regarded him as a very significant capture, "He was a player of the future, big and strong with a lot of speed for such a big man. Featherstone had been playing him in the centre but we saw him as a forward."

Harrison was cup-tied for the play-offs, which began for Trinity on a wet and cold Friday night at Belle Vue on 23 April. Their opponents were local rivals Castleford, for whom Alan Hardisty would be making his last appearance if his team were ousted. Trinity's performance was more like the team Neil was striving to create. Terry Ramshaw, returning after a long absence, played a stormer and Keith Slater claimed two magnificent tries, after receiving the club's Player of the Year award before the kick-off. Neil, who landed a solitary goal, acted as a substitute, replacing winger Eddie McDonagh.

Neil was back in the starting line-up at centre for the quarter final clash with Challenge Cup finalists Leigh at Hilton Park on 2 May. On a sun-drenched afternoon Trinity played with great restraint in the face of provocative tactics and, for once, Alex Murphy had a nightmare match. Alex missed five drop-goal attempts and provided both of Trinity's tries. The first came after 14 minutes when Eddie McDonagh intercepted one of his long passes near half-way to give Wakefield the lead. Stuart Ferguson kicked a goal for Leigh after 33 minutes and on 68 minutes winger Tony Barrow scored at the corner to give Leigh the lead. Neil levelled the scores with a penalty after Morgan had been fouled but narrowly failed with two attempts to drop a goal and as injury time approached a replay seemed inevitable. However, from a tap re-start on the Leigh '25' Murphy fired out another misdirected pass which Mick Morgan intercepted to score the winning try. Trinity had performed exceptionally well, particularly in defence, to emerge victorious by 8-5 and earn winning pay of £35 a man.

The semi-final took Trinity to Central Park to meet top-of-the-league Wigan on 9 May. Few people outside Wakefield expected a victory for Neil's team but eight minutes into the game an improbable drop-goal from Rob Valentine gave them the lead. A try by full-back Colin Tyrer in the 10th minute put Wigan ahead and Trinity stand-off Jack Marston was lucky to stay on the field after trying to trip the try scorer. With quarter of an hour gone Trinity's cause was lost, when Marston was sent off by Eric Clay for another trip on centre Bill Francis. Joe Humphreys of the *Sunday Mirror* wrote, "Marston's departure was like opening the pantry door to a pack of hungry wolves." By half-time Trinity were 26-7 down and the final score of 49-15 represented Wigan's highest score of the season and Trinity's heaviest defeat for 13 years.

It was a wretched way to end a season in which Trinity had exceeded all reasonable expectations. But the true test of Neil's men, many critics believed, would be in the following season, when Trinity would have to face all the other top 15 sides. Yet for now Neil could await 1971-72 with a good deal of satisfaction at a job well done. While bad luck with injuries had disrupted the latter half of his season, Neil had recovered his scoring touch again in no uncertain fashion. He had scored a dozen tries for Trinity despite playing in and out of the pack. Only Keith Slater with 31 and Dave Topliss with 22 had scored more. His 110 goals had given him eighth place in the leading goalkickers' list and his 256 points put him in seventh spot in the points' list.

In spite of Trinity's notable improvement and Neil's return to prolific scoring form, some critics were dubious about the advisability of Neil's willingness to carry on playing. Jack Bentley of the *Daily Express* and 'Left Footer' in the *Rugby Leaguer* were among those expressing such sentiments. After Trinity's ill-fated Championship semi-final at Wigan, Bentley wrote, "Neil Fox will have to crack the whip over his mates who will find themselves back in the top playing section of the league next season. He will also have to ask himself seriously whether it is time he himself confines his activities to coaching." 'Left Footer' wrote: "There is one big problem Neil has yet to solve and this is himself. Let's face it, in the last few matches he was only a shadow of his former self and at Wigan he was the poorest of the Trinity backs. It poses the problem of a player-coach – who is to tell the coach to take himself off?"

There is little doubt that these criticisms were well meant. The writers were clearly anxious that Neil's continued playing did not devalue his status as one of the game's greatest exponents. They obviously believed in the dictum "Go out on top". It was evident that Neil had similar thoughts from time to time. He had now reached 32 years of age and it all had to end some time. He had done more than enough to establish himself as one of the greatest figures in the rugby league pantheon. If he chose to, he could rest happily on his laurels. However, he chose to carry on playing and coaching.

On 30 May, Neil took a squad to Headingley for the annual Leeds Sevens tournament, but did not play himself. His side won the competition, beating Leigh 16-3, Barrow 13-11 and Hull KR 19-13 in the final. It was believed to be Wakefield Trinity's first ever success in a rugby league sevens competition – another feather in Neil's cap. The squad was Cooper, Slater, Topliss, Marston, Hawley (captain), Morgan, West and McDonagh (substitute). Unfortunately, the risks of taking part in such events were too evident with injuries to Brooke, Hawley and McDonagh. There was more bad news as Harry Wilkinson, Trinity's great former prop forward and captain and a stalwart member of the coaching and back-room staff at Belle Vue, had died on the same day, aged 61.

Neil and his charges returned to training on 29 June. The unusually early start was caused by the decision to open the season with the Yorkshire Cup ties on 1 August, the earliest ever kick-off to a rugby league season. The decision was anathema to Leeds, who withdrew from the competition – not the response expected by the organisers.

As well as seeing the professionals return to training, Neil instituted a summer school for 15 to 18 year-olds at Belle Vue and down the road at Eastmoor. The course lasted six weeks and was a bridge between school and open-age rugby for boys who may otherwise be lost to the game in those uncatered for years. Neil, Ken Rollin and Don Robinson organised the courses. Despite his concerns about the first team, he did not forget the importance of developing young talent for the club.

Wakefield Trinity 1970-71

Wakefield Trinity finished 5th in the league: P34, W24, L9, D1, For 760, Against 330
Fox scored 12 tries, 110 goals, 256 points for Wakefield

Date	Opponent	Score	Fox	Crowd	
22 Aug	Rochdale H	35-9	6G	2,525	
24 Aug	**Hull KR**	27-5	9G	5,485	
29 Aug	**Leeds**	10-20	2G	7,641	YC1
31 Aug	**Dewsbury**	7-10	2G	4,317	
5 Sep	Workington T	22-12	5G	2,020	
9 Sep	**Doncaster**	30-13	6G	3,651	
12 Sep	York	46-18	T, 5G	2,182	
15 Sep	Doncaster*	9-2		1,170	
19 Sep	Barrow	30-14	3G	3,644	
23 Sep	**Keighley**	20-8	T, 4G	4,706	
26 Sep	**Huyton**	63-0	6G	4,053	
29 Sep	Huddersfield	14-16	dnp	2,781	FT Prel
3 Oct	Bramley	23-7	dnp	2,000	
7 Oct	**Wigan**	5-18		8,202	
10 Oct	**Rochdale H**	21-8	dnp	4,348	
14 Oct	**Batley**	26-10	T, 6G	4,375	
16 Oct	Salford	10-25	T, 2G	7,644	
26 Oct	Oldham	15-15	3G	2,587	
14 Nov	**Oldham**	38-2	T, 7G	3,751	
21 Nov	Hunslet	28-4	T, 5G	1,700	
29 Nov	Halifax	16-11	2T, 2G	2,174	
13 Dec	**Blackpool B**	44-8	2T, 7G	4,832	
19 Dec	**Workington T**	42-6	12G	4,117	
26 Dec	Batley	12-4	2G	3,307	
2 Jan	Hull KR	10-12	2G	3,841	
10 Jan	**Salford**	14-7	4G	10,606	
17 Jan	**Halifax**	14-8	T, 4G	6,343	
24 Jan	Salford	6-6	dnp	14,278	Ch Cup 1
27 Jan	**Salford**	8-15	dnp	11,733	Replay
6 Feb	**Hunslet**	72-8	dnp	2,976	
13 Feb	Blackpool B	12-5	dnp	600	
6 Mar	Wigan	5-11	G	6,629	
13 Mar	Huyton	0-5		950	
20 Mar	**Barrow**	11-22	T, G	3,259	
26 Mar	**Bramley**	14-4	dnp	2,688	
2 Apr	Keighley	7-10	dnp	2,544	
12 Apr	Dewsbury	15-22	dnp	3,500	
18 Apr	**York**	17-7	dnp	3,482	
23 Apr	**Castleford***	10-4	G	2,786	CH1
2 May	Leigh	8-5	G	11,460	CH2
9 May	Wigan	15-49	2G	16,506	CH semi

* Substitute

Neil playing for Bradford Northern against Wakefield Trinity.

Neil scoring for Bradford against Hull at Odsal.

20. 1971-72: Trials and tribulations at Trinity

Rugby league in the early 1970s was in deep trouble. Attendances had been falling for many years, as they had in other spectator sports. The 1970-71 season had seen a drop of almost 265,000 in total attendances at league fixtures to 1,170,060. When Neil had begun his career as a professional in 1955-56 the total attendance had been 3,245,305. Clubs and the RFL had tried everything to stem the fall in crowds – they had changed the rules *ad nauseam*, they had tried two divisions, they had invested in floodlights and they had begun to play on Friday nights and Sunday afternoons, rather than on Saturday afternoons. Nothing seemed to work. The fans continued to abandon the game. Remarkably, however, Trinity were one of only four clubs to show an improvement in support during the 1970-71 season, along with Huddersfield, Leigh and Wigan. Even so, Trinity's home crowds averaged less than 5,000 – not enough to pay their way. Good off-the-field management and improved performances on the field under Neil contributed to a profit of £1,652 on the 1970-71 season and home receipts rose by £8,026.

Trinity, so opposed to the notion of Sunday rugby originally, now saw playing on Sunday as their financial saviour and most of the fixtures for 1971-72 were set for that day. Trinity also had a new chairman, their former centre John Leighton Davies taking over from Les Pounder. John Lindley became vice-chairman. On the playing side, Neil had taken note of David Jeanes' good attitude and ability, and decided to make him team captain, although Neil would obviously still have a major say in what happened on the field whenever he played. David handsomely repaid Neil's faith in him and during the course of the season he played in four tests for Great Britain against New Zealand and France.

Neil had problems with selection from the beginning of the season. Eleven men were injured or unavailable for the first game, a home Yorkshire Cup tie against Huddersfield on Sunday 1 August. The biggest blow had befallen Ian Brooke, who had severely ruptured his Achilles tendon in a friendly sevens game against Salford in a 'Sports Spectacular' staged at Belle Vue in July. Ian would be out for at least six months, according to his surgeon. John Hegarty and Dave Hawley were key players also on the long term injured list.

Neil started the season at left-centre and little seemed to have changed when the *Wakefield Express* ran the headline "One Flash of Fox Magic". The game against Huddersfield was pretty dreary but Frank Jeffrey noted, "Neil Fox, the man some critics love to write off, performed yet another of his match-winning feats". At half-time Trinity were 4-2 down and it took a piece of inspiration to breathe the kiss of life into the game. Neil had brought the teams level after 46 minutes with a close-in drop-goal. A few minutes later he created the match's only try, when he dummied and cut through from 30 yards out before sending out a perfect long pass to winger Backhouse, who scored in the corner. Neil converted and two minutes from time landed his fourth goal from an angled penalty to give Trinity an 11-4 win. Unfortunately, full-back Gary Cooper was added to the injury list when his forearm was broken after 30 minutes.

If the game against Huddersfield had been dull, the second-round tie at Castleford the following Friday was sensational, albeit for the wrong reasons. Neil certainly did his bit, Frank Jeffrey reporting, "Fox scored all Trinity's points and led the side superbly". Neil opened the scoring with a third minute penalty and followed with a howitzer of a goal from the half-way line before dropping a goal in the 10th minute. After 13 minutes he extended Trinity's lead to 8-0, when Castleford prop Ian van Bellen was sent off for punching. There followed a crazy quarter of an hour in which referee Eric Lawrinson sent off five more players – Trinity's Geoff Wraith, David Jeanes and Keith Slater and Cas forwards Dennis

Hartley and Alan Dickinson. The last 50 minutes were thus played 10-a-side. Neil dropped another goal in the 34th minute to give Trinity a 10-0 lead but 10-a-side obviously suited Castleford better and they played some spectacular football in the second half to win 13-10, the winning try being scored by Alan Ackroyd four minutes from time. Neil recalls, "It was obvious that Castleford were giving away lots of penalties by their tactics. I told the lads just to carry on trying to play rugby but you can only take so much. Tempers were lost and Kevin Harkin had to go off with concussion. Cas had three forwards sent off, while we had two backs and a forward sent off. It suited them better in the end. Eric Lawrinson told me later that the second half produced the best rugby he had seen for a long time. In one incident Lawrinson had sent off Steve 'Knocker' Norton for hitting Keith Slater but brought him back on the intervention of a touch judge. Keith did retaliate eventually but normally he wouldn't say boo to a goose."

Trinity's dismissal from the Yorkshire Cup meant that the final between Castleford and Hull KR could be staged at Belle Vue on 21 August. However, the whole competition proved farcical. Not only had Leeds withdrawn, but Dewsbury had too, because of a players' pay dispute. The six first-round ties had drawn an aggregate of less than 14,000 paying fans and the final itself attracted a worst-ever 5,536. As an advertisement for summer rugby – a recurring proposition in rugby league circles – it had been a catastrophic turn-off.

Neil's team had to wait almost three weeks for their opening league fixture – a home game against Wigan on 25 August. It was another rip-roaring affair under the control of Eric Lawrinson, who earned the wrath of Wakefield fans and their slow handclap by continually giving penalties to Wigan in the second half. Wigan hooker Colin Clarke was sent off after 32 minutes after a clash with Neil and the *Wakefield Express* headlines shouted "Fabulous Fox and mighty Morgan whip Wigan". By half-time Trinity led 18-7, Neil having kicked wonderfully – three penalties, two drop-goals and a conversion to add to two scintillating tries from loose-forward Mick Morgan. They were hanging on like grim death, however, to an 18-16 lead before Neil made the game safe in the second minute of injury time with his seventh goal.

Neil added to the club's register by signing David Smith, a very promising 18 year-old centre from Shaw Cross. Smith was one of Neil's best captures but made his name as a flying winger. The Wakefield committee was obviously highly pleased with Neil because they gave him a new three-year contract, in which they dispensed with the committee-style team selection, which had always been the preferred method at the club. From now on Neil was the sole selector, with the chairman acting in an advisory capacity.

On 27 August, Trinity hammered York 32-3 at Belle Vue. Neil's kicking was again immaculate – seven successes, including a drop-goal. David Smith appeared as a substitute in the 58th minute and made his mark immediately with tries in the 64th and 79th minutes. On the other wing Keith Slater made his 100th appearance for the club and Mick Morgan, in a rich vein of form, scored another sensational try. Three days later Neil displayed tremendous leadership of a much-depleted team at Featherstone. He made two tries and kicked four goals in a 20-15 victory, his 70th-minute drop-goal wrapping up the spoils.

A seriously exciting game followed at Hull KR on 3 September. Neil landed another five goals and Andrew Collomosse reported in the *Wakefield Express:* "Fox's mighty boot seemed to have won the match for Trinity when he kicked a long-range penalty 10 minutes from time to give his side a 16-15 lead". Minutes later, however, Roger Millward slotted a 35-yard angled penalty for Rovers and, despite a furious finale from Trinity, they ran out winners 17-16. The teams went off to a standing ovation, reminiscent of the previous season, when Trinity had also lost to a late goal. The *Wakefield Express* observed, "Behind the pack, Fox was always looking for openings and, with better support, his passes must have seriously worried KR's well organised defence."

On 8 September Wakefield returned to winning ways at Leigh. Losing hooker Tom Hill injured after only 10 minutes, Trinity played beautifully to win 22-7, scoring four sparkling tries, one of which was Neil's 300th in first-class fixtures. Neil thus became only the fifth player in history to perform the 300 tries and 300 goals double, following in the giant footsteps of James Lomas, who played between 1900 and 1923, Jim Leytham (1901 to 1912), Ike Southward (1952 to 1969) and Eric Ashton (1955 to 1969). Since Neil achieved this feat, only Garry Schofield has joined this select band of players.

The following Saturday evening Wakefield, severely depleted in the pack, found themselves trailing 13-4 to St Helens at half-time at Belle Vue, Neil having potted two goals. A brave effort saw them pipped 13-12 and the injury bogey struck Neil this time. Ten minutes from time he retired, having broken two bones in his hand.

There was an overwhelming necessity for the club to enter the transfer market. It was reported that Trinity were interested in Castleford scrum-half Keith Hepworth but he eventually moved to Leeds to renew his partnership with Alan Hardisty. Neil recalls: "With so many injuries we signed Mick Major from Huddersfield – swapping him for Eddie McDonagh. Mick did well for us on the wing. He had plenty of speed and was very experienced. One of our best signings was Steve Lyons, a prop from Featherstone. Steve added a bit more grit to the team and was a tireless worker in defence and attack. He was a great buy for us. Moving the other way was Terry Ramshaw, who went to Salford. He had done well for us but he got itchy feet and wanted to go."

Neil missed the next four games and Dave Topliss took over as temporary skipper, leading Wakefield to a whopping 53-9 home win against Workington Town, when Lyons and Major made their debuts and full-back Terry Crook landed nine goals. Trinity then went out of the BBC2 Floodlit Trophy in the first round at Hull and lost depressingly at Keighley. Neil was not at all happy at the standard of the team's handling and called them in for extra training again. The next game, a 38-10 rout of Barrow, seemed to indicate that a positive effect had been achieved. There was more bad news, however, on the injury front. The club announced that Ian Brooke's playing career was over, because his Achilles problem would not allow him to resume playing first class rugby again. Neil says, "This was a terrible loss to Trinity and a great disappointment to Ian. At such a young age he would surely have gained many more caps for Yorkshire and Great Britain. A testimonial was sanctioned for him by the RFL and lots of events were organised for him." Neil was quick to get Ian involved in coaching Trinity's under-19 side.

Neil came back to action in a 27-5 'A' team victory over Keighley 'A' on 8 October, claiming a hat-trick of tries and landing a touchline conversion. He was not as happy after his next appearance, back in the first team, a heavy loss at Salford, when Dave Topliss limped off after 10 minutes and subsequently sat out the next six games. There was an unusual incident in the second half when a Salford player broke down the middle and turned a sharp inside pass straight to the referee, J. Wharton of Mirfield. Frank Jeffrey called it, "the most unusual interception I have ever seen". For the next game, at home to Halifax, Neil went into the second-row for his first appearance of the season in the pack. On an evening of torrential rain, the first half was a surprisingly attractive affair. Neil created the opening score with a sublimely delayed pass to John Hegarty, which Barney Ward converted. By half-time Trinity led 10-3 but within a few minutes of returning were pulled back to 10-8. As the game wore on, tempers became frayed and it was left to Neil to settle the issue. In the 70th minute he hoisted a monster penalty from 45 yards before

Lyons and Halifax's John Martin were sent off for fighting. Minutes later Halifax scrum-half Gordon Baker followed them and three minutes from time Neil landed a 25-yard penalty to allow Trinity to emerge 14-8 winners.

A strange match followed at York on Saturday, 23 October. The home side led 8-2 at half-time, thanks to four penalties from John Maloney. Neil, still playing second-row, then turned the game on its head, fashioning tries for Barends and Ward and by the time he substituted himself Trinity were 17-8 ahead. However, by the end of the game they were happy to have sneaked a 17-13 victory. Within 24 hours, Trinity were entertaining the touring New Zealanders in a fine, open game. Tony Handforth's 25-13 scrum superiority was a big factor in keeping Wakefield in the game. Neil converted a 40-yard Mick Major try in the first half but the Kiwis led 12-5 at the break. By the 67th minute a try by Morgan and two penalties from Neil had the tourists rocking at 15-12 but tries for Mocky Brereton and Murray Eade, and a conversion by Henry Tatana in the last four minutes gave the scoreline of 23-12 a somewhat misleading appearance. The match had been a very good advert for rugby league. At the civic reception for the Kiwis, their captain Roy Christian said the game was the fastest played on the tour.

At Thrum Hall the following Saturday, Neil brought himself on after half an hour with Halifax – the worst defensive team in the game – leading 8-0. Trinity lost 19-5 and Wakefield did not score until the 78th minute. Frank Jeffrey described the performance as "embarrassingly inept". A better show with a weakened team was forthcoming at Castleford when Neil, playing loose-forward, kicked his 1,600th goal for Trinity but they still lost 12-5. The *Wakefield Express* reported, "Fox set his side a good lead. He was constantly in action and made two great try-saving tackles in the second half."

A heart-stopping match against Leigh at a rain-lashed Belle Vue followed on 7 November. Stuart Ferguson kicked Leigh into a 4-0 lead with penalties in the 17th and 58th minutes, the latter after Neil had kicked the ball straight out from a goal-line drop-out. Trinity looked well beaten as the game went into its 82nd minute. Then a scrum was formed on Leigh's '25'. Trinity scrum-half Kevin Harkin took the ball from the scrum and whizzed round the blind-side to score mid-way between the posts and the touchline. Under the circumstances - a sodden ground, a heavy ball and the pressure of the kick being the last act of the match - Neil hardly had the easiest of conversions. The roar of the crowd at the Agbrigg Road end of the ground, however, left no one in any doubt that Neil had again landed a match-winner. The crowd's reaction seemed to be a mixture of relief and triumph.

Rugby league had a new knock-out competition in 1971-72, the Player's No. 6 Trophy, which was worth £5,000 to the winners. Wakefield had drawn a tough first-round tie at Widnes on Sunday, 14 November, which seemed to be going Widnes's way for most of the game. By the 68th minute they led 10-3 but Neil began a fightback when he delivered one of those trademark long passes which shattered the defensive line. Harkin and Wraith continued the movement to get Marston over near the flag. Neil made light of the difficult conversion and in the 72nd minute piloted a straight penalty over to level the scores at 10-10 and Trinity lived to fight another day. Neil, though, did not make the replay having twisted his knee. Three days later at Belle Vue the teams again followed a similar pattern. With six minutes remaining Terry Crook landed a penalty to level the scores at 10-10 again but this time Kevin Harkin produced an injury-time winner with a close-in drop-goal, which miraculously found its way through a crowd of players.

Neil missed a good 10-3 win at Barrow in truly abominable conditions but was able to play in the last 20 minutes of a bruising game at Bramley in the second round of the Player's No.6 Trophy. Trinity won 10-5 but were under all sorts of pressure while holding out. Neil did not play in a 59-9 home romp against Batley on 5 December, when Dave Topliss bagged a wondrous 80-yard try and Terry Crook did a passable impression of Neil with a try and 10 goals. The following week Trinity met Blackpool Borough in the third round of the Player's No.6 Trophy at Belle Vue and, true to the tradition of cup ties between the two teams, Borough gave Trinity, who were on £35 a man to win, a heck of a fight. Wakefield were losing 10-7 after 42 minutes, at which point Topliss scored a fantastic 40-yard try to make the score 10-10. Neil came on as a substitute only to see his side fall behind to a drop-goal from Bishop after 51 minutes. A Hegarty try on 64 minutes gave Trinity a 13-12 advantage before Neil stretched it to 15-12 with a penalty goal. Blackpool were finally nailed down in the 72nd minute when a scrum was formed near half-way. An incident occurred between Mick Morgan and Joe Egan, after which Egan chased Mick and kicked out at him. Referee Eric Lawrinson sent Egan off and then dispatched prop Loughlin for protesting. Down to 11 men, Borough mishandled after winning a 78th-minute scrum near their own line and presented Dave Hawley with a gift try to wrap up the game for Wakefield at 18-12.

If Trinity's progress to the semi-finals had been something of a struggle, they could be expected to be even more sorely tested when they drew St Helens, albeit at Belle Vue. Wakefield entered the semi-final on the back of five straight victories and an unbeaten run of seven games but that paled in comparison to St Helens's recent record. Saints had won the Floodlit Trophy just four days earlier and had won their last 11 games, scoring 238 points in the process while conceding only 31, including a mere three tries. Unfortunately for Saints, they came up against Neil at his most imperious. John Robinson wrote in the *Sunday People*: "Player-coach Neil Fox was left nursing a broken nose and what looked like the beginning of a black eye. But it couldn't stop him from grinning ear-to-ear at leading Trinity into the Player's No 6 competition final. Fox collected his shiner from a head-high tackle by Stephens 10 minutes after the interval – an incident which led to the prompt dismissal of the St Helens forward substitute. Fox went off [injured] at the same time... but he was already the hero, with the game safely in the bag. Tactically, everything went exactly the way Fox had hoped. Four goals rocked the champions – one was a superb long-distance drop-goal. Yet his master stroke had come near the end of the first half. From a scrum 10 yards out, he fooled the Saints' cover with a dummy to plunge in for a try. This sent Trinity 12-4 ahead and well on their way to a crack at the final's £5,000 prize money."

When Neil left the field Trinity led 14-4 and were in complete control. Saints did not manage to score a try until the 78th minute and were beaten much more convincingly than the 14-9 final scoreline suggested. Neil had masterminded Trinity's memorable victory but it had also been a triumph of teamwork. Frank Jeffrey called the first half "the most satisfying 40 minutes of rugby in years" and reported, "I am reliably informed that the cheering could be heard at Eastmoor!" Neil had set Wakefield on their way with a close-in drop-goal before Kel Coslett equalised with a penalty. In the 27th minute good passing had put David Barends over in the corner and Neil's colossal conversion was a real fillip for his side. Coslett pulled back two points with another penalty before Neil's killer try. Geoff Cudworth wrote: "Both tries were beauties. In fact, I doubt whether, in his long and distinguished playing career, Neil Fox has produced greater shrewdness than he packed into the play that produced Wakefield's second try and the virtual knock-out blow for Saints. So completely did he bluff the opposition that he strode to the try-line unchallenged." Neil agrees that the defeat of Saints was one of his greatest performances, "I seemed to run the game from the start, prompting and probing all the time. Then later on in the game I put in a grubber kick between two players. Just as I went to pick up the ball I was hit from behind and my nose was shattered."

His broken nose did not prevent him from turning out for a televised game at Leeds on Boxing Day, although he may well have wished it had because the Loiners won 13-2. The New Year began with Neil kicking five goals and a David Topliss hat-trick in a 22-4 home win over Huddersfield. St Helens gained some measure of revenge on 8 January with an 18-12 success over Trinity at Knowsley Road, but Wakefield put on a good show after arriving late for the game, when their bus blew a gasket near Huddersfield and they had to wait for a replacement.

Around this time Gary Cooper was released to join York as assistant coach but on the positive side Trinity signed Castleford full-back Les Sheard on a free transfer.

On 16 January, Trinity met the 'Bank of England' team, Salford, at Belle Vue and emerged with a fine 9-2 victory. It was a game of tremendous tackling and few chances. The only scores of the first half were a penalty each to Neil and David Watkins. Trinity dominated the second half, however. The only try of the match arrived in the 53rd minute when a gem of a long pass from Neil caught Salford out of position and launched a movement which culminated in a try by Slater at the corner. Neil rounded the victory off with a second penalty goal and dropped another goal just before the end.

Trinity entered the Player's No.6 Trophy final as firm favourites. Their opponents Halifax had surprised everyone with a stunning semi-final victory over Leeds at Headingley but were languishing at 21st in the league table, 11 places lower than Trinity. The final, at Odsal on 22 January, was played on a very heavy pitch but it did not seem to bother Wakefield much, at least in the first half. Michael Crossley of the *Sunday Telegraph* wrote, "It was a classic cup tie, played incredibly hard – no surprise, of course, to Yorkshiremen, with so much brass at stake." Trinity seemed to have the measure of their opponents from the kick-off and by the 30th minute were leading 8-2. Topliss shot over after only three minutes and quarter of an hour later Slater finished off an 80-yard movement with a try under the bar, which Neil converted. Just before the interval Halifax pulled back to 8-7, however, and the second half saw them take control, running to a match-winning 22-8 lead before Valentine scored a late try. A 22-11 defeat was not what Wakefield had expected.

Some credit had to be given to Neil's opposing coach, Les Pearce. Pearce had anticipated the heavy conditions at Odsal and had made his players play a full-scale match on Thrum Hall's own muddy pitch on the Wednesday night preceding the final, "to give them their mud-larking legs", and telling them that it would be even worse at Odsal in the final. After the final Pearce said, "I was worried at the beginning when Neil Fox kept out of the scrums and became an extra man in the passing chain, so I got a message out on to the field telling [Halifax's loose-forward] Tony Halmshaw to take his position in the pack only when Neil did. It seemed to work." Losing the inaugural Player's No. 6 Final was a big disappointment for Neil and the Wakefield fans.

There was also some surprise for Trinity's followers when Bryan West and Dave Hawley were allowed to join York before the Challenge Cup register closed. The *Wakefield Express* reported that in the case of Hawley, Neil had not been consulted, contrary to his agreement with the club, and also that he would not have agreed to allow Hawley to depart for such a small fee - £1,000. Neil says of Hawley, "Dave had been with Trinity since 1966 and had given us great service as a utility player, scoring 18 tries in 161 games. As I could not promise him a regular place in the team he wanted to leave. So now only David Jeanes and myself remained of the Championship-winning sides of 1967 and 1968."

Neil reverted to centre for the visit to Wigan two days after the Odsal defeat, needing just two points to pass the 4,000 mark for Wakefield. On a freezing night, replete with a blinding hailstorm, he reached the target when he converted a second-half try by Peter Harrison and finished the game on 4,002 points, but his side were whacked 27-10.

The annual struggle to reach Wembley began for Trinity on 29 January. The bookies had installed Leeds as favourites for the Challenge Cup at 9-2, with St Helens at 5-1 and Wakefield and Wigan at 6-1. Trinity's opponents Doncaster were the rank outsiders, along with Huyton, at 5,000-1. Tattersfield could be a great leveller though, especially when it was partially waterlogged and there was snow on the ground and in the air. Trinity got the shock of their lives as the Dons' short passing game seemed to be more effective than the open game the visitors tried to employ. It was a good job that Tony Handforth won the scrums 24-13 for all Trinity had to show was a 14th-minute try, coming when David Jeanes rushed 30 yards for the touchdown after Mick Morgan had made the break. Neil converted but the Dons hit back eight minutes later with an unimproved try by winger Ian Fortis. That concluded the scoring but Trinity were mightily relieved when full-back David Towle failed with a penalty in the 67th minute and then with a late attempt to drop an equalising goal.

Another desperate struggle followed at Huddersfield on 6 February. The first half was a comedy of errors and the only score was a penalty to Huddersfield. There seemed unlikely to be any addition to the score as the game entered its 72nd minute. At that point Neil and Terry Crook whipped the ball out to Dave Barends 30 yards out. The winger seemed completely bottled up but casually wrong-footed two men, shrugged off another and romped over to be mobbed by his team-mates. Neil hit a brilliant conversion. Two minutes later Morgan demoralised the Fartowners with a baffling solo try followed two minutes after that by Neil bursting through on Huddersfield's '25' to send his co-centre Stephen Davies in for his first try in senior rugby. Eddie McDonagh scored a last minute try for Huddersfield and what had been a mediocre game had produced an exciting ending.

A crowd exceeding 9,000 was at Belle Vue for the visit of Leeds on 13 February and Neil surprised everyone by making himself a substitute. Trinity produced their worst display of the season and were hammered 26-3. Wingers Alan Smith and John Atkinson scored hat-tricks as Leeds won at Belle Vue for the first time in 11 years. It was not the preparation Trinity wanted for the second-round Challenge Cup match against Wigan the following Sunday. Nor was the decision by the Wakefield football committee, on a 7-1 vote, to appoint an assistant coach for the forwards, without consulting Neil. The players were reported to be solidly behind Neil as coach and he told Geoff Cudworth and readers of the *Wakefield Express*, "I do not want to work with a lot of 'yes men' on the committee, but I want to feel that I have the full backing of them all. I know I have not. In fact, it's been like that ever since I came back to Belle Vue as coach. If I find I do not gain the full confidence of the whole committee, I shall resign and take the free transfer they said would be available to me if things came to a head." He said that if there was to be an assistant coach, he would choose and he would not have interference by the committee.

In the meantime there was the small matter of Wigan at Belle Vue in the Cup. A crowd of 13,700 was treated to a dramatic Trinity-Wigan clash in the best traditions of the fixture and Neil gave a timely reminder to his detractors that he still had much to offer. After 12 minutes both hookers were sent off. Trinity, on £50 a man to win, prospered as a result, winning the scrums 23-8. However, they were caned 12-2 in the penalty count and did not receive a penalty until the 63rd minute, which tended to offset the advantage in the tight. Wigan took the lead after 23 minutes with a Bill Ashurst drop-goal but nine minutes later fell behind. On the fourth tackle, according to Patrick O'Hara in the *Yorkshire Post*, "Fox dummied and swerved, bewildering the Wigan defence [25 yards out] before slicing through two tackles to touch down in the corner". Two minutes later he put up a sky-high punt which saw the Wigan full-back tackled over his own line by Kevin Harkin. From the drop-out the ball was swept towards the right wing and a pass from Steve Lyons sent Geoff Wraith over and Trinity led 6-2 at the break. A pulsating second period produced a solitary try, in the 44th minute, to Wigan by Bill Francis. A minute from time Bill Ashurst sliced a drop-goal attempt and Trinity won 6-5.

Trinity's forwards had been tremendous but Geoff Cudworth singled out Neil, who had been making his 500th appearance in first-class rugby league, "What an answer Fox gave to his critics. His superbly created try was just the inspiration his side needed and his experience played a big part in the triumph. He was constantly in the picture, both in attack and defence, leading his men by personal example. 'We have been out-generalled by an old head', was one Wigan supporter's verdict."

On the political front Neil appeared to have a victory, of sorts. In his column "Talking Points" on 3 March, Geoff Cudworth reported, "Wakefield announced that Fox would be brought into all future discussions concerning coaching policy and players. Not all the committee felt able, however, to associate themselves with a vote of confidence in Fox, I gather. My information is that there were five in favour with three abstentions."

Meanwhile, Neil had Trinity's third round Challenge Cup tie against Leeds on his agenda. Although Trinity had fallen to 14th in the league, they still harboured high hopes of another trip to Wembley and knew anything could happen in a Challenge Cup tie between such rivals as Wakefield and Leeds, even though the game was at Headingley and Leeds were top of the table. The game was Leeds's first ever home game on a Sunday and drew a crowd of 21,127, their best for six years. It was a taut, bad-tempered match and Trinity, on £75 a man to win, never got in front. Leeds went seven points ahead within 13 minutes and led 9-5 at half-time. Trinity had the satisfaction of creating the best try of the game through a David Topliss special, goaled by Neil, but the only score of the second half was a drop-goal by John Holmes, as Leeds won 11-5. Neil came in for some criticism for not taking a series of penalty kicks at goal in the second half. Neil's view was that the penalties awarded were difficult long shots with no certainty of being turned into goals and it was therefore better to keep the pressure on Leeds in the hope of scoring tries.

Out of the Cup, Trinity had to make progress up the league table, if there was to be any silverware at Belle Vue. Their next fixture was at Dewsbury, who had beaten Trinity five times in a row and were 3-0 ahead at half-time. Trinity, with Les Sheard making his debut, made a rousing rally in the second half to win 16-3, Neil scoring two tries and two goals. The *Wakefield Express* said: "Their fightback was inspired by Neil Fox, whose leadership and personal contribution played a big part in this somewhat unexpected victory ... It was Fox who made the vital breakthrough in the second half after seeing earlier efforts wasted by indifferent finishing, and he was constantly urging his men to greater efforts."

A defeat at Workington, who had lost their last nine games, prompted Neil to return to the forwards for the home game against Hull on 24 March, which precipitated a run of six consecutive victories. Hull were beaten handsomely and Neil kicked two goals before taking himself off. His goalkicking had been below par for some weeks and for the remainder of the season he left the task predominantly to scrum-half Barney Ward.

On Good Friday, 31 March, Neil made his 600th appearance in first-class rugby league in a thrilling game against Castleford at Belle Vue. Trinity won 12-9 but the result became almost meaningless. In the last minute Wakefield's dashing, 22-year-old second-rower Peter Harrison fell awkwardly and was carried from the field with a broken leg.

Complications arose after surgeons could not connect two veins which had been severed and on 6 April Peter's leg had to be amputated. It was a dreadful reminder of the dangers of playing rugby but an incredibly rare tragedy. The game rallied round immediately and a testimonial fund, which would run until 31 October, was opened. The Mayor of Wakefield, Alderman A. E. Lofthouse headed the testimonial committee, which included John Lindley, John Leighton Davies, Jim Bowden and David Jeanes from the club, Frank Jeffrey of the *Wakefield Express*, representatives of the Wakefield Trinity Supporters' Club, the Wakefield & District Amateur Rugby League, the Wakefield Schools Rugby League and representatives from the Castleford and Featherstone Rovers clubs.

Neil had had high hopes for Peter Harrison, "I believe he would have played for Great Britain, had it not been for that tragic injury. It was a great shock to the whole club. He had such a promising future. When the news of the amputation was released, Ian Brooke, great sportsman that he is, ordered all the money he had raised from his own benefit to be transferred to the Peter Harrison Testimonial Fund and asked that all the planned events for the rest of his benefit season should be devoted instead to Peter's. That was a wonderful thing to do and Ian was and still is a very popular guy. Peter had played in the Players No. 6 Final at Odsal earlier in the season. I had taken him off after 65 minutes and substituted Ray Spencer for him, which probably disappointed him a bit. He had left the field by the time the game was over and gone up to the dressing rooms, which were miles away from the pitch, of course. Consequently, he had not collected his runners-up medal. None of us knew that at the time. Years later, Peter's brother Paul was talking to Mick Morgan and mentioned the fact that Peter had never got the medal. Mick approached the RFL to see if Peter's medal could be found and presented to him. Almost miraculously, someone knew where it was, although the RFL didn't know who it belonged to. So, Peter finally got his medal 20-odd years late."

Between 3 and 9 April, Trinity played and won four league games. By the end of that run the players were clearly almost out on their feet. Neil abandoned Tuesday training before the game at Batley and replaced it with a trip to the Turkish baths in Leeds. The season petered out disappointingly, however, with home defeats by Dewsbury and Featherstone Rovers. Those losses cost Wakefield a home tie in the Championship play-offs, as they finished in ninth position. They had to visit Rochdale in the opening round and after 32 minutes were 8-3 ahead, only to run out of steam and capitulate 18-13. Neil, back at loose-forward, made two tries and landed the 1,900th and 1,901st goals of his career.

A season which had promised so much ended rather tamely. There had been progress, however. Ninth position in the league was not a bad performance, bearing in mind the improved quality of the opposition, and on a better day Trinity could have been inaugural winners of the Player's No. 6 Trophy. But it was evident that the club's forward strength needed attention. David Jeanes and Mick Morgan had been outstanding and Tony Handforth had proved a tremendously successful hooker. However, the loss of the unfortunate Harrison and of Hawley, West and Ramshaw had not helped. In the backs the burgeoning talents of Geoff Wraith and David Topliss, scorer of 23 tries, promised better things ahead. Neil's personal scoring had dropped to 186 points, with 84 goals and six tries, but Frank Jeffrey noted, "Fox's tactical skill played a big part in some of the side's notable wins. He looked well on the way to a century of goals at Christmas, but subsequently lost his touch and eventually handed over to Ward."

Wakefield Trinity 1971-72

Wakefield Trinity finished 9th in the league: P34, W21, L13, For 587, Against 414
Fox scored 6 tries, 84 goals, 186 points for Wakefield

Date	Opponent	Score	Fox	Crowd	
1 Aug	**Huddersfield**	11-4	4G	3,415	YC1
6 Aug	Castleford	10-13	5G	4,655	YC2
25 Aug	**Wigan**	20-16	7G	5,340	
27 Aug	**York**	32-3	7G	3,079	
30 Aug	Featherstone R	20-15	4G	3,306	
3 Sep	Hull KR	16-17	5G	4,496	
8 Sep	Leigh	22-7	T, 5G	7,026	
11 Sep	**St Helens**	12-13	2G	6,373	
18 Sep	**Workington T**	53-9	dnp	2,860	
21 Sep	Hull	16-23	dnp	3,456	FT1
24 Sep	Keighley	7-16	dnp	2,132	
2 Oct	**Barrow**	38-10	dnp	3,239	
10 Oct	Salford	5-25		8,836	
15 Oct	**Halifax**	14-8	2G	2,185	
23 Oct	York	17-13	2G	1,659	
24 Oct	**New Zealand**	12-23	3G	5,367	
30 Oct	Halifax*	5-19	G	2,238	
3 Nov	Castleford	5-12	G	4,053	
7 Nov	**Leigh**	5-4	G	3,665	
14 Nov	Widnes	10-10	2G	3,614	PT1
17 Nov	**Widnes**	12-10	dnp	2,499	Replay
20 Nov	Barrow	10-3	dnp	1,885	
28 Nov	Bramley*	10-5		3,700	PT2
5 Dec	**Batley**	59-9	dnp	3,301	
12 Dec	**Blackpool B***	18-12	G	4,260	PT3
18 Dec	**St Helens**	14-9	T, 4G	3,964	PT semi
27 Dec	Leeds	2-13	G	15,362	
2 Jan	**Huddersfield**	22-4	5G	3,530	
8 Jan	St Helens	12-18	3G	4,593	
16 Jan	**Salford**	9-2	3G	6,185	
22 Jan	Halifax	11-22	G	7,975	JP Final (at Odsal)
24 Jan	Wigan	10-27	2G	6,345	
29 Jan	Doncaster	5-3	G	1,550	Ch Cup 1
6 Feb	Huddersfield	11-5	G	3,796	
13 Feb	**Leeds***	3-26		9,201	
20 Feb	**Wigan**	6-5	T	13,700	Ch Cup 2
5 Mar	Leeds	5-11	G	21,127	Ch Cup 3
12 Mar	Dewsbury	16-3	2T, 2G	3,700	
18 Mar	Workington T	10-13	2G	900	
24 Mar	**Hull**	26-5	2G	3,011	
31 Mar	**Castleford**	12-9		4,396	
3 Apr	Hull	20-13	G	3,905	
5 Apr	**Hull KR**	20-8		3,173	
7 Apr	**Keighley**	44-14	T	2,822	
9 Apr	Batley*	18-12		2,429	
14 Apr	**Dewsbury**	8-17		4,147	
16 Apr	**Featherstone R**	4-16	G	5,170	
23 Apr	Rochdale H	13-18	2G	3,376	CH1

* Substitute

21. 1972-73: 5,000 points and counting

The close season of 1972 was anything but quiet on all fronts throughout the sport of rugby league. The rule makers were back in action, as the game fell ever deeper into the mire of falling attendances. Most critics still believed there were too many scrums. The four-tackle rule had at first been generally welcomed, but after six years there was disenchantment. Forwards now seemed to rule the roost and the days of free-scoring wingers regularly topping 50 tries in a season appeared long gone. In 1970-71 former Trinity second-rower Bob Haigh of Leeds had amazed the sport by finishing joint top try-scorer with 40 tries and a couple of years earlier Hull KR stand-off Roger Millward had been top scorer with 38 tries. The answer, the law makers felt, was to extend the four tackle rule to six tackles for the 1972-73 season, in the hope that the backs might see more of the ball and teams could play more constructively. Also, hookers were to be allowed to strike with either foot for the ball, instead of only the foot furthest from the scrum-half. Another innovation for the season was the introduction of official time-keepers, Trinity conferring the job on Peter Harrison.

Neil was happy to see the change in the tackle rule. In an interview with Trevor Watson in the *Yorkshire Evening Post* shortly before the new rule was adopted he observed that he "regrets the introduction of the four tackle rule... It has brought a panic element into the play ... If you drop on a loose ball, that's one tackle gone. Two more and you are trying to kick the ball clear. We would be better trying six tackles as they are in Australia."

The RFL also passed a bye-law compelling all teams to enter all competitions for which they were eligible, a result of Leeds's withdrawal from the previous season's Yorkshire Cup. They also decided to revert to a fixture system which involved all clubs playing all the other clubs in their county, plus three from Yorkshire or Lancashire and Cumberland. This was met with dismay from Wakefield Trinity's committee. Chairman John Leighton Davies realised that the more attractive fixture list of the top 15 teams playing each other was more profitable. Trinity had managed to make a profit of £769 on the previous season and gate money had risen by £4,199, despite a declining membership and a fall in aggregate home crowds of 9,867. There would be dire financial consequences, unless Trinity were able to win major trophies. Trinity had needed home gates bringing in £900 in 1971-72 to break even but had only averaged about £812. They estimated that they would now need £1,000 per home game. Much of the increased cost emanated from the necessity to pay players an extra £5, win or lose, for appearing in Sunday games. The RFL had made another innovation in declaring that home teams could say what day of the week games should be played, overriding any objection from the visiting club. This was a blow for the anti-Sunday clubs such as Leeds and St Helens. Trinity consequently arranged for most of their games to be played on Sundays, knowing that bigger crowds could be attracted than on Saturdays with all its attendant distractions, particularly televised sport.

There was change at Belle Vue too. On 7 July the *Wakefield Express* ran the headline "'Constitutional' stand by chairman over Fox". Neil had asked the chairman whether he would be granted a free transfer if he resigned. It was only an inquiry, however, because he had no intention of leaving. That did not stop the rumours, of course, which told of him leaving to join York. Mr Davies thought it unlikely that a free transfer would be allowed.

The following week the *Wakefield Express* reported that Johnny Malpass was to be relieved of his post of trainer and was to be succeeded by Gary Cooper, who was returning from York. Trinity handled the business badly and Johnny felt he had been shabbily treated after service which had stretched back 36 years.

Don Froggett had resigned as 'A' team coach because he had joined the Prison Service. The committee had decided not to replace him. Henceforth the first and second teams would train under Neil and Gary Cooper. On match days the 'A' team would be under the aegis of the captain and two committee members. Once again, the first-team would be selected by a committee of five – Neil, Gary, J. L. Davies, Jim Bowden and Les Pounder. Such an arrangement smacked of a return to older ways.

July also brought the sad news of the death of John L. Allen, who, as 'The Pinder' in the *Wakefield Express*, had covered Neil's career until he left for Bradford in 1969.

Neil's first-teamers agreed playing terms of £18 for a home win, £20 for an away win and £8 for a defeat, plus that extra £5 for playing in Sunday matches. Six weeks before the season began Neil had his charges running to Sharlston where they ran up and down the slag heaps. He was determined they would be fit for a long and arduous campaign. There was also an added burden of bringing success to Belle Vue in the club's centenary season.

Play got under way with a 71-10 romp against the Wakefield & District Amateur League on Thursday, 10 August. Neil kicked 13 goals. The real business began, however, eight days later with a 35-10 home win over Castleford. Dave Topliss bagged four tries and Neil was straight into his stride. Frank Jeffrey reported, "The amazing Fox, in his 17th season, looked anything but over the hill as he ran in two tries and landed six goals from seven attempts – his only failure was an ambitious long range penalty – for a total of 18 points." Neil ran 40 yards for his first try, shaking off a late challenge from winger Briggs. His second came after he combined in a movement with Topliss 20 yards inside his own half and was there in support to finish after a run of 70 yards.

Defeat at Widnes followed before Keighley were dispatched in a Yorkshire Cup tie at Belle Vue on the day that the Munich Olympics opened. Onlookers remarked that it hardly seemed like a cup tie, as the players struggled to come to terms with the new laws and the lack of scrums. Neil kicked four goals before retiring from the fray with a knee injury in a 38-17 win. The injury kept him out of a resounding 35-11 home victory against Featherstone, which was followed by an exhilarating 33-15 win at Halifax. Neil played only the last seven minutes at Thrum Hall but had enough time to make a try for Jackie Marston. Two days later, Trinity played their sixth game in only 18 days when they drew 7-7 with Hull at Belle Vue in a preliminary-round, first-leg Floodlit Trophy tie. The 1,867 crowd was the lowest for a long time at the ground. Neil came on for the second half and was soon running 30 yards to touch down after beating two tacklers, only to be denied a try as David Jeanes and Len Casey were fighting, which resulted in a penalty for Hull.

On 7 September, Halifax beat Trinity 11-9 at Belle Vue in a thrilling second-round Yorkshire Cup match, after Neil failed to convert a 78th minute try by Les Sheard, which would have forced a replay. Two days later, in Trinity's fourth game in a week, they beat Bramley 13-7 at Belle Vue. Only 1,351 fans turned up and only 449 of them paid for admission, the rest being season ticket holders. The *Wakefield Express* described the affair as "devoid of atmosphere" and railed against the insanity of the fixture list which was now so congested with sponsored competitions. The early weeks of the season were a catalogue of Floodlit Trophy ties, Player's No. 6 Trophy matches and county cup games, all running side-by-side with league fixtures. The attraction of prize money in the sponsored competitions was, of course, irresistible for cash-strapped clubs. However, if a club was dismissed early in the proceedings, it lost even more money from unprofitable extra fixtures. No-one seemed too worried about the wear and tear on the players or the damage to keen supporters' bank balances.

Trinity were in a classic 'catch 22' situation. They had to win trophies to make money or they had to sell off their assets. Neil was mortified that Trinity had to part with David Jeanes to help balance the books. David was transferred to Leeds for £8,000, the Bramley game being his 168th and last for the club. Neil had been playing in the centre up to this point in the season but the departure of Jeanes prompted his return to the pack, initially in the second row. Neil knew that there was a crying need for more pace out wide and, at Hull on Friday, 15 September, he moved Topliss into the centres. It did not work. Trinity let in three tries in the first 20 minutes but fought back to 11-10 with tries from Lyons and Topliss, which Neil converted. Hull pulled away to win 18-10, their first victory of the season in eight games. Frank Jeffrey noted, "Most of Trinity's moves stemmed from Fox, but they looked short of pace."

Four days later there was redemption for Trinity at The Boulevard, where they beat Hull 11-3 in the second leg of the Floodlit Trophy preliminary round. Neil was in sublime form. He landed a goal from the centre spot in the first minute, kicked another from the touchline in the 20th minute and carved out an opening for Topliss to score in the 34th minute, converting the try. Trinity led 9-0 at the break and went to 11-0 when Topliss dropped a goal in the second half. *Hull Daily Mail* reporter Richard Tingle wrote: "Neil Fox inspired, drove and led Trinity into the first round of the BBC Floodlit Trophy... when he almost single-handedly beat Hull on their own ground. The key to his success was the way he paced himself. In Friday's game he burnt himself out in a 20 minute spell, but on Tuesday he played a completely different game and lasted the full 80 minutes. Fox found plenty of support, especially from stand off-half Topliss."

On Sunday 24 September, Wakefield went to Wigan for a first round Player's No. 6 Trophy match with an under-strength team and recorded a staggering 34-10 success. The first half was a miserable affair in which Trinity finally grabbed a 9-5 lead after trailing for most of it. The second half was simply stunning, however, as Trinity inspired by Joe Bonnar, romped away. Neil was in fantastic form with the boot, landing eight goals and hit the post with a long-range drop-goal attempt, while tactically he was at his masterful best.

Trinity's committee was on the lookout for players and went to Wales in search of a forward but ended up signing David Knowles from Upper Wharfedale RUFC instead. Neither Neil nor Gary Cooper had watched him. Wigan were reported to have been chasing Knowles and were also reported to have offered Trinity £4,000 for Mick Morgan. Neil recalls: "David Knowles settled in well at second-row and kept his place with his determination and willingness to learn the game. He had a good turn of pace for a big lad. We also signed Geoff Wriglesworth from York at this period. Geoff, a test player, was a good signing for the centres. His experience helped us a lot and with him in the centre I could play in the pack."

Unbeaten Leeds visited Belle Vue on 1 October and attracted Trinity's biggest home crowd of the season of just over 8,000. It proved to be an incident-packed encounter with a frenetic finish. The game began controversially when Terry Clawson took a fifth-minute penalty shot, which the Trinity players believed missed. They went to the '25' for the drop-out but were astonished to find that the referee had given a goal. After 16 minutes Neil and Topliss created a try for Bonnar, which Neil improved. Leeds regained the lead on 33 minutes, when Hardisty took a short ball from Hepworth to race 35 yards for a converted try. A minute before the break Trinity took an 8-7 lead, when Neil dummied his way through before sending Wraith over for a try. That lead was extended to 11-7 when Neil initiated a movement with a long pass on his own line. Sheard sold a classic dummy before sending Barends roaring to the corner for a stupendous score. John Holmes and Neil (from

40 yards out) then exchanged penalties for Trinity to lead 13-9. The game was in the third minute of injury time when Leeds won a scrum about 40 yards out. Holmes surprised everyone by kicking to the corner for Les Dyl to score but the former failed to convert with the last act of the game. For the first time the *Wakefield Express* could say, "The klaxon sounded for time and relieved Wakefield supporters acclaimed a memorable [13-12] win."

David Knowles made his debut as a 70th-minute substitute in the victory over Leeds and Geoff Wriglesworth made his first appearance a week later at Swinton, when Trinity were disappointing in a 17-7 defeat. Despite some good performances Trinity were lying in 10th position in the league. Things were still in flux, though. David Barends went on the transfer list at his own request and Barney Ward was transferred to Bramley for £1,000. There was disappointment, too, for Dave Topliss and Steve Lyons, who were both ruled out of Yorkshire's team for the Roses Match at Castleford, although Geoff Wraith played. Topliss was rewarded, however, with selection for Great Britain's World Cup squad in France, along with his former Trinity colleague David Jeanes.

Trinity's form vacillated. Neil missed a last-gasp home win against Huddersfield and returned at loose-forward in a frustrating defeat at Bramley, when he kicked three good goals but had a try disallowed and hit the post with a penalty attempt from 50 yards, as Johnny Wolford inspired the Villagers to a surprise 13-9 victory. An 18-6 win at Swinton in the first round of the Floodlit Trophy with another depleted team was a much more palatable performance. Neil excelled with his distribution and landed three goals but the man of the match was Knowles, who scored a try and made two more. Four days later Swinton were at Belle Vue for a league game. Neil was substituted in the 62nd minute, by which time he had scored a try and six goals as Trinity won 33-10. The *Wakefield Express* match report was headlined "Swinton 'Foxed' into collapse", a variation on a theme which had now lasted for almost two decades.

On 5 November, Trinity went to Rochdale Hornets and won 22-12. The *Wakefield Express* reported, "Neil Fox staged his own fireworks display at Rochdale ... This game was dominated by Trinity's player-coach. Apart from his personal contribution of five goals and a try, his know-how and experience repeatedly outwitted Hornets. Without his skill Trinity would have been struggling." The main headline of the sports pages, however, was almost unbelievable, running "Crisis Looms at Belle Vue: Neil Fox 'sickened' by a 'conspiracy'." After Neil's eye-catching display against Rochdale he told the *Wakefield Express* that a committee man had said in front of some Trinity players, "We cannot carry Neil Fox any longer: he just won't tackle". The *Express* added, "Fox is convinced there is a conspiracy to get him out of the side... He said he went home on Sunday depressed and told his wife he was thinking of retiring. There were always men ready to put the knife in... If I had a real shocker I am sure it would delight some of them." Neil wanted to clear the air.

Needless to say, subsequent letter columns of the *Wakefield Express* were filled with missives from members and non-members alike, overwhelmingly in support of Neil. One perhaps summed matters up, when he opined: "If they sack Neil Fox, they might as well sack the turnstile operators!" Matters settled down for a while but the Machiavellian machinations of this 100-year-old members club would rumble on for some time yet.

A heavy cold forced Neil to miss a great win at Hull KR, when an injury-time try by reserve centre Ray Layton gave Trinity their first victory at Craven Park since 1965. Neil was back for the second round of the Floodlit Trophy, a 19-2 success against Keighley at Belle Vue on a freezing Tuesday night. Frank Jeffrey observed, "Fox landed only two goals from seven attempts, but gave TV viewers a sample of his artistry with some astute breaks." But on 18 November he was in better kicking form with four goals, including a drop, in a convincing 23-5 home win against Widnes. Trinity had now advanced to sixth place in the league behind Warrington, Leeds, Oldham, St Helens and Widnes. There was also excellent news for all at the club when it was revealed that the final total raised for Peter Harrison amounted to £11,550, a phenomenal achievement by Trinity's fans, the fundraisers and the wider rugby league public.

On 24 November, Trinity visited Hull for the third time this season and lost 9-4 in the second round of the Player's No. 6 Trophy in a dour encounter. Neil tried his level best to galvanise his side and almost rescued his team a couple of minutes from time but stumbled just short of the line. Clive Sullivan scored the game's only try after 35 minutes.

At this time Don Fox took over as coach at Batley and perhaps uniquely three brothers held senior coaching posts simultaneously, Peter being in charge at Featherstone. By a strange coincidence, Don's first game as coach was at Featherstone on 3 December, when Peter's Rovers won 36-14. On the same afternoon a few miles away Neil was making hay with seven goals and a blockbusting try in Trinity's 44-13 pummelling of York at Belle Vue.

On Tuesday, 12 December, Trinity faced a big game at Widnes in the semi-final of the Floodlit Trophy. The first half was all Wakefield. Neil kicked a seventh-minute 30-yard penalty and then converted a typically weaving try from Topliss in the 23rd minute. By half-time they led 9-3, Neil having added a fine angled penalty. The second half was a disaster. After only three minutes Neil tried to get David Smith away from a scrum 15 yards out but his pass struck Widnes winger McDonnell on the shoulder and the ball rebounded into his arms for a gift try. Around the hour, Widnes substitute Mick George ran in two quick-fire tries and Widnes proceeded to a place in the final with a 16-9 victory. The game became very unpleasant in the closing stages and was marred by stone throwing, as the curse of crowd hooliganism began to emerge in the 1970s, although never on the same catastrophic scale as in association football.

The *Wakefield Express* of 15 December declared "Neil Fox thinks of quitting as a player". Geoff Cudworth wrote that Neil was considering retiring at the end of the season: "Neil (now 33) said he was finding the strain of playing weighing more heavily on him week by week. The last three matches, he said, had taken a lot out of him. He was expected and wanted to do so much on the field that the commitment seemed overwhelming at times... If he did give up at first-team level, he might still play with the 'A' team to bring young players on".

If his burden was becoming unbearable it did not show a couple of days later in a 44-11 thrashing of Hull KR at Belle Vue. Neil booted five goals before retiring for the last 20 minutes, as Wakefield strode into the top four. His second goal was his 1,700th for Wakefield. On Christmas Eve, Trinity went to Mount Pleasant to face a Batley side which was well up the league and found themselves trailing by 9-0 after only 15 minutes. They struck back to lead 10-9 after 28 minutes, Neil converting tries by Hegarty and Wraith, but were 11-10 behind at the break. Batley centre Keith Toohey had been acting like Neil Fox, having scored all his side's points. Trinity had to summon up all their resources and energy to win an exciting clash 20-13. It took an acutely angled penalty goal by Neil in the 76th minute to finally kill off the challenge of the Gallant Youths.

Boxing Day took Wakefield to Leeds and into a very scrappy and ill-tempered contest, which ended in a 20-7 success for the Loiners. Neil played well enough, landing a first-half penalty goal and adding a magnificent conversion to a try by David Smith, which he had begun himself. He also had a try disallowed for taking a tap too quickly. Mick Morgan was sent off after half an hour when Trinity were already 10-0 down. However, they seemed to play better with 12 men on this occasion. The last quarter was scarred by "a disgusting brawl", according to Frank Jeffrey, and there were some very bad images for the game transmitted on BBC television's *Grandstand*. Commentator Eddie Waring was not popular in politically correct rugby league circles when he declared that Mick Morgan had delivered a "Sandal feaster" to Keith Hepworth, before he was dismissed, although it's doubtful if anyone outside a 10-mile radius of Wakefield knew what Eddie was talking about.

Wakefield's first fixture of the New Year on 6 January yielded a 57-5 rout of Doncaster at Belle Vue. Neil landed five goals before retiring with the score at 31-5. A teenage trialist hooker from Castleford under-19s took over the kicking, landed four goals from six shots and was duly signed. He would go far in the game, as anyone who has followed rugby league over the last three decades knows. The young man was Gary Hetherington, founder of Sheffield Eagles and currently chief executive of Leeds Rhinos. Another massacre took place at Hunslet the following week, where Trinity won 48-10. Neil had a field day with the boot, landing nine goals, while David Topliss added to his growing number of hat-tricks.

Off the field there were further developments at Belle Vue. Eddie Thomas announced he would be retiring as club secretary after 21 years in office. He would leave on his 65th birthday on 5 April. It was also decided that Neil would become sole team selector, the five-man committee being scrapped. He was also to become the team's trainer after Gary Cooper resigned. Stuart Kelley was put in charge of the 'A' team on match days. At the club's half-yearly meeting Neil had agreed to be sole selector, saying, "I am paid as coach and if I pick a wrong team, it's my neck at stake". The committee voted overwhelmingly in favour. At the same time that Neil announced that he was to stay for at least the remaining 18 months of his contract, the *Sydney Sun* ran a story that he was about to emigrate to Australia as a player. Life is full of surprises.

On 27 January, Trinity went to Huyton for a first round Challenge Cup tie and fell behind to a 7th-minute try but by half-time led 12-3, with Neil contributing three goals, before winning 18-6. A 32-14 win at York followed. Trinity were impressive and there was a promising debut for 19-year-old forward Roy Bratt but Neil took the plaudits from Frank Jeffrey, who wrote, "Trinity were well led by Fox, whose deadly accurate goalkicking brought him a seven-out-of-seven return, including two superb touchline shots".

Sunday, 11 February 1973 was set aside for Wakefield Trinity's official centenary game against Bradford Northern. Prior to the game there was a buffet lunch at the Theatre Club attended by many of the club's great past players, who were later paraded on the pitch to the delight of those who remembered their deeds. It was somehow completely appropriate that Neil, arguably the club's greatest player, should be in charge of the team on this historic occasion and he did not disappoint. Unfortunately, the game was not worthy of the occasion, Frank Jeffrey describing the first half as "sordid". Steve Lyons was ordered off after 20 minutes and Bradford prop Kel Earl followed in the 30th, while late in the game the referee spoke to both captains in an effort to calm matters. The *Wakefield Express* headline for the match report ran "Fox provides only spice on the centenary cake". Trinity won 19-7 and Neil kicked sublimely – eight goals from nine attempts. Geoff Wraith scored Trinity's only try after 25 minutes, to which Neil tacked on the conversion. It was his third goal of the game and his 100th goal of the season. His second goal had brought up his 2,000th in first-class rugby league.

Trinity faced a difficult second round in the Challenge Cup at Leigh on 17 February. The bookies rated both teams as 14-1 shots for the trophy. *Grandstand* viewers must have been glad that they were watching the game from home. Four inches of snow had to be removed before the kick-off and the pitch was a real glue-pot. A gruelling game was the result but Trinity were much better than their 5-0 victory suggests. Neil, now in the second row, gave his side the lead with a well-judged penalty after 20 minutes and the only try of the game was a beauty. Geoff Wraith made the extra man at a scrum and unleashed winger Mick Major who sped to the corner for the touchdown.

A terrific 36-2 home win over Halifax followed, which included a blast of 25 points in the space of 20 minutes in the second half. The game came at a cost, however, as David Topliss limped off after 47 minutes and was unavailable for the Challenge Cup third round on 4 March. Trinity had been drawn away to Dewsbury. The bookies had clearly not yet recognised how good a team Dewsbury had become for they were, at 12-1, the longest odds in the Challenge Cup quarter-finals. The favourites at 3-1 were Warrington and Wigan, while Trinity and Castleford were the next best bets at 6-1. As a measure of their ability, Dewsbury went on to become League Champions that season. The cup tie drew the biggest crowd for years to Crown Flatt – 14,496. Wakefield were on almost £60 a man to win, but must have known that the odds had turned against them when they went in for half-time level at 4-4, having already had the benefit of Dewsbury's notorious slope. Neil had piloted penalty goals in the 14th and 31st minutes, the latter a monster. As the teams came out for the second half a rainstorm blew up into the faces of Trinity and within a minute Dewsbury got the lead they sought. David Knowles put out a pass which went to ground. Nigel Stephenson nipped in, kicked the ball forward, gathered and scored. Four minutes later he dropped a goal, and then landed two penalties. The scoring concluded with a 67th-minute try by winger Jeff Yoward. Dewsbury fully merited their 16-4 victory.

Although Neil and his troops were disappointed, there was still a very good chance that they could make a good showing in the Championship play-offs. Trinity were fifth in the table and were well enough placed to harbour thoughts of finishing second. The home game against Rochdale Hornets on 10 March, however, was a shocker. Trinity won 28-25 but gave their worst defensive performance of the season. Neil schemed three first-half tries and kicked five goals but the *Wakefield Express* reported, "Neil Fox had rung the changes after the Dewsbury defeat but this performance hardly inspired confidence". Neil continued to experiment for the home game against Batley, when debutant winger Barry Lumb kicked seven goals in a 29-16 victory. At half-time though the teams had been level at 9-9 and Neil's leadership on the field was being missed. He came on for the second half and quickly scored a try to put his side on the way to victory.

On Friday 23 March, Wakefield astonishingly went down 9-0 to Keighley, who were the first team to beat Trinity at home in the league. Neil again came on after the break but this time could do nothing to alter the pattern of the game. Defeats at Bradford Northern and Huddersfield followed and suddenly Trinity were struggling to ensure a place in the top eight for a home play-off. The rot was stopped with a brilliant 28-12 win at Featherstone on 1 April, when Trinity players earned £40 pay packets. Rovers had won 12 games in a row and were entrenched in the top four but had not reckoned on a masterly performance from Neil. Geoff Cudworth had this to say in his "Talking Points" column, under the heading "The Mighty Fox", Cudworth was "privileged to see his extraordinary performance at Featherstone on Sunday. I don't think I have ever seen one player stamp his authority on a game as did Fox in this triumph over a Featherstone side that had carried all before it for weeks and weeks. Operating from his old position at centre and giving 10 years and more to most of the players opposed to him, he had them in a state of perplexity whenever he received the ball – and that was often. Somehow, Fox always had that little extra time in which to work. He pulled out his whole repertoire of ploys that, in the end, amounted to three tries opened up to other people and one for himself. The pass cutting out two men early in the second half was one of the most effective I have seen. It was all of 15 yards –

and travelled like a bullet. Some Trinity supporters appear to enjoy knocking Fox these days. They should, instead, realise he is a footballing genius and enjoy watching what is left of his playing career. Thanks, Neil, and thanks to the players of both Featherstone and Trinity for a tingling derby game played in admirable spirit."

On 4 April, David Topliss zipped over for four tries in a 47-9 home win over Hunslet. Neil kicked five goals and then substituted himself after 52 minutes. Four days later a 15-2 win at Doncaster brought him another three goals, the second of which took him past the 5,000 points mark in all games. Only 1,000 more or so and he would be close to Jim Sullivan's record of the 'greatest-scorer-in-history' title. No-one, however, thought this was feasible, as Neil had often intimated that he saw his career drawing to a close.

Neil contracted enteritis and missed Wakefield's last three league fixtures, which began with another shock defeat at Keighley but ended with good wins against Castleford and Hull. Warrington (on 56 points), Featherstone (54) and Leeds (53) finished in the top three positions and four clubs – St Helens, Trinity, Salford and Castleford - finished on 50. Saints pipped Trinity for fourth place by 0.05 of a point on scoring average. Trinity's 814 points in league fixtures was bettered only by Warrington, who piled up 816.

Neil resumed in his old left centre berth for the first-round play-off clash with Widnes at Belle Vue on 29 April. Wakefield played delightfully to run out winners 33-6. Neil crashed over for the game's last try and converted it – his sixth goal of the afternoon. The conversion brought his points tally for Wakefield during the season to 300, an amazing achievement for a player approaching 34 and continually being written off.

It all came to naught, though. Wakefield went to St Helens for the quarter-final and were blitzed 28-0, after trailing 18-0 at half-time. There were some tough exchanges, however, and Neil and Kel Coslett, two unlikely villains, were both warned by the referee. Neil moved himself to loose-forward for the second half but to no avail. He told the press, "I was bitterly disappointed with our performance. Except for a short period in the second half we did not seem capable of putting up a fight." He added that he wanted to have a long rest and think things over in the summer.

In truth Neil had little, if anything, for which to reproach himself. His personal form had been excellent. He had finished sixth in the leading goalkickers list – David Watkins of Salford had topped it with a record 221 goals. His 300 points had been exceeded by only four players and he had ended the season with Trinity's Player of the Year award. He had led Wakefield, on relatively meagre financial and playing resources, to fifth place in the league and they had played some wonderfully entertaining rugby league into the bargain.

In his end-of-season summary in the *Wakefield Express*, Frank Jeffrey wrote, "Neil Fox, who has given such fine service to the club, again led the side with distinction and fully deserved the Supporters' Club's player-of-the-year award. This was a fitting reply to the strange and, in my view, totally unjustified criticism of him, alleged to have been made by a committee man after he had played a blinder at Rochdale, which almost led to Fox resigning. Trinity never played with the same confidence when he was missing and there are bound to be many problems when he decides to retire."

Confirmation of Neil's incontestable place in Trinity's history came when he was named in the *Wakefield Express* 'Team of All Time' centenary season competition. The team was: Charlie Pollard, Dennis Boocker, Alan Skene, Neil Fox, Stanley Smith, Harold Poynton, Jonty Parkin, Jack Wilkinson, Harry Field, A. K. (Nealy) Crosland, Bill Horton, Harry Murphy, Derek Turner.

Wakefield Trinity 1972-73

Wakefield Trinity finished 5th in the league: P34, W25, L9, For 814, Against 398
Fox scored 8 tries, 138 goals, 300 points for Wakefield

Date	Opponent	Score	Fox	Crowd	
18 Aug	**Castleford**	35-10	2T, 6G	3,964	
23 Aug	Widnes	3-17		3,900	
26 Aug	**Keighley**	38-17	4G	2,178	YC1
28 Aug	**Featherstone R**	35-11	dnp	3,661	
3 Sep	Halifax*	33-15		3,009	
5 Sep	**Hull***	7-7		1,867	FT Prel, 1st leg
7 Sep	**Halifax**	9-11		2,461	YC2
9 Sep	**Bramley**	13-7		1,351	
15 Sep	Hull	10-18	2G	2,348	
19 Sep	Hull	11-3	3G	2,350	FT Prel, 2nd leg
24 Sep	Wigan	34-10	8G	4,000	PT1
1 Oct	**Leeds**	13-12	2G	8,041	
8 Oct	Swinton	7-17	2G	3,528	
15 Oct	**Huddersfield**	15-12	dnp	3,440	
22 Oct	Bramley	9-13	3G	1,800	
25 Oct	Swinton	18-6	3G	1,761	FT1
29 Oct	**Swinton**	33-10	T, 6G	2,929	
5 Nov	Rochdale H	22-12	T, 5G	2,632	
12 Nov	Hull KR	11-8	dnp	3,110	
14 Nov	**Keighley**	19-2	2G	1,827	FT2
18 Nov	**Widnes**	23-5	4G	2,464	
24 Nov	Hull	4-9	2G	2,064	PT2
3 Dec	**York**	44-13	T, 7G	3,153	
12 Dec	Widnes	9-16	3G	3,914	FT semi
17 Dec	**Hull KR**	44-11	5G	2,307	
24 Dec	Batley	20-13	4G	1,983	
26 Dec	Leeds	7-20	2G	10,644	
6 Jan	**Doncaster**	57-5	5G	1,041	
14 Jan	Hunslet	48-10	9G	1,550	
27 Jan	Huyton	18-6	3G	750	Ch Cup 1
4 Feb	York	32-14	7G	4,237	
11 Feb	**Bradford N**	19-7	8G	4,594	
17 Feb	Leigh	5-0	G	4,862	Ch Cup 2
25 Feb	**Halifax**	36-2	G	3,747	
4 Mar	Dewsbury	4-16	2G	14,496	Ch Cup 3
10 Mar	**Rochdale H**	28-25	5G	2,451	
17 Mar	**Batley***	29-16	T	2,260	
23 Mar	**Keighley***	0-11		1,917	
25 Mar	Bradford N	9-17	3G	5,609	
28 Mar	Huddersfield	10-24	2G	1,683	
1 Apr	Featherstone R	28-12	T, 5G	4,690	
4 Apr	**Hunslet**	47-9	5G	1,481	
8 Apr	Doncaster	15-2	3G	915	
13 Apr	Keighley	14-15	dnp	1,416	
21 Apr	Castleford	13-5	dnp	1,922	
23 Apr	**Hull**	52-0	dnp	1,714	
29 Apr	**Widnes**	33-6	T, 6G	4,072	CH1
2 May	St Helens	0-28		6,329	CH2

* Substitute

Neil with 11 year-old ball-boy Dennis Jones at half-time
at the 1962 Championship Final at Odsal.

22. 1973-74: End of an era

In many ways the 1973-74 season was a pivotal one for both Neil and the game. Rugby league's spectator base was still in freefall. The 1972-73 season had attracted only 1,013,675 paying customers to league fixtures – the lowest aggregate on record – and the overall average per game stood at a mere 1,987. The average league fixture had attracted more than 6,200 when Neil began as a professional. It had been as high as 11,500 in 1948-49. Portents of doom were exacerbated when the government decided to apply a 10 per cent VAT levy on games for 1973-74 and most clubs' treasurers were at their wits' end. In the late weeks of the previous season the clubs had voted to adopt two divisions for 1973-74 as panic buttons were hit all around rugby league land. Hunslet were the most prominent sign of the parlous state of the game. They folded before the season started but were quickly revived as New Hunslet, although they lost their venerable Parkside ground to developers. At least the Trinity committee was pleased that the new First Division fixture list against the bigger clubs was bound to improve attendances at Belle Vue.

Jim Bowden became chairman at Wakefield, with Don Robinson as vice-chairman. At the AGM in late July Ron Rylance, chairman of the Finance Committee, spelled out some bad news, declaring that the club's future was at stake unless finances improved. There had been a loss of £4,765 on the previous season and the club's overdraft had risen to £18,272. The reasons cited were a winning team, a poor fixture formula and poor support. Neil had provided the winning team, but he could hardly be expected to do anything about the other factors. Money was certainly tight and the only signing of any note was Barry Parker, a winger from Leeds, who cost a mere £750. The club raised the basic admission charge from 35p to 40p but once again season ticket sales fell.

Missing from the club now was, of course, the familiar face of secretary Eddie Thomas, whose retirement in April had been a sad loss for many at Belle Vue. Neil recalls, "Eddie had been like a father figure to many of the younger players at Trinity down the years. He had signed me on all those years ago and had really been the first person at Trinity I got to know. He was a nice man and did a good job for Wakefield. I remember when I returned from Bradford Northern, Eddie made a point of welcoming me back." Eddie's position was filled by Michael Bennett. Eddie was honoured by being made a life member of the club.

At the AGM Neil had told the audience that he wanted to stop playing but he had been training for most of the summer. He said, "I suppose I will play but the time is approaching when I will have to hang up my boots. I hope the team will come on sufficiently for me to retire about Christmas time." The *Wakefield Express* reported that "there was a reaction of disappointment in the audience". Playing at Neil's age – he was now 34 – had become more problematic with the change to limited tackle football but he had been encouraged by the previous season's change from four to six tackles, declaring "Six tackles was better than four. Under four tackles there was never enough time to settle moves. Six gave players a bit more time. The four tackle rule was ridiculous. There was no pattern to the game. A couple of drives and you were forced into moves that you were not really ready for. The extension to six tackles meant you could plan your moves a bit better". At this stage in his playing career the less hectic style of play was a godsend to players like Neil.

Problems arose before a ball was kicked or passed. Neil was in the middle of a dispute over playing terms. The committee had offered £25 for an away win, £20 for a home win and £8 for a defeat. It was an improvement on the previous season's terms but the players wanted £28 and £24. They refused to budge at first but eventually accepted the new terms on 14 August. Four days earlier they would have been lucky to be offered anything at all, according to spectators who attended Trinity's annual altercation with the Wakefield & District Amateur League. The amateurs led for most of the game, leading 20-9 after 50 minutes. Trinity went ahead on 68 minutes but with five minutes left the score was 25-25. In the last few seconds Neil won the game with a try, which he converted.

The First Division fixtures began on a much better note on Friday, 17 August. A fast, lively game at Castleford was locked at 11-11 with less than a quarter of an hour remaining. Hooker Mick Morgan turned the game Trinity's way with two tries from the play-the-ball in the 66th and 71st minutes. Neil, playing loose-forward, led his side well, converted both and Trinity won 21-14. The following week Rochdale Hornets were overwhelmed 42-8 at Belle Vue. Neil substituted himself in the second half having kicked superbly for seven goals. Two days later Wakefield visited champions Dewsbury for a clash which the *Wakefield Express* described "as good an advertisement for rugby league as one is likely to see all season". The tackling by both sides was wonderful – "as much as man and muscle can stand", according to Frank Jeffrey. Dewsbury's own version of Neil Fox, Nigel Stephenson, scored a try and goal after only two minutes. Five minutes later Neil pulled back two points with a penalty. Then, at third man out from a play-the-ball, he whizzed out an extraordinary 20-yard pass, cutting out three men, which ended with a try for new winger Parker. It was not until the 70th minute that Trinity edged ahead, Neil converting a fine try by Geoff Wriglesworth. Neil stopped Nigel Stephenson from equalising with a desperate flying tackle before an electric run by Dave Topliss, who hoodwinked four men, wrapped the game up in the fifth minute of injury time. Neil's conversion gave Trinity a great 15-5 victory.

On 2 September, Wakefield opened their Yorkshire Cup campaign with a 39-7 home rout of Doncaster. The Dons put up a tough struggle though and trailed only 8-7 at the break. Neil opened the scoring after blasting through two tackles from a play-the-ball and then converted a try by Ray Layton. After the interval he moved to centre and began to create havoc. He followed up a sizzling move by Wraith and Knowles, received the ball 25 yards out, sent the full-back the wrong way with a beguiling dummy and "stepped out majestically for his second try". His conversion put Trinity 13-7 ahead and the Dons fell apart after losing a man through dissent. David Smith scored three tries in the last 10 minutes but was overshadowed by Neil, who finished with 21 points from three tries and six goals. Geoff Cudworth observed, "That points haul in no way exaggerated Fox's influence on the game. His was a giant-sized performance, beside which all other contributions paled."

After four victories Trinity came a cropper 30-9 at St Helens, for whom Geoff Pimblett booted nine goals. Neil missed the disaster but was back at loose-forward for the second-round Yorkshire Cup tie at Keighley on 9 September, landing six goals in a 39-4 win.

Trinity's playing strength was depleted with the transfer of Dave Barends to York. He had not figured in the first-team that season and had scored 22 tries for Trinity in 65 games since his dramatic signing three years previously. Neil recalls, "Dave was a very strong, determined wingman – not the fastest of wingers – and he was very hard to bring down. At Trinity he probably did not fulfil his potential but we had to start from scratch with him. We gave him his start and he must have gained good experience with Trinity because later he won a Lions tour place and I played with him again at York and Bradford."

On 16 September, Neil had a field day in a 47-13 thumping of Blackpool Borough at Belle Vue. He bagged 20 points from a couple of tries and seven goals bringing his tally from just six appearances to 79 points (five tries and 32 goals). His first goal had taken him to the 1,800 mark for Trinity. Late in the game, however, Neil went down awkwardly scoring Wakefield's last try. A Blackpool player fell across his back and Neil's shoulder was dislocated. It had to be strapped for three weeks but Neil told the press he could be back in time for the Yorkshire Cup Final in five weeks, if Trinity got that far. He also announced that he was now considering playing through the season.

Neil remembers that Blackpool match well: "That dislocated shoulder actually kept me out for 12 games. So the pressure was on the lads to keep up the good performances. While I was being attended to in the dressing-room, the great Ces Mountford, a New Zealand player who starred with Wigan, came in to ask me if I would go to New Zealand. He wanted me to help out there, playing and coaching one of the teams. Not feeling too good, I said to him, 'I'm not going anywhere and will you just leave me alone'. This was probably the worst injury I have had. I did see him later and apologised and he realised then that it had not been the right time to ask. I did take up his offer 12 months later and went to New Zealand for about 10 weeks."

In Neil's absence Mick Morgan acted as captain and the team fulfilled all the coach's expectations, beating Oldham and Warrington in the league and winning an intensely exciting Yorkshire Cup semi-final against Castleford within a week. They also put up a brave performance against the Kangaroos at Belle Vue before going down 13-9. It was the first time since 1956 that Neil had missed appearing against a touring side. If that was a disappointment for him the next few days proved even more disappointing and disturbing.

On 5 October the *Wakefield Express* noted, "Wakefield Trinity have developed an unfortunate penchant in recent years for washing their dirty linen in public. I would not suggest this week's episode has been as distasteful as some, but it certainly has put at risk the splendid team spirit developed among the players at Belle Vue." The piece referred to the fact that a Sunday paper had reported that Wakefield Trinity had sounded out Derek Turner as a possible successor to Neil, whose contract would expire the following August. Unsurprisingly, the *Express* continued, "The reaction of Neil Fox, having that same day seen the Trinity side he himself shaped, beat league leaders Warrington on their own ground, was one of indignation."

The local press was clearly on Neil's side. They thought the move premature and that Wakefield were providing the goods on the playing field. Derek Turner had told the *Wakefield Express* he was "not interested" in the Trinity coaching job. He had recently been given the boot at Leeds and was in no hurry to return to coaching rugby league. The *Express* added, "Neil Fox claimed any man would be upset to learn that his job was under review nearly 12 months before his contract was due to expire and against results as good as any in rugby league. 'What do they want?' was his wry comment."

The paper noted that Neil had postponed his decision to retire at Christmas, feeling able to continue as a player longer than he had originally thought. Trinity chairman Jim Bowden said, "I have not always seen eye to eye with Neil, but so far as I am concerned if we have good results and a successful season there is no reason why the contract should not be renewed." He did concede that the committee had discussed the coaching position.

Trinity had a great 18-9 win at home to Leeds on Sunday, 7 October, Dave Topliss scoring the decisive try – his 100th for the club – five minutes from time. Three days later it was all different as Bramley ousted them from the Floodlit Trophy when a last-gasp drop-goal from John Wolford gave them a 10-9 victory at Belle Vue. Unfancied Bramley went on to win the Trophy – one of the most romantic and popular triumphs in league's history.

On the night of the Bramley match, club politics took a dramatic turn, when a Trinity member, Derek Pickering, handed in a petition to the committee calling for an Extraordinary General Meeting, signed by 390 members, when the rules required only 50 to call a meeting. The petition wanted: To investigate events leading up to the newspaper report on the approach to Derek Turner; to pass a vote of confidence in Neil Fox as coach and to establish the committee's attitude over the possible sale of leading players, notably Dave Topliss. It also wanted the EGM to take place on 20 October, after Trinity's Yorkshire Cup Final encounter with Leeds and required that Neil and the press should attend.

Neil's predicament with the Wakefield Trinity committee was clearly exercising many supporters' minds and they wanted a rapid and satisfactory solution. The committee had no option but to agree to meet the petitioners but refused to do so within such a short time scale and the EGM was eventually set for 21 November.

In the meantime Neil had a team to prepare for the Yorkshire Cup Final. Playing Leeds would have been a big enough task in itself but it had been decided before the competition even began that the final would be played at Headingley – at the insistence of Esso, the sponsors. The fact that Leeds were playing at home in a major final rankled with most fair-minded followers of rugby league. Neil was no different, believing that the game should be played on a neutral ground. He had no choice, of course, but to lump it. Neil had his players put in three training sessions before the final and they did him proud before eventually losing 7-2. Neil's side lacked the services of injured Geoff Wriglesworth and Steve Lyons, not forgetting himself, and Ernest Holmes took Neil's place at loose-forward.

Unfortunately, off-field matters were putting the on-field action in the shade. In the run-up to the EGM, Trinity confounded the form book by losing at home to Bramley and Featherstone while recording super wins at Wigan and Widnes. Neil returned to action on 27 October with the 'A' team at Huddersfield and continued his comeback with further outings at that level against York, Hull KR and Batley.

On 2 November the *Wakefield Express* ran the headline "Fox will not seek contract renewal". Neil was clearly very unhappy. The committee had, once again, decided to relieve him of team selection duties. He told Geoff Cudworth, "They aren't satisfied with my team selection; they criticise my coaching; I don't know why they don't sack me." The committee decided that "for an experimental period up to the end of the year the team would be selected by the full committee." Trinity's committee then announced that they had received a letter signed by 13 'A' teamers alleging that Neil was unfair in his selection and was guilty of favouritism. It was claimed that too many men were being played out of position and that first-teamers were switched instead of drafting in 'A' teamers. There was also criticism of certain aspects of Neil's coaching. The committee also told the press that Neil had ignored a request to go on a scouting mission to Northumberland on 27 October to watch a Yorkshire County rugby union player.

In hindsight it appears clear that the anti-Neil Fox faction on the Trinity committee was getting in its retaliation first. Neil responded by telling the *Wakefield Express* that the letter from the 'A' teamers probably reflected frustration caused by the pay disparity compared to the first-team, which was roughly £5 against £25 for a win. He had, he felt, given most of the 'A' teamers who deserved it a run-out with the first-team. However, he also stressed to them that under Ken Traill players like Mick Morgan and Geoff Wraith had had to wait patiently before clinching first-team places. Regarding the scouting mission to Northumberland, he said he had been told about it by telephone on the preceding Tuesday night but had wanted to test out his shoulder with the reserves and no one had even subsequently mentioned the trip at Thursday's training session. Besides, he or the committee could see the player concerned any time they wanted to without travelling to Northumberland, as he played his club rugby union in Yorkshire.

Neil found all this very unsettling. Letters flooded into the *Wakefield Express* about the "Fox affair", mostly taking the committee to task. Even Molly was provoked into sending a letter in Neil's defence. The *Express* ran it under the heading "'Undermined' says Mrs Fox". Molly wrote, "I don't think there is another coach in any game who has had so much pressure put on him from people who are supposed to be working for the club... A member told Neil he was against him no matter what he did. About a year ago it was suggested Neil's coaching was all wrong – just before a cup tie... What do they want – blood?

It has been wrongly alleged of Neil that he is anti-rugby union players. Neil picks the best men available, whether they cost thousands or hundreds. I could go on and on... Even Ken Traill had the same trouble with 'A' teams. If any team ever repaid and supported their coach, Trinity did by reaching the Yorkshire Cup Final against Leeds this year. They were magnificent in their response. In fact, if Neil did not realise he had the backing of the players and supporters he would have long since packed up at Wakefield. How long will it be before they dishearten him completely? I just don't know."

Neil recalls: "In the week before the EGM Trevor Woodward, one of the committee and a good friend of mine and one-time business partner, came and told me, 'They are going to sack you on Tuesday. They have had a vote. I have to be honest and say I suggested Derek Turner for coach. But that was because if they lost you they would need someone as good as Derek to replace you, someone the fans could look up to. They were trying to soften the blow for the supporters by getting Derek. I thought the discussion was just a bit of speculation in case you ever left. Your Peter was also mentioned as a possibility'. After Trevor told me I went down to training expecting to get the sack but no one said anything. I went again on Thursday thinking it would be my last time training at Belle Vue but again nothing was said."

The EGM took place on Wednesday, 21 November at the Unity Hall in the city centre and it was a riotous affair. The *Wakefield Express* reported, "Anger and bad manners were often demonstrated to an embarrassing degree. One felt it was a sad night for a great club. May Trinity be spared such pains in the future." About 300 members, out of about 1,400, were present. Neil was on the platform with the entire committee, except for Eddie Sugden who had suffered a bereavement. The committee said it believed that the team's forwards were giving inadequate performances and admitted that they had discussed appointing Derek Turner or Peter Fox in Neil's place for the following August. They admitted too that Neil had not been informed of the approach to Turner. Calls of "resign" began to echo around Unity Hall and a protracted argument developed. According to the *Wakefield Express*, it became a straight coach-versus-committee issue as the uproar intensified. Neil recalls, "I never got the chance to say a word. It was basically a case of the supporters demanding to know why the committee wanted to get rid of Neil Fox."

Eventually a vote of confidence in Neil as coach was taken. Only seven votes against him were recorded out of the 300 or so present. The anti-Fox brigade were urged to resign and five of them soon did – Jim Bowden, Don Robinson, J. L. Davies, Ken Croft and secretary-manager Mike Bennett. The following Tuesday Trevor Woodward announced he would resign if Jim Bowden remained on the committee but Mr Bowden stood down "for the good of the club". Mr Bennett, a tax consultant, had already intimated that he would not be carrying on at the end of the year but he later returned in a managerial capacity. Effectively the Wakefield Trinity committee was reduced to four – Les Pounder, who became chairman, Ronnie Rylance (vice-chairman), Trevor Woodward and John Sellers. Eddie Sugden resigned in early December.

The immediate upshot was the restoration of Neil as sole selector. Although later the chairman and vice-chairman were to nominally share selection duties with Neil, he was essentially left in sole charge.

Neil returned to the first-team on 25 November for the second round of another new competition, the Captain Morgan trophy, when Trinity lost 20-14 at Featherstone. He opened the scoring with a prodigious drop-goal and added three place goals. Frank Jeffrey reported, "Fox, who made a surprise comeback at centre, did well in his first senior game since 16 September, creating one try and setting up most of Trinity's moves."

On 9 December, Neil booted another four goals in a drab game against Leigh at Belle Vue. Frank Jeffrey noted, "Fox's craft shone like a beacon and Valentine, whose passes created two tries, had another excellent game." Trinity were fourth in the table at this point in the season and as the three-day-week, power cuts and industrial strife bit the nation Neil and his men at least were brightening up their locality. Home victories over Workington Town and Warrington followed, in both of which Neil claimed outrageous tries with his beguiling dummies. On Boxing Day at Headingley against Leeds, Trinity took a 12-7 first half lead, Neil landing three goals, but fell away to lose 19-14.

Three days later they met St Helens at Belle Vue in a televised third-round Player's No.6 Trophy match. It was a see-saw thriller which ended in an 18-18 draw. Trinity, who held 10-2 and 15-7 leads, should have won after scoring four magnificent tries. Neil had kicked a couple of goals in the first half, but damaged a muscle in the second half and felt unable to take a 73rd-minute penalty which could have won the match, handing the kick to loose-forward Ian Ellis, who missed the angled shot. The replay took place on 6 January and was another cracking game, but ended in a 16-10 knock-out for Trinity.

A week later Trinity, now third in the league, visited league leaders Salford and were soundly beaten 22-7. After the defeat Neil declared it was time for changes to the team and said he shared the responsibility. He felt he needed a rest and intended to relegate himself to substitute for the visit to Whitehaven on 20 January. In the event, circumstances forced him to turn out at centre and he kicked four goals in a 29-18 success. It was to be the last time Neil would ever play centre for Trinity. The home crowd howled in derision when Neil failed with two relatively simple penalties in the first half but he had the last laugh. By half-time he had kicked three goals as Trinity led 18-6 and he substituted himself. With 10 minutes remaining Trinity were hanging on to a 21-18 lead and he returned to the fray, making the break which resulted in a try for Ellis and finished off Whitehaven. He ended the match with a touchline conversion of a last-gasp Joe Bonnar try.

However, nothing could conceal the fact that Trinity were operating on meagre playing resources, as 13 of their 37 registered players were unavailable through injury or other causes. Three – Geoff Wraith, Kevin Harkin and Steve Lyons – were due to leave for Australia in a deal brokered by the Queensland Rugby League, which would eventually bring a welcome £10,000 into the Wakefield coffers. For now though Neil was limited to signing winger John Archer from Wakefield RUFC and half-back Barry Langton, whose brother Terry was already on the club's playing staff. Archer scored five tries on his debut for the 'A' team against New Hunslet and made his first-team debut in the win at Whitehaven, scoring a try.

Neil and Trinity entered a desperate time in the following weeks, as their season appeared to be falling apart. Seven consecutive games were lost, including a first-round Challenge Cup tie at Widnes. The run culminated in a 21-0 home defeat to Wigan on 3 March. Frank Jeffrey wrote, "Like a never-ending nightmare, the sad saga of Trinity's alarming decline goes on and on". Trinity were not as bad as the score suggested but suddenly they went from the top four to the fringes of the relegation struggle. However, Neil's problems were put into perspective, when his old Sharlston headmaster Job Musgrave died and Neil, his brother Don, Joe Mullaney and another old boy of the school, John Ackroyd, acted as pallbearers for their old scholastic and rugby league mentor.

On 10 March, Trinity took on Hull KR at Belle Vue and won 10-9 in vile conditions. Neil was the game-breaker, the *Wakefield Express* remarking, "Trinity's success was master minded by Neil Fox, who scored his side's first seven points, laid on the second try and created several openings". His first goal, a ninth-minute conversion of his own try after he had broken through from 25 yards and sent the full-back in completely the wrong direction, was the 2,100th of his first class career. His second, a drop, and his last goal for the club, gave Trinity a 7-4 lead after 30 minutes, while his 45th-minute surge through the defence enabled him to release David Smith for his 27th try of the season. The victory erased any mathematical possibility of Trinity being relegated and they finally ended up in a creditable seventh position in the First Division.

Only a reported 2,190 saw the victory over the Robins and the reality was that there were probably even fewer because only 790 actually paid for the privilege of seeing Neil's last game for Wakefield. The remaining 1,400 were members, who may or may not have actually attended but were always included in the official attendances. For the record, the teams for Neil's last game as a Trinitarian were:

Wakefield Trinity: Les Sheard, David Smith, Terry Crook, Geoff Wriglesworth, Ernest Holmes, Dave Topliss, Barry Langton, Norman Cooper, Tony Handforth (sub Alan Tonks), Roy Bratt, Neil Goodwin, Ken Endersby, Neil Fox.
Non-playing substitute: John Hegarty
Hull KR: Phil Coupland (sub Brian Pinkney), Steve Leighton, Paul Longstaff, David Hall, Ged Dunn, Roger Millward, Terry Hudson, Neil Dawson, Ian Madley, Paul Rose, Steve Wiley, Gordon Young (sub Roy Holdstock), Joe Brown.
Referee: Billy Thompson (Huddersfield)

The following Friday, 15 March, the *Wakefield Express* carried a massive headline, several inches tall, declaring "Fox resigns bombshell".

Neil had finally had enough. The *Express* reported that he had told the committee on Tuesday, "It's been a very hard decision to make. The trouble is that I cannot say anything specifically has made me make up my mind. I've no desire to create trouble at Belle Vue. I just feel I must make a clean break now that I consider the team to be free from relegation worries. It will be hard after 19 years with Trinity, but I imagine they will be able to get along all right without me." It continued, "Neil added that should another offer in the game come along he would be obliged to consider it. His heart remained in rugby league." The committee agreed in principle to release Neil from his contract, making him a free agent.

Neil gave the *Wakefield Express* a letter for the clubs' supporters explaining his decision: "I think the time has come after our unfortunate defeats of late for my resignation. No doubt many of you will think the captain is deserting his ship, but that is not the case, as people who really know me will realise. After last week's win over Hull KR we should be clear of any relegation worries now. I can leave knowing that the players I am leaving, some of whom will go far with just that turn of luck, have not such a threat hanging over their heads.

After working hard together over the past four seasons and knowing how sickened some of the players have been with recent results and the knowledge that chances of honours were evading them, I think it only fair for me to resign and make way for a solution that some people think could come with the appointment of a new coach. I hope Trinity will go from strength to strength in the coming weeks and will pull together next time. I shall miss the club for it has been my life for so long and holds so many happy memories. I would like to thank all the supporters for loyalty through the good and difficult times, and also express my appreciation for the help I have received from the players and staff."

To anyone who knows Neil, such consideration for the fans who had supported, cheered and adored him, would have come as no surprise.

Another of Trinity's true greats, Dave Topliss, was appointed Neil's successor as captain but the club announced that they would appoint a caretaker coach for the remainder of the season. 'A' team coach David Lamming took over the first-team duties for the short term and two weeks after Neil's resignation they brought in Nick Whitehead, a senior lecturer in PE at Carnegie College and a former Olympic sprinter, to help with fitness. Finally, and ironically, they appointed Peter Fox as coach. Peter took up his post on 10 June, having led Featherstone Rovers to Wembley finals in 1973 and 1974.

Neil had been granted a free transfer on 24 May. Dewsbury, Huddersfield and York were reported to have approached him but he decided to throw in his lot with Hull Kingston Rovers. A letter soon appeared in the *Wakefield Express* from a fan, who had spotted Neil haring around local country lanes obviously intent on being fit for his next challenge.

Neil's time at Wakefield Trinity had been extraordinary by any standards. Belle Vue could hardly expect to see his like again. In cold statistics he had made 574 appearances (12 as a substitute) for the club and amassed 272 tries, 1,836 goals and 4,488 points. Those figures were a monumental testimony to his match-winning powers, his durability and loyalty. Neil had at one time or another held all the club records for tries, goals and points scored in a match, a season and a career. The only major club record which escaped him was Harry Wilkinson's 605 games (between 1930 and 1949) for Trinity. Neil's first-class career record stood at a phenomenal 669 games (15 as a substitute), 321 tries, 2,101 goals and 5,165 points. He was already established in the pantheon of rugby league's greatest players, standing shoulder to shoulder with the legendary Welshman Jim Sullivan as the only two men to have piled up more than 5,000 points. Neil's test career was over but he remains to this day Great Britain's most prolific goalkicker with 93 and highest points scorer with 228. His 321 career tries also constituted a record for any non-winger. If his career had ended at this point, he would still have walked into the Rugby League Hall of Fame on those achievements alone.

There is little doubt that those fans and critics, who had been so royally captivated, entertained and thrilled by Neil's performances for the best part of two decades, believed that his days of record-breaking had passed and that his retirement was merely being delayed for a year or so. How wrong they all were.

Wakefield Trinity 1973-74

Wakefield Trinity finished 7th in Division 1: P30, W16, L14, For 470, Against 411
Fox scored 8 tries, 62 goals, 148 points for Wakefield

Date	Opponent	Score	Fox	Crowd	
17 Aug	Castleford	21-14	3G	2,789	
25 Aug	**Rochdale H**	42-8	7G	2,693	
27 Aug	Dewsbury	15-5	3G	4,800	
2 Sep	**Doncaster**	39-7	3T, 6G	2,578	YC1
7 Sep	St Helens	9-30	dnp	4,513	
9 Sep	Keighley	39-4	6G	2,680	YC2
16 Sep	**Blackpool B**	47-13	2T, 7G	2,473	PT1
23 Sep	**Oldham**	22-0	dnp	3,462	
26 Sep	**Castleford**	19-18	dnp	4,642	YC semi
30 Sep	Warrington	13-10	dnp	8,029	
3 Oct	**Australians**	9-13	dnp	5,863	
7 Oct	**Leeds**	18-9	dnp	7,845	
10 Oct	**Bramley**	9-10	dnp	1,393	FT1
20 Oct	Leeds	2-7	dnp	7,621	YC Final (at Leeds)
24 Oct	**Batley**	24-5	dnp	2,010	CM1
27 Oct	**Bramley**	13-18	dnp	2,632	
7 Nov	Wigan	18-12	dnp	4,142	
11 Nov	**Featherstone R**	13-17	dnp	4,770	
18 Nov	Widnes	28-13	dnp	2,756	
25 Nov	Featherstone R	14-20	4G	4,148	CM2
9 Dec	**Leigh**	26-8	4G	2,596	
16 Dec	**Workington T**	10-7	T, G	1,835	PT2
23 Dec	**Warrington**	26-15	T, 4G	3,448	
26 Dec	Leeds	14-19	3G	9,711	
29 Dec	**St Helens**	18-18	2G	2,890	PT3
6 Jan	St Helens	10-16	2G	7,181	Replay
13 Jan	Salford	7-22	2G	7,127	
20 Jan	Whitehaven	29-18	4G	1,450	
27 Jan	**Widnes***	7-12		3,284	
3 Feb	Widnes	7-27	G	5,525	Ch Cup 1
10 Feb	Leigh	8-16	dnp	2,505	
16 Feb	Oldham	2-9	G	1,482	
24 Feb	**Castleford**	14-15	dnp	3,575	
3 Mar	**Wigan**	0-21		3,504	
10 Mar	**Hull KR**	10-9	T, 2G	2,190	
17 Mar	Hull KR	17-10	dnp	2,807	
24 Mar	Bramley	35-5	dnp	2,100	
31 Mar	**Salford**	13-32	dnp	4,915	
3 Apr	Rochdale H	6-15	dnp	1,703	
6 Apr	**Whitehaven**	24-12	dnp	2,022	
10 Apr	**St Helens**	2-15	dnp	3,328	
15 Apr	**Dewsbury**	10-3	dnp	3,727	
16 Apr	Featherstone R	8-19	dnp	3,297	
21 Apr	**Dewsbury**	26-11	dnp	4,150	CC1
28 Apr	Featherstone R	19-16	dnp	4,419	CC2
5 May	Warrington	7-12	dnp	10,007	CC semi

* Substitute

Teams from the 1970s

Hull KR 1974-75 side with the Yorkshire Cup.

York versus Dewsbury, February 1976. Back: Gary Hetherington, Ted Campbell, Billy Harris, Geoff Clarkson, Mike Marshall, Alan Rhodes, Jackie Marston. Front: Tony Handforth, Dave Barends, Peter Inns, Neil Fox, Adrian Rushton, John Hughes.

Player-coach Neil with his Huddersfield squad for the 1977-78 season.
Back: David Jeanes, Ian van Bellen, Trevor Leathley, Mick Keean, Malcolm Branch, Derek Wroe, Steve Mullaney, Tony Johnson, Mick Redfearn, Tom Davies, Jon Morton, Joe Cyrus. Middle: Frank Hutton, Andy Wilson, Les Shaw, Ken Senior, Dave Hooson, Tony Clegg, Tommy Nelmes, Mike Smith, Neil Fox, Peter Cramp, Alan Forster, Peter Rowe. Front: Mick Shepherd, Dave Schofield, Roger Armitage, Alan Ruddock, Alan Greenwood, John Hartley, Chris Leese.

23. 1974-75: Records for the rocking Robins

Neil's move to Hull Kingston Rovers probably surprised many observers of the game. It was an unusual step for a 35-year-old player from the West Riding to decide to join a club in the far east of the county, which had also just been relegated. Neil explains: "During the summer I got a call from Colin Hutton, the general manager at Hull Kingston. He asked if I would come and have a chat about joining Rovers. I had got to know Colin well after being on tour with him in 1962, when he was the coach. I always found him to be a gentleman and trustworthy. After I indicated that I was interested in joining Rovers at the first meeting, another was organised between me, Colin and the chairman Wilf Spaven, to discuss terms. I did not want to travel to Hull two nights a week for training. There was no motorway then. I said I would go once a week and train by myself in Horbury. This was agreed, so I went and signed for them. To make sure I was ready for the pre-season training, I went out nearly every night pounding the streets of Horbury. People who were Trinity supporters used to shout at me and encourage me by saying things like, 'Hey, Neil. It looks like you're going to show the Trinity committee they were wrong to let you go'. They were right, as well. I was bursting for the season to start.

Before it did start Molly and I took Mandy and Jonathan to Spain on holiday for a couple of weeks. I think this was the first holiday I ever took my training gear with me. Every morning I went for a run before breakfast and kept it up for the whole two weeks. That was how important it was for me to help Hull KR back to Division 1."

Rovers had been relegated the previous season having finished 14th in the First Division, five points adrift of safety. It was difficult to fathom how they had ended up in the Second Division, as they had some wonderful players and provided two Lions for the 1974 tour in skipper Roger Millward and Paul Rose. It was clear, however, that they intended to remain in the lower division for as little time as possible. Apart from Neil, they acquired the services of former Great Britain winger and captain, Clive Sullivan, from Hull. Bernard Watson, a fine centre, was signed from Bradford Northern and forward Cliff Wallis was re-signed for a third time, from Castleford. Bob Smithies, a cracking full-back and Grand Final winner in Sydney with Balmain in 1969, returned to Craven Park after an injury-ruined spell at the club the previous year. To most observers of the sport the Rovers' squad seemed to possess enough talent and class to win promotion. Arthur Bunting, a popular half-back for the Robins for more than a decade, had been coach since 1972.

In their never-ending attempt to improve the game and win back bigger crowds, the RFL had commissioned a committee under Lord Derby to investigate how best to achieve their objectives. Their proposals seemed modest - a change to seven forwards and six backs, better scrummaging and a speeding up of the play-the-ball. Referees were to be instructed to apply the scrummaging laws to the letter. There was one substantial change to the laws, however, with the reduction in the value of a drop-goal to a single point. The Australians had introduced one-point drop-goals in 1971. Another major change came with a new RFL secretary. David Oxley, a Rovers follower, took over from Bill Fallowfield at Chapeltown Road and began a quiet revolution in the game, which in 1973-74 had experienced a catastrophic all-time low in attendances at league matches of just 825,771 an average of 1,957 per game.

Neil's new routine included travelling by car to Hull for training with team-mates Terry Ramshaw, Terry Hudson and Bob Woodhead, who were all from the Featherstone area. Later these players left Hull KR and instead he travelled with Bernard Watson, Steve Lyons and George Kirkpatrick.

Rovers fans had their first sight of Neil in his new robin redbreast jersey in a pre-season sevens tournament at Craven Park on Saturday, 10 August. The *Hull Daily Mail* reported that the "playing highlights were a 75-yard try by prop John Millington, the goalkicking of Neil Fox, who landed nine out of nine, the form of scrum-halves Terry Hudson and Brian Pinkney, and a typical try from Peter Flanagan." On Sunday, 18 August Neil got his first taste of a Humberside derby, when Rovers beat Hull 24-13 at The Boulevard in the annual Eva Hardaker Memorial Trophy. Neil kicked six goals but saw his winger Ged Dunn and Hull forward Alan Wardell sent off by referee Fred Lindop.

Neil's official debut came on the following Sunday at Doncaster. He had been signed as a centre, despite his conversion to the pack in recent years, but he was confident he still had the skill and nous to unlock defences in the threequarters, particularly Second Division defences. Rovers won easily, 33-3, with full-back Smithies running in a hat-trick. John Sexton reported in the *Hull Daily Mail*, "Fox paced his game intelligently, and used his skill to good effect, particularly when creating the first try with a piece of football wizardry." Neil's kicking was pretty good too, with six successes from seven attempts.

The following Friday in a home Yorkshire Cup tie against Batley, however, Neil had a nightmare match with his boot, missing five shots, four of which should have been easy for a kicker of his calibre. He finally landed a goal late in the game as Rovers won 16-0. He had more success in the next round which took place at Craven Park on Wednesday, 4 September. First Division Bramley were the visitors, but Rovers looked more like a team from the higher reaches racing to a 23-2 lead by half-time. Neil hoisted a 40-yard penalty after seven minutes and five minutes later hit a tremendous touchline conversion after his winger Ged Dunn had scored. He converted two more tries, the second in first-half injury time after one of his mighty charges set up a try for Paul Rose. Unfortunately, the game deteriorated alarmingly after a 20th minute tackle by Johnny Wolford that knocked out Rovers prop John Millington for fully five minutes, causing him to spend the night in Hull Royal Infirmary. Rovers won 23-10.

Two days later the *Hull Daily Mail* headline for Rovers' home league game against Workington Town proclaimed "Neil Fox gets all the points in KR win". In a tough struggle four penalties from Neil, one from 45 yards, gave Rovers an 8-4 interval lead. By the hour he had added another and a tired Rovers were hanging on to a 10-6 lead, when Town stand-off John Dobie was sent off for a high tackle on Roger Millward. Five minutes later Rovers took a scrum 10 yards out for Hudson and Millward to send Neil crashing through for the only try of the night, which he converted to give his side a 15-8 victory.

Rovers lost their first match of the season to a last-minute drop-goal by Tony Wainwright at Watersheddings, where Oldham scraped home 8-7 in a first-leg, preliminary round of the BBC2 Floodlit Trophy. Neil kicked two goals to add to a try by Millward and a one-point defeat was regarded as pretty satisfactory with a home second leg to come.

On 15 September, Neil and his colleagues received an almighty shock when they went down 21-20 at lowly Huyton – hardly a result to conjure up visions of promotion. Huyton stunned Rovers by scoring four tries from less than five yards and when hooker Don Parry dropped a 79th-minute goal to give his side a 21-17 lead, no one begrudged them their success. Neil had kicked four goals and was given a last-gasp chance to win the match in the fifth minute of injury time when he combined with Millward and Watson to get Dunn over at the flag. His conversion attempt narrowly missed its mark, however, and one of the shocks of the season caused a few blushes for Craven Park devotees.

Neil moved to loose-forward, taking over from the injured Joe Brown, for the return Floodlit Trophy match against Oldham two days after the disaster at Alt Park. Rovers again struggled to impose their authority. Neil kicked two first-half goals but by the 65th minute Oldham were only 14-11 down (21-20 on aggregate) and looking as likely to win as Rovers. There was no further score until the 79th minute when, according to John Sexton, "Fox again cut through cleverly using all his skill and strength and Stephenson backed up to take the pass and score by the posts, Millward's goal completing victory." Sexton also observed, "Fox looked much more at home at loose-forward, and although he has done an adequate job at centre, quite obviously it is in the pack where he must play." Coach Arthur Bunting must have agreed because for the remainder of the season, apart from one game, Neil operated at second-row with occasional outings at loose-forward.

Three days after dismissing Oldham from the Floodlit Trophy, Rovers faced them again at Craven Park in the league. If Rovers had had a fault so far in the season it had been an almost compulsive urge to play open rugby, which was fine when it came off but often risky against less accomplished but determined sides. Yet, everything came off in the first half against Oldham, after which the Robins led 12-2 but might have been much further ahead. Neil had kicked three goals and kick-started a wonderful try for Dunn. In the second half, however, they simply could not gain any possession and were wilting with a lead of only 12-6 before Millington made a late try for Millward, which Neil converted. Their 17-8 win took them to the top of the Second Division.

Thoughts then turned to the small matter of a Yorkshire Cup semi-final at First Division Bradford Northern on 24 September. Bradford took the lead with a first-minute try from winger Rudy Francis and played all over Rovers during the first half but squandered innumerable chances. Almost unbelievably, Rovers ended the first period 13-7 ahead, in large measure due to Neil's brilliance. On 12 minutes George Kirkpatrick touched down at the corner flag for Neil to land a mighty conversion. Two Keith Mumby penalties gave Northern the lead again by the 26th minute but Rovers struck back hard. The *Hull Daily Mail* reported, "Then came a remarkable spell. At last finding the sort of cohesion expected, Fox almost made it to the line and then the ever-willing Brown stormed in to support. Brown played the ball and Fox dummied, then cut through smartly, outwitting five defenders to force his way over and then kick the goal. On the stroke of half-time, Fox again made the break, cutting through the defence and turning an inside pass which Millward snapped up to round Mumby and score." Two more Mumby penalties early in the second half put the game on a knife-edge at 13-11 before Smithies raced over to make it 16-11 on 53 minutes. Neil was subbed on the hour and was as aghast as the Rovers followers when, in the last minute, Dave Redfearn raced through for a try, goaled from a difficult angle by Mumby to force a replay.

Rovers decided to rest Millward and Neil in readiness for the replay and so left them out of their side for a first-round John Player Trophy match at Rochdale, which they won 16-12. The replay with Bradford was a genuine thriller, full of exciting football despite a drizzly evening, a wet ball and a slippery pitch. Rovers suffered a blow when John Millington was taken off after only seven minutes with a cut head. The Rovers forwards excelled, however, with some tremendous tackling and 'Flash' Flanagan's scrum superiority of 22-12. Neil kicked a simple but ultimately crucial penalty after 11 minutes and the lead was extended to 5-0 three minutes later when an exquisite move involving Millward, Ramshaw, Wallis, Smithies and Stephenson created a stunning try for Kirkpatrick. In the 32nd minute, good forward play put Bill Ramsey over for a try for Northern and that completed the scoring. Bradford almost stole the game in the last minute but Kirkpatrick pulled off a miraculous tackle to take winger Mike Lamb into touch and to take Rovers into their fifth Yorkshire Cup Final in 12 years. Neil had extra incentive to make sure he was in the team for the final because the previous evening Wakefield Trinity had beaten Hull 8-6 at The Boulevard in the other semi-final.

The final was more than three weeks away and in the meantime Rovers hardly looked like potential winners of the trophy. On Sunday, 6 October they made their first ever visit to Blackpool Borough. Neil kicked three penalty goals but Rovers trailed 14-12 as the game entered its last minute. They got out of jail with a 40-yard try from Ged Dunn to win 15-14, but they had been awful. They were still top of the table but the following Friday met second-placed Whitehaven at Craven Park. After taking a 5-0 lead Rovers were blitzed in the forwards, losing the scrums 21-8 and the match 10-5. John Sexton was forced to comment, "After last night's game, which touched every aspect of entertainment, farce, comedy, drama and tragedy, with long intervals of nothing in particular, the Robins must realise that unless they add strength to their forwards they will never win promotion."

Neil was put into the centre for the next game at Swinton but again Rovers lost. With 14 minutes left, Ian Madley was sent off for a high tackle but eight minutes later a drop-goal by Joe Brown levelled the scores at 6-6, only for Swinton to score two late tries and a conversion to win 14-6. Neil, who had not wanted to return to the threequarters, had probably the worst game for Rovers of the 59 he would play for them.

The only good news coming out of Craven Park in this dark spell had been the announcement of a whopping profit of £6,038 by the club on the previous season.

The Yorkshire Cup Final took place at Headingley on 26 October and there was much interest in how Neil would perform against his former team-mates, who were now under the direction of his brother Peter. Coincidentally, Neil's team had also knocked out his other brother Don's team in the first round. Neil told the *Hull Daily Mail*, "It means a great deal to me to win this one, especially after having been coach to most of the players who will be in their side... I know a lot about the Wakefield players obviously, but with my brother being there, I can be certain that they will have learned some new tricks." Rovers coach Arthur Bunting arranged for extra training sessions leading up to the final and caused a few eyebrows to be raised by bringing in Clive Sullivan on the wing for leading try-scorer Ged Dunn. Sully had missed the last nine games through injury and had only played half a match for the 'A' team since. They were, however, glad to have skipper Roger Millward back in the side following a shoulder problem. Neil, himself, proved the surprise selection as Bunting put him into the second-row for the first time at Rovers. John Sexton was a little sceptical about the move, writing, "Putting Fox back in the pack is a controversial selection as the Robins have again got Cliff Wallis, Fox and Joe Brown together in the back three, a trio which has not made a great deal of impression in earlier games. There is, however, one subtle difference. Whereas Fox was made loose-forward and pack leader earlier in the season, Brown retains both roles for this match". The teams were:

Hull Kingston Rovers: Bob Smithies, Clive Sullivan, Bernard Watson, Phil Coupland, George Kirkpatrick, Roger Millward, captain, Mike Stephenson, John Millington, Dave Heslop, Paul Rose, Cliff Wallis, Neil Fox, Joe Brown.
Substitutes: Ged Dunn, Ian Madley (both played).
Wakefield Trinity: Les Sheard, David Smith, Terry Crook, John Hegarty, John Archer, David Topliss, captain, Joe Bonnar, George Ballantyne, Tony Handforth, Roy Bratt, Trevor Skerrett, Alan Tonks, Mick Morgan.
Substitutes: Ernest Holmes, Neil Goodwin (both played).

Trinity, as a First Division side, started as favourites but Rovers had enough men of class to worry any team, if things went their way. The game, Neil's fifth Yorkshire Cup Final but his first since 1964, was attended by a paltry 5,639. They were treated to a classic, certainly one of the best county finals anyone could remember. Paul Rylance of the *Daily*

Telegraph wrote: "It was a tremendous battle, providing some of the best and most exhilarating football I have seen for a long time." Alfred Drewry in the *Yorkshire Post* observed: "The main impression left was of two bold, quick-thinking sides prepared to take risks in the hope of making openings and the result was a fast, stirring contest in which the winners made nonsense of their Second Division status by twice coming from behind."

Things looked bad for Rovers when they went 5-0 down in the first eight minutes. Crook banged over a 45-yard penalty goal and then Neil flung out a long pass which Rose could not hold and Hegarty grabbed the ball to run in for a try from 30 yards. He made up for his lapse four minutes later. Millington, Coupland and Watson worked a sweet movement to get Kirkpatrick in at the corner and Neil's towering conversion levelled the scores. Rovers were cock-a-hoop when Millward crossed but crestfallen when referee Mick Naughton ruled a forward pass. Another piece of bad luck followed in the 25th minute when a mighty penalty from the touchline by Neil hit the post and bounced out. There was more frustration for Neil and his team when he tackled Sheard, who lost the ball. Mr Naughton decided it had been stolen and Crook's easy penalty goal sent Trinity into the dressing-rooms 7-5 up at the break.

Six minutes after the break Neil brought Rovers level when he kicked a penalty after Bonnar fed the pack illegally near the posts. Two minutes later Rovers took the lead after great work by Brown, Neil and Millward sent Watson over at the flag. Neil missed the conversion and had a drop-goal attempt charged down. Just when Trinity seemed to be on their last legs they conjured up a glorious equalising try, when Morgan made a tremendous break before sending Smith, who was playing with 19 stitches in his nose, careering over from near half-way. A minute later, Rovers were back in front when a long pass from Millward enabled Dunn to touch down and in the 69th minute Smithies burst down the right-hand side of the field, kicked ahead causing confusion in Wakefield's defence as the ball bobbled near their goal-line and allowed Watson to score a simple try. Neil was taken off for the last five minutes with the score at 16-10 but there was a late scare when Roy Bratt forced his way over for a try to reduce Rovers' winning score to 16-13.

It had been a tremendous triumph for Hull KR. Roger Millward took the White Rose Trophy as man-of-the-match but, as John Sexton noted: "The foundations for the win were firmly laid by the pack. The Robins produced six forwards willing to run, work and tackle for victory and this was just too much power for Wakefield to cope with. Cliff Wallis... epitomised the whole pack with his non-stop efforts and it is to his credit that he missed the man-of-the-match award by one point. But Wallis was not alone. Joe Brown was superb at loose-forward, John Millington and Paul Rose worked tirelessly at prop, David Heslop proved elusive and hard-working at hooker – and also won the scrums 10-8 – while Neil Fox provided the link that meant all the good work counted. After the forwards had driven enormous gaps down the middle of the Wakefield defence, it was often Fox who provided the pass or took the ball wide into the stretched Trinity cover and allowed Roger Millward to work his magic."

The final had been a tough game and Rovers suffered as a consequence. Bernard Watson broke a thumb and Clive Sullivan suffered a back injury which put him out of the next five games, while Roger Millward lost a tooth. Neil, naturally enough, was delighted to be once more in a trophy-winning team. Geoff Cudworth wrote in the *Wakefield Express:* "Neil said he thought Rovers were lucky over one of their tries. At the same time, he recalled one or two missed scoring chances in the first half. His...Yorkshire Cup-winning medal was of very special significance, he added, partly as an answer to some of his critics at Belle Vue but more importantly as a vindication of the faith invested in him by the

Rovers' board. 'I wanted to be on the winning side as much as any time in my playing career', said Neil."

Four days after winning the Yorkshire Cup, Rovers took another notable First Division scalp. Wigan came to Craven Park in the BBC2 Floodlit Trophy first-round and quickly took a 10-2 lead. By half-time Rovers trailed 10-4, Neil having landed two penalties. The second half was all Rovers, however. Tries by Dunn and Kirkpatrick brought them level at 10-10 with 11 minutes remaining. With five minutes to go Kirkpatrick scored again, Neil converting. In the last minute Neil swept through after receiving a reverse pass from Heslop to score the final try, added the conversion and Rovers had won 20-10. The forwards had been brilliant, John Saxton writing, "Behind it all, again, was the incomparable Neil Fox, providing that link between the pack and the half-backs."

Rovers faced another potentially tough encounter on 3 November, when they went to Division Two leaders Huddersfield. It proved no contest really, as they hauled themselves back into the promotion race with a convincing 29-8 victory and looked several classes better than the Fartowners. Neil kicked four goals. He added another four the following week at York, where Rovers knocked another First Division side out of the John Player Trophy with a resounding 26-12 triumph. Neil, Cliff Wallis and Roger Millward were in scintillating form and Ged Dunn ran in three tries. Batley were hammered 47-0 at Craven Park on Sunday, 17 November, Neil grabbing 11 points before retiring at half-time. The following Saturday Rovers went to Leigh with Neil being rested and due to act as a substitute. However, Watson and Kirkpatrick failed to turn up by kick-off time and Neil found himself on the left wing for the first half. Leigh took a 5-0 lead on 32 minutes, when Neil's lack of pace was exploited. Just before the interval, however, quick Rovers handling got Neil over in the corner and his prodigious conversion levelled the scores at 5-5. Rovers ran away with the second half to win 23-5, leapt over Leigh in the table and took over on points average at the top of the league, ahead of Huddersfield and Whitehaven, all three clubs having won seven of their 10 fixtures.

A sizzling second-round Floodlit Trophy match at Halifax was Rovers' next triumph. Cliff Wallis was sent off in the 56th minute at which point Rovers were 24-17 down and looking as if they were about to depart from the tournament. Eleven points in the last 11 minutes, however, brought Rovers a seventh consecutive win, 28-24, to take them into their second semi-final of the season. John Sexton singled out Neil's performance: "Once again, it was a team effort that won the day, but for me Fox was the outstanding player. Although he landed two goals from eight attempts – mostly from the touchline – his play in the loose was superb and his tackling first-class."

Returning to league fare Rovers entertained Blackpool on Sunday, 1 December, giving a debut to prop Steve Lyons, a former colleague of Neil at Wakefield. Steve had returned home from his stint with the Brisbane Souths club and Rovers had paid a hefty £4,500 transfer fee for his services. In view of their imminent Floodlit Trophy semi-final at Salford two days later, Rovers took the precaution of substituting Neil and Roger Millward at half-time, when they led 24-3, finally winning 32-16.

Salford, second in the First Division and current holders of the Championship, would have been a hard enough nut to crack under any circumstances but Rovers must have sensed it was not going to be their night. First Roger Millward withdrew with an ankle injury and then the team coach broke down en route on the motorway. When they did get on the pitch Rovers simply failed to deliver and went down 27-10. Salford winger Keith Fielding terrorised them with four tries and John Sexton remarked, "Only Joe Brown and Neil Fox, who worked really hard, defended consistently well".

Within four days Rovers had another crack at Salford, this time at Craven Park in the third round of the John Player Trophy. This game was entirely different from the previous clash. Rovers swept Salford aside in the first half and raced to a 17-2 lead, Neil kicking four goals. The real stars of the show, however, were the Robins half-backs Steve Hartley and Millward, the latter putting on a performance of near genius. Salford monopolised possession in the second half but were fortunate to come as close to Rovers as a final score of 25-17. Second Division Rovers had thus qualified for their third semi-final of the campaign and Neil's move to Humberside was looking ever more fortuitous.

Although no-one was in any doubt that Rovers on song were the outstanding team in the Second Division, a real dogfight had begun to develop for the leading positions. Rovers went to Oldham on 15 December, became mired in an ankle-deep morass of a pitch and went down 15-6. Oldham consequently moved to the top of the table and Rovers, with a couple of games in hand, were now fifth, all five of the top teams having lost four games. Neil failed to score for the first time in his career with Rovers, having so far piled up 68 goals, five tries and 151 points in 24 appearances.

Boxing Day brought Hull to Craven Park and the ground's and the Second Division's biggest crowd of the season so far – 5,395. On form Rovers were sure to win, Hull languishing fifth from bottom and without an away win to their credit. But Humberside derbies were notoriously unpredictable, as everyone knew. No-one had shown the Airlie Birds the script and with quarter of an hour to go they led 12-11. They had led 5-0 within minutes of the kick-off but Neil had remedied matters by scorning a kickable penalty and instead performing his party piece by forcing himself over for a try at the corner. Neil recalls, "I fooled the Hull players who were not really paying attention. Fred Lindop awarded a penalty to us wide on the Hull '25'. Fred came over to me and asked, 'What are you doing?' I pointed up in the air but said, 'I'm taking a tap'. So he said, 'Get on with it then'. But the Hull players had seen my hand go up and turned their backs. I tapped the ball, picked up and scored in the corner. Fred pointed for the try and nearly all the Hull players complained, because they said I was going for goal. But Fred told them from the start he had been told I was taking a tap. The Hull players would have learned a lesson – never turn your backs in such a situation." Neil magnified their misery by landing the touchline conversion and by half-time had added three penalties to give his side an 11-9 advantage. There had been little flow to the game as Lindop issued 24 first-half penalties and another 13 after the break. Winger Howard Firth gave Hull a late lead with a try but in the end tries from Rose on 65 minutes and Hall on 78 sealed a 19-12 victory, Neil converting the last try to bring his tally to 13 points.

Neil was rested for the return at the Boulevard on New Year's Day, when a crowd of 6,752, saw Rovers establish a 10-0 interval lead, only to settle for a 10-10 draw in the face of a sterling fightback by Hull, the first drawn Hull derby in a competitive match since 1950.

The day after the Hull game, Rovers went to Cleveleys on the west coast for a couple of days to prepare for their John Player Trophy semi-final against a redoubtable Widnes at Naughton Park. Rovers were now used to giant-killing acts and half-time arrived with the teams locked at 6-6, no goals having been kicked. Neil had struck the post in the dying seconds of the half attempting to convert Steve Hartley's try at the corner. Five minutes after half-time Chris Anderson scored a try to give Widnes the lead but three minutes later Millward backed up Rose to score and Neil added the match's first goal, giving Rovers an 11-9 lead. Ray Dutton levelled the scores with a penalty on 54 minutes but around the hour mark Rovers again took the lead, when Millward shot down the blind side of a scrum to feed Watson who put Sullivan over at the flag. Neil's conversion was wide and with only eight minutes remaining, Widnes snatched the game when Reg Bowden scored under the posts for Dutton to convert.

Rovers' status as a team of First Division class playing in the Second Division was enhanced when Roger Millward, now operating at scrum-half, was selected as captain of the England team to play France in Perpignan on 19 January and there was also a debut for prop John Millington. Hull KR were still keen to improve their playing strength though and signed hooker Clive Dickinson from Castleford for £1,500 and welcomed back their former Great Britain centre or winger Alan Burwell, who had left Rovers to play for Canterbury-Bankstown in Sydney five years earlier. Burwell had played on the wing outside Neil in four tests against France in 1968 and 1969. One player to leave Craven Park, however, was scrum-half Terry Hudson, who moved to Wakefield.

Dickinson made his debut in a 24-13 home win over Huyton on 19 January, when David Hall scored three excellent tries. It was Glyn Turner, a trialist scrum-half from Ebbw Vale, however, who made the biggest impression on Rovers supporters and he was soon signed, though with a view to him eventually taking the stand-off spot. Another signing for the future was 17 year-old English Schools centre or loose-forward Mike Smith.

Rovers completed a league double over New Hunslet, who had given them a stern struggle at Elland Road but were crushed 56-5 at Craven Park, when Ged Dunn scored six tries and Clive Sullivan three. On 8 February, Rovers went to play the amateurs Dewsbury Celtic at Batley in the first round of the Challenge Cup. Rovers did what was necessary in winning 31-15 but Celtic put up a good show, although Millington and Celtic's 22 stone prop Trevor 'The Tank' Walker were sent off for fighting at a second-half scrum. Neil ran 30 yards for a try after scooping up a loose ball and kicked five goals.

On Sunday, 16 February, Rovers had a vital appointment with Huddersfield at Craven Park. The Fartowners were league leaders and seven points ahead of Rovers, who had three games in hand. Although Rovers were unquestionably going to win one of the four promotion positions, they also wanted to go up as champions so a win was a necessity. Neil was making the 700th appearance of his career (including 15 as a substitute) and began in inimitable style. He scored nine points in the first 13 minutes, forcing his way over from a few yards for a try, kicking the conversion and adding two penalties. With the score at 9-2 Huddersfield prop Ian van Bellen was sent off in the 29th-minute for fouling Roger Millward, when he did not have the ball. Rovers took full advantage to run out 28-2 winners, Neil producing 13 points.

Big games seemed to occur every week for Rovers now and the following Sunday they hosted Workington Town in the second round of the Challenge Cup before 7,087 spectators – Craven Park's biggest crowd of the season. Arthur Bunting had taken his team to Bridlington for a couple of days' preparation and it seemed to work. Town presented a formidable physical challenge, their main focus apparently to get rid of Roger Millward. Roger eventually limped off near the end to a standing ovation. Rovers led 7-2 at the break, Neil booting two penalties, one from 40 yards, to add to a 32nd-minute try by David Hall. He landed a third penalty in the 55th minute and eight minutes later improved a super try by Clive Sullivan near the corner to make the score 14-2. Sullivan capitalised on great play by Millward for a second try after 71 minutes before Town gained a consolation converted try. Neil had the last word, however, with his fifth goal, a penalty in injury time. Five minutes from time Paul Rose was sent off along with Town prop Ralph Calvin.

The quality of Rovers' side was shown two days after the Challenge Cup tie when Roger Millward and Ged Dunn played for England against Wales, while Glyn Turner represented Wales. Rovers' next fixture was a 28-14 home win against promotion rivals Swinton. The highlight was a magnificent 80-yard combined movement, which ended in a score for Millward. Neil "was again the perfect link, as well as picking up his now customary try", according to John Sexton. His five goals took him past the century mark for the season.

The third round of the Challenge Cup took Neil back to Belle Vue, where it was like the good old days with 14,514 crowding the terraces and stands. Wakefield Trinity proved the Robins' nemesis on this occasion, winning 27-10. Rovers put up tremendous resistance, however. They were level at 7-7 after 32 minutes, Neil potting a couple of penalties and Ged Dunn racing 60 yards to equal the club's post-war try-scoring record with his 34th of the season. With 20 minutes remaining they trailed just 12-10 and were looking likely to snatch yet another improbable win, even though they had been shorn of Roger Millward's presence from the 25th to the 62nd minute. He had suffered a badly cut eyebrow. Trinity generated 15 unanswered points in the last quarter to give the score a totally misleading impression of the run of play.

The run-in to the end of the league programme began on 12 March with a comprehensive 29-7 rout of Leigh. Neil kicked brilliantly to land seven goals from eight shots. Nine days later Rovers smashed bottom-of-the-league Doncaster 45-12 at Craven Park and Neil was in top form with a try and six goals. Ged Dunn's brace of tries gave him 36 for the season - a new post-war record, surpassing Chris Young's 34 in 1966-67.

On Good Friday, 28 March, Hull KR went to Barrow seeking the win which would ensure promotion. It was the popular Bob Smithies's last game for the Robins before he returned home to Australia to play for Dapto. Neil kicked Rovers into a 2-0 lead after a couple of minutes but Barrow were leading 7-5 when the first half entered its final moments. At that crucial point Neil outwitted the Barrow defence with a couple of mesmerising dummies allowing second-row forward Mike Hughes to put Steve Hartley over for a try to give his team an 8-7 advantage. In the second half, with Clive Dickinson taking 80 per cent possession in the scrums and props Millington and Lyons terrorising the home defence, Rovers stretched away to win 24-10. Smithies scored the last Rovers try - an appropriate going-away present - as promotion was sealed.

On Easter Tuesday, 1 April, Rovers swamped Batley 43-2 at Mount Pleasant. There were hat-tricks for half-backs Millward and Hartley and a last-minute try on a plate from Millward for Dunn, allowing him to equal Gilbert Austin's club record of 37 tries. Neil contributed six place goals and the first one-point drop-goal of his career, which he landed early in the second half to stretch Rovers' lead to 9-2 before an avalanche of attacking play crushed the Gallant Youths.

Rovers now had three games left to play and victory in all of them would give them the Second Division Championship – a solitary point more than Huddersfield. Neil had targets too. Rovers' points-in-a-season record was 290, achieved by Cyril Kellett twice – in 1962-63 and 1966-67. Cyril also held the goals-in-a-season record with 145 in 1966-67. Neil had amassed 126 goals and 11 tries for a total of 284 points so far. Kellett's points record was an almost certain casualty but the goals record would be a tough mark to reach, even if Rovers played a few extra games in the end-of-season Premiership play-offs.

On 6 April Rovers travelled to Workington Town, where they had never won a league fixture. When the 80 minutes were up, nothing had changed. Town, with only pride and winning pay to play for, gave their best performance of the season to win 16-7. Neil kicked penalties in the 20th and 44th minutes and was substituted with nine minutes to play, when Rovers were 11-4 in arrears. The *Hull Daily Mail* lamented, "Key men Roger Millward, Neil Fox and Joe Brown were all off form together, and provided little or no leadership for the rest", as Rovers' hopes of the title disintegrated. It was the Robins' first league defeat since they lost at Oldham on 15 December, a run of 11 games.

A week later it was all smiles again. Rovers turned on a devastating performance at home against Barrow to win 42-15. Roger Millward received the club's player-of-the-year award before scoring a hat-trick, Ged Dunn broke Gilbert Austin's try-scoring record which had stood since 1924-25 with his 38th and 39th tries of the season and Neil passed Cyril Kellett's record 290 points in a season. Although he came off with quarter of an hour remaining, Neil had extended his new club record to 299 points, having passed Kellett's mark with the first of four goals, after converting a 16th-minute try by Roy Holdstock. Neil's try in the 37th minute came from one of his bewildering dummying runs.

Rovers' final league fixture took them to Whitehaven, another ground where they had never won. That ghost was laid with a hard-fought 15-7 victory, all the points being scored in the first half. Neil and Roger Millward were the dominant figures. Millward scored the first try after 15 minutes and Neil's conversion took him past the 300 points mark. John Sexton reported, "After 24 minutes, Fox dummied beautifully to split Whitehaven's defence and, although he appeared to lose the chance by dummying again when he should have put Millward over, he managed to get in his pass to Dickinson, who charged over. Fox again added the goal. Then, with five minutes to go to the break, Lyons changed the direction of the attack, Millward fed Fox and, in a curving run, he showed deceptive pace to race through to the corner, adding a superb touchline goal to make it 15-2."

At the close of the league fixtures the Second Division's top four, who all gained promotion, had the following records:

	P	W	D	L	Pts	For	Agst
Huddersfield	26	21	0	5	42	489	213
Hull Kingston Rovers	26	20	1	5	41	628	249
Oldham	26	19	0	7	38	406	223
Swinton	26	17	1	8	35	399	254

Rovers' season was not ended, however. The RFL had introduced a new competition, the Premiership Trophy. While St Helens had topped the First Division and were awarded the old Championship Cup, the Premiership was a new knock-out competition contested by the top 12 First Division clubs and the top four from the Second Division. Bizarrely for rugby league's end-of-season competition, the draw was random, as in normal cup competitions. Consequently, Rovers found themselves with the chance to prove who really was the best team in Division 2 with a fixture at Huddersfield.

At Fartown on 27 April Huddersfield received their trophy for winning the division prior to kick-off, but it was Rovers who left the field smiling after winning 35-18. To be fair, Huddersfield had not played since Easter and were short of several leading players. Even so, Rovers put on a wonderful display and Neil was in particularly sharp form before he was substituted with the score at 27-5. He had kicked Rovers into a 4-0 lead by the 14th minute and went on to add another four goals and a blockbusting try in the second half, when he went clean through two tacklers to score under the posts. A minute after Neil left the field, Steve Lyons and Fartown hooker Tony Miller were sent off and Huddersfield were able to make the scoreline somewhat more respectable.

Fortune and the luck of the draw favoured Rovers in the second round which brought a weakened Keighley – 10th in the First Division - to Craven Park. Rovers won 29-10, John Sexton describing it as "a bloodless victory". Keighley did not score until the 79th minute.

By half-time Rovers led 15-0, Neil converting all three of their tries. He converted their fourth early in the second half, which brought him level with Cyril Kellett's record of 145 goals but frustratingly missed three further conversions and saw a 70th-minute penalty attempt strike the post and bounce out. Glyn Turner grabbed a hat-trick and Ged Dunn extended his club try-scoring record to 42 with two more touchdowns.

Almost unbelievably, Rovers found themselves in the semi-final draw with the First Division's top three – St Helens, Wigan and Leeds. They were rewarded with a trip to Headingley, where no side had beaten Leeds during the season. The game took place on Sunday, 4 May – Neil's 36th birthday. Raymond Fletcher in the *Yorkshire Post* was captivated by the encounter, reporting: "When rugby league is played as it was at Headingley yesterday it is difficult to imagine any other sport packing as many thrills and spills into one game... The intention of both teams seemed to be to run the other off the field. The result was no tame exhibition but rugby played at breakneck speed. Defences were frequently disorganised, yet there was never any likelihood of a high-scoring spree because of countless last-ditch tackles. Only a perfectionist would want to find fault with either performance."

Rovers were still firmly in the game with 13 minutes left, just 13-8 down. Leeds had an 8-3 advantage at the break, having scored tries through Les Dyl and Alan Smith, one of which was converted from the touchline by John Holmes. Rovers had replied with a beautiful try from Millward after great work by Lyons. Neil could not convert, however, and also failed with a penalty. He had made his presence felt, though, with a tremendous 40-yard break and some exquisite ball-handling. In the 49th minute Neil booted a penalty to make the score 8-5 and in so doing passed Cyril Kellett's club record with his 146th goal of the campaign. Mel Mason stretched Leeds's advantage with a converted try to 13-5 but Rovers were not done. Dickinson won the ball at a scrum and Millward, Hall and Smith combined sweetly to send Sullivan over at the corner for his 28th try of the season for Rovers. Five points down, Rovers seemed to have a legitimate claim for a try ruled out by referee Vince Moss, when Dunn swept downfield, kicked ahead and was blatantly obstructed by Holmes. The Leeds full-back rubbed salt in the Robins' wounds by kicking a simple penalty in the 67th minute and a Ray Batten try sealed an 18-8 victory for Leeds.

It had been a magnificent season for Rovers. Neil had helped them to the Yorkshire Cup, to promotion and the semi-finals of the BBC2 Floodlit Trophy, the John Player Trophy and the Premiership Trophy. Rovers had scored more points than anyone else in the Second Division and in all competitive games had piled up 1,001 points, a tally never before achieved by the club. Neil's form had belied his age and the predictions of his detractors. He had smashed two club records and had finished the season as the league's leading goal-kicker with 146 and its leading points scorer with 333, completing the double he had achieved in 1959-60 and 1961-62. He also topped the points-scorers in 1963-64.

Anyone would think he should take a rest...

Hull Kingston Rovers 1974-75

Hull Kingston Rovers finished 2nd in Division 2: P26, W20, L5, D1, For 628, Against 249
Fox scored 14 tries, 145 goals, 1 drop goal, 333 points for Hull KR

Date	Opponent	Score	Fox	Crowd	
25 Aug	Doncaster	33-3	6G	588	
30 Aug	**Batley**	16-0	G	3,151	YC1
4 Sep	**Bramley**	23-10	4G	3,086	YC2
6 Sep	**Workington T**	15-8	T, 6G	2,286	
10 Sep	Oldham	7-8	2G	1,081	FT Prel, 1st leg
15 Sep	Huyton	20-21	4G	290	
17 Sep	**Oldham**	19-11	2G	2,752	FT Prel, 2nd leg
20 Sep	**Oldham**	17-8	4G	1,933	
24 Sep	Bradford N	16-16	T, 2G	2,942	YC semi
29 Sep	Rochdale H	16-12	dnp	1,813	PT1
2 Oct	**Bradford N**	5-3	G	4,047	YC semi Replay
6 Oct	Blackpool B	15-14	3G	258	
11 Oct	**Whitehaven**	5-10	G	1,892	
20 Oct	Swinton	6-14	G	987	
26 Oct	Wakefield T	16-13	2G	5,639	YC Final (at Leeds)
30 Oct	**Wigan**	20-10	T, 4G	2,009	FT1
3 Nov	Huddersfield	29-8	4G	1,729	
10 Nov	York	26-12	4G	3,299	PT2
17 Nov	**Batley**	47-0	T, 4G	2,478	
23 Nov	Leigh	23-5	T, G	912	
26 Nov	Halifax	28-24	2G	752	FT2
1 Dec	**Blackpool B**	32-16	3G	2,911	
3 Dec	Salford	10-27	2G	3,727	FT semi
7 Dec	**Salford**	25-17	5G	3,927	PT3
15 Dec	Oldham	6-15		1,690	
26 Dec	**Hull**	19-12	T, 5G	5,395	
1 Jan	Hull	10-10	dnp	6,752	
4 Jan	Widnes	14-16	G	3,624	PT semi
19 Jan	**Huyton**	24-13	2G	2,846	
26 Jan	New Hunslet	10-2	2G	909	
2 Feb	**New Hunslet**	56-5	T, 3G	3,838	
8 Feb	Dewsbury Celtic	31-15	T, 5G	1,937	Ch Cup 1 (at Batley)
16 Feb	**Huddersfield**	28-2	T, 5G	4,829	
23 Feb	**Workington T**	19-7	5G	7,087	Ch Cup 2
2 Mar	**Swinton**	28-14	T, 5G	4,818	
9 Mar	Wakefield T	10-27	2G	14,514	Ch Cup 3
12 Mar	**Leigh**	29-7	7G	2,586	
21 Mar	**Doncaster**	45-12	T, 6G	2,574	
28 Mar	Barrow	24-10	3G	1,136	
1 Apr	Batley	43-2	6G, DG	439	
6 Apr	Workington T	7-16	2G	483	
13 Apr	**Barrow**	42-15	T, 4G	3,365	
18 Apr	Whitehaven	15-7	T, 3G	593	
27 Apr	Huddersfield	35-18	T, 6G	2,924	Prem 1
30 Apr	**Keighley**	29-10	4G	4,861	Prem 2
4 May	Leeds	8-18	G	7,448	Prem semi

24. 1975: Showing the Kiwis

Instead of resting like most of his fellow players in the close season of 1975, Neil took an opportunity to play on the other side of the globe. He recalls: "I got a call from Bernie Wood, the secretary of the Wellington League, asking if I was interested in going to New Zealand to do some playing and coaching. I told him it might be possible but would have to talk it over with Molly first. We discussed it and I asked Jack Pearson, the turf accountant for whom I worked at the time, if he would give me some time off – about 10 weeks. Straightaway Jack said yes and that it would be good experience for me. Our only problem was that Mandy, who was 12, and Jonathan, who was 10, did not want to go. That looked like stopping Molly and me from going until Molly's parents said they would stay at our house and look after the children if we really wanted to go. So it was settled and the two of us were off to New Zealand.

When Bernie rang back later, he was over the moon that we were coming to Wellington, especially because I had missed out 12 months earlier due to my shoulder injury. But I told him he would have to wait until Rovers had finished their season, which meant we did not leave until early May.

We were met at the airport by Wellington Rugby League officials and officials from the Marist club, who were paying part of my expenses. I was to play for them and the Wellington representative team. The coach at Marist was the former Kiwi hooker Colin O'Neil. Bernie took us to his house, where we stayed for the first week, so that we could settle in and get our bearings. It had been Molly's first long-haul flight and we were both really tired. So it was a bit of a surprise when one of the Wellington officials who was chairman of the St George's club said he would like to pick us up and take us to a presentation to Phil Orchard, a winger who had been selected for the 1975 World Championship squad. We went but after a couple of hours we were shattered and got a lift back to Bernie's to finally get some sleep."

The next afternoon Marist played Petone, the current Air New Zealand Championship holders, at the aptly named Rugby League Park. Neil did not play but witnessed the game from the stand and was introduced to the players by Colin O'Neil. The local paper, the *Evening Post,* ran the headline "Was his trip really necessary?" after Marist's smashing 27-11 victory. The report began, "Marist played such driving and tactical rugby league on Saturday that there was more than one joke going round about sending Neil Fox home... On the sideline watching and weighing up his future team-mates was Neil Fox... Fox was highly elated with what he saw, and was the first to tell the team: 'I might as well pack my bags – you don't need me'."

It was a good victory, but Neil was not, in reality, wholly convinced. He recalls: "During the match Molly whispered to me, 'Do you know what you have let yourself in for?' She was referring to the way the team played. They were trying to prove who were the toughest. They were playing one-up rugby, not letting the ball do the work. I told her, 'Don't worry. I can look after myself, as I have done for nearly the last 20 years in England. They will play the way I want them to play'. That meant a more attractive game, keeping the ball moving and not just knocking hell out of the other team."

In a press interview Neil said he believed there was insufficient variety in New Zealand rugby league. He told the interviewer that there was plenty of good raw material, but the young players were not being taught to maximise their abilities. He said, "Your forwards – like the Australians – run full tilt into the tackler and almost always die with the ball... Why charge a brick wall when there is a gate to go through?... English teams are constantly trying something new, particularly set moves, to break through the defence. I want to see my team here moving the ball away from the immediate vicinity of the play-the-ball much more frequently." He was not impressed either with the amount of rough play in Wellington, commenting: "Last weekend I saw more stiff-arm tackles, elbows, fists and off-the-ball niggling than in two whole seasons in Britain... At present good players are hanging back to avoid a bit of stick. Remove that fear and they will be able to produce the higher quality football the public pays to see."

The press were interested in Neil's profession, the *Evening Post's* rugby league article for 10 May declaring, "Legal Bookmaker Will Play Here". Betting was illegal in New Zealand, except in government-sanctioned turf accountancies. However, Neil was in Wellington for the rugby. He recalls, "Training was two nights a week and Colin left the footballing side to me. I brought in a few moves we used at Hull KR but only a couple at a time. After three or four weeks we could put the moves on at any given time and we looked good compared to some of the other teams who were still playing one-up rugby.

The Marist club was a very close family-type club. Everyone made us welcome from day one. After every match it was back to the local hotel, which was the club's headquarters. The guitars came out and everyone sang. That was the first time Molly had ever seen people ordering big jugs of beer, which was how New Zealanders drank – communally.

Marist had several up and coming players and I was pleased I was able to help in raising their playing to higher and representative levels. The Henry brothers, Whetu and Whare, were both picked for the Kiwis in 1977. Both played in the pack and were good with the ball. Paul Te Ariki was another of our forwards who played for New Zealand and toured Europe in 1980. Then there was the veteran prop Roy Roberts, who had played with Auckland and Manawatu before joining Marist. He must have been at least 39 when I played with him. The work he did in and out of the scrums though was unbelievable. Roy never looked fit but always did the work of two men."

The Wellington Championship was contested by eight teams – Marist, Miramar, Petone, Porirua City, Randwick, St George, Upper Hutt and Waterside. All the teams played each other three times in the Championship. In 2005 Bernie Wood remembered: "The game in Wellington has always had a large Maori participation and nowadays a very large Polynesian player base including Maori, Samoan, Tongan, Tokelau and Rarotongan... In the competition were a number of current, past and future Kiwis, Bill Harrison, Gary Woollard, Eric Carson, Phillip Orchard, Nolan Tupaea, Kevin Tamati, Don Munro, Peter Mellars and John Whittaker. So the games were truly competitive in the main... It would be fair to say that when Neil arrived he found a game here in Wellington very confrontational, lacking the best skills the game offered. Players tended to run at each other, rather than into gaps. Neil concentrated on getting players to run on to the ball and into gaps. It is noteworthy that three of his Marist club-mates became Kiwis not long after. They became top players because of Neil's influence." He added: "Neil and Molly endeared themselves to the entire rugby league community in Wellington, so much so that they are still very fondly remembered by a host of people and former players."

Neil agrees that there were some fine players in the competition, recalling: "St George had Phil Orchard and Eric Carson. I think Phil still holds the Kiwi record for tries on a tour and it was a shame that he packed in playing at 30 due to injury. Eric was the brains of the St George side – a very good footballer. He and his wife Claire became great friends to us during our stay in the city and we still keep in touch. Eric used to supply Molly and me with meat from the butcher's shop he managed. Alongside Eric was Nolan Tupaea, a stand-off with electrifying pace, who was a New Zealand tourist in 1980. Porirua had Don Munro, a strong runner who scored plenty of tries and made the 1975 World Championship squad. Randwick had John Whittaker, the test full-back, a very skilful player and a great attacking force. At Waterside there was Ron Farrell, a good pack leader and fine distributor. He was very unlucky in not gaining international honours but he played for Wellington more than 80 times - a record. Petone had a good team but one player who shone with his work rate was a young bloke called Kevin Tamati. You could see from the start what a great player Kevin was going to be. He played in more than 20 tests and had a successful career with Widnes and Warrington."

Neil made his debut for Marist - known as the 'Greens' - on Saturday 17 May. The *Evening News* ran the headline "Fox boots Marist to glory in league clash" and observed, "Fox kicked and played well as the much improved Marist side survived a strong rally by Randwick in the third quarter to win 32-18 at Rugby League Park". Neil landed five goals and Marist jumped to joint top of the league with Waterside. However, the unnamed correspondent was more impressed by Neil's leadership qualities, shrewdness and ability to keep the ball on the move.

Neil did not get much rest because the following day he was in the Pakehas (white men) XIII against the Wellington Maoris at Natone Park, Porirua. The Pakehas had not beaten the Maoris for 14 years, but Neil got them off to a flying start when he intercepted a wayward pass after only 30 seconds before rushing 30 yards to score near the corner flag. By half-time, however, the Maoris led 13-5, Neil having added a penalty goal. The second half saw him convert one of his side's two added tries but the Maoris ran away with the game 38-13.

On 24 May, Marist came a cropper against Waterside, going down 19-5. Neil converted his side's try but his pack was overwhelmed. A week later, on Sunday, 1 June, there was a return to form with a hard earned 16-13 win against Upper Hutt at Whakatiki Street, when Neil bagged the opening try and landed two conversions. The following day Neil made his debut for Wellington (the Lions) against Canterbury in the National Provincial Competition in Christchurch. At one stage Wellington led 13-9 but crumbled to a 50-23 defeat. A young second-rower, Mark Broadhurst was the star of the match. He went on to become one of the greatest front-rowers in New Zealand history and an icon at Hull KR.

Neil kicked four goals for Wellington, but he was not enamoured of Wellington's way of operating. He says: "The problem with the Wellington representative team was our inability to play the likes of Orchard, Munro and Whittaker because of their World Championship commitments. When the team was picked, players did not want to play. They were talked out of playing by their club coaches and the League would allow them to play for their clubs. It was completely different to what happened back in England.

The Wellington coach was Bud Lisle, but while I was there he let me do the coaching. Bud also coached the New Zealand Students and was a real workaholic for rugby league. He had played for St George, helping them to six championships, and played for Wellington from 1953 to 1963. He did a phenomenal amount of work as a coach and selector for all sorts of teams. Molly and I got on well with Bud and his wife Ruth. He is another we keep in touch with."

Bud Lisle has fond memories of Neil, whom he describes as "a highly respected ambassador of our great game". He says, "During that period I was the Wellington representative team selector and coach. I believe we were very fortunate to have Neil playing for us and for him to be able to assist me. As we say, you never stop learning during your life and I was grateful for the advice and tips he shared with me. His Wellington team-mates all enjoyed playing beside Neil... Players and administrators both had a high regard and respect for Neil and Molly... Neil may have been near the end of his outstanding career, but the experience he brought, along with his many skills, including ball skills, distribution, positional play, direction and kicking, was a huge asset to our side and rubbed off on our players."

On 7 June, Neil did not play in Marist's 46-18 rout of winless, bottom-of-the-league Miramar, but he was back the next Saturday for a tougher encounter with Porirua City at Rugby League Park in dreadful conditions. Neil converted two tries in a 13-2 win which kept his side in second place behind Waterside. The *Evening Post* noted: "It was [Fox's] clever link work and tactics that gave Marist the winning edge in a match that never really got going as the wind and rain lashed the players."

On Wednesday 18 June, Neil had the unexpected experience of captaining Wellington against Wales, who were in New Zealand competing in the World Championship. It was their first game in New Zealand and there were about 2,000 fans at the Basin Reserve ground hoping for a Wellington victory. However, it was no contest. By half-time Wales led 21-0 and finished up 52-8 victors. At times the game was ugly, one brawl just before the break lasting a full minute. Wellington lost the scrums 14-5, but had the advantage of a 26-11 penalty count. Neil converted a try by Whare Henry, made by Neil and Eric Carson, while Ron Farrell, equalling Colin O'Neil's record of 74 appearances for Wellington, scored their other try.

Three days later there was more disappointment for Neil when St George beat Marist 9-5 at Natone Park, Neil converting his own try. However, on Sunday, 29 June, at the same venue he was much happier. Wellington obliterated Taranaki 51-14. Neil landed nine goals from 12 attempts and *The Dominion* reported: "In the forwards, former English international Neil Fox and experienced John Hona and Ron Farrell got excellent support from the Henry brothers and Bill Smith... Just before half-time Fox began a brilliant move and the Wellington forwards took the ball 50 metres upfield for Whetu Henry to crash across". Although Taranaki were annihilated, Neil recalls, "They had a star forward – Graham West, who later played for and coached Wigan. He was all over the field, tackling and backing up in open play. Anyone could see he was a great player in the making."

The following week Neil failed to land a last-minute, 45-yard penalty, as Wellington lost 20-19 to Northland at Whangarei. He had landed a couple of goals in the first 10 minutes, when Wellington led 13-0, but by half-time the lead had been cut to 16-8. A bumper crowd of around 3,000 watched in perfect conditions, but they were watching Neil's fourth and last appearance for the Lions.

There were, however, still club games for Marist to negotiate. Neil missed a 23-23 draw with Randwick the day after the Northland fixture but returned to the fray on 12 July, when the Greens overran table-toppers Waterside 25-11. Neil turned in a towering performance to claim 13 of their points, through a try, three conversions, a penalty and two late drop-goals. It was a great victory because Marist were so severely hit by injuries that Colin O'Neil was forced out of retirement to play. Neil's try came from one of Colin's passes and he had "easily his best match in Wellington", according to the *Evening Post*.

On Wednesday 16 July, a crunch game against Petone at the Hutt Recreation Ground seemed to be going Marist's way. Marist established a 6-0 lead after half an hour, thanks to a try by winger Reg Christian and a penalty and a drop-goal from Neil. By the break, however, Petone led 8-6 and dominated the second half to win 18-11, although Neil booted a penalty in the second half. The Championship was a real dog-fight at this stage with Waterside leading on 21 points from 15 games, Marist and Petone on 19 points (both from 14), Porirua City on 18 and Randwick on 18 (both from 15).

Neil played his last game for Marist on 19 July against Upper Hutt. The *Evening Post* reported: "Marist had a battle on their hands – against an inspired Upper Hutt side – but were too good and went on to give Neil Fox a farewell gift of a 34-23 win." Neil contributed a try and five conversions, as the Greens held on to their second place in the table with four more games to play.

During his time in Wellington Neil had found a part-time job with the New Zealand Post Office checking television licences. Neil was being paid for his services as player-coach, but all rugby league in New Zealand was strictly amateur under normal circumstances. He recalls: "They gave me a car and I went to different areas armed with a computer sheet of houses where I had to call. If the television set was rented the hire firm paid the licence fee. Otherwise, the owner had to pay. On one of my calls in a suburb called Titahi Bay, I rang the bell and couldn't believe it when Reg Cooke, the New Zealand centre, came to the door. I had played against him in 1961 and 1962. We recognised each other immediately. He invited me in for a coffee and we talked for ages about the different players we had encountered and the great times we had had in rugby league. I didn't get through too much work that day!"

Another episode of New Zealand life that Neil readily recalls, but with mixed feelings, was his day trip from Wellington to the South Island to coach some university students. The day prior to the trip Neil and Molly went to a function at the school attended by Bernie Wood's children. People began to ask Molly if she was intending to go with Neil on the trip to South Island. At the same time they warned her that it could be a very rough trip by boat, which took a good couple of hours and the forecast was poor. Sensibly, Molly decided that she would rather spend the morning shopping with Trish Wood. Neil says, "I was picked up about six in the morning by the Wellington Victoria University group and we took the ferry from Wellington to Picton. At first it wasn't too bad, but then we hit rough water in the Cook Strait. Soon I was as sick as a dog. It was really awful. Somehow the captain had discovered I was on board and invited me on to the bridge. He said that eating something would help. It didn't. Bernie Wood says I left my previous night's dinner, my breakfast and lunch floating in the water. Funnily enough, once we reached Picton Sound the sea became like a mill pond and I was fine again.

However, when we got ashore I told Bud Lisle that I was not going back by sea. I expected he would arrange two flights to get back home, whatever happened. I conducted the coaching course and then the University played a game against the Marlborough representative side in Blenheim. I played for the University in the first half and then for the other side in the second half and everyone had a good time. After the match though I went straight to Bud and asked him if he had booked the flights. He said the last plane had already gone and I would have to go back on the ferry. I am not kidding, I was not happy. The University lads had a real party going home and kept offering me beer, but I said no because I knew what was likely to happen and I stayed up on the bridge with the captain. Was I happy to get off that boat."

Although Neil played for just over two months in the country, the 1975 *New Zealand Rugby League Annual* selected him as one of their five Wellington players of the year alongside his Marist club-mate Roy Roberts, Kiwi winger Don Munro of Porirua City, Waterside's prop Ron Farrell and their player-coach John Hona. The *Annual* commented, "Physical crunches are not [Fox's] forte now, which is not surprising seeing he has over 700 games of professional league behind him. But there could be no doubt that his tactical astuteness and ball distribution ability would be of immense value to any team with the ability to take advantage of his build-up work. Fox's Wellington and Marist team-mates needed quite a long time to get used to his English style of play. But by the time he left to return to Hull Kingston Rovers, Marist were beginning to cotton on and to anticipate the pass into the gap. During his stay, Fox spent some time with a number of Wellington's promising players. It will be interesting to see next year whether they are able to put some aspects of the heady Englishman's style into practice."

Neil and Molly enjoyed New Zealand. Neil sums up their stay: "Our time in Wellington was very good. The people we met couldn't do enough for us to make our stay a happy one. We met a lot of people who had emigrated there years ago and both Molly and I thought that we could have happily moved to New Zealand. We had lovely times with people like Eric and Claire Carson, Bud and Ruth Lisle and the St George club chairman, Barry Readman, who was also the Wellington team manager, and his wife, Sally. But we owe most thanks to Bernie and Trish Wood, who visit us when they come to England. Bernie was, of course, secretary of the Wellington RL but he later became a New Zealand RL Board member and for many years edited the *New Zealand Rugby League Annual*.

My only regret was not being able to take part in the play-offs for Marist, who eventually finished third and were knocked out by Waterside. It might have been different if I had stayed but we'll never know. I had arranged for a fortnight's holiday for Molly and me in Fiji. I had promised Hull KR I would be back for the new season but I needed a rest. Wellington asked me if I would come back on a full-time basis and I admit I was eager. On arriving home to Mandy and Jonathan though, we could not make up our minds. They were settled in school so we turned the chance down. If we had been younger, I think we would have settled in easily to life in New Zealand. By the way, it belted down all the first week in 'sunny' Fiji, so we cut the holiday short and returned to a heat wave in Horbury."

Neil's playing record in New Zealand

Date	Fixture	Neil Fox
17 May	Marist 32 Randwick 18	5G
18 May	Pakehas 13 Maoris 38	T, 2G
24 May	Marist 5 Waterside 19	G
1 June	Marist 16 Upper Hutt 13	T, 2G
2 June	Wellington 23 Canterbury 50	4G
14 June	Marist 13 Porirua City 2	2G
18 June	Wellington 8 Wales 52	G
21 June	Marist 5 St George 9	T, G
29 June	Wellington 51 Taranaki 14	9G
6 July	Wellington 19 Northland 20	2G
12 July	Marist 25 Waterside 11	T, 4G, 2DG
16 July	Marist 11 Petone 18	2G, DG
19 July	Marist 34 Upper Hutt 23	T, 5G

Summary:

	A	T	G	DG	P
Marist	8	4	22	3	59
Wellington	4	-	16	-	32
Pakehas	1	1	2	-	7
Totals	**13**	**5**	**40**	**3**	**98**

NB: These figures are not included in Neil's official record total of appearances, tries, goals and points. The figures are the work of Bernie Wood and differ slightly from previously given figures in the author's book *Rugby League Hall of Fame* (Tempus Publishing, 2003)

25. 1975-76: From Craven Park to Clarence Street

Neil had not been the only Hull KR player who had spent the summer in the southern hemisphere. Roger Millward and Ged Dunn had been to Australia and New Zealand with England for the World Championship and Clive Sullivan and Glyn Turner had travelled with Wales. They were all back for the start of the 1975-76 season, however. Paul Rose was still in Australia playing for Dapto, Bob Smithies' club, in New South Wales country football but there was a welcome addition in John Cunningham, who had also spent the summer in Sydney playing for Balmain. Cunningham was a second-rower, who was signed from Barrow for £8,000 and much was expected from a man who had been capped the previous season for England.

Unusually, there were no significant alterations to the laws of the game in the close season but the Premiership Trophy competition was reduced to a top-eight play-off. Rovers were quite confident that they had the firepower necessary to qualify for it.

They got off to an excellent start. Their season began with a visit to Huddersfield on Saturday 16 August, when Neil partnered Cunningham in the second-row. After taking an 11-point lead with some thoroughly enterprising rugby in the early stages, Rovers went to sleep and by half-time the score was 11-11. Neil had contributed a penalty goal, bringing his career points total to 5,500. Rovers re-established their superiority in the second half, Neil adding a couple of goals, and ran out 26-16 victors.

A week later Premiership holders Leeds were the opposition at Craven Park. Neil gave Rovers the lead on two minutes with an angled penalty after Keith Hepworth was penalised for feeding at the scrum. Within five minutes Heppy committed the same sin and Neil landed a monstrous penalty from five yards inside Leeds's half. After 10 minutes Neil strode into the Leeds attacking line on his own '25' to intercept a pass and surged 50 yards upfield. Just as he was tackled he expertly unloaded to Burwell, who raced the remaining 25 yards to score. Neil added the goal. By half-time Rovers had added further tries by Millward, improved by Neil, and Sullivan to lead 17-7. Millward's try equalled the club record of Gilbert Austin who played between 1919 and 1928, who had claimed 160. A frantic second half saw Roy Holdstock and Tony Fisher sent off for trading blows after a scrum and there was no further scoring until the 74th minute, when John Atkinson sped over for a converted try to leave Rovers sweating at 17-12. In the 80th minute Bernard Watson made the game safe with a drop-goal and in injury time Neil made doubly sure by shrugging off a tackler to score a try, which he converted to make the final score 23-12.

Neil came up against his old colleagues from Wakefield again in the first round of the Yorkshire Cup on 31 August. Trinity gave Rovers a hard time in the first half, holding them to 4-4, Neil landing penalties after 15 and 39 minutes. Five minutes into the second half, the former Trinity pair of Steve Lyons and Neil opened up the defence to send Millward skipping through for the try which broke Gilbert Austin's record. Neil converted, then kicked a penalty, made a try for Lyons and finished with seven goals, as Rovers entered the second round 26-9.

After three good victories Rovers travelled to Wigan on 6 September. They were soon 12-3 in arrears but staged a superb rally before the interval to lead 13-12, Neil converting two tries. In the second half, however, they collapsed and Wigan emerged winners by 34-13 – not a happy debut for Dick Wallace, a full-back on loan from York, who later signed for the Robins. John Cunningham, who had just been selected along with Millward for England, suffered a bad ligament injury which was to put him out for several months.

The second round of the Yorkshire Cup on Sunday 14 September, brought a better result but a hard struggle at Elland Road Greyhound Stadium, which was the home of New Hunslet. John Sexton reckoned that the pitch was 12 yards narrower than Craven Park and Rovers' expansive game was unsuited to the constrictions imposed by it. A 15-7 win was a satisfactory result, however, Neil's four goals being a major factor, as was Clive Dickinson's 22-9 success in the scrums. The semi-final pitted Rovers against Featherstone at Post Office Road on Monday, 23 September, and constituted Neil's 50th game as a Robin. His team looked home and dry at half-time, having had all the ball and establishing a 15-2 lead. Neil had landed four out of four place goals and dropped another. But Featherstone reversed the scrummaging domination in the second half and ran in four tries to set up a nail-biting finale. The Robins owed everything in the end to Neil's wonderful marksmanship, his two additional penalties giving him a 100 per cent success rate and Hull KR a nerve-shredding 19-16 victory.

Five days later Rovers had another cup tie to negotiate when Rochdale Hornets visited Craven Park in the first round of the John Player Trophy. Loose-forward Len Casey, a £6,000 transfer from Hull, made his debut for the Robins but the star of the show was Neil. The game was won 33-10, Neil landed eight out of eight shots at goal, made several tries, won the official man-of-the-match award and passed the 400 points mark in his Rovers career. Hornets cut up very rough towards the close of the game and Rovers lost Dunn with a suspected broken nose, Smith with a broken ankle and Moore with a depressed fracture of the cheekbone.

A leg strain kept Neil out of Rovers 24-13 league victory at Castleford, when Paul Rose made his return to Rovers' team after returning from Australia. On Tuesday, 7 October, Neil and Paul were partners in the second-row for Rovers' home first-round Floodlit Trophy tie against Huddersfield, who were bottom of Division 1. Neil kicked well enough, landing four goals but the whole team had an off day and Huddersfield won 12-11.

On 12 October, Rovers owed plenty to Neil's kicking prowess, as he booted six goals in a 25-10 win over Swinton at Craven Park, while the following week the *Hull Daily Mail* headline told it all: "Neil's magic boot saves sad Robins", as Bradford Northern fell 11-10 at Craven Park. Rovers just about deserved their win. Neil kicked magnificently, his five goals from six attempts, plus a Dick Wallace drop-goal, making up Rovers' 11 points.

A groin strain kept Neil out of the team at Widnes on 26 October in a 33-11 defeat. He returned for a second-round Player's No.6 Trophy game against Second Division Leigh on 7 November. Rovers struck better form to win comfortably 23-8. Neil kicked a towering 45-yard penalty on 11 minutes to edge Rovers into a 2-1 lead. Soon afterwards Turner scored the opening try at the corner. Neil's wonderful touchline conversion gave him his 2,300th career goal, while in the 36th minute his conversion of a try from Burwell was his 200th goal for Rovers. In general play Neil also impressed, John Sexton remarking, "Neil Fox showed the benefits of the rest between games, looking far sharper, and his tactical awareness brought more width to the Robins' game".

Rovers' next fixture was the Yorkshire Cup Final against Leeds on Saturday 15 November. Facing Leeds on neutral territory would have been hard enough but, as in the 1974 final, the Loiners would have home advantage, because well-appointed Headingley was the only ground acceptable to the sponsors. Both teams had injury worries, but a bombshell exploded at Craven Park five days before the final. Robins coach Arthur Bunting had resigned with immediate effect. He told the *Hull Daily Mail*, "I have done so because of constant interference from a very small minority of the board of directors. I feared that this interference, which was an urge to run the whole show, by this small section of the club, would make an always difficult job almost impossible."

This was not ideal preparation for a major final and in the meantime Rovers placed John Moore in charge of training and gave responsibility for tactics to Roger Millward. The team was taken to a Harrogate hotel for a couple of days to be in complete readiness for the final. Leeds, on the other hand, had the disadvantage of having to play against Hull in a replayed John Player Trophy tie, just as Rovers settled in at Harrogate. Hull beat them 23-11 at Headingley, which must have been a spur to Rovers and a blow to the Loiners only 48 hours before the big game.

The final began with a light drizzle falling, the floodlights on and a ghostly mist hovering around Headingley. Rovers opened brightly though and went ahead after four minutes when Burwell and Rose combined well to send Sullivan shooting over for a try in the corner. Neil missed the conversion. After 20 minutes Leeds took a 5-3 lead, John Holmes converting a well-worked try by Phil Cookson. They extended their advantage to 7-3 with a penalty from Holmes after Millward was penalised at a scrum and at the interval Rovers trailed by four points, having had more of the ball from the scrums and playing just as well as their opponents. Three minutes into the second half Neil and Paul Rose sent Sullivan careering over for another try, only for the touch judge to rule that Sullivan had started his run with a foot on the touchline, even though, as John Sexton ruefully noted, "He was the only man on the ground who thought so". It did not matter too much because within a minute Neil put his team in the lead. Taking the ball about 15 yards out, he dummied, found a gap, beat full-back David Marshall's tackle and took Leeds skipper Syd Hynes over with him for a tremendous try, which he converted to give Hull KR a one-point lead.

Leeds regained their one-point advantage in the 50th minute when Lyons was caught offside and Holmes potted a simple penalty. This gripping game continued to fluctuate as Millward popped over a drop-goal to make it 9-9 after 63 minutes. Two minutes later Leeds were penalised for offside and Neil teed up the penalty attempt just five yards inside the Loiners' half and blasted a massive kick between the posts for an 11-9 lead. Rovers entered the last five minutes looking likely winners. They only had to play sensibly and the trophy was theirs. Unfortunately for them, Leeds kept going and when Paul Rose, in possession of the ball, was penalised for pushing Graham Eccles at a play-the-ball, the resultant kick gave Leeds good field position. Leeds centre Les Dyl suddenly appeared at dummy-half as Rovers' defensive line momentarily adjusted itself. Dyl spotted a sliver of space, threw a dummy and sliced through for the match-winning try. Holmes converted and in injury time added a drop-goal to seal a 15-11 victory, which was barely deserved. Neil, appearing in his sixth Yorkshire Cup Final, was awarded the White Rose Trophy as player-of-the-match.

Rovers' next game was a third-round John Player tie against formidable Widnes at Craven Park on 23 November. It was another thriller, which Rovers again lost unluckily. Neil's kicking was stupendous. Widnes were penalised a yard inside their own half after 30 seconds and Neil's successful kick was an absolute beauty. Widnes struck back in the second minute with a converted try before Neil landed another huge penalty from 50 yards in the fourth minute. Another Widnes try on eight minutes stretched their lead to 8-4 before Neil added a third penalty after 12 minutes. On 20 minutes Bernard Watson dropped a goal which went in off a post before Neil failed narrowly with a penalty from two yards inside his own half. A penalty to Widnes and a Ged Dunn try locked the teams 10-10 before a fourth successful penalty from Neil in the 38th minute gave his side a half-time lead. The second half was a catalogue of mishaps for Rovers. Widnes full-back Ray Dutton's 45th-minute penalty levelled the scores, Glyn Turner had a try disallowed and

Millward limped off in the 51st minute before Mick Adams dropped a goal for Widnes. Neil got over, but failed to ground the ball properly and then slammed a 45-yard penalty into the wind against the post. The game looked lost when Eric Hughes scored at the corner and Dutton's superb conversion took Widnes clear at 18-12. In the 70th minute Neil's fifth penalty goal raised Rovers' spirits, but Widnes held out against a final barrage which almost engulfed them.

On 30 November the Robins got back on the winning trail with an 18-8 home victory over Keighley. Neil kicked three goals but very few people saw them because the game was played in varying thicknesses of fog throughout. Many spectators left well before the end, unable to see what was happening.

Three weeks after losing Arthur Bunting as coach, Rovers appointed their former test loose-forward Harry Poole to the post. Poole had been Rovers' skipper when they went to Wembley in 1964 and was the first Rovers coach to have full control over the team, including selection. His arrival precipitated Neil's departure. His first game in charge saw Rovers play abysmally at Warrington on 14 December, going down 23-11. No one played well for Rovers, but Neil was the sole player to lose his place for the next fixture at home to St Helens on 28 December, the now-recovered John Cunningham taking his place.

Neil recalls: "The week after the Warrington defeat, I turned up for training as usual and Harry asked me to go through our moves for Len Casey, who was still new to the team. Then he sent me to the dressing room for an early bath and I thought no more about it until I was in the car going home with Bernard Watson and George Kirkpatrick. I asked them what the team was for Sunday's game against St Helens. They told me what it was and I wasn't in the 15, not even as sub. What a shock. I remember that was the only time I ever wanted a club that I played for to lose. I couldn't believe after doing so well for Rovers that a new coach didn't have the guts or courtesy to tell me I was not playing. I drove to the game in my own car and when I got to the ground people were assuming that I was injured. Even the directors were shocked that Harry had not said anything to me. I suppose I did get my wish. Rovers lost badly to a weakened St Helens team.

I spoke to the directors and told them I would still come to training and to see what Harry would say to me. He did not say anything. So I went back to the directors and told them if he didn't want me in the team I would move on.

A week later, on New Year's Eve, I got a call from the Rovers' secretary Ron Turner telling me Harry wanted me to stand by for the game at Leeds on New Year's Day, because I might be needed if Len Casey did not recover from 'flu. I told him, 'If Harry wants me, ask him to ring. Hasn't he got the decency to talk to me? He has avoided me for the last two weeks'. He didn't ring. That week I went and picked up my gear and said goodbye to my team-mates. Harry followed me out and asked if I wanted a word with him. What do you think I said?

I had enjoyed my time at the club and got on well with the people there. I was sorry to leave, as I also got on well with the directors. The supporters were great and were really behind the team. All I wanted to do was play out the rest of the season but the coach had other ideas. With Phil Lowe due to return from Australia the following season the pack would have been very strong, including Lowe, Casey, Millington, Rose, Lyons, Cunningham and Holdstock. What ball-handler wouldn't want to play with that lot? There was a good team spirit at Rovers and a few perks. For example, the players never went short of fish because we always called at a wholesale fish merchants' shop on the docks, which belonged to one of the directors and stuffed the team coach boot full of fish. Another director was a pork wholesaler, so meat was also on our list. Then there was the time we went by coach to Cumberland. I always sat with the directors at the front of the coach because I was a poor bus traveller. Those winding roads in the Lake District always made me feel sick. I was sitting with Peter Frankland, the pork seller, and next to us was David Wilkinson, a director of a firm that manufactured caravans. A couple of the lads had bought caravans from him. All of a sudden from the back of the bus a voice piped up, 'Eh, it looks like Foxy's the next to get a caravan.' Then John Millington, the joker of the team, yelled out, 'Aye, and it looks like he'll get some pigs to pull it too.' Of course, there was uproar on the bus. Everybody fell about laughing, including the directors."

Ironically, the man Neil for whom had been dropped, John Cunningham suffered a bad injury in the St Helens defeat and did not play again that season. Irrespective of this, Rovers agreed to let Neil leave on a free transfer, thereby honouring their original agreement with him. Chairman Wilf Spaven said, "We will never be able to forget what Neil did for us. He played a big part in getting us promotion and giving us such a wonderful season. We will always be grateful for that, and if he can do the same for whatever club he goes to... then we wish him the best of luck."

Neil had certainly done well for Rovers. In 59 matches he had accumulated 470 points from 16 tries, 210 goals and two drop-goals, and had failed to score in only one game.

His next move was a little nearer home. He recalls: "A week or so after I left Hull, I got a call from my old mate Gary Cooper at York, asking me if I would help him out there. I agreed but stipulated that if I was not happy there I should be allowed to move on. Gary agreed. At York he did not have anyone who could change the direction of play. When I played with him at Wakefield, Don and I used to throw long passes to him on the blind side. He scored plenty of tries and made others for team-mates. But he couldn't get the York players to read this part of the game before I came. I remember, he had a bell with him in the trainer's box and when he saw an opening on the blind side he rang it to tell the ball-handler and the full-back that the move was on. It was that bad. No wonder he wanted me on the field to dictate play."

York were struggling in the Second Division and Neil must have thought that he had arrived at some sort of Wakefield Trinity Old Boys club. Apart from Gary Cooper, former Trinity colleagues included Dave Barends, Gary Hetherington, Geoff Clarkson, Jackie Marston, Ted Campbell, Tony Handforth and Kevin Harkin. When he arrived at Wiggington Road, or Clarence Street, as the old-timers still called York's ground, the club was running ninth in the division, having won only six of 17 games. They had lost 10 of their last 11 matches. Neil had certainly not taken an easy option.

He made his debut on Sunday 11 January, in a home game against Bramley, partnering Alan Rhodes in the second-row. In the first few minutes he landed a fine 40-yard penalty goal and after 10 minutes converted a try by centre Terry Day. York were 7-6 up at the interval but soon fell behind to a try by Bramley centre Billy Rowett. Neil brought York level with a penalty after 51 minutes and then landed another superb goal to give his new team an 11-9 lead. Another former Trinity colleague, Jack Austin put Bramley back in the lead with a try, superbly converted by full-back John Hay. Two minutes from time Australian loose-forward Peter Howlett strode over near the right corner to equalise at 14-14. Neil, who had kicked very well, failed with the conversion but at least York had taken a point.

A week later, York visited Blackpool Borough. Neil had spent the last two days in bed suffering from a severe cold but was still fit enough to hoof five goals in a sound 19-7 victory, York's first away win in more than three months. The crowd of a mere 112 souls was probably the lowest before which Neil had ever played first-class rugby league. Robert Mills in the *Yorkshire Evening Press* was satisfied with York's performance, writing, "York provided plenty of hope for the future with a much improved collective display... York's improved spirit, reflected in the dressing room as well as on the field, was apparent as they moved forward with greater method and determination than in 1975."

Neil moved back to loose-forward for the visit of promotion hopefuls Huyton on 8 February. York gave debuts that day to new signings Barry Hollis and Billy Harris, who filled the prop positions. The highlight of the game was a terrific 75-yard try by Barends, converted by Neil. The lowlight was a brawl in the 68th minute following the flooring of York's Welsh wingman Mike Marshall. Robert Mills regarded York's 21-9 victory as their best of the season so far.

A week later Mills had to revise his opinion as York surprised First Division Dewsbury by beating them 25-15 in the first round of the Challenge Cup. The *Yorkshire Evening Press* match report headline blared, "Wily Fox outwits Dewsbury", as Neil produced a virtuoso performance. Mills reported "It was man-of-the-match Fox, producing two breathtaking bursts, who steered his side to a 12-6 lead and a standing ovation at half-time." His breaks provided tries for Barends after 15 minutes and debutant stand-off John Hughes on 32 minutes, while his three penalty goals cancelled out three landed by Dewsbury centre Nigel Stephenson. However, by the hour mark Dewsbury, spurred by Stephenson's brains and Jeff Grayshon's brawn, had edged ahead 13-12 and with little time remaining led 15-12. The fat lady had not yet sung, however. Robert Mills became lyrical: "York rose from the dead at Clarence Street to win a compelling Cup tie with three dramatic tries in the final six minutes. Veteran Neil Fox was the man who breathed new life into a jaded, labouring York side which had seen a 12-6 interval lead slip away into almost certain defeat – and which seemed incapable of combating Dewsbury's simple but effective methods. Fox, the seasoned general, kicked his tiring troops into a rare attacking pose after 74 minutes. As if sensing a last chance of glory, York for the first time in the half moved the ball slickly along the line and Jackie Marston created a telling overlap. So Dave Barends' second try of the match levelled the score at 15-15. And the crowd's low murmurs of relief turned to howls of jubilation as Fox's left boot hoisted over a touchline conversion, which the tension alone should have made impossible. More drama two minutes later. The veteran forward, throwing caution to the wind, scythed through three tackles and passed inside for Tony Handforth to ensure York's passage into the second round. Fox's easy conversion put York, incredibly, 22-15 ahead. Dewsbury were numb with disbelief and it showed on time, when Alan Bates, who would have been one of the architects of York's defeat, lobbed a pass into Marston's path and the debutant centre scored from half-way."

York rested Neil and Geoff Clarkson at Huyton the following week but had clearly caught a winning habit to triumph 18-6. Both returned for the second round Challenge Cup tie at another First Division club, Oldham, on 29 February. It proved to be an epic clash. Neil hit a splendid touchline penalty in the fourth minute but struck the post with another after 28 minutes, while Jackie Marston slipped to the ground five yards out with a try in the offing. Oldham centre Phil Larder potted penalties after 23 and 26 minutes and York went in 4-2 down after having most of the play. A third Larder penalty made the score 6-2 after 49 minutes but York still looked the likely winners, especially when Barends scored the game's only try in the 67th minute. Neil missed the conversion, however. Six minutes from time he had another chance from a penalty only 20 yards out but agonisingly hooked it wide and York lost 6-5. Gary Cooper was not happy, declaring to the *Yorkshire Evening Press*, "It was a diabolical end to a game we should have won. They never seemed to have us in real trouble. When we got that kick, I seriously thought of shouting for Hetherington to take it. Fox was tired after a gruelling match and I knew it was a risk that he would lose concentration at the vital moment. I still can't believe it." Robert Mills summed matters up well, "They always say that nothing is certain in the Cup, but at least York now know they have the makings of a good side."

A 58-2 home drubbing of Blackpool Borough followed. York ran in 12 tries and Neil scored 21 points from a try and nine goals, just one point short of the club record held jointly by Vic Yorke in 1958 and Steve Quinn in 1972, while the match score was only two short of the club record league win of 60-0 against Barrow in 1972. Robert Mills reported, "At the heart of most of York's good work was Fox, although his first-half display was an exercise in contrasts. He compensated for some wild long passing with brainpower and subtlety in close-in situations to set up tries for Harkin and Harris. His kicking also was unpredictable – a hideous miss from in front of the posts after 26 minutes being followed by the sort of touchline conversion that makes those aberrations all the more annoying."

After seven undefeated league games since Neil joined the club, York had jumped up to seventh in the Second Division but with only four games remaining and a four-point gap between them and New Hunslet above them, there was precious little hope of a higher finish. They were able, however, to gauge how much improvement they had made on 14 March when they visited Barrow, who needed to win to virtually guarantee themselves the Championship. York certainly gave a good account of themselves but lost 21-12 in a game described by the *Yorkshire Evening Press* as, "uncompromisingly hard for the participants but totally absorbing for the spectators". York won the scrums 15-3 but conceded four stoppable tries yet remained in contention until the 76th minute. Neil made a try for Harkin and landed three goals.

A trip to lowly Halifax on 21 March produced an 11-9 victory, as Thrum Hall threw "clinging mud, driving snow and biting cold" at the contestants and the fans. York refused to bow to the conditions and "Neil Fox was forever urging his side to play football". Halifax's only try did not arrive until the 78th minute and York were much easier winners than the scoreline suggested. Neil was heavily involved in all three of York's tries, scoring one himself in the 43rd minute after hooker Ronnie Wileman put him into the clear. Neil wanted support but none arrived so he strode through full-back Colin Shires's tackle and his momentum on the muddy surface carried him over for a try he converted. In claiming the try he passed the 5,700 points mark in first-class rugby league.

On 28 March, Whitehaven were despatched 23-15 at Clarence Street. It was not a great performance by the team but Neil provided the goods. As well as kicking four goals, Neil made four of the five tries. Robert Mills wrote, "Key man in this new collective style, which Cooper sees as demanded by the cramped Clarence Street arena, is Neil Fox. His ability to find a position under the enemy's posts and create gaping chasms in their defence with seemingly innocuous passes was the bright spot yesterday."

York's last game of the season was against runners-up Rochdale Hornets at Clarence Street on 11 April and Neil was the centre of a sensation. The local paper's headline was "York fade away after Fox is sent off". Neil had been playing professional rugby league for 20 years and had never been sent off, despite the provocation which from time to time was aimed at him. Robert Mills wrote after York's 23-10 loss, "Never was skipper Neil Fox's influence on his side so vividly demonstrated as in the seething, tension-filled atmosphere of Clarence Street yesterday. York prospered with him, but simply could not exist without him... York were left to reflect on Fox's fatal loss of temper that led to his 53rd-minute dismissal. Fox, who had masterminded a display of controlled aggression from York in the first half, was sent off with Hornets' Peter Clarke after an ugly off-the-ball clash which appeared to start with Clarke's late tackle and end with Fox tripping the hooker and then kicking him on the floor."

York had led 8-2 at half-time and were still leading when Neil left the field. Hornets ran in 21 points in the second half. Neil's version of events is interesting: "I remember that game particularly well. On running out for the kick-off we were met with a great cheer from a large group of Hull supporters. As far as I remember, we had to beat Rochdale to give Hull a chance of promotion. While the game was progressing we were always in charge and while I was on the field we were always going to win. Rochdale had twigged that. I was dictating play and putting our lads through all the time. Peter Clarke, the Rochdale hooker, kept running into me and being a complete nuisance. I said to Stan Wall, the referee: 'Are you going to sort him out or shall I do it?' He replied, 'Leave him to me'. Half-time came and went. When I had another brush with him I chased him. He ran away and threw himself on the ground. I did a silly thing and kicked him up the arse - but not hard. I shouted at him to get up and have a go. The ref blew his whistle and sent me off. He said Peter would be following me. I made a personal appearance at the RFL's Disciplinary Committee meeting, taking with me a letter Peter had sent to the club stating that he had been put up to his antics to try to get me sent off. The plan obviously worked – they won and we lost. The chairman of the disciplinary committee was Jack Grindrod, who was chairman of Rochdale Hornets. I gave him the letter, which he put onto one side and said, 'It's the referee's report we will be looking at, not the letter of the other player'. That was a bit rich, I thought. I came away with a one-match suspension. In view of my record, I think just about everyone thought I would be given sending off sufficient." Perversely, the self-confessed instigator of the trouble, who had a far worse disciplinary record than Neil, also received a one-match suspension.

So Neil's season of change ended on a sour note. Overall though, Neil had been pretty successful. In 25 games for Hull KR and York he had scored four tries, 102 goals and 215 points. His century of goals was the 12th of his career but it would be his last. Only seven players had landed more goals or amassed more points during that season. Neil's move to York may have seemed like a backward step, but it presented a new challenge for him. There was no doubt that his arrival at Clarence Street had buoyed up the club. Their league record of played 17, won 6, lost 11, when he arrived, and their record of played 9, won 6, drawn 1, lost 2, in the period afterwards proclaimed his influence and character.

On transferring to York in January 1976, Neil was interviewed by Raymond Fletcher for the *Yorkshire Post*. Raymond pointed out that Neil might just be able to threaten Jim Sullivan's all-time points record, a figure which only a couple of seasons ago had seemed unattainable. Neil replied: "I never give records a thought. It's nice to break them, but as long as the team and I are playing well, I just keep putting them over." He did concede, "Sullivan's figure probably does interest me more than others. But, of course, the nearer I get to it, the older I get. I always said it was one figure that could not be beaten. But who knows? I thought I was finished when I went to Rovers, but I seemed to take on a new lease of life." He then asked: "By the way, what are the York scoring records?"

Neil's points tally stood at 5,713 at the close of the 1975-76 season and he was just about to turn 37. The best estimate of Jim Sullivan's record was 6,206 points, although records were imprecise then. It was likely that Neil was nearer to Sullivan's record than it seemed because Jim's figures included points in non-competitive games. It was interesting to speculate whether age, injury or exhaustion would get to Neil before he got to that fabulous record, whatever Sullivan's final total was. Whatever the real record was, Neil definitely needed to play a couple more seasons to take it.

Hull Kingston Rovers 1975-76

Hull Kingston Rovers finished 8th in Division 1: P30, W17, L13, For 446, Against 472
Fox scored 2 tries, 65 goals, 1 drop goal, 137 points for Hull KR before signing for York

Date	Opponent	Score	Fox	Crowd	
16 Aug	Huddersfield	26-16	3G	966	
23 Aug	**Leeds**	23-12	T, 5G	3,371	
31 Aug	**Wakefield T**	26-9	7G	6,407	YC1
6 Sep	Wigan	13-34	2G	2,500	
14 Sep	New Hunslet	15-7	4G	2,206	YC2
23 Sep	**Featherstone R**	19-16	6G, DG	6,481	YC semi
28 Sep	**Rochdale H**	33-10	8G	5,274	PT1
3 Oct	Castleford	24-13	dnp	2,095	
7 Oct	**Huddersfield**	11-12	4G	4,155	FT1
12 Oct	**Swinton**	25-10	6G	3,671	
19 Oct	**Bradford N**	11-10	5G	5,002	
26 Oct	Widnes	11-33	dnp	3,966	
7 Nov	**Leigh**	23-8	4G	3,764	PT2
15 Nov	Leeds	11-15	T, 2G	5,304	YC Final (at Leeds)
23 Nov	**Widnes**	14-18	5G	6,594	PT3
30 Nov	**Keighley**	18-8	3G	2,199	
14 Dec	Warrington	11-23	G	2,603	

York 1975-76

York finished 7th in Division 2: P26, W12, L13, D1, for 447, Against 394
Fox scored 2 tries, 36 goals, 78 points for York

Date	Opponent	Score	Fox	Crowd	
11 Jan	**Bramley**	14-14	4G	1,742	
18 Jan	Blackpool B	19-7	5G	112	
8 Feb	**Huyton**	21-9	3G	1,583	
15 Feb	**Dewsbury**	25-15	5G	3,487	Ch Cup 1
22 Feb	Huyton	18-6	dnp	263	
29 Feb	Oldham	5-6	G	6,190	Ch Cup 2
7 Mar	**Blackpool B**	58-2	T, 9G	1,781	
14 Mar	Barrow	12-21	3G	2,732	
21 Mar	Halifax	11-9	T, G	1,323	
28 Mar	**Whitehaven**	23-15	4G	1,709	
11 Apr	**Rochdale H**	10-23	G	3,198	

1979 Testimonial match at Belle Vue

The Wakefield Trinity team, captained by Neil.
Back: Keith Holliday, Geoff Wriglesworth, Ted Campbell, David Jeanes, Terry Ramshaw,
David Wakefield, Geoff Oakes, David Blakeley, Geoff Clarkson, Malcolm Sampson. Front: Don Fox,
Joe Bonnar, Ken Hirst, Mick Major, Harold Poynton, Eric Ingham, Neil Fox, Ken Rollin, Fred Smith.

The Great Britain team who provided the opposition.
Back: Geoff Gunney, Colin Dixon, Sammy Lloyd, Jimmy Thompson, Rob Valentine, Ken Roberts,
Alan Davies, John Etty, Billy Boston, Johnny Whiteley, Graham Idle, Ray French.
Front: Alan Buckley, Vince Farrar, Tommy Smales, Keith Hepworth, Arthur Keegan.
(Both photos: Brian Robinson)

26. 1976-77: The Bramley Foxes

After years of falling attendances rugby league had, it seemed, turned the corner in attracting back the fans, if only marginally. Part of the recovery was due to the stabilisation brought about by the new regime at Chapeltown Road, following the departure of Bill Fallowfield. It also helped that the mania for change was brought under control. The only significant law change for the 1976-77 season was the introduction of the differential penalty at scrummages. It was no longer permissible to kick for goal after a technical scrum infringement – only a penalty for off-side at the scrum could now result in an attempt at goal. For kickers like Neil, the new law would obviously mean fewer opportunities for kicking goals.

York opened the season on 22 August by losing at Halifax in the first round of the Yorkshire Cup. Neil was missing, serving out his suspension. He was back for the first league fixture on 5 September at home to Halifax. This time York won 20-11 but were unimpressive. Robert Mills commented, "Neil Fox, in the centre, and David Barends were asked to survive on a starvation diet of ball - a pity since York were at their most dangerous when Fox got into the game." Neil kicked four goals and created two tries.

Neil was missing a week later when York lost 9-8 at Huyton. Neil recalls, "The season began with Gary chopping and changing the team. He was playing players out of position instead of keeping the lads together so we could develop a settled team. I actually got a call from Gary saying he was going to prolong my career and he wanted to play me at full-back. I told him, 'No way'. His reply was, 'I'll put you on the transfer list if you don't play'. I just laughed and he put the phone down. Then I got a call from Robert Mills at the *Yorkshire Evening Press* saying I had refused to play. I told Robert that I had said I would not play full-back but would play in the pack or at centre, positions I was used to.

I went to training as usual and after it Gary said I was sub for the home match against Dewsbury. The lads couldn't believe he had left me out of the starting line-up. But knowing Gary, I knew anything could happen. During his team talk before the game he promised the players a bonus if we won. The players went out and I stayed behind for a while with Gary and said to him, 'We have to win this match, Gary, or the pressure will really be on you'. He replied, 'I know. That's why I have put them on a bonus!' The bonus, it seemed, was nothing to do with the board of directors. It was coming out of his own pocket.

I got on early when centre Ray Wilson was injured. Gary thought I was going on to play full-back, but I went to centre and stayed there. Nothing was said at half-time about it. We lost the game 18-2 and after the match Gary went straight home to Pontefract, feeling the pressure. I joined the other players in the bar for a drink and heard rumours that Gary's job was not safe. I decided I would go to his house in Pontefract to tell him what I had heard. He said they wouldn't dare sack him. I told him if he went I would not stay.

After training on Tuesday he was called into the directors' room and they said they wanted a change of coach and that he was going to be sacked. On hearing that, I went to the directors' and said I wanted to leave. They said they thought I might be interested in the coaching job, but I said I had only come to York because of Gary. How could I take his job? I said I would play against New Hunslet but that would be my last match for them. So sticking up for Gary put me back on the road, not knowing where I would end up."

That final game at New Hunslet on 26 September was something of a shambles. Neil played in the second-row, but the side was clearly shell-shocked and went down to a wretched 30-5 defeat. Neil's career at York amounted to a mere 13 appearances in which he claimed 90 points. The turnaround in the team's fortunes was pretty staggering. York had some talented players, whose performances just a few months earlier had suggested they were heading for promotion but their bad start to the season set them back. Under new coach Malcolm Dixon, they began to play nearer to their obvious potential but finished in fifth place in the Second Division, three points short of a promotion place.

Within a week of playing his last game for York, Neil had joined Bramley. Already at McLaren Field as coach was his brother Peter, who had left Wakefield Trinity under similar circumstances to those Neil experienced. Peter had been told he was not to be re-engaged at Wakefield shortly before the season ended, despite protests from the supporters and the Trinity players. So Bramley appointed Peter as their coach after the team had made a poor start to the 1976-77 season, winning only one of their first five league fixtures. He replaced Arthur Keegan, a wonderful full-back, who had graced the game with Hull, Bramley and Great Britain and had led Bramley to their only major triumph, when they lifted the BBC2 Floodlit Trophy in 1973-74. Peter was given full control over all playing matters at McLaren Field and believed that he could deliver promotion within two seasons.

Neil recalls: "I got a call from Peter asking if I would be willing to help him out at Bramley. He needed a pack leader and I was his choice. I told him I would meet him and Doug Alton, the chairman, to discuss it. I told them that if I couldn't settle, I wanted to be able to leave on a free transfer, as I had with Hull KR and York. The chairman agreed to that, because they had not paid a fee for me. I went to Bramley specifically because Peter wanted me there. When I arrived one of the first people I came across was one of the main causes of the troubles I had had at Wakefield. He had resigned at Trinity but was now on the board at Bramley. He said to me, 'Let's forget what went off at Wakefield, shall we?' I couldn't believe his cheek. I certainly wasn't going to forget it but I wouldn't let it worry me. If I had known he was at Bramley, I don't think I would have gone there."

Bramley had some useful backs in full-back John Hay, wingers Jack Austin, Billy Rowett and Keith Waites, centres Derek Parker, Keith Bollon and Trevor Briggs and scrum-half Barry Langton, who had been at Wakefield in Neil's time. They needed strengthening in the pack and that was Peter Fox's priority. Bramley had already spent a club-record £6,000 on Salford's clever prop Jimmy Fiddler, and Peter soon added Geoff Clarkson, Alan Maskill and the Australian Lou Lardi, as well as Neil. There were also another couple of good men on the books in club skipper Dave Sampson, yet another old Trinity colleague of Neil, and the up-and-coming loose-forward Steve Bond. If Peter could get this collection of players to perform to their potential, the future would be bright for Bramley. With his tactical insight, skills in man-management, attention to detail, penchant for devising planned moves and ability to spot a good player, Peter Fox was certainly the man for the job.

Neil made his debut on 3 October in a home game against Hull, who led the Second Division. Winger Peter Goodchild, a 38-year-old former Yorkshire cap, also made his first appearance of the season for Bramley – a sure indication that Peter Fox appreciated the old dictum, "If they're good enough, they're young enough." The *Pudsey News* heralded Neil's first game with the headline "Big Neil transforms Bramley: Fox has Hull on the run." It reported: "Fox completely transformed the McLaren Field men in his debut game, creating three tries through vintage handling, which had rugged league leaders Hull reeling to their first defeat of the season... Fox proved the inspiration Bramley have sadly lacked this season. He caused trouble whenever Hull allowed him space in which to move and he landed three goals, including two magnificent efforts from the touchline... This was the sort of display Bramley fans have been wanting to see from their side for a long time. The team now has the correct balance of youth and experience, and with the redoubtable and effervescent Peter Fox in charge, the future looks surprisingly bright at Bramley after all the early season gloom." Hull were beaten 18-13.

The following week Bramley hosted Swinton and lost 16-13, Neil landing two goals and making a try for Rowett. Bramley lost the scrums 16-3 and were never in the lead, but might have snatched victory late on after a marvellous length-of-the-field move by Goodchild and Austin. A trip to Fartown on 17 October proved more fruitful. Neil and Fiddler were the outstanding figures, although Neil failed to score. Huddersfield took a 3-0 lead after only two minutes with a fine try by Trevor Leathley but Neil wiped that out by creating a try for Briggs. Fiddler dropped two goals but a penalty by Dave Hooson tied the scores at 5-5. Steve Bond stole a 6-5 victory for Bramley with a last gasp drop-goal.

League leaders Dewsbury visited McLaren Field in the John Player Trophy and came a real cropper, losing 33-5. The *Pudsey News* described Bramley's performance as their best for years and was ecstatic about the quality of their six tries. Neil kicked three first-half goals to help his side to a 9-2 half-time lead but hurt a hamstring and did not play in the second half. The highlight of the game was an extraordinary 60-yard try by Jimmy Fiddler, who kicked ahead twice and dribbled "like a soccer veteran" before outpacing two chasers for the final touchdown. The *News* declared of Bramley, "The transformation in their confidence and attitude since the arrival of new coach Peter Fox has been unbelievable."

Neil's injury caused him to miss two games, both of which were lost. The defeats at York and Workington, in the second round of the John Player Trophy, were super games. The latter, in which Bramley came near to a tremendous upset victory over a First Division side, saw the debuts of hooker Alan Maskill from New Hunslet and Geoff Clarkson. Maskill dislocated his shoulder and was unable to play again until January. Neil recalls, "During this early period at Bramley I asked Peter to go back to York for Geoff Clarkson to strengthen our team. He was just getting over a cartilage operation but he was a great buy for us. Geoff played for a lot of teams but he did a good job at all of them. Everyone spoke highly of Geoff." Ironically, Clarkson's knee was damaged again and he was again committed to the surgeon's care. Like Maskill, he did not return until the New Year.

On 14 November at Batley, the Villagers found themselves in trouble but, according to the *Pudsey News*, "A pep talk behind the posts by Neil Fox after Batley had taken a 12-3 lead had precisely the right effect on Bramley". They scored four tries in quick succession, all of which Neil converted, including a couple of siege-gun proportions almost from touch. It was a fast and furious clash in which "Bramley had been inspired, not only by Fox's determination and craft, but also by that of Jack Austin and Steve Bond." The 23-17 victory was only marred by former Bramley hero Arthur Keegan's broken jaw, which ended his illustrious career after only six games for Batley.

At this stage in the season Bramley were lying ninth in the league but Peter Fox's influence had been noticeable enough to secure the job of coaching England in the forthcoming triangular series with France and Wales, which was an impressive achievement for a man coaching a lowly Second Division club.

Peter was not impressed by his side's defence in a 26-18 home win against Huyton on 21 November. Neil converted four tries and performed well enough for the *Pudsey News* to comment that "again the wily Fox proved that there is no substitute for experience and an eye for an opening". One highlight was a typical Jack Austin try in which he "ploughed through several Huyton defenders like a bulldozer through a brick wall".

The next week Bramley went to The Boulevard to take on champions-elect Hull. Neil describes the conditions as "some of the worst I have ever experienced". Deep mud was exacerbated by a torrential downpour at half-time and referee Peter Oliver abandoned the match after 56 minutes when Bramley were leading 7-5, thanks to a 50-yard try from Billy Rowett and two goals from Neil. Neil says, "There was no way that Hull were going to score again and I'm sure we would have won. The referee said he couldn't see who was who in all the mud. He said he would continue the match if Hull could change into a fresh kit but they said they couldn't. They must have realised they had no chance of winning that afternoon." The referee's decision was contentious but, to be fair, Hull had changed their kit at half-time and Bramley had not brought a change of kit at all. The Bramley chairman Doug Alton wanted to claim victory, saying 63 minutes had actually been played, including first-half injury time – scores in abandoned games which lasted 60 minutes or more were sometimes allowed to stand. Peter Fox was adamant that "Hull didn't want to play. We had beaten them on their own midden at their own game. I can't believe that a club as big as Hull do not have three sets of jerseys". His team had tackled Hull to a standstill.

Bramley's season was then brought to a halt for six weeks. Four of their next six games were postponed through severe weather and on two weekends they had no scheduled fixtures. They were the worst affected team in the league, having completed only 10 of their 26 league fixtures by the time they resumed activities with a home game against Halifax in freezing conditions on 9 January. After their long lay-off Bramley struggled to win 15-13, Neil kicking three goals. A fortnight later they encountered Dewsbury at McLaren Field in a game which was vital to both clubs' hopes of promotion. The game looked lost when Dewsbury led 13-5 but a Barry Langton try, improved by Neil, gave them a late vestige of hope. As the whistle drew ever nearer Jack Austin, 'the McLaren Field folk hero', capitalised on good work by Dave Sampson to take the ball at full pelt and launch himself spectacularly over for a heart-stopping try. Neil, playing his 750th first-class game, nervelessly converted from wide out and the *Pudsey News* joyfully observed, "The goal provoked the biggest roar of the season from the Bramley crowd", as their team snatched a memorable 15-13 win.

On 30 January Bramley went to Blackpool and won 21-2. Neil landed three first-half penalties and converted all three second-half tries, giving him a 100 per cent kicking return, despite carrying an injury from the Dewsbury match. At Doncaster the following week Neil claimed six goals and a try in a 33-24 success, although the win should have been bigger as the Dons rattled up 12 late points. Austin scored a hat-trick and Clarkson had his best game for the club. Neil's last goal brought his career points record to 5,800.

Bramley faced a huge hurdle in the first round of the Challenge Cup on 13 February, when Widnes visited McLaren Field. A crowd of 5,092, the biggest of the season, paid ground record receipts of £2,817 and Bramley certainly gave them value for money. Hooker Keith Elwell gave Widnes the lead with a drop-goal after two minutes, although many thought Widnes had already taken six tackles. Neil sent a towering 35-yard penalty between the sticks three minutes later to give his side a 2-1 lead but Ray Dutton's simpler penalty goal restored Widnes's lead. Before the break Dave Sampson levelled matters with a neat drop-goal. Crucially, Widnes won the scrums 16-10 but it was not until the 58th minute that Jim Mills scored the first try, through brute strength. On 70 minutes McLaren Field exploded when Peter Goodchild crashed over at the corner for an equalising try. Then followed perfect silence as Neil lined up the most difficult of conversions. The *Pudsey News* captured the drama: "Bramley supporters looked on with anticipation; Widnes supporters feared the worst. But it was too much to ask of even a great player like Fox, and his touchline effort drifted wide." At 6-6 Bramley deserved a replay but their hopes evaporated with five minutes remaining, when Bill Ramsey bludgeoned his way over for the winning try, converted by Dutton. Neil almost salvaged a draw in the dying minutes, when he broke through and sent Billy Rowett on a run before centre Mal Aspey brought him down.

A week later Bramley went to Halifax seeking a seventh consecutive league victory and were successful by 20-8. Thrum Hall was about as unwelcoming as it could be, pitting the players against fog, slush, sleet and snow and the spectators and press against exceedingly low visibility. Halifax could not cope with the second-row pairing of Neil and Geoff Clarkson and Bramley established a 15-1 lead before half-time. The *Pudsey News* noted, "Neil Fox again showed his value in terms of experience. His astute passing created much-needed space on a heavy pitch, and again he was in fine goal-kicking form, landing four shots."

Bramley were now on the fringes of the promotion race and a 22-5 home win against Huddersfield pushed them into sixth position. Neil kicked five goals from six attempts, his fourth being his 2,400th career goal. There was, however, a big blow, when captain Dave Sampson broke his arm and was ruled out for the remainder of the season.

On Friday 11 March, Bramley visited Whitehaven in search of a 10th consecutive league victory, a post-war club record. The mission was successful, a 17-12 win taking Bramley into the top four – but only for 48 hours. The *Pudsey News* ran a familiar headline: "Fox too cunning for Whitehaven". Neil scored four goals and two tries, one from an interception and the other after racing through a gap before the opposition had time to close it. Peter thought he had done enough by the 63rd minute and pulled him off.

Nine days later, Bramley faced a crunch clash at York. Neil was keen to show what his former team was missing. He created the first try with a huge downfield kick, which centre Derek Parker took on the first bounce to score. He then converted a try scored by Austin at the corner flag and followed with another touchline conversion of a second try by Parker, adding a penalty to give his side an unassailable 15-0 lead. The Bramley pack performed brilliantly and a rock-like defence conceded only a late converted try.

Although Peter Fox's charges were now in the top four, there was some personal disappointment for Bramley's coach when the RFL chose Welshman David Watkins to coach Great Britain's World Cup squad for the summer tournament in Australia. His Bramley team kept winning, however. Their next victims were Keighley who were beaten 17-9 at McLaren Field on 27 March, ending their promotion hopes. Neil had a big game, the *Pudsey News* reporting, "Neil Fox was the instigator of Bramley's most dangerous moves, switching the point of attack regularly. He was also again in deadly goal-kicking form, recovering from his now familiar easy miss early in the game, to land four long-range shots."

On Sunday 3 April Bramley were coasting to a comfortable victory at Swinton, when they led 13-2 at half-time but allowed the Lions to come back to 13-12. Two old-timers finally nailed down Bramley's 12th consecutive league win, however. Peter Goodchild crossed for his second try and Neil's conversion from near touch sealed an 18-12 success.

Four days later New Hunslet came to McLaren Field at the fifth time of asking, the game having been postponed four times during the season. Bramley were not happy at having to play on the Thursday evening, rather than the following day, Good Friday, when this local derby would surely have drawn a bigger crowd than 1,722. Bramley won 14-9 in a desperately fought match with Neil contributing his usual share of the points and entertainment. Trevor Watson wrote in the *Yorkshire Evening Post:* "It took what is a typical Neil Fox performance these days to steer them through. He doesn't gambol around like a spring lamb, but his influence cannot be ignored. Fox bundled his way over, despite three defenders, from Alan Maskill's pass for the first try and added the goal. Then he landed a marvellous 45-yard angled penalty and kicked two other easier ones in the second half. He also sent out the well-judged pass which full-back John Hay plucked from his own winger's grasp to catch Hunslet napping for the second try. Fox did not top the tackle count, yet in the dying seconds he popped up to make the save which prevented Ken Endersby probably snatching a point. That is how legends are made."

Easter Monday saw Bramley win comfortably, 22-11, at Huyton. Neil kicked two goals but Jimmy Fiddler provided the game's high spot with an 80-yard interception try. The victory was Bramley's 14th in a row in the league – possibly the best winning run in the club's entire history. Neil seemed to have had a talismanic effect on the team. Raymond Fletcher wrote in the *Yorkshire Post*, "[Peter] Fox's shrewdest move was in persuading his brother, Neil, to join him from York. The former-centre-turned-forward has been the pivot of Peter Fox's set moves and been on the losing side only once in the 15 league matches he has played for them. 'This is one of the best winning runs I have had,' said Neil Fox... 'Wakefield did have a better one and that ended at Batley when our Peter played for them. I'm enjoying my rugby at Bramley. I try to make the openings and let the younger ones do the running. My kicking is also the best it has been for some time. I usually miss the first one, but once I've broken my duck they get easier'."

Bramley had four games left and needed one victory to ensure promotion. Their next opponents, however, were championship-chasing Hull at The Boulevard on Friday 15 April. This was the replay of the abandoned fixture back in November. Peter Fox caused consternation, when he complained to the referee – Mr Oliver again – that the pitch was unplayable, being rock-hard, devoid of grass and rutted. Mr Oliver declared it was playable but he told the teams he would call 'held' early to avoid injuries. After the pre-match sparring a fast game ensued. Bramley ended the first half one point behind, Derek Parker having scored a fine try and Neil had scored a second. However, the second half saw Hull pull away to win 26-10 and halt Bramley's record-breaking sequence of victories.

Two days later Bramley achieved promotion with a 42-10 thumping of Batley at McLaren Field, scoring 10 tries and recording their highest score in a league match for nine years. Neil came off at half-time after landing a couple of goals. He had already done enough damage in the first half, as Trevor Watson in the *Yorkshire Evening Post* observed, "The crafty hand of Neil Fox was in three of the scores as he fanned the ball around and only bad finishing prevented another score after his 20-yard break had set things up". The *Pudsey News* announced joyously, "They're up – and now it's a fight to keep Fox."

So the Fox brothers had achieved their target a year earlier than Peter's initial estimate. It did not matter that they lost their away game at New Hunslet two days later, when Neil was missing from the side. They finished off this highly successful campaign with an 18-12 win at Doncaster, Neil gathering half the side's points. Bramley's final position was third, behind Hull and Dewsbury.

Neil topped Bramley's scorers with 164 points from six tries and 73 goals but had played his last game for them. Bramley were already reeling from the shock of losing Peter Fox, who had gone to Bradford on a three-year contract, having said goodbye at a celebration evening on 25 April. Neil says, "The job of getting Bramley into Division 1 had been done and after Peter left I was approached by Huddersfield to become their player-coach. I informed the Bramley directors that I was leaving. To my astonishment they said Huddersfield would have to pay a fee of £3,000. I reminded the chairman of our agreement when I signed for Bramley that said I would be granted a free transfer. He denied ever saying they would give me such a deal. Huddersfield wanted me so badly though that they paid £2,500. That was the first time in my experience that anyone had gone back on their word. I was not happy about that. Anyway, I was going to the club I had supported as a youngster, which was something to be happy about."

York 1976-77

York finished 5th in Division 2: P26, W17, L 9, For 422, Against 279
Fox scored 6 goals, 12 points for York before signing for Bramley

Date	Opponent	Score	Fox	Crowd	
22 Aug	Halifax	11-21	dnp	1,245	YC1
5 Sep	**Halifax**	20-11	4G	1,637	
12 Sep	Huyton	8-9	dnp	208	
19 Sep	**Dewsbury***	2-18	G	2,173	
26 Sep	New Hunslet	5-30	G	1,166	

* Substitute

Bramley 1976-77

Bramley finished 3rd in Division 2: P26, W19, L7, For 464, Against 377
Fox scored 6 tries, 73 goals, 164 points for Bramley

Date	Opponent	Score	Fox	Crowd	
3 Oct	**Hull**	18-13	3G	1,174	
10 Oct	**Swinton**	13-16	2G	1,160	
17 Oct	Huddersfield	6-5		1,346	
24 Oct	**Dewsbury**	33-5	3G	2,168	PT1
31 Oct	**York**	19-21	dnp	1,499	
7 Nov	Workington T	13-17	dnp	2,051	PT2
14 Nov	Batley	23-17	4G	770	
21 Nov	**Huyton**	26-18	4G	2,121	
28 Nov	Hull+	7-5	2G	3,847	
9 Jan	**Halifax**	15-13	3G	1,029	
23 Jan	**Dewsbury**	15-13	3G	1,637	
30 Jan	Blackpool B	21-2	6G	236	
6 Feb	**Doncaster**	33-24	T, 6G	970	
13 Feb	**Widnes**	6-11	G	5,092	Ch Cup 1
20 Feb	Halifax	20-8	4G	1,145	
6 Mar	**Huddersfield**	22-5	5G	1,388	
11 Mar	Whitehaven	17-12	2T, 4G	556	
20 Mar	York	15-5	3G	4,013	
27 Mar	**Keighley**	17-9	4G	1,966	
3 Apr	Swinton	18-12	3G	877	
7 Apr	**New Hunslet**	14-9	T, 4G	1,722	
11 Apr	Huyton	22-11	2G	240	
15 Apr	Hull	10-26	T, 2G	3,015	
17 Apr	**Batley**	42-10	2G	1,191	
19 Apr	New Hunslet	7-26	dnp	1,760	
24 Apr	Doncaster	18-12	T, 3G	355	

+ Match abandoned

291

Neil captaining Bradford Northern in 1978.
Back: Tony Fisher, Derek Parker, Les Gant, Jeff Grayshon, Ian van Bellen, Dennis Trotter,
Colin Forsyth. Front: Dave Barends, Nigel Stephenson, Neil Fox, Keith Mumby,
David Redfearn, Kevin Harkin.

Neil clasps the Holliday Cup after Underbank's 16-2 victory over St Joseph's at
Fartown in 1982. His former Wakefield Trinity team-mates David Jeanes
(with beard) and Ian Brooke on David's left shared in the triumph.

27. 1977-78: World-record points scorer

If anyone thought that helping Bramley to attain First Division status was a tall order, it was probably no taller than doing the same for Huddersfield. True enough, Huddersfield had much more potential to be a big name in rugby league than the perennial minnows of Bramley; Fartown was one of the game's great venues and the Fartowners had a glorious history but that was all they had – a history, and its glories were fast receding in their fans' memories. Huddersfield had been champions in 1962, as Neil would all too readily and ruefully remember. In the 15 intervening years the club's fortunes had slumped dramatically. Mid-table had become the norm for them in the old one division system which operated until 1973 and apart from winning promotion in 1974-75, followed by immediate relegation, mediocrity was all the Fartown supporters had experienced. In 1976-77 they had finished seventh in Division 2, so Neil was taking over as player-coach at a time when the club was in a parlous state. The appointment could well have been regarded as a poisoned chalice. Neil was Huddersfield's third coach within a year, following quickly on the heels of Keith Goulding and Bob Tomlinson. Moreover, even as he signed his contract, the club was in the early throes of a takeover bid, as the venerable institution of the Huddersfield Cricket & Athletic Club prepared to become a limited company.

Neil arrived at Fartown at the beginning of August and the *Huddersfield Daily Examiner* announced "Fox spells it out: he wants success". He told John Huxley, "I believe that we can do well and I'm aiming for promotion this season". The following day the club announced Neil's first capture, David Jeanes, Neil's former colleague at Wakefield. Neil says, "My first move was for David, who had not played for a couple of years after finishing at Leeds to concentrate on his job. But he had kept himself fit and was eager to play again. He would certainly make a difference to the lads who were already on Fartown's books."

Jeanes and Neil both turned out in the Charity Cup match against Halifax at Thrum Hall on Sunday, 14 August and John Huxley reported, "A large ray of hope dawned on Huddersfield Rugby League Club's horizon yesterday". Huddersfield won 20-12 and Huxley continued, "The whole team responded well to the leadership of player-coach Neil Fox; new signing David Jeanes shone with his power play; and there was an extra enthusiasm for the game by the rest of the players... Fox dictated the whole of Huddersfield's game. He stood 10 yards back at play-the-balls, encouraging players to seek the gaps and his voice was always to be heard cajoling, persuading when the Fartowners were tackling." Neil, playing at loose-forward, booted four goals and, although happy with the performance, was left in no doubt that he had much hard work ahead of him.

The season began in earnest with a home first-round Yorkshire Cup tie against York on 21 August. Things were going very well for Neil and his side, who led 17-4 with only 19 minutes remaining. Their tackling had been ferocious and victory was in the bag until all concentration seemed to desert them and York stormed back to win 20-17 with four unanswered tries. Their next game was against Wigan at home in a Floodlit Trophy preliminary round tie, when no-one seriously expected a Huddersfield win. At half-time Wigan were coasting along 21-4 in front, Neil having landed a couple of penalties. A dramatic turning point occurred when Neil was subjected to a particularly violent three-man tackle. He was so incensed that he uncharacteristically complained to the referee, Ken Spencer, only to be penalised for dissent. The incident appeared to fire up his colleagues, who were transformed into a rampaging host of avenging angels. By the 76th minute Wigan were hanging on for dear life at 21-18 and with seconds to go were grateful for a drop-goal by scrum-half Jimmy Nulty to give them a 22-18 victory.

The league programme began with another home game against Leigh, one of the promotion favourites, on 4 September. Huddersfield again played well for most of the game and led 11-7 after 46 minutes, only to collapse to a 22-11 defeat through some slipshod tackling and a complete lack of possession. Neil knew the team had capabilities but also knew that the Second Division would prove possibly the hardest competition since its introduction in 1973.

On 11 September, Huddersfield finally won a competitive fixture, 27-13 at Swinton. Huddersfield should have won much more easily, especially after Derek Wroe won the scrums 25-7. Neil moved to second-row and used Malcolm Branch at loose-forward. Branch profited by scoring two tries, while Neil was spot-on with his kicking and landed six goals.

However, Neil was unhappy about the overall playing strength of the club. He wanted forwards who could tackle and a better balance in the pack, telling John Huxley, "Ian van Bellen, Dave Heppleston and myself all play at about the same speed and candidly there is not room in the same pack for us all". He solved this quandary by letting van Bellen go to Bradford Northern, where his fortunes blossomed, and by playing Heppleston at open-side prop and also entrusting the 'A' team coaching to his care. Yet despite correcting the faulty balance of the pack, there were simply not enough players available at Fartown. On 16 September, Huddersfield pulled out of their first round Yorkshire Senior Competition Challenge Cup tie at Featherstone. Huddersfield 'A' had won the competition the previous season and Neil railed, "I think it is disgraceful that as holders we should have to pull out without playing but we've got no option. We simply can't find enough players in time". Neil had been scouting at seven amateur games in the past three weeks for players, besides fulfilling his playing and coaching duties. He issued an invitation for local amateurs to trial at Fartown, realising that the club needed to recruit youngsters. One player he wanted to sign, but could not afford, was John Taylor, who he later recruited at Underbank.

On 18 September, Huddersfield crushed Huyton 44-0 at Fartown. Three veterans dominated the show. Dave Heppleston dictated matters up front and former test winger Ken Senior scored two tries to bring his tally for the club to 200. Both had been Fartowners for 15 years. The third veteran, Neil, scored six goals before being substituted after 65 minutes. The *Huddersfield Daily Examiner* reported, "Intercepting the ball just inside his own half, 38-year-old Fox won the 55-yard sprint to the line, just touching down by the posts as the Huyton defenders got their hands on him." Ironically, Neil's points scoring progress, which was taking him ever closer Jim Sullivan's world record, would no longer be observed by 'Peerless Jim', who died four days before the Huyton fixture.

A week later Neil kicked six goals in a 33-15 win at Blackpool Borough, while Malcolm Branch scored two tries for the third match in a row. Neil was unhappy, however, because the second-half performance, after leading 25-0, had been lamentable. He was much happier on 2 October after a hard-earned 18-10 home win against Keighley, a team likely to be challenging for promotion. Branch scored a hat-trick and Senior claimed the other try, to which Neil added three goals. Branch's form earned him a place in Yorkshire's team to meet Cumbria and most critics were quick to spot the improvement in his game since Neil had arrived at Fartown. Another Fartowner to win county honours was scrum-half Mick Shepherd, who also won Great Britain under-24 caps during the season. After the win against Keighley, Huddersfield stood third in the table below Rochdale Hornets and York.

A trip to fourth-placed Leigh on 9 October proved tough. Neil had no luck with his kicking but the Fartowners had looked likely winners for much of the game. A 7-1 beating in the second-half scrums was too great a handicap, however, and Leigh won 20-14, Branch and winger Joe Cyrus both grabbing two tries in a losing cause. A week later

Huddersfield rose to the occasion in beating Barrow 15-13 at Fartown, when stand-off Glen Knight, signed from Oldham, made his debut. Knight had previously been at Fartown before transferring to Warrington and on his day was a brilliant footballer. The game was one of the best seen at Huddersfield for years, the lead changing hands five times. Malcolm Branch scored his 13th try of the season to take over at the top of the try-scoring chart, a remarkable feat for a loose-forward. Neil kicked three goals and created a try just before half-time when he ploughed through three tackles to put Shepherd over under the posts.

Neil's impact at Fartown was increasingly evident. John Huxley wrote in the *Huddersfield Daily Examiner* on 15 October: "Something is stirring at Fartown. Like somebody emerging from a 15-year coma, there are signs that life is flowing back into Fartown's sadly withered limbs. The takeover group led by three Huddersfield businessmen, Colin Wood, Roy Brook and Jack Pearson, are firmly entrenched in the running of the club, while Neil Fox is quite clearly in command in the dressing-room... It is pleasant to report that the atmosphere in the dressing-room is approaching the spirit that was there when the Fartowners were on their way to the Second Division Championship in 1974-75. And it is on that happy basis that the interest within the club itself is on the increase. It has to be said that the dramatic improvement must be down to Neil Fox... As well as inspiring better performances on the field, Fox has demanded and received a more professional attitude in the administration." Neil, incidentally, was the first Fartown coach to have complete powers in team selection.

After early dismissals from the Yorkshire Cup and BBC2 Floodlit Trophy, Neil was hoping for something better from the Players No.6 Trophy and he got it in the first round, when Whitehaven were trounced 33-13 at Fartown. Alan Irving, Whitehaven correspondent for the *Rugby Leaguer*, wrote, "Neil Fox almost single-handedly put the skids under Whitehaven and spotlighted one of the Cumbrians' biggest needs. That is for an on-the-field general who can dictate the tempo of the team's play... Fox was never one of the game's quickest players, even in his heyday as a centre, but what a brain! Even at the age of 38, the legendary Yorkshireman possessed too much speed of thought and sheer football ability for Whitehaven. He masterminded that 33-13 Fartown success by scoring the best try of the match, and scheming three others, as well as banging over six goals."

Neil added to the club's forward strength by signing Steve Lyons from Hull KR. Steve had played with Neil at Rovers and Trinity, so Neil knew exactly what he was getting – a no-frills, workaholic prop, who would drive the ball in and tackle all afternoon. Steve made a try-scoring debut in a 44-10 thrashing of Doncaster on 30 October, when Neil added another 17 points to his monumental tally. John Huxley noted, "Fox is making Huddersfield tick. His distribution had Doncaster reeling and with such powerful men as David Jeanes, Andy Wilson and Malcolm Branch, he had the men capable of bursting open any defence."

The second round of the Players No.6 Trophy brought Oldham to Fartown and the club's biggest crowd of the season so far – 3,900. They were treated to an enthralling cup tie in which Huddersfield trailed 9-0, 11-5 at half-time and 11-10 by the 52nd minute when David Jeanes was sent off. The 12 remaining men, however, produced a period of brilliant rugby to stun Oldham and run out 21-11 winners. Neil played his usual influential role. Apart from landing three goals he pushed his way over for a vital try in the 71st minute and converted it to make the score 18-11. Three minutes later his pass to centre Peter Rowe sent the Welshman through two tackles for the final score.

Another tremendous triumph followed when Huddersfield won 14-0 at York. Neil regarded this win as Huddersfield's best performance of the season, because of the stern defence his men produced. His conversion of the first try by Glen Knight, off Neil's pass from a play-the-ball, gave him his 50th goal of the season and his 6,000th career point. He also converted a Trevor Leathley try and struck a monster of a drop-goal.

Huddersfield's biggest game of the season followed – a home third round Players No.6 Trophy tie against brother Peter's First Division leaders Bradford. Of course, such a family affair attracted much press coverage. Peter told the *Yorkshire Post*, "Neil doesn't even think without my knowing and we have plans to stop him... There is no better player in the game than our Neil... We have got to cut him out and above all make sure we do not give him opportunities for goals." Neil's response was, "Peter has got it all wrong. He knows my style and thinks he knows what to expect but we have a few surprises for him. We will force them into making mistakes and cash in." Naturally, Huddersfield were not the bookies' favourites, although Warrington coach Alex Murphy tipped them as winners.

The game drew more than 6,000 to Fartown, the largest crowd there since 1968, on 19 November. There was a heavy ground and a wet and windy afternoon. Neil would have preferred firmer going. His team played bravely but were 8-0 down at half-time and, despite having the benefit of the elements for the second half, lost 11-0. Peter was proved right – Neil never got a kick at goal and Northern made no mistakes.

Returning to league fare a fortnight later, Doncaster were dispatched 31-8 at Tattersfield. Neil engineered two tries and hoofed three goals but had to retire with a hamstring injury in the second half. It caused him to miss his first game of the season, a 9-5 defeat at Whitehaven on 10 December. Three days earlier the Huddersfield takeover had been completed and the club became a limited company, although Jack Pearson, a turf accountant for whom Neil worked, had stood down from the three-man consortium.

Christmas arrived with Huddersfield lying fifth in the league. They faced a couple of traditional holiday derbies against Halifax, who had not won a game all season. Huddersfield won both games. Neil landed five goals in the 22-5 Boxing Day win at Fartown and the following day, Tuesday, 27 December, 1977, at Thrum Hall he broke Jim Sullivan's record points aggregate of 6,022 points. Of course, no-one realised it at the time. He began the game at Thrum Hall on 6,020 points. Huddersfield led 6-0 through tries by Peter Rowe and Joe Cyrus, which Neil had failed to convert. Neil missed four attempts in all but as half-time approached he equalled Sullivan's world record. Branch made a telling break and fed Shepherd with a suspiciously forward-looking pass for the scrum-half to scamper between the posts. Neil landed the easy conversion and broke the record with a penalty goal in the 67th minute to extend Huddersfield's lead to 13-0.

Huddersfield, although still winning games, had gone off the boil since the clash with Bradford. A crucial match against Oldham - the two teams were level on points - would arguably have a big influence on the promotion race. It took place at Fartown on 2 January and for the first 40 minutes Oldham had Neil's men on the rack to lead 12-3. The second half was a complete reversal as the Fartowners ran the Roughyeds into the ground with some splendid play to win 22-15. Neil kicked four goals and popped out a peach of a pass to put Glen Knight over for a 65th-minute try, which sealed the victory.

On 8 January, Huddersfield gave an indifferent display against Batley but won 24-17. Ian Laybourne, who had succeeded John Huxley as the *Examiner's* rugby league correspondent, wrote, "The Fartown leader had had a crucial hand in all three first-half tries with superbly timed passes but when he missed his third conversion it meant Huddersfield still trailed. Right on half-time, however, Fox landed a penalty to put his team ahead for the first time and, two minutes after the restart, scored a further five points when he chipped over the defence and regathered to touch down and goaled the try to make it 16-12." No-one noticed that the score had been Neil's 350th career try.

A week later Huddersfield unaccountably lost 12-5 at Huyton. Ian Laybourne described it as a "shabby display" and fulminated that "Huddersfield were not just beaten. They were given a lesson in open football and tactics". On 29 January they returned to winning ways with a 12-5 success at Batley. Neil landed three goals, the second of which took him to another incredible milestone – his 2,500th.

With things going so satisfactorily at Fartown, Neil's immediate future seemed mapped out – finish the job of winning promotion and take stock of the situation thereafter. Suddenly everything changed and Neil recalls, "Wakefield had parted company with their coach Brian Lockwood. They had appointed my friend Ian Brooke as team manager. Trevor Woodward, my ex-business partner, was Trinity's chairman and he phoned me to ask if I would go back to Trinity for a third time as player-coach to work with Ian. I was tempted to return and thought long and hard about it. In the end, I said no. If it did not work there was a danger that Ian and I might fall out. I valued our friendship too much and did not want to risk losing it."

Neil was, however, on his way out of Fartown. On 1 February 1978 the Bradford *Telegraph & Argus* announced on its back page "Odsal after all for Fox". Brian Smith reported: "Bradford Northern have beaten Wakefield Trinity in the chase to sign Huddersfield player-coach Neil Fox." Smith reported that the deal would be completed the following day and was costing Northern just over £2,000, according to director Ronnie Firth, who handled the negotiations. Mr Firth had made more than 70 calls in the last few days in pursuit of the deal. Neil told the *Telegraph & Argus:* "I decided there would be too many problems going back to Trinity... I worked with my brother Peter at Bramley last season and we didn't have a single argument. There is no reason why we shouldn't get on together at Odsal. He knows not to expect too much of me but he expects that I shall play the rest of this season and next season. Then I hope to look for a coaching job."

Peter told the press: "I'm looking to him as the manipulator in the pack. He will help take weight off Johnny Wolford in this respect and he will also ease the pressure on Keith Mumby with his goalkicking." Like the rest of the rugby league fraternity, Peter was unaware that Neil had already become the most prolific scorer in the sport's history and added, "He is going to break that record [of Sullivan] and he has a better chance of doing it with a better team. That has been a big factor in his decision to join us."

When Neil left Huddersfield his team was in fourth place in Division 2 and he reckoned that they would only need to win a couple more games to clinch promotion. He says, "The only reason I was walking away from Huddersfield was that I knew we would get promotion so I asked the directors if there would be money for strengthening the side. One player I was interested in was Wakefield's Graham Idle. The fee quoted was £6,000, but the directors said there was no money at all and that I would have to work with what I had. I thought I had done a good job with the players I had but there needed to be additions if there was to be any progress. I was sorry to be leaving Fartown and the players and supporters, who had been great during my short time at the club." Huddersfield, under Dave Heppleston as caretaker coach and skipper Trevor Leathley, won promotion in fourth position and Neil could look back with satisfaction on a job well done.

Neil had gone from being player-coach at an aspiring Second Division club with crowds of fewer than 2,000 to being a player at a club which had hopes of winning major trophies. Northern had spent more than £30,000 on players since the start of the season. They had also wanted to buy test loose-forward Steve Norton from Castleford but he had gone to Hull for £25,000. Neil was considered the next best buy, if only short term. Northern had forked out £8,000 to Bramley for centre Derek Parker and had signed Jimmy Thompson for a club record £10,000 from Featherstone, David Barends for £7,500 from York, Dean Raistrick at £2,500 from Keighley, Ian van Bellen for £1,500 from Huddersfield and Jack Austin for £1,000 from Bramley. Peter Fox was building a team which meant business.

Neil made his debut for Bradford on Sunday, 5 February, in a home game against Hull, playing second-row alongside Dennis Trotter. Also making his debut in the centre was new signing Lee Greenwood from Halifax. The *Telegraph & Argus* headline "Fox misses make Odsal fans wince" may not have been flattering but Neil did miss seven out of eight shots at goal. However, he sent Jimmy Thompson over for the opening try after 90 seconds and had a major impact in the general play, giving his side a lot of width with his long passing. It appeared that Steve Norton's brilliant solo try after 51 minutes had won the game for Hull at 13-11 but a try by Dean Raistrick after good work from Ian van Bellen with five minutes remaining gave Northern a dramatic 14-13 victory.

After the game Neil told the *Yorkshire Post's* Raymond Fletcher that he had not been troubled by the step up from Division 2: "I always pace myself and did not feel that there was all that much difference. In fact, I think I was more involved than at Huddersfield. I had a hand in a couple of tries, so I can't have done too badly." Fletcher noted, "Fox was just one of several players of class on both sides whose handling ability was a joy to watch in a game packed with movement and interest despite the very greasy conditions."

However, it would be three weeks before Bradford played again following a spell of Arctic weather. Second Division Barrow visited Odsal for a first round Challenge Cup tie, which had all the makings of a classic upset when they took a 13-4 lead in the 49th minute. Neil had kicked a couple of penalties but Barrow had shrugged off a 7-1 first-half scrum deficit to run in three tries. However, Peter Fox made a masterful tactical move after 53 minutes by switching Wolford to scrum-half and bringing in Ian Slater at stand-off. The crowd expressed their unhappiness but were won over when Northern roared in for 17 points in 13 minutes. Neil and Graham Joyce made a try for Mumby, which Neil converted in the 61st minute. Four minutes later his conversion of a storming try from Thompson put his side 14-13 up and then he added a penalty. His sixth goal, a conversion of a final try from Barends, sealed a 21-13 success. Neil's combination with the creative John Wolford played a huge part in driving Northern to victory and his goalkicking was decisive.

Northern were running third in Division 1, one point behind joint leaders St Helens and Widnes, with a game in hand. Their game at Widnes on 1 March, therefore, would have a significant impact on the Championship race. Unfortunately, Bradford took a weakened team to Naughton Park and were beaten 19-2. Neil scored the team's only points with a penalty and the pack did well enough "with Thompson putting in a mighty stint and Fox constantly probing for the openings". The result showed how much Northern would have to improve to be real Championship contenders. Four days later at Odsal, Neil came up against Wakefield Trinity, who had won three games on the trot since Ian Brooke's appointment as manager but were still mired in the relegation struggle. In the first minute he suffered a knee strain but played on for about 50 minutes before coming off with Northern leading 8-5 after their best display for weeks. In first-half injury time, according to Brian Smith, "Fox produced a vintage piece of play, storming through two tackles from 10 yards to score." Bradford won 18-10 but Neil's injury caused him to miss three games.

In his absence Northern gave a commanding performance in knocking Wigan out of the Cup at Central Park, their first win there since 1952, but went out at Leeds in the third round. The Headingley tie was a cracker and Northern played well but not well enough in front of the biggest rugby league crowd of the season so far of almost 19,000. Neil missed a home win against New Hunslet but returned as a substitute in a 34-4 spanking of Workington Town at Odsal, dummying his way over for a try after 67 minutes.

Bad weather had caused a fixture pile-up for Northern of nine league games in 31 days, which was a tall order for a young player, let alone a man of Neil's age. Neil was again selected at substitute for a must-win game at St Helens on Thursday, 30 March, but suffered a rib injury after replacing Francis Jarvis after 52 minutes, as Northern went down 28-13. He missed another defeat, 21-13 at Salford, the following Wednesday as Northern's hopes of the Championship disintegrated.

There was, however, a compelling end to the season. Two days after losing at Salford, Northern went to fifth-placed Hull KR, giving debuts to Derek Parker, who had finally recovered from a groin injury, and Great Britain Colts forward Kenny Roberts. Parker scored a splendid try after four minutes from his first pass and two goals from Neil gave Northern a 7-5 half-time lead. Colin Forsyth crashed over for his 17th try of the campaign to equal the record for tries scored by a prop forward in a season, set by Dewsbury's Trevor Walker in 1969-70. Neil converted and there was a final try from skipper Bob Haigh after some typical jiggery-pokery from John Wolford to clinch victory by 15-7. The win ensured that Northern would finish in the top four and was the first for Bradford at Craven Park for 10 years. Peter Fox could turn round to his critics, who had accused him of buying too many veterans, and say, "The old men didn't do too badly, did they?"

On 12 April, Northern hosted St Helens requiring a point to ensure at least third place in the league. Neil booted three penalties to give his side a 6-3 lead at the break, when the light suddenly faded and it began to snow. Saints subsequently improved and took a 9-6 lead but in the last minute of normal time Wolford put Mumby over for an equalising try, which Neil failed to convert. In injury time both sets of fans had palpitations, when Saints' Harry Pinner dropped for goal, missed and Les Jones almost scored a try from the aftermath. Neil then struck a valiant long-distance drop-goal attempt, which missed as the hooter sounded. A 9-9 draw had achieved Bradford's objective and was a fair result.

Four days later Dewsbury, already relegated, visited Odsal and were walloped 33-3. Keith Mumby was given the first conversion, which brought him his 1,000th point for the club, and David Redfearn scored his 150th try for Bradford. The last try of the game by Jack Austin was Northern's 100th league try of the season. Among all these milestones, Neil was busy on his own account, bagging two tries and hoisting five goals.

On 19 April, Bradford went to Headingley and beat Leeds 18-10, the Loiners scoring eight of their points in the last eight minutes. It was Northern's first win at Leeds in 12 attempts and their first double over them since 1964-65. Leeds needed to win to qualify for the Premiership play-off and had the advantage of a 13-8 scrum count and a 13-4 penalty count but could not cope with the wiles of Wolford, Alan Redfearn and Neil. The *Telegraph & Argus* reported, "Fox turned the clock back once with a superb storming run which would have brought a try just before the interval, but for an excellent tackle by Kevin Dick."

Northern were due to finish their league season on 23 April with a tough game at Featherstone Rovers, who had already qualified for the play-offs. The Rovers players, however, were on strike and the club could not raise a team. Gordon Appleyard, Rovers' chairman, had resigned because he felt he did not have the support of the rest of the club's committee. The players supported him and had threatened to strike if he was not reinstated. The committee did not back down and cancelled the game against Bradford. They were subsequently ejected from the play-offs and ninth-placed Warrington took their place. St Helens had finished with 45 points from 30 games. Northern, due to the cancellation of the Featherstone fixture, had 44 points from 29. However, the RFL decided that Northern had finished second to Champions Widnes, who had 50 points, on a percentage basis, with Wembley-bound Saints third.

Northern's Premiership challenge began with a home tie against Leeds on Sunday, 30 April, an appalling afternoon, which left Odsal in one of its vilest states for play. Under the circumstances a remarkably good game ensued. Northern took a 10-0 lead through two Bob Haigh tries, which were converted by Neil, but Leeds had fought back to 13-5 by half-time, Jimmy Thompson having added a third try to Northern's cause, plunging through from 15 yards after a tap penalty. Parker extended the lead to 18-5 with a fourth try converted by Mumby after 58 minutes before Les Dyl's 75th-minute try brought Leeds some respectability at 18-10. Neil's four points had taken him past a career total of 6,100.

The semi-finals were played on a home-and-away basis. Northern's opponents were St Helens. Neil damaged a knee against Leeds and missed the first leg at Knowsley Road on Wednesday, 3 May, along with Alan Redfearn, Thompson and Forsyth. Bradford scored a moral victory in losing only 14-10. Peter Fox reckoned it was as good a performance as Northern had produced in his stewardship. Van Bellen, Trotter, Peter Roe and Paul Harkin were outstanding. The player of the match though was Keith Mumby, who gave a faultless display, prompting Peter Fox to comment, "Mumby was like a brick wall, 12 feet high". His tackling was wonderful and he kicked his 100th goal of the season. It was no surprise that he was Northern's Player of the Year the third time, despite being only 21.

The second leg took place at Odsal on Sunday, 7 May, and it soon looked as if all Northern's heroics had been in vain as Saints took an 8-0 lead by the eighth minute. Northern were effectively 12-0 down. However, the Northern spirit burned brightly and after 10 minutes Haigh raced over after good work by Joyce and Mumby's conversion reduced the deficit to seven points, only for Saints full-back Geoff Pimblett to drop two goals within two minutes and then slot a penalty to stretch the lead to 12-5. On the half hour good passing put Austin over for a converted try and Northern had a lifeline at 12-10. The first half saw only three penalties and seven scrums, which Saints took 4-3, although Northern did not win one until the 32nd minute. On 47 minutes Derek Parker smashed through two tackles to score and Mumby improved before adding a penalty in the 66th minute to nose Northern ahead 17-12. One point up on aggregate, Northern brought Neil on for van Bellen. He immediately dropped a goal and another drop-goal from Wolford finished the scoring at 19-12 and sealed a famous victory for Bradford.

The *Telegraph & Argus* observed: "In pure footballing terms Northern were never at their best... but they all helped each other up the mountain with a mighty team achievement and every one of the men on duty in the two matches did themselves and Bradford proud." Peter Fox said, "After five minutes I felt physically sick. I just could not believe that we were 12-0 down on aggregate after that marvellous effort on Wednesday. Had we started at that score, I couldn't honestly have hoped to win... these lads are fighters and showed their character by the way they ... kept going."

So, 20 years after his first, Neil had yet another major final to look forward to. The Premiership Final pitted Northern against champions Widnes at Swinton on Saturday, 20 May, where the teams were:

Bradford Northern: Keith Mumby, Dave Barends, Peter Roe, Jack Austin, Dave Redfearn, John Wolford, Alan Redfearn, Ian van Bellen, Dean Raistrick, Jimmy Thompson, Dennis Trotter, Graham Joyce, Bob Haigh (captain). Substitutes: Neil Fox, Colin Forsyth.

Widnes: Dave Eckersley, Stuart Wright, Eric Hughes, Mal Aspey, Paul Woods, Ken Gill, Reg Bowden (captain), Jim Mills, Keith Elwell, Glyn Shaw, Mick Adams, Dave Hull, Dougie Laughton. Substitutes: Mick George, Bill Ramsey.

Referee: J. E. Jackson (Pudsey)

The game proved a humdinger. Following on from a wonderful Wembley final between Leeds and St Helens, Phil Lyon of the *Halifax Evening Courier* wrote, "Every few years, rugby league serves up a vintage Wembley. But for a single season to produce two such fine games as the 1978 Challenge Cup and Premiership finals is a pleasurable and unexpected bonus... From start to finish the tackling was of such ferocity that it was clear that neither side was taking prisoners. And in the end Bradford won because they had the ability and the patience to soak up the punishment better than Widnes and take their chances when they sensed the Chemics' guard had dropped."

Widnes were unlucky enough to lose Glyn Shaw after 20 minutes and his replacement Bill Ramsey after 40, while Mick Adams played with a pulled muscle. But Northern were undoubtedly worthy winners, overcoming an early five point deficit and a penalty count of 10-13. After conceding a try by Aspey, improved by Woods after 10 minutes, Alan Redfearn sent Haigh careering over for a 20th-minute try, goaled by Mumby. They edged ahead on 30 minutes with a spectacular try, begun by van Bellen, developed by Haigh and finished by Roe, who sprinted clear from near halfway. Five minutes before the break Wolford smartly dropped a goal to give Northern a 9-5 lead. Early in the second half both Bradford substitutes were introduced but it was Widnes who struck, when Laughton sent Aspey through for a 55th-minute try. Neil put in a couple of hefty clearing kicks and another attacking kick had Thompson touching down only for the try to be disallowed. Raymond Fletcher in the *Yorkshire Post* noted: "Neil Fox replaced van Bellen. Widnes, having braced themselves for the battering runs of the latter, fell for the bluffing of the old Fox. Eighteen years after playing in his first play-off final he treated us to 26 minutes of memories."

Bradford effectively sealed their victory after 62 minutes, when fine play by Wolford and Trotter enabled Dave Redfearn to cross at the corner for a try, magnificently converted by Mumby. In the last minute Barends flung himself over for a final try to make the score 17-8. The pitch had to be cleared of jubilant Northern fans before Mumby could attempt the conversion, which he missed. Northern's Premiership success heralded the start of a mini golden age for the club under Peter Fox and an unexpected bonus for his youngest brother. Neil told the press: "That's another medal to put in the safe. I have lost count of how many I have got, but this is my first Premiership one. I usually find it harder going on as substitute, because the pressure is on you to do something special. But today it was easier. Widnes seemed to open up every time I moved forward." Mighty Ian van Bellen, the man Neil released from Huddersfield earlier in the year, and whom he replaced during the final, told the *Telegraph & Argus*, "I couldn't have imagined anything like this at the start of the season". Pointing to Neil Fox, he said, "I couldn't even get in at Huddersfield when he took over, but now we've shared this together. Everything's worked like a dream for me."

Brian Smith's end of season summary in the *Telegraph & Argus* noted, "[the semi-finals] typified the spirit Peter Fox has given the side this season, and Saturday's display against Widnes not only had all the grit and determination but also skill and flair and signalled Northern's emergence as a side that is going to take some stopping. One could perhaps wish that the clock could be turned back a few years for some of the players who have done so well this season, for men like Haigh, van Bellen, Wolford, Forsyth, Fox, Austin, Thompson, etc., cannot be expected to go on for ever".

Neil was not ready for retirement just yet. During the 1977-78 season he had made 34 appearances for Huddersfield and Bradford, running up 215 points. Anyway, he could hardly let down Peter, having promised to play the 1978-79 season for him, when he first returned to Odsal.

Huddersfield 1977-78

Huddersfield finished 4th in Division 2: P26, W18, L8, For 502, Against 324
Fox scored 5 tries, 72 goals, 1 drop goal, 160 points for Huddersfield before signing for Bradford Northern

Date	Opponent	Score	Fox	Crowd	
21 Aug	**York**	17-20	4G	1,497	YC1
30 Aug	**Wigan**	18-22	3G	1,282	FT Prel
4 Sep	**Leigh**	11-22	G	1,087	
11 Sep	Swinton	27-13	6G	905	
18 Sep	**Huyton**	44-0	T, 6G	958	
25 Sep	Blackpool B	33-15	6G	721	
2 Oct	**Keighley**	18-10	3G	1,771	
9 Oct	Leigh	14-20	G	2,030	
16 Oct	**Barrow**	15-13	3G	1,340	
23 Oct	**Whitehaven**	33-13	T, 6G	1,832	PT1
30 Oct	**Doncaster**	44-10	T, 7G	1,163	
6 Nov	**Oldham**	21-11	T, 3G	3,900	PT2
13 Nov	York	14-0	2G, DG	3,861	
19 Nov	**Bradford N**	0-11		6,094	PT3
4 Dec	Doncaster	31-8	3G	725	
10 Dec	Whitehaven	5-9	dnp	441	
26 Dec	**Halifax**	22-5	5G	1,399	
27 Dec	Halifax	16-5	2G	2,383	
2 Jan	**Oldham**	22-15	4G	2,921	
8 Jan	**Batley**	24-17	T, 3G	1,830	
15 Jan	Huyton	5-12	G	300	
29 Jan	Batley	12-5	3G	913	

Bradford Northern 1977-78

Bradford Northern finished 2nd in Division 1: P29, W21, L6, D2, For 500, Against 291
Fox scored 4 tries, 21 goals, 1 drop goal, 55 points for Bradford

Date	Opponent	Score	Fox	Crowd	
5 Feb	**Hull**	14-13	G	4,735	
26 Feb	**Barrow**	21-13	6G	7,276	Ch Cup 1
1 Mar	Widnes	2-19	G	7,187	
5 Mar	**Wakefield T**	18-10	T	8,379	
11 Mar	Wigan	22-10	dnp	9,426	Ch Cup 2
19 Mar	Leeds	8-16	dnp	18,895	Ch Cup 3
24 Mar	**New Hunslet**	18-6	dnp	5,724	
27 Mar	**Workington T***	34-4	T	6,063	
30 Mar	St Helens*	13-28		5,881	
5 Apr	Salford	13-21	dnp	3,961	
7 Apr	Hull KR	15-7	3G	5,069	
12 Apr	**St Helens**	9-9	3G	6,262	
16 Apr	**Dewsbury**	33-3	2T, 5G	6,042	
19 Apr	Leeds	18-10		4,676	
23 Apr	Featherstone R++				
30 Apr	**Leeds**	18-10	2G	7,268	Prem 1
3 May	St Helens	10-14	dnp	6,827	Prem semi, 1st leg
7 May	**St Helens***	19-12	DG	12,822	Prem semi, 2nd leg
20 May	Widnes*	17-8		16,813	Prem Final (at Swinton)

* Substitute
++ This game was not played because of a threatened strike by the Featherstone players.

28. 1978-79: Bowing out

Neil had finished the 1977-78 season on a high with his capture of a Premiership winners' medal. English rugby league, too, had reason to be pleased. The slow recovery in attendances was continuing. Season 1977-78 had seen a rise from 1,190,498 to 1,354,887 in total league attendances, with an average crowd of 3,218. The latter figure represented an increase of almost 1,300 fans per match on the 1973-74 figures. Bradford Northern were setting the pace in attendance figures, especially in Yorkshire. Total league crowds at Odsal passed the 100,000 mark for the first time since 1969-70 – coincidentally, the season Neil had first played for them. Their average crowd for 1977-78 was 7,237, an increase of more than 2,500. Only Widnes, with 7,487, could boast better crowds than Northern. Administratively the game was certainly in better hands with David Oxley and David Howes giving both stability and dynamism at the RFL after the upheavals of the latter part of Bill Fallowfield's tenure at Chapeltown Road. The fans were spared more changes in the laws and were becoming accustomed to the six-tackle rule.

The season would culminate in a Lions tour and although Neil was hardly likely to be anything more than an interested bystander, many of his team-mates would be vying for tour berths, while Peter Fox could reasonably expect to be in the running for the Lions coaching job. His hopes were heightened when he was given the job of coaching Great Britain for the 1978 Ashes tests in England. Indeed, Bradford Northern supplied the coach, the Great Britain manager Harry Womersley and the Great Britain physio Ronnie Barritt.

There were a few changes at Odsal as the pre-season friendlies began. Jimmy Thompson took over the captaincy from Bob Haigh and veteran hooker Tony Fisher was signed from Castleford on a free transfer. Francis Jarvis was sold to Featherstone for £5,500 and Northern pulled in a similar amount from Halifax for Jimmy Birts, Graham Garrod and Derek Howard. Another £5,000 was banked in a package deal which took Lee Greenwood and Kevin Farrell to Keighley. Revenue was also pouring into the club's coffers from increased season-ticket sales, £18,000 accruing from 3,100 tickets, double the previous season. The fans expected big signings, but would have to wait for a while.

Neil played in both of Northern's friendlies. He kicked four goals in a 26-10 win at Batley on 6 August and five goals in a 36-23 home success against Doncaster a week later. Those games saw the first appearances of a precocious Ellery Hanley, first at full-back and then at centre. The season proper began with a pulsating home Yorkshire Cup tie against Leeds. Neil, in the second-row, played a big part in a 24-23 win before a crowd of 8,523, the biggest at a Yorkshire Cup tie since 1970. Northern recovered from deficits of 15-5 and 23-14 to snatch a breathtaking last-gasp victory. Neil's first goal brought him his 100th point for Northern and his sixth and last, a conversion of Alan Redfearn's winning try, brought the victory. Neil had kicked six from six but could have lost the game for Northern in injury time, when he conceded a penalty. Fortunately, Gibson's attempt from half-way fell short.

A week later, Neil turned out in a second-round Yorkshire Cup tie at home against Hull KR. It was his 800th appearance in first-class rugby league and he celebrated by landing another half-dozen goals in an easy 28-17 win. On 3 September, Northern won their first league game, a 35-10 rout at promoted Barrow, despite lacking their entire first choice threequarter line. A debutant was 17-year-old winger Henderson Gill who, like Ellery Hanley, would make a huge impact on the sport. Neil played for the last 32 minutes and kicked three goals. Three days later Leigh were dispatched 38-7 at Odsal, Dave Barends scoring a hat-trick, while Neil added four goals before being substituted after 52 minutes.

Northern's winning run came to a halt at Warrington on 10 September but Neil was missing thanks to a heavy cold. The *Telegraph & Argus* noted that in his absence there appeared to be no link between the pack and the backs. He was back, however, for the Yorkshire Cup semi-final against Hull at Odsal on 13 September. Northern were the only First Division team in the semis, Halifax and York contesting the other match. Despite a 5.45pm kick-off, as Northern did not have floodlights, the game attracted a crowd of 10,239, the highest of the season so far at any game. There was tremendous traffic congestion and many Hull fans were still stranded on the M606 long after the game had started. One Hull journalist arrived 30 minutes after kick-off having left Hull at 4pm, usually enough time for the trip along the motorway. The *Telegraph & Argus* described "supporters leaping out of coaches and racing across fields and the [South Bradford] golf course in an effort to get to the match on time."

The game was an intriguing struggle but Northern progressed to the final, winning more comfortably than a 12-7 scoreline suggested. Scrum-half Alan Redfearn was man-of-the-match but Neil stole many of the headlines. The *Yorkshire Post* reported: "Neil Fox celebrated... in the best possible way... by guiding Bradford Northern to their first Yorkshire Cup final since 1965. It was not his goalkicking which put him in the spotlight, but his masterly work in the loose... Fox shrugged off his 39 years as he showed younger players how it was done. No one handled better, and when it was needed, he could always find the extra speed and energy. It was from a couple of dummies by Fox that Haigh scored the first try after six minutes. Amazingly, Fox's kick at goal from almost in front of the posts hit an upright, but although he also missed with two other shots, he was always making an impact in the pack. He finally turned the game entirely Bradford's way after 66 minutes with a superb try which Mumby improved. After slipping through two tackles he stretched out to plant the ball over the line."

There was anti-climax four days later at Odsal in the league, where Castleford triumphed 31-19. Neil, who kicked three goals, had to turn out at blind-side prop because of injuries, while Paul Starbuck, a £3,000 signing from Oldham, made his debut in the second-row. The following week in a John Player Trophy match Neil came off the bench at Barrow, with Northern leading 12-5. Within six minutes he had orchestrated a try for Mumby. Neil converted it and went on to add three more goals in an ultimately comfortable 26-8 success. A bad Friday followed at Salford. Northern were injury-hit and took the field with six players under the age of 21. The weather was wretched and Northern arrived late because of traffic chaos. A 17-8 defeat was their third consecutive in the league.

Centre Graham Evans was sold to Keighley for £5,000 and Northern splashed out a club record £14,000 for Dewsbury test forward Jeff Grayshon. The latter was signed in time to make his debut against the Kangaroos at Odsal on 8 October. The Australians had opened their tour with three big wins against Blackpool Borough, Cumbria and the Great Britain under-24 side and had not conceded a try. The Bradford crowd expected an Australian victory but Northern, and Neil in particular, gave the Australians a nasty shock. Jack Bentley in the *Daily Express* reported: "Neil Fox, the oldest man on the field who first showed Australians what British Rugby League skill could do 22 years ago, gave Britain's test selectors some guidance here. He stormed in for the first try against the powerful Kangaroos after a mere 30 seconds following an interception 25 yards out. Then 20 minutes later it was 39-year-old Fox tormenting the tourists once more. He pushed off one defender before thrusting over the line between their posts in full-back Alan McMahon's tackle for Northern's second try. Another veteran, test ace hooker Tony Fisher, revelled with Fox in the battle. And the 15,755 crowd erupted with euphoria and enthusiasm as

Northern, tackling superbly, went on to chalk up an 11-5 lead just before half-time. Fox had landed two goals to make his personal contribution 10 points and Fisher dropped a goal from a Fox pass. Both had demonstrated how the Kangaroos can be tied down by hard, low tackling and how Australians can always be baffled by British football skill."

Neil was replaced by Colin Forsyth after 51 minutes, after almost scoring two more tries. The crowd gave him a standing ovation. At that point Northern were still ahead at 11-10 but subsided against the superior fitness and pace of the tourists in the last quarter to lose 21-11. The game against the 1978 Kangaroos unquestionably represented one of Neil's most impressive exhibitions as a forward. He told Raymond Fletcher in the *Yorkshire Post:* "I always seem to save something for the Australians. They have written me off many times in the past, but that was another performance to give me great pleasure. I first played against the Australians 22 years ago, but this was my farewell song against them. It probably rates with my other displays against them, but I used to last longer! I think I showed that they can still be beaten by brains."

The game against the Australians was the last time Neil was to score either two tries or 10 points in a match at first-class level. He also had the distinction of being one of only two players to bag two tries against the tourists, who conceded just 12 tries in 16 fixtures in Britain. Great Britain winger Stuart Wright, in the second test at Odsal, was the other.

A fortnight later Neil kicked two goals in a 19-8 home win over Wigan, although two spectacular late tries from Dave Barends stole the limelight. Another big game followed on Saturday 28 October, as Northern encountered York at Headingley in the Yorkshire Cup Final. The teams were:

Bradford Northern: K. Mumby, D. Barends, L. Gant, D. Parker, D. Redfearn, I. Slater, A. Redfearn, J. Thompson, A. Fisher, C. Forsyth, N. Fox, D. Trotter, R. Haigh.
Substitutes: J. Wolford (For Slater), M. Joyce (for Forsyth).
York: G. Smith, T. Morgan, T. Day, D. Foster, G. Nicholson, B. Banks, K. Harkin, D. Dunkerley, R. Wileman, W. Harris, A. Rhodes, B. Hollis, S. Cooper.
Substitutes: J. Crossley (for Day), T. Ramshaw (for Hollis).

Hot favourites Northern took the lead with a try from Alan Redfearn, goaled by Neil, but were held to 5-5 at half-time after York landed two penalties and a drop-goal. On the resumption Peter Fox introduced John Wolford, who had flown in just the previous day after working in Singapore, at stand-off. It was the catalyst that turned the match. Two minutes into the half Wolford conjured a try for Haigh, who won the White Rose Trophy as man-of-the-match. Neil converted and Bradford subsequently never lost their grip. After 53 minutes, Wolford, Neil and Parker combined to put Gant over but Neil's conversion struck a post and bounced out. An 80-yard interception try by Parker, improved by Neil, stretched their lead to 18-5 before full-back Gary Smith finally scored for York after 70 minutes. The game was Neil's seventh Yorkshire Cup Final, five of which had been won, and his three goals gave him an aggregate of 53 points, a record for the county cup, as was his 19 goals. Neil was replaced by Colin Forsyth for the final five minutes. Although happy with another winners' medal, Neil said: "It was the worst final I have played in. Perhaps it was because it was against Second Division opposition, but it did not have the feel of a final and I never really got worked up for it."

Despite winning the Yorkshire Cup and running the Kangaroos so close, Northern were making little headway in the league. After going down unluckily in a stirring match at unbeaten league leaders Hull KR, they found themselves in 12th place in the table. However, it was still a surprise when Peter Fox decided to part with John Wolford, who, along with Jack Austin, was transferred to Dewsbury in exchange for centre or stand-off Nigel Stephenson, a very gifted and clever player, who crucially was five years younger than Wolford. Peter Fox's wheeling and dealing in this period also saw the departures of Graham Joyce and Ian Slater to Leeds and Dean Raistrick to Halifax, for a combined total estimated at £27,000.

Stephenson made his debut at stand-off at Leigh on 19 November and Bradford could now boast a trio of players, who collectively had amassed well over 9,000 points in Neil (6,000), Stephenson (2,000) and Mumby (1,000) – possibly a unique situation. Northern won 13-7, Neil claiming two goals and a 32nd-minute try. Brian Smith described the score as "a sample of vintage play by Neil Fox, who scored a try reminiscent of his second against Australia recently at Odsal, dummying his way through and crashing past two defenders." It was Neil's last try for Northern and his last in first class rugby league – his 358th overall.

On 26 November, Neil booted four goals in a scratchy 30-18 home win over Rochdale Hornets. The match was notable for being Ellery Hanley's first-class debut. He substituted for Les Gant after 71 minutes and scored his side's last try. When Ellery entered the fray, however, Neil had been replaced by Bob Haigh 15 minutes earlier, so these two great icons of their respective eras never actually played together in a first class fixture. Hanley did not make any further first-team appearances during the season.

The following week Bradford won a second-round John Player Trophy match at Hull. Neil kicked two goals before leaving the field after 62 minutes, but the hero was Alan Redfearn, who played brilliantly. An 18-7 win at Featherstone on 10 December brought Neil two more landmarks. His first of three goals took his career points total to 6,200 and his third goal gave him his 100th point of the season. It was the 22nd time he had scored 100 or more points in a season - his only failure to reach that in a complete season was with Northern in 1969-70.

On 17 December, Neil played 56 minutes of a third-round John Player Trophy tie against Wakefield Trinity after replacing Bob Haigh. He did not score, but made a try for Forsyth, which gave Northern an 11-10 lead after they had trailed for much of the game. Henderson Gill scored the winning try three minutes from time to give a 16-13 scoreline and Neil was looking forward to yet another semi-final.

On Boxing Day, Bradford won convincingly at Huddersfield, Neil's major contribution being a long pass which put Barends over, but he was only brought on to steady the team for the last 13 minutes of a splendid 10-5 win at Headingley on 6 January. The game was notable for Len Casey's debut for Bradford. He had cost Northern a large fee plus scrum-half Paul Harkin. The deal was estimated at £23,000, a new club record. Peter Fox was increasingly using Neil in smaller but more judicious doses. Northern had risen to seventh in the table but had played fewer league games than anyone. This created a difficult situation for the club because bad weather soon became as much a problem as opposing teams. The John Player Trophy semi-finals fell victim to the weather and the final, which was scheduled for 27 January, was moved to the end of April.

Neil missed a league game against the semi-final opponents Widnes on Wednesday 17 January. Northern lost 17-0, their first 'nilling' for three years. Blizzards hit the West Riding and Northern were so desperate to whittle down their fixture backlog that they arranged to switch venues for their game against Workington Town on 21 January, leaving behind the Arctic weather at Odsal for Cumbria, where conditions were spring-like. A tremendous try by Barends gave Northern a 3-1 interval lead and five minutes after the break Neil hoisted a huge, steepling kick, which forced Workington to drop-out. Northern immediately engineered a try for David Redfearn at the corner, which Neil converted with a superb kick.

Their 13-6 win was well deserved and Brian Smith noted, "The return of Alan Redfearn and Fox provided the attacking links missing so badly at Widnes last Wednesday".

Three days later Northern finally played their John Player Trophy semi-final at Widnes, but a wretched night brought a wretched result with a 21-3 defeat, Neil again missing the debacle. He was back for a desperately close-run win at bottom club Barrow and for Northern's first-round Challenge Cup tie at Swinton, which had already been postponed twice. He landed a fine angled penalty in the first minute, but was substituted after 48 minutes, as Northern struggled to win 8-2 after losing the penalty count 19-5.

The second round brought table-toppers Hull KR to Odsal and a crowd of almost 14,000 was spellbound by a thrilling cup tie, laced with exciting movements and continuous full-blooded tackling. Although Northern were caned 18-7 on penalties and had three tries disallowed, they were demonstrably the better team and fully deserved their 14-7 victory. The third round on 11 March attracted a crowd of more than 19,000 to Odsal for the visit of Hull, who were going through the Second Division with a perfect record of 26 victories from 26 games. Northern seemed to have their measure and tries by Casey and Grayshon, the latter improved by Neil, gave them an 8-0 half-time lead. But it was 8-8 when Neil was substituted in the 61st minute and remained so at full-time. Neil was a substitute for the replay three days later but was not used as Northern won 8-4. Hull had led 4-0 at the break but tries from David Redfearn and Parker demonstrated the difference in class and strong defence saw off Hull's challenge before an all-ticket crowd of 16,979. Stephenson and Ian van Bellen added drop-goals for Northern.

Northern continued to have difficulties fulfilling fixtures, owing to the weather and their success in the knock-out competitions. It was a relief to them when the RFL extended the deadline for the First Division season from 22 April to 2 May and later to 13 May, with the Premiership Final pushed back to 27 May. In order to get a league fixture against Featherstone out of the way on 25 March because Odsal was snowbound, they conceded ground advantage. Featherstone had only won twice in their last 16 games and Bradford probably thought ceding ground advantage would not prevent them from winning. Their decision backfired. Heavy rain did not deter the fans and Featherstone got their biggest gate of the season. Neil played 73 minutes of the game and landed a solitary goal but Rovers won 25-11. The *Telegraph & Argus* noted "the heavy going which gradually reduced the game to a farce and made the Eton wall game seem a sophisticated affair".

Bradford faced Widnes in the Challenge Cup semi-final at Swinton on 31 March. Widnes had won the Lancashire Cup and the Floodlit Trophy and qualified for the upcoming final of the John Player Trophy. They did not seem to need luck. They had it in spades, however, in the semi-final. Every ball seemed to bounce for them but they ruthlessly took their chances. Northern hooker Tony Fisher withdrew injured just before the game and his side lost the scrums 14-7, while scrum-half Alan Redfearn was suffering from 'flu and did not return after half-time. Northern scored three tries to two but could not kick their goals.

Widnes's biggest stroke of luck, however, was Northern's delay in getting Neil onto the field. They were 14-3 ahead before he was introduced. The *Yorkshire Post's* Raymond Fletcher wrote, "Bradford's magnificent fightback began in the 61st minute, when Neil Fox replaced van Bellen. Twenty two years after making his Cup debut, Fox called on all his vast experience to start spraying out a succession of defence–splitting passes. They had Widnes reeling with a series of brilliant attacks that produced two late tries to add to the 18th minute try by Mumby." Brian Smith in the *Telegraph & Argus* concurred: "It was veteran substitute Fox who really began to make the difference in the last quarter, moving the ball wide and helping to bring the match-winning potential of the backs into action...

Fox turned the clock back with a superb brief outing as he tried for a dream return to Wembley which he first graced in 1960." Even so, Northern lost 14-11. Five more minutes with Neil on the pitch could have made the difference.

Neil recalls: "Widnes were in front at half-time and I kept asking Peter to let me go on but he kept saying 'just a minute'. He finally sent me on with less than 20 minutes left and we began to get back into the game. Keith Mumby missed a couple of goals, one of which hit the post and bounced out, and with my only shot at goal after Nigel Stephenson's try I missed by about six inches. Basically we just ran out of time. If only I could have got on 10 minutes earlier, I think we would have been going to Wembley in place of Widnes."

Northern, seventh in the table, still had the Premiership in their sights but luck was not going their way. As March drew to its close they had played only 16 of their 30 league fixtures, while Leeds had played 25 and Leigh 24. They now had 14 fixtures to be played between 3 April and 12 May, nine at Odsal. The fixture list had been contorted by postponements and cup competitions, which had resulted in them staging only six home league games in the first eight months of the season and with nine to come in the last five weeks. Unfortunately, Neil would miss most of them.

He was in the second-row alongside Jeff Grayshon for a disappointing home defeat against Salford on 3 April. Two days later he came off the bench at Rochdale after 51 minutes and helped turn the tide in a 16-8 win. On the hour he kicked a sensational penalty from just inside Hornets' half, only for the referee to disallow it because Dave Barends had stepped offside. A minute later Neil got another penalty in more or less the same position and potted it again. This time Northern made sure Dave was somewhere near his own goal line. On 10 April he again came off the bench in the familiar surroundings of Belle Vue. He had originally been ruled out, but the injury situation was so severe that he was forced to play. The game was notable for being the debut of Bradford Northern's new signing, test hooker Keith Bridges, who had cost them yet another club record fee of £24,500 from Featherstone. Northern beat Trinity 8-6 and the *Telegraph & Argus* commented, "The Fox appearance was timely... for it marked the 23rd anniversary of his professional debut with Trinity, who acknowledged the occasion with a pre-match presentation. And Fox duly got his name on the scoresheet with a second half goal." The goal was his 50th of the season and his 200th and 201st career points for Bradford.

That goal was the last he kicked in the 1978-79 season. Neil had been suffering with cartilage trouble and a foot injury, which kept him out for the rest of the campaign. In his absence Northern struggled against their fixture pile-up and just qualified for the Premiership in eighth place. They then surprised the rugby league fraternity by winning at Hull KR and Warrington, the top two teams, to reach the Premiership Final, but they went down 24-2 to Leeds at Fartown. If that was disappointing to coach Peter Fox, it was probably no more so than his exclusion from the Great Britain coaching post for the 1979 Lions tour, with Eric Ashton getting the appointment. Five Northern players did win Lions places: Dave Barends, Len Casey, Jeff Grayshon, Keith Mumby and Alan Redfearn.

Early in April the RFL announced that Neil was now officially to be recognised as the game's record points scorer. They had decided that Neil had indeed surpassed Jim Sullivan's previous record, although they were still not quite sure of Jim's figures. David Oxley said: "We congratulate Neil Fox on his magnificent achievement. The delay in recognition is unfortunate, but we wanted to be certain about Sullivan's total... We now intend to make an award to Fox for scaling the Everest of scoring records." Of course, Neil would like to have known when exactly he had broken the record. He said: "It's a pity because it was a moment I wanted to treasure. But it's a relief to know that I am now the official record holder. At least I don't have to go on playing for ever now." He told Brian Smith of the *Telegraph & Argus*, "I have known deep down for some time that I must have set a new record but it's nice to have the matter settled once and for all. The saddest thing is that it happened without realising it at the time. It would have been better to have had a definite target to have aimed at on a particular day but it's too late... I have no intention of packing in just yet, but I will be thinking things over at the end of the season."

Neil decided to continue playing with Bradford for the forthcoming 1979-80 season, his 25th as a professional. He was granted a testimonial by the RFL to mark his remarkable longevity and his breaking of the points scoring record. The major event of the testimonial was a match at Belle Vue between a Great Britain Past XIII and a Wakefield Trinity Past XIII on Sunday, 12 August. Neil was in two minds as to which team to play for but chose Trinity. Thirty-six former greats, some still playing, took part in an entertaining affair. That game was preceded by a sevens tournament contested by teams from the six professional clubs Neil had served, plus Yorkshire County and Hull. After the testimonial a reception was held at the Ship Inn, Kirkgate, paid for by the landlords, Geoff and Joan Hamill.

A testimonial brochure was produced for Neil by his friends Terry Kelly and John Lindley. Terry had done a wonderful job organising sponsorship and advertising, and on 24 September there was a sportsman's dinner in Neil's honour, organised by Wakefield Trinity Players' Association at the Painthorpe House Country Club. Neil was presented with a gold watch by Bob Oliver, chairman of the Players' Association. Speakers W. H. (George) Hirst, Jack Charlton, Ian McGeechan and Ian Brooke paid tributes to "the big fella" and an auction by Mick Morgan realised £245 for the testimonial fund. Neil told the audience that he still had an ambition, to play in four decades - from the 1950s to the 1980s.

That ambition was under threat when Neil announced it. He had already become one of the few men who had played professional rugby league when past their 40th birthday. He achieved that when he played in Bradford Northern's opening game of the season on Sunday 19 August 1979 in a first round Yorkshire Cup tie at Huddersfield. Fartown was as appropriate as any ground, other than Belle Vue, for Neil to pass that landmark. Moreover, Huddersfield were coached by his great friend Ian Brooke. A young hooker, Brian Noble, made his first class debut for Northern that afternoon. Northern got off to a flying start when Eddie Okulicz went under the pots for a ninth minute try, goaled by Neil. Three minutes later he converted a try by Alan Redfearn. It was the last goal he would land as a professional player – his 2,575th and his 6,220th point. After 56 minutes he was replaced by Paul Starbuck and limped off into history. Neil had suffered a knee cartilage injury, which required surgery and it was reported that he would be out of action for six to eight weeks. Northern defeated Huddersfield 22-7. The teams in Neil's last first-class game were:

Huddersfield: Adrian Rushton, Peter Cramp, Trevor Leathley, Mick Ward, Ken Senior, Mick Shepherd, Alan Bates, Andy Wilson, David Schofield, Steve Lyons, Chris Burton, Ian Hobson, Malcolm Branch. Substitutes: Dave Hooson, Tony Johnson.
Bradford Northern: Keith Mumby, Peter Roe, Steve Ferres, Eddie Okulicz, Henderson Gill, David Redfearn, Alan Redfearn, Ian van Bellen, Brian Noble, Dave Mordue, Alan Spencer, Neil Fox, Jeff Grayshon. Substitute: Paul Starbuck.
Referee: Vince Moss (Manchester)

Neil's injury was problematic and he next played on 1 March 1980 – a 14-8 defeat for Bradford Northern 'A' at Dewsbury. He thus achieved his ambition of playing in four decades as a professional, but it was his last game as a pro. He says, "I got through the game OK but I could tell that my knee was not right and I decided that it was time to give up the game at professional level." Neil had certainly had a good innings. He could now look to life beyond professional rugby league although he was not done with the game yet.

Bradford Northern 1978-79

Bradford Northern finished 8th in Division 1: P30, W16, L14, For 523, Against 416
Fox scored 4 tries, 50 goals, 112 points for Bradford

Date	Opponent	Score	Fox	Crowd	
20 Aug	**Leeds**	24-23	6G	8,523	YC1
27 Aug	**Hull KR**	28-17	6G	8,273	YC2
3 Sep	**Barrow***	35-10	3G	7,312	
6 Sep	**Leigh**	38-7	4G	5,503	
10 Sep	Warrington	16-24	dnp	5,820	
13 Sep	**Hull**	12-7	T	10,239	YC semi
17 Sep	**Castleford**	19-31	3G	8,871	
24 Sep	Barrow*	26-8	4G	3,800	PT1
29 Sep	Salford	8-17		4,258	
8 Oct	**Australians**	11-21	2T, 2G	15,755	
22 Oct	**Wigan**	19-8	2G	7,876	
28 Oct	York	18-8	3G	10,429	YC Final (at Leeds)
12 Nov	Hull KR*	6-10		7,742	
19 Nov	Leigh	13-7	T, 2G	4,277	
26 Nov	**Rochdale H**	30-18	4G	6,882	
3 Dec	Hull	18-12	2G	8,622	PT2
10 Dec	Featherstone R	18-7	3G	4,276	
17 Dec	**Wakefield T***	16-13		8,377	PT3
26 Dec	Huddersfield	28-10		5,294	
6 Jan	Leeds*	10-5		6,818	
17 Jan	Widnes	0-17	dnp	6,403	
21 Jan	Workington T	13-6	G	2,060	
24 Jan	Widnes	3-21	dnp	7,911	PT semi
4 Feb	Barrow	12-11		2,179	
20 Feb	Swinton	8-2	G	2,230	Ch Cup 1
4 Mar	**Hull KR**	14-7		13,828	Ch Cup 2
11 Mar	**Hull**	8-8	G	19,609	Ch Cup 3
14 Mar	Hull	8-4	dnp	16,979	Replay
25 Mar	**Featherstone R**	11-25	G	6,325	
31 Mar	Widnes*	11-14		14,324	Ch Cup semi (at Swinton)
3 Apr	**Salford**	8-12		5,129	
5 Apr	Rochdale H*	16-8	G	1,708	
10 Apr	Wakefield T*	8-6	G	4,309	
13 Apr	**Leeds**	10-13	dnp	7,924	
15 Apr	Castleford	12-28	dnp	4,701	
18 Apr	**Warrington**	14-22	dnp	5,449	
27 Apr	**Wakefield T**	50-5	dnp	4,893	
29 Apr	**St Helens**	12-13	dnp	5,930	
30 Apr	St Helens	15-31	dnp	3,722	
1 May	**Workington T**	16-3	dnp	4,161	
3 May	Wigan	3-23	dnp	2,829	
8 May	**Huddersfield**	38-8	dnp	4,545	
10 May	**Hull KR**	26-4	dnp	4,668	
12 May	**Widnes**	19-27	dnp	5,618	
15 May	Hull KR	18-17	dnp	8,075	Prem 1
19 May	Warrington	14-11	dnp	5,441	Prem semi
27 May	Leeds	2-24	dnp	19,486	Prem Final (at Fartown)

* Substitute

Bradford Northern 1979-80

19 Aug	Huddersfield	22-7	2G	3,737	YC1

29. Post-professional days

Life after a career in professional sport often presents problems for those whose main focus has always been on the next match. Retirement can leave a big void. Neil's sporting career had been much longer than most, but there was not much chance that he would idle the rest of his life away. His children, Mandy and Jonathan, had reached their teens by the time Neil played his last game for Bradford Northern in 1979. It was now time for family and work to take precedence over sport, although Neil had never neglected either.

Neil's career as a turf accountant had taken a few turns over the past decade. He recalls: "After Trevor Woodward and I sold our betting shops in South Yorkshire, Trevor wanted to go back into the pub business. He bought a run-down pub in Methley, ripped everything out and transformed it into a lovely hostelry called *The Viking*. It served meals and there were facilities for private parties and weddings. I stayed in the betting business and went to work for one of the biggest chains of shops in the country. That was Jim Windsor's of Leeds. Jim had about 250 shops at that time and he set me on as one of his area managers. He was a lovely man and was always helping amateur rugby league clubs in the area with donations and sponsorships. He had played for Bramley as a young man and later on he brought players over from South Africa, his home in winter. Louie Neumann joined Leeds on Jim's recommendation and Dave Barends came to Trinity through Jim. Every morning when I went in to head office, he would call me in and have a chat about rugby. He wanted to know what was going on in the game. Molly and I often went to his house, because we were invited to his dinner parties.

In his later years most of his work was done by his daughter and son-in-law. I was there for a couple of years. When Jim died the company was sold to William Hill's. I left the company then, after a couple of years there, because I felt I was just a number in the new organisation rather than an employee. I was still playing then and was told that I would have to end my rugby career and concentrate on the job. I must admit I found that hard to believe because sport was obviously what William Hill's was supposed to be about."

Neil left William Hill's in April 1973. He stayed in the business, however: "I rang Jack Pearson in Huddersfield. He was an old pal who had about 26 betting shops around the area. I had got to know Jack years before through Dave Valentine, the Great Britain skipper in the 1954 World Cup. I explained my situation and he invited me over for a chat about what I had done at Windsor's. After that he told me I could start work with him on the following Monday. What a difference there was between working for a family firm and a huge business. Jack told me if ever I wanted time off for rugby, it was fine by him. What a nice gesture. It was Jack who let me take all that time off in 1975 to go to play with Marist in New Zealand. He was a great guy, one of the best I have met. I worked with Richard, Jack's son, organising the staff and making sure the shops were open on time and that the cleaning staff were doing their jobs properly. I still keep in touch with Jack and Richard, although I don't see them that often. But when I do call, I am made very welcome. I was sorry to leave Pearson's but I had a different challenge to face."

Neil took a new tack in his working life in 1979, roughly at the same time as he had stopped playing as a professional. He went to work for Worthington Sports as a company representative. Worthington Sports, a company selling sports equipment, had been set up by Bob Worthington, brother of the soccer player Frank, his father-in-law and a couple of other business people. Other directors were Neil's old playing colleague David Jeanes, Malcolm Russell, another former professional footballer, and Phil Carrick, the former Yorkshire cricket spinner and captain.

Not long after taking this new challenge on, Neil took on another quite unexpectedly. On 19 June, 1980 a small article appeared in the *Yorkshire Post* sports pages, headlined "Fox on the move". It read, "Neil Fox, at 41 still on Bradford Northern's books, will be on the move again next season as player-coach to top amateur club Underbank. Underbank are one of the most progressive amateur clubs and recently opened a new £20,000 club house at Holmfirth. Fox... will be in charge of two open-age sides. Fox has turned down approaches from two professional clubs and said he did not now have time to do a full-time coaching job. He has been told by Northern that he can have a free transfer although he may stay on the register in case of emergencies and play under permit for Underbank. 'I want to keep going,' said Fox. 'It will help keep me fit and help the players on the field. My experience may brush off on to them'."

Nowadays Holmfirth may well be most famous as the idyllic setting for the television comedy programme *Last of the Summer Wine*, but its local team, Underbank Rangers, has a long and distinguished history as a breeding ground for rugby league players. Among its former players it can boast the iconic Harold Wagstaff, "the Prince of Centres", who was among the first batch of inductees into the Rugby League Hall of Fame in 1988, followed a year later by Neil. Another notable Underbank old boy was Maurice Oldroyd, a former scrum-half, who became national administrator, chief executive and latterly chairman of BARLA. When Neil joined them, however, Underbank had been relegated from the Premier League to Division One of the Pennine League. Instead of facing teams such as Wigan and Leeds, Neil was about to face up to Park Amateurs, Siddal, Worth Village, Wyke, Fitton Hill, Spotland Rangers, Mixenden, Illingworth and Saddleworth Rangers – all clubs which were situated in the towns which clung to either side of the Pennines, such as Bradford, Halifax, Huddersfield, Keighley, Oldham and Rochdale.

Neil dropped a goal on his debut, a 30-20 home win over Saddleworth Rangers at Underbank's Cross ground. Neil played the last 30 minutes of the game, which drew a crowd of 300. Neil recalls, "Underbank wanted to get back into the Premier Division as soon as possible. It took two years but not until a lot of hard work had been put in. It wasn't easy getting players to training two nights a week in the winter months – it snowed a lot up there in those days. Players came from all parts of the district. Not everyone had cars and a lot relied on getting lifts from others. Underbank is not the easiest of places to get to without transport. I must say, though, that when the team played they put in a lot of effort and listened to the advice I gave.

I also got two of my old team-mates from Wakefield to play for Underbank – Ian Brooke and David Jeanes. Ian played in most of the games while I was there and gave the lads a lot of useful tips. He had not played rugby at all since he had to pack in as a pro' with his Achilles injury, so he really enjoyed playing again. Due to his work commitments, David did not play often but he would always be there for a lot of the harder games when needed. It was great having the two around and it helped me tremendously."

Underbank just missed promotion in 1980-81, finishing third behind Siddal and Saddleworth Rangers. They did, however, win the prestigious Holliday Challenge Cup, contested by the clubs in the Huddersfield & District League. Neil led them to a 14-3 victory over St Joseph's in the final. Underbank also reached the semi-finals of the Pennine Challenge Cup, losing 10-8 at home to the eventual winners, Dudley Hill.

The following season Neil had Underbank firing on all cylinders. Rangers won the Division 1 title, winning 17 of their 18 games, and were promoted with Oldham St Anne's. They retained the Holliday Cup with a 16-2 victory in the final against St Joseph's, who finished third in the Premier Division. Other successes came in the Huddersfield & District competitions for the reserves, who won the Open Age Supplementary Cup, and the under-17 side, who won their Youth final.

Neil was still, therefore, drawing the attention of the local scribes. Ian Laybourne of the *Huddersfield Examiner* went to see him at work "on the sleepy hills above Holmfirth". He wrote, "Gone are the shimmering skills of a speedy centre-threequarter... but there's still a touch of class about him. That long, bullet-like pass, the mighty boot and that outrageous dummy are very much in evidence. He's rarely tackled with the ball these days and you won't see him running half the length of the field. But, of course, you wouldn't expect him to now." Neil told the reporter, however, that "I don't think I'll be playing next year. The time has come to call it a day. It's ridiculous playing at my age... I can last 80 minutes, though I am still carrying the knee injury that forced me to pack in at Bradford. From time to time it swells up and gives me some jip." Surprisingly, Neil was by no means the oldest player in open age amateur rugby league, BARLA having 39 players registered who were older than 40, with the oldest aged 52. Neil did, however, carry on playing for Underbank, although with decreasing regularity, for the best part of two more seasons, during which time Underbank retained their Premier Division status. When he left, he was succeeded as coach by Malcolm Branch, while Ian van Bellen later followed Malcolm as coach.

As if playing for Underbank was not enough, Neil turned out every three or four weeks with Worthington Sports All Stars XIII, which played in games to raise money for charities. The list of players who represented the team rolls off Neil's tongue like a veritable Hall of Fame in its own right: Ian Brooke, David Jeanes, Drew Broatch, Geoff Wriglesworth, Tommy Smales, Dennis Hartley, Tony Fisher, Kenny Eyre, Geoff Gunney, Rob Valentine, Colin Dixon, Alan Hardisty, Vince Farrar, Cliff Williams, John Holmes, John Atkinson, Arthur Keegan, Dave Topliss, Mick Morgan, Geoff Wraith, Terry Hollindrake, Steve Lyons and "our Don", plus a good many more. Neil reckons, "The Worthington Sports team played about 25 games over a couple of years. We only lost twice - to Castleford Colts at Headingley and to the British Universities at Keighley. Most teams, usually open-age sides, thought that they would be able to run us off our feet, because some of us were getting on a bit but it actually worked the other way round. We just played good rugby, threw the ball about and won the games. Some thought a bit of the rough stuff might put us off but with blokes like Dennis Hartley and Tony Fisher in our team, that was a pretty dicey option."

Neil talks fondly of his days in the amateur ranks at Underbank: "We brought three exceptional under-18 players into the first team– Brian Blacker, David Bootland and Paul Dixon. With Ian, David and me looking after them on the field, they went from strength to strength, scoring plenty of tries by following the right people, being put into gaps and exhibiting a real willingness to learn the game. David was the first to sign as a pro'. I took him to Bradford and I thought he would make it to the top. He was a good goal-kicker and had a football brain. Things didn't go well for him though, as the second team coach at the time was playing his own son ahead of David. So he came back to us on a permit and played at Underbank all the time I was there. Paul and Brian went on to better things. Brian played for Hull, Huddersfield and Barrow. Paul played at Huddersfield, Oldham, Halifax, Leeds and Bradford, turning into a great forward who toured as a Lion and won 15 test caps. Underbank was lucky to have two good sponsors in Jack Brook, who owned a couple of hotels in the area, and John Wray from St Andrew's Motor Company. Both were keen supporters, who were very generous financially. When I look back on my days with Underbank and remember what we achieved with the club and how a couple of the lads made good as professionals, it makes me very proud and happy."

Back in the world of business, there was a change at Worthington Sports, which had expanded to four shops. Neil says, "A family dispute arose among the Worthingtons. David and Malcolm suggested that the three of us should buy the Bradford and Horsforth shops. We did so and then bought another shop in Doncaster and the business went from strength to strength. We changed the company name to Worthington Sports (1982) Limited and then formed two other companies - Sports Bulk Suppliers and Replica World. SBS sold equipment and clothing to schools and clubs, while Replica World was a mail order business selling replica football shirts, shorts and stockings all over the globe. David was our accountant and ran Replica World. Malcolm was in charge of all the company's advertising and promotion, while I ran SBS, using my name to promote the business.

In 1989, by which time the business had really built up, we moved into a warehouse in Low Moor, Bradford and ran the company from there. We later sold the Bradford and Doncaster shops. The Horsforth shop was closed in 1996, so all our business was eventually under one roof and easier to manage. We remained at Low Moor until 2000, when we sold out to Chris Crowther. He had been with us since we started in 1979. Chris moved the business to smaller premises nearer the centre of Bradford. I stayed with him for a couple of years doing two or three days a week, helping until his son Scott joined him and later another son, Russ, came into the business. At that stage I moved out and I am pleased to say that the company is doing well for them all. During our 21 years in the company David, Malcolm and I had a great time going to sports shows and meeting sporting personalities, who were contracted to Umbro, Adidas and Nike. That meant people such as Bruce Grobbelaar, Bryan Robson, Viv Richards, Ian Botham, Fran Cotton, Steve Smith, Bill Beaumont, Frank Worthington and Geoff Capes, just to mention a few. I am pleased to say that the three of us never fell out in all our time with the company."

Neil's playing career might have ended but he was still a respected figure in the game, always willing to make appearances in good causes and popular everywhere he went. Honours and awards seemed to follow Neil around. On 12 July 1977, two years before he retired, he and Molly were invited to a dinner at Leeds Civic Hall to celebrate Queen Elizabeth II's Silver Jubilee. A lot of the region's great and good were in attendance and Neil renewed acquaintance with the Queen and Duke of Edinburgh. He was back in Her Majesty's company six years later. On 3 May 1983 he had received a letter from the Principal Private Secretary at 10, Downing Street informing him that he was being considered for the MBE and that he should reply by return of post as to whether he would accept the honour, which Neil was thrilled to do.

On 13 September a letter was sent to Neil from Major General D. H. G. Rice, Central Chancery of the Orders of Knighthood, St James's Palace, giving him details of the investiture, which was to take place at Buckingham Palace on the morning of Thursday 20 October 1983. He recalls, "Molly and I went to London with Mandy, her boyfriend and future husband, Mick, and Molly's mum. We stayed at the Regent's Park Hotel and went to see *Fiddler on the Roof*, starring Topol, on the night before the ceremony. Only two guests were allowed at the investiture and in my case that meant Molly and Mandy. On the morning of the investiture we took a taxi to Buckingham Palace. I told the taxi driver where we were going and told him I had a pass for Buckingham Palace. He took us right into the Palace grounds, after depositing Molly's mum and Mick at the gates. They waited outside and took in some of the sights while we were at the investiture. During the presentations, which were made by the Queen, you only got a few words of conversation. When it was my turn to be presented, the Queen began by remarking, 'You are the rugby player.' I replied, 'Yes, ma'am.' She said, 'But you are not the one, who...?' I replied, 'No, ma'am.

That was my brother Don'. And that was it. When we came out of the Palace, we found Molly's mum and Mick, who had been talking to a Dutch chap, telling him all about what was happening. He was very interested and offered to take our pictures together and also photographed the MBE. He said he would send us copies of the photos and took our address. We thought he would probably forget but to our surprise and delight the photos duly arrived. We have still got them but still don't know who he is. It was a lovely gesture."

Neil was the sixth rugby league player to be awarded an MBE, following in the footsteps of Eric Ashton, Geoff Gunney, Clive Sullivan, Chris Hesketh and Roger Millward. By any standards, Neil was in pretty good company.

If receiving the MBE was Neil's greatest honour in life, it was followed six years later by the highest accolade the sport of rugby league can bestow on a player – induction into the Rugby League Hall of Fame. The Hall of Fame had been inaugurated on 24 October 1988 with nine entrants – Billy Batten, Brian Bevan, Billy Boston, Alex Murphy, Jonty Parkin, Gus Risman, Albert Rosenfeld, Jim Sullivan and Harold Wagstaff. Neil would have been among the first inductees but for the stipulation that a player must have been retired for 10 years before he could be considered for the Hall of Fame. Neil fell a year outside that regulation. It was, however, decided that as soon as he became eligible he should be admitted. Thus, on 29 August 1989 Neil was inducted into the pantheon of the game's greatest players, receiving his gold Hall of Fame medal from the Earl of Derby, life-president of the Rugby Football League. Molly, Don and Peter and their wives, Neil's mother and daughter and his first grandchild, seven-months-old Lisa, were all present to see Neil's induction.

In an interview with Ian Proctor for the Wakefield Trinity match programme, Neil said, "It was certainly an occasion to match the honour. The celebration was low key but very personal, and I was so pleased that the whole family was included. The atmosphere was just right. The Rugby League have done a lot for the game in recent years and they know just how to set the right mood. Being in such exalted company is very gratifying, something of which I'm obviously very proud."

Neil says: "The game has been very good to me. I don't just mean in financial terms or in winning caps and medals. It has made Molly and me hundreds of friends, not just in England but as far away as Australia and New Zealand, and we still keep in touch with lots of them. Our closest friends, however, are Ian Brooke and his wife Janice. We see them every week and have now been friends for over 40 years." Neil is right; the game had been good to Neil but the reverse also applied.

Neil was again given a place of honour in the rugby league centenary year of 1995, when *Open Rugby* magazine selected a Great Britain Immortals team, which spanned the entire history of the game. The team was: Jim Sullivan; Billy Boston, Harold Wagstaff, Neil Fox, Mick Sullivan; Roger Millward, Alex Murphy; Alan Prescott, Joe Egan, Brian McTigue, Martin Hodgson, Dick Huddart, Ellery Hanley.

In 1998 Neil was appointed to the Rugby League's Advisory Panel, serving for several years on the Disciplinary Committee, alongside such people as former referees, Derek Fox and Eric Lawrinson, and ex-players Colin Clarke and Alan McInnes, plus various club officials. The committee met every Thursday, three members being on the panel. Neil says, "More players were sent off in those days than now. That was because there was less video evidence available and putting suspected offenders on report was not so prevalent. In the end I resigned because I did not agree with the appeals system. When a bigger club's player was suspended, they would appeal and the appeal was always heard the following day by a completely different panel. The cost to the appealing club was, maybe, £100-£200 – hardly anything to such clubs. There was never any new evidence – how could there be? Yet, I would say that on the majority of occasions the big clubs were successful with their appeals, getting their players' sentences reduced or even gaining a 'sending-off sufficient' verdict. Certainly sentences were rarely increased. The less fashionable clubs hardly ever appealed because £100-£200 to them was a lot of money. In the end I felt I was wasting my time and resigned."

In 2000 Neil received a very unexpected honour when he was invited to Rugby School, which played a key role in the development of rugby football, along with Billy Boston and Trevor Foster. Rugby School and Rugby Borough Council had decided to create a Rugby Pathway of Fame in the town, honouring 58 of rugby's most notable figures, mainly from the union code, with plaques set in and around the town's pavements and had decided to include Neil, Billy and the late Brian Bevan from rugby league – a rare distinction indeed.

In 2004 Neil joined a very select band of players when the British Rugby League Lions Association gave him the Tom Mitchell Lion of the Year award, joining such luminaries as Roger Millward, Billy Boston, Trevor Foster, Mick Sullivan, Johnny Whiteley and Alex Murphy.

One of Neil's regrets is the fact that he only made one tour of Australia as a player. Recent years, however, have compensated him in that respect. He says, "Peter Banner, the former Salford, Leeds, Featherstone and Wales scrum-half, was one of the first people to organise supporters' tours down-under. Molly and I have been lucky enough to have been on several trips with his company as couriers and have had some wonderful times in Australia and New Zealand. We first went out in 1992, which was when the Lions had their last proper tour. We went to the Melbourne test, when Britain murdered the Aussies, and to the third test at Lang Park in Brisbane. We also took parties to the games against Parramatta and Newcastle. That tour enabled us to meet up with former Trinity players, Ken Batty, Brian Briggs and Geoff Steel, who had all emigrated to Australia. In 1996 the tour was called off because of the Super League war but we still took a party out in the summer and saw Andy Platt and Denis Betts playing for Auckland.

In 1999 we went to the Tri-Series and saw both games in Australia and New Zealand, where we also attended a Kiwis reunion. The last time we went was in 2002, when State of Origin was the main attraction although we did take in Parramatta against the Broncos. Those trips included, among the visitors, lots of past players and friends of ours – too many to mention really – but they also enabled me to meet up with old Aussie opponents like Johnny Raper, Reg Gasnier and Johnny Riley from the 1959 tour, as well as blokes like Ron Coote, Kevin Ryan and Wally Lewis. They were great times."

Nowadays Neil and Molly are proud parents and doting grandparents, living in the quiet outskirts of Wakefield at Kirkhamgate. In 1985 their daughter Mandy married Michael Staszewsky and the couple have provided Neil and Molly with grandchildren, Lisa and James, who are now teenagers. Their son Jonathan married Sue Leitch in 1990 and subsequently doubled the number of Fox grandchildren, with Daniel and Joshua.

Neil still attends Wakefield Trinity home matches regularly, and is often joined in the directors' box by David Topliss, Ian Brooke, Don Robinson, Don Froggett and David Hinchliffe. He also meets former playing colleagues and opponents at social functions. Now aged 66, he can reflect on his time in the game, a career that undoubtedly placed him among the great names of both rugby league and British sport in the latter half of the 20th century.

Appendix: Statistics and records

Playing record:

Wakefield Trinity
Debut 10 April 1956 versus Keighley (away)

	A	T	G	P
1955-56	2	-	6	12
1956-57	23	10	54	138
1957-58	37	32	124	344
1958-59	40	26	146	370
1959-60	40	30	140	370
1960-61	32	18	81	216
1961-62	42	27	163	407
1962-63	30	10	100	230
1963-64	34	20	108	276
1964-65	35	12	113	262
1965-66	29	11	94	221
1966-67	37	15	132	309
1967-68	29	17	88	227
1968-69	29	9	87	201
1969-70	2	1	6	15
1970-71	28+2	12	110	256
1971-72	36+5	6	84	186
1972-73	38+4	8	138	300
1973-74	19+1	8	62	148
TOTALS	562+12	272	1,836	4,488

Last game 10 March 1974 versus Hull KR (home)

Bradford Northern
Debut 23 August 1969 versus Dewsbury (home)
Second debut 5 February 1978 versus Hull (home)

	A	T	G	P
1969-70	26+1	4	11	34
1977-78	9+4	4	22(1)	55
1978-79	21+8	4	50	112
1979-80	1	-	2	4
Totals	57+13	12	85(1)	205

Last game – 19 August 1979 versus Huddersfield (away), Yorkshire Cup

Hull Kingston Rovers
Debut 25 August 1974 versus Doncaster (away)

	A	T	G	P
1974-75	44	14	146(1)	333
1975-76	15	2	66(1)	137
Totals	59	16	212(2)	470

Last game 14 December 1975 versus Warrington (away)

York
Debut 11 January 1976 versus Bramley (home)

	A	T	G	P
1975-76	10	2	36	78
1976-77	2+1	-	6	12
Totals	12+1	2	42	90

Last game 26 September 1976 versus New Hunslet (away)

Bramley
Debut 3 October 1976 versus Hull (home)

	A	T	G	P
1976-77	23	6	73	164

Last game 24 April 1977 versus Doncaster (away)

Huddersfield
Debut 21 August 1977 versus York (home), Yorkshire Cup

	A	T	G	P
1977-78	21	5	73(1)	160

Last game 29 January 1978 versus Batley (away)

Career Record	A	T	G	P
Wakefield Trinity	562+12	272	1,836	4,488
Bradford Northern	57+13	2	85(1)	205
Hull KR	59	6	212(2)	470
York	12+1	2	42	90
Bramley	23	6	73	164
Huddersfield	21	5	73(1)	160
Great Britain tests	29	14	93	228
England	1	1	3	9
Yorkshire	17	9	60	147
Representative games	2	-	6	12
1962 Tour*	14+2	17	73	197
1962 GB in South Africa	3	4	19	50
Totals	800+28	358	2,575(4)	6,220

* Excluding tests

Neil played in 13 games and scored 5 tries, 43 goals (3 drop goals), 98 points while player-coach to Marist and Wellington (New Zealand) in 1975. These are not included in the above figures.

Figures in brackets represent one-point drop goals, which are included in the total of goals preceding them.

Representative record:

Tests (29)

	Date	Venue	Fox
Great Britain 15 France 24	5 April 1959	Grenoble	2 tries
Great Britain 11 Australia 10	21 November 1959	Leeds	Try, goal
Great Britain 18 Australia 12	12 December 1959	Wigan	Try, 6 goals
Great Britain 18 France 20	6 March 1960	Toulouse	2 tries, 3 goals
Great Britain 17 France 17	26 March 1960	St Helens	Try, 4 goals
Great Britain 21 France 10	11 December 1960	Bordeaux	2 tries, 2 goals
Great Britain 23 New Zealand 10	21 October 1961	Bradford	4 goals
Great Britain 35 New Zealand 19	4 November 1961	Swinton	7 goals
Great Britain 15 France 20	17 February 1962	Wigan	3 goals
Great Britain 13 France 23	11 March 1962	Perpignan	2 goals
Great Britain 31 Australia 12	9 June 1962	Sydney	5 goals
Great Britain 17 Australia 10	30 June 1962	Brisbane	3 goals
Great Britain 17 Australia 18	14 July 1962	Sydney	Try, 4 goals
Great Britain 0 New Zealand 19	28 July 1962	Auckland	
Great Britain 8 New Zealand 27	11 August 1962	Auckland	Try
Great Britain 12 France 17	2 December 1962	Perpignan	Try, 3 goals
Great Britain 42 France 4	3 April 1963	Wigan	Try, 9 goals
Great Britain 2 Australia 28	16 October 1963	Wembley	Goal
Great Britain 12 Australia 50	9 November 1963	Swinton	3 goals
Great Britain 39 France 0	18 March 1964	Leigh	Try, 9 goals
Great Britain 17 France 7	23 January 1965	Swinton	7 goals
Great Britain 13 France 18	16 January 1966	Perpignan	2 goals
Great Britain 16 France 13	22 January 1967	Carcassonne	2 goals
Great Britain 13 France 23	4 March 1967	Wigan	2 goals
Great Britain 11 Australia 17	3 November 1967	White City	3 goals
Great Britain 22 France 13	11 February 1968	Paris	
Great Britain 19 France 8	2 March 1968	Bradford	
Great Britain 34 France 10	30 November 1968	St Helens	5 goals
Great Britain 9 France 13	2 February 1969	Toulouse	3 goals

England (1)

	Date	Venue	Fox
England 18 France 6	17 November 1962	Leeds	Try, 3 goals

County games (17)

	Date	Venue	Fox
Yorkshire 7 Cumberland 29	15 September 1958	Whitehaven	2 goals
Yorkshire 47 Australians 15	28 September 1959	York	Try, 10 goals
Yorkshire 38 Lancashire 28	11 November 1959	Leigh	Try, 7 goals
Yorkshire 20 Lancashire 21	31 August 1960	Wakefield	4 goals
Yorkshire 19 Cumberland 43	14 September 1960	Whitehaven	5 goals
Yorkshire 21 New Zealanders 11	6 September 1961	Hull KR	Try
Yorkshire 8 Cumberland 23	11 September 1961	Wakefield	Try, goal
Yorkshire 12 Lancashire 14	9 October 1961	Leigh	Try, 3 goals
Yorkshire 11 Cumberland 2	19 September 1962	Workington	Try, goal
Yorkshire 22 Lancashire 8	26 September 1962	Wakefield	5 goals
Yorkshire 11 Australians 5	18 September 1963	Hull KR	4 goals
Yorkshire 14 Cumberland 6	9 September 1964	Whitehaven	Try, goal
Yorkshire 16 Lancashire 13	10 November 1965	Swinton	2 goals
Yorkshire 17 Cumberland 17	7 September 1966	Workington	4 goals
Yorkshire 17 Lancashire 22	21 September 1966	Leeds	Try, 4 goals
Yorkshire 15 Australians 14	4 October 1967	Wakefield	Try, 3 goals
Yorkshire 17 Lancashire 23	24 January 1968	Widnes	4 goals

Season by season figures

	A	T	G	Pts	FTS
1955-56	2	-	6	12	1
1956-57	23	10	54	138	5
1957-58	37	32	124	344	2
1958-59	42	28	148	380	-
1959-60	46	37	171	453	1
1960-61	36	20	94	248	3
1961-62	49	30	183	456	-
1962 Tour*	22+2	23	104	277	1
1962-63	36	14	125	292	1
1963-64	38	21	125	313	2
1964-65	37	13	121	281	2
1965-66	31	11	98	229	1
1966-67	41	16	144	336	1
1967-68	34	18	98	250	2
1968-69	31	9	95	217	2
1969-70	28+1	5	17	49	17
1970-71	28+2	12	110	256	3
1971-72	36+5	6	84	186	7
1972-73	38+4	8	138	300	7
1973-74	19+1	8	62	148	2
1974-75	44	14	146(1)	333	1
1975-76	25	4	102(1)	215	-
1976-77	25+1	6	79	176	1
1977-78	30+4	9	95(2)	215	4
1978-79	21+8	4	50	112	9
1979-80	1	-	2	4	-
TOTALS	**800+28**	**358**	**2,575(4)**	**6,220**	**75**

* Includes all games played in Australia, New Zealand and South Africa.
The 1975 period in New Zealand is not included here (see chapter 24)
Figures in brackets represent one-point drop goals, which are included in the total of goals preceding them.

Record in British club rugby league

Opponents	A	T	G	P	FTS
Ackworth	1	-	10	20	-
Australia	5	3	19	47	-
Barrow	14	2	33	72	2
Batley	31	18	110(1)	273	3
Blackpool B	12	7	54	129	1
Bradford N	25	15	71	187	3
Bramley	27	18	86	226	3
Castleford	31	12	104	244	2
Dewsbury	36	19	121	299	1
Dewsbury Celtic	1	1	5	13	-
Doncaster	33	32	121	338	5
Featherstone R	34	11	112(1)	256	1
Halifax	36	16	95	238	3
Huddersfield	32	9	80	187	8
Hull	42	14	129	300	1
Hull KR	39	16	106	260	5
Hunslet/New Hunslet	32	10	101	232	2
Huyton/Liverpool C	11	1	35	73	1
Keighley	32	11	114	261	4
Leeds	40	17	121	293	5
Leigh	14	4	37	86	-
New Zealand	3	2	11	28	-
Oldham	19	3	44	97	1
Rochdale H	11	2	44	94	-
St Helens	36	5	86(1)	186	4
Salford	12	4	35	82	3
Swinton	25	6	75	168	-
Wakefield T	7	1	12	27	2
Warrington	11	8	27	78	1
Whitehaven	8	5	29	73	-
Widnes	17	3	34	77	4
Wigan	31	9	74	175	4
Workington T	18	11	68	169	1
York	34	18	118(1)	289	2
Totals	**760**	**313**	**2,321(4)**	**5,577**	**72**
Representative rugby	68	45	254	643	3
Grand totals	**828**	**358**	**2,575(4)**	**6,220**	**75**